F
7X7
100V Set 2

JOHN MARSHALL

From the portrait by Chester Harding

THE LIFE

OF

JOHN MARSHALL

BY

ALBERT J. BEVERIDGE

VOLUME III

CONFLICT AND CONSTRUCTION

1800–1815

BOSTON AND NEW YORK

HOUGHTON MIFFLIN COMPANY

The Riverside Press Cambridge

1919

PREFACE

MARSHALL'S great Constitutional opinions grew out of, or were addressed to, serious public conditions, national in extent. In these volumes the effort is made to relate the circumstances that required him to give to the country those marvelous state papers: for Marshall's opinions were nothing less than state papers and of the first rank. In order to understand the full meaning of his deliverances and to estimate the just value of his labors, it is necessary to know the historical sources of his foremost expositions of the Constitution, and the historical purposes they were intended to accomplish. Without such knowledge, Marshall's finest pronouncements become mere legal utterances, important, to be sure, but colorless and unattractive.

It is worthy of repetition, even in a preface, that the history of the times is a part of his greatest opinions; and that, in the treatment of them a résumé of the events that produced them must be given. For example, the decision of Marbury *vs.* Madison, at the time and in the manner it was rendered, was compelled by the political situation then existing, unless the principle of judicial supremacy over legislation was to be abandoned. The Judiciary Debate of 1802 in Congress — one of the most brilliant as well as most important legislative engagements in parliamentary history — can no more be overlooked by the student of American Constitutional development, than the opinion of Marshall in Marbury *vs.* Madison can be disregarded.

Again, in Cohens *vs.* Virginia, the Chief Justice rises to heights of exalted — almost emotional — eloquence. Yet the case itself was hardly more than a police court controversy. If the trivial fine of itinerant peddlars of lottery tickets were alone involved, Marshall's splendid passages become unnecessary and, indeed, pompous rhetoric. But when the curtains of history are raised, we see the heroic part that Marshall played and realize the meaning of his powerful language. While Marshall's opinion in M'Culloch *vs.* Maryland, even taken by itself, is a major treatise on constitutional government, it becomes a fascinating chapter in an engaging story, when read in connection with an account of the situation which compelled that outgiving.

The same thing is true of his other historic utterances. Indeed, it may be said that his weightiest opinions were interlocking parts of one great drama.

Much space has been given to the conspiracy and trials of Aaron Burr. The combined story of that adventure and of those prosecutions has not hitherto been told. In the conduct of the Burr trials, Marshall appears in a more intimate and personal fashion than in any other phase of his judicial career; the entire series of events that make up that page of our history is a striking example of the manipulation of public opinion by astute politicians, and is, therefore, useful for the self-guidance of American democracy. Most important of all, the culminating result of this dramatic episode was the definitive establishment of the American law of treason.

In narrating the work of a jurist, the temptation is very strong to engage in legal discussion, and to cite and comment upon the decisions of other courts and the opinions of other judges. This, however, would be the very negation of biography; nor would it add anything of interest or enlightenment to the reader. Such information and analysis are given fully in the various books on Constitutional law and history, in the annotated reports, and in the encyclopædias of law upon the shelves of every lawyer. Care, therefore, has been taken to avoid making any part of the *Life of John Marshall* a legal treatise.

The manuscript of these volumes has been read by Professor Edward Channing of Harvard; Professor Max Farrand of Yale; Professor Edward S. Corwin of Princeton; Professor William E. Dodd of Chicago University; Professor Clarence W. Alvord of the University of Illinois; Professor James A. Woodburn of Indiana University; Professor Charles H. Ambler of the University of West Virginia; Professor Archibald Henderson of the University of North Carolina; Professor D. R. Anderson of Richmond (Va.) College; and Dr. H. J. Eckenrode of Richmond, Virginia.

The manuscript of the third volume has been read by Professor Charles A. Beard of New York; Dr. Samuel Eliot Morison of Harvard; and Mr. Harold J. Laski of Harvard. The manuscript of both the third and fourth volumes has been read, from

the lawyer's point of view, by Mr. Arthur Lord of
Boston, President of the Massachusetts Bar Association, and by Mr. Charles Martindale of Indianapolis.

The chapters on the Burr conspiracy and trials
have been read by Professor Walter Flavius McCaleb
of New York; Professor Isaac Joslin Cox of the University of Cincinnati; and Mr. Samuel H. Wandell
of New York. Chapter Three of Volume Three (Marbury vs. Madison) has been read by the Honorable
Oliver Wendell Holmes, Associate Justice of the Supreme Court of the United States; by the Honorable Philander Chase Knox, United States Senator;
and by Mr. James M. Beck of New York. Other
special chapters have been read by the Honorable
Henry Cabot Lodge, United States Senator; by
Professor J. Franklin Jameson of the Department
of Historical Research of the Carnegie Institution
of Washington; by Professor Charles H. Haskins of
Harvard; by Dr. William Draper Lewis of Philadelphia, former Dean of the Law School of the University of Pennsylvania; and by Mr. W. B. Bryan of
Washington.

All of these gentlemen have made valuable suggestions of which I have availed myself, and I gratefully
acknowledge my indebtedness to them. The responsibility for everything in these volumes, however, is,
of course, exclusively mine; and, in stating my appreciation of the comment and criticism with which
I have been favored, I do not wish to be relieved of
my burden by allowing the inference that any part
of it should be assigned to others.

I also owe it to myself again to express my heavy

obligation to Mr. Worthington Chauncey Ford,
Editor of the Massachusetts Historical Society.
As was the case in the preparation of the first two
volumes of this work, Mr. Ford has extended to me
the resources of his ripe scholarship; while his wise
counsel, steady encouragement, and unselfish assistance, have been invaluable in the prosecution of
a long and exacting task.

I also again acknowledge my indebtedness to Mr.
Lindsay Swift, Editor of the Boston Public Library,
who has read with critical care not only the many
drafts of the manuscript, but also the proofs of the
entire work. Mr. Swift has given, unstintedly, his
rare literary taste and critical accomplishment to the
examination of these pages.

I also tender my hearty thanks to Dr. Gardner
Weld Allen of Boston, who has generously directed
the preparation of the bibliography and personally
revised it.

Mr. David Maydole Matteson of Cambridge,
Massachusetts, has made the index of these volumes
as he made that of the first two volumes, and has
combined both indexes into one. In rendering this
service, Mr. Matteson has also searched for points
where text and notes could be made more accurate;
and I wish to express my appreciation of his kind-
ness.

My thanks are also owing to the staff of The Riverside Press, and particularly to Mr. Lanius D. Evans,
to whose keen interest and watchful care in the production of this work I am indebted for much of
whatever exactitude it may possess.

The manuscript sources have been acknowledged, in all instances, in the footnotes where references to them have been made, except in the case of the letters of Marshall to his relatives, for which I again thank those descendants and connections of the Chief Justice named in the preface to Volumes One and Two. The Hopkinson manuscripts are in the possession of Mr. Edward Hopkinson of Philadelphia, to whom I am indebted for the privilege of inspecting this valuable source and for furnishing me with copies of important letters.

In preparing these volumes, Mr. A. P. C. Griffin, Assistant Librarian, and Mr. John Clement Fitzpatrick, of the Manuscript Division of the Library of Congress, have been even more obliging, if possible, than they were in the preparation of the first part of this work. The officers and their assistants of the Boston Public Library, the Boston Athenæum, the Massachusetts State Library, the Massachusetts Historical Society, the Pennsylvania Historical Society, the Virginia State Library, the Indiana State Library, and the Indianapolis City Library, have assisted whole-heartedly in the performance of my labors; and I am glad of the opportunity to thank all of them for their interest and help.

ALBERT J. BEVERIDGE

CONTENTS

the Federalist Judiciary act — They also suspend the sessions of the Supreme Court for fourteen months — This done to prevent Marshall from overthrowing the Republican repeal of the Federalist Judiciary Act of 1801 — Marshall proposes to his colleagues on the bench that they refuse to sit as Circuit Judges — They reject his proposal — The New England Federalist leaders begin to talk secession — The jubilation of the Republican press: "Huzza for the *Washington Judiciary!*"

CONTENTS

CONTENTS

lessly assail Marshall and the Supreme Court — The fight for the
passage of a bill to relieve the New England investors is renewed —
Marshall's opinion and the decision of the court influential in securing the final passage of the measure.

APPENDIX

ILLUSTRATIONS

LIST OF ABBREVIATED TITLES MOST FREQUENTLY CITED

All references here are to the List of Authorities at the end of this volume

Adams: *U.S.* *See* Adams, Henry. History of the United States.

Ames. *See* Ames, Fisher. Works.

Channing: *Jeff. System.* *See* Channing, Edward. Jeffersonian System, 1801–11.

Channing: *U.S.* *See* Channing, Edward. History of the United States.

Chase Trial. *See* Chase, Samuel. Trial.

Corwin. *See* Corwin, Edward Samuel. Doctrine of Judicial Review.

Cutler. *See* Cutler, William Parker, and Julia Perkins. Life, Journals, and Correspondence of Manasseh Cutler.

Dillon. *See* Marshall, John. Life, Character, and Judicial Services. Edited by John Forrest Dillon.

Eaton: Prentiss. *See* Eaton, William. Life.

Jay: Johnston. *See* Jay, John. Correspondence and Public Papers.

Jefferson Writings: Washington. *See* Jefferson, Thomas, Writings. Edited by Henry Augustine Washington.

King. *See* King, Rufus. Life and Correspondence.

McCaleb. *See* McCaleb, Walter Flavius. Aaron Burr Conspiracy.

McMaster: *U.S.* *See* McMaster, John Bach. History of the People of the United States.

Marshall. *See* Marshall, John. Life of George Washington.

Memoirs, J.Q.A.: Adams. *See* Adams, John Quincy. Memoirs.

Morris. *See* Morris, Gouverneur. Diary and Letters.

N.E. Federalism: Adams. *See* New-England Federalism, 1800–1815, Documents relating to. Edited by Henry Adams.

Plumer. *See* Plumer, William. Life.

Priv. Corres.: Colton. *See* Clay, Henry. Private Correspondence. Edited by Calvin Colton.

Records Fed. Conv.: Farrand. *See* Records of the Federal Convention of 1787.

Story. *See* Story, Joseph. Life and Letters.

Trials of Smith and Ogden. See Smith, William Steuben, and Ogden, Samuel Gouverneur. Trials for Misdemeanors.

Wharton: *Social Life. See* Wharton, Anne Hollingsworth. Social Life in the Early Republic.

Wharton: *State Trials. See* Wharton, Francis. State Trials of the United States during the Administrations of Washington and Adams.

Wilkinson: *Memoirs. See* Wilkinson, James. Memoirs of My Own Times.

Works: Colton. *See* Clay, Henry. Works.

Works: Ford. *See* Jefferson, Thomas. Works. Federal Edition. Edited by Paul Leicester Ford.

Writings, J. Q. A.: Ford. *See* Adams, John Quincy. Writings. Edited by Worthington Chauncey Ford.

THE LIFE OF JOHN MARSHALL

THE LIFE OF JOHN MARSHALL

CHAPTER I

DEMOCRACY: JUDICIARY

Rigorous law is often rigorous injustice. (Terence.)

The Federalists have retired into the Judiciary as a stronghold, and from that battery all the works of republicanism are to be battered down.
(Jefferson.)

There will be neither justice nor stability in any system, if some material parts of it are not independent of popular control. (George Cabot.)

A STRANGE sight met the eye of the traveler who, aboard one of the little river sailboats of the time, reached the stretches of the sleepy Potomac separating Alexandria and Georgetown. A wide swamp extended inland from a modest hill on the east to a still lower elevation of land about a mile to the west.[1] Between the river and morass a long flat tract bore clumps of great trees, mostly tulip poplars, giving, when seen from a distance, the appearance of "a fine park." [2]

Upon the hill stood a partly constructed white stone building, mammoth in plan. The slight elevation north of the wide slough was the site of an apparently finished edifice of the same material, noble in its dimensions and with beautiful, simple lines,[3] but "surrounded with a rough rail fence 5 or 6 feet high unfit for a decent barnyard." [4] From the river

[1] Gallatin to his wife, Jan. 15, 1801, Adams: *Life of Albert Gallatin*, 252; also Bryan: *History of the National Capital*, I, 357–58.

[2] *First Forty Years of Washington Society*: Hunt, 11.

[3] *Ib.*; and see Wolcott to his wife, July 4, 1800, Gibbs: *Administrations of Washington and John Adams*, II, 377.

[4] Plumer to Thompson, Jan. 1, 1803, Plumer MSS. Lib. Cong.

nothing could be seen beyond the groves near the banks of the stream except the two great buildings and the splendid trees which thickened into a seemingly dense forest upon the higher ground to the northward.[1]

On landing and making one's way through the underbrush to the foot of the eastern hill, and up the gullies that seamed its sides thick with trees and tangled wild grapevines,[2] one finally reached the immense unfinished structure that attracted attention from the river. Upon its walls laborers were languidly at work.

Clustered around it were fifteen or sixteen wooden houses. Seven or eight of these were boarding-houses, each having as many as ten or a dozen rooms all told. The others were little affairs of rough lumber, some of them hardly better than shanties. One was a tailor shop; in another a shoemaker plied his trade; a third contained a printer with his hand press and types, while a washerwoman occupied another; and in the others there was a grocery shop, a pamphlets-and-stationery shop, a little dry-goods shop, and an oyster shop. No other human habitation of any kind appeared for three quarters of a mile.[3]

A broad and perfectly straight clearing had been made across the swamp between the eastern hill and the big white house more than a mile away to the westward. In the middle of this long opening ran a roadway, full of stumps, broken by deep mud holes in the rainy season, and almost equally deep with

[1] Gallatin to his wife, Jan. 15, 1801, Adams: *Gallatin*, 252-53.
[2] Hunt, 10.   [3] Gallatin to his wife, *supra*.

dust when the days were dry. On either border was a path or "walk" made firm at places by pieces of stone; though even this "extended but a little way." Alder bushes grew in the unused spaces of this thoroughfare, and in the depressions stagnant water stood in malarial pools, breeding myriads of mosquitoes. A sluggish stream meandered across this avenue and broadened into the marsh.[1]

A few small houses, some of brick and some of wood, stood on the edge of this long, broad embryo street. Near the large stone building at its western end were four or five structures of red brick, looking much like ungainly warehouses. Farther westward on the Potomac hills was a small but pretentious town with its many capacious brick and stone residences, some of them excellent in their architecture and erected solidly by skilled workmen.[2]

Other openings in the forest had been cut at various places in the wide area east of the main highway that connected the two principal structures already described. Along these forest avenues were scattered houses of various materials, some finished and some in the process of erection.[3] Here and there unsightly gravel pits and an occasional brick kiln added to the raw unloveliness of the whole.

Such was the City of Washington, with Georgetown near by, when Thomas Jefferson became President and John Marshall Chief Justice of the United States — the Capitol, Pennsylvania Avenue, the

[1] Bryan, I, 357–58.
[2] A few of these are still standing and occupied.
[3] Gallatin to his wife, *supra;* also Wharton: *Social Life in the Early Republic*, 58–59.

"Executive Mansion" or "President's Palace," the
department buildings near it, the residences, shops,
hostelries, and streets. It was a picture of sprawl-
ing aimlessness, confusion, inconvenience, and utter
discomfort.

When considering the events that took place in
the National Capital as narrated in these volumes,
— the debates in Congress, the proclamations of
Presidents, the opinions of judges, the intrigues of
politicians, — when witnessing the scenes in which
Marshall and Jefferson and Randolph and Burr and
Pinkney and Webster were actors, we must think
of Washington as a dismal place, where few and
unattractive houses were scattered along muddy
openings in the forests.

There was on paper a harmonious plan of a splendid city, but the realization of that plan had scarcely
begun. As a situation for living, the Capital of the
new Nation was, declared Gallatin, a "hateful
place." [1] Most of the houses were "small miserable
huts" which, as Wolcott informed his wife, "present
an awful contrast to the public buildings." [2]

Aside from an increase in the number of residences
and shops, the "Federal City" remained in this
state for many years. "The *Chuck* holes were not
bad," wrote Otis of a journey out of Washington in
1815; "that is to say they were none of them much
deeper than the Hubs of the hinder wheels. They
were however exceedingly frequent." [3] Pennsylvania

---

[1] Gallatin to his wife, Aug. 17, 1802, Adams: *Gallatin*, 304.

[2] Wolcott to his wife, July 4, 1800, Gibbs, II, 377.

[3] Otis to his wife, Feb. 28, 1815, Morison: *Life and Letters of
Harrison Gray Otis*, II, 170–71. This letter is accurately descriptive

Avenue was, at this time, merely a stretch of "yellow, tenacious mud," [1] or dust so deep and fine that, when stirred by the wind, it made near-by objects invisible.[2] And so this street remained for decades. Long after the National Government was removed to Washington, the carriage of a diplomat became mired up to the axles in the sticky clay within four blocks of the President's residence and its occupant had to abandon the vehicle.

John Quincy Adams records in his diary, April 4, 1818, that on returning from a dinner the street was in such condition that "our carriage in coming for us . . was overset, the harness broken. We got home with difficulty, twice being on the point of oversetting, and at the Treasury Office corner we were both obliged to get out . . in the mud. . . It was a mercy that we all got home with whole bones." [3]

of travel from the National Capital to Baltimore as late as 1815 and many years afterward.

"The Bladensburg *run, before we came to the bridge,* was happily in no one place *above* the Horses bellies. — As we passed thro', the driver pointed out to us the spot, right under our wheels, where all the stage horses last year were drowned, but then he consoled us by shewing the tree, on which all the Passengers *but one,* were saved. Whether that one was gouty or not, I did not enquire. . .

"We . . arriv'd safe at our first stage, Ross's, having gone at a rate rather exceeding two miles & an half per hour. . . In case of a *break Down* or other accident, . . I should be sorry to stick and freeze in over night *(as I have seen happen to twenty waggons)* for without an extraordinary thaw I could not be dug out in any reasonable dinner-time the next day."

Of course conditions were much worse in all parts of the country, except the longest and most thickly settled sections.

[1] Parton: *Life of Thomas Jefferson,* 622.

[2] Plumer to his wife, Jan. 25, 1807, Plumer MSS. Lib. Cong.

[3] *Memoirs of John Quincy Adams:* Adams, IV, 74; and see Quincy: *Life of Josiah Quincy,* 186.

Bayard wrote to Rodney: "four months [in Washington] almost

Fever and other malarial ills were universal at certain seasons of the year.[1] "No one, from the North or from the high country of the South, can pass the months of August and September there without intermittent or bilious fever," records King in 1803.[2] Provisions were scarce and Alexandria, across the river, was the principal source of supplies.[3] "My God! What have I done to reside in such a city," exclaimed a French diplomat.[4] Some months after the Chase impeachment[5] Senator Plumer described Washington as "a little village in the midst of the woods."[6] "Here I am in the wilderness of Washington," wrote Joseph Story in 1808.[7]

Except a small Catholic chapel there was only one church building in the entire city, and this tiny wooden sanctuary was attended by a congregation which seldom exceeded twenty persons.[8] This absence of churches was entirely in keeping with the

killed me." (Bayard to Rodney, Feb. 24, 1804, N. Y. Library Bulletin, IV, 230.)

[1] Margaret Smith to Susan Smith, Dec. 26, 1802, Hunt, 33; also Mrs. Smith to her husband, July 8, 1803, *ib.* 41; and Gallatin to his wife, Aug. 17, 1802, Adams: *Gallatin*, 304–05.

[2] King to Gore, Aug. 20, 1803, *Life and Correspondence of Rufus King:* King, IV, 294; and see Adams: *History of the United States*, IV, 31.

[3] Gallatin to his wife, Jan. 15, 1801, Adams: *Gallatin*, 253.

[4] Wharton: *Social Life*, 60.   [5] See *infra*, chap. IV.

[6] Plumer to Lowndes, Dec. 30, 1805, Plumer: *Life of William Plumer*, 244.

"The wilderness, alias the federal city." (Plumer to Tracy, May 2, 1805, Plumer MSS. Lib. Cong.)

[7] Story to Fay, Feb. 16, 1808, *Life and Letters of Joseph Story:* Story, I, 161.

[8] This was a little Presbyterian church building, which was abandoned after 1800. (Bryan, I, 232; and see Hunt, 13–14.)

inclination of people of fashion. The first Republican administration came, testifies Winfield Scott, in "the spring tide of infidelity. . . At school and college, most bright boys, of that day, affected to regard religion as base superstition or gross hypocricy." [1]

Most of the Senators and Representatives of the early Congresses were crowded into the boarding-houses adjacent to the Capitol, two and sometimes more men sharing the same bedroom. At Conrad and McMunn's boarding-house, where Gallatin lived when he was in the House, and where Jefferson boarded up to the time of his inauguration, the charge was fifteen dollars a week, which included service, "wood, candles and liquors." [2] Board at the Indian Queen cost one dollar and fifty cents a day, "brandy and whisky being free." [3] In some such inn the new Chief Justice of the United States, John Marshall, at first, found lodging.

Everybody ate at one long table. At Conrad and McMunn's more than thirty men would sit down at the same time, and Jefferson, who lived there while he was Vice-President, had the coldest and lowest place at the table; nor was a better seat offered him

[1] *Memoirs of Lieut.-General Scott*, 9–10. Among the masses of the people, however, a profound religious movement was beginning. (See Semple: *History of the Rise and Progress of the Baptists in Virginia;* and Cleveland: *Great Revival in the West.*)

A year or two later, religious services were held every Sunday afternoon in the hall of the House of Representatives, which always was crowded on these occasions. The throng did not come to worship, it appears; seemingly, the legislative hall was considered to be a convenient meeting-place for gossip, flirtation, and social gayety. The plan was soon abandoned and the hall left entirely to profane usages. (Bryan, I, 606–07.)

[2] Gallatin to his wife, Jan. 15, 1801, Adams: *Gallatin*, 253.

[3] Wharton: *Social Life*, 72.

on the day when he took the oath of office as Chief Magistrate of the Republic.[1] Those who had to rent houses and maintain establishments were in distressing case.[2] So lacking were the most ordinary conveniences of life that a proposal was made in Congress, toward the close of Jefferson's first administration, to remove the Capital to Baltimore.[3] An alternative suggestion was that the White House should be occupied by Congress and a cheaper building erected for the Presidential residence.[4]

More than three thousand people drawn hither by the establishment of the seat of government managed to exist in "this desert city."[5] One fifth of these were negro slaves.[6] The population was made up of people from distant States and foreign countries[7] — the adventurous, the curious, the restless, the improvident. The "city" had more than the usual proportion of the poor and vagrant who, "so far as I can judge," said Wolcott, "live like fishes

[1] Hunt, 12.

[2] See Merry to Hammond, Dec. 7, 1803, as quoted in Adams: *U.S.* ii, 362.

Public men seldom brought their wives to Washington because of the absence of decent accommodations. (Mrs. Smith to Mrs. Kirkpatrick, Dec. 6, 1805, Hunt, 48.)

"I do not perceive how the members of Congress can possibly secure lodgings, unless they will consent to live like scholars in a college or monks in a monastery, crowded ten or twenty in a house; and utterly excluded from society." (Wolcott to his wife, July 4, 1800, Gibbs, ii, 377.)

[3] Plumer to Thompson, March 19, 1804, Plumer MSS. Lib. Cong. And see *Annals*, 8th Cong. 1st Sess. 282–88. The debate is instructive. The bill was lost by 9 yeas to 19 nays.

[4] Hildreth: *History of the United States*, v, 516–17.

[5] Plumer to Lowndes, Dec. 30, 1805, Plumer, 337.

[6] Channing: *History of the United States*, iv, 245.

[7] Bryan, i, 438.

by eating each other." [1] The sight of Washington filled Thomas Moore, the British poet, with contempt.

"This embryo capital, where Fancy sees
Squares in morasses, obelisks in trees;
Where second-sighted seers, even now, adorn
With shrines unbuilt and heroes yet unborn,
Though nought but woods and Jefferson they see,
Where streets should run and sages *ought* to be." [2]

Yet some officials managed to distill pleasure from materials which one would not expect to find in so crude a situation. Champagne, it appears, was plentiful. When Jefferson became President, that connoisseur of liquid delights [3] took good care that the "Executive Mansion" was well supplied with the choicest brands of this and many other wines. [4] Senator Plumer testifies that, at one of Jefferson's dinners, "the wine was the best I ever drank, particularly the champagne which was indeed delicious." [5] In fact, repasts where champagne was served seem to have been a favorite source of enjoyment and relaxation. [6]

[1] Wolcott to his wife, July 4, 1800, Gibbs, II, 377.

"The workmen are the refuse of that class and, nevertheless very high in their demands." (La Rochefoucauld-Liancourt: *Travels Through the United States of North America*, III, 650.)

[2] "To Thomas Hume, Esq., M.D.," Moore: *Poetical Works*, II, 83.

[3] See Jefferson to Short, Sept. 6, 1790, *Works of Thomas Jefferson*: Ford, VI, 146; same to Mrs. Adams, July 7, 1785, *ib.* IV, 432-33; same to Peters, June 30, 1791, *ib.* VI, 276; same to Short, April 24, 1792, *ib.* 483; same to Monroe, May 26, 1795, *ib.* VIII, 179; same to Jay, Oct. 8, 1787, *Memoir, Correspondence, and Miscellanies, from the Papers of Thomas Jefferson*: Randolph, II, 249; also see Chastellux: *Travels in North America in the Years 1780-81-82*, 299.

[4] See Singleton: *Story of the White House*, I, 42-43.

[5] Plumer to his wife, Dec. 25, 1802, Plumer, 246.

[6] "Mr. Granger [Jefferson's Postmaster-General] . . after a few

Scattered, unformed, uncouth as Washington was, and unhappy and intolerable as were the conditions of living there, the government of the city was torn by warring interests. One would have thought that the very difficulties of their situation would have compelled some harmony of action to bring about needed improvements. Instead of this, each little section of the city fought for itself and was antagonistic to the others. That part which lay near the White House [1] strove exclusively for its own advantage. The same was true of those who lived or owned property about Capitol Hill. There was, too, an "Alexandria interest" and a "Georgetown interest." These were constantly quarreling and each was irreconcilable with the other. [2]

In all respects the Capital during the first decades of the nineteenth century was a representation in miniature of the embryo Nation itself. Physical conditions throughout the country were practically the same as at the time of the adoption of the Constitution; and popular knowledge and habits of thought had improved but slightly. [3]

A greater number of newspapers, however, had profoundly affected public sentiment, and demo-

bottles of champagne were emptied, on the observation of Mr. Madison that it was the most delightful wine when drank in moderation, but that more than a few glasses always produced a headache the next day, remarked with point that this was the very time to try the experiment, as the next day being Sunday would allow time for a recovery from its effects. The point was not lost upon the host and bottle after bottle came in." (S. H. Smith to his wife, April 26, 1803, Hunt, 36.)

[1] At that time it was called "The Executive Mansion" or "The President's Palace."

[2] Bryan, I, 44; also see La Rochefoucauld-Liancourt, III, 642–51.

[3] See vol. I, chaps. VI and VII, of this work.

cratic views and conduct had become riotously dominant. The defeated and despairing Federalists viewed the situation with anger and foreboding. Of all Federalists John Marshall and George Cabot were the calmest and wisest. Yet even they looked with gloom upon the future. "There are some appearances which surprize me," wrote Marshall on the morning of Jefferson's inauguration to his intimate friend, Charles Cotesworth Pinckney.

"I wish, however, more than I hope that the public prosperity & happiness will sustain no diminution under Democratic guidance. The Democrats are divided into speculative theorists & absolute terrorists. With the latter I am disposed to class Mr. Jefferson. If he ranges himself with them it is not difficult to foresee that much difficulty is in store for our country — if he does not, they will soon become his enemies and calumniators." [1]

After Jefferson had been President for four months, Cabot thus interpreted the Republican victory of 1800: "We are doomed to suffer all the evils of *excessive* democracy through the United States. . . Maratists and Robespierrians everywhere raise their heads. . . There will be neither justice nor stability in any system, if some material parts of it are not independent of popular control" [2] — an opinion

[1] Marshall to Pinckney, March 4, 1801, MS. furnished by Dr. W. S. Thayer of Baltimore.

[2] Cabot to Wolcott, Aug. 3, 1801, Lodge: *Life and Letters of George Cabot*, 322.

George Cabot was the ablest, most moderate and far-seeing of the New England Federalists. He feared and detested what he called "excessive democracy" as much as did Ames, or Pickering, or Dwight, but, unlike his brother partisans, did not run to the opposite extreme himself and never failed to assert the indispensability of the democratic

which Marshall, speaking for the Supreme Court of
the Nation, was soon to announce.

Joseph Hale wrote to King that Jefferson's election meant the triumph of "the wild principles of up-
roar & misrule" which would produce "anarchy." [1]
Sedgwick advised our Minister at London: "The
aristocracy of virtue is destroyed." [2] In the course
of a characteristic Federalist speech Theodore
Dwight exclaimed: "The great object of Jacobinism
is . . to force mankind back into a savage state. . . .
We have a country governed by blockheads and
knaves; our wives and daughters are thrown into the
stews. . . Can the imagination paint anything more
dreadful this side of hell." [3]

The keen-eyed and thoughtful John Quincy
Adams was of the opinion that "the basis of it all is
democratic popularity. . . There never was a system
of measures [Federalist] more completely and irrev-
ocably abandoned and rejected by the popular
voice. . . Its restoration would be as absurd as to
undertake the resurrection of a carcass seven years in
its grave." [4] A Federalist in the *Commercial Gazette*
of Boston,[5] in an article entitled "Calm Reflections,"
mildly stated that "democracy teems with fanati-

element in government. Cabot was utterly without personal ambition
and was very indolent; otherwise he surely would have occupied a
place in history equal to that of men like Madison, Gallatin, Hamilton,
and Marshall.

[1] Hale to King, Dec. 19, 1801, King, IV, 39.
[2] Sedgwick to King, Dec. 14, 1801, *ib.* 34–35.
[3] Dwight's oration as quoted in Adams: *U.S.* I, 225.
[4] J. Q. Adams to King, Oct. 8, 1802, *Writings of John Quincy Adams:*
Ford, III, 8–9. Within six years Adams abandoned a party which offered
such feeble hope to aspiring ambition. (See *infra*, chap. IX.)
[5] J. Russell's *Gazette-Commercial and Political*, January 28, 1799.

cism." Democrats "love liberty . . and, like other
lovers, they try their utmost to debauch . . their
mistress."

There was among the people a sort of diffused ego-
tism which appears to have been the one characteristic common to Americans of that period. The most
ignorant and degraded American felt himself far
superior to the most enlightened European. "Behold the universe," wrote the chronicler of Congress
in 1802. "See its four quarters filled with savages or
slaves. Out of nine hundred millions of human beings but four millions [Americans] are free." [1]

William Wirt describes the contrast of fact to pretension: "Here and there a stately aristocratick
palace, with all its appurtenances, strikes the view:
while all around for many miles, no other buildings
are to be seen but the little smoky huts and log
cabins of poor, laborious, ignorant tenants. And
what is very ridiculous, these tenants, while they
approach *the great house*, cap in hand, with all the
fearful trembling submission of the lowest feudal
vassals, boast in their court-yards, with obstreper-
ous exultation, that they live in a land of freemen, a
land of equal liberty and equal rights." [2]

[1] *History of the Last Session of Congress Which Commenced 7th Dec.
1801* (taken from the *National Intelligencer*). Yet at that time in
America manhood suffrage did not exist excepting in three States, a
large part of the people could not read or write, imprisonment for
debt was universal, convicted persons were sentenced to be whipped
in public and subjected to other cruel and disgraceful punishments.
Hardly a protest against slavery was made, and human rights as we
now know them were in embryo, so far as the practice of them was
concerned.

[2] Wirt: *Letters of the British Spy*, 10–11.
These brilliant articles, written by Wirt when he was about thirty

Conservatives believed that the youthful Republic was doomed; they could see only confusion, destruction, and decline. Nor did any nation of the Old World at that particular time present an example of composure and constructive organization. All Europe was in a state of strained suspense during the interval of the artificial peace so soon to end. "I consider the whole civilized world as metal thrown back into the furnace to be melted over again," wrote Fisher Ames after the inevitable resumption of the war between France and Great Britain.[1] "Tremendous times in Europe!" exclaimed Jefferson when cannon again were thundering in every country of the Old World. "How mighty this battle of lions & tygers! With what sensations should the common herd of cattle look upon it? With no partialities, certainly!"[2]

Jefferson interpreted the black forebodings of the defeated conservatives as those of men who had been thwarted in the prosecution of evil designs: "The

years old, were published in the Richmond *Argus* during 1803. So well did they deceive the people that many in Gloucester and Norfolk declared that they had seen the British Spy. (Kennedy: *Memoirs of the Life of William Wirt*, I, 111, 113.)

[1] Ames to Pickering, Feb. 4, 1807, Pickering MSS. Mass. Hist. Soc.

[2] Jefferson to Rush, Oct. 4, 1803, *Works:* Ford, x, 32.

Immediately after his inauguration, Jefferson restated the American foreign policy announced by Washington. It was the only doctrine on which he agreed with Marshall.

"It ought to be the very first object of our pursuits to have nothing to do with European interests and politics. Let them be free or slaves at will, navigators or agricultural, swallowed into one government or divided into a thousand, we have nothing to fear from them in any form. . . To take part in their conflicts would be to divert our energies from creation to destruction." (Jefferson to Logan, March 21, 1801, *Works:* Ford, IX, 219–20.)

clergy, who have missed their union with the State, the Anglo men, who have missed their union with England, the political adventurers who have lost the chance of swindling & plunder in the waste of public money, will never cease to bawl, on the breaking up of their sanctuary." [1]

Of all the leading Federalists, John Marshall was the only one who refused to "bawl," at least in the public ear; and yet, as we have seen and shall again find, he entertained the gloomy views of his political associates. Also, he held more firmly than any prominent man in America to the old-time Federalist principle of Nationalism — a principle which with despair he watched his party abandon.[2] His whole being was fixed immovably upon the maintenance of order and constitutional authority. Except for his letter to Pinckney, Marshall was silent amidst the clamor. All that now went forward passed before his regretful vision, and much of it he was making ready to meet and overcome with the affirmative opinions of constructive judicial statesmanship.

Meanwhile he discharged his duties — then very light — as Chief Justice. But in doing so, he quietly began to strengthen the Supreme Court. He did

[1] Jefferson to Postmaster-General (Gideon Granger), May 3, 1801, *Works:* Ford, IX, 249.

The democratic revolution that overthrew Federalism was the beginning of the movement that finally arrived at the abolition of imprisonment for debt, the bestowal of universal manhood suffrage, and, in general, the more direct participation in every way of the masses of the people in their own government. But in the first years of Republican power there was a pandering to the crudest popular tastes and passions which, to conservative men, argued a descent to the sansculottism of France.

[2] See *infra*, chaps. III and VI; also vol. IV, chap. I.

this by one of those acts of audacity that later marked the assumptions of power which rendered his career historic. For the first time the Chief Justice disregarded the custom of the delivery of opinions by the Justices *seriatim*, and, instead, calmly assumed the function of announcing, himself, the views of that tribunal. Thus Marshall took the first step in impressing the country with the unity of the highest court of the Nation. He began this practice in Talbot *vs*. Seeman, familiarly known as the case of the Amelia,[1] the first decided by the Supreme Court after he became Chief Justice.

During our naval war with France an armed merchant ship, the Amelia, owned by one Chapeau Rouge of Hamburg, while homeward bound from Calcutta, was taken by the French corvette, La Diligente. The Amelia's papers, officers, and crew were removed to the French vessel, a French crew placed in charge, and the captured ship was sent to St. Domingo as a prize. On the way to that French port, she was recaptured by the American frigate, Constitution, Captain Silas Talbot, and ordered to New York for adjudication. The owner demanded ship and cargo without payment of the salvage claimed by Talbot for his rescue. The case finally reached the Supreme Court.

In the course of a long and careful opinion the Chief Justice held that, although there had been no formal declaration of war on France, yet particular acts of Congress had authorized American warships to capture certain French vessels and had provided

[1] 1 Cranch, 1 *et seq.*

for the payment of salvage to the captors. Virtually, then, we were at war with France. While the Amelia was not a French craft, she was, when captured by Captain Talbot, "an armed vessel commanded and manned by Frenchmen," and there was "probable cause to believe" that she was French. So her capture was lawful.

Still, the Amelia was not, in fact, a French vessel, but the property of a neutral; and in taking her from the French, Talbot had, in reality, rescued the ship and rendered a benefit to her owners for which he was entitled to salvage. For a decree of the French Republic made it "extremely probable" that the Amelia would be condemned by the French courts in St. Domingo; and that decree, having been "promulgated" by the American Government, must be considered by American courts "as an authenticated copy of a public law of France interesting to all nations." This, said Marshall, was "the real and only question in the case." The first opinion delivered by Marshall as Chief Justice announced, therefore, an important rule of international law and is of permanent value.

Marshall's next case [1] involved complicated questions concerning lands in Kentucky. Like nearly all of his opinions, the one in this case is of no historical importance except that in it he announced for the second time the views of the court. In United States *vs.* Schooner Peggy,[2] Marshall declared that, since the Constitution makes a treaty a "supreme law of the land," courts are as much bound by it as

---

[1] Wilson *vs.* Mason, 1 Cranch, 45–101.   [2] 1 Cranch, 102–10.

by an act of Congress. This was the first time that
principle was stated by the Supreme Court. Another case [1] concerned the law of practice and of
evidence. This was the last case in which Marshall
delivered an opinion before the Republican assault
on the Judiciary was made — the causes of which
assault we are now to examine.

At the time of his inauguration, Jefferson apparently meant to carry out the bargain [2] by which his
election was made possible. "We are all Republicans, we are all Federalists," were the reassuring
words with which he sought to quiet those who already were beginning to regret that they had yielded
to his promises.[3] Even Marshall was almost favorably impressed by the inaugural address. "I have
administered the oath to the Presdt.," he writes
Pinckney immediately after Jefferson had been in-
ducted into office. "His inauguration speech . . is in
general well judged and conciliatory. It is in direct
terms giving the lie to the violent party declamation
which has elected him, but it is strongly characteristic of the general cast of this political theory." [4]

It is likely that, for the moment, the President
intended to keep faith with the Federalist leaders.
But the Republican multitude demanded the spoils
of victory; and the Republican leaders were not
slow or soft-spoken in telling their chieftain that he
must take those measures, the assurance of which

---

[1] Turner *vs.* Fendall, 1 Cranch, 115–30.

[2] See vol. II, 531–47, of this work.

[3] See Adams: *U.S.* I, chaps. IX and X, for account of the revolutionary measures which the Republicans proposed to take.

[4] Marshall to Pinckney, March 4, 1801, "four o'clock," MS.

had captivated the popular heart and given "the party of the people" a majority in both House and Senate.

Thus the Republican programme of demolition was begun. Federalist taxes were, of course, to be abolished; the Federalist mint dismantled; the Federalist army disbanded; the Federalist navy beached. Above all, the Federalist system of National courts was to be altered, the newly appointed Federalist National judges ousted and their places given to Republicans; and if this could not be accomplished, at least the National Judiciary must be humbled and cowed. Yet every step must be taken with circumspection — the cautious politician at the head of the Government would see to that. No atom of party popularity [1] must be jeopardized; on the contrary, Republican strength must be increased at any cost, even at the temporary sacrifice of principle.[2] Unless these facts are borne in mind, the curious blending of fury and moderation — of violent attack and sudden quiescence — in the Re-

[1] "It is the sole object of the Administration to acquire popularity." (Wolcott to Cabot, Aug. 28, 1802, Lodge: *Cabot*, 325.)

"The President has .. the itch for popularity." (J. Q. Adams to his father, November, 1804, *Writings, J. Q. A.*: Ford, III, 81.)

" The mischiefs of which his immoderate thirst for .. popularity are laying the foundation, are not immediately perceived." (Adams to Quincy, Dec. 4, 1804, Quincy, 64.)

"It seems to be a great primary object with him never to pursue a measure if it becomes unpopular." (Plumer's Diary, March 4, 1805, Plumer MSS. Lib. Cong.)

" In dress, conversation, and demeanor he studiously sought and displayed the arts of a low demagogue seeking the gratification of the democracy on whose voices and votes he laid the foundation of his power." (Quincy's Diary, Jan. 1806, Quincy, 93.)

[2] Ames to Gore, Dec. 13, 1802, *Works of Fisher Ames:* Ames, I, 309.

publican tactics during the first years of Jefferson's Administration are inexplicable.

Jefferson determined to strike first at the National Judiciary. He hated it more than any other of the "abominations" of Federalism. It was the only department of the Government not yet under his control. His early distrust of executive authority, his suspicion of legislative power when his political opponents held it, were now combined against the National courts which he did not control.

Impotent and little respected as the Supreme Court had been and still was, Jefferson nevertheless entertained an especial fear of it; and this feeling had been made personal by the thwarting of his cherished plan of appointing his lieutenant, Spencer Roane of Virginia, Chief Justice of the United States.[1] The elevation of his particular aversion, John Marshall, to that office, had, he felt, wickedly robbed him of the opportunity to make the new régime harmonious; and, what was far worse, it had placed in that station of potential, if as yet undeveloped, power, one who, as Jefferson had finally come to think, might make the high court of the Nation a mighty force in the Government, retard fundamental Republican reforms, and even bring to naught measures dear to the Republican heart.

It seems probable that, at this time, Jefferson was the only man who had taken Marshall's measure correctly. His gentle manner, his friendliness and conviviality, no longer concealed from Jefferson the

[1] Dodd in *American Historical Review*, XII, 776; and see next chapter.

courage and determination of his great relative; and Jefferson doubtless saw that Marshall, with his universally conceded ability, would find means to vitalize the National Judiciary, and with his fearlessness, would employ those means.

"The Federalists," wrote Jefferson, "have retired into the judiciary as a stronghold . . and from that battery all the works of republicanism are to be beaten down and erased." [1] Therefore that stronghold must be taken. Never was a military plan more carefully devised than was the Republican method of capturing it. Jefferson would forthwith remove all Federalist United States marshals and attorneys; [2] he would get rid of the National judges whom Adams had appointed under the Judiciary Act of 1801. [3] If this did not make those who remained on the National Bench sufficiently tractable, the sword of impeachment would be held over their obstinate heads until terror of removal and disgrace should render them pliable to the dominant political will.

[1] Jefferson to Dickinson, Dec. 19, 1801, *Writings of Thomas Jefferson:* Washington, iv, 424.

[2] "The only shield for our Republican citizens against the federalism of the courts is to have the attorneys & Marshals republicans." (Jefferson to Stuart, April 8, 1801, *Works:* Ford, ix, 248.)

[3] "The judge of course stands until the law [Judiciary Act of 1801] shall be repealed which we trust will be at the next Congress." (Jefferson to Stuart, April 8, 1801, *Works:* Ford, ix, 247.) For two weeks Jefferson appears to have been confused as to the possibility of repealing the Judiciary Act of 1801. A fortnight before he informed Stuart that this course would be taken, he wrote Giles that "the courts being so decidedly federal and irremovable," it was "indispensably necessary" to appoint "republican attorneys and marshals." (Jefferson to Giles, March 23, 1801, MSS. Lib. Cong. as quoted by Carpenter in *American Political Science Review,* ix, 522.)

But the repeal had been determined upon within six weeks after Jefferson's inauguration as his letter to Stuart shows.

Thus by progressive stages the Supreme Court would be brought beneath the blade of the executioner and the obnoxious Marshall decapitated or compelled to submit.

To this agreeable course, so well adapted to his purposes, the President was hotly urged by the foremost leaders of his party. Within two weeks after Jefferson's inauguration, the able and determined William Branch Giles of Virginia, faithfully interpreting the general Republican sentiment, demanded "the removal of all its [the Judiciary's] executive officers indiscriminately." This would get rid of the Federalist marshals and clerks of the National courts; they had been and were, avowed Giles, "the humble echoes" of the "vicious schemes" of the National judges, who had been "the most unblushing violators of constitutional restrictions." [1] Again Giles expressed the will of his party: "The revolution [Republican success in 1800] is incomplete so long as that strong fortress [the Judiciary] is in possession of the enemy." He therefore insisted upon "the absolute repeal of the whole judiciary system." [2]

The Federalist leaders quickly divined the first part of the Republican purpose: "There is nothing which the [Republican] party more anxiously wish than the destruction of the judicial arrangements made during the last session," wrote Sedgwick.[3] And Hale, with dreary sarcasm, observed that "the independence of our Judiciary is to be confirmed

[1] Giles to Jefferson, March 16, 1801, Anderson: *William Branch Giles — A Study in the Politics of Virginia 1790–1830*, 77.

[2] Same to same, June 1, 1801, *ib.* 80.

[3] Sedgwick to King, Dec. 14, 1801, King, IV, 36.

by being made wholly subservient to the will of the legislature & the caprice of Executive visions." [1]

The judges themselves had invited the attack so soon to be made upon them.[2] Immediately after the Government was established under the Constitution, they took a position which disturbed a large part of the general public, and also awakened apprehensions in many serious minds. Persons were haled before the National courts charged with offenses unknown to the National statutes and unnamed in the Constitution; nevertheless, the National judges held that these were indictable and punishable under the common law of England.[3]

This was a substantial assumption of power. The Judiciary avowed its right to pick and choose among the myriad of precedents which made up the common law, and to enforce such of them as, in the opinion of the National judges, ought to govern American citizens. In a manner that touched directly the lives and liberties of the people, therefore, the judges

[1] Hale to King, Dec. 19, 1801, King, IV, 39.

[2] It must be carefully kept in mind that from the beginning of the Revolution most of the people were antagonistic to courts of any kind, and bitterly hostile to lawyers. (See vol. I, 297–99, of this work.)

Braintree, Mass., in 1786, in a town meeting, denounced lawyers and demanded by formal resolution the enactment of "such laws . . as may crush or, at least, put a proper check of restraint" upon them.

Dedham, Mass., instructed its members of the Legislature to secure the passage of laws that would "check" attorneys; and if this were not practicable, then "you are to endeavor [to pass a bill declaring] that the order of Lawyers be totally abolished." (Warren: *History of the American Bar*, 215.) All this, of course, was the result of the bitter hardships of debtors.

[3] For an able defense of the adoption by the National courts of the British common law, see *Works of the Honourable James Wilson:* Wilson, III, 384.

became law-givers as well as law-expounders. Not
without reason did the Republicans of Boston drink
with loud cheers this toast: "The Common Law of
England! May wholesome statutes soon root out
this engine of oppression from America." [1]

The occasions that called forth this exercise of
judicial authority were the violation of Washington's Neutrality Proclamation, the violation of the
Treaty of Peace with Great Britain, and the numberless threats to disregard both. From a strictly legal
point of view, these indeed furnished the National
courts with plausible reasons for the position they
took. Certainly the judges were earnestly patriotic
and sincere in their belief that, although Congress
had not authorized it, nevertheless, that accumulation of British decisions, usages, and customs called
"the common law" was a part of American National
jurisprudence; and that, of a surety, the assertion of
it in the National tribunals was indispensable to the
suppression of crimes against the United States. In
charging the National grand jury at Richmond, May
22, 1793, Chief Justice John Jay first announced this
doctrine, although not specifically naming the common law. [2] Two months later, Justice James Wilson
claimed the same inclusive power in his address to
the grand jury at Philadelphia. [3]

In 1793, Joseph Ravara, consul for Genoa, was in-

[1] *Columbian Centinel*, July 11, 1801, as quoted in Warren, 225–27.
[2] *Correspondence and Public Papers of John Jay:* Johnston, III,
478–85.
[3] Wharton: *State Trials of the U.S. during the Administrations of
Washington and Adams*, 60 *et seq.*; and see Wilson's law lecture on
the subject, Wilson, III, 384.

dicted in the United States District Court of Pennsylvania for sending an anonymous and threatening letter to the British Minister and to other persons in order to extort money from them. There was not a word in any act of Congress that referred even indirectly to such a misdemeanor, yet Justices Wilson and Iredell of the Supreme Court, with Judge Peters of the District Court, held that the court had jurisdiction,[1] and at the trial Chief Justice Jay and District Judge Peters held that the rash Genoese could be tried and punished under the common law of England.[2]

Three months later Gideon Henfield was brought to trial for the violation of the Neutrality Proclamation. The accused, a sailor from Salem, Massachusetts, had enlisted at Charleston, South Carolina, on a French privateer and was given a commission as an officer of the French Republic. As such he preyed upon the vessels of the enemies of France. One morning in May, 1793, Captain Henfield sailed into the port of Philadelphia in charge of a British prize captured by the French privateer which he commanded.

Upon demand of the British Minister, Henfield was seized, indicted, and tried in the United States Circuit Court for the District of Pennsylvania.[3] In the absence of any National legislation covering the

---

[1] 2 Dallas, 297–99.

[2] *Ib.* Ravara was tried and convicted by the jury under the instructions of the bench, "but he was afterward pardoned on condition that he surrender his commission and Exequatur." (Wharton: *State Trials*, 90–92.)

[3] For the documents preceding the arrest and prosecution of Henfield, see Wharton: *State Trials*, footnotes to 49–52.

subject, Justice Wilson instructed the grand jury that Henfield could, and should, be indicted and punished under British precedents.[1] When the case was heard the charge of the court to the trial jury was to the same effect.[2]

The jury refused to convict.[3] The verdict was "celebrated with extravagant marks of joy and exultation," records Marshall in his account of this memorable trial. "It was universally asked," he says, "what law had been offended, and under what statute was the indictment supported? Were the American people already prepared to give to a proclamation the force of a legislative act, and to subject themselves to the will of the executive? But if they were already sunk to such a state of degradation, were they to be punished for violating a proclamation which had not been published when the offense was committed, if indeed it could be termed an offense to engage with France, combating for liberty against the combined despots of Europe?" [4]

In this wise, political passions were made to strengthen the general protest against riveting the common law of England upon the American people by judicial fiat and without authorization by the National Legislature.

Isaac Williams was indicted and tried in 1799, in the United States Circuit Court for the District of

[1] See Wilson's charge, Wharton: *State Trials*, 59–66.
[2] See Wharton's summary of Wilson's second charge, *ib.* footnote to 85.
[3] *Ib.* 88.
[4] Marshall: *Life of George Washington*, 2d ed. II, 273–74. After the Henfield and Ravara cases, Congress passed a law applicable to such offenses. (See Wharton: *State Trials*, 93–101.)

Connecticut, for violating our treaty with Great Britain by serving as a French naval officer. Williams proved that he had for years been a citizen of France, having been "duly naturalized" in France, "renouncing his allegiance to all other countries, particularly to America, and taking an oath of allegiance to the Republic of France." Although these facts were admitted by counsel for the Government, and although Congress had not passed any statute covering such cases, Chief Justice Oliver Ellsworth practically instructed the jury that under the British common law Williams must be found guilty.

No American could cease to be a citizen of his own country and become a citizen or subject of another country, he said, "without the consent .. of the community." [1] The Chief Justice announced as American law the doctrine then enforced by European nations — "born a subject, always a subject." [2] So the defendant was convicted and sentenced "to pay a fine of a thousand dollars and to suffer four months imprisonment." [3]

These are examples of the application by the National courts of the common law of England in cases

---

[1] Wharton: *State Trials*, 653–54.

[2] This was the British defense for impressment of seamen on American ships. It was one of the chief points in dispute in the War of 1812. The adherence of Federalists to this doctrine was one of the many causes of the overthrow of that once great party. (See *infra*, vol. IV, chap. I, of this work.)

[3] Wharton: *State Trials*, 654. Upon another indictment for having captured a British ship and crew, Williams, with no other defense than that offered on his trial under the first indictment, pleaded guilty, and was sentenced to an additional fine of a thousand dollars, and to further imprisonment of four months. (*Ib.*; see also vol. II, 495, of this work.)

where Congress had failed or refused to act. Crime
must be punished, said the judges; if Congress would
not make the necessary laws, the courts would act
without statutory authority. Until 1812, when the
Supreme Court put an end to this doctrine,[1] the
National courts, with one exception,[2] continued to
apply the common law to crimes and offenses which
Congress had refused to recognize as such, and for
which American statutes made no provision.

Practically all of the National and many of the
State judges were highly learned in the law, and, of
course, drew their inspiration from British precedents and the British bench. Indeed, some of them
were more British than they were American.[3] "Let
a stranger go into our courts,' wrote Tyler, "and he

[1] U.S. *vs.* Hudson, 7 Cranch, 32–34. "Although this question is
brought up now for the first time to be decided by this court, we consider it as having been long since settled in public opinion. . . The legislative authority of the Union must first make an act a crime, affix a
punishment to it and declare the court that shall have jurisdiction of
the offense." (Justice William Johnson delivering the opinion of the
majority of the court, *ib.*)

Joseph Story was frantic because the National judges could not
apply the common law during the War of 1812. (See his passionate
letters on the subject, vol. IV, chap. I, of this work; and see his
argument for the common law, Story, I, 297–300; see also Peters to
Pickering, Dec. 5, 1807, March 30, and April 14, 1816, Pickering
MSS. Mass. Hist. Soc.)

[2] The opinion of Justice Chase, of the Supreme Court of Philadelphia, sitting with Peters, District Judge, in the case of the United
States *vs.* Robert Worral, indicted under the common law for attempting to bribe a United States officer. Justice Chase held that English
common law was not a part of the jurisprudence of the United States
as a Nation. (Wharton: *State Trials,* 189–99.)

[3] This was notably true of Justice James Wilson, of the Supreme
Court, and Alexander Addison, President Judge of the Fifth Pennsylvania (State) Circuit, both of whom were born and educated in the
United Kingdom. They were two of the ablest and most learned men
on the bench at that period.

would almost believe himself in the Court of the King's Bench." [1]

This conduct of the National Judiciary furnished Jefferson with another of those "issues" of which that astute politician knew how to make such effective use. He quickly seized upon it, and with characteristic fervency of phrase used it as a powerful weapon against the Federalist Party. All the evil things accomplished by that organization of "monocrats," "aristocrats," and "monarchists" — the bank, the treaty, the Sedition Act, even the army and the navy — "have been solitary, inconsequential, timid things," avowed Jefferson, "in comparison with the audacious, barefaced and sweeping pretension to a system of law for the U.S. without the adoption of their legislature, and so infinitely beyond their power to adopt." [2]

But if the National judges had caused alarm by treating the common law as though it were a statute of the United States without waiting for an act of Congress to make it so, their manners and methods in the enforcement of the Sedition Act [3] aroused against them an ever-increasing hostility.

Stories of their performances on the bench in such cases — their tones when speaking to counsel, to accused persons, and even to witnesses, their immoderate language, their sympathy with one of the European nations then at war and their animosity

---

[1] Message of Governor John Tyler, Dec. 3, 1810, Tyler: *Letters and Times of the Tylers*, I, 261; and see Tyler to Monroe, Dec. 4, 1809, *ib.* 232.

[2] Jefferson to Randolph, Aug. 18, 1799, *Works*: Ford, IX, 73.

[3] See vol. II, chaps. X and XI, of this work.

toward the other, their partisanship in cases on trial before them — tales made up from such material flew from mouth to mouth, until finally the very name and sight of National judges became obnoxious to most Americans. In short, the assaults upon the National Judiciary were made possible chiefly by the conduct of the National judges themselves.[1]

The first man convicted under the Sedition Law was a Representative in Congress, the notorious Matthew Lyon of Vermont. He had charged President Adams with a "continual grasp for power . . an unbounded thirst for ridiculous pomp, foolish adulation and selfish avarice." Also, Lyon had permitted the publication of a letter to him from Joel Barlow, in which the President's address to the Senate and the Senate's response[2] were referred to as "the bullying speech of your President" and "the stupid answer of your Senate"; and expressed wonder "that the answer of both Houses had not

[1] The National judges, in their charges to grand juries, lectured and preached on religion, on morality, on partisan politics.

"On Monday last the Circuit Court of the United States was opened in this town. The Hon. Judge Patterson . . delivered a most elegant and appropriate charge.

"The *Law* was laid down in a masterly manner: *Politics* were set in their true light by holding up the Jacobins [Republicans] as the disorganizers of our happy country, and the only instruments of introducing discontent and dissatisfaction among the well meaning part of the community. *Religion & Morality* were pleasingly inculcated and enforced as being necessary to good government, good order, and good laws; for 'when the righteous [Federalists] are in authority, the people rejoice.' . .

"After the charge was delivered the Rev. Mr. Alden addressed the Throne of Grace in an excellent and well adapted prayer." (*United States Oracle of the Day*, May 24, 1800, as quoted by Hackett, in *Green Bag*, II, 264.)

[2] Adams's War Speech of 1798; see vol. II, 351, of this work.

been an order to send him [Adams] to the mad house." [1]

Lyon was indicted under the accusation that he had tried "to stir up sedition and to bring the President and Government of the United States into contempt." He declared that the jury was selected from his enemies. [2] Under the charge of Justice Paterson of the Supreme Court he was convicted. The court sentenced him to four months in jail and the payment of a fine of one thousand dollars. [3]

In the execution of the sentence, United States Marshal Jabez G. Fitch used the prisoner cruelly. On the way to the jail at Vergennes, Vermont, he was repeatedly insulted. He was finally thrown into a filthy, stench-filled cell without a fireplace and with nothing "but the iron bars to keep the cold out." It was "the common receptacle for horse-thieves . . runaway negroes, or any kind of felons." He was subjected to the same kind of treatment that was accorded in those days to the lowest criminals. [4] The people were deeply stirred by the fate of Matthew Lyon. Quick to realize and respond to public feeling, Jefferson wrote: "I know not which mortifies me most, that I should fear to write what I think, or my country bear such a state of things." [5]

One Anthony Haswell, editor of the *Vermont Ga-*

[1] Wharton: *State Trials*, 333–34.   [2] *Ib.* 339.

[3] *Ib.* 337. Paterson sat with District Judge Hitchcock and delivered the charge in this case. Luther Martin in the trial of Justice Chase (see *infra*, chap. IV) said that Paterson was "mild and amiable," and noted for his "suavity of manners." (*Trial of the Hon. Samuel Chase:* Evans, stenographer, 187–88.)

[4] See Lyon to Mason, Oct. 14, 1798, Wharton: *State Trials*, 339–41.

[5] Jefferson to Taylor, Nov. 26, 1798, Jefferson MSS. Lib. Cong.

zette published at Bennington, printed an advertisement of a lottery by which friends of Lyon, who was a poor man, hoped to raise enough money to pay his fine. This advertisement was addressed "to the enemies of political persecutions in the western district of Vermont." It was asserted that Lyon "is holden by the oppressive hand of usurped power in a loathsome prison, deprived almost of the right of reason, and suffering all the indignities which can be heaped upon him by a hard-hearted savage, who has, to the disgrace of Federalism, been elevated to a station where he can satiate his barbarity on the misery of his victims." [1] The "savage" referred to was United States Marshal Fitch. In the same paper an excerpt was reprinted from the *Aurora* which declared that "the administration publically notified that Tories .. were worthy of the confidence of the government." [2]

Haswell was indicted for sedition. In defense he established the brutality with which Lyon had been treated and proposed to prove by two witnesses not then present (General James Drake of Virginia, and James McHenry, President Adams's Secretary of War) that the Government favored the occasional appointment of Tories to office. Justice Paterson ruled that such evidence was inadmissible, and charged the jury that if Haswell's intent was defamatory, he should be found guilty. Thereupon he was convicted and sentenced to two months' imprisonment and the payment of a fine of two hundred dollars. [3]

[1] Wharton: *State Trials*, 684.   [2] *Ib.* 685.   [3] *Ib.* 685–86.

Dr. Thomas Cooper, editor of the *Sunbury and Northumberland Gazette* in Pennsylvania, in the course of a political controversy declared in his paper that when, in the beginning of Adams's Administration, he had asked the President for an office, Adams "was hardly in the infancy of political mistake; even those who doubted his capacity thought well of his intentions. . . Nor were we yet saddled with the expense of a permanent navy, or threatened . . with the existence of a standing army. . . Mr. Adams . . had not yet interfered . . to influence the decisions of a court of justice." [1]

For this "attack" upon the President, Cooper was indicted under the Sedition Law. Conducting his own defense, he pointed out the issues that divided the two great parties, and insisted upon the propriety of such political criticism as that for which he had been indicted.

Cooper was himself learned in the law, [2] and during the trial he applied for a subpœna *duces tecum* to compel President Adams to attend as a witness, bringing with him certain documents which Cooper alleged to be necessary to his defense. In a rage Justice Samuel Chase of the Supreme Court, before whom, with Judge Richard Peters of the District Court, the case was tried, refused to issue the writ. For this he was denounced by the Republicans. In the trial of Aaron Burr, Marshall was to issue this very writ to President Thomas Jefferson and, for doing so, to be rebuked, denounced, and abused by the very parti-

[1] Wharton: *State Trials*, 661–62. Cooper was referring to the case of Jonathan Robins. (See vol. II, 458–75, of this work.)

[2] Cooper afterward became a State judge.

sans who now assailed Justice Chase for refusing to grant it.[1]

Justice Chase charged the jury at intolerable length: "If a man attempts to destroy the confidence of the people in their officers . . he effectually saps the foundation of the government." It was plain that Cooper "intended to provoke" the Administration, for had he not admitted that, although he did not arraign the motives, he did mean "to censure the conduct of the President"? The offending editor's statement that "our credit is so low that we are obliged to borrow money at 8 per cent. in time of peace," especially irritated the Justice. "I cannot," he cried, "suppress my feelings at this gross attack upon the President." Chase then told the jury that the conduct of France had "rendered a loan necessary"; that undoubtedly Cooper had intended "to mislead the ignorant . . and to influence their votes on the next election."

So Cooper was convicted and sentenced "to pay a fine of four hundred dollars, to be imprisoned for six months, and at the end of that period to find surety for his good behavior himself in a thousand, and two sureties in five hundred dollars each."[2]

"Almost every other country" had been "convulsed with . . war," desolated by "every species of vice and disorder" which left innocence without protection and encouraged "the basest crimes." Only in America there was no "grievance to complain of." Yet our Government had been "as

[1] See *infra*, chap. VIII.

[2] Wharton: *State Trials*, 679. Stephen Girard paid Cooper's fine. (McMaster: *Life and Times of Stephen Girard*, I, 397–98.)

grossly abused as if it had been guilty of the vilest
tyranny" — as if real "republicanism" could "only
be found in the happy soil of France" where "Liberty, like the religion of Mahomet, is propagated by
the sword." In the "bosom" of that nation "a dagger was concealed." [1] In these terms spoke James
Iredell, Associate Justice of the Supreme Court,
in addressing the grand jury for the District of
Pennsylvania. He was delivering the charge that
resulted in the indictment for treason of John
Fries and others who had resisted the Federalist
land tax. [2]

The triumph of France had, of course, nothing
whatever to do with the forcible protest of the Pennsylvania farmers against what they felt to be Federalist extortion; nevertheless upon the charge of
Justice Iredell as to the law of treason, they were
indicted and convicted for that gravest of all offenses. A new trial was granted because one of the
jury, John Rhoad, "had declared a prejudice against
the prisoner after he was summoned as a juror." [3] On
April 29, 1800, the second trial was held. This time
Justice Chase presided. The facts were agreed to by
counsel. Before the jury had been sworn, Chase
threw on the table three papers in writing and announced that these contained the opinion of the
judges upon the law of treason — one copy was for
the counsel for the Government, one for the defendant's counsel, and one for the jury.

William Lewis, leading attorney for Fries, and one

---

[1] Wharton: *State Trials*, 466–69.
[2] See vol. II, 429 *et seq.* of this work.
[3] Wharton: *State Trials*, 598–609.

of the ablest members of the Philadelphia bar,[1] was enraged. He looked upon the paper, flung it from him, declaring that "his hand never should be polluted by a prejudicated opinion," and withdrew from the case, although Chase tried to persuade him to "go on in any manner he liked." Alexander J. Dallas, the other counsel for Fries, also withdrew, and the terrified prisoner was left to defend himself. The court told him that the judges, personally, would see that justice was done him. Again Fries and his accomplices were convicted under the charge of the court. "In an aweful and affecting manner"[2] Chase pronounced the sentence, which was that the condemned men should be "hanged by the neck *until dead*." [3]

The Republicans furiously assailed this conviction and sentence. President Adams pardoned Fries and his associates, to the disgust and resentment of the Federalist leaders.[4] On both sides the entire proceeding was made a political issue.

On the heels of this "repetition of outrage," as the Republicans promptly labeled the condemnation of Fries, trod the trial of James Thompson Callender for sedition, over which it was again the fate of the unlucky Chase to preside. *The Prospect Before Us*, written by Callender under the encouragement of Jefferson,[5] contained a characteristically vicious

---

[1] For sketch of Lewis see Wharton: *State Trials*, 32–33.
[2] *Independent Chronicle*, Boston, May 12, 1800.
[3] Wharton: *State Trials*, 641 *et seq.*
[4] See vol. II, 429 *et seq.* of this work.
[5] Jefferson to Mason, Oct. 11, 1798, *Works:* Ford, VIII, 449–50; same to Callender, Sept. 6, 1799, *ib.* IX, 81–82; same to same, Oct. 6, 1799, *ib.* 83–84; Pickering to Higginson, Jan. 6, 1804, Pickering MSS. Mass. Hist. Soc.

screed against Adams. His Administration had been "a tempest of malignant passions"; his system had been "a French war, an American navy, a large standing army, an additional load of taxes." He "was a professed aristocrat and he had proved faithful and serviceable to the British interest" by sending Marshall and his associates to France. In the President's speech to Congress,[1] "this hoary headed incendiary . . bawls to arms! then to arms!"

Callender was indicted for libel under the Sedition Law.

Before Judge Chase started for Virginia, Luther Martin had given him a copy of Callender's pamphlet, with the offensive passages underscored. During a session of the National court at Annapolis, Chase, in a "jocular conversation," had said that he would take Callender's book with him to Richmond, and that, "if Virginia was not too depraved" to furnish a jury of respectable men, he would certainly punish Callender. He would teach the lawyers of Virginia the difference between the liberty and the licentiousness of the press.[2] On the road to Richmond, James Triplett boarded the stage that carried the avenging Justice of the Supreme Court. He told Chase that Callender had once been arrested in Virginia as a vagrant. "It is a pity," replied Chase, "that they had not hanged the rascal." [3]

[1] War speech of Adams to Congress in 1798, see vol. II, 351, of this work.

[2] Testimony of James Winchester (*Annals*, 8th Cong. 2d Sess. 246–47); of Luther Martin (*ib.* 245–46); and of John T. Mason (*ib.* 216); see also *Chase Trial*, 63.

[3] Testimony of James Triplett, *Chase Trial*, 44–45, and see *Annals*, 8th Cong. 2d Sess. 217–19.

But the people of Virginia, because of their hatred of the Sedition Law, were ardent champions of Callender. Richmond lawyers were hostile to Chase and were the bitter enemies of the statute which they knew he would enforce. Jefferson was anxious that Callender "should be substantially defended, whether in the first stages by public interference or private contributors." [1]

One ambitious young attorney, George Hay, who seven years later was to act as prosecutor in the greatest trial at which John Marshall ever presided,[2] volunteered to defend Callender, animated to this course by devotion to "the cause of the Constitution," in spite of the fact that he "despised" his adopted client.[3] William Wirt was also inspired to offer his services in the interest of free speech. These Virginia attorneys would show this tyrant of the National Judiciary that the Virginia bar could not be borne down.[4] Of all this the hot-spirited Chase

[1] Jefferson to Monroe, May 26, 1800, *Works:* Ford, IX, 136. By "public interference" Jefferson meant an appropriation by the Virginia Legislature. (*Ib.* 137.)

[2] The trial of Aaron Burr, see *infra*, chaps. VI, VII, VIII, and IX.

[3] See testimony of George Hay, *Annals*, 8th Cong. 2d Sess. 203; and see especially Luther Martin's comments thereon, *infra*, chap. IV.

[4] The public mind was well prepared for just such appeals as those that Hay and Wirt planned to make. For instance, the citizens of Caroline County subscribed more than one hundred dollars for Callender's use.

The subscription paper, probably drawn by Colonel John Taylor, in whose hands the money was placed, declared that Callender "has a cause closely allied to the preservation of the Constitution, and to the freedom of public opinion; and that he ought to be comforted in his bonds."

Callender was "a sufferer for those principles." Therefore, and "because also he is poor and has three infant children who live by his daily labor" the contributors freely gave the money "to be applied

was advised; and he resolved to forestall the passionate young defenders of liberty. He was as witty as he was fearless, and throughout the trial brought down on Hay and Wirt the laughter of the spectators.

But in the court-room there was one spectator who did not laugh. John Marshall, then Secretary of State, witnessed the proceedings [1] with grave misgivings.

Chase frequently interrupted the defendant's counsel. "What," said he, "must there be a departure from common sense to find out a construction favorable" to Callender? The Justice declared that a legal point which Hay attempted to make was "a wild notion." [2] When a juror said that he had never seen the indictment or heard it read, Chase declared that of course he could not have formed or delivered an opinion on the charges; and then denied the request that the indictment be read for the information of the juror. Chase would not permit that eminent patriot and publicist, Colonel John Taylor of Caroline, to testify that part of Callender's statement was true; "No evidence is admissible," said the Justice, "that does not . . justify the whole charge." [3]

William Wirt, in addressing the jury, was arguing that if the jury believed the Sedition Act to be unconstitutional, and yet found Callender guilty, they

---

to the use of James T. Callender, and if he should die in prison, to the use of his children." (*Independent Chronicle*, Boston, July 10, 1800.)

[1] See *infra*, chap. IV.

[2] Wharton: *State Trials*, 692.

[3] *Ib.* 696–98; and see testimony of Taylor, *Chase Trial*, 38–39.

"would violate their oath." Chase ordered him to sit down. The jury had no right to pass upon the constitutionality of the law — "such a power would be extremely dangerous. Hear my words, I wish the world to know them." The Justice then read a long and very able opinion which he had carefully prepared in anticipation that this point would be raised by the defense.[1] After another interruption, in which Chase referred to Wirt as " the *young gentleman* " in a manner that vastly amused the audience, the discomfited lawyer, covered with confusion, abandoned the case.

When Hay, in his turn, was addressing the jury, Chase twice interrupted him, asserting that the beardless attorney was not stating the law correctly. The reporter notes that thereupon "Mr. Hay folded up and put away his papers . . and refused to proceed." The Justice begged him to go on, but Hay indignantly stalked from the room.

Acting under the instructions of Chase, Callender was convicted. The court sentenced him to imprisonment for nine months, and to pay a fine of two hundred dollars.[2]

The proceedings at this trial were widely published. The growing indignation of the people at the courts rose to a dangerous point. The force of popu-

[1] Wharton: *State Trials*, 717–18. Chase's charge to the jury was an argument that the constitutionality of a law could not be determined by a jury, but belonged exclusively to the Judicial Department. For a brief *précis* of this opinion see chap. III of this volume. Chase advanced most of the arguments used by Marshall in Marbury *vs.* Madison.

[2] *Ib.* 718. When Jefferson became President he immediately pardoned Callender. (See next chapter.)

lar wrath was increased by the alarm of the bar, which generally had been the stanch supporter of the bench.[1]

Hastening from Richmond to New Castle, Delaware, Justice Chase emphasized the opinion now current that he was an American Jeffreys and typical of the spirit of the whole National Judiciary. Upon opening court, he said that he had heard that there was a seditious newspaper in the State. He directed the United States Attorney to search the files of all the papers that could be found, and to report any abusive language discovered. It was the haying season, and the grand jury, most of whom were farmers, asked to be discharged, since there was no business for them to transact. Chase refused and held them until the next day, in order to have them return indictments against any printer that might have criticized the Administration.[2] But the prosecutor's investigation discovered nothing "treasonable" except a brief and unpleasant reference to Chase himself. So ended the Delaware visit of the ferret of the National Judiciary.

Thus a popular conviction grew up that no man was safe who assumed to criticize National officials. The persecution of Matthew Lyon was recalled, and the punishment of other citizens in cases less widely known [3] became the subject of common talk, — all

[1] Wharton: *State Trials*, footnote to 718.

[2] See testimonies of Gunning Bedford, Nicholas Vandyke, Archibald Hamilton, John Hall, and Samuel P. Moore, *Chase Trial*, 98–101.

[3] For example, one Charles Holt, publisher of a newspaper, *The Bee*, of New London, Connecticut, had commented on the uselessness of enlisting in the army, and reflected upon the wisdom of the Admin-

adding to the growing popular wrath against the
whole National Judiciary. The people regarded
those brought under the lash of justice as martyrs
to the cause of free speech; and so, indeed, they
were.

The method of securing indictments and convictions also met with public condemnation. In many
States the United States Marshals selected what
persons they pleased as members of the grand juries
and trial juries. These officers of the National courts
were, without exception, Federalists; in many cases
Federalist politicians. When making up juries they
selected only persons of the same manner of thinking
as that of the marshals and judges themselves.[1] So
it was that the juries were nothing more than
machines that registered the will, opinion, or even
inclination of the National judges and the United
States District Attorneys. In short, in these prose-

istration's policy; for this he was indicted, convicted, and sentenced
to three months' imprisonment, and the payment of a fine of two
hundred dollars. (Randall: *Life of Thomas Jefferson*, ii, 418.)

When President Adams passed through Newark, New Jersey, the
local artillery company fired a salute. One of the observers, a man
named Baldwin, idly remarked that "he wished the wadding from
the cannon had been lodged in the President's backside." For this
seditious remark Baldwin was fined one hundred dollars. (Hammond:
History of Political Parties in the State of New York, i, 130–31.)

One Jared Peck, a New York State Senator, circulated among his
neighbors a petition to Congress to repeal the Alien and Sedition
Laws. This shocking act of sedition was taken up by the United
States District Attorney for New York, who procured the indictment
of Peck; and upon bench warrant, the offender was arrested and
taken to New York for trial. It seems that such were the demonstra-
tions of the people, wherever Peck appeared in custody of the officer,
that the case was dropped. (Randall, ii, 420.)

[1] They were supposed to select juries according to the laws of the
States where the courts were held. As a matter of fact they called
the men they wished to serve.

cutions, trial by jury in any real sense was not to be had.[1]

Certain State judges of the rabid Federalist type, apostles of "the wise, the rich, and the good" political religion, were as insulting in their bearing, as immoderate in their speech, and as intolerant in their conduct as some of the National judges; and prosecutions in some State courts were as bad as the worst of those in the National tribunals.

In Boston, when the Legislature of Massachusetts was considering the Kentucky and Virginia Resolutions, John Bacon of Berkshire, a Republican State Senator, and Dr. Aaron Hill of Cambridge, the leader of the Republicans in the House, resisted the proposed answer of the Federalist majority. Both maintained the ground upon which Republicans everywhere now stood — that any State might disregard an act of Congress which it deemed unconstitutional.[2] Bacon and Hill were supported by the solid Republican membership of the Massachusetts Legislature, which the *Columbian Centinel* of Boston, a Federalist organ, called a "contemptible minority," every member of which was "worse than an infidel."[3]

The *Independent Chronicle*, the Republican newspaper of Boston, observed that "It is difficult for the

[1] McMaster: *History of the People of the United States*, II, 473; and see speech of Charles Pinckney in the Senate, March 5, 1800, *Annals*, 6th Cong. 1st and 2d Sess. 97.

[2] See speech of Bacon in the *Independent Chronicle*, Feb. 11–14, 1799; and of Hill, *ib.* Feb. 25, 1799.

[3] *Columbian Centinel*, Feb. 16, 1799; also see issue of Jan. 23, 1799. For condensed account of this incident see Anderson in *Am. Hist. Rev.* v, 60–62, quoting the *Centinel* as cited. A Federalist mob stoned the house of Dr. Hill the night after he made this speech. (*Ib.*) See also *infra*, chap. III.

common capacities to conceive of a sovereignty so situated that the *Sovereign shall have no right to decide on any invasion of his constitutional powers.*" Bacon's speech, said the *Chronicle*, "has been read with delight by all true Republicans, and will always stand as a monument of his firmness, patriotism, and integrity... The name of an *American* Bacon will be handed down to the latest generations of freemen with high respect and gratitude, while the names of such as have aimed a *death wound* to the Constitution of the United States will rot *above ground* and be unsavoury to the nostrils of every lover of Republican freedom." [1]

The *Massachusetts Mercury* of February 22, 1799, reports that "On Tuesday last.. Chief Justice Dana.. commented on the contents of the *Independent Chronicle* of the preceding day. He properly stated to the Jury that though he was not a subscriber to the paper, he obtained *that one* by accident, that if he was, his conscience would charge him with assisting to support a traitorous enmity to the Government of his Country."

Thereupon Thomas Adams, the publisher, and Abijah Adams, a younger brother employed in the office, were indicted under the common law for attempting "to bring the government into disrespect, hatred, and contempt," and for encouraging sedition. Thomas Adams was fatally ill and Abijah only was brought to trial. Under the instructions of the court he was convicted. In pronouncing sentence Chief Justice Dana delivered a political lecture.

[1] *Independent Chronicle*, Feb. 18, 1799.

The Virginia and Kentucky Resolutions, he said, had attempted "to establish the monstrous position" that the individual States had the right to pass upon the constitutionality of acts of Congress. He then gave a résumé of the reply of the majority of the Massachusetts Legislature to the Virginia Resolutions. This reply asserted that the decisions of all questions arising under the Constitution and laws of the United States "are exclusively vested in the Judicial Courts of the United States," and that the Sedition Act was "wise and necessary, as an audacious and unprincipled spirit of falsehood and abuse had been too long unremittingly exerted for the purpose of *perverting* public opinion, and threatened to undermine the whole fabric of government." The irate judge declared that the *Chronicle's* criticism of this action of the majority of the Legislature and its praise of the Republican minority of that body was an "indecent and outrageous calumny."

"Censurable as the libel may be in itself," Dana continued, the principles stated by Adams's counsel in conducting his defense were equally "dangerous to public tranquility." These daring lawyers had actually maintained the principle of the liberty of the press. They had denied that an American citizen could be punished under the common law of England. "Novel and disorganizing doctrines," exclaimed Dana in the midst of a long argument to prove that the common law was operative in the United States.[1]

[1] *Columbian Centinel*, March 30, 1799. The attorneys for Adams also advanced the doctrines of the Kentucky and Virginia Resolutions.

In view of the fact that Abijah Adams was not the author of the libel, nor even the publisher or editor of the *Chronicle*, but was "the only person to whom the public can look for retribution," the court graciously sentenced him to only one month's imprisonment, but required him to find sureties for his good behavior for a year, and to pay the costs of the trial.[1]

Alexander Addison, the presiding judge of one of the Pennsylvania State courts, was another Federalist State judge whose judicial conduct and assaults from the bench upon democracy had helped to bring courts into disrepute. Some of his charges to grand juries were nothing but denunciations of Republican principles.[2]

His manner on the bench was imperious; he bul-

---

so far, at least, as to assert that any State ought to protest against and resist any act of Congress that the Commonwealth believed to be in violation of the National Constitution. (Anderson, in *Am. Hist. Rev.* v, 226–27.)

[1] *Columbian Centinel*, March 27, 1799.
Another instance of intolerant and partisan prosecutions in State courts was the case of Duane and others, indicted and tried for getting signatures to a petition in Congress against the Alien and Sedition Laws. They were acquitted, however. (Wharton: *State Trials*, 345–89.)

[2] These charges of Judge Addison were, in reality, political pamphlets. They had not the least reference to any business before the court, and were no more appropriate than sermons. They were, however, written with uncommon ability. It is doubtful whether any arguments more weighty have since been produced against what George Cabot called "excessive democracy." These grand jury charges of Addison were entitled: "Causes and Error of Complaints and Jealousy of the Administration of the Government"; "Charges to the Grand Juries of the County Court of the Fifth Circuit of the State of Pennsylvania, at December Session, 1798"; "The Liberty of Speech and of the Press"; "Charge to Grand Juries, 1798"; "Rise and Progress of Revolution," and "A Charge to the Grand Juries of the State of Pennsylvania, at December Session, 1800."

lied counsel, browbeat witnesses, governed his associate judges, ruled juries. In one case,[1] Addison forbade the Associate Judge to address the jury, and prevented him from doing so.[2]

Nor did the judges stop with lecturing everybody from the bench. Carrying with them the authority of their exalted positions, more than one of them, notably Justice Chase and Judge Addison, took the stump in political campaigns and made partisan speeches.[3]

So it fell out that the manners, language, and conduct of the judges themselves, together with their use of the bench as a political rostrum, their partisanship as to the European belligerents, their merciless enforcement of the common law — aroused that public fear and hatred of the courts which gave Jefferson and the Republicans their opportunity. The questions which lay at the root of the Republican assault upon the Judiciary would not of themselves, and without the human and dramatic incidents of which the cases mentioned are examples, have wrought up among citizens that fighting spirit essential to a successful onslaught upon the

[1] Coulter *vs.* Moore, for defamation. Coulter, a justice of the peace, sued Moore for having declared, in effect, that Coulter "kept a house of ill fame." (*Trial of Alexander Addison, Esq.*: Lloyd, stenographer, 38; also Wharton: *State Trials*, 32 *et seq.*)

[2] This judge was John C. B. Lucas. He was a Frenchman speaking broken English, and, judging from the record, was a person of very inferior ability. There seems to be no doubt that he was the mere tool of another judge, Hugh H. Brackenridge, who hated Addison virulently. From a study of the case, one cannot be surprised that the able and erudite Addison held in greatest contempt the fussy and ignorant Lucas.

[3] Wharton: *State Trials*, 45; Carson: *Supreme Court of the United States, Its History*, I, 193.

National system of justice, which the Federalists had made so completely their own.[1]

Those basic questions thus brought theatrically before the people's eyes, had been created by the Alien and Sedition Laws, and by the Virginia and Kentucky Resolutions which those undemocratic statutes called forth. Freedom of speech on the one hand and Nationalism on the other hand, the crushing of "sedition" as against that license which Localism permitted — such were the issues which the imprudence and hot-headedness of the Federalist judges had brought up for settlement. Thus, unhappily, democracy marched arm in arm with State Rights, while Nationalism found itself the intimate companion of a narrow, bigoted, and retrograde conservatism.

Had not the Federalists, arrogant with power and frantic with hatred of France and fast becoming zealots in their championship of Great Britain, passed the drastic laws against liberty of the press and freedom of speech; had not the Republican protest against these statutes taken the form of the assertion that individual States might declare uncon-

---

[1] The uprising against the Judiciary naturally began in Pennsylvania where the extravagance of the judges had been carried to the most picturesque as well as obnoxious extremes. For a faithful narrative of these see McMaster: *U.S.* III, 153–55.

On the other hand, wherever Republicans occupied judicial positions, the voice from the bench, while contrary to that of the Federalist judges, was no less harsh and absolute.

For instance, the judges of the Supreme Court of New Hampshire refused to listen to the reading of British law reports, because they were from "musty, old, worm-eaten books." One of the judges declared that "not Common Law — not the quirks of Coke and Blackstone — but common sense" controlled American judges. (Warren, 227.)

stitutional and disregard the acts of the National
Legislature; and finally, had not National tribunals
and some judges of State courts been so harsh and
insolent, the Republican assault upon the National
Judiciary,[1] the echoes of which loudly sound in our
ears even to the present day, probably never would
have been made.

But for these things, Marbury *vs*. Madison [2] might
never have been written; the Supreme Court might
have remained nothing more than the comparatively
powerless institution that ultimate appellate judicial
establishments are in other countries; and the career
of John Marshall might have been no more notable
and distinguished than that of the many ghostly
figures in the shadowy procession of our judicial history. But the Republican condemnations of the severe punishment that the Federalists inflicted upon
anybody who criticized the Government, raised fundamental issues and created conditions that forced
action on those issues.

[1] See next chapter.

[2] See *infra*, chap. III, for a résumé of the conditions that forced
Marshall to pronounce his famous opinion in the case of Marbury *vs*.
Madison, as well as for a full discussion of that controversy

CHAPTER II

THE ASSAULT ON THE JUDICIARY

The angels of destruction are making haste.   Our judges are to be as independent as spaniels.   (Fisher Ames.)

The power which has the right of passing, without appeal, on the validity of your laws, is your sovereign.   (John Randolph.)

ON January 6, 1802, an atmosphere of intense but suppressed excitement pervaded the little semicircular room where the Senate of the United States was in session.[1] The Republican assault upon the Judiciary was about to begin and the Federalists in Congress had nerved themselves for their last great fight. The impending debate was to prove one of the permanently notable engagements in American legislative history and was to create a situation which, in a few months, forced John Marshall to pronounce the first of those fundamental opinions which have helped to shape and which still influence the destiny of the American Nation.

The decision of Marbury *vs.* Madison was to be made inevitable by the great controversy to which we are now to listen. Marshall's course, and, indeed, his opinion in this famous case, cannot be understood without a thorough knowledge of the notable debate in Congress which immediately preceded it.[2]

Never was the effect of the long years of party

[1] The Senate then met in the chamber now occupied by the Supreme Court.

[2] See *infra*, chap. III.

training which Jefferson had given the Republicans better manifested than now. There was unsparing party discipline, perfect harmony of party plan. The President himself gave the signal for attack, but with such skill that while his lieutenants in House and Senate understood their orders and were eager to execute them, the rank and file of the Federalist voters, whom Jefferson hoped to win to the Republican cause in the years to come, were soothed rather than irritated by the seeming moderation and reasonableness of the President's words.

"The Judiciary system . . and especially that portion of it recently enacted, will, of course, present itself to the contemplation of Congress," was the almost casual reference in the President's first Message to the Republican purpose to subjugate the National Judiciary. To assist Senators and Representatives in determining "the proportion which the institution bears to the business it has to perform" Jefferson had "procured from the several states . . an exact statement of all the causes decided since the first establishment of the courts and of the causes which were pending when additional courts and judges were brought to their aid." This summary he transmitted to the law-making body.

In a seeming spirit of impartiality, almost of indifference, the President suggested Congressional inquiry as to whether jury trials had not been withheld in many cases, and advised the investigation of the manner of impaneling juries.[1]

---

[1] Jefferson to Congress, Dec. 8, 1801, *Works:* Ford, ix, 321 *et seq.*; also *Messages and Papers of the Presidents:* Richardson, i, 331.

Thus far and no farther went the comments on the National Judiciary which the President laid before Congress. The status of the courts — a question that filled the minds of all, both Federalists and Republicans — was not referred to. But the thought of it thrilled Jefferson, and only his caution restrained him from avowing it. Indeed, he had actually written into the message words as daring as those of his cherished Kentucky Resolutions; had boldly declared that the right existed in each department "to decide on the validity of an act according to its own judgment and uncontrolled by the opinions of any other department"; had asserted that he himself, as President, had the authority and power to decide the constitutionality of National laws; and had, as President, actually pronounced, in official form, the Sedition Act to be 'in palpable and unqualified contradiction to the Constitution." [1]

This was not merely a part of a first rough draft of this Presidential document, nor was it lightly cast aside. It was the most important paragraph of the completed Message. Jefferson had signed it on December 8, 1801, and it was ready for transmission to the National Legislature. But just before sending the Message to the Capitol, he struck out this passage,[2] and thus notes on the margin of the draft his reason for doing so: "This whole paragraph was omitted as capable of being chicaned, and furnishing something to the opposition to make a handle of.

[1] Jefferson, Jefferson MSS. Lib. Cong., partly quoted in Beard: *Economic Origins of Jeffersonian Democracy*, 454–55.

[2] For full text of this exposition of Constitutional law by Jefferson see Appendix A.

It was thought better that the message should be clear of everything which the public might be made to misunderstand."

Although Jefferson's programme, as stated in the altered message which he finally sent to Congress, did not arouse the rank and file of Federalist voters, it did alarm and anger the Federalist chieftains, who saw the real purpose back of the President's colorless words. Fisher Ames, that delightful reactionary, thus interpreted it: "The message announces the downfall of the late revision of the Judiciary; economy, the patriotism of the shallow and the trick of the ambitious. . . The U. S. Gov't . . is to be dismantled like an old ship. . . The state gov'ts are to be exhibited as alone safe and salutary." [1]

The Judiciary Law of 1801, which the Federalist majority enacted before their power over legislation passed forever from their hands, was one of the best considered and ablest measures ever devised by that constructive party.[2] Almost from the time of the organization of the National Judiciary the National judges had complained of the inadequacy and positive evils of the law under which they performed their duties. The famous Judiciary Act of 1789, which has received so much undeserved praise, did not entirely satisfy anybody except its author, Oliver Ellsworth. "It is a child of his and he defends

---

[1] Ames to King, Dec. 20, 1801, King, IV, 40.

Like most eminent Federalists, except Marshall, Hamilton, and Cabot, Fisher Ames was soon to abandon his Nationalism and become one of the leaders of the secession movement in New England. (See vol. IV, chap. I, of this work.)

[2] See vol. II, 531, 547–48, 550–52, of this work.

it . . with wrath and anger," wrote Maclay in his diary.[1]

In the first Congress opposition to the Ellsworth Act had been sharp and determined. Elbridge Gerry denounced the proposed National Judiciary as "a tyranny." [2] Samuel Livermore of New Hampshire called it "this new fangled system" which "would . . swallow up the State Courts." [3] James Jackson of Georgia declared that National courts would cruelly harass "the poor man." [4] Thomas Sumter of South Carolina saw in the Judiciary Bill "the iron hand of power." [5] Maclay feared that it would be "the gunpowder plot of the Constitution." [6]

When the Ellsworth Bill had become a law, Senator William Grayson of Virginia advised Patrick Henry that it "wears so monstrous an appearance that I think it will be *felo-de-se* in the execution. . . Whenever the Federal Judiciary comes into operation, . . the pride of the states . . will in the end procure its destruction" [7] — a prediction that came near fulfillment and probably would have been realized but for the courage of John Marshall.

While Grayson's eager prophecy did not come to pass, the Judiciary Act of 1789 worked so badly that it was a source of discontent to bench, bar, and people. William R. Davie of North Carolina, a member of the Convention that framed the Constitution and one of the most eminent lawyers of his time, condemned the Ellsworth Act as "so defective

---

[1] *Journal of Samuel Maclay:* Meginness, 90.
[2] *Annals*, 1st Cong. 1st Sess. 862.   [3] *Ib.* 852.
[4] *Ib.* 833–34.   [5] *Ib.* 864–65.   [6] *Maclay's Journal*, 98.
[7] Grayson to Henry, Sept. 29, 1789, Tyler, I, 170–71.

.. that .. it would disgrace the composition of the meanest legislature of the States." [1]

It was, as we have seen,[2] because of the deficiencies of the original Judiciary Law that Jay refused reappointment as Chief Justice. "I left the bench," he wrote Adams, "perfectly convinced that under a system so defective it would not obtain the energy, weight, and dignity which are essential to its affording due support to the national government, nor acquire the public confidence and respect which, as the last resort of the justice of the nation, it should possess." [3]

The six Justices of the Supreme Court were required to hold circuit courts in pairs, together with the judge of the district in which the court was held. Each circuit was to be thus served twice every year, and the Supreme Court was to hold two sessions annually in Washington.[4] So great were the distances between places where courts were held, so laborious, slow, and dangerous was all travel,[5] that

[1] Davie to Iredell, Aug. 2, 1791, *Life and Correspondence of James Iredell:* McRee, II, 335.

[2] Vol. II, 552–53, of this work.

[3] Jay to Adams, Jan. 2, 1801, *Jay:* Johnston, IV, 285.

[4] *Annals,* 1st Cong. 2d and 3d Sess. 2239.

[5] See vol. I, chap. VI, of this work. The conditions of travel are well illustrated by the experiences of six members of Congress, when journeying to Philadelphia in 1790. "Burke was shipwrecked off the Capes; Jackson and Mathews with great difficulty landed at Cape May and traveled one hundred and sixty miles in a wagon to the city; Burke got here in the same way. Gerry and Partridge were overset in the stage; the first had his head broke, .. the other had his ribs sadly bruised... Tucker had a dreadful passage of sixteen days with perpetual storms." (Letter of William Smith, as quoted by Johnson: *Union and Democracy,* 105–06.)

On his way to Washington from Amelia County in 1805, Senator Giles was thrown from a carriage, his leg fractured and his knee badly injured. (Anderson, 101.)

the Justices — men of ripe age and studious habits — spent a large part of each year upon the road.[1] Sometimes a storm would delay them, and litigants with their assembled lawyers and witnesses would have to postpone the trial for another year or await, at the expense of time and money, the arrival of the belated Justices.[2]

A graver defect of the act was that the Justices, sitting together as the Supreme Court, heard on appeal the same causes which they had decided on the Circuit Bench. Thus, in effect, they were trial and appellate judges in identical controversies. Moreover, by the rotation in riding circuits different judges frequently heard the same causes in their various stages, so that uniformity of practice, and even of decisions, was made impossible.

The admirable Judiciary Act, passed by the Federalists in 1801, corrected these defects. The membership of the Supreme Court was reduced to five after the next vacancy, the Justices were relieved of the heavy burden of holding circuit courts, and their duties were confined exclusively to the Supreme Bench. The country was divided into sixteen circuits, and the office of circuit judge was created for

[1] This arrangement proved to be so difficult and vexatious that in 1792 Congress corrected it to the extent of requiring only one Justice of the Supreme Court to hold circuit court with the District Judge; but this slight relief did not reach the serious shortcomings of the law. (*Annals*, 2d Cong. 1st and 2d Sess. 1447.)

See Adams: *U.S.* I, 274 *et seq.*, for good summary of the defects of the original Judiciary Act, and of the improvements made by the Federalist Law of 1801.

[2] See statement of Ogden, *Annals*, 7th Cong. 1st Sess. 172; of Chipman, *ib.* 123; of Tracy, *ib.* 52; of Griswold, *ib.* 768; of Huger, *ib.* 672.

each of these. The Circuit Judge, sitting with the District Judge, was to hold circuit court, as the Justices of the Supreme Court had formerly done. Thus the prompt and regular sessions of the circuit courts were assured. The appeal from decisions rendered by the Supreme Court Justices, sitting as circuit judges, to the same men sitting as appellate judges, was done away with.[1]

In establishing these new circuits and creating these circuit judges, this excellent Federalist law gave Adams the opportunity to fill the offices thus created with stanch Federalist partisans. Indeed, this was one motive for the enactment of the law. The salaries of the new circuit judges, together with other necessary expenses of the remodeled system, amounted to more than fifty thousand dollars every year — a sum which the Republicans exaggerated in their appeals to the people and even in their arguments in Congress.[2]

Chiefly on the pretext of this alleged extravagance, but in reality to oust the newly appointed Federalist judges and intimidate the entire National Judiciary, the Republicans, led by Jefferson, determined to re-

---

[1] Of course, to some extent this evil still continued in the appeals to the Circuit Bench; but the ultimate appeal was before judges who had taken no part in the cause.

The soundness of the Federalist Judiciary Act of 1801 was demonstrated almost a century later, in 1891–95, when Congress reënacted every essential feature of it. (See "Act to establish circuit courts of appeals and to define and regulate in certain cases the jurisdiction of the courts of the United States, and for other purposes," March 3, 1891, chap. 517, amended Feb. 18, 1895, chap. 96.)

[2] For example, Senator Cocke of Tennessee asserted the expense to be $137,000. (*Annals*, 7th Cong. 1st. Sess. 30.) See especially Prof. Farrand's conclusive article in *Am. Hist. Rev.* v, 682–86.

peal the Federalist Judiciary Act of 1801, upon the faith in the passage of which John Marshall, with misgiving, had accepted the office of Chief Justice.

On January 6, 1802, Senator John Breckenridge of Kentucky pulled the lanyard that fired the opening gun.[1] He was the personification of anti-Nationalism and aggressive democracy. He moved the repeal of the Federalist National Judiciary Act of 1801.[2] Every member of Senate and House — Republican and Federalist — was uplifted or depressed by the vital importance of the issue thus brought to a head; and in the debate which followed no words were too extreme to express their consciousness of the gravity of the occasion.[3]

In opening the debate, Senator Breckenridge confined himself closely to the point that the new Federalist judges were superfluous. "Could it be necessary," he challenged the Federalists, "to *increase* courts when suits were *decreasing?* . . to multiply

[1] It was to Breckenridge that Jefferson had entrusted the introduction of the Kentucky Resolutions of 1798 into the Legislature of that State. It was Breckenridge who had led the fight for them. At the time of the judiciary debate he was Jefferson's spokesman in the Senate; and later, at the President's earnest request, resigned as Senator to become Attorney-General.

[2] Breckenridge's constituents insisted that the law be repealed, because they feared that the newly established National courts would conflict with the system of State courts which the Legislature of Kentucky had just established. (See Carpenter, *Am. Pol. Sci. Rev.* IX, 523.)

Although the repeal had been determined upon by Jefferson almost immediately after his inauguration (see Jefferson to Stuart, April 8, 1801; *Works:* Ford, IX, 247), Breckenridge relied upon that most fruitful of Republican intellects, John Taylor "of Caroline," the originator of the Kentucky Resolutions (see vol. II, 397, of this work) for his arguments. See Taylor to Breckenridge, Dec. 22, 1801, *infra*, Appendix B.

[3] *Annals*, 7th Cong. 1st Sess. 31–46, 51–52, 58, 513, 530.

judges, when their duties were diminishing?" No!
"The time never will arrive when America will stand
in need of thirty-eight Federal Judges." [1] The Federalist Judiciary Law was "a wanton waste of the
public treasure." [2] Moreover, the fathers never intended to commit to National judges "subjects of
litigation which . . could be left to State Courts."
Answering the Federalist contention that the Constitution guaranteed to National judges tenure of
office during "good behavior" and that, therefore,
the offices once established could not be destroyed
by Congress, the Kentucky Senator observed that
"sinecure offices, . . are not permitted by our laws
or Constitution." [3]

James Monroe, then in Richmond, hastened to inform Breckenridge that "your argument . . is highly
approved here." But, anxiously inquired that foggy
Republican, "Do you mean to admit that the legislature [Congress] has not a right to repeal the law
organizing the supreme court for the express purpose of dismissing the judges when they cease to possess the public confidence?" If so, "the people have
no check whatever on them . . but impeachment."
Monroe hoped that "the period is not distant" when
any opposition to "the sovereignty of the people"
by the courts, such as "the application of the principles of the English common law to our constitution," would be considered "good cause for impeachment." [4] Thus early was expressed the Republican
plan to impeach and remove Marshall and the entire

[1] *Annals*, 7th Cong. 1st Sess. 26.   [2] *Ib*. 25.   [3] *Ib*. 28.
[4] Monroe to Breckenridge, Jan. 15, 1802, Breckenridge MSS. Lib.
Cong.

Federal membership of the Supreme Court so soon
to be attempted.[1]

In reply to Breckenridge, Senator Jonathan
Mason of Massachusetts, an accomplished Boston
lawyer, promptly brought forward the question in
the minds of Congress and the country. "This,"
said he, "was one of the most important questions
that ever came before a Legislature." Why had the
Judiciary been made "as independent of the Legislature as of the Executive?" Because it was their
duty "to expound not only the laws, but the Constitution also; in which is involved the power of
checking the Legislature in case it should pass any
laws in violation of the Constitution."[2]

The old system which the Republicans would now
revive was intolerable, declared Senator Gouverneur
Morris of New York. "Cast an eye over the extent
of our country" and reflect that the President, "in
selecting a character for the bench, must seek less
the learning of a judge than the agility of a post
boy." Moreover, to repeal the Federal Judiciary
Law would be "a declaration to the remaining
judges that they hold their offices subject to your
[Congress's] will and pleasure." Thus "the check
established by the Constitution is destroyed."

Morris expounded the conservative Federalist
philosophy thus: "Governments are made to provide against the follies and vices of men. . . Hence,
checks are required in the distribution of power
among those who are to exercise it for the benefit of

---

[1] See *infra*, chaps. III and IV.
[2] *Annals*, 7th Cong. 1st Sess. 31–32.

the people." The most efficient of these checks was the power given the National Judiciary — "a check of the first necessity, to prevent an invasion of the Constitution by unconstitutional laws — a check which might prevent any faction from intimidating or annihilating the tribunals themselves." [1]

Let the Republican Senators consider where their course would end, he warned. "What has been the ruin of every Republic? The vile love of popularity. *Why are we here? To save the people from their most dangerous enemy; to save them from themselves.*" [2] Do not, he besought, "commit the fate of America to the mercy of time and chance." [3]

"Good God!" exclaimed Senator James Jackson of Georgia, "is it possible that I have heard such a sentiment in this body? Rather should I have expected to have heard it sounded from the despots of Turkey, or the deserts of Siberia.[4] .. I am more afraid of an army of judges, .. than of an army of soldiers. .. Have we not seen sedition laws?" The Georgia Senator "thanked God" that the terrorism of the National Judiciary was, at last, overthrown. "That we are not under dread of the patronage of judges, is manifest, from their attack on the Secretary of State." [5]

---

[1] *Annals*, 7th Cong. 1st Sess. 38.

[2] This unfortunate declaration of Morris gave the Republicans an opportunity of unlimited demagogic appeal. See *infra*. (Italics the author's.)

[3] *Annals*, 7th Cong. 1st Sess. 40–41.

Morris spoke for an hour. There was a "large audience, which is not common for that House." He prepared his speech for the press. (*Diary and Letters of Gouverneur Morris:* Morris, II, 417.)

[4] *Annals*, 7th Cong. 1st Sess. 49.

[5] *Ib.* 47–48. Senator Jackson here refers to the case of Marbury *vs.*

Senator Uriah Tracy of Connecticut was so concerned that he spoke in spite of serious illness. "What security is there to an individual," he asked, if the Legislature of the Union or any particular State, should pass an *ex post facto* law? "None in the world" but revolution or "an appeal to the Judiciary of the United States, where he will obtain a decision that the law itself is unconstitutional and void." [1]

That typical Virginian, Senator Stevens Thompson Mason, able, bold, and impetuous, now took up Gouverneur Morris's gage of battle. He was one of the most fearless and capable men in the Republican Party, and was as impressive in physical appearance as he was dominant in character. He was

Madison, then pending before the Supreme Court. (See *infra*, chap. III.) This case was mentioned several times during the debate. It is plain that the Republicans expected Marshall to award the mandamus, and if he did, to charge this as another act of judicial aggression for which, if the plans already decided upon did not miscarry, they would make the new Chief Justice suffer removal from his office by impeachment. (See *infra*, chap. IV.)

[1] *Annals*, 7th Cong. 1st Sess. 58. Tracy's speech performed the miracle of making one convert. After he closed he was standing before the glowing fireplace, "half dead with his exertions." Senator Colhoun of South Carolina came to Tracy, and giving him his hand, said: "You are a stranger to me, sir, but by —— you have made me your friend." Colhoun said that he "had been told a thousand lies" about the Federalist Judiciary Act, particularly the manner of passing it, and he had, therefore, been in favor of repealing it. But Tracy had convinced him, and Colhoun declared: "I shall be with you on the question." "May we depend upon you?" asked Tracy, wringing the South Carolina Senator's hand. "By —— you may," was the response. (Morison: *Life of the Hon. Jeremiah Smith*, footnote to 147.) Colhoun kept his word and voted with the Federalists against his party's pet measure. (*Annals*, 7th Cong. 1st Sess. 185.)

The correct spelling of this South Carolina Senator's name is *Colhoun*, and not Calhoun, as given in so many biographical sketches of him. (See *South Carolina Magazine* for July, 1906.)

just under six feet in height, yet heavy with fat; he had extraordinarily large eyes, gray in color, a wide mouth with lips sternly compressed, high, broad forehead, and dark hair, thrown back from his brow. Mason had "wonderful powers of sarcasm" which he employed to the utmost in this debate.[1]

It was true, he said, in beginning his address, that the Judiciary should be independent, but not "independent of the nation itself." Certainly the Judiciary had not Constitutional authority "to control the other departments of the Government." [2] Mason hotly attacked the Federalist position that a National judge, once appointed, was in office permanently; and thus, for the second time, Marbury *vs.* Madison was brought into the debate. "Have we not heard this doctrine supported in the memorable case of the mandamus, lately [3] before the Supreme Court? Was it not there said [in argument of counsel] that, though the law had a right to establish the office of a justice of the peace, yet it had not a right to abridge its duration to five years?" [4]

[1] See Grigsby: *Virginia Convention of 1788*, II, 260–262.
This was the same Senator who, in violation of the rules of the Senate, gave to the press a copy of the Jay Treaty which the Senate was then considering. The publication of the treaty raised a storm of public wrath against that compact. (See vol. II, 115, of this work.) Senator Mason's action was the first occurrence in our history of a treaty thus divulged.
[2] *Annals*, 7th Cong. 1st Sess. 59.
[3] In that case Marshall had issued a rule to the Secretary of State to show cause why a writ of mandamus should not be issued by the court ordering him to deliver to Marbury and his associates commissions as justices of the peace, to which offices President Adams had appointed them. (See *infra*, chap. III.)
[4] *Annals*, 7th Cong. 1st Sess. 61.

The true principle, Mason declared, was that
judicial offices like all others "are made for the good
of the people and not for that of the individual who
administers them." Even Judges of the Supreme
Court should do something to earn their salaries; but
under the Federalist Judiciary Act of 1801 "what
have they got to do? To try ten suits, [annually] for
such is the number now on their docket."

Mason now departed slightly from the Republican
programme of ignoring the favorite Federalist theory
that the Judiciary has the power to decide the constitutionality of statutes. He fears that the Justices
of the Supreme Court "will be induced, from want
of employment, to do that which they ought not to
do. . . They may . . hold the Constitution in one
hand, and the law in the other, and say to the departments of Government, so far shall you go and no
farther." He is alarmed lest "this independence
of the Judiciary" shall become "something like supremacy." [1]

Seldom in parliamentary contests has sarcasm, always a doubtful weapon, been employed with finer
art than it was by Mason against Morris at this
time. The Federalists, in the enactment of the Judiciary Act of 1801, had abolished two district courts
— the very thing for which the Republicans were
now assailed by the Federalists as destroyers of the
Constitution. Where was Morris, asked Mason,
when his friends had committed that sacrilege?
"Where was the *Ajax Telamon* of his party" at that
hour of fate? "Where was the hero with his seven-

[1] *Annals*, 7th Cong. 1st Sess. 63.

fold shield — not of bull's hide, but of brass — prepared to prevent or to punish this Trojan rape?"[1]

Morris replied lamely. He had been criticized, he complained, for pointing out "the dangers to which popular governments are exposed, from the influence of designing demagogues upon popular passion." Yet "'t is for these purposes that all our Constitutional checks are devised." Otherwise "the Constitution is all nonsense." He enumerated the Constitutional limitations and exclaimed, "Why all these multiplied precautions, unless to check and control that impetuous spirit . . which has swept away every popular Government that ever existed?"[2]

Should all else fail, "the Constitution has given us . . an independent judiciary" which, if "you trench upon the rights of your fellow citizens, by passing an unconstitutional law . . will stop you short." Preserve the Judiciary in its vigor, and in great controversies where the passions of the multitude are aroused, "instead of a resort to arms, there will be a happier appeal to argument."[3]

Answering Mason's fears that the Supreme Court, "having little else to do, would do mischief," Morris avowed that he should "rejoice in that mischief," if it checked "the Legislative or Executive departments in any wanton invasion of our rights. . . I know this doctrine is unpleasant; I know it is more popular to appeal to public opinion — that equivocal, transient being, which exists nowhere and every-

---

[1] *Annals,* 7th Cong. 1st Sess. 66. The eloquence of the Virginia Senator elicited the admiration of even the rabidly Federalist *Columbian Centinel* of Boston. See issue of February 6, 1802.

[2] *Ib.* 77.   [3] *Ib.* 83.

where. But if ever the occasion calls for it, I trust the Supreme Court will not neglect doing the great mischief of saving this Constitution." [1]

His emotions wrought to the point of oratorical ecstasy, Morris now made an appeal to "the good sense, patriotism, and . . virtue" of the Republic, in the course of which he became badly entangled in his metaphors. "Do not," he pleaded, "rely on that popular will, which has brought us frail beings into political existence. That opinion is but a changeable thing. It will soon change. This very measure will change it. You will be deceived. Do not . . commit the dignity, the harmony, the existence of our nation to the wild wind. Trust not your treasure to the waves. Throw not your compass and your charts into the ocean. Do not believe that its billows will waft you into port. Indeed, indeed, you will be deceived.

"Cast not away this only anchor of our safety. I have seen its progress. I know the difficulties through which it was obtained. I stand in the presence of Almighty God, and of the world; and I declare to you, that if you lose this charter, never, no, never will you get another! We are now, perhaps, arrived at the parting point. Here, even here, we stand on the brink of fate. Pause — Pause! For Heaven's sake, pause!" [2]

Senator Breckenridge would not "pause." The "progress" of Senator Morris's "anchor," however, dragged him again to "the brink of fate." The Senate had "wandered long enough" with the Federal-

---

[1] *Annals*, 7th Cong. 1st Sess. 89.   [2] *Ib.* 91–92.

ist Senators "in those regions of fancy and of terror, to which they [have] led us." He now insisted that the Senate return to the real subject, and in a speech which is a model of compact reasoning, sharpened by sarcasm, discussed all the points raised by the Federalist Senators except their favorite one of the power of the National Judiciary to declare acts of Congress unconstitutional. This he carefully avoided.[1]

On January 15, 1802, the new Vice-President of the United States, Aaron Burr, first took the chair as presiding officer of the Senate.[2] Within two weeks[3] an incident happened which, though seemingly trivial, was powerfully and dramatically to affect the course of political events that finally encompassed the ruin of the reputation, career, and fortune of many men.

Senator Jonathan Dayton of New Jersey, in order, as he claimed, to make the measure less objectionable, moved that "the bill be referred to a select committee, with instructions to consider and report the alterations which may be proper in the judiciary system of the United States."[4] On this motion the Senate tied; and Vice-President Burr, by his deciding vote, referred the bill to the select committee. In doing this he explained that he believed the Federalists sincere in their wish "to ameliorate the provisions of the bill, that it might be rendered more

---

[1] *Annals*, 7th Cong. 1st Sess. 99.

[2] Morris notes in his diary that, on the same day, the Senate resolved "to admit a short-hand writer to their floor. This is the beginning of mischief." (Morris, ɪɪ, 416–17.)

[3] January 27, 1802.   [4] *Annals*, 7th Cong. 1st Sess. 149.

acceptable to the Senate." But he was careful to warn them that he would "discountenance, by his vote, any attempt, if any such should be made, that might, in an indirect way, go to defeat the bill." [1]

Five days later, one more Republican Senator, being present, and one Federalist Senator, being absent, the committee was discharged on motion of Senator Breckenridge; and the debate continued, the Federalists constantly accusing the Republicans of a purpose to destroy the independence of the National Judiciary, and asserting that National judges must be kept beyond the reach of either Congress or President in order to decide fearlessly upon the constitutionality of laws.

At last the steady but spirited Breckenridge was so irritated that he broke away from the Republican plan to ignore this principal article of Federalist faith. He did not intend to rise again, he said, but "an argument had been so much pressed" that he felt it must be answered. "I did not expect, sir, to find the doctrine of the power of the courts to annul the laws of Congress as unconstitutional, so seriously insisted on. . . I would ask where they got that

---

[1] *Annals*, 7th Cong. 1st Sess. 150.

Burr's action was perfectly correct. As an impartial presiding officer, he could not well have done anything else. Alexander J. Dallas, Republican Attorney-General of Pennsylvania, wrote the Vice-President a letter approving his action. (Dallas to Burr, Feb. 3, 1802, Davis: *Memoirs of Aaron Burr*, II, 82.) Nathaniel Niles, a rampant Republican, sent Burr a letter thanking him for his vote. As a Republican, he wanted his party to be fair, he said. (Niles to Burr, Feb. 17, 1802, *ib.* 83–84.) Nevertheless, Burr's vote was seized upon by his enemies as the occasion for beginning those attacks upon him which led to his overthrow and disgrace. (See chaps. VI, VII, VIII, and IX of this volume.)

power, and who checks the courts when they violate the Constitution?"

The theory that courts may annul legislation would give them "the absolute direction of the Government." For, "to whom are they responsible?" He wished to have pointed out the clause which grants to the National Judiciary the power to overthrow legislation. "Is it not extraordinary," said he, "that if this high power was intended, it should nowhere appear? .. Never were such high and transcendant powers in any Government (much less in one like ours, composed of powers specially given and defined) claimed or exercised by construction only." [1]

Breckenridge frankly stated the Republican philosophy, repeating sometimes word for word the passage which Jefferson at the last moment had deleted from his Message to Congress.[2] "The Constitution," he declared, "intended a separation of the powers vested in the three great departments, giving to each exclusive authority on the subjects committed to it. .. Those who made the laws are presumed to have an equal attachment to, and interest in the Constitution; are equally bound by oath to support it, and have an equal right to give a construction to it. .. The construction of one department of the powers vested in it, is of higher authority than the construction of any other department.

"The Legislature," he continued, "have the exclusive right to interpret the Constitution, in what

---

[1] *Annals*, 7th Cong. 1st Sess. 178–79.
[2] See Appendix A to this volume.

regards the law-making power, and the judges are
bound to execute the laws they make. For the Legislature would have at least an equal right to annul
the decisions of the courts, founded on their construction of the Constitution, as the courts would
have to annul the acts of the Legislature, founded on
their construction.[1] . . In case the courts were to
declare your revenue, impost and appropriation laws
unconstitutional, would they thereby be blotted out
of your statute book, and the operations of Government arrested? . . Let gentlemen consider well before
they insist on a power in the Judiciary which places
the Legislature at their feet." [2]

The candles [3] now dimly illuminating the little
Senate Chamber shed scarcely more light than radiated from the broad, round, florid face of Gouverneur Morris. Getting to his feet as quickly as his
wooden leg would permit, his features beaming with
triumph, the New York Senator congratulated "this
House, and all America, that we have at length got
our adversaries upon the ground where we can fairly
meet." [4]

The power of courts to declare legislation invalid
is derived from "authority higher than this Constitution . . from the constitution of man, from the
nature of things, from the necessary progress of
human affairs," [5] he asserted. In a cause on trial
before them, it becomes necessary for the judges to

[1] *Annals*, 7th Cong. 1st Sess. 179.   [2] *Ib.* 180.

[3] It was five o'clock (*ib.* 178) when Senator Breckenridge began to
speak; it must have been well after six when Senator Morris rose
to answer him.

[4] *Ib.* 180.   [5] *Ib.* 180.

"declare what the law is. They must, of course, determine whether that which is produced and relied on, has indeed the binding force of law."

Suppose, said Morris, that Congress should pass an act forbidden by the Constitution — for instance, one laying "a duty on exports," and "the citizen refuses to pay." If the Republicans were right, the courts would enforce a collection. In vain would the injured citizen appeal to the Supreme Court; for Congress would "defeat the appeal, and render final the judgment of inferior tribunals, subjected to their absolute control." According to the Republican doctrine, "the moment the Legislature . . declare themselves supreme, they become so . . and the Constitution is whatever they choose to make it." [1] This time Morris made a great impression. The Federalists were in high feather; even the Republicans were moved to admiration. Troup reported to King that "the democratical paper at Washington pronounced his speech to be the greatest display of eloquence ever exhibited in a deliberative assembly!" [2]

Nevertheless, the Federalist politicians were worried by the apparent indifference of the rank and file of their party. "I am surprized," wrote Bayard, "at the public apathy upon the subject. Why do not those who are opposed to the project, express in the public papers or by petitions their disapprobation? . . It is likely that a public movement would have great effect." [3] But, thanks to the former conduct of

[1] *Annals*, 7th Cong. 1st Sess. 181.

[2] Troup to King, April 9, 1802, King, IV, 103.

[3] Bayard to Bassett, Jan. 25, 1802, *Papers of James A. Bayard:* Donnan, 146-47.

the judges themselves, no "public movement" developed. Conservative citizens were apprehensive; but, as usual, they were lethargic.

On February 3, 1802, the Senate, by a strictly party vote[1] of 16 to 15, passed the bill to repeal the Federalist Judiciary Act of 1801.[2]

When the bill came up in the House, the Federalist leader in that body, James A. Bayard of Delaware, moved to postpone its consideration to the third Monday in March, in order, as he said, to test public opinion, because "few occasions have occurred so important as this."[3] But in vain did the Federalists plead and threaten. Postponement was refused by a vote of 61 to 35.[4] Another plea for delay was denied by a vote of 58 to 34.[5] Thus the solid Republican majority, in rigid pursuance of the party plan, forced the consideration of the bill.

The Federalist organ in Washington, which Marshall two years earlier was supposed to influence and to which he probably contributed,[6] saw little hope of successful resistance. "What will eventually be the issue of the present high-handed, overbearing proceedings of Congress it is impossible to determine," but fear was expressed by this paper that conditions

---

[1] Except Colhoun of South Carolina, converted by Tracy. See *supra*, 62.

[2] *Annals*, 7th Cong. 1st Sess. 183.

[3] *Ib.* 510. A correspondent of the *Columbian Centinel*, reporting the event, declared that "the stand which the Federal Senators have made to preserve the Constitution, has been manly and glorious. They have immortalized their names, while those of their opposers will be execrated as the assassins of the Constitution." (*Columbian Centinel*, Feb. 17, 1802.)

[4] *Annals*, 7th Cong. 1st Sess. 518–19.   [5] *Ib.* 521–22.

[6] See vol. II, 532, 541.

would be created "which impartial, unbiased and reflecting men consider as immediately preceding the total destruction of our government and the introduction of disunion, anarchy and civil war." [1]

This threat of secession and armed resistance, already made in the Senate, was to be repeated three times in the debate in the House which was opened for the Federalists by Archibald Henderson of North Carolina, whom Marshall pronounced to be "unquestionably among the ablest lawyers of his day" and "one of the great lawyers of the Nation." [2] "The monstrous and unheard of doctrine . . lately advanced, that the judges have not the right of declaring unconstitutional laws void," was, declared Henderson, "the very definition of tyranny, and wherever you find it, the people are slaves, whether they call their Government a Monarchy, Republic, or Democracy." If the Republican theory of the Constitution should prevail, "better at once to bury it with all our hopes." [3]

Robert Williams of the same State, an extreme but unskillful Republican, now uncovered his party's scheme to oust Federalist judges, which thus far had carefully been concealed: [4] "Agreeably to our Constitution a judge may be impeached," said he, but this punishment would be minimized if judges could declare an act of Congress unconstitutional. "However he may err, he commits no crime; how, then, can he be impeached?" [5]

[1] *Washington Federalist*, Feb. 13, 1802.
[2] Henderson in *North Carolina Booklet*, xvii, 66.
[3] *Annals*, 7th Cong. 1st Sess. 529–30.
[4] See *infra*, chap. iv.   [5] *Annals*, 7th Cong. 1st Sess. 531.

Philip R. Thompson of Virginia, a Republican, was moved to the depths of his being: "Give the Judiciary this check upon the Legislature, allow them the power to declare your laws null and void, . . and in vain have the people placed you upon this floor to legislate.[1] . . This is the tree where despotism lies concealed. . . Nurture it with your treasure, stop not its ramifications, and . . your atmosphere will be contaminated with its poisonous effluvia, and your soaring eagle will fall dead at its root." [2]

Thomas T. Davis of Kentucky, deeply stirred by this picture, declared that the Federalists said to the people, you are "incapable" of protecting yourselves; "in the Judiciary alone you find a safe deposit for your liberties." The Kentucky Representative "trembled" at such ideas. "The sooner we put men out of power, who [sic] we find determined to act in this manner, the better; by doing so we preserve the power of the Legislature, and save our nation from the ravages of an uncontrolled Judiciary." [3] Thus again was revealed the Republican purpose of dragging from the National Bench all judges who dared assert the right, and to exercise the power to declare an act of Congress unconstitutional.[4]

The contending forces became ever more earnest as the struggle continued. All the cases then known in which courts directly or by inference had held legislative acts invalid were cited; [5] and all the argu-

[1] *Annals*, 7th Cong. 1st Sess. 552–53.   [2] *Ib.* 554.
[3] *Ib.* 558.   [4] See *infra*, chap. IV.
[5] See, for example, the speeches of Thomas Morris of New York (*Annals*, 7th Cong. 1st Sess. 565–68); Calvin Goddard of Connecticut (*ib.* 727–34); John Stanley of North Carolina (*ib.* 569–78); Roger Griswold of Connecticut (*ib.* 768–69).

ments that ever had been advanced in favor of the
principle of the judicial power to annul legislation
were made over and over again.

All the reasons for the opinion which John Marshall, exactly one year later, pronounced in Marbury
vs. Madison were given during this debate. Indeed,
the legislative struggle now in progress and the result of it, created conditions which forced Marshall
to execute that judicial *coup d'état*. It should be repeated that an understanding of Marbury *vs.* Madison is impossible without a thorough knowledge of
the debate in Congress which preceded and largely
caused that epochal decision.

The alarm that the repeal was but the beginning of Republican havoc was sounded by every
Federalist member. "This measure," said John
Stanley of North Carolina, "will be the first link
in that chain of measures which will add the name
of America to the melancholy catalogue of fallen
Republics."[1]

William Branch Giles, who for the next five years
bore so vital a part in the stirring events of Marshall's life, now took the floor and made one of the
ablest addresses of his tempestuous career.[2] He was
Jefferson's lieutenant in the House.[3] When the Federalists tried to postpone the consideration of the
bill,[4] Giles admitted that it presented a question
"more important than any that ever came before

---

[1] *Annals*, 7th Cong. 1st Sess. 579.

[2] Anderson, 83. Grigsby says that "Mr. Jefferson pronounced
him (Giles) the ablest debater of the age." His speech on the Repeal Act, Grigsby declares to have been "by far his most brilliant
display." (Grigsby: *Virginia Convention of 1829–30*, 23, 29.)

[3] Anderson, 76–82.   [4] See *supra*, 72.

this house." [1] But there was no excuse for delay, because the press had been full of it for more than a year and the public was thoroughly informed upon it. [2]

Giles was a large, robust, "handsome" Virginian, whose lightest word always compelled the attention of the House. He had a very dark complexion, black hair worn long, and intense, "retreating" brown eyes. His dress was "remarkably plain, and in the style of Virginia carelessness." His voice was "clear and nervous," his language "powerfully condensed." [3]

This Republican gladiator came boldly to combat. How had the Federalists contrived to gain their ends? Chiefly by "the breaking out of a tremendous and unprecedented war in Europe," which had worked upon "the feelings and sympathies of the people of the United States" till they had neglected their own affairs. So it was, he said, that the Federalists had been able to load upon the people an expensive army, a powerful navy, intolerable taxes,

---

[1] This statement, coming from the Virginia radical, reveals the profound concern of the Republicans, for Giles thus declared that the Judiciary debate was of greater consequence than those historic controversies over Assumption, the Whiskey Rebellion, the Bank, Neutrality, the Jay Treaty, the French complication, the army, and other vital subjects. In most of those encounters Giles had taken a leading and sometimes violent part.

[2] *Annals*, 7th Cong. 1st Sess. 512.

[3] Story's description of Giles six years later: Story to Fay, Feb. 13, 1808, Story, i, 158–59. Also see Anderson, frontispiece and 238.

Giles was thirty-nine years of age. He had been elected to the House in 1790, and from the day he entered Congress had exasperated the Federalists. It is an interesting though trivial incident that Giles bore to Madison a letter of introduction from Marshall. Evidently the circumspect Richmond attorney was not well impressed with Giles, for the letter is cautious in the extreme. (See Anderson, 10; also *Annals*, 7th Cong. 1st Sess. 581.)

and the despotic Alien and Sedition Laws. But at last, when, as the result of their maladministration, the Federalists saw their doom approaching, they began to "look out for some department of the government in which they could entrench themselves . . and continue to support those favorite principles of irresponsibility which they could never consent to abandon."

For this purpose they had selected the Judiciary Department: "Not only because it was already filled" with rabid Federalists, "but because they held their offices by indefinite tenures, and of course were further removed from any responsibility to the people than either of the other departments." Thus came the Federalist Judiciary Act of 1801 which the Republicans were about to repeal.

Giles could not resist a sneer at Marshall. Referring to the European war, to which "the feelings and sympathies of the people of the United States were so strongly attracted . . that they considered their own internal concerns in a secondary point of view," Giles swiftly portrayed those measures used by the Federalists as a pretext. They had, jeered the sharp-tongued Virginia Republican, "pushed forward the people to the X, Y, Z, of their political alphabet, before they had well learned . . the A, B, C, of the principles of the [Federalist] Administration." [1]

But now, when blood was no longer flowing on European battle-fields, the interests of the American people in that "tremendous and unprecedented" combat of nations "no longer turn their attention

[1] *Annals*, 7th Cong. 1st Sess. 580–81.

from their internal concerns; arguments of the highest consideration for the safety of the Constitution and the liberty of the citizens, no longer receive the short reply, French partisans! Jacobins! Disorganizers!" [1] So "the American people and their Congress, in their real persons, and original American characters" were at last "engaged in the transaction of American concerns." [2]

Federalist despotism lay prostrate, thank Heaven, beneath the conquering Republican heel. Should it rise again? Never! Giles taunted the Federalists with the conduct of Federalist judges in the sedition cases,[3] and denounced the attempt to fasten British law on the American Nation — a law "unlimited in its object, and indefinite in its character," covering "every object of legislation."

Think, too, of what Marshall and the Supreme Court have done! "They have sent a . . process leading to a mandamus, into the Executive cabinet, to examine its concerns." [4] The real issue between Federalists and Republicans, declared Giles, was "the doctrine of irresponsibility against the doctrine of responsibility. . . . The doctrine of despotism in opposition to the representative system." The Federalist theory was "an express avowal that the people were incompetent to govern themselves."

A handsome, florid, fashionably attired man of thirty-five now took the floor and began his reply to the powerful speech of the tempestuous Virginian.

---

[1] *Annals,* 7th Cong. 1st Sess. 582.   [2] *Ib.* 583.

[3] See *supra,* chap. I.

[4] Marbury *vs.* Madison (see *infra,* chap. III). For Giles's great speech see *Annals,* 7th Cong. 1st Sess. 579–602.

His complexion and stoutness indicated the generous manner in which all public men of the time lived, and his polished elocution and lofty scorn for all things Republican marked him as the equal of Gouverneur Morris in oratorical finish and Federalist distrust of the people.[1] It was James A. Bayard, the Federalist leader of the House.

He asserted that the Republican "designs [were] hostile to the powers of this government"; that they flowed from "state pride [which] extinguishes a national sentiment"; that while the Federalists were in charge of the National Administration they struggled "to maintain the Constitutional powers of the Executive" because "the wild principles of French liberty were scattered through the country. We had our Jacobins and disorganizers, who saw no difference between a King and a President; and, as the people of France had put down their King, they thought the people of America ought to put down their President.

"They [Federalists] who considered the Constitution as securing all the principles of rational and practicable liberty, who were unwilling to embark upon the tempestuous sea of revolution, in pursuit of visionary schemes, were denounced as monarchists. A line was drawn between the Government

---

[1] Bayard is "a fine, personable man . . of strong mental powers. . . Nature has been liberal to him. . . He has, in himself, vast resources . . a lawyer of high repute . . and a man of integrity and honor. . . He is very fond of pleasure . . a married man but fond of wine, women and cards. He drinks more than a bottle of wine each day. . . He lives too fast to live long. . . He is very attentive to dress and person." (Senator William Plumer's description of James A. Bayard, March 10, 1803, "Repository," Plumer MSS. Lib. Cong.)

and the people, and the friends of the Government [Federalists] were marked as the enemies of the people." [1] This was the spirit that was now triumphant; to what lengths was it to carry the Republicans? Did they include the downfall of the Judiciary in their plans of general destruction? Did they propose to make judges the mere creatures of Congress? [2]

Bayard skillfully turned the gibe at Marshall into a tribute to the Chief Justice. What did Giles mean by his cryptic X. Y. Z. reference? "Did he mean that the dispatches . . were impostures?" Though Giles "felt no respect" for Marshall or Pinckney — "two characters as pure, as honorable, and exalted, as any the country can boast of" — yet, exclaimed Bayard, "I should have expected that he would have felt some tenderness for Mr. Gerry." [3]

The Republicans had contaminated the country with falsehoods against the Federalist Administrations; and now the target of their "poisoned arrows" was the National Judiciary. "If . . they [the judges] have offended against the Constitution or laws of the country, why are they not impeached? The gentleman now holds the sword of justice. The judges are not a privileged order; they have no shelter but their innocence." [4]

In detail Bayard explained the facts in the case of Marbury vs. Madison. That the Supreme Court had been "hardy enough to send their mandate into the Executive cabinet" [5] was, said he, "a strong proof

---

[1] *Annals*, 7th Cong. 1st Sess. 605.   [2] *Ib.* 606.
[3] *Ib.* 609.   [4] *Ib.* 611.   [5] *Ib.* 614.

of the value of that Constitutional provision which makes them independent. They are not terrified by the frowns of Executive power, and dare to judge between the rights of a citizen and the pretensions of a President." [1]

Contrast the defects of the Judiciary Act of 1789 with the perfection of the Federalist law supplanting it. Could any man deny the superiority of the latter? [2] The truth was that the Republicans were "to give notice to the judges of the Supreme Court of their fate, and to bid them to prepare for their end." [3] In these words Bayard charged the Republicans with their settled but unavowed purpose to unseat Marshall and his Federalist associates.[4]

Bayard hotly denied the Republican accusation that President Adams had appointed to the bench Federalist members of Congress as a reward for their party services; but, retorted he, Jefferson had done that very thing.[5] He then spoke at great length on

[1] *Annals*, 7th Cong. 1st Sess. 615.

[2] Bayard's summary of the shortcomings of the Ellsworth Act of 1789 and the excellence of the Judiciary Act of 1801 (*Annals*, 7th Cong. 1st Sess. 616–27) was the best made at that time or since.

[3] *Ib.* 632.   [4] See *infra*, chap. iv.

[5] Bayard pointed out that Charles Pinckney of South Carolina, whose "zeal and industry" decided the Presidential vote of his State, had been appointed Minister to Spain; that Claiborne of Tennessee held the vote of that State and cast it for Jefferson, and that Jefferson had conferred upon him "the high degree of Governor of the Mississippi Territory"; that Mr. Linn of New Jersey, upon whom both parties depended, finally cast his deciding vote in favor of Jefferson and "Mr. Linn has since had the profitable office of supervisor of his district conferred upon him"; and that Mr. Lyon of Vermont neutralized the vote of his State, but since "his character was low . . Mr. Lyon's son has been handsomely provided for in one of the Executive offices." (*Annals*, 7th Cong. 1st Sess. 640.) Bayard named other men who had influenced the vote in the House and who had thereafter been rewarded by Jefferson.

the nature of the American Judiciary as distinguished from that of British courts, gave a vivid account of the passage of the Federalist Judiciary Act under attack, and finally swung back to the subject which more and more was coming to dominate the struggle — the power of the Supreme Court to annul acts of Congress.

Again and again Bayard restated, and with power and eloquence, all the arguments to support the supervisory power of courts over legislation.[1] At last he threatened armed resistance if the Republicans dared to carry out their plans against the National Judiciary. "There are many now willing to spill their blood to defend that Constitution. Are gentlemen disposed to risk the consequences? . . Let them consider their wives and children, their neighbors and their friends." Destroy the independence of the National Judiciary and "the moment is not far when this fair country is to be desolated by civil war."[2]

Bayard's speech aroused great enthusiasm among the leaders of his party. John Adams wrote: "Yours is the most comprehensive masterly and compleat argument that has been published in either house. and will have, indeed . . has already had more effect and influence on the public mind than all other publications on the subject."[3] The *Washington Federalist* pronounced Bayard's performance to be "far superior, not only to . . the speeches of Mr. Morris

[1] *Annals*, 7th Cong. 1st Sess. 645–48.

[2] *Ib.* 648–50. This was the second open expression in Congress of the spirit that led the New England Federalist leaders into their futile secession movement. (See *infra*, chaps. iii and vi; also vol. iv, chap. i, of this work.)

[3] Adams to Bayard, April 10, 1802; *Bayard Papers:* Donnan, 152.

and Mr. Tracy in the Senate, but to any speech of a
Demosthenes, a Cicero, or a Chatham." [1]

Hardly was Bayard's last word spoken when the
man who at that time was the Republican master of
the House, and, indeed, of the Senate also, was upon
his feet. Of medium stature, thin as a sword, his
straight black hair, in which gray already was beginning to appear, suggesting the Indian blood in his
veins, his intense black eyes flaming with the passion
of combat, his high and shrilling voice suggesting
the scream of an eagle, John Randolph of Roanoke —
that haughty, passionate, eccentric genius — personi-
fied the aggressive and ruthless Republicanism of
the hour. He was clad in riding-coat and breeches,
wore long riding-boots, and if the hat of the Virginia
planter was not on his head, it was because in his
nervousness he had removed it; [2] while, if his riding-
whip was not in his hand, it was on his desk where
he had cast it, the visible and fitting emblem of this
strange man's mastery over his partisan followers. [3]

[1] *Washington Federalist*, Feb. 20, 1802.

[2] Members of Congress wore their hats during the sessions of House
and Senate until 1828. For a description of Randolph in the House, see
Tyler, I, 291. Senator Plumer pictured him as "a pale, meagre, ghostly
man," with "more popular and effective talents than any other member of his party." (Plumer to Emery, Plumer, 248.) See also Plumer's letter to his son, Feb. 22, 1803, in which the New Hampshire
Senator says that "Randolph goes to the House booted and spurred,
with his whip in his hand, in imitation, it is said, of members of the
British Parliament. He is a very slight man, but of the common
stature." At a distance he looks young, but "upon a nearer approach
you perceive his wrinkles and grey hairs. He is, I believe, about
thirty." (*Ib.* 256.)

[3] The personal domination which John Randolph of Roanoke
wielded over his party in Congress, until he broke with Jefferson (see
infra, chaps. IV and X), is difficult to realize at the present day.
Nothing like it has since been experienced, excepting only the merci-

"He did not rise," he said, his voice quivering and body trembling,[1] "for the purpose of assuming the gauntlet which had been so proudly thrown by the Goliah of the adverse party; not but that he believed even his feeble powers, armed with the simple weapon of truth, a sling and a stone, capable of prostrating on the floor that gigantic boaster, armed cap-a-pie as he was." Randolph sneered, as only he could sneer, at the unctuous claims of the Federalists, that they had "nobly sacrificed their political existence on the altar of the general welfare"; he refused "to revere in them the self-immolated victims at the shrine of patriotism." [2]

As to the Federalist assertion that "the common law of England is the law of the United States in their confederate capacity," Randolph observed that the meaning of such terms as "court," "jury," and the like must, of course, be settled by reference to common-law definitions, but "does it follow that that indefinite and undefinable body of law is the irrepealable law of the land? The sense of a most important phrase, 'direct tax,' as used in the Constitution, has been . . settled by the acceptation of Adam Smith; an acceptation, too, peculiar to himself. Does the Wealth of Nations, therefore, form a part of the Constitution of the United States?"

And would the Federalists inform the House what phase of the common law they proposed to adopt for the United States? Was it that "of the reign of

less rule of Thaddeus Stevens of Pennsylvania from 1862 until 1868. (See Woodburn: *Life of Thaddeus Stevens*, 247 *et seq.*)

[1] *Washington Federalist*, Feb. 22, 1802.
[2] *Annals*, 7th Cong. 1st Sess. 650–51.

Elizabeth and James the first; or . . that of the time
of George the Second?" Was it that "of Sir Walter
Raleigh and Captain Smith, or that which was im-
ported by Governor Oglethorpe?" Or was it that
of some intermediate period? "I wish especially to
know," asked Randolph, "whether the common law
of libels which attaches to this Constitution, be the
doctrine laid down by Lord Mansfield, or that which
has immortalized Mr. Fox?" Let the Federalists
reflect on the persecution for libel that had been
made under the common law, as well as under the
Sedition Act.[1]

Proper restraint upon Congress, said Randolph,
was not found in a pretended power of the Judiciary
to veto legislation, but in the people themselves,
who at. the ballot box could "apply the Constitutional corrective. That is the true check; every
other is at variance with the principle that a free
people are capable of self-government." Then the
imperious Virginian boldly charged that the Federalists intended to have John Marshall and his associates on the Supreme Bench annul the Republican
repeal of the Federalist Judiciary Act.

"Sir," cried Randolph, "if you pass the law, the
judges are to put their veto upon it by declaring it
unconstitutional. Here is a new power of a dangerous and uncontrollable nature. . . The decision of a
Constitutional question must rest somewhere. Shall
it be confided to men immediately responsible to the
people, or to those who are irresponsible? . . From
whom is a corrupt decision most to be feared? . .

---

[1] *Annals*, 7th Cong. 1st Sess. 652.

The power which has the right of passing, without appeal, on the validity of your laws, is your sovereign. . . Are we not as deeply interested in the true exposition of the Constitution as the judges can be?" inquired Randolph. "Is not Congress as capable of forming a correct opinion as they are? Are not its members acting under a responsibility to public opinion which can and will check their aberrations from duty?"

Randolph referred to the case of Marbury *vs*. Madison and then recalled the prosecution of Thomas Cooper in which the National court refused "to a man under criminal prosecution . . a subpœna to be served on the President, as a witness on the part of the prisoner.[1] . . This court, which it seems, has lately become the guardian of the feeble and oppressed, against the strong arm of power, found itself destitute of all power to issue the writ. . .

"No, sir, you may invade the press; the courts will support you, will outstrip you in zeal to further this great object; your citizens may be imprisoned and amerced, the courts will take care to see it executed; the helpless foreigner may, contrary to the express letter of your Constitution, be deprived of compulsory process for obtaining witnesses in his defense; the courts in their extreme humility cannot find authority for granting it."

Again Marbury *vs*. Madison came into the de-

[1] See *supra*, chap. I, 33; also *infra*, chap. IX, where Marshall, during the trial of Aaron Burr, actually issued such a subpœna. Randolph was now denouncing the National court before which Cooper was tried, because it refused to grant the very writ for the issuing of which Marshall in a few years was so rancorously assailed by Jefferson personally, and by nearly all Republicans as a party.

bate: [1] "In their inquisitorial capacity," the Supreme Court, according to Marshall's ruling in that case, could force the President himself to discharge his executive functions "in what mode" the omnipotent judges might choose to direct. And Congress! "For the amusement of the public, we shall retain the right of debating but not of voting." [2] The judges could forestall legislation by "inflammatory pamphlets," as they had done. [3]

As the debate wore on, little that was new was adduced. Calvin Goddard of Connecticut reviewed the cases in which judges of various courts had asserted the Federalist doctrine of the judicial power to decide statutes unconstitutional, [4] and quoted from Marshall's speech on the Judiciary in the Virginia Convention of 1788. [5]

John Rutledge, Jr., of South Carolina, then delivered one of the most distinguished addresses of this notable discussion. Suppose, he said, that Congress were to pass any of the laws which the Constitution forbids, "who are to decide between the Constitution and the acts of Congress? . . If the people . . [are] not shielded by some Constitutional checks" their liberties will be "destroyed . . by demagogues, who filch the confidence of the people by pretending

---

[1] At the time Marshall issued the rule against Madison he apparently had no idea that Section 13 of the Ellsworth Judiciary Act was unconstitutional. (See next chapter.)

[2] *Annals*, 7th Cong. 1st Sess. 662–63.

[3] The Federalist organ tried, by ridicule, to minimize Randolph's really strong speech. "The speech of Mr. Randolph was a jumble of disconnected declamation. . . He was horribly tiresome to the ear and disgusting to the taste." (*Washington Federalist*, Feb. 22, 1802.)

[4] *Annals*, 7th Cong. 1st Sess. 727.

[5] *Ib.* 737. See also vol. I, 452, of this work.

to be their friends; .. demagogues who carry daggers in their hearts, and seductive smiles in their hypocritical faces."[1]

Rutledge was affected by the prevailing Federalist pessimism. "This bill," said he, "is an egg which will produce a brood of mortal consequences... It will soon prostrate public confidence; it will immediately depreciate the value of public property. Who will buy your lands? Who will open your Western forests? Who will build upon the hills and cultivate the valleys which here surround us?" The financial adventurer who would take such risks "must be a speculator indeed, and his purse must overflow .. if there be no independent tribunals where the validity of your titles will be confirmed.[2] ..

"Have we not seen a State [Georgia] sell its Western lands, and afterwards declare the law under which they were sold made null and void? Their nullifying law would have been declared void, had they had an independent Judiciary."[3] Here Rutledge anticipated by eight years the opinion delivered by Marshall in Fletcher vs. Peck.[4]

"Whenever in any country judges are dependent, property is insecure." What had happened in France? "Frenchmen received their constitution as the followers of Mahomet did their Koran, as though it came to them from Heaven. They swore on their standards and their sabres never to abandon it. But, sir, this constitution has vanished; the swords which were to have formed a rampart around it, are now

---

[1] *Annals*, 7th Cong. 1st Sess. 747–55.   [2] *Ib.* 759.
[3] *Ib.* 760.   [4] See *infra*, chap. x.

worn by the Consular janissaries, and the Republican standards are among the trophies which decorate the vaulted roof of the Consul's palace.[1] Indeed . . [the] subject," avowed Rutledge with passionate earnestness, "is perhaps as awful a one as any on this side of the grave. This attack upon our Constitution will form a great epoch in the history of our Government." [2]

Forcible resistance, if the Republican assault on the Judiciary succeeded, had twice been intimated during the debate. As yet, however, actual secession of the Northern and Eastern States had not been openly suggested, although it was common talk among the Federalists; [3] but now one of the boldest and frankest of their number broadly hinted it to be the Federalist purpose, should the Republicans persist in carrying out their purpose of demolishing the National courts.[4] In closing a long, intensely partisan and wearisome speech, Roger Griswold of Connecticut exclaimed: "There are states in this Union who will never consent and are not doomed to become the humble provinces of Virginia." [5]

Joseph H. Nicholson of Maryland, Republican, was hardly less prolix than Griswold. He asked whether the people had ever approved the adoption of the common law by the Judiciary. "Have they ever sanctioned the principle that the judges should make laws for them instead of their Representatives?" [6] Tiresome as he was, he made a conclusive

[1] *Annals*, 7th Cong. 1st Sess. 760.   [2] *Ib.* 760.
[3] See *infra*, chaps. III and VI.
[4] *Annals*, 7th Cong. 1st Sess. 767–94.
[5] *Ib.* 793.   [6] *Ib.* 805–06.

argument against the Federalist position that the National Judiciary might apply the common law in cases not provided for by acts of Congress.

The debate ran into the month of March.[1] Every possible phase of the subject was gone over time and again. All authorities which the ardent and tireless industry of the contending partisans could discover were brought to light. The pending case of Marbury *vs.* Madison was in the minds of all; and it was repeatedly dragged into the discussion. Samuel W. Dana of Connecticut examined it minutely, citing the action of the Supreme Court in the case of the application for a mandamus to the Secretary of War upon which the court acted February 14, 1794: "There does not appear to have been any question respecting the general power of the Supreme Court, to issue a mandamus to the Secretary of War, or any other subordinate officer." That was "a regular mode for obtaining a decision of the Supreme Court. . . When such has been the unquestioned usage heretofore, is it not extraordinary that there has not been prudence enough to say less about the case of Marbury against the Secretary of State?"[2]

---

[1] In sour disgust Morris notes in his diary: "The House of Representatives have talked themselves out of self-respect, and at headquarters [White House] there is such an abandonment of manner and such a pruriency of conversation as would reduce even greatness to the level of vulgarity." (March 10, 1802, Morris, II, 421.)

[2] *Annals,* 7th Cong. 1st Sess. 904.

Dana's statement is of first importance and should be carefully noted. It was at the time the universally accepted view of the power of the Supreme Court to issue writs of mandamus. Neither Federalists nor Republicans had ever questioned the Constitutional right of the Supreme Court to entertain original jurisdiction of mandamus proceedings in proper cases. Yet just this was what Marshall was so soon to deny in Marbury *vs.* Madison. (See *infra,* chap. III.)

Dana then touched upon the general expectation that Marshall would declare void the Repeal Act. Because of this very apprehension, the Republicans, a few days later, suspended for more than a year the sessions of the Supreme Court. So Dana threatened that if the Republicans should pass the bill, the Supreme Court would annul it; for, said he, the Judiciary were sworn to support the Constitution, and when they find that instrument on one side and an act of Congress on the other, "what is their duty? Are they not to obey their oath, and judge accordingly? If so, they necessarily decide, that your act is of no force; for they are sworn to support the Constitution. This is a doctrine coeval with the existence of our Government, and has been the uniform principle of all the constituted authorities." [1] And he cited the position taken by National judges in 1792 in the matter of the pension commission. [2]

John Bacon, that stanch Massachusetts Republican, [3] asserted that "the Judiciary have no more right to prescribe, direct or control the acts of the other departments of the Government, than the other departments of the Government have to prescribe or direct those of the Judiciary." [4]

The Republicans determined to permit no further delay; for the first time in its history the House was kept in session until midnight. [5] At twelve o'clock, March 3, 1802, the vote was taken on the final passage of the bill, the thirty-two Federalists voting against and the fifty-nine Republicans for the meas-

---

[1] *Annals*, 7th Cong. 1st Sess. 920.   [2] *Ib.* 923–26.
[3] See *supra*, chap. i, 43.
[4] *Annals*, 7th Cong. 1st Sess. 983.   [5] Hildreth, v, 441.

ure.[1] "Thus ended this gigantic debate," chronicles
the historian of that event.[2] No discussion in Congress had hitherto been so widely reported in the
press or excited such general comment. By the great
majority of the people the repeal was received with
enthusiasm, although some Republicans believed
that their party had gone too far.[3] Republican papers, however, hailed the repeal as the breaking of
one of those judicial fetters which shackled the people, while Federalist journals bemoaned it as the beginning of the annihilation of all that was sane and
worthy in American institutions.

"The fatal bill has passed; our Constitution is no
more," exclaimed the *Washington Federalist* in an
editorial entitled

"FAREWELL, A LONG FAREWELL, TO ALL OUR GREATNESS."

The paper despaired of the Republic — nobody
could tell "what other acts, urged by the intoxication of power and the fury of party rage" would be
put through. But it announced that the Federalist
judges would disregard the infamous Republican
law: "The judges will continue to hold their courts
as if the bill had not passed. 'T is their solemn duty
to do it; their country, all that is dear and valuable,
call upon them to do it. By the judges this bill will
be declared null and void. . . And we now ask the

[1] Bayard to Bassett, March 3, 1802, *Bayard Papers*: Donnan, 150;
and see *Annals*, 7th Cong. 1st Sess. 982. One Republican, Dr. William
Eustis of Boston, voted with the Federalists.

[2] *Hist. Last Sess. Cong. Which Commenced 7th Dec. 1801* (taken
from the *National Intelligencer*), 71.

[3] Tucker: *Life of Thomas Jefferson*, II, 114.

mighty victors, what is your triumph? . . What is the triumph of the President? He has gratified his malice towards the judges, but he has drawn a tear into the eye of every thoughtful patriot . . and laid the foundation of infinite mischief." The Federalist organ declared that the Republican purpose was to force a "dissolution of the Union," and that this was likely to happen.

This significant editorial ended by a consideration of the Republican purpose to destroy the Supreme Court: "Should Mr. Breckenridge now bring forward a resolution to repeal the law establishing the Supreme Court of the United States, we should only consider it a part of the system to be pursued. . . We sincerely expect it will be done next session. . . Such is democracy." [1]

Senator Plumer declared, before the final vote, that the passage of the Republican Repeal Bill and of other Republican measures meant "anarchy." [2]

The ultra-Federalist *Palladium* of Boston lamented: "Our army is to be less and our navy nothing: Our Secretaries are to be aliens and our Judges as independent as spaniels. In this way we are to save everything, but our reputation and our rights.[3] . . Has Liberty any citadel or fortress, has mob despotism any impediments?" [4]

---

[1] *Washington Federalist*, March 3, 1802. Too much importance cannot be attached to this editorial. It undoubtedly expressed accurately the views of Federalist public men in the Capital, including Marshall, whose partisan views and feelings were intense. It should not be forgotten that his relations with this newspaper were believed to be intimate. (See vol. II, 532, 541, of this work.)

[2] Plumer to Upham, March 1, 1802, Plumer MSS. Lib. Cong.

[3] March 12, 1802.   [4] March 23, 1802.

The *Independent Chronicle*, on the other hand, "congratulated the public on the final triumph of *Republicanism*, in the repeal of the late obnoxious judiciary law." [1] The Republicans of Boston and Cambridge celebrated the event with discharges of artillery.

Vans Murray reported to King that "the principle of . . disorganizing . . goes on with a destructive zeal. Internal Taxes — Judicial Sanctity — all are to be overset." [2] Sedgwick was sure that no defense was left against "legislative usurpation." [3] "The angels of destruction . . are making haste," moaned Fisher Ames. [4]

"The angels of destruction " lost no time in striking their next blow. On March 18, two weeks after the threat of the *Washington Federalist* that the Supreme Court would declare unconstitutional the Republican Repeal Act, a Senate committee was appointed to examine further the National Judiciary establishment and report a bill for any improvements considered necessary. [5] Within a week the committee laid the measure before the Senate, [6] and on April 8 it was passed [7] without debate.

When it reached the House, however, the Federalists had taken alarm. The Federalist Judiciary Act of 1801 had fixed the terms of the Supreme Court in December and June instead of February and August. This new bill, plainly an afterthought, abolished the

[1] March 15, 1802.
[2] Vans Murray to King, April 5, 1802, King, IV, 95.
[3] Sedgwick to King, Feb. 20, 1802, *ib.* 73.
[4] Ames to Dwight, April 16, 1802, Ames, I, 297.
[5] *Annals*, 7th Cong. 1st Sess. 201.   [6] *Ib.* 205.   [7] *Ib.* 257.

June session of the Supreme Court, directed that, thereafter, that tribunal should convene but once each year, and fixed the second Monday of February as the time of this annual session.

Thus did the Republicans plan to take away from the Supreme Court the opportunity to pass upon the repeal of the Federalist Judiciary Act of 1801 until the old and defective system of 1789, which it restored, was again in full operation. Meanwhile, the wrath of the new National judges, whom the repeal left without offices, would wear itself down, and they would accept the situation as an accomplished fact.[1] John Marshall should have no early opportunity to overturn the Repeal Act, as the Republicans believed he would do if given the chance. Neither should he proceed further with the case of Marbury *vs.* Madison for many months to come.[2]

Bayard moved that the bill should not go into effect until July 1, thus permitting the Supreme Court to hold its June session; but, said Nicholson, that was just what the Republicans intended to prevent. Was a June session of the Supreme Court "a source of alarm?" asked Bayard. "The effect of the present bill will be, to have no court for fourteen months. . . Are gentlemen afraid of the judges? Are they afraid that they will pronounce the repealing law void?"[3]

Nicholson did not care whether the Supreme

[1] They never occupied the bench under the Federalist Act of 1801. They were appointed, but the swift action of Jefferson and the Republicans prevented them from entering upon the discharge of their duties.

[2] This case was before the Supreme Court in December, 1801, and, ordinarily, would have been decided at the next term, June, 1802.

[3] *Annals*, 7th Cong. 1st Sess. 1228–29.

Court "pronounced the repealing law unconstitutional or not." The Republican postponement of the session for more than a year "does not arise from any design . . to prevent the exercise of power by the judges." But what of the Federalists' solicitude for an early sitting of the court? "We have as good a right to suppose gentlemen on the other side are as anxious for a session in June, that this power may be exercised, as they have to suppose we wish to avoid it, to prevent the exercise.". [1]

Griswold could not credit the Republicans with so base a purpose: "I know that it has been said, out of doors, that this is the great object of the bill. I know there have been slanders of this kind; but they are too disgraceful to ascribe to this body. The slander cannot, ought not to be admitted." So Griswold hoped that Republicans would permit the Supreme Court to hold its summer session. He frankly avowed a wish for an early decision that the Repeal Act was void. "I think the speedier it [usurpation] is checked the better." [2]

Bayard at last flatly charged the Republicans with the purpose of preventing the Supreme Court from holding the Repeal Act unconstitutional. "This act is not designed to amend the Judicial system," he asserted; "that is but pretense. . . It is to prevent that court from expressing their opinion upon the validity of the act lately passed . . until the act has gone into full execution, and the excitement of the public mind is abated. . . Could a less motive induce gentlemen to agree to suspend

---

[1] *Annals*, 7th Cong. 1st Sess. 1229.   [2] *Ib.* 1229–30.

the sessions of the Supreme Court for fourteen months ?" [1]

But neither the pleading nor the denunciation of the Federalists moved the Republicans. On Friday, April 23, 1802, the bill passed and the Supreme Court of the United States was practically abolished for fourteen months. [2]

At that moment began the movement that finally developed into the plan for the secession of the New England States from the Union. It is, perhaps, more accurate to say that the idea of secession had never been entirely out of the minds of the extreme New England Federalist leaders from the time Theodore Sedgwick threatened it in the debate over the Assumption Bill. [3]

Hints of withdrawing from the Union if Virginia should become dominant crop out in their correspondence. The Republican repeal of the Judiciary Act immediately called forth many expressions in Federalist papers such as this from the Boston *Palladium* of March 2, 1802: "Whether the rights and interests of the Eastern States would be perfectly safe when Virginia rules the nation is a problem easy to solve but terrible to contemplate. . . As ambitious *Virginia* will not be just, let valiant *Massachusetts* be zealous."

Fisher Ames declared that "the federalists must entrench themselves in the State governments, and endeavor to make State justice and State power a

---

[1] *Annals*, 7th Cong. 1st Sess. 1235-36.
[2] *Ib.* 1236. See also Channing, *U.S.* IV, 280-81.
[3] See vol. II, 62, of this work.

shelter of the wise, and good, and rich, from the wild destroying rage of the southern Jacobins." [1] He thought the Federalists had neglected the press. "It is practicable," said he, "to rouse our sleeping patriotism — sleeping, like a drunkard in the snow. . . The newspapers have been left to the lazy or the ill-informed, or to those who undertook singly work enough for six." [2]

Pickering, the truculent, brave, and persistent, anticipated "a new confederacy. . . There will be — and our children at farthest will see it — a separation. . . The British Provinces, even with the assent of Britain, will become members of the Northern Confederacy." [3]

The more moderate George Cabot, on the contrary, thought that the strong defense made by the Federalists in Congress would induce the Republicans to cease their attacks on the National courts. "The very able discussions of the Judiciary Question," he wrote, " & great superiority of the Federalists in all the debates & public writings have manifestly checked the career of the *Revolutionists*." [4] But for once Cabot was wrong; the Republicans were jubilant and hastened to press their assault more vigorously than ever.

[1] Ames to Gore, Dec. 13, 1802, Ames, I, 310.

[2] *Ib.* Here is another characteristic passage from Ames, who accurately expressed New England Federalist sentiment: "The second French and first American Revolution is now commencing. . . The extinction of Federalism would be followed by the ruin of the wise, rich, and good." (Ames to Smith, Dec. 14, 1802, *ib.* 313–16.)

[3] Pickering to Peters, Dec. 24, 1803, *New-England Federalism:* Adams, 338.

[4] Cabot to King, March 27, 1802, King, IV, 94.

The Federalist newspapers teemed with long arguments against the repeal and laboriously strove, in dull and heavy fashion, to whip their readers into fighting humor. These articles were little more than turgid repetitions of the Federalist speeches in Congress, with a passage here and there of the usual Federalist denunciation. For instance, the *Columbian Centinel*, after restating the argument against the Repeal Act, thought that this "refutes all the absurd doctrines of the Jacobins upon that subject, . . and it will be sooner or later declared by the people, in a tone terrible to the present disorganizing party, to be the true construction of their constitution, and the only one compatible with their safety and happiness." [1]

The *Independent Chronicle*, on the other hand, was exultant. After denouncing "the impudence and scurrility of the Federal faction," a correspondent of that paper proceeded in this fashion: "The Judiciary! The Judiciary! like a wreck on Cape Cod is dashing at every wave"; but, thank Heaven, "instead of the 'Essex Junto's' Judiciary we are sailing by the grace of God in the Washington *Frigate* — our judges are as at first and Mr. Jefferson has thought fit to practice the old navigation and steer with the same compass by which *Admiral Washington* regulated his log book. The Essex Junto may be afraid to trust themselves on board but every true Washington American will step on board in full confidence of a prosperous voyage. Huzza for the *Washington Judiciary* — no windows

[1] *Columbian Centinel*, April 7, 1802.

broke — no doors burst in — free from leak — tight and dry." [1]

Destiny was soon again to call John Marshall to the performance of an imperative duty.

[1] "Bowling" in the *Independent Chronicle* of April 26, 1802. An example of Jefferson's amazing skill in directing public opinion is found in the fact that the people were made to feel that the President was following in Washington's footsteps.

CHAPTER III

MARBURY VERSUS MADISON

To consider the judges as the ultimate arbiters of all constitutional questions, would place us under the despotism of an oligarchy. (Jefferson.)

The constitution is either a superior paramount law, unchangeable by ordinary means, or it is on a level with ordinary legislative acts alterable when the legislature shall please to alter it. It is emphatically the province and duty of the judicial department to say what the law is. This is the very essence of judicial duty. (Marshall.)

To have inscribed this vast truth of conservatism upon the public mind, so that no demagogue not in the last stages of intoxication denies it — this is an achievement of statesmanship which a thousand years may not exhaust or reveal all that is good. (Rufus Choate.)

"RAWLEIGH, Jan? 2ᵈ 1803

"MY DEAREST POLLY

"You will laugh at my vexation when you hear the various calamaties that have befallen me. In the first place when I came to review my funds, I had the mortification to discover that I had lost 15 silver dollars out of my waist coat pocket. They had worn through the various mendings the pocket had sustained & sought their liberty in the sands of Carolina.

"I determined not to vex myself with what coud not be remedied & orderd Peter to take out my cloaths that I might dress for court when to my astonishment & grief after fumbling several minutes in the portmanteau, staring at vacancy, & sweating most profusely he turned to me with the doleful tidings that I had no pair of breeches. You may be sure this piece of inteligence was not very graciously receivd; however, after a little scolding I determined to make the best of my situation & immediately set out to get a pair made.

"I thought I should be a sans culotte only one day & that for the residue of the term I might be well enough dressd for the appearance on the first day to be forgotten. But, the greatest of evils, I found, was followed by still greater! Not a taylor in town coud be prevaild on to work for me. They were all so busy that it was impossible to attend to my wants however pressing they might be, & I have the extreme mortification to pass the whole time without that important article of dress I have mentiond. I have no alleviation for this misfortune but the hope that I shall be enabled in four or five days to commence my journey homeward & that I shall have the pleasure of seeing you & our dear children in eight or nine days after this reaches you.

"In the meantime I flatter myself that you are well & happy.

"Adieu my dearest Polly

I am your ever affectionate

J MARSHALL." [1]

With the same unfailing light-heartedness which, nearly a quarter of a century before, had cheered his comrades at Valley Forge, John Marshall, Chief Justice of the United States, thus went about his duties and bore his troubles. Making his circuit in a battered gig or sulky, which he himself usually drove, absent-minded and laughing at himself for the mishaps that his forgetfulness and negligence

---

[1] Marshall to his wife, Jan. 2, 1803, MS.

continually brought upon him, he was seemingly
unperturbed in the midst of the political upheaval.

Yet he was not at ease. Rufus King, still the
American Minister to Great Britain, had finally
settled the controversy over the British debts, upon
the very basis laid down by Marshall when Secretary of State.[1] But Jefferson's Administration now
did not hesitate to assert that this removal of one
cause of conflict with Great Britain was the triumph
of Republican diplomacy. Marshall, with unreserve
so unlike him, reveals to King his disgust and sense
of injury, and in doing so portrays the development
of political conditions.

"The advocates of the present administration
ascribe to it great praise," wrote Marshall to our
Minister in London, "for having, with so much dex-
terity & so little loss, extricated our country from
a debt of twenty-four million of dollars in which a
former administration had involved it. . . The mor-
tifying reflection obtrudes itself, that the reputation
of the most wise & skilful conduct depends, in this
our capricious world, so much on accident. Had
Mr. Adams been reelected President of the United
States, or had his successor been [a Federalist] . . a
very different reception . . would have been given
to the same measure.

"The payment of a specific sum would then have
been pronounced, by those who now take merit to
themselves for it, a humiliating national degradation, an abandonment of national interest, a free
will offering of millions to Britain for her grace &

[1] See vol. II, 502–05, of this work.

favor, by those who sought to engage in a war with France, rather than repay, in part, by a small loan to that republic, the immense debt of gratitude we owe her."

So speaks with bitter sarcasm the new Chief Justice, and pessimistically continues: "Such is, & such I fear will ever be human justice!" He tells King that the Federalist "disposition to coalesce" with the Republicans, which seemed to be developing during the first few months after Jefferson's inauguration, had disappeared; "but," he adds, "the minority [Federalist Party] is only recovering its strength & firmness. It acquires nothing." Then, with the characteristic misgivings of a Federalist, he prophesies: "Our political tempests will long, very long, exist, after those who are now toss'd about by them shall be at rest." [1]

For more than five years [2] Marshall had foreseen the complicated and dangerous situation in which the country now found itself; and for more than a year [3] he had, in his ample, leisurely, simple manner of thinking, been framing the constructive answer which he was at last forced to give to the grave question: Who shall say with final authority what is and what is not law throughout the Republic? In his opinion in the case of Marbury *vs.* Madison, to which this chapter is devoted, we shall see how John Marshall answered this vital question.

[1] Marshall to King, May 5, 1802, King, IV, 116–18.
[2] Since the adoption of the Kentucky and Virginia Resolutions in 1798. (See vol. II, chaps. X, XI, XII, of this work.)
[3] Since the Republican repeal of the Federalist Judiciary Act was proposed. See *supra*, 51.

The philosophy of the Virginia and Kentucky Resolutions had now become the ruling doctrine of the Republican Party. The writer of the creed of State Rights sat in the Executive chair, while in House and Senate Virginia and her daughter Kentucky ruled the Republican majority. The two States that had declared the right and power of any member of the Union to pronounce a National law unconstitutional, and that had actually asserted a National statute to be null and void, had become the dominant force in the National Government.

The Federalist majority in the legislatures of ten States,[1] it is true, had passed resolutions denouncing that anti-National theory, and had vigorously asserted that the National Judiciary alone had the power to invalidate acts of Congress.[2] *But in none of*

[1] Maryland, Pennsylvania, New Jersey, Delaware, New York, Vermont, New Hampshire, Massachusetts, Connecticut, Rhode Island.

[2] The Federalist majority in Vermont resolved that: "It belongs not to *State Legislatures* to decide on the constitutionality of laws made by the general government; this power being exclusively vested in the *Judiciary Courts of the Union*." (*Records of Governor and Council of Vermont*, IV, 529.)

The Federalist majority in the Maryland Legislature asserted that "no state government .. is competent to declare an act of the federal government unconstitutional, .. that jurisdiction .. is exclusively vested in the courts of the United States." (Anderson, in *Am. Hist. Rev.* v, 248.)

The New York Federalists were slow to act, but finally resolved "that the right of deciding on the constitutionality of all laws passed by Congress .. appertains to the judiciary department." (*Ib.* 248–49.)

Connecticut Federalists declared that the Kentucky and Virginia plan was "hostile to the existence of our national Union." (*Ib.* 247.)

In Delaware the then dominant party decided that the Kentucky and Virginia Resolutions were "not a fit subject" for their consideration. (*Ib.* 246.)

The Pennsylvania Federalist majority resolved that the people

these States had the Republican minority concurred.
In all of them the Republicans had vigorously fought
the Federalist denial of the right and power of the
States to nullify National laws, and had especially
resisted the Federalist assertion that this power was
in the National Judiciary.

In the New York Legislature, forty-three Republicans voted solidly against the Federalist reply to
Virginia and Kentucky, while the Federalists were
able to muster but fifty votes in its favor. In Massachusetts, Pennsylvania, and Maryland, the Republican opposition was determined and outspoken.

The thirty-three Republicans of the Vermont
Legislature cited, in their protest, the position
which Marshall had taken on the Sedition Law in his
campaign for Congress: [1] "We have ever been of an
opinion, with that much and deservedly respected
statesman, Mr. Marshall, (whose abilities and in-

"have committed to the supreme judiciary of the nation the high authority of ultimately and conclusively deciding the constitutionality
of all legislative acts." (Anderson, in *Am. Hist. Rev.* v, 245.)

On February 8, 1799, Massachusetts replied to the Virginia Resolutions that: "This legislature are persuaded that the decision of all
cases in law or equity, arising under the Constitution of the United
States, and the construction of all laws made in pursuance thereof,
are exclusively vested by the people in the Judicial Courts of the
U. States." (*Mass. Senate Journal, 1798–99*, xix, 238, MS. volume
Mass. State Library.)

Such was the general tenor of the Federalists' pronouncements upon
this grave problem. But because the people believed the Sedition
Law to be directed against free speech, the Federalist supremacy in
many of the States that insisted upon these sound Nationalist principles was soon overthrown.

The resolutions of the Republican minorities in the Legislatures of
the Federalist States were emphatic assertions that any State might
declare an act of Congress unconstitutional and disregard it, and *that
the National Judiciary did not have supervisory power over legislation.*

[1] See vol. ii, 387–89, of this work.

tegrity have been doubted by no party, and whose spirited and patriotic defence of his country's rights, has been universally admired) [1] that 'it was calculated to create *unnecessarily*, discontents and jealousies, at a time, when our very existence as a nation may depend on our union.'" [2]

In Southern States, where the Federalists were dominant when Kentucky and Virginia adopted their famous Resolutions, the Republicans were, nevertheless, so strong that the Federalist majority in the Legislatures of those States dared not attempt to deny formally the new Republican gospel. [3]

So stood the formal record; but, since it had been written, the Jeffersonian propaganda had drawn scores of thousands of voters into the Republican ranks. The whole South had now decisively repudiated Federalism. Maryland had been captured; Pennsylvania had become as emphatically Republican as Virginia herself; New York had joined her forces to the Republican legions. The Federalists still held New England and the States of Delaware and New Jersey, but even there the incessant Republican assaults, delivered with ever-increasing strength, were weakening the Federalist power. Nothing was plainer than that, if the Kentucky and Virginia Resolutions had been submitted to the Legislatures of the various States in 1801–1803, most of them would have enthusiastically endorsed them.

Thus the one subject most discussed, from the campaign of 1800 to the time when Marshall deliv-

[1] Referring to Marshall's conduct in the French Mission. (See vol. II, chaps. VII, VIII, IX, of this work.)

[2] Anderson, in *Am. Hist. Rev.* v, 249.   [3] *Ib.* 235-37.

ered his opinion in Marbury *vs.* Madison, was the all-important question as to what power, if any, could annul acts of Congress.[1] During these years popular opinion became ever stronger that the Judiciary could not do so, that Congress had a free hand so far as courts were concerned, and that the individual States might ignore National laws whenever those States deemed them to be infractions of the Constitution. As we have seen, the Republican vote in Senate and House, by which the Judiciary Act of 1801 was repealed, was also a vote against the theory of the supervisory power of the National Judiciary over National legislation.

Should this conclusion go unchallenged? If so, it would have the sanction of acquiescence and soon acquire the strength of custom. What then would become the condition of the country? Congress might pass a law which some States would oppose and which they would refuse to obey, but which other States would favor and of which they would demand the enforcement. What would this entail? At the very least it would provoke a relapse into the chaos of the Confederation and more probably civil war. Or a President might take it upon himself to pronounce null and void a law of Congress, as Jefferson had already done in the matter of the Sedition Law,[2] and if House and Senate were of a hostile political party, Congress might insist upon

---

[1] The questions raised by the Kentucky and Virginia Resolutions were principal themes of debate in State Legislatures, in the press, in Congressional campaigns, and in the Presidential contest of 1800. The Judiciary debate of 1802 was, in part, a continuance of these popular discussions.

[2] See *supra*, 52.

the observance of its legislation; but such a course would seriously damage the whole machinery of the National Government.

The fundamental question as to what power could definitely pass upon the validity of legislation must be answered without delay. Some of Marshall's associates on the Supreme Bench were becoming old and feeble, and death, or resignation enforced by illness, was likely at any moment to break the Nationalist solidarity of the Supreme Court; [1] and the appointing power had fallen into the hands of the man who held the subjugation of the National Judiciary as one of his chief purposes.

Only second in importance to these reasons for Marshall's determination to meet the issue was the absolute necessity of asserting that there was one department of the Government that could not be influenced by temporary public opinion. The value to a democracy of a steadying force was not then so well understood as it is at present, but the Chief Justice fully appreciated it and determined at all hazards to make the National Judiciary the stabilizing power that it has since become. It should be said, however, that Marshall no longer "idolized democracy," as he declared he did when as a young man he addressed the Virginia Convention of 1788. [2] On the contrary, he had come to distrust popular rule as much as did most Federalists.

[1] Within a year after Marbury *vs.* Madison was decided, Albert Moore, one of the Federalist Associate Justices of the Supreme Court, resigned because of ill health and his place was filled by William Johnson, a Republican of South Carolina.

[2] See vol. I, 410, of this work.

A case was then pending before the Supreme Court the decision of which might, by boldness and ingenuity, be made to serve as the occasion for that tribunal's assertion of its right and power to invalidate acts of Congress and also for the laying-down of rules for the guidance of all departments of the Government. This was the case of Marbury *vs.* Madison.

Just before his term expired,[1] President Adams had appointed forty-two persons to be justices of the peace for the Counties of Washington and Alexandria in the District of Columbia.[2] The Federalist Senate had confirmed these nominations,[3] and the commissions had been signed and sealed, but had not been delivered. When Jefferson was inaugurated he directed Madison, as Secretary of State, to issue commissions to twenty-five of the persons appointed by Adams, but to withhold the commissions from the other seventeen.[4]

Among the latter were William Marbury, Dennis Ramsay, Robert Townsend Hooe, and William Harper. These four men applied to the Supreme Court for a writ of mandamus compelling Madison to deliver their commissions. The other thirteen did not join in the suit, apparently considering the office of justice of the peace too insignificant to be worth the expense of litigation. Indeed, these offices were deemed so trifling that one of Adams's appointees to

---

[1] March 2, 1801.

[2] *Journal of the Executive Proceedings of the Senate,* I, 388.

[3] *Ib.* 390.

[4] *Ib.* 404. Jefferson did this because, as he said, the appointees of Adams were too numerous.

whom Madison delivered a commission resigned, and
five others refused to qualify.[1]

When the application of Marbury and his associates came before Marshall he assumed jurisdiction, and in December, 1801, issued the usual rule
to Madison ordering him to show cause at the next
term of the Supreme Court why the writ of mandamus should not be awarded against him. Soon afterward, as we have seen, Congress abolished the June
session of the Supreme Court;[2] thus, when the court
again convened in February, 1803, the case of Marbury *vs.* Madison was still pending.

Marshall resolved to make use of this unimportant litigation to assert, at the critical hour when
such a pronouncement was essential, the power of the
Supreme Court to declare invalid acts of Congress
that violate the Constitution.

Considering the fact that Marshall was an experienced politician, was intimately familiar with the
political methods of Jefferson and the Republican
leaders, and was advised of their purposes, he could
not have failed to realize the probable consequences
to himself of the bold course he now determined to
take. As the crawling months of 1802 wore on, no
signs appeared that the Republican programme for
overthrowing the independence of the Judiciary
would be relinquished or modified. On the contrary,
the coming of the new year (1803) found the second
phase of the Republican assault determined upon.

At the beginning of the session of 1803 the House
impeached John Pickering, Judge of the United

---

[1] *Journal, Exec. Proc. Senate,* I, 417.   [2] See *supra,* 94-97.

States District Court for the District of New Hampshire. In Pennsylvania, the recently elected Republican House had impeached Judge Alexander Addison, and his conviction by a partisan vote was assured. Already the Republican determination to remove Samuel Chase from the Supreme Bench was frankly avowed.[1]

Moreover, the Republicans openly threatened to oust Marshall and his Federalist associates in case the court decided Marbury *vs.* Madison as the Republicans expected it would. They did not anticipate that Marshall would declare unconstitutional that section of the old Federalist Judiciary Act of 1789 under which the suit had been brought. Indeed, nobody imagined that the court would do that.

Everybody apparently, except Marshall and the Associate Justices, thought that the case would be decided in Marbury's favor and that Madison would be ordered to deliver the withheld commissions. It was upon this supposition that the Republican threats of impeachment were made. The Republicans considered Marbury's suit as a Federalist partisan maneuver and believed that the court's decision and Marshall's opinion would be inspired by motives of Federalist partisanship.[2]

---

[1] See *infra*, chap. IV.

[2] This belief is strikingly shown by the comment of the Republican press. For example, just before Marshall delivered his opinion, a correspondent of the *Independent Chronicle* of Boston sent from Washington this article:

"The efforts of *federalism* to exalt the Judiciary over the Executive and Legislature, and to give that favorite department a political character & influence, may operate for a time to come, as it has already, to the promotion of one party and the depression of the other; but

There was a particular and powerful reason for
Marshall to fear impeachment and removal from
office; for, should he be deposed, it was certain that
Jefferson would appoint Spencer Roane of Virginia
to be Chief Justice of the United States. It was
well known that Jefferson had intended to appoint
Roane upon the death of Chief Justice Ellsworth.[1]
But Ellsworth had resigned in time to permit Adams
to appoint Marshall as his successor and thus thwart
Jefferson's purpose. If now Marshall were removed,
Roane would be given his place.

Should he be succeeded by Roane, Marshall knew
that the great principles of Nationalism, to the car-

will probably terminate in the degradation and disgrace of the Judiciary.

"Politics are more improper and dangerous in a Court of Justice, if
possible, than in the pulpit. Political charges, prosecutions, and similar modes of official influence, ought never to have been resorted to by
any party. The fountains of justice should be unpolluted by party
passions and prejudices.

"The *attempt* of the Supreme Court of the United States, by a mandamus, to control the Executive functions, is a new experiment. It
seems to be no less than a commencement of war between the constituted departments.

"The Court must be defeated and retreat from the attack; or march
on, till they incur an impeachment and removal from office. But our
Republican frame of Government is so firm and solid, that there is
reason to hope it will remain unshaken by the assaults of opposition,
& the conflicts of interfering departments.

"The will of the nation, deliberately and constitutionally expressed,
must and will prevail, the predictions and exertions of *federal* monarchists and aristocrats to the contrary notwithstanding." (*Independent Chronicle*, March 10, 1803.)

Marshall's opinion was delivered February 24. It took two weeks
of fast traveling to go from Washington to Boston. Ordinary mail required a few days longer. The article in the *Chronicle* was probably
sent while Marbury *vs.* Madison was being argued.

[1] Dodd, in *Am. Hist. Rev.* xii, 776. Under the law Marshall's successor must come from Virginia or North Carolina.

rying-out of which his life was devoted, would never
be asserted by the National Judiciary. On the contrary, the Supreme Court would become an engine
for the destruction of every theory of government
which Marshall held dear; for a bolder, abler, and
more persistent antagonist of those principles than
Spencer Roane did not exist.[1] Had he become Chief
Justice those cases in which Marshall delivered opinions that vitalized the Constitution would have been
decided in direct opposition to Marshall's views.[2]

But despite the peril, Marshall resolved to act.
Better to meet the issue now, come what might, than
to evade it. If he succeeded, orderly government
would be assured, the National Judiciary lifted to
its high and true place, and one element of National
disintegration suppressed, perhaps destroyed. If he
failed, the country would be in no worse case than
that to which it was rapidly tending.

No words in the Constitution gave the Judiciary
the power to annul legislation. The subject had
been discussed in the Convention, but the brief and
scattering debate had arisen upon the proposition to
make the President and Justices of the Supreme

[1] As President of the Court of Appeals of Virginia he later challenged Marshall and brought about the first serious conflict between
the courts of a State and the supreme tribunal of the Nation; and as
a pamphleteer he assailed Marshall and his principles of Nationalism
with unsparing rigor. (See vol. IV, chaps. III, and VI, of this work.)

[2] For example, in Fletcher vs. Peck, Roane would have held that
the National Courts could not annul a State statute; in Martin vs.
Hunter's Lessees and in Cohen vs. Virginia, that the Supreme Court
could not review the judgment of a State court; in McCulloch vs.
Maryland, that Congress could not exercise implied powers, but only
those expressly granted by the specific terms of the Constitution, etc.
All this we know positively from Roane's own writings. (See vol. IV,
chaps. III, VI, and VII, of this work.)

Court members of a Council of Revision with power to negative acts of Congress. No direct resolution was ever offered to the effect that the Judiciary should be given power to declare acts of Congress unconstitutional. In the discussion of the proposed Council of Revision there were sharp differences of opinion on the collateral question of the right and wisdom of judicial control of legislative acts.[1] But,

[1] It seems probable, however, that it was generally understood by the leading men of the Convention that the Judiciary was to exercise the power of invalidating unconstitutional acts of Congress. (See Corwin: *Doctrine of Judicial Review*, 10–11; Beard: *Supreme Court and the Constitution*, 16–18; McLaughlin: *The Courts, the Constitution and Parties*, 32–35.)

In the Constitutional Convention, Elbridge Gerry of Massachusetts asserted that the judicial function of expounding statutes "involved a power of deciding on their Constitutionality." (*Records of the Federal Convention of 1787:* Farrand, I, 97.) Rufus King of Massachusetts — later of New York — was of the same opinion. (*Ib.* 109.)

On the other hand, Franklin declared that "it would be improper to put it in the power of any Man to negative a Law passed by the Legislature because it would give him the controul of the Legislature." (*Ib.*)

Madison felt "that no Man would be so daring as to place a veto on a Law that had passed with the assent of the Legislature." (*Ib.*) Later in the debate, Madison modified his first opinion and declared that "a law violating a constitution established by the people themselves, would be considered by the Judges null & void." (*Ib.* II, 93.)

George Mason of Virginia said that the Judiciary "could declare an unconstitutional law void. . . He wished the further use to be made of the Judges of giving aid in preventing every improper law." (*Ib.* 78.)

Gouverneur Morris of Pennsylvania — afterwards of New York — dreaded "legislative usurpations" and felt that "encroachments of the popular branch . . ought to be guarded agst." (*Ib.* 299.)

Gunning Bedford, Jr., of Delaware was against any "check on the Legislative" with two branches. (*Ib.* I, 100–01.)

James Wilson of Pennsylvania insisted that power in the Judiciary to declare laws unconstitutional "did not go far enough" — the judges should also have "Revisionary power" to pass on bills in the process of enactment. (*Ib.* II, 73.)

Luther Martin of Maryland had no doubt that the Judiciary had "a negative" on unconstitutional laws. (*Ib.* 76.)

John Francis Mercer of Maryland "disapproved of the Doctrine

in the end, nothing was done and the whole subject was dropped.

Such was the record of the Constitutional Convention when, by his opinion in Marbury *vs*. Madison, Marshall made the principle of judicial supremacy over legislation as much a part of our fundamental law as if the Constitution contained these specific words: the Supreme Court shall have the power to declare invalid any act of Congress which, in the opinion of the court, is unconstitutional.

In establishing this principle Marshall was to contribute nothing new to the thought upon the subject. All the arguments on both sides of the question had been made over and over again since the Kentucky and Virginia Resolutions had startled the land, and had been freshly stated in the Judiciary debate in the preceding Congress. Members of the Federalist majority in most of the State Legislatures had expressed, in highly colored partisan rhetoric, every sound reason for the theory that the National Judiciary should be the ultimate interpreter of the Constitution. Both Federalist and Republican newspapers had printed scores of essays for and against that doctrine.

In the Virginia Convention of 1788 Marshall had announced as a fundamental principle that if Con-

that the Judges as expositors of the Constitution should have authority to declare a law void." (*Records, Fed. Conv.*: Farrand, 298.)

John Dickinson of Delaware "thought no such power ought to exist," but was "at a loss what expedient to substitute." (*Ib.* 299.)

Charles Pinckney of South Carolina "opposed the interference of the Judges in the Legislative business." (*Ib.* 298.)

The above is a condensed *précis* of all that was said in the Constitutional Convention on this vital matter.

gress should pass an unconstitutional law the courts would declare it void,[1] and in his reply to the address of the majority of the Virginia Legislature [2] he had elaborately, though with much caution and some mistiness, set forth his views.[3] Chief Justice Jay and his associates had complained that the Judiciary Act of 1789 was unconstitutional, but they had not had the courage to announce that opinion from the Bench.[4] Justices Iredell and Paterson, sitting as circuit judges, had claimed for the National Judiciary the exclusive right to determine the constitutionality of laws. Chief Justice Jay in charging a grand jury, and Associate Justice Wilson in a carefully prepared law lecture, had announced the same conclusion.

Various State judges of the Federalist faith, among them Dana of Massachusetts and Addison of Pennsylvania, had spoken to like effect. At the trial of Callender [5] Marshall had heard Chase deliver the opinion that the National Judiciary had the exclusive power to declare acts of Congress unconstitutional.[6] Jefferson himself had written Meusnier, the year before the National Constitution was framed, that the Virginia Legislature had passed unconstitutional laws,[7] adding: "I have not heard that in the other states they have ever infringed their con-

---

[1] See vol. I, 452, of this work.   [2] The Virginia Resolutions.
[3] Address of the Minority, Jan. 22, 1799, *Journal of the House of Delegates of Virginia, 1798–99*, 90–95.
[4] Jay to Iredell, Sept. 15, 1790, enclosing statement to President Washington, *Iredell:* McRee, 293–96; and see letter of Jay to Washington, Aug. 8, 1793, *Jay:* Johnston, III, 488–89.
[5] See *supra,* 40, footnote 1.   [6] Wharton: *State Trials,* 715–18.
[7] Jefferson to Meusnier, Jan. 24, 1786, *Works:* Ford, v, 31–32.

stitution; . . *as the judges would consider any law as void* which was contrary to the constitution." [1]

Just as Jefferson, in writing the Declaration of Independence, put on paper not a single new or original idea, but merely set down in clear and compact form what had been said many times before,[2] so Marshall, in his opinion in Marbury *vs.* Madison, did nothing more than restate that which had previously been declared by hundreds of men. Thomas Jefferson and John Marshall as private citizens in Charlottesville and Richmond might have written Declarations and Opinions all their lives, and to-day none but the curious student would know that such men had ever lived. It was the authoritative position which these two great Americans happened to occupy and the compelling emergency for the announcement of the principles they expressed, as well as the soundness of those principles, that have given immortality to their enunciations.

Learned men have made exhaustive research for legal decisions by which Marshall's footsteps may have been guided, or which, at least, would justify his conclusion in Marbury *vs.* Madison.[3] The cases thus discovered are curious and interesting, but it is

---

[1] Jefferson to Meusnier, Jan. 24, 1786, *Works:* Ford, v, 14–15. (Italics the author's.)

[2] For instance, the Legislature of Rhode Island formally declared Independence almost two months before Congress adopted the pronouncement penned by Jefferson, and Jefferson used many of the very words of the tiny colony's defiance. In her Declaration of Independence in May, 1776, Virginia set forth most of the reasons stated by Jefferson a few weeks later in similar language.

[3] For these cases and references to studies of the question of judicial supremacy over legislation, see Appendix C.

probable that Marshall had not heard of many of them. At any rate, he does not cite one of them in the course of this opinion, although no case ever was decided in which a judge needed so much the support of judicial precedents. Neither did he know anything whatever of what was said on the subject in the Constitutional Convention, unless by hearsay, for its sessions were secret [1] and the Journals were not made public until 1819 — thirty years after the Government was established, and sixteen years after Marbury *vs.* Madison was decided.[2] Nor was Marshall informed of the discussions of the subject in the State Conventions that ratified the Constitution, except of those that took place in the Virginia Convention.[3]

On the other hand, he surely had read the Judiciary debate in Congress, for he was in the Capital when that controversy took place and the speeches were fully reported in the Washington press. Marshall probably was present in the Senate and the House when the most notable arguments were made.[4] More important, however, than written decisions or printed debates in influencing Marshall's mind was *The Federalist*, which we know he read carefully. In number seventy-eight of that work, Hamilton stated the principle of judicial supremacy which Marshall whole-heartedly adopted in Marbury *vs.* Madison.

[1] See vol. I, 323, of this work.
[2] See *Records Fed. Conv.*: Farrand, I, Introduction, xii.
[3] Elliot's *Debates* were not published until 1827–30.
[4] Until very recently Justices of the Supreme Court often came to the Senate to listen to debates in which they were particularly interested.

"The interpretation of the laws," wrote Hamilton, "is the proper and peculiar province of the courts. A constitution is, in fact, and must be regarded by the judges, as a fundamental law. It therefore belongs to them to ascertain its meaning, as well as the meaning of any particular act proceeding from the legislative body. If there should happen to be an irreconcilable variance between the two, . . the Constitution ought to be preferred to the statute, the intention of the people to the intention of their agents." [1]

In this passage Hamilton merely stated the general understanding of nearly all the important framers of the Constitution. Beyond question, Marshall considered that principle to have been woven into the very fiber of the Nation's fundamental law.

In executing his carefully determined purpose to have the Supreme Court formally announce the exclusive power of that tribunal as the authority of last resort to interpret the Constitution and determine the validity of laws by the test of that instrument, Marshall faced two practical and baffling difficulties, in addition to those larger and more forbidding ones which we have already considered.

The first of these was the condition of the Supreme Court itself and the low place it held in the public esteem; from the beginning it had not, as a body, impressed the public mind with its wisdom, dignity, or force.[2] The second obstacle was techni-

---

[1] *The Federalist:* Lodge, 485–86. Madison also upheld the same doctrine. Later he opposed it, but toward the end of his life returned to his first position. (See vol. IV, chap. X, of this work.)

[2] John Jay had declined reappointment as Chief Justice because,

cal and immediate. Just how should Marshall declare the Supreme Court to be the ultimate arbiter of conflicts between statutes and the Constitution? What occasion could he find to justify, and seemingly to require, the pronouncement as the judgment of the Supreme Court of that opinion now imperatively demanded, and which he had resolved at all hazards to deliver?

among other things, he was "perfectly convinced" that the National Judiciary was hopelessly weak. (See *supra*, 55.) The first Chief Justice of the United States at no moment, during his occupancy of that office, felt sure of himself or of the powers of the court. (See Jay to his wife, *Jay:* Johnston, III, 420.) Jay had hesitated to accept the office as Chief Justice when Washington tendered it to him in 1789, and he had resigned it gladly in 1795 to become the Federalist candidate for Governor of New York.

Washington offered the place to Patrick Henry, who refused it. (See Henry: *Patrick Henry — Life, Correspondence and Speeches*, II, 562–63; also Tyler, I, 183.) The office was submitted to William Cushing, an Associate Justice of the Supreme Court, and he also refused to consider it. (Wharton: *State Trials*, 33.) So little was a place on the Supreme Bench esteemed that John Rutledge resigned as Associate Justice to accept the office of Chief Justice of the Supreme Court of South Carolina. (*Ib.* 35.)

Jefferson considered that the government of New Orleans was "the second office in the United States in importance." (Randal, III, 202.) For that matter, no National office in Washington, except the Presidency, was prized at this period. Senator Bailey of New York actually resigned his seat in the Senate in order to accept the office of Postmaster at New York City. (*Memoirs, J. Q. A.*: Adams, I, 290.) Edmund Randolph, when Attorney-General, deplored the weakening of the Supreme Court, and looked forward to the time when it should be strengthened. (Randolph to Washington, Aug. 5, 1792, *Writings of George Washington:* Sparks, X, 513.)

The weakness of the Supreme Court, before Marshall became Chief Justice, is forcibly illustrated by the fact that in designing and building the National Capitol that tribunal was entirely forgotten and no chamber provided for it. (See Hosea Morrill Knowlton in *John Marshall — Life, Character and Judicial Services:* Dillon, I, 198–99.) When the seat of government was transferred to Washington, the court crept into an humble apartment in the basement beneath the Senate Chamber.

When the Republicans repealed the Federalist
Judiciary Act of 1801, Marshall had actually proposed to his associates upon the Supreme Bench
that they refuse to sit as circuit judges, and "risk
the consequences." By the Constitution, he said,
they were Judges of the Supreme Court only; their
commissions proved that they were appointed solely
to those offices; the section requiring them to sit in
inferior courts was unconstitutional. The other
members of the Supreme Court, however, had not
the courage to adopt the heroic course Marshall
recommended. They agreed that his views were
sound, but insisted that, because the Ellsworth
Judiciary Act had been acquiesced in since the adoption of the Constitution, the validity of that act
must now be considered as established.[1] So Marshall reluctantly abandoned his bold plan, and in
the autumn of 1802 held court at Richmond as circuit judge. To the end of his life, however, he held
firmly to the opinion that in so far as the Republican Judiciary Repeal Act of 1802 deprived National
judges of their offices and salaries, that legislation
was unconstitutional.[2]

Had the circuit judges, whose offices had just been
taken from them, resisted in the courts, Marshall
might, and probably would, have seized upon the
issue thus presented to declare invalid the act by
which the Republicans had overturned the new
Federalist Judiciary system. Just this, as we have

---

[1] *New York Review*, III, 347. The article on Chief Justice Marshall
in this periodical was written by Chancellor James Kent, although his
name does not appear.

[2] See vol. IV, chap. IX.

seen, the Republicans had expected him to do, and therefore had so changed the sessions of the Supreme Court that it could not render any decision for more than a year after the new Federalist courts were abolished.

Certain of the deposed National judges had, indeed, taken steps to bring the "revolutionary" Republican measure before the Supreme Court,[1] but their energies flagged, their hearts failed, and their only action was a futile and foolish protest to the very Congress that had wrested their judicial seats from under them.[2] Marshall was thus deprived of that opportunity at the only time he could have availed himself of it.

A year afterward, when Marbury *vs.* Madison came up for decision, the entire National Judiciary had submitted to the Republican repeal and was holding court under the Act of 1789.[3] This case,

---

[1] See Tilghman to Smith, May 22, 1802, Morison: *Smith*, 148–49.

"A general arrangement [for action on behalf of the deposed judges] will be attempted before we separate. It is not descrete to say more at present." (Bayard to Bassett, April 19, 1802, *Bayard Papers:* Donnan, 153.)

[2] See "Protest of Judges," *American State Papers, Miscellaneous*, I, 340.

Writing to Wolcott, now one of the displaced National circuit judges (Wolcott's appointment was secured by Marshall; see vol. II, 559, of this work), concerning "the outrage committed by Congress on the Constitution" (Cabot to Wolcott, Dec. 20, 1802, Lodge: *Cabot*, 328), Cabot said: " I cannot but approve the intention of your judicial corps to unite in a memorial or remonstrance to Congress." He considered this to be "a manifest duty" of the judges, and gave Wolcott the arguments for their action. (Cabot to Wolcott, Oct. 21, 1802, *ib.* 327–28.)

A proposition to submit to the Supreme Court the constitutionality of the Repeal Act was rejected January 27, 1803. (*Annals*, 7th Cong. 2d Sess. 439.)

[3] See *infra*, 130, 131.

then, alone remained as the only possible occasion for announcing, at that critical time, the supervisory power of the Judiciary over legislation.

Marshall was Secretary of State when President Adams tardily appointed, and the Federalist Senate confirmed, the forty-two justices of the peace for the District of Columbia,[1] and it was Marshall who had failed to deliver the commissions to the appointees. Instead, he had, with his customary negligence of details, left them on his desk. Scarcely had he arrived at Richmond, after Jefferson's inauguration, when his brother, James M. Marshall, wrote him of the plight in which the newly appointed justices of the peace found themselves as the result of Marshall's oversight.

The Chief Justice replied: "I learn with infinite chagrin the 'development of principle' mentioned in yours of the 12th," — sarcastically referring to the Administration's conduct toward the Judiciary, — "& I cannot help regreting it the more as I fear some blame may be imputed to me. . .

"I did not send out the commissions because I apprehended such as were for a fixed time to be completed when signed & sealed & such as depended on the will of the President might at any time be revoked. To withhold the commission of the Marshal is equal to displacing him which the President, I presume, has the power to do, but to withhold the commissions of the Justices is an act of which I entertaind no suspicion. I should however have sent out the commissions which had been signed & sealed

[1] See *supra*, 110.

but for the extreme hurry of the time & the absence of Mr. Wagner [Clerk of the State Department] who had been called on by the President to act as his private secretary." [1]

Marshall, it thus appears, was thoroughly familiar with the matter when the application of Marbury and his three associates came before the Supreme Court, and took in it a keen and personal interest. By the time [2] the case came on for final disposition the term had almost half expired for which Marbury and his associates had been appointed. The other justices of the peace to whom Madison had delivered commissions were then transacting all the business that required the attention of such officials. It was certain, moreover, that the Administration would not recognize Marbury and his associates, no matter what Marshall might decide. In fact, these appointees must have lost all interest in the contest for offices of such slight dignity and such insignificant emoluments.

So far, then, as practical results were concerned, the case of Marbury *vs.* Madison had now come to the point where it was of no consequence whatever to any one. It presented only theoretical questions, and, on the face of the record, even these were as simple as they were unimportant. This controversy, in fact, had degenerated into little more than "a moot case," as Jefferson termed it twenty years later. [3]

At the hearing it was proved that the commissions

[1] Marshall to James M. Marshall, March 18, 1801, MS.
[2] February, 1803.
[3] Jefferson to Johnson, June 12, 1823, *Works:* Ford, xii, footnote to 256.

had been signed and sealed. One witness was Marshall's brother, James M. Marshall. Jefferson's Attorney-General, Levi Lincoln, was excused from testifying as to what finally became of them. Madison refused to show cause and denied, by utterly ignoring, the jurisdiction of the Supreme Court to direct or control him in his administration of the office of Secretary of State.[1]

Charles Lee, former Attorney-General, counsel for the applicants, argued the questions which he and everybody else thought were involved. He maintained that a mandamus was the proper remedy, made so not only by the nature of the relation of the Supreme Court to inferior courts and ministerial officers, but by positive enactment of Congress in the Judiciary Law of 1789. Lee pointed out that the Supreme Court had acted on this authority in two previous cases.

Apparently the court could do one or the other of two things: it could disavow its power over any branch of the Executive Department and dismiss the application, or it could assert this power in cases like the one before it and command Madison to deliver the withheld commissions. It was the latter course that the Republicans expected Marshall to take.

If the Chief Justice should do this, Madison undoubtedly would ignore the writ and decline to obey the court's mandate. Thus the Executive and Judicial Departments would have been brought into direct conflict, with every practical advantage in the hands of the Administration. The court had no

[1] See 1 Cranch, 137–80.

physical means to compel the execution of its order. Jefferson would have denounced the illegality of such a decision and laughed at the court's predicament. In short, had the writ to Madison been issued, the court would have been powerless to enforce obedience to its own mandate.

If, on the contrary, the court dismissed the case, the Republican doctrines that the National courts could not direct executives to obey the laws, and that the Judiciary could not invalidate acts of Congress, would by acquiescence have been admitted.

No matter which horn of the dilemma Marshall selected, it was hard to see how his views could escape impalement. He chose neither. Instead of allowing his cherished purpose of establishing the principle of supervisory power of the Judiciary over legislation to be thus wounded and perhaps fatally injured, he made the decision of this insignificant case — about which the applicants themselves no longer cared — the occasion for asserting that principle. And he did assert that principle — asserted it so impressively that for more than a century his conclusion has easily withstood repeated assaults upon it, which still continue.

Marshall accomplished his purpose by convincing the Associate Justices of the unconstitutionality of that section of the Ellsworth Judiciary Act of 1789 [1]

[1] Section 13 provided, among other things, that "the Supreme Court .. shall have power to issue writs of prohibition to the district courts .. and writs of *mandamus*, in cases warranted by the principles and usages of law, to any courts appointed, or persons holding office, under the authority of the United States." (*U.S. Statutes at Large*, I, 73; *Annals*, 1st Cong. 2d Sess. 2245.)

which expressly conferred upon the Supreme Court
the power to issue writs of mandamus and prohibition, and in persuading them to allow him to announce that conclusion as the opinion of the court.
When we consider that, while all the Justices agreed
with Marshall that the provision of the Ellsworth
Judiciary Law requiring them to sit as circuit judges
was unconstitutional, and yet refused to act upon
that belief as Marshall wanted them to act, we can
realize the measure of his triumph in inducing the
same men to hold unconstitutional another provision
of the same act — a provision, too, even less open
to objection than the one they had sustained.

The theory of the Chief Justice that Section 13
of the old Judiciary Law was unconstitutional was
absolutely new, and it was as daring as it was novel.
It was the only original idea that Marshall contributed to the entire controversy. Nobody ever
had questioned the validity of that section of the
statute which Marshall now challenged. Ellsworth,
who preceded Marshall as Chief Justice, had drawn
the act when he was Senator in the First Congress; [1]
he was one of the greatest lawyers of his time and
an influential member of the Constitutional Convention.

One of Marshall's associates on the Supreme
Bench at that very moment, William Paterson, had
also been, with Ellsworth, a member of the Senate
Committee that reported the Judiciary Act of 1789,
and he, too, had been a member of the Constitutional Convention. Senators Gouverneur Morris of

[1] See *supra*, 53–54.

PATERSON   CUSHING

CHASE

MOORE   WASHINGTON

Associate Justices sitting with Marshall in the case of Marbury *versus* Madison

New York, William S. Johnson of Connecticut, Robert Morris of Pennsylvania, William Few of Georgia, George Read and Richard Bassett of Delaware, and Caleb Strong of Massachusetts supported the Ellsworth Law when the Senate passed it; and in the House James Madison and George Wythe of Virginia, Abraham Baldwin of Georgia, and Roger Sherman of Connecticut heartily favored and voted for the act. Most of these men were thorough lawyers, and every one of them had also helped to draft the National Constitution. Here were twelve men, many of them highly learned in the law, makers of the Constitution, draftsmen or advocates and supporters of the Ellsworth Judiciary Act of 1789, not one of whom had ever dreamed that an important section of that law was unconstitutional.[1]

Furthermore, from the organization of the Supreme Court to that moment, the bench and bar had accepted it, and the Justices of the Supreme Court, sitting with National district judges, had recognized its authority when called upon to take action in a particular controversy brought directly under it.[2] The Supreme Court itself had held that it had jurisdiction, under Section 13, to issue a mandamus in a proper case,[3] and had granted a writ of prohibition by authority of the same section.[4] In two other cases this section had come before the Supreme

[1] See Dougherty: *Power of the Federal Judiciary over Legislation*, 82. Professor Corwin says that not many years later Marshall concurred in an opinion of the Supreme Court which, by analogy, recognized the validity of it. (Corwin, 8–9.)

[2] U.S. *vs.* Ravara, 2 Dallas, 297.

[3] U.S. *vs.* Lawrence, 3 Dallas, 42.   [4] U.S. *vs.* Peters, *ib.* 121.

Court, and no one had even intimated that it was unconstitutional.[1]

When, to his great disgust, Marshall was forced to sit as a circuit judge at Richmond in the winter of 1802, a case came before him that involved both the validity of the Republican Repeal Act and also the constitutionality of that provision of the Ellsworth Judiciary Law requiring justices of the Supreme Court to sit as circuit judges. This was the case of Stuart *vs.* Laird. Marshall held merely that the plea which raised these questions was insufficient, and the case was taken to the Supreme Court on a writ of error. After extended argument Justice Paterson delivered the opinion of the court, Marshall declining to participate in the decision because he had "tried the cause in the court below." [2]

At the same term, then, at which Marbury *vs.* Madison was decided, and immediately after Marshall's opinion in that case was delivered, all the justices of the Supreme Court except the Chief Justice, held "that practice and acquiescence under it [the Judiciary Act of 1789] for a period of several years, commencing with the organization of the

[1] In the argument of Marbury *vs.* Madison, Charles Lee called Marshall's attention to the case of U.S. *vs.* Hopkins, in the February term, 1794, in which a motion was made for a mandamus to Hopkins as loan officer for the District of Virginia, and to the case of one John Chandler of Connecticut, also in February, 1794, in which a motion was made in behalf of Chandler for a mandamus to the Secretary of War. These cases do not seem to have been reported, and Lee must have referred to manuscript records of them. (See 1 Cranch, 148–49.)

Samuel W. Dana of Connecticut also referred to the Chandler case during the Judiciary debate in the House, March, 1802. (See *Annals,* 7th Cong. 1st Sess. 903–04.)

[2] 1 Cranch, 308.

judicial system . . has fixed the construction. It is
a contemporary interpretation of the most forcible
nature. This practical exposition is too strong and
obstinate to be shaken or controlled. Of course, the
question is at rest, and ought not now to be disturbed." [1]

But the exigency disclosed in this chapter required immediate action, notwithstanding the ob-
stacles above set forth. The issue raised by the
Republicans — the free hand of Congress, unrestrained by courts — must be settled at that time or
be abandoned perhaps forever. The fundamental
consideration involved must have a prompt, firm,
and, if possible, final answer. Were such an answer
not then given, it was not certain that it could ever
be made. As it turned out, but for Marbury vs.
Madison, the power of the Supreme Court to annul
acts of Congress probably would not have been
insisted upon thereafter. For, during the thirty-
two years that Marshall remained on the Supreme
Bench after the decision of that case, and for twenty
years after his death, no case came before the court
where an act of Congress was overthrown; and
none had been invalidated from the adoption of the
Constitution to the day when Marshall delivered his
epochal opinion. So that, as a matter of historical
significance, had he not then taken this stand,
nearly seventy years would have passed without
any question arising as to the omnipotence of Congress.[2] After so long a period of judicial acquiescence

[1] Stuart vs. Laird, 1 Cranch, 309.
[2] The next case in which the Supreme Court overthrew an act of

in Congressional supremacy it seems likely that opposition to it would have been futile.

For the reasons stated, Marshall resolved to take that step which, for courage, statesmanlike foresight, and, indeed, for perfectly calculated audacity, has few parallels in judicial history. In order to assert that in the Judiciary rested the exclusive power [1] to declare any statute unconstitutional, and to announce that the Supreme Court was the ultimate arbiter as to what is and what is not law under the Constitution, Marshall determined to annul Section 13 of the Ellsworth Judiciary Act of 1789. In taking such a step the Chief Justice made up his mind that he would sum up in final and conclusive form the reasoning that sustained that principle.

Marshall resolved to go still further. He would announce from the Supreme Bench rules of procedure which the Executive branch of the Government must observe. This was indispensable, he correctly thought, if the departments were to be harmonious branches of a single and National Government, rather than warring factions whose dissensions must in the end paralyze the administration of the Nation's affairs. [2]

Congress was that of Scott *vs.* Sandford — the famous Dred Scott case, decided in 1857. In this case the Supreme Court held that Congress had no power to prohibit slavery in the territory purchased from France in 1803 (the Louisiana Purchase), and that the Act of March 6, 1820, known as the Missouri Compromise, was unconstitutional, null, and void. (See Scott *vs.* Sandford, 19 Howard, 393 *et seq.*)

[1] The President can veto a bill, of course, on the ground of unconstitutionality; but, by a two thirds vote, Congress can pass it over the Executive's disapproval.

[2] Carson, I, 203; and see especially Adams: *U.S.* I, 192.

It was not, then, Marshall's declaring an act of Congress to be unconstitutional that was innovating or revolutionary. The extraordinary thing was the pretext he devised for rendering that opinion — a pretext which, it cannot be too often recalled, had been unheard of and unsuspected hitherto. Nothing but the emergency compelling the insistence, at this particular time, that the Supreme Court has such a power, can fully and satisfactorily explain the action of Marshall in holding this section void.

In his opinion the Chief Justice spoke of "the peculiar delicacy of this case, the novelty of some of its circumstances, and the real difficulty attending the points which occur in it." [1] He would follow, he said, the points of counsel in the order in which they had been made.[2] Did the applicants have a right to the commissions? This depended, he said, on whether Marbury had been appointed to office. If so, he was entitled to the commission which was merely the formal evidence of the appointment. The President had nominated him to the Senate, the Senate had confirmed the nomination, the President had signed the commission, and, in the manner directed by act of Congress, the Secretary of State had affixed to it the seal of the United States.[3]

The President could not recall his appointment if "the officer is not removable." Delivery of the commission was not necessary to the consummation of the appointment which had already been effected;

[1] 1 Cranch, 154.
[2] This seems to have been inaccurate. Compare Lee's argument with Marshall's opinion.
[3] 1 Cranch, 158.

otherwise "negligence, . . fraud, fire or theft, might deprive an individual of his office." But the truth was that "a copy from the record . . would be, to every intent and purpose, equal to the original." [1] The appointment of Marbury "vested in the officer legal rights . . of his country," and "to withhold his commission is an act . . not warranted by law, but violative of a vested legal right. . ." [2]

"The very essence of civil liberty," continues Marshall, "certainly consists in the right of every individual to claim the protection of the laws, whenever he receives an injury. One of the first duties of government is to afford that protection." Ours has been "emphatically termed a government of laws, and not of men. It will certainly cease to deserve this high appellation, if the laws furnish no remedy for the violation of a vested legal right. . ." [3]

"The act of delivering or withholding a commission" is not "a mere political act, belonging to the executive department alone," but a ministerial act, the performance of which is directed by statute. Congress had ordered the Secretary of War to place the names of certain persons on the pension rolls; suppose that he should refuse to do so? "Would the wounded veteran be without remedy? . . Is it to be contended that the heads of departments are not amenable to the laws of their country?" [4]

Would any person whatever attempt to maintain that a purchaser of public lands could be deprived of his property because a Secretary of State withheld his patent? [5] To be sure, the President had certain

---

[1] 1 Cranch, 160.   [2] *Ib.* 162.   [3] *Ib.* 163.   [4] *Ib.* 164.   [5] *Ib.* 165.

political powers and could appoint agents to aid him
in the exercise of them. The courts had no authority
to interfere in this sphere of Executive action. For
example, the conduct of foreign affairs by the Secretary of State, as the representative of the President,
can never be examinable by the courts. But the
delivery of a commission to an office or a patent
to land was a different matter.

When Congress by statute peremptorily directs
the Secretary of State or any other officer to perform
specific duties on which "the rights of individuals
are dependent . . he cannot at his discretion sport
away the vested rights of others." If he attempts to
do so he is answerable to the courts. "The question whether a right has vested or not, is, in its nature, judicial, and must be tried by the judicial authority." The court therefore was empowered to decide
the point; and held that Madison's refusal to deliver
Marbury's commission was "a plain violation of that
right, for which the laws of his country afford him a
remedy." [1]

But was this remedy the writ of mandamus for
which Marbury had applied? It was, said Marshall;
but could such an order be directed to the Secretary
of State? This was a task "peculiarly irksome,
as well as delicate," [2] for, he observed, there were
those who would at first consider it "as an attempt
to intrude into the cabinet, and to intermeddle with
the prerogatives of the executive." Far be it from
John Marshall to do such a thing. He need hardly
"disclaim all pretensions to such jurisdiction." Not

[1] 1 Cranch, 166–68.   [2] *Ib.* 169.

"for a moment" would he entertain "an extravagance so absurd and excessive. . . Questions in their nature political, . . can never be made in this court." But if the case before him presented only questions concerning legal rights of an individual, "what is there in the exalted station" of the Secretary of State which "exempts him from . . being compelled to obey the judgment of the law"? The only remaining question, therefore, was whether a mandamus could issue from the Supreme Court.[1]

In such manner Marshall finally arrived at the examination of the constitutionality of Section 13, which, he said, fitted the present case "precisely"; and "if this court is not authorized to issue a writ of mandamus" to Madison, "it must be because the law is unconstitutional, and therefore absolutely incapable of conferring the authority."[2] In reaching this point Marshall employs almost seven thousand words. Fifteen hundred more words are used before he takes up the principle of judicial supremacy over legislation.

The fundamental law of the Nation, Marshall explained, expressly defined the original jurisdiction of the Supreme Court and carefully limited its authority. It could take original cognizance only of specific cases. In all others, the court was given nothing but "appellate jurisdiction." But he omitted the words that immediately follow in the same sentence — "with such exceptions . . as the Congress shall make." Yet this language had, for fourteen years, apparently been considered by the whole bench and

[1] 1 Cranch, 170.   [2] Ib. 173.

bar as meaning, among other things, that while Congress could *not take from* the Supreme Court original jurisdiction in the cases specifically named in Article Three of the Constitution, Congress *could add* other cases to the original jurisdiction of the Supreme Court.

Marshall was quite conscious of all this, it would seem. In the argument, counsel had insisted that since "the clause, assigning original jurisdiction to the Supreme Court, contains no negative or restrictive words, the power remains to the legislature, to assign original jurisdiction to that court in other cases than those specified." [1] But, reasons Marshall, in answer to this contention, if Congress could thus enlarge the original jurisdiction of the Supreme Court, "the subsequent part of the section [2] is mere surplusage, is entirely without meaning, . . is form without substance. . . Affirmative words are often . . negative of other objects than those affirmed; and in this case, a negative or exclusive sense must be given to them, *or they have no operation at all*." [3]

That is to say, when the Constitution conferred upon the Supreme Court original jurisdiction in specified cases, it thereby excluded all others — denied to Congress the power to add to the jurisdiction thus affirmatively granted. And yet, let it be repeated, by giving original jurisdiction in cases specifically named, the Constitution put it beyond the power of Congress to interfere with the Supreme

[1] 1 Cranch, 174.

[2] In all "other cases . . the Supreme Court shall have appellate jurisdiction . . with such exceptions . . as the Congress shall make."

[3] *Ib.* 174. (Italics the author's.)

Court in those cases; but Marshall asserted that
the specific grant of jurisdiction has "*no operation
at all*" unless "a negative or exclusive sense" be
given it.[1]

Marshall boldly held, therefore, that Section 13 of
the Ellsworth Judiciary Act was "not warranted by
the Constitution." Such being the case, ought the
Supreme Court to act under this unconstitutional
section? As the Chief Justice stated the question,
could "an act, repugnant to the constitution .. become the law of the land"? After writing nearly
nine thousand words, he now reached the commanding question: Can the Supreme Court of the United
States invalidate an act which Congress has passed
and the President has approved?

Marshall avowed that the Supreme Court can
and must do that very thing, and in so doing made
Marbury *vs.* Madison historic. In this, the vital
part of his opinion, the Chief Justice is direct, clear,
simple, and convincing. The people, he said, have
an elemental right to establish such principles for
"their future government, as .. shall most conduce
to their own happiness." This was "the basis on
which the whole American fabric had been erected."
These "permanent" and "fundamental" principles,
in the instance of the American Government, were
those limiting the powers of the various departments: "That those limits may not be mistaken,
or forgotten, the constitution is written. To what
purpose are powers limited .. if these limits may,

[1] 1 Cranch, 176. This particular part of the text adopts Professor
Edward S. Corwin's careful and accurate analysis of Marshall's opinion
on this point. (See Corwin, 4–10.)

at any time, be passed by those intended to be restrained?" [1]

If Congress or any other department of the Government can ignore the limitations of the Constitution, all distinction between government of "limited and unlimited powers" is done away with. To say that "acts prohibited and acts allowed are of equal obligation" is to deny the very purpose for which our fundamental law was adopted. "The constitution controls any legislative act repugnant to it." Congress cannot alter it by legislation.[2] All this, said Marshall, was too clear to admit of discussion, but he proceeded, nevertheless, to discuss the subject at great length.

There is "no middle ground." The Constitution is either "a superior paramount law" not to be changed by legislative enactment, or else "it is on a level with the ordinary legislative acts" and, as such, "alterable" at the will of Congress. If the Constitution is supreme, then an act of Congress violative of it is not law; if the Constitution is not supreme, then "written constitutions are absurd attempts, on the part of the people, to limit a power in its own nature illimitable." Three times in a short space Marshall insists that, for Congress to ignore the limitations which the Constitution places upon it, is to deny the whole theory of government under written constitutions.

Although the contention that the Judiciary must consider unconstitutional legislation to be valid was "an absurdity too gross to be insisted on," Marshall

[1] 1 Cranch, 176.   [2] *Ib.* 176–77.

would, nevertheless, patiently examine it.[1] This he did by reasoning so simple and so logical that the dullest citizen could not fail to understand it nor the most astute intellect escape it. But in the process he was tiresomely repetitious, though not to so irritating an extent as he at times became.

If two laws conflict, the courts must decide between them. Where the Constitution and an act of Congress apply to a case, "the court must determine which . . governs [it]. This is of the very essence of judicial duty. . . If, then, . . the constitution is superior to any ordinary act of the legislature," the Judiciary must prefer it to a mere statute. Otherwise "courts must close their eyes on the constitution," and see only the legislative enactment.[2]

But to do this "would subvert the very foundation of all written constitutions." It would be to "declare that an act which . . is entirely void, is yet . . completely obligatory," and that Congress may do "what is expressly forbidden." This would give to the legislature "a practical and real omnipotence, with the same breath which professes to restrict their powers within narrow limits." It would be "prescribing limits, and declaring that those limits may be passed at pleasure." This "reduces to nothing" both the letter and the theory of the Constitution.

That instrument expressly extends the judicial power to cases "arising under the constitution." Must the courts decide such a case "without examining the instrument under which it arises?" If the

[1] 1 Cranch, 177.　　　　　[2] *Ib.* 178.

courts must look into the Constitution at all, as assuredly they must do in some cases, "what part of it are they forbidden to read or to obey?"

Marshall cites hypothetical examples of legislation in direct conflict with the fundamental law. Suppose that Congress should place an export duty on cotton, tobacco, flour, and that the Government should bring suit to recover the tax. "Ought judgment to be rendered in such a case?" Or if a bill of attainder should be passed and citizens prosecuted under it, "must the court condemn to death those victims whom the constitution endeavors to preserve?"

Take, for example, the crime of treason: the Constitution emphatically prescribes that nobody can be convicted of this offense "unless on the testimony of two witnesses to the same overt act, or on confession in open court." The Judiciary particularly are addressed — "it prescribes, directly for them, a rule of evidence not to be departed from." Suppose that Congress should enact a law providing that a citizen might be convicted of treason upon the testimony of one witness or by a confession out of court? Which must the court obey — the Constitution or the act altering that instrument?

Did not these illustrations and many others that might be given prove that the Constitution must govern courts as well as Congress? If not, why does the Constitution require judges "to take an oath to support it"? That solemn obligation "applies in an especial manner to their conduct in their official character." How "immoral" to direct them to take this oath "if they were to be used as the instruments, and the knowing instruments, for violating what they swear to support!" Such contradictions and confusions would make the ceremony of taking the oath of judicial office "a solemn mockery" and even "a crime."

There is, then, said Marshall, no escape from the conclusion "that a law repugnant to the constitution is void," and that the judicial as well as other departments are bound by the Constitution.[1] The application of Marbury and others must therefore be dismissed.

Thus, by a coup as bold in design and as daring in execution as that by which the Constitution had been framed,[2] John Marshall set up a landmark in American history so high that all the future could take bearings from it, so enduring that all the shocks the Nation was to endure could not overturn it. Such a decision was a great event in American history. State courts, as well as National tribunals, thereafter fearlessly applied the principle that Marshall announced, and the supremacy of written constitutions over legislative acts was firmly established.

This principle is wholly and exclusively American. It is America's original contribution to the science of law.[3] The assertion of it, under the conditions related in this chapter, was the deed of a great man. One of narrower vision and smaller courage never

[1] 1 Cranch, 178-80.   [2] See vol. I, 323, of this work.

[3] It must be borne in mind that the American Constitution declares that, in and of itself, it is law — the supreme law of the land; and that no other written constitution makes any such assertion.

would have done what Marshall did. In his management and decision of this case, at the time and under the circumstances, Marshall's acts and words were those of a statesman of the first rank.

His opinion gave fresh strength to the purpose of the Republican leaders to subdue the Federalist Judiciary. It furnished Jefferson and his radical followers a new and concrete reason for ousting from the National Bench, and especially from the Supreme Court, all judges who would thus override the will of Congress. Against himself, in particular, Marshall had newly whetted the edge of Republican wrath, already over-keen.

The trial of John Pickering, Judge of the United States Court for the District of New Hampshire, brought by the House before the bar of the Senate, was now pushed with cold venomousness to what Henry Adams calls "an infamous and certainly an illegal conviction"; and then Marshall's associate on the Supreme Bench, Justice Samuel Chase, was quickly impeached for high crimes and misdemeanors. If the Republican organization could force from its partisans in the Senate a verdict of "guilty" in Chase's case also, Marshall's official head would be the next to fall.[1]

Concerning Marshall's assertion of the power of the National Judiciary to annul acts of Congress and to direct administrative officers in the discharge of their legal duties, Jefferson himself said nothing at the time. But the opinion of the Chief Justice was another ingredient thrown into the caldron of

[1] See *infra*, chap. IV.

Jefferson's heart, where a hatred was brewed that poisoned the great politician to his latest day.

Many months after the decision in the Marbury case, Jefferson first broke his silence. "Nothing in the Constitution has given them [the Supreme Court] a right to decide for the Executive, more than to the Executive to decide for them," he wrote. "The opinion which gives to the judges the right to decide what laws are constitutional, and what not, not only for themselves in their own sphere of action, but for the Legislature & Executive also, in their spheres, would make the judiciary a despotic branch." [1]

Again, during the trial of Aaron Burr,[2] Jefferson denounced Marshall for his opinion in Marbury vs. Madison; and toward the close of his life he returned again and again with corroding words to the subject regarding which, at the moment it arose, he concealed, so far as written words were concerned, his virulent resentment. For instance, seventeen years later Jefferson wrote that "to consider the judges as the ultimate arbiters of all constitutional questions . . would place us under the despotism of an oligarchy." [3]

· But for the time being, Jefferson was quiescent.

---

[1] Jefferson to Mrs. Adams, Sept. 11, 1804, *Works:* Ford, x, footnote to 89.

[2] See *infra*, chap. VIII.

[3] Jefferson to Jarvis, Sept. 28, 1820, *Works:* Ford, XII, 162. Yet, at the time when he was founding the Republican Party, Jefferson had written to a friend that "the laws of the land, administered by upright judges, would protect you from any exercise of power unauthorized by the Constitution of the United States." (Jefferson to Rowan, Sept. 26, 1798, *ib.* VIII, 448.)

His subtle mind knew how, in political controversies, to control his tongue and pen. It could do no good for him, personally, to make an outcry now; and it might do harm. The doctrine which Marshall announced had, Jefferson knew, a strong hold on all Federalists, and, indeed, on many Northern Republicans; the bar, especially, upheld it generally.

The Presidential campaign was drawing near, and for the President openly to attack Marshall's position would create a political issue which could win none to the Republican cause not already fighting for it, and might keep recruits from joining the Republican colors. Jefferson was infinitely concerned about his reëlection and was giving practical attention to the strengthening of his party for the approaching contest.

"I am decidedly in favor of making all the banks Republican, by sharing deposits among them in proportion to the [political] dispositions they show," he wrote to his Secretary of the Treasury three months after Marshall's bold assertion of the dignity and power of the National courts. "It is," he continued, "material to the safety of Republicanism to detach the mercantile interests from its enemies and incorporate them into the body of its friends." [1]

Furthermore, Jefferson was, at that particular moment, profoundly troubled by intimate personal

[1] Jefferson to Gallatin, July 12, 1803, *Works:* Ford, x, 15–16. It should be remembered that most of the banks and the financial and commercial interests generally were determined opponents of Jefferson and Republicanism. As a sheer matter of "practical politics," the President cannot be fairly criticized for thus trying to weaken his remorseless foes.

matters and vast National complications. He had
been trying, unsuccessfully, to adjust our dispute
with France; the radical West was becoming clamorous for a forward and even a militant policy concerning the control of the Mississippi River, and especially of New Orleans, which commanded the mouth
of that commercial waterway; while the Federalists,
insisting upon bold measures, had a fair prospect of
winning from Jefferson's support those aggressive
and predatory frontiersmen who, until now, had
stanchly upheld the Republican standard.

Spain had ceded Louisiana to France upon the
condition that the territory never should be transferred to any other government; but neither New
Orleans nor any part of Louisiana had actually been
surrendered by the Spanish authorities. Great
Britain informed the American Government that
she would not consent to the occupation by the
French of any part of Spain's possessions on the
American continent.

Hating and distrusting the British, but also in
terror of Napoleon, Jefferson, who was as weak in
the conduct of foreign affairs as he was dexterous
in the management of political parties, thought to
escape the predicament by purchasing the island of
Orleans and perhaps a strip on the east side of the
Mississippi River.[1]

A series of events swiftly followed the decision of
Marbury *vs.* Madison which enthralled the eager
attention of the whole people and changed the destiny of the Republic. Three months after Marshall

[1] See Channing: *U.S.* IV, 313–14.

delivered his opinion, Napoleon, yielding to "the empire of circumstances," as Talleyrand phrased it,[1] offered, and Livingston and Monroe accepted, the whole of Louisiana for less than fifteen million dollars. Of course France had no title to sell — Louisiana was still legally owned and actually occupied by Spain. The United States bought nothing more than a pretension; and, by force of propinquity and power, made it a fact.[2]

The President was amazed when the news reached him. He did not want Louisiana [3] — nothing was further from his mind than the purchase of it.[4] The immorality of the acquisition affected him not at all; but the inconvenience did. He did not know what to do with Louisiana. Worse still, the treaty of cession required that the people living in that territory should be admitted into the Union, "according to the principles of the Federal Constitution."

So, to his infinite disgust, Jefferson was forced to deal with the Louisiana Purchase by methods as vigorous as any ever advocated by the abhorred Hamilton — methods more autocratic than those which, when done by others, he had savagely denounced as unconstitutional and destructive of liberty.[5] The President doubted whether, under the Constitution, we could acquire, and was sure that we

---

[1] Talleyrand to Decrès, May 24, 1803, as quoted in Adams: *U.S.* II, 55.

[2] Morison: *Otis*, I, 262; see also Adams: *U.S.* II, 56.

[3] See instructions to Livingston and Monroe, *Am. State Papers, Foreign Relations*, II, 540.

[4] Adams: *U.S.* I, 442-43.   [5] *Ib.* II, 120-28.

could not govern, Louisiana, and he actually prepared amendments authorizing the incorporation
into the Republic of the purchased territory.[1] No
such legal mistiness dimmed the eyes of John Marshall who, in time, was to announce as the decision
of the Supreme Court that the Republic could acquire territory with as much right as any monar-
chical government.[2]

To add to his perturbations, the high priest of
popular rights found himself compelled to abandon
his adored phrase, "the consent of the governed,"
upon which he had so carefully erected the structure
of his popularity, and to drive through Congress a
form of government over the people of Louisiana
without consulting their wishes in the least.[3]

The Jeffersonian doctrine had been that the Union
was merely a compact between sovereign States, and
that new territory and alien peoples could not be
added to it without the consent of all the partners.
The Federalists now took their stand upon this
indefensible ground,[4] and openly threatened the
secession at which they had hinted when the Federalist Judiciary Act was repealed.

[1] *Works:* Ford, x, 3–12.

[2] American Insurance Company *et al. vs.* Canter, 1 Peters, 511–46;
and see vol. IV, chap. III, of this work.

[3] See *U.S. Statutes at Large*, II, 283; and *Annals*, 8th Cong. 2d
Sess. 1597.

[4] For instance, Senator Plumer, two years later, thus stated the old
Republican doctrine which the Federalists, in defiance of their party's
creed and traditions, had now adopted as their own: "We cannot admit a new partner into the Union, from without the original limits
of the United States, without the consent, first obtained, of each of
the partners composing the firm." (Plumer to Smith, Feb. 7, 1805,
Plumer, 328.)

Jefferson was alive to the danger: "Whatever Congress shall think it necessary to do [about Louisiana]," he cautioned one of the Republican House leaders, "should be done with as little debate as possible." [1] A month earlier he wrote: "The Constitution has made no provision for our holding foreign territory, still less for incorporating foreign nations into our Union. The Executive .. have done an act beyond the Constitution." [2]

Therefore, he declared, "the less we say about constitutional difficulties respecting Louisiana the better. . . What is necessary for surmounting them must be done sub-silentio." [3] The great radical favored publicity in affairs of state only when such a course was helpful to his political plans. On other occasions no autocrat was ever more secretive than Thomas Jefferson. [4] Seemingly, however, the President was concerned only with his influence on the destiny of the world. [5]

At first the Federalist leaders were too dazed to do more than grumble. "The cession of Louisiana .. is like selling us a Ship after she is surrounded by a

---

[1] Jefferson to Nicholas, Sept. 7, 1803, *Works:* Ford, x, 10.

[2] Jefferson to Breckenridge, Aug. 12, 1803, *ib.* 7.

[3] Jefferson to Madison, Aug. 18, 1803, *ib.* 8.

[4] "The medicine for that State [North Carolina] must be very mild & secretly administered." (Jefferson to Nicholas, April 7, 1800, *ib.* IX, 129; and see Adams: *U.S.* III, 147.)

[5] "The millenium was to usher in upon us as the irresistible consequence of the goodness of heart, integrity of mind, and correctness of disposition of Mr. Jefferson. All nations, even pirates and savages, were to be moved by the influence of his persuasive virtue and masterly skill in diplomacy." (Eaton's account of a call on President Jefferson, 1803, *Life of the Late Gen. William Eaton:* Prentiss, 263; also quoted in Adams: *U.S.* II, 431.)

British Fleet," shrewdly observed George Cabot, when the news was published in Boston.[1] Fisher Ames, of course, thought that "the acquiring of territory by money is mean and despicable," especially when done by Republicans. "The less of it [territory] the better. . . By adding an unmeasured world beyond that river [Mississippi], we rush like a comet into infinite space." [2]

Soon, however, their dissatisfaction blew into flame the embers of secession which never had become cold in their bosoms. "I am convinced," wrote Uriah Tracy, "that the accession of Louisiana will accelerate a division of these States; whose whenabouts is uncertain, but somewhen is inevitable." [3] Senator Plumer thought that the Eastern States should form a new nation: "Adopt this western world into the Union," he said, "and you destroy at once the weight and importance of the Eastern States, and compel them to establish a separate and independent empire." [4] A few days' reflection brought Ames to the conclusion that "our country is too big for union, too sordid for patriotism, too democratic for liberty." [5] Tapping Reeve of Connecticut made careful inquiry among the Federalists in his vicinity and informed Tracy that "all . .

[1] Cabot to King, July 1, 1803, King, IV, 279. The Louisiana Purchase was first publicly announced through the press by the *Independent Chronicle* of Boston, June 30, 1803. (Adams: *U.S.* II, 82–83.)

[2] Ames to Gore, Oct. 3, 1803, Ames, I, 323–24.

[3] Tracy to McHenry, Oct. 19, 1803, Steiner: *Life and Correspondence of James McHenry*, 522.

[4] Oct. 20, 1803, Plumer, 285.

[5] Ames to Dwight, Oct. 26, 1803, Ames I, 328.

believe that we must separate, and that this is the most favorable moment." [1]

Louisiana, however, was not the only motive of the foremost New England Federalists for their scheme of breaking up the Republic. As we have seen, the threat of secession was repeatedly made during the Republican assault on the Judiciary; and now, as a fundamental cause for disunion, the Northern Federalists speedily harked back to Jefferson's purpose of subverting the National courts. The Republicans were ruling the Nation, Virginia was ruling the Republicans, Jefferson was ruling all. Louisiana would permanently turn the balance against the Northern and Eastern States, already outweighed in the National scales; and the conquest of the National Judiciary would remove from that section its last protection against the pillaging hands of the Huns and Vandals of Republicanism. So reasoned the Federalists.

What could be done to save the rights and the property of "the wise, the rich and the good"? By what pathway could the chosen escape their doom? "The principles of our Revolution point to the remedy," declared the soured and flint-hearted Pickering. "The independence of the judges is now directly assailed. . . I am not willing to be sacrificed by such popular tyrants. . . I do not believe in the practicability of a long-continued union." [2]

---

[1] Reeve to Tracy, Feb. 7, 1804, *N.E. Federalism*: Adams, 342; and see Adams: *U.S.* II, 160.

Members of Congress among the Federalists and Republicans became so estranged that they boarded in different houses and refused to associate with one another. (Plumer, 245, 336.)

[2] Pickering to Cabot, Jan. 29, 1804, Lodge: *Cabot*, 338.

For the same reasons, Roger Griswold of Connecticut avowed that "there can be no safety to the Northern States *without a separation from the confederacy*." [1] The Reverend Jedediah Morse of New Hampshire wrote Senator Plumer that "our empire .. must .. break in pieces. Some think the sooner the better." [2] And the New Hampshire Senator replied: "I hope the time is not far distant when .. the sound part will separate from the corrupt." [3]

With the exception of John Adams, only one eminent New England Federalist kept his head steady and his patriotism undefiled: George Cabot, while sympathizing with his ancient party friends, frankly opposed their mad project. Holding that secession was impracticable, he declared: "I am not satisfied that the thing itself is to be desired. My habitual opinions have been always strongly against it." [4]

But the expressions of such men as Pickering, Ames, and Griswold indicated the current of New England Federalist thought and comment. Their secession sentiment, however, did not appeal to the young men, who hailed with joy the opportunity to occupy these new, strange lands which accident, or Providence, or Jefferson had opened to them. Knowledge of this was indeed one cause of the anger of some Federalist managers who owned immense tracts in New England and in the Ohio Valley and wanted them purchased and settled by those now

[1] Griswold to Wolcott, March 11, 1804, *N.E. Federalism:* Adams, 356.
[2] Morse to Plumer, Feb. 3, 1804, Plumer, 289.
[3] Plumer to Morse, March 10, 1804, *ib.*
[4] Cabot to King, March 17, 1804, Lodge: *Cabot*, 345.

turning their eyes to the alluring farther western country.[1] They saw with something like fury the shifting of political power to the South and West.

The management of the unwelcome Louisiana windfall, the conduct of the National campaign, the alarming reports from New England, left Jefferson no time to rail at Marshall or to attack that "subtle corps of sappers and miners" who were then beginning "to undermine . . our confederated fabric," as Jefferson declared seventeen years later.[2] For the present the great public duty of exposing Marshall's decision in Marbury *vs.* Madison must be deferred.

But the mills of democracy were grinding, and after he was reëlected certain impeachments would be found in the grist that would make all right. The defiant Marshall would at least be humbled, perhaps — probably — removed from office. But all in good time! For the present Jefferson had other work to do. He himself must now exercise powers which, according to his philosophy and declarations, were far beyond those conferred upon him by the Constitution.

So it came about that the first of Marshall's great Constitutional opinions received scant notice at the time of its delivery. The newspapers had little to say about it. Even the bench and the bar of the country, at least in the sections remote from Washington, appear not to have heard of it,[3] or, if they

---

[1] See Morison: *Otis*, I, 262.

[2] Jefferson to Ritchie, Dec. 25, 1820, *Works:* Ford, XII, 177.

[3] For instance, in 1808, the United States District Court of Massachusetts, in the decision of a case requiring all possible precedents like that of Marbury *vs.* Madison, did not so much as refer to Marshall's

had, to have forgotten it amid the thrilling events
that filled the times.

Because popular interest had veered toward and
was concentrated upon the Louisiana Purchase and
the renewal of war in Europe, Republican newspapers, until then so alert to discover and eager
to attack every judicial "usurpation," had almost
nothing to say of Marshall's daring assertion of judicial supremacy which later was execrated as the
very parent of Constitutional evil. An empire had
been won under Jefferson; therefore Jefferson had
won it — another proof of the far-seeing statesmanship of "The Man of the People." Of consequence

---

opinion, although every other case that could be found was cited.
Marbury *vs.* Madison, long afterwards, was added in a footnote to the
printed report. (McLaughlin, 30, citing *Am. Law Journal*, old series,
II, 255–64.)

Marshall's opinion in Marbury *vs.* Madison was first referred to by
counsel in a legal controversy in *Ex Parte* Burford, 1806 (3 Cranch,
448). Robert Goodloe Harper next cited it in his argument for Bollmann (4 Cranch, 86; and see *infra*, chap. VII). Marshall referred to it
in his opinion in that case, and Justice William Johnson commented
upon it at some length.

A year later Marshall's opinion in Marbury *vs.* Madison was cited
by Jefferson's Attorney-General, Cæsar A. Rodney. In the case *Ex
Parte* Gilchrist *et al. vs.* The Collector of the Port of Charleston, S.C.
(5 Hughes, 1), the United States Court for that circuit, consisting of
Johnson, Associate Justice of the Supreme Court, and the Judge of the
District Court, granted a mandamus under the section of the Judiciary
Act which Marshall and the entire court had, five years before, declared to be unconstitutional, so far as it conferred original jurisdiction upon the Supreme Court in applications for mandamus.

Rodney wrote to the President a letter of earnest protest, pointing out
the fact that the court's action in the Gilchrist case was in direct antagonism to the opinion in Marbury *vs.* Madison. But Jefferson was
then so savagely attacking Marshall's rulings in the Burr trial (see
infra, chaps. VII, VIII, IX) that he was, at last, giving public expression of
his disapproval of the opinion of the Chief Justice in Marbury *vs.*
Madison. He did not even answer Rodney's letter.

he must be reëlected. Such was the popular logic; and reëlected Jefferson was — triumphantly, almost unanimously.

Circumstances which had shackled his hands now suddenly freed them. Henceforth the President could do as he liked, both personally and politically. No longer should John Marshall, the abominated head of the National Judiciary, rest easy on the bench which his audacity had elevated above President and Congress. The opinion of the "usurping" Chief Justice in Marbury *vs.* Madison should have answer at last. So on with the impeachment trial of Samuel Chase! Let him be deposed, and then, if Marshall would not bend the knee, that obdurate judicial defender of Nationalism should follow Chase into desuetude and disgrace.

The incessant clamor of the Federalist past-statesmen, unheard by the popular ear, had nevertheless done some good — all the good it ought to have done. It had aroused misgivings in the minds of certain Northern Republican Senators as to the expediency, wisdom, and justice of the Republican plan to shackle or overthrow the National Judiciary. This hesitation was, however, unknown to the masters of the Republican organization in Congress. The Federalists themselves were totally unaware of it. Only Jefferson, with his abnormal sensibility, had an indistinct impression that somewhere, in the apparently perfect alignment of the Republican forces, there was potential weakness.

Marshall was gifted with no such divination. He knew only the fate that had been prepared for him.

A crisis was reached in his career and a determinative phase of American history entered upon. His place as Chief Justice was to be made secure and the stability of American institutions saved by as narrow a margin as that by which the National Constitution had been established.

CHAPTER IV

IMPEACHMENT

The judges of the Supreme Court must fall. Our affairs approach an important crisis. (William Plumer.)

These articles contained in themselves a virtual impeachment of not only Mr. Chase but of all the Judges of the Supreme Court.
(John Quincy Adams.)

We shall bring forward such a specimen of judicial tyranny, as, I trust in God, will never be again exhibited in our country. (John Randolph.)

We appear for an ancient and infirm man whose better days have been worn out in the service of that country which now degrades him.
(Joseph Hopkinson.)

Our property, our liberty, our lives can only be protected by independent judges. (Luther Martin.)

"WE *want your offices,* for the purpose of giving them to men who will fill them better." In these frank words, Senator William Branch Giles [1] of Virginia stated one of the purposes of the Republicans in their determined attack on the National Judiciary. He was speaking to the recently elected young Federalist Senator from Massachusetts, John Quincy Adams. [2]

They were sitting before the blazing logs in the wide fireplace that warmed the Senate Chamber. John Randolph, the Republican leader of the House, and Israel Smith, a Republican Senator from Vermont, were also in the group. The talk was of the

---

[1] Giles was appointed Senator August 11, 1804, by the Governor to fill the unexpired term of Abraham Venable who resigned in order that Giles might be sent to the Senate. In December the Legislature elected him for the full term. Upon taking his seat Giles immediately became the Republican leader of the Senate. (See Anderson, 93.)

[2] Dec. 21, 1804, *Memoirs, J. Q. A.*: Adams, I, 322–23.

approaching trial of Samuel Chase, Associate Justice of the Supreme Court of the United States, whom the House had impeached for high crimes and misdemeanors. Giles and Randolph were, "with excessive earnestness," trying to convince the doubting Vermont Senator of the wisdom and justice of the Republican method of ousting from the National Bench those judges who did not agree with the views of the Republican Party.

Giles scorned the idea of " an *independent* judiciary!" The independence claimed by the National judges was "nothing more nor less than an attempt to establish an aristocratic despotism in themselves." The power of the House to impeach, and of the Senate to try, any public officer was unlimited.

"If," continued Giles, "the Judges of the Supreme Court should dare, *as they had done*, to declare acts of Congress unconstitutional, or to send a mandamus to the Secretary of State, *as they had done*, it was the undoubted right of the House to impeach them, and of the Senate to remove them for giving such opinions, however honest or sincere they may have been in entertaining them." He held that the Senate, when trying an impeached officer, did not act as a court. "Removal by impeachment was nothing more than a declaration by Congress to this effect: You hold dangerous opinions, and if you are suffered to carry them into effect you will work the destruction of the Nation." [1]

Thus Giles made plain the Republican objective.

[1] Dec. 21, 1804, *Memoirs, J. Q. A.*: Adams I, 322-23.

Judges were to be removed for any cause that a dominant political party considered to be sufficient.[1] The National Judiciary was, in this manner, to be made responsive to the popular will and responsible to the representatives of the people in the House and of the States in the Senate.[2]

Giles, who was now Jefferson's personal representative in the Senate,[3] as he had been in the House, bore down upon his mild but reluctant fellow partisan from Vermont in a "manner dogmatical and peremptory." Not only must the aggressive and irritating Chase be stripped of his robes, but the same fate must fall upon "all other Judges of the Supreme Court except the one last appointed," [4] who, being a Republican, was secure.[5] Adams rightly concluded that the plan was

[1] Plumer, 274–75; and see especially Plumer, Jan. 5, 1804, "Congress," Plumer MSS. Lib. Cong.

[2] The powerful Republican organ, the *Aurora*, of Philadelphia, thus indicted the National Judiciary: Because judges could not be removed, "many wrongs are daily done by the courts to humble, obscure, or poor suitors. . . It is a prodigeous monster in a free government to see a class of men set apart, not simply to administer the laws, but who exercise a legislative and even an executive power, directly in defiance and contempt of the Constitution." (*Aurora*, Jan. 28, 1805, as quoted in Corwin, 41.) Professor Corwin says that this utterance was approved by Jefferson.

[3] "Mr. Giles from Virginia . . is the Ministerial leader in the Senate." (Plumer to Thompson, Dec. 23, 1804, Plumer MSS. Lib. Cong.)

"I considered Mr. Giles as the ablest *practical* politician of the whole party enlisted under Mr. Jefferson's banners." (Pickering to Marshall, Jan. 24, 1826, Pickering MSS. Mass. Hist. Soc.)

[4] William Johnson of South Carolina, appointed March 26, 1804, vice William Moore, resigned. Johnson was a stanch Jeffersonian when appointed. He was thirty-three years old at the time he was made Associate Justice.

[5] It is impossible to put too much emphasis on Giles's avowal. His statement is the key to the Chase impeachment.

to "have swept the supreme judicial bench clean at a stroke." [1]

For a long time everybody had understood that the impeachment of Chase was only the first step in the execution of the Republican plan to replace with Republicans Marshall and the four Federalist Associate Justices. "The judges of the Supreme Court are all Federalists," wrote Pickering six weeks before Johnson's appointment. "They stand in the way of the ruling power. . . The Judges therefore, are, if possible, to be removed," by impeachment. [2]

Nearly two years before, Senator William Plumer of New Hampshire had accurately divined the Republican plan: "The judges of the Supreme Court must fall," he informed Jeremiah Mason. "They are *denounced* by the Executive, as well as the House. They must be removed; they are obnoxious unyielding men; & why should they remain to awe & embarrass the administration? Men of more flexible nerves can be found to succeed them. Our affairs seem to approach an important crisis." [3] The Federalists rightly believed that Jefferson was the directing mind in planning and effecting the subjugation of the National Judiciary. That, said Bayard, "has been an object on which Mr. Jefferson has long been resolved, at least ever since he has been in office." [4]

[1] Adams to his father, March 8, 1805, *Writings, J. Q. A.*: Ford, III, 108.

[2] Pickering to Lyman, Feb. 11, 1804, *N.E. Federalism:* Adams, 344; Lodge: *Cabot,* 444; also see Plumer, 275.

[3] Plumer to Mason, Jan. 14, 1803, Plumer MSS. Lib. Cong.

[4] Bayard to Bassett, Feb. 12, 1802, *Bayard Papers:* Donnan, 148.

Samuel Chase

John Marshall especially must be overthrown.[1] He had done all the things of which Giles and the Republicans complained. He had "dared to declare an act of Congress unconstitutional," had "dared" to order Madison to show cause why he should not be compelled to do his legal duty. Everybody was at last awake to the fact that Marshall had become the controlling spirit of the Supreme Court and of the whole National Judiciary.

Every one knew, too, that he was the most determined Nationalist in the entire country, and that Jefferson and the Republican Party had no more unyielding enemy than the Chief Justice. And he had shown by his management of the Supreme Court and by his opinion in Marbury *vs.* Madison, how powerful that tribunal could be made. The downfall of Samuel Chase was a matter of small importance compared with the removal of John Marshall.

"They hate Marshall, Paterson, etc. worse than they hate Chase because they are men of better character," asserted Judge Jeremiah Smith of New Hampshire. "To be safe in these times good men must not only resign their offices but they must resign their good names. . . They will be obnoxious as long as they retain *either*. If they will neither die nor resign they give Mr J the trouble of correcting the *procedure*. . . Tell me what the judges say — are they frightened?" he anxiously inquired of Plumer.[2] Frightened they were — and very badly

[1] Channing: *Jeffersonian System*, 119–20; Adams: *U.S.* ii, 225–27, 235; Anderson, 93, 95.

[2] Smith to Plumer, Feb. 11, 1804, Plumer MSS. Lib. Cong.

frightened. Even John Marshall, hitherto imperturbable and dauntless, was shaken.[1]

In addition to his "heretical" opinion in Marbury *vs.* Madison, Marshall had given the Republicans, and Jefferson especially, another cause for complaint. A year after the decision of that case, he had again gone out of his way to announce from the Supreme Bench the fallacy of Jefferson's Constitutional views and the soundness of the Nationalist theory. During the February term of the Supreme Court for the year 1804, that tribunal, in the case of the United States *vs.* Fisher,[2] was called upon to decide whether the United States was a preferred creditor of an insolvent, under the Bankruptcy Act of 1800, which Marshall had helped to draw.[3] Among other objections, it was suggested by counsel for Fisher, the insolvent, that the Bankruptcy Law was unconstitutional and that the priority which that act gave the Nation over other creditors of the bankrupt would prevent the States from making similar laws for their own protection.

But, said Marshall, this is "the necessary consequence of the supremacy of the laws of the United States on all subjects to which the legislative power of the United States extends... The Constitution did not prohibit Congress" from enacting a bankruptcy law and giving the Nation preference as a creditor. On the contrary, Congress was expressly authorized "to make all laws which shall be necessary and proper to carry into execution the powers

[1] See *infra*, 176–77, 196.   [2] 2 Cranch, 358–405.
[3] See vol. II, 481–82, of this work.

vested by the Constitution in the National Government." To say that "no law was authorized which was not indispensably necessary .. would produce endless difficulties... Congress must possess the choice of means and must be empowered to use any means which are, in fact, conducive to the exercise of a power granted by the Constitution."

This was an emphatic denial of Jefferson's famous opinion on the power of Congress to charter a bank, and an outright assertion of the views of Hamilton on that celebrated question.[1] The case could have been decided without such an expression from the court, but it presented an opportunity for a judicial statement of liberal construction which might not soon come again,[2] and Marshall availed himself of it.

For two years no part of the Republican plans against the Judiciary had miscarried. Close upon the very day when John Breckenridge in the Senate had moved to repeal the National Judiciary Act of 1801, a petition signed by the enraged Republicans of Alleghany County, Pennsylvania, had been sent to the Legislature of that State, demanding the impeachment of Alexander Addison; and almost simultaneously with the passage of the Judiciary Repeal Act of Congress, the Pennsylvania House of Representatives transmitted to the State Senate articles charging the able but arrogant Federalist judge with high crimes and misdemeanors.

[1] See vol. II, 71–74, of this work.

[2] Fifteen years passed before a critical occasion called for another assertion by Marshall of the doctrine of implied powers; and that occasion produced one of Marshall's greatest opinions — in the judgment of many, the greatest of all his writings. (See McCulloch *vs.* Maryland, vol. IV, chap. VI, of this work.)

Addison's trial speedily followed; and while the evidence against him, viewed through the perspective of history, seems trivial, the Republican Pennsylvania Senate pronounced judgment against him and deposed him from the bench. With notable ability, Addison conducted his own defense. He made a powerful speech which is a classic of conservative philosophy.[1] But his argument was unavailing. The Republican theory, that a judge might be deposed from office for any conduct or opinion of which the Legislature disapproved, was ruthlessly carried out.[2]

Almost as soon as Congress convened after the overthrow of the obnoxious Pennsylvania Federalist judge, the Republicans in the National House, upon representations from Jefferson, took steps to impeach John Pickering, Judge of the United States Court for the District of New Hampshire.[3] This

[1] Addison's address is historically important; it perfectly shows the distrust of democracy which all Federalist leaders then felt. Among other things, he pleaded for the independence of the Judiciary, asserted that it was their exclusive province to decide upon the constitutionality of laws, and stoutly maintained that no judge could be impeached except for an offense for which he also could be indicted. (*Addison Trial*, 101–43.)

[2] The petition praying for the impeachment of Addison was sent to the Pennsylvania House of Representatives on January 11, 1802. On March 23, 1802, that body transmitted articles of impeachment to the State Senate. The trial was held in early January, 1803. Addison was convicted January 26, 1803. (*Ib.*)

[3] Jefferson's Message was transmitted to the House, February 4, 1803, nine days after the conviction of Addison. It enclosed a "letter and affidavits" setting forth Pickering's conduct on the bench in the case of the ship Eliza, and suggested that "the Constitution has confided [to the House] a power of instituting proceedings of redress." (*Annals*, 7th Cong. 2d Sess. 460.)

On March 2 the committee reported a resolution for Pickering's impeachment because of the commission by him of "high crimes and misdemeanors," and, though a few Federalists tried to postpone a vote, the resolution was adopted immediately.

judge had been hopelessly insane for at least three years and, as one result of his mental and nervous malady, had become an incurable drunkard.[1] In this condition he had refused to hear witnesses for the Government in the case of the ship *Eliza*, seized for violation of the revenue laws. He peremptorily ordered the vessel returned to its captain, and finally declined to allow an appeal from his decree. All this had been done with ravings, cursings, and crazed incoherences.[2]

That he was wholly incapacitated for office and unable to perform any act requiring intelligence was conceded by all. But the Constitution provided no method of removing an officer who had become insane.[3] This defect, however, gave the Republicans an ideal opportunity to put into practice their theory that impeachment was unrestricted and might be applied to any officer whom, for any reason, two thirds of the Senate deemed undesirable. "If the facts of his denying an appeal & of his intoxication, as stated in the impeachment, are proven, that will be sufficient cause for removal without further enquiry," asserted Jefferson when assured that Pickering was insane, and when asked "whether

---

[1] Depositions of Samuel Tenney, Ammi R. Cutter, Joshua Brackett, Edward St. Loe Livermore. (*Annals*, 8th Cong. 1st Sess. 334–42.)

[2] Testimony of John S. Sherburne, Thomas Chadbourne, and Jonathan Steele. (*Ib.* 351–56.)

[3] The wise and comprehensive Federalist Judiciary Act of 1801 covered just such cases. It provided that when a National judge was unable to discharge the duties of his office, the circuit judges should name one of their members to fill his place. (See *Annals*, 6th Cong. 2d Sess. 1545.) This very thing had been done in the case of Judge Pickering (see McMaster: *U.S.* III, 166). It is curious that, in the debate, the Republicans did not denounce this as unconstitutional.

insanity was good cause for impeachment & removal from office." [1]

The demented judge did not, of course, appear at his trial. Instead, a petition by his son was presented, alleging the madness of his father, and praying that evidence to that effect be received by the Senate.[2] This plea was stoutly resisted, and for two days the question was debated. "The most persevering and determined opposition is made against having evidence and counsel to prove the man insane," records John Quincy Adams, "only from the fear, that if insanity should be proved, he cannot be convicted of *high crimes and misdemeanors* by acts of decisive madness." [3] Finally the determined Republicans proceeded to the trial of the insane judge for high crimes and misdemeanors, evidence of his dethroned reason to be received "in mitigation." [4] In immense disgust the House managers withdrew, because "the Senate had determined *to hear evidence*" that the accused person was insane. Before they returned, they publicly denounced the Senators for their leniency; and thus Republican discipline was restored.[5]

Jefferson was impatient. "It will take two years to try this impeachment," he complained to Senator Plumer. "The Constitution ought to be altered,"

---

[1] Plumer, Jan. 5, 1804, "Congress," Plumer MSS. Lib. Cong.

[2] *Annals*, 8th Cong. 1st Sess. 328–30.

[3] *Memoirs*, J. Q. A.: Adams, I, 299–300.

[4] "This," records Adams, "had evidently been settled . . out of court. And this is the way in which these men administer justice." (*Ib.*)

[5] "In the House . . speeches are making every day to dictate to the Senate how they are to proceed; and the next morning they proceed accordingly." (*Ib.* 301–02.)

he continued, "so that the President should be authorized to remove a Judge from office, on the address of the two Houses." [1] But the exasperated Republicans hastened the proceedings; and the trial did not consume two weeks all told.

If an insane man should be condemned, "it will not hereafter be necessary," declared Senator Samuel Smith of Maryland, "that a man should be guilty of high crimes and misdemeanors," the commission of which was the only Constitutional ground for impeachment. Senator Jonathan Dayton of New Jersey denounced the whole proceeding as "a mere mockery of a trial." [2] Senator John Quincy Adams, in the flurry of debate, asserted that he should "speak until [his] mouth was stopped by force." [3] Senator Nicholas of Virginia shouted "Order! order! order!" when Samuel White of Delaware was speaking. So furious became the altercation that a duel seemed possible. [4] No delay was permitted and, on March 12, 1804, the demented Pickering was, by a strictly partisan vote of 19 to 7, [5] adjudged guilty of high crimes and misdemeanors.

An incident happened which was prophetic of a

[1] Feb. 18, 1803, Plumer, 253.

[2] *Annals*, 8th Cong. 1st Sess. 365.

[3] See *Memoirs, J. Q. A.*; Adams, I, 302–04, for a vivid account of the whole incident.

[4] Plumer, March 10, 1804, "Congress," Plumer MSS. Lib. Cong.

[5] *Annals*, 8th Cong. 1st Sess. 367. "The independence of our judiciary is no more. . . I hope the time is not far distant when the people east of the North river *will manage their own affairs in their own way;* . . and that the *sound* part will separate from the *corrupt.*" (Plumer to Morse, March 10, 1804, Plumer MSS. Lib. Cong.) On the unconstitutional and revolutionary conduct of the Republicans in the Pickering impeachment trial see Adams: *U.S.* II, 158.

decline in the marvelous party discipline that had kept the Republicans in Senate and House in solid support of the plans of the leaders. Three Republican Senators left the Chamber in order to avoid the balloting.[1] They would not adjudge an insane man to be guilty of high crimes and misdemeanors, but they were not yet independent enough to vote against their party.[2] This, however, did not alarm the Republican managers. They instantly struck

[1] Senators John Armstrong of New York, Stephen R. Bradley of Vermont, and David Stone of North Carolina. Jonathan Dayton of New Jersey and Samuel White of Delaware, Federalists, also withdrew. (*Annals*, 8th Cong. 1st Sess. 366.) And see *Memoirs, J. Q. A.*: Adams, I, 308–09; J. Q. Adams to his father, March 8, 1805, *Writings, J. Q. A.*: Ford, III, 110; Plumer to Park, March 13, 1804, Plumer MSS. Lib. Cong.

Senator John Brown of Kentucky, a Republican, "could not be induced to join the majority, but, unwilling to offend them, he obtained & has taken a leave of absence." (Plumer to Morse, March 10, 1804, Plumer MSS. Lib. Cong.) Senator Brown had been elected President *pro tem.* of the Senate, January 23, 1804.

Burr "abruptly left the Senate" to attend to his candidacy for the governorship of New York. (Plumer, March 10, 1804, "Congress," Plumer MSS. Lib. Cong.) Senator Franklin of North Carolina was then chosen President *pro tem.* and presided during the trial of Pickering. But Burr returned in time to arrange for, and preside over, the trial of Justice Chase.

[2] The Republicans even refused to allow the report of the proceedings to be "printed in the Appendix to the Journals of the Session." (*Memoirs, J. Q. A.*: Adams, I, 311.)

The conviction and removal of Pickering alarmed the older Federalists almost as much as did the repeal of the Judiciary Act. "The *demon* of party governed the decision. All who condemned were Jeffersonians, and all who pronounced the accused not guilty were Federalists." (Pickering to Lyman, March 4, 1804, *N.E. Federalism*: Adams, 358–59; Lodge: *Cabot*, 450.)

"I really wish those in New England who are boasting of the independence of our Judiciary would reflect on what a slender tenure Judges hold their offices whose political sentiments are at variance with the dominant party." (Plumer to Park, March 13, 1804, Plumer MSS. Lib. Cong.)

the next blow upon which they had determined
more than two years before. Within an hour after
John Pickering was convicted the House voted to
impeach Samuel Chase.

Marshall's irascible associate on the Supreme
Bench had given the Republicans a new and serious
cause for hostilities against him. In less than two
months after Marshall had delivered the unanimous
opinion of the Supreme Court in Marbury *vs*. Madison, Justice Chase, in charging the grand jury at
Baltimore, denounced Republican principles and
mercilessly assailed Republican acts and purposes.

This judicial critic of democracy told the grand
jury that "the bulk of mankind are governed by their
passions, and not by reason. . . The late alteration of
the federal judiciary . . and the recent change in our
state constitution, by the establishing of universal
suffrage, . . will . . take away all security for property and personal liberty . . and our republican
constitution will sink into a mobocracy, the worst
of all popular governments."

Chase condemned "the modern doctrines by our
late reformers, that all men, in a state of society,
are entitled to enjoy equal liberty and equal rights,
[which] have brought this mighty mischief upon us";
— a mischief which he feared "will rapidly progress,
until peace and order, freedom and property, shall
be destroyed. . . Will justice be impartially administered by judges dependent on the legislature for
their . . suport? Will liberty or property be protected or secured, by laws made by representatives
chosen by electors, who have no property in, or a

common interest with, or attachment to, the community?"[1]

Burning with anger, a young Republican member of the Maryland Legislature, John Montgomery, who had listened to this judicial tirade, forthwith savagely denounced Chase in the *Baltimore American*.[2] He demanded that the Justice be impeached and removed from the bench.[3] Montgomery hastened to send to the President[4] a copy of the paper.

Jefferson promptly wrote Nicholson: "Ought this seditious and official attack on the principles of our Constitution, and on the proceedings of a State, go unpunished? And, to whom so pointedly as yourself will the public look for the necessary measures?"

But Jefferson was not willing to appear openly. With that uncanny power of divining political currents to which coarser or simpler minds were oblivious, he was conscious of the uneasiness of Northern Republicans over ruthless impeachment and decided not to become personally responsible. "For myself," he cautioned Nicholson, "it is better that I should not interfere."[5]

Upon the advice of Nathaniel Macon,[6] Republican Speaker of the House, Nicholson concluded that it

---

[1] Exhibit VIII, *Chase Trial*, Appendix, 61–62; also see *Annals*, 8th Cong. 2d Sess. 675–76.

[2] June 13, 1803.   [3] See *Chase Trial*, 101 *et seq.*

[4] See McMaster: *U.S.* III, 162–70.

[5] Jefferson to Nicholson, May 13, 1803, *Jefferson Writings*: Washington, IV, 484.

[6] Macon to Nicholson, Aug. 6, 1803, Dodd: *Life of Nathaniel Macon*, 187–88. Macon seriously doubted the expediency and legality of the impeachment of Chase. However, he voted with his party.

would be more prudent for another to take the lead.
It was well understood that he was to have Chase's
place on the Supreme Bench,[1] and this fact would
put him at a disadvantage if he became the central
figure in the fight against the aged Justice. The procurement of the impeachment was, therefore, placed
in the eager hands of John Randolph, that "unusual
Phenomenon," as John Adams called him,[2] whose
lust for conspicuous leadership was insatiable.

The Republican managers had carefully moulded
public opinion into the belief that Chase was guilty
of some monstrous crime. Months before articles
of impeachment were presented to the House, *ex
parte* statements against him were collected, published in pamphlet form, and scattered throughout the country. To assure wider publicity all this
"evidence" was printed in the Republican organ
at Washington. The accused Justice had, therefore, been tried and convicted by the people before
the charges against him were even offered in the
House.[3]

This preparation of the popular mind accomplished, Chase was finally impeached. Eight articles
setting forth the Republican accusations were laid
before the Senate. Chase was accused of everything

---

[1] Dodd, 187–88.

[2] Adams to Rush, June 22, 1806, *Old Family Letters*, 100.

[3] Chase "is very obnoxious to the *powers that be* & must be *denounced*, but articles will not be exhibited agt him this session. The
Accusers have collected a volume of exparte evidence against him,
printed & published it in pamphlets, & now it is publishing in the
Court gazette to be diffused in every direction. . . If a party to a suit
at law, . . was to practice in this manner he would merit punishment."
(Plumer to Smith, March 11, 1804, Plumer MSS. Lib. Cong.)

of which anybody had complained since his appointment to the Supreme Bench. His conduct at the trials of Fries and Callender was set forth with tedious particularity: in Delaware he had stooped "to the level of an informer"; his charge to the grand jury at Baltimore was an "intemperate and inflammatory political harangue"; he had prostituted his "high judicial character . . to the low purpose of an electioneering partizan"; his purpose was "to excite . . odium . . against the government." [1]

This curious scramble of fault-finding, which was to turn out so fatally for the prosecution, was the work of Randolph. When the conglomerate indictment was drawn, no one, except perhaps Jefferson, had the faintest idea that the Republican plan would miscarry; Randolph's multifarious charges pleased those in Virginia, Pennsylvania, Delaware, and Maryland who had first made them; they were so drawn as to lay a foundation for the assault which was to follow immediately. "These articles," wrote John Quincy Adams, "contained in themselves a virtual impeachment not only of Mr. Chase, but of

---

[1] See *supra*, chap. I. For the articles of impeachment see *Annals*, 8th Cong. 2d Sess. 85–88; *Chase Trial*, 10–11.

The Republicans, for a time, contemplated the impeachment of Richard Peters, Judge of the United States Court for the District of Pennsylvania, who sat with Chase during the trial of Fries. (*Annals*, 8th Cong. 1st Sess. 823–24, 850, 873–74.) But his name was dropped because he had not "so acted in his judiciary capacity as to require the interposition of the Constitutional powers of this House." (*Ib.* 1171.)

Peters was terrified and turned upon his fellow judge. He showered Pickering and other friends with letters, complaining of the conduct of his judicial associate. "If I am to be immolated let it be with some other Victim — or for my own Sins." (Peters to Pickering, Jan. 26, 1804, Pickering MSS. Mass. Hist. Soc.)

all the Judges of the Supreme Court from the first establishment of the national judiciary." [1]

In an extended and carefully prepared speech, Senator Giles, who had drawn the rules governing the conduct of the trial in the Senate, announced the Republican view of impeachment which, he said, "is nothing more than an enquiry, by the two Houses of Congress, whether the office of any public man might not be better filled by another." Adams was convinced that "this is undoubtedly the source and object of Mr. Chase's impeachment, and on the same principle any officer may easily be removed at any time." [2]

From the time the House took action against Chase, the Federalists were in despair. "I think the Judge will be removed from Office," was Senator Plumer's opinion. [3] "The event of the impeachment is already determined," wrote Bayard before the trial began. [4] Pickering was certain that Chase would be condemned — so would any man that the House might impeach; such "measures . . are made questions of *party*, and therefore at all events to be carried into effect according to the wishes of the prime mover [Jefferson]." [5]

As the day of the arraignment of the impeached Justice approached, his friends were not comforted

[1] J. Q. Adams to his father, March 14, 1805, *Writings*, *J. Q. A.*: Ford, III, 116.

[2] Dec. 20, 1804, *Memoirs*, *J. Q. A.*: Adams, I, 321.

[3] Plumer to Cogswell, Jan. 4, 1805, Plumer MSS. Lib. Cong.; and see Plumer to Sheafe, Jan. 9, 1805, Plumer MSS. *loc. cit.*

[4] Bayard to Harper, Jan. 30, 1804, *Bayard Papers:* Donnan, 160.

[5] Pickering to Lyman, March 14, 1804, Lodge: *Cabot*, 450; also *N.E. Federalism:* Adams, 359.

by their estimate of the public temper. "Our public
. . will be as tame as Mr. Randolph can desire,"
lamented Ames. "You may broil Judge Chase and
eat him, or eat him raw; it shall stir up less anger
or pity, than the Six Nations would show, if Corn-
planter or Red Jacket were refused a belt of wam-
pum."[1]

When finally Chase appeared before the bar of the
Senate, he begged that the trial should be postponed
until next session, in order that he might have time
to prepare his defense. His appeal fell on remorseless
ears; the Republicans gave him only a month. But
this scant four weeks proved fatal to their purpose.
Jefferson's wise adjustment of the greatest financial
scandal in American history [2] came before the House
during this interval; and fearless, honest, but impolitic John Randolph attacked the Administration's
compromise of the Yazoo fraud with a ferocity all
but insane in its violence. Literally screaming with
rage, he assailed Jefferson's Postmaster-General
who was lobbying on the floor of the House for
the passage of the President's Yazoo plan, and delivered continuous philippics against that polluted
transaction out of which later came the third of
John Marshall's most notable opinions.[3]

In this frame of mind, nervously exhausted, physically overwrought and troubled, the most brilliant

---

[1] Ames to Dwight, Jan. 20, 1805, Ames, i, 338.

[2] The Yazoo fraud. No other financial scandal in our history
equaled this, if one considers the comparative wealth and population
of the country at the times other various great frauds were perpetrated.
For an account of it, see *infra*, chap. x.

[3] For Randolph's frantic speech on the Yazoo fraud and Marshall's
opinion in Fletcher *vs.* Peck, see *infra*, chap. x.

and effective Congressional partisan leader of our
early history came to the trial. Moreover, Randolph had broken with the Administration and
challenged Jefferson's hitherto undisputed partisan
autocracy. This was the first public manifestation
of that schism in the Republican Party which was
never entirely healed.

Such was the situation on the 4th of February,
1805, when the Senate convened to hear and determine the case of Samuel Chase, impeached by the
House for high crimes and misdemeanors, to settle
by the judgment it should render the fate of John
Marshall as Chief Justice of the United States, and
to fix forever the place of the National Judiciary in
the scheme of American government.

"Oyez! Oyez! Oyez! — All persons are commanded to keep silence on pain of imprisonment,
while the grand inquest of the nation is exhibiting
to the Senate of the United States, sitting as a Court
of Impeachments, articles of impeachment against
Samuel Chase, Associate Justice of the Supreme
Court of the United States." [1]

So cried the Sergeant-at-Arms of the National
Senate when, in the Chase trial, John Marshall, the
Supreme Court, and the whole National Judiciary
were called to judgment by Thomas Jefferson, on
the bleak winter day in dismal, scattered, and quarreling Washington. An audience crowded the Senate Chamber almost to the point of suffocation.
There were present not only the members of Senate

---

[1] This form was adopted in the trial of Judge Pickering. See *Annals*, 8th Cong. 1st Sess. 319.

and House, the officers of the Executive departments, and the men and women of the Capital's
limited society, but also scores of eminent persons
from distant parts of the country.[1]

Among the spectators were John Marshall and the
Associate Justices of the Supreme Court, thoroughly
conscious that they, and the institution of which
they were the highest representatives, were on trial
almost as much as their imprudent, rough, and outspoken fellow member of the Bench. It is not improbable that they were helping to direct the defense
of Chase,[2] in which, as officials, they were personally
interested, and in which, too, all their convictions
as citizens and jurists were involved.

Marshall, aroused, angered, and frightened by the
articles of the impeachment, had written his brother
a year before the Chase trial that they are "sufficient to alarm the friends of a pure, and, of course,
an independent Judiciary, if, among those who rule
our land there be any of that description."[3] At
the beginning of the proceedings Chase had asked
Marshall, who was then in Richmond, to write an
account of what occurred at the trial of Callender,
and Marshall promptly responded: "I instantly
applied to my brother[4] & to Mr. Wickham[5] to
state their recollection of the circumstances under
which Colo. Taylors testimony was rejected.[6] They
both declared that they remembred them very im-

---

[1] See Plumer, 323.   [2] Channing: *U.S.* IV, 287.

[3] Marshall to James M. Marshall, April 1, 1804, MS.

[4] William Marshall. See *infra*, 191-92.

[5] John Wickham, leader of the Richmond bar and one of Marshall's intimate friends.

[6] See *supra*, chap. I; and *infra*.

Richmond Jany 23^d 1804

My dear Sir

On receiving your letter of the 13th I instantly applied to my brother & to Mr Wickham requesting them to state their recollection of the circumstances under which Col^o Taylors testimony was rejected. They both declared that they remembered them very imperfectly but that they would endeavor to recollect what pasd & commit it to writing.

I shall bring it with me to Washington in February. At the same time I shall take with me a list of the Grand & petit jury; & a copy of the order of court directing Callenders arrest.

The foreman of the Jury was Col^o Gamble the juror who spoke to you was Mr John Basset. They are both men of character & intelligence.

Admitting it to be true that on legal principles Co^o Taylors testimony was admissible it certainly constitutes very extraordinary ground for an impeachment. Accord^g to the antient doctrine a jury finding a verdict against law of the case was liable to an attaint; & thus amounts the present doctrine seems to be that a Judge giving a legal opinion contrary to the opinion of the legislature liable to impeachment. As for convenience & humanity the old doctrine of attaint has yielded to the silent, modest but not less operative influence of new trials, I think the modern doctrine of impeachment should yield to an absolute jurisdiction in the legislature. A removal of those legal opinions deemed unsound by the legislature would certainly better comport with the mildness of our character than a removal of the judge who had rendered them unknowing of his fault. The other things except the 1st & 4th which I suppose to be altogether unfounded, seem still less to furnish cause for impeachment. But the little finger of ~~——————~~ is heavier than the loins of ————

I have not written to Mr. Moore because I count on his setting out for Washington before my letter could reach him

Farewell — with much respect & esteem

I am dear Sir your obedt

J Marshall

Mr Nelson is unfortunately dead

perfectly but that they woud endeavor to recollect what passed & commit it to writing. I shall bring it with me to Washington in february." Marshall also promised to bring other documents.

"Admitting it to be true," continues Marshall, "that on legal principles Colo. Taylors testimony was admissible, it certainly constitutes a very extraordinary ground for an impeachment. According to the antient doctrine a jury finding a verdict against the law of the case was liable to an attaint; & the amount of the present doctrine seems to be that a Judge giving a legal opinion contrary to the opinion of the legislature is liable to impeachment.

"As, for convenience & humanity the old doctrine of attaint has yielded to the silent, moderate but not less operative influence of new trials, I think the modern doctrine of impeachment should yield to an appellate jurisdiction in the legislature. A reversal of those legal opinions deemed unsound by the legislature would certainly better comport with the mildness of our character than [would] a removal of the Judge who has rendered them unknowing of his fault.

"The other charges except the 1st & 4th which I suppose to be altogether unfounded, seem still less to furnish cause for impeachment. But the little finger of [blotted out — probably "democracy"] is heavier than the loins of ——.[1]

"Farewell — With much respect and esteem. . .

"J. MARSHALL."[2]

[1] See 1 Kings, xii, 10.
[2] Marshall to Chase, Jan. 23, 1804, Etting MSS. Pa. Hist. Soc.

Marshall thus suggested the most radical method for correcting judicial decisions ever advanced, before or since, by any man of the first class. Appeals from the Supreme Court to Congress! Senators and Representatives to be the final judges of any judicial decision with which a majority of the House was dissatisfied! Had we not the evidence of Marshall's signature to a letter written in his well-known hand, it could not be credited that he ever entertained such sentiments. They were in direct contradiction to his reasoning in Marbury *vs.* Madison, utterly destructive of the Federalist philosophy of judicial control of legislation.

The explanation is that Marshall was seriously alarmed. By his own pen he reveals to us his state of mind before and on that dismal February day when he beheld Samuel Chase arraigned at the bar of the Senate of the United States. During the trial Marshall's bearing as a witness [1] again exhibited his trepidation. And, as we have seen, he had good cause for sharp anxiety.[2]

The avowed Republican purpose to remove him and his Federalist associates from the Supreme Bench, the settled and well-known intention of Jefferson to appoint Spencer Roane as Chief Justice when Marshall was ousted, and the certainty that this would be fatal to the execution of those fundamental principles of government to which Marshall was so passionately devoted — these important considerations fully warranted the apprehension which the Chief Justice felt and now displayed.

[1] See *infra*, 192–96.   [2] See *supra*, chap. III, 113.

Had he been indifferent to the peril that confronted him and the whole National Judiciary, he would have exhibited a woeful lack of sense and feeling. He was more than justified in resorting to any honorable expedient to save the great office he held from occupancy by a resolute and resourceful foe of those Constitutional theories, the application of which, Marshall firmly believed, was indispensable to the sound development of the American Nation.

The arrangements for the trial were as dramatic as the event itself was momentous.[1] The scenes of the impeachment prosecution of Warren Hastings were still vivid in the minds of all, and in imitation of that spectacle, the Senate Chamber was now bedecked with impressive splendor. It was aglow with theatrical color, and the placing of the various seats was as if a tragic play were to be performed.

To the right and left of the President's chair were two rows of benches with desks, the whole covered with crimson cloth. Here sat the thirty-four Senators of the United States. Three rows of benches, arranged in tiers, extended from the wall toward the center of the room; these were covered with green cloth and were occupied by the members of the House of Representatives. Upon their right an enclosure had been constructed, and in it were the members of Jefferson's Cabinet.

Beneath the permanent gallery to which the general public was admitted, a temporary gallery, supported by pillars, ran along the wall, and faced

---

[1] "Mr Burr had the sole power of making the arrangements . . for the trial." (Plumer to Sheafe, Jan. 9, 1805, Plumer MSS. Lib. Cong.)

the crimson-covered places of the Senators. At either end of it were boxes. Comfortable seats had been provided in this enclosure; and these were covered with green cloth, which also was draped over the balustrade.

This sub-gallery and the boxes were filled with ladies dressed in the height of fashion. A passageway was left from the President's chair to the doorway. On either side of this aisle were two stalls covered with blue cloth, as were also the chairs within them. They were occupied by the managers of the House of Representatives and by the lawyers who conducted the defense.[1]

A short, slender, elegantly formed man, with pallid face and steady black eyes, presided over this Senatorial Court. He was carefully dressed, and his manners and deportment were meticulously correct. Aaron Burr, fresh from his duel with Hamilton, and under indictment in two States, had resumed his duties as Vice-President. Nothing in the bearing of this playwright character indicated in the smallest degree that anything out of the ordinary had happened to him. The circumstance of his presence, however, dismayed even the most liberal of the New England Federalists. "We are indeed fallen on evil times," wrote Senator Plumer. "The high office of President is filled by an *infidel*, that of Vice-President by a *murderer*." [2]

For the first time since the Republican victory of 1800, which, but for his skill, courage, and energy in

---

[1] *Annals*, 8th Cong. 2d Sess. 100; *Chase Trial*, 2–5.
[2] Plumer to Norris, Nov. 7, 1804, Plumer, 329.

New York, would not have been achieved,[1] Burr
now found himself in favor with the Administration
and the Republican chieftains.[2] Jefferson determined that Aaron Burr must be captured — at least
conciliated. He could not be displaced as the presiding officer at the Chase impeachment trial; his
rulings would be influential, perhaps decisive; the
personal friendship and admiration of several Senators for him were well known; the emergency of
the Republican Party was acute. Chase must be
convicted at all hazards; and while nobody but
Jefferson then doubted that this would be the result,
no chances were to be taken, no precaution overlooked.

The President had rewarded the three principal
witnesses against Pickering with important and
lucrative offices [3] after the insane judge had been
removed from the bench. Indeed he had given the
vacated judgeship to one of these witnesses. But
such an example Jefferson well knew would have no
effect upon Burr; even promises would avail nothing
with the man who for nearly three years had suffered
indignity and opposition from an Administration
which he, more than any one man except Jefferson
himself, had placed in power.

[1] See *infra*, chap. VI.

[2] See J. Q. Adams to his father, Jan. 5, 1805, *Writings*, *J. Q. A.*:
Ford, III, 104.

[3] Plumer, 274. "John S. Sherburne, Jonathan Steele, Michael
McCleary and Richard Cutts Shannon were the principal witnesses
against Pickering. Sherburne was appointed Judge [in Pickering's
place]; Steele, District Attorney; McCleary, Marshal; and Shannon,
Clerk of the Court. . . Steele, expecting to have been Judge refused to
accept his appointment, assigning as the reason his agency in the removal of Pickering."

So it came about that Vice-President Aaron Burr, with only four weeks of official life left him, with the whole North clamorous against him because of his killing of Hamilton and an indictment of murder hanging over him in New Jersey, now found himself showered with favors by those who owed him so much and who, for nearly four years, had so grossly insulted him.

Burr's stepson, his brother-in-law, his most intimate friend, were forthwith appointed to the three most valuable and commanding offices in the new government of the Louisiana Territory, at the attractive city of New Orleans.[1] The members of the Cabinet became attentive to Burr. The President himself exercised his personal charm upon the fallen politician. Time after time Burr was now invited to dine with Jefferson at the Executive Mansion.

Nor were Presidential dinners, the bestowal of patronage hitherto offensively refused, and attentions of the Cabinet, the limit of the efforts to win the coöperation of the man who was to preside over the trial of Samuel Chase. Senator Giles drew a petition to the Governor of New Jersey begging that the prosecution of Burr for murder be dropped, and to this paper he secured the signature of nearly all the Republican Senators.[2]

Burr accepted these advances with grave and

---

[1] Plumer, 329–30; and see Adams: *U.S.* II, 220.

[2] Nov. 26, 1804, *Memoirs, J. Q. A.*: Adams, I, 317–18; and Adams, *U.S.* II, 220–22.

"Burr is flattered and feared by the administration." (Plumer to Thompson, Dec. 23, 1804, Plumer MSS. Lib. Cong.; and Plumer to Wilson, Dec. 7, 1804, Plumer MSS. *loc. cit.*)

reserved dignity; but he understood the purpose that inspired them, did not commit himself, and remained uninfluenced and impartial. Throughout the momentous trial the Vice-President was a model presiding officer. "He conducted with the dignity and impartiality of an angel, but with the rigor of a devil," records a Washington newspaper that was bitterly hostile to Burr personally and politically.[1]

When Chase took his place in the box, the Sergeant-at-Arms brought him a chair; but Burr, adhering to the English custom, which required

[1] Davis, II, 360; also Adams: *U.S.* 218–44.

"It must be acknowledged that Burr has displayed much ability, and since the first day I have seen nothing of partiality." (Cutler to Torrey, March 1, 1805, Cutler: *Life, Journals and Correspondence of Manasseh Cutler*, II, 193.)

At the beginning of the trial, however, Burr's rigor irritated the Senate: "Mr. Burr is remarkably testy — he acts more of the tyrant — is impatient, passionate — scolds — he is in a rage because we do not sit longer." (Plumer, Feb. 8, 1805, "Diary," Plumer MSS. Lib. Cong.)

"Just as the time for adjourning to morrow was to be put . . Mr. Burr said he wished to inform the Senate of some irregularities that he had observed in the Court.

"Some of the Senators as he said during the trial & while a witness was under examination walked between him & the Managers — others eat apples — & some eat cake in their seats.

"Mr. Pickering said he eat an apple — but it was at a time when the President had retired from the chair. Burr replied he did not mean him — he did not see him.

"Mr. Wright said he eat cake — he had a just right to do so — he was faint — but he disturbed nobody — He never would submit to be schooled & catechised in this manner.

"At this instance a motion was made by Bradley, who also had eaten cake, for an adjournment. Burr told Wright he was not in order — sit down. The Senate adjourned — & I left Burr and Wright scolding.

"Really, *Master Burr*, you need a ferule, or birch to enforce your lectures on polite behavior!" (*Ib.* Feb. 12, 1805; also *ib.* Jan. 2, 1805.) Burr was sharply criticized by the *Washington Federalist*, January 8, for his rude conduct at the beginning of the trial.

prisoners to stand when on trial in court, ordered
it to be taken away.[1] Upon the request of the elderly Justice, however, Burr quickly relented and the
desired seat was provided.[2]

Chase was, in appearance, the opposite of the
diminutive and graceful Vice-President. More than
six feet tall, with thick, broad, burly shoulders, he
was a picture of rugged and powerful physical manhood, marred by an accumulation of fat which his
generous manner of living had produced. Also he
was afflicted with an agonizing gout, with which it
seems so many of "the fathers" were cursed. His face
was broad and massive, his complexion a brownish
red.[3] "Bacon face" was a nickname applied to him
by the Maryland bar.[4] His head was large, his brow
wide, and his hair was thick and white with the snows
of his sixty-four winters.[5]

[1] Plumer to Sheafe, Jan. 1805, Plumer, 330–31.
[2] *Annals*, 8th Cong. 2d Sess. 92; *Chase Trial*, 4.
[3] Dwight: *Signers of the Declaration of Independence*, 245–52.
[4] Hudson: *Journalism in the United States, 1690–1872*, 214; and
see Story to Bramble, June 10, 1807, Story, i, 154.
[5] "In person, in manners, in unwieldy strength, in severity of reproof, in real tenderness of heart; and above all in intellect," he was
"the living, I had almost said the exact, image of Samuel Johnson."
(Story to Fay, Feb. 25, 1808, Story, i, 168.)

Chase's career had been stirring and important. Carefully educated
by his father, an Episcopal clergyman, and thoroughly grounded in
the law, he became eminent at the Maryland bar at a very early age.
From the first his aggressive character asserted itself. He was rudely
independent and, as a member of the Maryland House of Burgesses,
treated the royal governor and his Tory partisans with contemptuous
defiance. When the British attempted to enforce the Stamp Act, he
joined a band of high-spirited young patriots who called themselves
"The Sons of Liberty," and led them in their raids upon public offices,
which they broke open, seizing and destroying the stamps and burning in effigy the stamp distributor.

His violent and fearless opposition to British rule and officials

The counsel that surrounded the impeached Justice were brilliant and learned.[1] They were Joseph Hopkinson, who six years before, upon Marshall's return from France, had written "Hail Columbia; or, The President's March"; Philip Barton Key, brother of the author of "The Star-Spangled Banner";[2] Robert Goodloe Harper, one of the Federalist leaders in Congress during the ascendancy of that party; and Charles Lee, Attorney-General under President Adams when Marshall was Secretary of State, and one of Marshall's most devoted friends.[3]

But in the chair next to Chase sat a man who, single-handed and alone, was more than a match for

made young Chase so popular that he was elected as one of the five Maryland delegates to the first Continental Congress that assembled during the winter of 1774. He was reëlected the following year, and was foremost in urging the measures of armed defense that ended in the appointment of Washington as Commander-in-Chief of the American forces. Disregarding the instructions of his State, Chase hotly championed the adoption of the Declaration of Independence, and was one of the signers of that document.

On the floor of Congress he denounced a member as a traitor — one Zubly, a Georgia parson — who in terror fled the country. Chase continued in the Continental Congress until 1778 and was appointed a member of almost every important committee of that body. He became the leader of his profession in Maryland, was appointed Chief Justice of the Criminal Court of Baltimore, and elected a member of the Maryland Convention, called to ratify the National Constitution. Thereafter, he was made Chief Justice of the Supreme Court of the State. In 1796, President Washington appointed Chase as Associate Justice of the National Supreme Court of which he was conceded to be one of the ablest members. (Dwight, 245–52.)

[1] See Plumer to his brother, Feb. 25, 1805, Plumer MSS. Lib. Cong.

[2] *Maryland Historical Society Fund-Publication No. 24*, p. 20. Burr told Key that "he must not appear as counsel with his loose coat on." (Plumer, Feb. 11, 1805, "Diary," Plumer MSS. Lib. Cong.)

[3] Adams: *U.S.* II, 227–28. Bayard strongly urged Chase to have no counsel, but to defend himself. (Bayard to Harper, Jan. 30, 1804, *Bayard Papers:* Donnan, 159–60.)

all the managers of the House put together. Luther
Martin of Maryland — of medium height, broad-
shouldered, near-sighted, absent-minded, shabbily
attired, harsh of voice, now sixty-one years old,
with gray hair beginning to grow thin and a face
crimsoned by the brandy which he continually imbibed — was the dominating figure of this historic
contest.[1]

[1] See Story's description of Martin three years later, Story to Fay,
Feb. 16, 1808, Story, I, 163–64.

Luther Martin well illustrates the fleeting nature of the fame
of even the greatest lawyers. For two generations he was "an acknowledged leader of the American bar," and his preëminence in
that noble profession was brightened by fine public service. Yet
within a few years after his death, he was totally forgotten, and to-
day few except historical students know that such a man ever lived.

Martin began his practice of the law when twenty-three years of
age and his success was immediate and tremendous. His legal learning
was prodigious — his memory phenomenal.

Apparently, Martin was the heaviest drinker of that period of
heavy drinking men. The inexplicable feature of his continuous excesses was that his mighty drinking seldom appeared to affect his
professional efficiency. Only once in his long and active career did
intoxication interfere with his work in court. (See *infra*, 586.)

Passionate in his loves and hates, he abhorred Jefferson with all
the ardor of his violent nature; and his favorite denunciation of any
bad man was, "Sir! he is as great a scoundrel as Thomas Jefferson."

For thirty years Martin was the Attorney-General of Maryland.
He was the most powerful member of his State in the Convention that
framed the National Constitution which he refused to sign, opposing
the ratification of it in arguments of such signal ability that forty
years afterward John C. Calhoun quarried from them the material for
his famous Nullification speeches.

When, however, the Constitution was ratified and became the
supreme law of the land, Martin, with characteristic wholeearted-
ness, supported it loyally and championed the Administrations of
Washington and Adams.

He was the lifelong friend of the impeached justice, to whom he
owed his first appointment as Attorney-General of Maryland as well
as great assistance and encouragement in the beginning of his career.
Chase and he were also boon companions, each filled with admiration
for the talents and attainments of the other, and strikingly similar in

Weary and harried as he was, Randolph opened the trial with a speech of some skill. He contrasted the conduct of Chase in the trial of Callender with that of Marshall in a trial in Richmond in 1804 at which Marshall had presided. "Sir," said Randolph, "in the famous case of Logwood,[1] whereat the Chief Justice of the United States presided, I was present, being one of the grand jury who found a true bill against him. . . The government was as deeply interested in arresting the career of this dangerous and atrocious criminal, who had aimed his blow against the property of every man in society, as it could be in bringing to punishment a weak and worthless scribbler [Callender]."

But how had Marshall acted in the conduct of that trial? "Although," continued Randolph, "much testimony was offered by the prisoner, which did by no means go to his entire exculpation, although

their courage and fidelity to friends and principles. So the lawyer threw himself into the fight for the persecuted judge with all his astonishing strength.

When, in his old age, he was stricken with paralysis, the Maryland Legislature placed a tax of five dollars annually on all lawyers for his support. After Martin's death the bench and bar of Baltimore passed a resolution that "we will wear mourning for the space of thirty days." (*American Law Review*, I, 279.)

No biography of Martin has ever been written; but there are two excellent sketches of his life, one by Ashley M. Gould in *Great American Lawyers*: Lewis, II, 3–46; and the other by Henry P. Goddard in the *Md. Hist. Soc. Fund. Pub. No. 24.*

[1] *Annals*, 8th Cong. 2d Sess. 160–61. The case to which Randolph refers was that of the United States *vs.* Thomas Logwood, indicted in April, 1801, for counterfeiting. Logwood was tried in the United States Circuit Court at Richmond during June, 1804. Marshall, sitting with District Judge Cyrus Griffin, presided. Notwithstanding Marshall's liberality, Logwood was convicted and Marshall sentenced him to ten years' imprisonment at hard labor. (Order Book No. 4, 464, Records, U.S. Circuit Court, Richmond.)

much of that testimony was of a very questionable nature, none of it was declared *inadmissable*." Marshall suffered it "to go to the jury, who were left to judge of its weight and credibility"; nor had he required "any interrogatories to the witnesses . . to be reduced to writing," — such a thing never had been done in Virginia before the tyrannical ruling of Chase in the trial of Callender.

"No, Sir!" he cried. "The enlightened man who presided in Logwood's case knew that, although the basest and vilest of criminals, he was entitled to *justice*, equally with the most honorable member of society." Marshall "did not avail himself of the previous and great discoveries in criminal law, of this respondent [Chase]"; Marshall "admitted the prisoner's testimony to go to the jury"; Marshall "never thought it *his right* or *his duty* to require questions to be reduced to writing"; Marshall "gave the accused *a fair trial* according to law and usage, without any innovation or departure from the established rules of criminal jurisprudence in his country."

Marshall's gentle manner and large-minded, soft-spoken rulings as a trial judge were thus adroitly made to serve as an argument for the condemnation of his associate, and for his own undoing if Chase should be convicted. Randolph denounced "the monstrous pretension that an act to be impeachable must be indictable. Where? In the Federal Courts? There, not even robbery and murder are indictable."

A judge could not, under the National law, be indicted for conducting a National court while drunk,

JOHN RANDOLPH

and perhaps not in all State courts. "It is indictable nowhere for him to omit to do his duty, to refuse to hold a court. But who can doubt that both are impeachable offenses, and ought to subject the offender to removal from office?"

The autocrat of Congress then boldly announced to the Republican Senators that the House managers "confidently expect on his [Chase's] conviction. . . We shall bring forward . . such a specimen of judicial tyranny, as, I trust in God, will never be again exhibited in our country."[1]

Fifty-two witnesses were examined. It was established that, in the trial of Fries, Chase had written the opinion of the court upon the law before the jury was sworn, solely in order to save time; had withdrawn the paper and destroyed it when he found Fries's counsel resented the court's precipitate action; and, finally, had repeatedly urged them to proceed with the defense without restriction. Chase's inquisitorial conduct in Delaware was proved, and several witnesses testified to the matter and manner of his charge to the Baltimore grand jury.[2]

Every incident in the trial of Callender[3] was described by numerous witnesses.[4] George Hay,

[1] *Annals*, 8th Cong. 2d Sess. 163–65; *Chase Trial*, 18. Randolph disgusted the Federalists. "This speech is the most feeble — the most incorrect that I ever heard him make." (Plumer, Feb. 9, 1805, "Diary," Plumer MSS. Lib. Cong.)

[2] Two witnesses to the Baltimore incident, George Reed and John Montgomery, committed their testimony to memory as much "as ever a Presbyterian clergyman did his sermon — or an Episcopalian his prayer." (Plumer, Feb. 14, 1805, "Diary," Plumer MSS. Lib. Cong.)

[3] See *supra*, chap. I.

[4] Annals, 8th Cong. 2d Sess. 203–05; *Chase Trial*, 36–37.

who had been the most aggressive of Callender's counsel, was so anxious to help the managers that he made a bad impression on the Senate by his eagerness.[1] It developed that the whole attitude of Chase had been one of sarcastic contempt; and that Callender's counsel were more piqued by the laughter of the spectators which the witty sallies and humorous manner of the Justice excited, than they were outraged by any violence on Chase's part, or even by what they considered the illegal and oppressive nature of his rulings.

When, in defending Callender, Hay had insisted upon "a literal recital of the parts [of *The Prospect Before Us*] charged as libellous," Chase, looking around the court-room, said with an ironical smile: "It is contended .. that the book ought to be copied *verbatim et literatim*, I wonder, . . that *they* do not contend for *punctuatim* too." [2] The audience laughed. Chase's interruption of Wirt [3] by calling the young lawyer's "syllogistical" conclusion a "*non sequitur, sir*," was accompanied by an inimitable "bow" that greatly amused the listeners.

In short, the interruptions of the sardonic old Justice were, as John Taylor of Caroline testified, in "a very high degree imperative, satirical, and witty .. [and] extremely well calculated to abash and disconcert counsel." [4]

[1] Plumer, Feb. 11, 1805, "Diary," Plumer MSS. Lib. Cong.
[2] *Annals*, 8th Cong. 2d Sess. 200; *Chase Trial*, 35.
[3] See *supra*, chap. I.
[4] *Annals*, 8th Cong. 2d Sess. 207. John Quincy Adams's description of all of the evidence is important and entertaining:
"Not only the casual expressions dropped in private conversations among friends and intimates, as well as strangers and adversaries, in

Among the witnesses was Marshall's brother William, whom President Adams had appointed clerk of the United States Court at Richmond.[1] His testimony was important on one point. One John Heath, a Richmond attorney and a perfect stranger to Chase, had sworn that Chase, in his presence, had asked the United States Marshal, David M. Randolph, "if he had any of those creatures or people called democrats on the panel of the jury to try Callender"; that when the Marshal replied that he had "made no discrimination," the

the recess of a bed-chamber as well as at public taverns and in stage coaches, had been carefully and malignantly laid up and preserved for testimony in this prosecution; not only more witnesses examined to points of *opinion*, and called upon for discrimination to such a degree as to say whether the deportment of the Judge was *imperative* or *imperious*, but hours of interrogation and answer were consumed in evidence to *looks*, to *bows*, to *tones* of voice and modes of speech — to prove the insufferable grievance that Mr. Chase had more than once raised a laugh at the expense of Callender's counsel, and to ascertain the tremendous fact that he had accosted the ATTORNEY GENERAL *of Virginia* by the appellation of *Young Gentleman!!*

"If by the thumbscrews, the memory of a witness trace back for a period of five years the features of the Judge's face, it could be darkened with a frown, it was to be construed into rude and contumelious treatment of the Virginia bar; if it was found lightened with a smile, 'tyrants in all ages had been notorious for their pleasantry.'

"In short, sir, Gravity himself could not keep his countenance at the nauseating littlenesses which were resorted to for proof of atrocious criminality, and indignation melted into ridicule at the puerile perseverance with which *nothings* were accumulated, with the hope of making *something* by their multitude.

"All this, however, was received because Judge Chase would not suffer his counsel to object against it. He indulged his accusers with the utmost licence of investigation which they ever derived, and contented himself with observing to the court that he expected to be judged upon the *legal* evidence in the case." (J. Q. Adams to his father, March 8, 1805, *Writings, J. Q. A.*: Ford, III, 112–13.)

[1] This was the fourth member of the Marshall family upon whom offices were bestowed while Marshall was Secretary of State. (See vol. II, 560, of this work.)

Judge told him "to look over the panel and if there
were any of that description, strike them off."

William Marshall, on the contrary, made oath
that Chase told him that he hoped even Giles would
serve on the jury — "Nay, he wished that Callender
might be tried by a jury of his own politics."
David M. Randolph then testified that he had never
seen Heath in the Judge's chambers, that Chase
"never at any time or place" said anything to him
about striking any names from the jury panel, and
that he never received "any instructions, verbal,
or by letter, from Judge Chase in relation to the
grand jury." [1]

John Marshall himself was then called to the
stand and sworn. Friendly eye-witnesses record that
the Chief Justice appeared to be frightened. He
testified that Colonel Harvie, with whom he "was
intimately acquainted," [2] had asked him to get the
Marshal to excuse Harvie from serving on the jury
because "his mind was completely made up . . and
whatever the evidence might be, he should find the
traverser not guilty." When Marshall told this to
the court official, the latter said that Harvie must

---

[1] *Annals*, 8th Cong. 2d Sess. 251–62; *Chase Trial*, 65–69. "I was
unable to give credence to his [Heath's] testimony." (Plumer, Feb.
12, 1805, "Diary," Plumer MSS. Lib. Cong.) Although Heath's
story was entirely false, it has, nevertheless, found a place in serious
history.

Marshall's brother made an excellent impression on the Senate.
"His answers were both prompt & lucid — There was a frankness, a
fairness & I will add a firmness that did him much credit. His testimony was [on certain points] . . a complete defense of the accused."
(*Ib.* Feb. 15, 1805.)

[2] Harvie's son, Jacquelin B. Harvie, married Marshall's daughter
Mary. (Paxton: *Marshall Family*, 100.)

apply to the Judge, because he "was watched," and "to prevent any charge of improper conduct" he would not discharge any of the jury whom he had summoned. Marshall then induced Chase to release Harvie "upon the ground of his being sheriff of Henrico County and that his attendance was necessary" at the county court then in session.

Marshall said that he was in court during a part of the Callender trial and that "there were several circumstances that took place . . on the part both of the bar and the bench which do not always occur at trials. . . The counsel appeared . . to wish to argue to the jury that the Sedition Law was unconstitutional. Mr. Chase said that that was not a proper question to go to the jury"; and that whenever Callender's attorneys began to argue to the contrary the court stopped them.

The Chief Justice further testified that George Hay had addressed the court to the effect that in this ruling Chase was "not correct in point of law," and again the Judge "stopped him"; that "Mr. Hay still went on and made some political observations; Judge Chase stopped him again and the collision ended by Mr. Hay sitting down and folding up his papers as if he meant to retire."

Marshall did not recollect "precisely," although it appeared to him that "whenever Judge Chase thought the counsel incorrect in their points, he immediately told them so and stopped them short." This "began early in the proceedings and increased. On the part of the judge it seemed to be a disgust with regard to the mode adopted by the traverser's counsel, at least .. as to the part which Mr. Hay took in the trial."

Randolph asked Marshall whether it was the practice for courts to hear counsel argue against the correctness of rulings; and Marshall replied that "if counsel have not been already heard, it is usual to hear them in order that they may change or confirm the opinion of the court, when there is any doubt entertained." But there was "no positive rule on the subject and the course pursued by the court will depend upon circumstances: Where the judge believes that the point is perfectly clear and settled he will scarcely permit the question to be agitated. However, it is considered as decorous on the part of the judge to listen while the counsel abstain from urging unimportant arguments."

Marshall was questioned closely as to points of practice. His answers were not favorable to his Associate Justice. Did it appear to him that "the conduct of Judge Chase was mild and conciliatory" during the trial of Callender? Marshall replied that he ought to be asked what Chase's conduct was and not what he thought of it. Senator William Cocke of Tennessee said the question was improper, and Randolph offered to withdraw it. "No!" exclaimed Chase's counsel, "we are willing to abide in this trial by the opinion of the Chief Justice." Marshall declared that, except in the Callender trial, he never heard a court refuse to admit the testimony of a witness because it went only to a part and not to the whole of a charge.

Burr asked Marshall: "Do you recollect whether

the conduct of the judge at this trial was tyrannical, overbearing and oppressive?" "I will state the facts," cautiously answered the Chief Justice. "Callender's counsel persisted in arguing the question of the constitutionality of the Sedition Law, in which they were constantly repressed by Judge Chase. Judge Chase checked Mr. Hay whenever he came to that point, and after having resisted repeated checks, Mr. Hay appeared to be determined to abandon the cause, when he was desired by the judge to proceed with his argument and informed that he should not be interrupted thereafter.

"If," continued Marshall, "this is not considered tyrannical, oppressive and overbearing, I know nothing else that was so." It was usual for courts to hear counsel upon the validity of rulings "not solemnly pronounced," and "by no means usual in Virginia to try a man for an offense at the same term at which he is presented"; although, said Marshall, "my practice, while I was at the bar was very limited in criminal cases."

"Did you ever hear Judge Chase apply any unusual epithets — such as *young men* or *young gentlemen* — to counsel?" inquired Randolph. "I have heard it so frequently spoken of since the trial that I cannot possibly tell whether my recollection of the term is derived from expressions used in court, or from the frequent mention since made of them." But, remarked Marshall, having thus adroitly placed the burden on the irresponsible shoulders of gossip, "I am rather inclined to think

that I did hear them from the judge." Randolph
then drew from Marshall the startling and important fact that William Wirt was "about thirty years
of age and a widower." [1]

Senator Plumer, with evident reluctance, sets
down in his diary a description from which it would
appear that Marshall's manner affected the Senate
most unfavorably. "John Marshall is the Chief
Justice of the Supreme Court of the United States.
I was much better pleased with the manner in which
his brother testified than with him.

"The Chief Justice really discovered too much
caution — too much fear — too much cunning —
He ought to have been more bold — frank & explicit
than he was.

"There was in his manner an evident disposition
to accommodate the Managers. That dignified
frankness which his high office required did not appear. A cunning man ought never to discover the
arts of the *trimmer* in his testimony." [2]

Plainly Marshall was still fearful of the outcome
of the Republican impeachment plans, not only as
to Chase, but as to the entire Federalist membership of the Supreme Court. His understanding of
the Republican purpose, his letter to Chase, and his
manner on the stand at the trial leave no doubt as
to his state of mind. A Republican Supreme Court,
with Spencer Roane as Chief Justice, loomed for-
biddingly before him.

Chase was suffering such agony from the gout

---

[1] *Annals*, 8th Cong. 2d Sess. 262–67; *Chase Trial*, 71.
[2] Plumer, Feb. 16, 1805, "Diary," Plumer MSS. Lib. Cong.

that, when the testimony was all in, he asked to be released from further attendance.[1] Six days before the evidence was closed, the election returns were read and counted, and Aaron Burr "declared Thomas Jefferson and George Clinton to be duly elected to the respective offices of President and Vice-President of the United States." [2] For the first time in our history this was done publicly; on former occasions the galleries were cleared and the doors closed.[3]

Throughout the trial Randolph and Giles were in frequent conference — judge and prosecutor working together for the success of the party plan.[4] On February 20 the arguments began. Peter Early of Georgia spoke first. His remarks were "chiefly declamatory." [5] He said that the conduct of Chase exhibited that species of oppression which puts accused citizens "at the mercy of *arbitrary and overbearing judges*." For an hour and a half he reviewed the charges,[6] but he spoke so badly that "most of the members of the other House left the chamber & a large portion of the spectators the gallery." [7]

---

[1] Feb. 19, 1805, *Memoirs, J. Q. A.*: Adams, I, 354.

Chase did not leave Washington, and was in court when some of the arguments were made. (See Chase to Hopkinson, March 10, 1805; Hopkinson MSS. in possession of Edward P. Hopkinson, Phila.) .

[2] Feb. 13, 1805, *Memoirs, J. Q. A.*: Adams, I, 351.

[3] *Ib.* The motion to admit the public was carried by one vote only. (Plumer, Feb. 13, 1805, "Diary," Plumer MSS. Lib. Cong.)

[4] Feb. 13, 1805, *Memoirs, J. Q. A.*: Adams, I, 353.

[5] Feb. 20, 1805, *ib.* 355.

[6] Cutler, II, 183; also *Annals*, 8th Cong. 2d Sess. 313–29; *Chase Trial*, 101–07.

[7] Plumer, Feb. 20, 1805, "Diary," Plumer MSS. Lib. Cong.

George Washington Campbell of Tennessee argued "long and tedious[ly]" [1] for the Jeffersonian
idea of impeachment which he held to be "a kind
of an inquest into the conduct of an officer . . and the
effects that his conduct . . may have on society."
He analyzed the official deeds of Chase by which
"the whole community seemed shocked. . . Future
generations are interested in the event." [2] He spoke
for parts of two days, having to suspend midway in
the argument because of exhaustion.[3] Like Early,
Campbell emptied the galleries and drove the members of the House, in disgust, from the floor.[4]

Joseph Hopkinson then opened for the defense.
Although but thirty-four years old, his argument
was not surpassed,[5] even by that of Martin — in
fact, it was far more orderly and logical than that
of Maryland's great attorney-general. "We appear,"
began Hopkinson, "for an ancient and infirm man,
whose better days have been worn out in the service of that country which now degrades him." The
case was "of infinite importance," truly declared
the youthful attorney. "The faithful, the scrutiniz-
ing historian, . . without fear or favor" will render
the final judgment. The House managers were following the British precedent in the impeachment of
Warren Hastings; but that celebrated prosecution
had not been instituted, as had that of Chase, on

[1] Cutler, II, 183.

[2] *Annals*, 8th Cong. 2d Sess. 329–53; *Chase Trial*, 107 *et seq.*

[3] *Memoirs, J. Q. A.*: Adams, I, 355–56.

[4] Plumer, Feb. 21, 1805, " Diary," Plumer MSS. Lib. Cong.

[5] Adams: *U.S.* II, 231. Even Randolph praised him. (*Annals*, 8th
Cong. 2d Sess. 640.)

"a petty catalogue of frivolous occurrences, more calculated to excite ridicule than apprehension, but for the alleged murder of princes and plunder of empires"; yet Hastings had been acquitted.

In England only two judges had been impeached in half a century, while in the United States "seven judges have been prosecuted criminally in about two years." Could a National judge be impeached merely for "error, mistake, or indiscretion"? Absurd! Such action could be taken only for "an indictable offense." Thus Hopkinson stated the master question of the case. In a clear, closely woven argument, the youthful advocate maintained his ground.

The power of impeachment by the House was not left entirely to the "opinion, whim, or caprice" of its members, but was limited by other provisions of the fundamental law. Chase was not charged with treason, bribery, or corruption. Had any other "high crimes and misdemeanors" been proved or even stated against him? He could not be impeached for ordinary offenses, but only for "high crimes and high misdemeanors." Those were legal and technical terms, "well understood and defined in law... A misdemeanor or a crime .. is an act committed or omitted, in violation of a *public* law either forbidding or commanding it. By this test, let the respondent .. stand justified or condemned."

The very nature of the Senatorial Court indicated "the grade of offenses intended for its jurisdiction. .. Was such a court created .. to scan and punish paltry errors and indiscretions, too insignificant to have a name in the penal code, too paltry for the notice of a court of quarter sessions? This is indeed employing an elephant to remove an atom too minute for the grasp of an insect."

Had Chase transgressed any State or National statute? Had he violated the common law? Nobody claimed that he had. Could any judge be firm, unbiased, and independent if he might at any time be impeached "on the mere suggestions of caprice . . condemned by the mere voice of prejudice"? No! "If his nerves are of iron, they must tremble in so perilous a situation."

Hopkinson dwelt upon the true function of the Judiciary under free institutions. "All governments require, in order to give them firmness, stability, and character, some permanent principle, some settled establishment. The want of this is the great deficiency in republican institutions." In the American Government an independent, permanent Judiciary supplied this vital need. Without it "nothing can be relied on; no faith can be given either at home or abroad." It was also "a security from oppression."

All history proved that republics could be as tyrannical as despotisms; not systematically, it was true, but as the result of "sudden gust of passion or prejudice. . . If we have read of the death of a Seneca under the ferocity of a Nero, we have read too of the murder of a Socrates under the delusion of a Republic. An independent and firm Judiciary, protected and protecting by the laws, would have snatched the one from the fury of a despot, and preserved the other from the madness of a people." [1] So

[1] *Annals*, 8th Cong. 2d Sess. 354-94; *Chase Trial*, 116-49.

spoke Joseph Hopkinson for three hours,[1] made brief and brilliant by his eloquence, logic, and learning.

Philip Barton Key of Washington, younger even than Hopkinson, next addressed the Senatorial Court. He had been ill the day before [2] and was still indisposed, but made an able speech. He analyzed, with painstaking minuteness, the complaints against his client, and cleverly turned to Chase's advantage the conduct of Marshall in the Logwood case.[3] Charles Lee then spoke for the defense; but what he said was so technical, applying merely to Virginia legal practice of the time, that it is of no historical moment.[4]

When, on the next day, February 23, Luther Martin rose, the Senate Chamber could not contain even a small part of the throng that sought the Capitol to hear the celebrated lawyer. If he "*only* appeared in defense of a friend," said Martin, he would not be so gravely concerned; but the case was plainly of highest possible importance, not only to all Americans then living, but to "posterity." It would "establish a most important precedent as to future cases of impeachment." An error now would be fatal.

For what did the Constitution authorize the

---

[1] Feb. 21, 1805, *Memoirs, J. Q. A.*: Adams, I, 356.

"The effect on the auditory [was] prodigiously great." (Cutler, II, 184.)

"His argument . . was one of the most able . . I ever heard." (Plumer, Feb. 21, 1805, "Diary," Plumer MSS. Lib. Cong.)

[2] Feb. 22, 1805, *Memoirs, J. Q. A.*: Adams, I, 356.

[3] *Annals*, 8th Cong. 2d Sess. 394–413; see also *Chase Trial*, 149–62; and Cutler, II, 184.

[4] *Annals*, 8th Cong. 2d Sess. 413–29; *Chase Trial*, 162–72.

House to impeach and the Senate to try an officer of the National Government? asked Martin. Only for "an indictable offense." Treason and bribery, specifically named in the Constitution as impeachable offenses, were also indictable. It was the same with "other high crimes and misdemeanors," the only additional acts for which impeachment was provided. To be sure, a judge might do deeds for which he could be indicted that would not justify his impeachment, as, for instance, physical assault "provoked by insolence." But let the House managers name one act for which a judge could be impeached that did not also subject him to indictment. Congress could pass a law making an act criminal which had not been so before; but such a law applied only to deeds committed after, and not to those done before, its passage. Yet if an officer might, years after the event, be impeached, convicted, and punished for conduct perfectly legal at the time, "could the officers of Government ever know how to proceed?" Establish such a principle and "you leave your judges, and all your other officers, at the mercy of the prevailing party."

Had Chase "used *unusual*, rude and *contemptuous* expressions towards the prisoner's counsel" in the Callender case, as the articles of impeachment charged? Even so, this was "rather a violation of the principles of politeness, than the principles of law; rather the want of decorum, than the commission of a *high crime and misdemeanor*." Was a judge to be impeached and removed from office because his deportment was not elegant?

The truth was that Callender's counsel had not acted in his interest and had cared nothing about him; they had wished only "to hold up the prosecution as oppressive" in order to "excite public indignation against the court and the Government." Had not Hay just testified that he entertained "no hopes of convincing the court, and scarcely the faintest expectation of inducing the jury to believe that the sedition law was unconstitutional"; but that he had wished to make an "impression upon the public mind. . . What barefaced, what unequalled hypocrisy doth he admit that he practiced on that occasion! What egregious trifling with the court!" exclaimed Martin.

When Chase had observed that Wirt's syllogism was a "*non sequitur*," the Judge, it seems, had "bowed." Monstrous! But "as *bows*, sir, according to the manner they are *made*, may . . convey very different meanings," why had not the witness who told of it, "given us a *fac simile* of it?" The Senate then could have judged of "the propriety" of the bow. "But it seems this *bow*, together with the '*non sequitur*' entirely discomfitted poor Mr. Wirt, and down he sat 'and never word spake more!'" By all means let Chase be convicted and removed from the bench — it would never do to permit National judges to make bows in any such manner!

But alas for Chase! He had committed another grave offense — he had called William Wirt "*young* gentleman" in spite of the fact that Wirt was actually thirty years old and a widower. Perhaps Chase did not know "of these circumstances"; still, "if he had, considering that Mr. Wirt was a widower, he certainly erred on the right side .. in calling *him* a *young* gentleman." [1]

When the laughter of the Senate had subsided, Martin, dropping his sarcasm, once more emphasized the vital necessity of the independence of the Judiciary. "We boast" that ours is a "government of laws. But how can it be such, unless the laws, while they exist, are sacredly and impartially, without regard to popularity, carried into execution?" Only independent judges can do this. "Our property, our liberty, our lives, can only be protected and secured by such judges. With this honorable Court it remains, whether we shall have such judges!" [2]

Martin spoke until five o'clock without food or any sustenance, "except two glasses of wine and water"; he said he had not even breakfasted that morning, and asked permission to finish his argument next day.

When he resumed, he dwelt on the liberty of the press which Chase's application of the Sedition Law to Callender's libel was said to have violated. "My honorable client with many other respectable characters .. considered it [that law] as a wholesome and necessary restraint" upon the licentiousness of the press.[3] Martin then quoted with telling effect from Franklin's denunciation of newspapers.[4] "Franklin, himself a printer," had been "as great an advocate

[1] *Annals*, 8th Cong. 2d Sess. 429–82; *Chase Trial*, 173 *et seq.*
[2] *Annals*, 8th Cong. 2d Sess. 483.   [3] *Ib.* 484–87.
[4] See résumé of Franklin's indictment of the press in vol. i, 268–69, of this work.

for the liberty of the press, as any reasonable man ought to be"; yet he had "declared that unless the slander and calumny of the press is restrained by some other law, it will be restrained by club law." Was not that true?

If men cannot be protected by the courts against "base calumniators, they will become their own avengers. And to the bludgeon, the sword or the pistol, they will resort for that purpose." Yet Chase stood impeached for having, as a judge, enforced the law against the author of "one of the most flagitious libels ever published in America." [1]

Throughout his address Martin mingled humor with logic, eloquence with learning.[2] Granted, he said, that Chase had used the word "damned" in his desultory conversation with Triplett during their journey in a stage. "However it may sound elsewhere in the United States, I cannot apprehend it will be considered *very* offensive, *even* from the mouth of a judge on this side of the Susquehanna; — to the southward of that river it is in familiar use . . supplying frequently the place of the word 'very' . . connected with subjects the most pleasing; thus we say indiscriminately a very good or a damned good bottle of wine, a damned good dinner, or a damned clever fellow." [3]

Martin's great speech deeply impressed the Senate with the ideas that Chase was a wronged

---

[1] *Annals*, 8th Cong. 2d Sess. 488; *Chase Trial*, *223.

[2] "Mr. Martin really possesses much legal information & a great fund of good humour, keen satire & poignant wit . . he certainly has talents." (Plumer, Feb. 23, 1805, "Diary," Plumer MSS. Lib. Cong.)

[3] *Annals*, 8th Cong. 2d Sess. 489; *Chase Trial*, *224.

man, that the integrity of the whole National Judicial establishment was in peril, and that impeachment was being used as a partisan method of placing the National Bench under the rod of a political party. And all this was true.

Robert Goodloe Harper closed for the defense. He was intolerably verbose, but made a good argument, well supported by precedents. In citing the example which Randolph had given as a good cause for impeachment — the refusal of a judge to hold court — Harper came near, however, making a fatal admission. This, said Harper, would justify impeachment, although perhaps not an indictment. Most of his speech was a repetition of points already made by Hopkinson, Key, and Martin. But Harper's remarks on Chase's charge to the Baltimore grand jury were new, that article having been left to him.

"Is it not lawful," he asked, "for an aged patriot of the Revolution to warn his fellow-citizens of dangers, by which he supposes their liberties and happiness to be threatened?" That was all that Chase's speech from the bench in Baltimore amounted to. Did his office take from a judge "the liberty of speech which belongs to every citizen"? Judges often made political speeches on the stump — "What law forbids [them] to exercise these rights by a charge from the bench?" That practice had "been sanctioned by the custom of this country from the beginning of the Revolution to this day."

Harper cited many instances of the delivery by

judges of political charges to grand juries, beginning with the famous appeal to the people to fight for independence from British rule, made in a charge to a South Carolina grand jury in 1776.[1]

The blows of Chase's strong counsel, falling in unbroken succession, had shaken the nerve of the House managers. One of these, Joseph H. Nicholson of Maryland, now replied. Posterity would indeed be the final judge of Samuel Chase. Warren Hastings had been acquitted; "but is there any who hears me, that believes he was innocent?" The judgment of the Senate involved infinitely more than the fortunes of Chase; by it "must ultimately be determined whether justice shall hereafter be impartially administered or whether the rights of the citizen are to be prostrated at the feet of overbearing and tyrannical judges."

Nicholson denied that the House managers had "resorted to the forlorn hope of contending that an impeachment was not a criminal prosecution, but a mere inquest of office. . . If declarations of this kind have been made, in the name of the Managers, I here disclaim them. We do contend that this is a criminal prosecution, for offenses committed in the discharge of high official duties." [2]

The Senate was dumbfounded, the friends of Chase startled with joyful surprise; a gasp of amazement ran through the overcrowded Chamber! Nicholson had abandoned the Republican position — and at a moment when Harper had all but admitted it to be

[1] *Annals*, 8th Cong. 2d Sess. 556; *Chase Trial*, *205–44.
[2] *Annals*, 8th Cong. 2d Sess. 560–62; *Chase Trial*, 237 *et seq.*

sound. What could this mean but that the mighty
onslaughts of Martin and Hopkinson had discon-
certed the managers, or that Republican Senators
were showing to the leaders signs of weakening in
support of the party doctrine.

At any rate, Nicholson's admission was an irre-
trievable blunder. He should have stoutly championed his party's theory upon which Chase had
been impeached and thus far tried, ignored the
subject entirely, or remained silent. Sadly confused, he finally reversed his argument and swung
back to the original Republican theory.

He cited many hypothetical cases where an officer
could not be haled before a criminal court, but could
be impeached. One of these must have furnished
cause for secret mirth to many a Senator: "It is possible," said Nicholson, "that the day may arrive
when a President of the United States .. may endeavor to influence [Congress] by holding out threats
or inducements to them. . . The hope of an office
may be held out to a Senator; and I think it cannot
be doubted, that for this the President would be
liable to impeachment, although there is no positive
law forbidding it."

Lucky for Nicholson that Martin had spoken before him and could not reply; fortunate for Jefferson that the "impudent Federal Bulldog," [1] as the
President afterward styled Martin, could not now be
heard. For his words would have burned the paper
on which the reporters transcribed them. Every
Senator knew how patronage and all forms of

---

[1] See Jefferson to Hay, *infra*, chap. VIII.

Executive inducement and coercion had been used by the Administration in the passage of most important measures — the Judiciary repeal, the Pickering impeachment, the Yazoo compromise, the trial of Chase. From the floor of the House John Randolph had just denounced, with blazing wrath, Jefferson's Postmaster-General for offering Government contracts to secure votes for the Yazoo compromise.[1]

For two hours and a half Nicholson continued,[2] devoting himself mainly to the conduct of Chase during the trial of Fries. He closed by pointing out the inducements to a National judge to act as a tyrannical tool of a partisan administration — the offices with which he could be bribed, the promotions by which he could be rewarded. The influence of the British Ministry over the judges has been "too flagrant to be mistaken." For example, in Ireland "an overruling influence has crumbled [an independent judiciary] into ruins. The demon of destruction has entered their courts of justice, and spread desolation over the land. Execution has followed execution, until the oppressed, degraded and insulted nation has been made to tremble through every nerve, and to bleed at every pore."

The fate of Ireland would be that of America, if an uncontrolled Judiciary were allowed to carry out, without fear of impeachment, the will of a highhanded President, in order to win the preferments he had to offer. Already "some of our judges have

---

[1] See *infra*, chap. x.
[2] *Memoirs, J. Q. A.*: Adams, I, 358.

been elevated to places of high political importance... Let us nip the evil in the bud, or it may grow to an enormous tree, bearing destruction upon every branch." [1]

Cæsar A. Rodney of Delaware strove to repair the havoc Nicholson had wrought; he made it worse. The trial was, he said, "a spectacle truly solemn and impressive .. a trial of the first importance, because of the first impression; .. a trial .. whose novelty and magnitude have excited so much interest .. that it seems to have superseded for the moment, not only every other grave object or pursuit, but every other fashionable amusement or dissipation." [2]

Rodney flattered Burr, whose conduct of the trial had been "an example worthy of imitation." He cajoled the Senators, whose attitude he had "observed with heartfelt pleasure and honest pride"; and he warned them not to take as a precedent the case of Warren Hastings, "that destroyer of the people of Asia, that devastator of the East," — murderer of men, violator of *zenanas*, destroyer of sacred treaties, but yet acquitted by the British House of Lords.

Counsel for Chase had spoken with "the fascinating voice of eloquence and the deluding tongue of ingenuity"; but Rodney would avoid "everything

---

[1] *Annals*, 8th Cong. 2d Sess. 582; *Chase Trial*, 237–43.

[2] *Annals*, 8th Cong. 2d Sess. 583.
This was an under-statement of the facts; for the first time the celebration of Washington's birthday was abandoned in the National Capital. (Plumer, 326.) Plumer says that this was done because the celebration might hurt Chase, "for there are senators who for the veriest trifles may be brought to vote against him." (Feb. 22, 1805, "Congress," Plumer MSS. Lib. Cong.)

like declamation" and speak "in the temperate language of reason." [1] He was sure that "the weeping voice of history will be heard to deplore the oppressive acts and criminal excesses [of Samuel Chase]. . . In the dark catalogue of criminal enormities, perhaps few are to be found of deeper dye" than those named in the articles of impeachment. "The independence of the Judiciary, the political tocsin of the day, and *the alarm bell of the night*, has been rung through every change in our ears. . . The poor hobby has been literally rode to death." Rodney was for a "rational independence of the Judiciary," but not for the "inviolability of judges more than of Kings.[2] In this country I am afraid the doctrine has been carried to such an extravagant length, that the Judiciary may be considered like a spoiled child."

An independent Judiciary, indeed! "We all know that an associate justice may sigh for promotion, and may be created a Chief Justice,[3] while . . more than one Chief Justice has been appointed a Minister Plenipotentiary." [4] With what result? Had judges stood aloof from politics — or had they "united in the *Io triumphe* which the votaries and idolators of power have sung to those who were seated in the car of Government? Have they made no offerings at the shrine of party; have they not

[1] *Annals*, 8th Cong. 2d Sess. 583–84; *Chase Trial*, 243–56.

[2] *Annals*, 8th Cong. 2d Sess. 585–87.

[3] Rodney here refers to the Republican allegation that Chase tried to secure appointment as Chief Justice by flattering Adams through charges to juries, rulings in court, and speeches on the stump.

[4] John Jay to England and Oliver Ellsworth to France. (See vol. II, 113, 502, of this work.)

preached political sermons from the bench, in which they have joined chorus with the anonymous scribblers of the day and the infuriate instruments of faction?" [1]

In this fashion Rodney began a song of praise of Jefferson, for the beneficence of whose Administration "the lamentable annals of mankind afford no example." After passing through many "citadels" and "Scean gates," and other forms of rhetorical architecture, he finally discovered Chase "seated in a curricle of passion" which the Justice had "driven on, Phæton-like, . . with destruction, persecution, and oppression" following.

At last the orator attempted to discuss the law of the impeachment, taking the double ground that an officer could be removed for any act that two thirds of the Senate believed to be not "good behavior," and that the Chase impeachment was "a criminal prosecution." For parts of two days [2] Rodney examined every phase of the charges in a distracting mixture of high-flown language, scattered learning, extravagant metaphor, and jumbled logic. [3] His speech was a wretched performance, so cluttered with tawdry rhetoric and disjointed argument that it would have been poor even as a stump speech.

In an address that enraged the New England Federalists, Randolph closed for the House managers. [4] He was late in arriving at the Senate Cham-

[1] *Annals*, 8th Cong. 2d Sess. 587–89.
[2] *Memoirs, J. Q. A.*: Adams, I, 359.
[3] *Annals*, 8th Cong. 2d Sess. 583–641; *Chase Trial*, 243–56.
[4] Cutler announced it as "an outrageous, infuriated declamation,

ber. He had been so ill the day before that Nicholson, because of Randolph's "habitual indisposition," had asked the Senate to meet two hours later
than the usual time.[1] Sick as he was, without his
notes (which he had lost), Randolph nevertheless
made the best argument for the prosecution. Wast-
ing no time, he took up the theory of impeachment
upon which, he said, "the wildest opinions have
been advanced" — for instance, "that an offense,
to be impeachable, must be indictable." Why,
then, had the article on impeachment been placed
in the Constitution at all? Why "not have said,
at once, that any . . officer . . convicted on indictment should (*ipso facto*) be removed from office?
This would be coming at the thing by a short and
obvious way." [2]

Suppose a President should veto every act of
Congress "indiscriminately"; it was his Constitutional right to do so; he could not be indicted, but
would anybody say he could not be impeached? Or
if, at a short session, the President should keep back
until the last moment all bills passed within the previous ten days, as the Constitution authorized him
to do, so that it would be a physical impossibility
for the two Houses to pass the rejected measures
over the President's veto, he could not be indicted
for this abuse of power; but surely "he could be
impeached, removed and disqualified." [3]

which might have done honor to Marat, or Robespierre." (Cutler,
II, 184.)

[1] *Memoirs, J. Q. A.*: Adams, I, 359.
[2] *Annals*, 8th Cong. 2d Sess. 642; *Chase Trial*, 256.
[3] *Annals*, 8th Cong. 2d Sess. 644; *Chase Trial*, 257.

Randolph's Virginia soul was deeply stirred by what he considered Chase's alternate effrontery and cowardice. Is such a character "fit to preside in a court of justice? . . Today, haughty, violent, imperious; tomorrow, humble, penitent and submissive. . . Is this a character to dispense law and justice to this nation? No, Sir!" Randolph then drew an admirable picture of the ideal judge: "firm, indeed, but temperate, mild though unyielding, neither a blustering bravo, nor a timid poltroon." [1]

As far as he could go without naming him, Randolph described John Marshall. Not without result had the politically experienced Chief Justice conciliated the House managers in the manner that had so exasperated the Federalist Senators. He would not thereafter be impeached if John Randolph could prevent.

With keen pleasure at the annoyance he knew his words would give to Jefferson,[2] Randolph continued to praise Marshall. The rejection of Colonel Taylor's testimony at the Callender trial was contrary to "the universal practice of our courts." On this point "what said the Chief Justice of the United States," on whose evidence Randolph said he specially relied? "He never knew such a case [to] occur before. He never heard a similar objection advanced by any court, until that instance. And this is the cautious and guarded language of a man placed in the delicate situation of being compelled to give testimony against a brother judge."

[1] *Annals*, 8th Cong. 2d Sess. 644–45; *Chase Trial*, 258.
[2] See *infra*, chap. x.

With an air of triumph Randolph asked: "Can anyone doubt Mr. Marshall's thorough acquaintance with our laws? Can it be pretended that any man is better versed in their theory and practice? And yet in all his extensive reading, his long and extensive practice, in the many trials of which he has been spectator, and the yet greater number at which he has assisted, he had never witnessed such a case." Chase alone had discovered "this fatal novelty, this new and horrible doctrine that threatens at one blow all that is valuable in our criminal jurisprudence."

Had Martin shown that Chase was right in requiring questions to be reduced to writing? "Here again," declared Randolph, "I bottom myself upon the testimony of the same great man, yet more illustrious for his abilities than for the high station that he fills, eminent as it is." And he recited the substance of Marshall's testimony on this point. Consider his description of the bearing of Chase toward counsel! "I again ask you, what said the Chief Justice? . . And what did he *look?* [1] He felt all the delicacy of his situation, and, as he could not approve, he declined giving any opinion on the demeanor of his associate." [2] In such manner Randolph extolled Marshall.

Again he apostrophized the Chief Justice. If Fries and Callender "had had fair trials, our lips would have been closed in eternal silence. Look at the case of Logwood: The able and excellent judge whose

[1] See *supra*, 196.
[2] *Annals*, 8th Cong. 2d Sess. 651–52; *Chase Trial*, 266.

worth was never fully known until he was raised to the bench .. uttered not one syllable that could prejudice the defense of the prisoner." Once more he contrasted the judicial manners and rulings of Marshall with those of Chase: "The Chief Justice knew that, sooner or later, the law was an overmatch for the dishonest, and .. he disdained to descend from his great elevation to the low level of a public prosecutor."

The sick man spoke for two hours and a half, his face often distorted and his body writhing with pain. Finally his tense nerves gave way. Only public duty had kept him to his task, he said. "In a little time and I will dismiss you to the suggestions of your own consciences. My weakness and want of ability prevent me from urging my cause as I could wish, but" — here the overwrought and exhausted man broke into tears — "it is the last day of my sufferings and of yours."

Mastering his indisposition, however, Randolph closed in a passage of genuine power: "We adjure you, on behalf of the House of Representatives and of all the people of the United States, to exorcise from our Courts the baleful spirit of party, to give an awful memento to our judges. In the name of the nation, I demand at your hands the award of justice and of law." [1]

---

[1] *Annals*, 8th Cong. 2d Sess. 641–62. John Quincy Adams notes in his diary that Randolph spoke for more than two hours "with as little relation to the subject matter as possible — without order, connection, or argument; consisting altogether of the most hackneyed commonplaces of popular declamation." Throughout, records Adams, there was "much distortion of face and contortion of body, tears, groans and sobs." (*Memoirs, J. Q. A.*: Adams, I, 359.)

So ended this unequal forensic contest in one of the most fateful trials in American history. The whole country eagerly awaited tidings of the judgment to be rendered by the Senatorial tribunal. The fate of the Supreme Court, the character of the National Judiciary, the career of John Marshall, depended upon it. Even union or disunion was involved; for if Chase should be convicted, another and perhaps final impulse would be given to the secessionist movement in New England, which had been growing since the Republican attack on the National Judiciary in 1802.[1]

When the Senate convened at half-past twelve on March 1, 1805, a dense mass of auditors filled every inch of space in the Senate Chamber.[2] Down the narrow passageway men were seen bearing a couch on which lay Senator Uriah Tracy of Connecticut, pale and sunken from sickness. Feebly he rose and took one of the red-covered seats of the Senatorial judges.[3]

"The Sergeants-at-Arms will face the spectators and seize and commit to prison the first person who

"His speech . . was devoid of argument, method or consistency — but was replete with invective & even vulgarity. . . . I never heard him deliver such a weak feeble & deranged harangue." (Plumer to his wife, Feb. 28, 1805, Plumer MSS. Lib. Cong.)

"After he sat down — he threw his feet upon the table — distorted his features & assumed an appearance as disgusting as his harangue." (Plumer, Feb. 27, 1805, "Diary," Plumer MSS. Lib. Cong.)

[1] See *supra*, chaps. II and III; *infra*, chap. VI, and vol. IV, chap. I.

[2] "There was a vast concourse of people . . and great solemnity." (Cutler to Torrey, March 1, 1805, Cutler, II, 193.) "The galleries were crowded — many ladies. I never witnessed so general & so deep an anxiety." (Plumer to his wife, March 1, 1805, Plumer MSS. Lib. Cong.)

[3] Plumer, 323.

makes the smallest noise or disturbance," sternly ordered Aaron Burr.

"The secretary will read the first article of impeachment," he directed.

"Senator Adams of Massachusetts! How say you? Is Samuel Chase, the respondent, guilty of high crimes and misdemeanors as charged in the article just read?"

"Not guilty!" responded John Quincy Adams.

When the name of Stephen R. Bradley, Republican Senator from Vermont, was reached, he rose in his place and voted against conviction. The auditors were breathless, the Chamber filled with the atmosphere of suspense. It was the first open break in the Republican ranks. Two more such votes and the carefully planned battle would be lost to Jefferson and his party.

"Not guilty!" answered John Gaillard, Republican Senator from South Carolina.

Another Republican defection and all would be over. It came from the very next Senator whose name Aaron Burr pronounced, and from one whose answer will forever remain an enigma.

"Senator Giles of Virginia! How say you? Is Samuel Chase guilty of the high crimes and misdemeanors as charged in the articles just read?"

"Not guilty!"

Only sixteen Senators voted to impeach on the first article, nine Republicans aligning themselves with the nine Federalists.

The vote on the other articles showed varying results; on the fourth, fourteen Senators responded

"Guilty!"; on the fifth, the Senate was unanimous for Chase.

Upon the eighth article — Chase's political charge to the Baltimore grand jury — the desperate Republicans tried to recover, Giles now leading them. Indeed, it may be for this that he cast his first vote with his party brethren from the North — he may have thought thus to influence them on the one really strong charge against the accused Justice. If so, his stratagem was futile. The five Northern Republicans (Bradley and Smith of Vermont, Mitchell and Smith of New York, and John Smith of Ohio) stood firm for acquittal as did the obstinate John Gaillard of South Carolina.[1]

The punctilious Burr ordered the names of Senators and their recorded answers to be read for verification.[2] He then announced the result: "It appears that there is not a constitutional majority of votes finding Samuel Chase, Esq. guilty of any one article. It therefore becomes my duty to declare that Samuel Chase, Esq. stands acquitted of all the articles exhibited by the House of Representatives against him." [3]

The fight was over. There were thirty-four Senators, nine of them Federalists, twenty-five Republi-

---

[1] *Annals*, 8th Cong. 2d Sess. 665–69; *Memoirs, J. Q. A.*: Adams, I, 362–63.   [2] *Ib.* 363.

[3] *Annals*, 8th Cong. 2d Sess. 669. By this time Burr had changed to admiration the disapproval with which the Federalist Senators had, at first, regarded his conduct of the trial. "Mr. Burr has certainly, on the whole, done himself, the Senate, and the Nation honor by the dignified manner in which he has presided over this high and numerous court," testifies Senator Plumer, notwithstanding his deep prejudice against Burr. (Plumer, March 1, 1805, "Diary," Plumer MSS. Lib. Cong.)

cans. Twenty-two votes were necessary to convict. At their strongest the Republicans had been able to muster less than one fifth of their entire strength. Six of their number — the New York and Vermont Senators, together with John Gaillard of South Carolina and John Smith of Ohio — had answered "not guilty" on every article.

For the first time since his appointment, John Marshall was secure as the head of the Supreme Bench.[1] For the first time since Jefferson's election, the National Judiciary was, for a period, rendered independent. For the first time in five years, the Federalist members of the Nation's highest tribunal could go about their duties without fear that upon them would fall the avenging blade of impeachment which had for half a decade hung over them. One of the few really great crises in American history had passed.[2]

"The greatest and most important trial ever held in this nation has terminated justly," wrote Senator Plumer to his son. "The venerable judge whose head bears the frost of seventy winters,[3] is honorably acquitted. I never witnessed, in any place, such a display of learning as the counsel for the accused exhibited." [4]

Chagrin, anger, humiliation, raged in Randolph's heart. His long legs could not stride as fast as his

[1] See Adams: *U.S.* ii, 243.

[2] See Plumer, 324; *Memoirs, J. Q. A.*: Adams, i, 371; Adams: *John Randolph*, 131–32, 152; Channing: *Jeff. System*, 120; Adams: *U.S.* ii, 243.

[3] Plumer here adds six years to Chase's age — an unusual inaccuracy in the diary of that born newspaper reporter.

[4] Plumer to his son, March 3, 1805, Plumer, 325.

frenzy, when, rushing from the scene of defeat, he flew to the floor of the House. There he offered an amendment to the Constitution providing that the President might remove National judges on the joint address of both Houses of Congress.[1] "Tempest in the House," records Cutler.[2]

Nicholson was almost as frantic with wrath, and quickly followed with a proposal so to amend the Constitution that State Legislatures might, at will, recall Senators.[3]

Republicans now began to complain to their party foes of one another. Over a "rubber of whist" with John Quincy Adams, Senator Jackson of Georgia, even before the trial, had spoken "slightingly both of Mr. John Randolph and of Mr. Nicholson";[4] and this criticism of Republicans *inter se* now increased.

Jefferson's feelings were balanced between grief and glee; his mourning over the untoward result of his cherished programme of judicial reform was ameliorated by his pleasure at the overthrow of the unruly Randolph,[5] who had presumed to dissent from the President's Georgia land policy.[6] The great politician's cup of disappointment, which the acquittal of Chase had filled, was also sweetened by the knowledge that Republican restlessness in the Northern States would be quieted; the Federalists who were ready, on other grounds, to come to his

[1] *Annals*, 8th Cong. 2d Sess. 1213; and see *Annual Report, Am. Hist. Assn. 1896*, II, 64; also Adams: *U.S.* II, 240.

[2] Cutler, II, 185.

[3] *Annals*, 8th Cong. 2d Sess. 1213; and see J. Q. Adams to his father, March 14, 1805, *Writings, J. Q. A.*: Ford, III, 117.

[4] Jan. 30, 1805, *Memoirs, J. Q. A.*: Adams, I, 341.

[5] See Adams: *U.S.* II, 243.   [6] See *infra*, chap. x.

standard would be encouraged to do so; and the
New England secession propaganda would be deprived of a strong argument. He confided to the
gossipy William Plumer, the Federalist New Hampshire Senator, that "impeachment is a farce which
will not be tried again." [1]

The Chief Justice of the United States, his peril
over, was silent and again serene, his wonted composure returned, his courage restored. He calmly
awaited the hour when the wisdom of events should
call upon him to render another and immortal service to the American Nation. That hour was not to
be long delayed.

[1] Plumer, 325. Jefferson soon took Plumer into the Republican
fold.

CHAPTER V

BIOGRAPHER

Marshall has written libels on one side. (Jefferson.)

What seemed to him to pass for dignity, will, by his reader, be pronounced dullness. (Edinburgh Review.)

That work was hurried into the world with too much precipitation. It is one of the most desirable objects I have in this life to publish a corrected edition. (Marshall.)

ALTHOUGH the collapse of the Chase impeachment made it certain that Marshall would not be removed from office, and he was thus relieved from one source of sharp anxiety, two other causes of worry served to make this period of his life harried and laborious. His heavy indebtedness to Denny Fairfax [1] continuously troubled him; and, worse still for his peace of mind, he was experiencing the agonies of the literary composer temperamentally unfitted for the task, wholly unskilled in the art, and dealing with a subject sure to arouse the resentment of Jefferson and all his followers. Marshall was writing the "Life of Washington."

In a sense it is fortunate for us that he did so, since his long and tiresome letters to his publishers afford us an intimate view of the great Chief Justice and reveal him as very human. But the biography itself was to prove the least satisfactory of all the labors of Marshall's life.

Not long after the death of Washington, his nephew, Bushrod Washington, had induced Marshall

[1] See vol. II, 210–12, of this work.

to become the biographer of "the Father of his Country." Washington's public and private papers were in the possession of his nephew. Although it was advertised that these priceless original materials were to be used in this work exclusively, many of Washington's writings had already been used by other authors.

Marshall needed little urging to undertake this monumental labor. Totally unfamiliar with the exhausting toil required of the historian, he deemed it no great matter to write the achievements of his idolized leader. Moreover, he was in pressing need of money with which to pay the remaining $31,500 [1] which his brother and he still owed on the Fairfax purchase, as well as the smaller but yet annoying sum due their brother-in-law, Rawleigh Colston, for his share of the estate which the Marshall brothers had bought of him.[2] To discharge these obligations, Marshall had nothing but his salary and the income from his lands, which were wholly insufficient to meet the demands upon him. Some of his plantations, in fact, were "productive only of expense & vexation." [3]

Marshall and Bushrod Washington made extravagant estimates of the prospective sales of the biography and of the money they would receive. Everybody, they thought, would be eager to buy the true story of the life of America's "hero and sage." Perhaps the multitude could not afford volumes so expensive as those Marshall was to write, but there

[1] See *infra;* also vol. II, 211, of this work.
[2] Marshall to James M. Marshall, April 1, 1804, MS.
[3] Marshall to Peters, Oct. 12, 1815, Peters MSS. Pa. Hist. Soc.

would be tens of thousands of prosperous Federalists who could be depended upon to purchase at a generous price a definitive biography of George Washington.[1]

Nor was the color taken from these rosy expectations by the enthusiasm of those who wished to publish the biography. When it became known that the book was to be produced, many printers applied to Bushrod Washington "to purchase the copyright,"[2] among them C. P. Wayne, a successful publisher of Philadelphia, who made two propositions to bring out the work. After a consultation with Marshall, Bushrod Washington wrote Wayne: "Being ignorant of such matters . . we shall therefore decline any negotiation upon the subject for the present."[3]

After nearly two years of negotiation, Marshall and his associate decided that the biography would require four or five volumes, and arrived at the modest opinion that there would be "30,000 subscribers in America. . . . Less than a dollar a volume cannot be thought of," and this price should yield to the author and his partner "$150,000, supposing there to be five volumes. This . . would content us, whilst it would leave a very large profit" to the publisher. But, since the number of subscribers could not be foretold with exactness, Marshall and Bushrod Washington decided to "consent to receive

[1] Several persons were ambitious to write the life of Washington. David Ramsay and Mason Locke Weems had already done so. Noah Webster was especially keen to undertake the task, and it was unfortunate that he was not chosen to do it.

[2] Washington to Wayne, April 11, 1800, Dreer MSS. Pa. Hist. Soc.
[3] *Ib.*

$100,000 for the copyright in the United States";
and they sternly announced that, "less than this sum
we will not take." [1]

Wayne sought to reduce the optimism of Marshall and Washington by informing them that "the
greatest number of subscribers ever obtained for
any one publication in this country was . . 2000 and
the highest sum ever paid in for the copyright of
any one work . . was 30,000 Dollars." Wayne thinks
that Marshall's work may sell better, but is sure
that more than ten thousand sets cannot be disposed
of for many years. He gives warning that, if the
biography should contain anything objectionable
to the British Government, the sale of it would be
prevented in England, as was the case with David
Ramsay's "History of the Revolution." [2]

Marshall and Washington also "rec^d propositions
for the purchase of the right to sell in G^t. Britain,"
and so informed Wayne, calling upon him to "say
so" if he wished to acquire British, as well as American rights, "knowing the grounds upon which we
calculate the value in the United States." [3]

So we find Marshall counting on fifty thousand
dollars [4] at the very least from his adventure in the
field of letters. His financial reckoning was expan-
sive; but his idea of the time within which he could
write so important a history was grotesque. At first

[1] Bushrod Washington to Wayne, Dec. 11, 1801, Dreer MSS.
loc. cit.

[2] Wayne to Bushrod Washington, Dec. 10, 1801, Dreer MSS.
loc. cit.

[3] Bushrod Washington to Wayne, Dec. 11, 1801, Dreer MSS.
loc. cit.

[4] The division was to be equal between Marshall and Washington.

he counted on producing "4 or 5 volumes in octavos of from 4 to 500 pages each" in less than one year, provided "the present order of the Courts be not disturbed or very materially changed." [1]

It thus appears that Marshall expected the Federalist Judiciary Act of 1801 to stand; that he would not be called upon to ride the long, tiresome, time-consuming Southern circuit; and that, with no great number of cases to be disposed of by the Supreme Court, he would have plenty of leisure to write several large volumes of history in a single year.

But the Republican repeal of the act gave the disgusted Chief Justice "duties to perform," as John Randolph expressed it. Marshall was forthwith sent upon his circuit riding, and his fondly anticipated relief from official labors vanished. Although he had engaged to write the biography during the winter following Washington's death, not one line of it had he penned at the time the contract for publication was made in the autumn of 1802. He had, of course, done some reading of the various histories of the period; but he had not even begun the examination of Washington's papers, the subsequent study of which proved so irksome to him.

After almost two years of bartering, a contract was made with Wayne to print and sell the biography. This agreement, executed September 22, 1802, gave to the publisher the copyright in the United States and all rights of the authors "in any part of North and South America and in the West India

---

[1] Bushrod Washington to Wayne, Dec. 11, 1801, Dreer MSS. *loc. cit.*

Islands." The probable extent of the work was to be "four or five volumes in Octavo, from four to five hundred pages" each; and it was "supposed" that these would "be compleated in less than two years" — Marshall's original estimate of time having now been doubled.

Wayne engaged to pay "one dollar for every volume of the aforesaid work which may be subscribed for or which may be sold and paid for." It was further covenanted that the publisher should "not demand" of the public "a higher price than three dollars per volume in boards." [1] This disappointed Marshall, who had insisted that the volumes must be sold for four dollars each, a price which Wayne declared the people would not pay.[2]

It would seem that for a long time Marshall tried to conceal the fact that he was to be the author; and, when the first volume was about to be issued, strenuously objected to the use of his name on the title-page. However, Jefferson soon got wind of the project. The alert politician took swift alarm and promptly suggested measures to counteract the political poison with which he was sure Marshall's pen would infect public opinion. He consulted Madison, and the two picked out the brilliant and versatile Joel Barlow, then living in Paris, as the best man to offset the evil labor in which Marshall was engaged.

---

[1] "Articles of Agreement" between C. P. Wayne and Bushrod Washington, Sept. 22, 1802. (Dreer MSS. *loc. cit.*) Marshall's name does not appear in the contract, Washington having attended to all purely business details of the transaction.

[2] Wayne to Bushrod Washington, May 16, 1802, Dreer MSS. *loc. cit.*

"Mr. Madison and myself have cut out a piece of work for you," Jefferson wrote Barlow, "which is to write the history of the United States, from the close of the War downwards. We are rich ourselves in materials, and can open all the public archives to you; but your residence here is essential, because a great deal of the knowledge of things is not on paper, but only within ourselves for verbal communication."

Then Jefferson states the reason for the "piece of work" which he and Madison had "cut out" for Barlow: "John Marshall is writing the life of Gen. Washington from his papers. It is intended to come out just in time to influence the next presidential election." The imagination of the party manager pictured Marshall's work as nothing but a political pamphlet. "It is written therefore," Jefferson continues, "principally with a view to electioneering purposes; but it will consequently be out in time to aid you with information as well as to point out the perversions of truth necessary to be rectified." [1]

Thus Marshall's book was condemned before a word of it had been written, and many months before the contract with Wayne was signed — a circumstance that was seriously to interfere with subscriptions to the biography. Jefferson's abnormal sensitiveness to even moderate criticism finally led him to the preparation of the most interesting and untrustworthy of all his voluminous papers, as a reply to Marshall's "Washington." [2]

[1] Jefferson to Barlow, May 3, 1802, *Works:* Ford, ix, 372.
[2] The "Anas," *Works:* Ford, i, 163–430, see *infra.* The "Anas" was

News was sent to Republicans all over the country that Marshall's book was to be an attack upon their party. Wayne tells Marshall and Washington of the danger, but Washington testily assures the nervous publisher that he need have no fear: "The democrats may say what they please and I have expected they would say a great deal, but this is at least not intended to be a party work nor will any candid man have cause to make this charge." [1]

The contract signed, Wayne quickly put in motion the machinery to procure subscribers. Of this mechanism, the most important part should have been the postmasters, of whom Wayne expected to make profitable use. There were twelve hundred of them, "each acquainted with all the gentlemen of their respective neighborhoods . . and their neighbors would subscribe at request, when they would not to a stranger. . . . All letters to and from these men go free of postage," Wayne advised Marshall, while assuring the anxious author that "every Post Master in the United States holds a subscription paper." [2] But, thanks to Jefferson, the postmasters were to prove poor salesmen of the product of Marshall's pen.

Other solicitors, however, were also put to work:

Jefferson's posthumous defense. It was arranged for publication as early as 1818, but was not given to the public until after his death. It first appeared in the edition of Jefferson's works edited by his grandson, Thomas Jefferson Randolph. " It is the most precious mélange of all sorts of scandals you ever read." (Story to Fay, Feb. 5, 1830, Story, II, 33.)

[1] Bushrod Washington to Wayne, Nov. 19, 1802, Dreer MSS. *loc. cit.*

[2] Wayne to Marshall, Feb. 17, 1803, Dreer MSS. *loc. cit.*

among them the picturesque Mason Locke Weems,
part Whitefield, part Villon, a delightful mingling
of evangelist and vagabond, lecturer and politician,
writer and musician.[1] Weems had himself written a
"Life of Washington" which had already sold ex-
tensively among the common people.[2] He had long

[1] Weems is one of the most entertaining characters in American
history. He was born in Maryland, and was one of a family of nineteen children. He was educated in London as a physician, but abandoned medicine for the Church, and served for several years as rector
of two or three little Episcopal churches in Maryland and ministered
occasionally at Pohick Church, in Truro Parish (sometimes called
Mount Vernon Parish), Virginia. In this devout occupation he could
not earn enough to support his very large family. So he became a
professional book agent — the greatest, perhaps, of that useful fra-
ternity.

On horseback he went wherever it seemed possible to sell a book,
his samples in his saddlebags. He was a natural orator, a born enter-
tainer, an expert violinist; and these gifts he turned to good account
in his book-selling activities.

If a political meeting was to be held near any place he happened
upon, Weems would hurry to it, make a speech, and advertise his
wares. A religious gathering was his joy; there he would preach and
exhort — and sell books. Did young people assemble for merrymak-
ing, Weems was in his element, and played the fiddle for the danc-
ing. If he arrived at the capital of a State when the Legislature
was in session, he would contrive to be invited to address the Solons
— and procure their subscriptions.

[2] Weems probably knew more of the real life of the country, from
Pennsylvania southward, than any other one man; and he thoroughly
understood American tastes and characteristics. To this is due the
unparalleled success of his *Life of Washington*. In addition to this
absurd but engaging book, Weems wrote the *Life of Gen. Francis
Marion* (1805); the *Life of Benjamin Franklin* (1817); and the *Life
of William Penn* (1819). He was also the author of several tem-
perance pamphlets, the most popular of which was the *Drunkard's
Looking Glass*. Weems died in 1825.

Weems's *Life of Washington* still enjoys a good sale. It has been one
of the most widely purchased and read books in our history, and has
profoundly influenced the American conception of Washington. To
it we owe the grotesque and wholly imaginary stories of young Washington and the cherry tree, the planting of lettuce by his father to
prove to the boy the designs of Providence, and other anecdotes that

been a professional book agent with every trick of
the trade at his fingers' ends, and was perfectly acquainted with the popular taste.

First, the parson-subscription agent hied himself
to Baltimore. "I average 12 sub[s] pr day. *Thank
God for that*," he wrote to his employer. He is on
fire with enthusiasm: "If the Work be done handsomely, you will sell at least 20,000," he brightly
prophesies. Within a week Weems attacks the postmasters and insists that he be allowed to secure
sub-agents from among the gentry: "The Mass of
Riches and of Population in America lie in the
Country. There is the wealthy Yeomanry; and
there the ready Thousands who w[d.] instantly second
you were they but duly stimulated." [1]

Almost immediately Weems discovered a popular
distrust of Marshall's forthcoming volumes: "The
People are very fearful that it will be prostituted to
party purposes," he informs Wayne. "*For Heaven's
Sake, drop now and then a cautionary Hint to John
Marshall Esq.* Your all is at stake with respect to
this work. If it be done in a generally acceptable
manner you will make your fortune. Otherwise the
work will fall an Abortion from the press." [2]

Weems's apprehension grew. Wayne had written
that the cities would yield more subscribers than
the country. "For a moment, admit it," argues
Weems: "Does it follow that the Country is a mere

make that intensely human founder of the American Nation an impossible and intolerable prig.

The only biography of Weems is *Parson Weems*, by Lawrence C.
Wroth, a mere sketch, but trustworthy and entertaining.

[1] Weems to Wayne, Dec. 10, 1802, Dreer MSS. *loc. cit.*

[2] Same to same, Dec. 14, 1802, Dreer MSS. *loc. cit.*

blank, a cypher not worth your notice? Because there are 30,000 wealthy families in the City and but 20,000 in the Country, must nothing be tried to enlist 5000, at least of these 20,000??? *If the Fed^s sh^d be disappointed*, and the Demo^s disgusted with Genl· Marshals performance, will it not be very convenient to have 4 to 5000 good Rustic Blades to lighten your shelves & to shovel in the Dol^s." [1]

The dean of book agents evidently was having a hard time, but his resourcefulness kept pace with his discouragement: "Patriotic Orations — Gazetter Puffs — Washingtonian Anecdotes, Sentimental, Moral Military and Wonderful—All sh^d be Tried," he advises Wayne.[2] Again, he notes the failure of the postmasters to sell Marshall's now much-talked-of book. "In six months," he writes from Martinsburg, Virginia, "the P. Master here got 1. In ½ day. *I thank God*, I've got 13 sub^s." [3]

The outlook for subscriptions was even worse in New England. Throughout the whole land, there was, it seems, an amazing indifference to Washington's services to the Nation. "I am sorry to inform you," Wayne advised Marshall and his associate, "that the Prospect of an extensive Subscription is gloomy in N. England, particularly they argue it is too Expensive and wait for a cheaper Edition — 'tis like Americans, Mr. Wolcott and Mr. Pickering say they are loud in their professions, but attempt to touch their purses and they shut them in a moment." [4]

[1] Weems to Wayne, Dec. 17, 1802, Dreer MSS. *loc. cit.*
[2] Same to same, Dec. 22, 1802, Dreer MSS. *loc. cit.*
[3] Same to same, April 2, 1803, Dreer MSS. *loc. cit.*
[4] Wayne to Bushrod Washington, Jan. 23, 1803, Dreer MSS. *loc. cit.*

Writing from Fredericksburg, Virginia, Weems at last mingles cheer with warning: "Don't indulge a fear — let no sigh of thine arise. Give *Old Washington fair play* and all will be well. Let but the *Interior* of the Work be Liberal & the *Exterior Elegant*, and a Town House & a Country House, a Coach and Sideboard and Massy Plate shall be thine." Still, he declared, "I sicken when I think how much may be marr[d]." [1]

A week later found the reverend solicitor at Carlisle, Pennsylvania, and here the influence of politics on the success of Marshall's undertaking again crops out: "The place had been represented to me," records Weems, "as a Nest of Anti Washingtonian Hornets who w[d] draw their Stings at mention of his name — and the Fed [torn] Lawyers are all gone to York– However, I dash[d] in among them and *thank God* have obtain[d] already 17 good names." [2]

By now even the slow-thinking Bushrod Washington had become suspicious of Jefferson's postmasters: "The postmasters being (I believe) Democrats.[3] Are you sure they will feel a disposition to advance the work?" [4] Later he writes: "I would not give one honest soliciting agent for 1250 quiescent postmasters." [5]

---

[1] Weems to Wayne, April 8, 1803, Dreer MSS. *loc. cit.*

[2] Same to same, April 18, 1803, Dreer MSS. *loc. cit.*

[3] Bushrod Washington, like the other Federalists, would not call his political opponents by their true party name, Republicans: he styled them "democrats," the most opprobrious term the Federalists could then think of, excepting only the word "Jacobins." (See vol. II, 439, of this work.)

[4] Washington to Wayne, March 1, 1803, Dreer MSS. *loc. cit.*

[5] Same to same, March 23, 1803, Dreer MSS. *loc. cit.*

A year passed after the first subscriptions were made, and not even the first volume had appeared. Indeed, no part of the manuscript had been finished and sent to the publisher. Wayne was exasperated. "I am extremely anxious on this subject," he complains to Bushrod Washington, "as the Public evince dissatisfaction at the delay. Each hour I am questioned either verbally or by letter relative to it & its procrastination. The subscription seems to have received a check in consequence of an opinion that it is uncertain when the work will go to press. *Twelve thousand* dollars is the Total Cash yet rece^d — not quite 4,000 subscribers." [1]

By November, 1803, many disgusted subscribers are demanding a refund of the money, and Wayne wants the contract changed to the payment of a lump sum. The "Public [are] exclaiming against the price of 3 Doll^s per vol.," and his sanguine expectations have evaporated: "I did hope that I should realize *half* the number of subscribers you contemplated, *thirty thousand;* . . but altho' *two active*, and twelve hundred other agents have been employed 12 months, the list of names *does* not amount to *one seventh* of the contemplated number." [2]

[1] Wayne to Washington, Oct. 23, 1803, Dreer MSS. *loc. cit.*

An interesting sidelight on the commercial methods of the times is displayed by a circular which Wayne sent to his agents calling for money from subscribers to Marshall's *Life of Washington:* "The remittance may be made through the Post Office, and should any danger be apprehended, you can cut a Bank note in two parts and send each by separate mails." (Wayne's Circular, Feb. 17, 1803, Dreer MSS. *loc. cit.*)

[2] This list was published in the first edition. It is a good directory of the most prominent Federalists and of the leading Republican politicians of the time. "T. Jefferson, P.U.S." and each member of

Wayne insists on purchasing the copyright "for a *moderate, specifick* sum" so that he can save himself from loss and "that the Publick disgust may be removed." He has heard, he says, and quite directly, that the British rights have been sold "at two thousand doll^s !!!" — and this in spite of the fact that, only the previous year, Marshall and Washington "expected *Seventy* Thousand." [1]

At last, more than three years after Marshall had decided to embark upon the uncertain sea of authorship, he finished the first of the five volumes. And such a mass of manuscript! "It will make *at least* Eight hundred pages !!!!" moaned the distraught publisher. At that rate, considering the small number of subscribers and the greatly increased cost of paper and labor,[2] Wayne would be ruined. No titlepage had been sent, and Marshall's son, who had brought the manuscript to Philadelphia, "astonished" Wayne by telling him "that his father's name was not to appear in the Title." [3]

When Marshall learned that the publisher demanded a title-page bearing his name, he insisted

his Cabinet subscribed; Marshall himself was a subscriber for his own book, and John C. Calhoun, a student at Yale College at the time, was another. In the cities most of the lawyers took Marshall's book.

[1] Wayne to Bushrod Washington, Nov. 3, 1803, Dreer MSS. *loc. cit.*

It would seem from this letter that Marshall and Washington had reduced their lump cash price from $100,000 to $70,000. In stating his expenses, Wayne says that the painter "Gilbert Stuart demanded a handsome sum for the privilege of Engraving from his Original" portrait of Washington.

[2] See letter last cited.

[3] Wayne to Bushrod Washington, Dec. 16, 1803, Dreer MSS. *loc. cit.*

that this was unnecessary and not required by the copyright law. "I am unwilling," he hastened to write Wayne, "to be named in the book or in the clerk's office as the author of it, if it be avoidable." He cannot tell how many volumes there will be, or even examine, before some time in May, 1804, Washington's papers relating to the period of his two administrations. The first volume he wants "denominated *an introduction*." It is too long, he admits, and authorizes Wayne to split it, putting all after "the peace of 1763" into the second volume.[1]

Marshall objects again to appearing as the author: "My repugnance to permitting my name to appear in the title still continues, but it shall yield to your right to make the best use you can of the copy." He does not think that "the name of the author being given or withheld can produce any difference in the number of subscribers"; but, since he does not wish to leave Wayne "in the Opinion that a real injury has been sustained," he would "submit scruples" to Wayne and Washington, "only requesting that [his] name may not be given but on mature consideration and conviction of its propriety." In any case, Marshall declares: "I wish not my title in the judiciary of the United States to be annexed to it."

He writes at great length about punctuation, paragraphing, capital letters, and spelling, giving minute directions, but leaves much to Wayne's judgment. As to spelling: "In any doubtful case I woud de-

[1] Marshall to Wayne, Dec. 23, 1803, Dreer MSS. *loc. cit.*

cidedly prefer to follow Johnson." [1] Two other long letters about details of printing the first volume followed. By the end of March, 1804, his second volume was ready. [2]

He now becomes worried about "the inaccuracies . . the many and great defects in composition" of the first two volumes; but "the hurried manner in which it is press^d forward renders this inevitable." He begs Bushrod Washington to "censure and alter freely. . . You mistake me very much if you think I rank the corrections of a friend with the bitter sarcasms of a foe, or that I shou^d feel either wounded or chagrined at my inattentions being pointed out by another." [3]

Once more the troubled author writes his associate, this time about the spelling of "Chesapeak" and "enterprise," the size of the second volume, and as to "the prospects of subscribers." [4] Not until June, 1804, did Marshall give the proof-sheets of the first volume even "a hasty reading" because of "the pressure of . . official business." [5] Totally forgotten was the agreed plan to publish maps in a separate volume, although it was thus "stated in the prospectus." [6] He blandly informs the exasperated publisher that he must wait a long time after publishing the volumes describing the Revolution and those on the Presidency of Washington before

[1] Marshall to Wayne, Jan. 10, 1804, Dreer MSS. *loc. cit.*

[2] Marshall to Bushrod Washington, March 25, 1804, Dreer MSS. *loc. cit.*

[3] Same to same, April, 1804, Dreer MSS. *loc. cit.*

[4] Same to same, April 29, 1804, Dreer MSS. *loc. cit.*

[5] Marshall to Wayne, June 1, 1804, Dreer MSS. *loc. cit.*

[6] Same to same, June 6, 1804, Dreer MSS. *loc. cit.*

the manuscript of the last volume can be sent to press — this when many subscribers were clamoring for the return of the money they had paid, and the public was fast losing interest in the book. Large events had meanwhile filled the heavens of popular interest, and George Washington's heroic figure was already becoming dim and indistinct.

The proof-sheets of the second volume were now in Marshall's hands; but the toil of writing, "super-intending the copying," and various other avoca-tions "absolutely disabled" him, he insists, from giving them any proper examination. He had no idea that he had been so careless in his writing and is anxious to revise the work for a second edition. He complains of his health and says he must spend the summer in the mountains, where, of course, he "cannot take the papers with [him] to prosecute the work." He will, however, read the pages of the first two volumes while on his vacation.

The manuscript of the third he had finished and sent to Bushrod Washington.[1] When Wayne saw the length of it, his Quaker blood was heated to wrath. Did Marshall's prolixity know no limit? The first two volumes had already cost the publisher far more than the estimate — would not Washington persuade Marshall to be more concise?[2]

By midsummer of 1804 the first two volumes ap-peared. They were a dismal performance. Never-theless, one or two Federalist papers praised them,

[1] Marshall to Wayne, June 10, July 5, July 8, 1804, Dreer MSS. *loc. cit.*

[2] Wayne to Bushrod Washington, Aug. 20, 1804, Dreer MSS. *loc. cit.*

and Marshall was as pleased as any youthful writer by a first compliment. He thanks Wayne for sending the reviews and comments on one of them: "The very handsome critique in the 'Political and Commercial Register' was new to me." He modestly admits: "I cou^d only regret that there was in it more of panuegyric than was merited. The editor . . manifests himself to be master of a style of a very superior order and to be, of course, a very correct judge of the composition of Others."

Marshall is somewhat mollified that his parentage of the biography has been revealed: "Having, Heaven knows how reluctantly, consented against my judgement to be known as the author of the work in question I cannot be insensible to the opinions entertained of it. But, I am much more solicitous to hear the strictures upon it" — than commendation of it — because, he says, these would point out defects to be corrected. He asks Wayne, therefore, to send to him at Front Royal, Virginia, "every condemnatory criticism. . . I shall not attempt to polish every sentence; that wou^d require repeated readings & a long course of time; but I wish to correct obvious imperfections & the animadversions of others wou^d aid me very much in doing so." [1]

Within three weeks Marshall had read his first volume in the form in which it had been delivered to subscribers, and was "mortified beyond measure to find that it [had] been so carelessly written." He had not supposed that so many "inelegancies . . cou^d have appeared in it," and regrets that he must re-

[1] Marshall to Wayne, July 20, 1804, Dreer MSS. *loc. cit.*

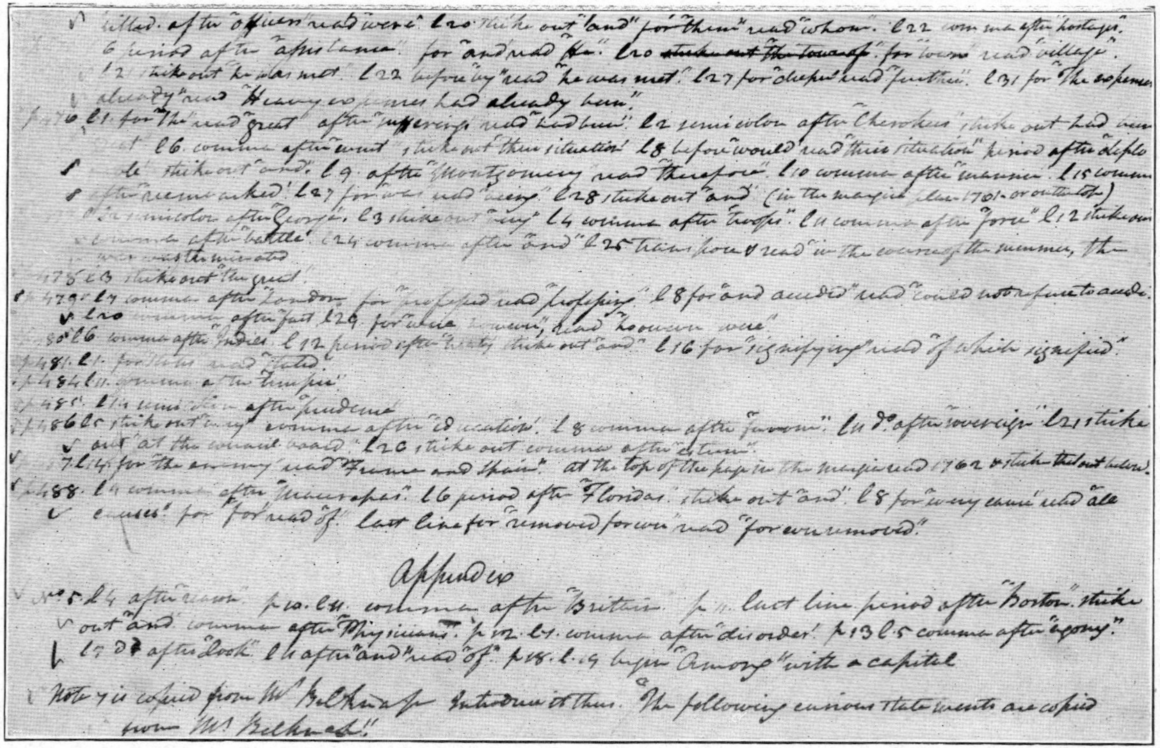

quire Wayne to reset the matter "so materially."
He informs his publisher, nevertheless, that he is
starting on his vacation in the Alleghanies; and he
promises that when he returns he "will . . review
the corrections" he has made in the first volume,
although he would "not have time to reperuse the
whole volume."[1]

Not for long was the soul of the perturbed author
to be soothed with praise. He had asked for "strictures"; he soon got them. Wayne promptly sent him
a "Magazine[2] containing a piece condemnatory of
the work." Furthermore, the books were not going
well; not a copy could the publisher sell that had
not been ordered before publication. "I have all
those on hand which I printed over the number
of subscribers," Wayne sourly informs the author.

In response to Marshall's request for time for revision, Wayne is now willing that he shall take all he
wishes, since "present prospects would not induce
[him] to republish," but he cautions Marshall to "let
the idea of a 2d edit. revised and corrected remain
a secret"; if the public should get wind of such a
purpose the stacks of volumes in Wayne's printing
house would never be sold. He must have the
manuscript of the "*fourth* vol. by the last of September at furthest. . . Can I have it? — or must I dismiss my people."

At the same time he begs Marshall to control
his redundancy: "The first and second vols. have

[1] Marshall to Wayne, Aug. 10, 1804, Dreer MSS. *loc. cit.*

[2] *Literary Magazine and American Register of Philadelphia*, July,
1804. The reviewer makes many of the criticisms that appeared on
the completion of the biography. (See *infra*, 261–79.)

cost me (1500) fifteen hundred dollars more than calculated!" [1]

It was small wonder that Marshall's first two bulky books, published in the early summer of 1804, were not hailed with enthusiasm. In volume one the name of Washington was mentioned on only two minor occasions described toward the end.[2] The reader had to make his way through more than one hundred thousand words without arriving even at the cradle of the hero. The voyages of discovery, the settlements and explorations of America, and the history of the Colonies until the Treaty of Paris in 1763, two years before the Stamp Act of 1765, were treated in dull and heavy fashion.

The author defends his plan in the preface: No one connected narrative tells the story of all the Colonies and "few would .. search through the minute details"; yet this he held to be necessary to an understanding of the great events of Washington's life. So Marshall had gathered the accounts of the various authorities[3] in parts of the country and in England, and from them made a continuous history. If there were defects in the book it was due to "the impatience .. of subscribers" which had so hastened him.

The volume is poorly done; parts are inaccurate.[4]

---

[1] Wayne to Marshall, Aug. 20, 1804, Dreer MSS. *loc. cit.*

[2] The affair at Little Meadows and the defeat of Braddock. (Marshall: *Life of George Washington*, 1st ed. i, 356–58, 368–71.)

[3] These were: Belknap, Belsham, Chalmers, Dodsley, Entick or Entinck, Gordon, Hutchinson, Minot, Ramsay, Raynal, Robertson, Russell, Smith, Stedman, Stith, Trumbull.

[4] For example, Marshall's description of Sir William Berkeley, who was, the reader is informed, "distinguished .. by the mildness of

To Bacon's Rebellion are given only four pages.[1]
The story of the Pilgrims is fairly well told.[2] A page
is devoted to Roger Williams and six sympathetic
lines tell of his principles of liberty and toleration.[3]
The Salem witchcraft madness is well treated.[4] The
descriptions of military movements constitute the
least disappointing parts of the volume. The beginnings of colonial opposition to British rule are tiresomely set out; and thus at last, the reader arrives
within twelve years of Bunker Hill.

Marshall admits that every event of the Revolutionary War has been told by others who had examined Washington's "immensely voluminous correspondence," and that he had copied these authors,
sometimes using their very language. Still, he promises the reader "a particular account of his [Wash-
ington's] own life." [5]

One page and three lines at the beginning of the
second volume are all that Marshall gives of the ancestry, birth, environment, upbringing, education,
and experiences of George Washington, up to the
nineteenth year of his age. On the second page the
hero, fully uniformed and accoutred, is plunged
into the French and Indian Wars. Braddock's defeat, already described in the first volume, is repeated and elaborated.[6] Six lines, closing the first
chapter, disposes of Washington in marriage and
describes the bride.[7]

his temper, the gentleness of his manners and .. popular virtues."
(Marshall, 1st ed. I, 72.)

[1] *Ib.* 188–92; and see vol. I, 6, of this work.
[2] *Ib.* 1st ed. I, 86–89.   [3] *Ib.* 111–12.   [4] *Ib.*; see Notes, 9–18.
[5] *Ib.* x.   [6] *Ib.* 1st ed. II, 14–20.   [7] *Ib.* 67.

About three pages are devoted to the Stamp Act speeches in the British Parliament; while but one short paragraph is given to the immortal resolutions of Patrick Henry and the passage of them by the Virginia House of Burgesses. Not a word describes the "most bloody" debate over them, and Henry's time-surviving speech is not even referred to.[1] All mention of the fact that Washington was a fellow member with Henry and voted for the resolutions is omitted. Henry's second epoch-making speech at the outbreak of the Revolution is not so much as hinted at, nor is any place found for the Virginia Resolutions for Arming and Defense, which his unrivaled eloquence carried.

The name of the supreme orator of the Revolution is mentioned for the second time in describing the uprising against Lord Dunmore,[2] and then Marshall adds this footnote: "The same gentleman who had introduced into the assembly of Virginia the·original resolution against the stamp act."[3]

Marshall's account of the development of the idea of independence is scattered.[4] He gives with unnecessary completeness certain local resolutions favoring it,[5] while to the great Declaration less than two pages[6] are assigned. It is termed "this important paper"; and a footnote disposes of the fact that "Mr. Jefferson, Mr. John Adams, Mr. Franklin, Mr. Sherman, and Mr. R. R. Livingston, were appointed to prepare this declaration; and the draft reported by the committee has been generally at-

---

[1] Marshall, 1st ed. II, 82–83; and see vol. I, 66, of this work.
[2] See vol. I, 74–79, of this work. [3] Marshall, 1st ed. II, 193.
[4] *Ib.* 160–69. [5] *Ib.* 374–75. [6] *Ib.* 377–78.

tributed to Mr. Jefferson." [1] A report of the talk
between Washington and Colonel Paterson of the
British Army, concerning the title by which Washington insisted upon being addressed,[2] is given one
and one third times the space that is bestowed upon
the Declaration of Independence.

Marshall is satisfactory only when dealing with
military operations. He draws a faithful picture of
the condition of the army; [3] quotes Washington's
remorseless condemnations of the militia,[4] short en-
listments, and the democratic spirit among men and
officers.[5] When writing upon such topics, Marshall
is spirited; his pages are those of the soldier that,
by nature, he was.

The earliest objection to Marshall's first two volumes came from American Tories, who complained
of the use of the word "enemy" as applied to the
British military forces. Wayne reluctantly calls
Marshall's attention to this. Marshall replies:
"You need make no apology for mentioning to me
the criticism of the word 'enemy.' I will endeavor
to avoid it where it can be avoided." [6]

Unoffended by such demands, Marshall was
deeply chagrined by other and entirely just criticisms. Why, he asks, had not some one pointed out
to him "some of those objections .. to the plan
of the work" before he wrote any part of it? He
wishes "very sincerely" that this had been done.
He "should very readily have relinquished [his own]

---

[1] Marshall, 1st ed. II, 377.   [2] *Ib.* 386-89.   [3] *Ib.* 390-94.
[4] *Ib.* 417-18, 445-46; and see vol. I, 83-86, of this work.
[5] Marshall, 1st ed. II, 259-61.
[6] Marshall to Wayne, Aug. 10, 1804, Dreer MSS. *loc. cit.*

opinion . . if [he] had perceiv^d that the public taste required a different course." Thus, by implication, he blames Wayne or Bushrod Washington, for his own error of judgment.

Marshall also reproaches himself, but in doing so he saddles on the public most of the burden of his complaints: "I ought, indeed, to have foreseen that the same impatience which precipitated the publication wou^d require that the life and transactions of Mr. Washington should be immediately entered upon." Even if he had stuck to his original plans, still, he "ought to have departed from them so far as to have composed the introductory volume at leizure after the principal work was finished."

Marshall's "mortification" is, he says, also "increased on account of the careless manner in which the work has been executed." For the first time in his life he had been driven to sustained and arduous mental labor, and he found, to his surprise, that he "had to learn that under the pressure of constant application, the spring of the mind loses its elasticity. . . But regrets for the past are unavailing," he sighs. "There will be great difficulty in retrieving the reputation of the first volume. . . I have therefore some doubts whether it may not be as well to drop the first volume for the present — that is not to speak of a republication of it."

He assures Wayne that he need have no fears that he will mention a revised edition, and regrets that the third volume is also too long; his pen has run away with him. He would shorten it if he had the copy once more; but since that cannot be, perhaps

Wayne might omit the last chapter. Brooding over the "strictures" he had so confidently asked for, he grows irritable. "Whatever might have been the execution, the work wou^d have experienced unmerited censure. We must endeavor to rescue what remains to be done from such [criticism] as is deserved. I wish you to consult Mr. Washington." [1]

Another very long letter from Front Royal quickly follows. Marshall again authorizes the publisher himself to cut the bulk of the third volume, in the hope that it "will not be so defective. . . It shall be my care to render the 4th more fit for the public eye." He promises Wayne that, in case of a second edition,[2] he will shorten his interminable pages which shall also "receive very material corrections." But a corrected and improved edition! "On this subject . . I remain silent. . . Perhaps a free expression of my thoughts . . may add to the current which seems to set against it." Let the public take the first printing "before a second is spoken of." [3]

Washington drew on the publisher [4] and wrote Wayne that "the disappointment will be very great if it is not paid." In December, 1804, Wayne sent the first royalty. It amounted to five thousand dollars.[5]

[1] Marshall to Wayne from Front Royal, Virginia, Sept. 3, 1804, Dreer MSS. *loc. cit.*

[2] Marshall spent many years preparing this second edition of his *Washington*, which appeared in 1832, three years before Marshall's death. See *infra*, 272–73.

[3] Marshall to Wayne, Sept. 8, 1804, Dreer MSS. *loc. cit.*

[4] The amount of this draft is not stated.

[5] This would seem to indicate that Wayne had been able to collect payment on the first two volumes, from only two thousand five hundred subscribers, since, by the contract, Marshall and Washington together were to receive one dollar for each book sold.

Our author needed money badly. "I do not wish to press you upon the subject of further remittances but they will be highly acceptable," Washington tells Wayne, "particularly to Mr. Marshall, whose arrangements I know are bottomed upon the expectation of the money he is to receive from you." [1] In January, 1805, Wayne sent Washington another thousand dollars — "which I have paid," says Washington, "to Mr. Marshall as I shall also do of the next thousand you remit." [2] Thus pressed, Wayne sends more money, and by January 1, 1805, Marshall and Washington have received the total sum of eight thousand seven hundred and sixty dollars. [3]

Toward the end of February, 1805, Marshall completed the manuscript of the fourth volume. He was then in Washington, and sent two copies from there to Philadelphia by Francis Hopkinson who had just finished his notable work in the Chase impeachment trial. "They are both in a rough state; too rough to be sent . . but it was impossible to have them recopied," Marshall writes Wayne. He admits they are full of errors in capitalization, punctuation, and spelling, but adds, "it has absolutely been impossible to make corrections in these respects." [4] This he "fears will produce considerable difficulty." Small wonder, with the Chase trial absorbing his every thought and depressing him with heavy anxiety.

Marshall's relief from the danger of impeachment

---

[1] Washington to Wayne, Dec. 25, 1804, Dreer MSS. *loc. cit.*
[2] Same to same, Jan. 15, 1805, Dreer MSS *loc. cit.*
[3] Same to same, Dec. 30, 1804, Dreer MSS. *loc. cit.*
[4] Marshall to Wayne, Feb. 27, 1805, Dreer MSS. *loc. cit.*

is at once reflected in his correspondence with Wayne. Two weeks after the acquittal of Chase, he placidly informs his publisher that the fifth volume will not be ready until the spring of 1806 at the earliest. It is "not yet commenced," he says, "but I shall however set about it in a few days." He explains that there will be little time to work on the biography. "For the ensuing twelve months I shall scarcely have it in my power to be five in Richmond." [1] Three months later he informs Wayne that it will be "absolutely impossible" to complete the final volume by the time mentioned. "I regret this very seriously but it is a calamity for which there is no remedy."

The cause of this irremediable calamity was "a tour of the mountains" — a journey to be made "for [his] own health and that of [his] family" from which he "cannot return till October." He still "laments sincerely that an introductory volume was written because [he] finds it almost impossible to compress the civil administration into a single volume. In doing it," he adds, "I shall be compelled to omit several interesting transactions & to mutilate others." [2]

At last Marshall's eyes are fully opened to what should have been plain to him from the first. Nobody wanted a tedious history of the discovery and settlement of America and of colonial development, certainly not from his pen. The subject had been dealt with by more competent authors.

But the terrible years following the war, the Con-

[1] Marshall to Wayne, March 16, 1805, Dreer MSS. *loc. cit.*
[2] Same to same, June 29, 1805, Dreer MSS. *loc. cit.*

stitutional period, the Administrations of Washington and the first half of that of Adams, the decisive part played by Washington throughout this critical time of founding and constructing — all these were virgin fields. They constituted, too, as vital an epoch in American history as the Revolution itself. Marshall's own life had been an important part of it, and he was not unequipped to give it adequate treatment.

Had Marshall written of these years, it is probable that the well-to-do Federalists alone would have purchased the thirty thousand sets that Marshall originally counted on to be sold. He would have made all the money he had expected, done a real public service, and achieved a solid literary fame. His "Life of Washington" might have been the great social, economic, political, and Constitutional history of the foundation processes of the Government of the American Nation. His entire five volumes would not have been too many for such a work.

But all this matter relating to the formative years of the Nation must now be crowded between two covers and offered to an indifferent, if not hostile, public — a public already "disgusted," as the publisher truly declared, by the unattractive rehash of what had already been better told.

Wayne again presses for a change in the contract; he wants to buy outright Marshall's and Washington's interests, and end the bankrupting royalty he is paying them: "If you were willing to take 70000$ for 30000 Sub^s I thought it would not be deemed

illiberal in offering twenty thousand dollars for four
thousand subscribers — this was two-sevenths of
the original sum for less than *one-seventh* of the subscribers contemplated." Wayne asks Marshall and
Washington to "state the lowest sum" they will
take. Subscriptions have stopped, and in three
years he has sold only "*two* copies . . to non-sub-
scribers." But the harried publisher sends two
thousand dollars more of royalty.[1]

In the autumn of 1805, upon returning from his
annual vacation, Marshall is anxious to get to work,
and he must have the *Aurora* and *Freneau's Gazette*
quickly. His "official duties recommence . . on the
22d of November from which time they continue 'till
the middle of March." Repeating his now favorite
phrase, he says, "It is absolutely impossible to get
the residue of the work completed in the short time
which remains this fall." He has been sorely vexed
and is a cruelly overworked man: "The unavoidable
delays which have been experienced, the immense
researches among volumes of manuscript, & chests
of letters & gazettes which I am compelled to make
will impede my progress so much that it is absolutely
impossible" to finish the book at any early date.[2]

Want of money continually embarrasses Marshall:
"What payments my good Sir, will it be in your
power to make us in the course of this & the next
month?" Bushrod Washington asks Wayne. "I
am particularly anxious," he explains, "on account
of Mr. M. . . His principal dependence is upon this

---

[1] Wayne to Washington, July 4, 1804, Dreer MSS. *loc. cit.*
[2] Marshall to Wayne, Oct. 5, 1805, Dreer MSS. *loc. cit.*

fund." [1] Marshall now gets down to earnest and continuous labor and by July, 1806, actually finishes the fifth and only important volume of the biography. [2]

During all these years the indefatigable Weems continued his engaging career as book agent, and, like the subscribers he had ensnared, became first the victim of hope deferred and then of unrealized expectations. The delay in the publication of Marshall's first volumes and the disfavor with which the public received them when finally they appeared, had, it seems, cooled the ardor of the horseback-and-saddlebag distributer of literary treasures. At all events, he ceases to write his employer about Marshall's "Life of Washington," but is eager for other books. [3] Twice only, in an interval of two years, he

[1] Washington to Wayne, April 1, 1806, Dreer MSS. *loc. cit.* It was in this year that the final payments for the Fairfax estate were made and the deed executed to John and James M. Marshall and their brother-in-law Rawleigh Colston. See vol. II, footnote to 211, and vol. IV, chap. III, of this work.

[2] Same to same, July 14, 1806, Dreer MSS. *loc. cit.*

[3] Weems's orders for books are trustworthy first-hand information concerning the literary tastes of the American people at that time, and the extent of education among the wealthy. Writing from Savannah, Georgia, August, 1806, he asks for "Rippons hymns, Watts D?, Newton's D?, Methodist D?, Davies Sermons, Massillons D?, Villiage D?, Whitfields D?, Fuller [the eminent Baptist divine,] Works, viz. His Gospel its own evidence, Gospel Worthy of all Acceptation, Pilgrim's progress, Baxter's Sts Rest, Call to the Unconverted, Alarm, by Allein, Hervey's Works, Rushe's Medical Works; All manner of School Books, Novels by the cart load, particularly Charlotte Temple . . 2 or 300 of Charlotte Temple . . Tom Paines Political Works, Johnson's Poets bound in green or in any handsome garb, particularly Miltons Paradise lost, Tompsons Seasons, Young's N. Thoughts wou'd do well." (Weems to Wayne, Aug. 1806, Dreer MSS. *loc. cit.*)

Another order calls for all the above and also for "Websters Spell^g book, Universal D?, Fullers Backslider, Booths reign of Grace, Looking Glass for the mind, Blossoms of Morality, Columbian Orator,

mentions Marshall's biography, but without spirit
or enthusiasm.[1] In the autumn of 1806, he queru-
lously refers to Marshall and Washington: "I did not
call on *you* [Wayne] for increase of Diurnal Salary.
I spoke to Judge W. I hope and expect that he and
Gen. M.[2] will do me something."

Marshall's third volume, which had now appeared, is an improvement on the first two. In it he
continues his narrative of the Revolutionary War
until 1779, and his statement of economic and financial conditions[3] is excellent. The account of the
battles of Brandywine and Germantown, in both of
which he had taken part,[4] is satisfactory,[5] and his
picture of the army in retreat is vivid.[6] He faithfully
relates the British sentiment among the people.[7]
Curiously enough, he is not comprehensive or stirring in his story of Valley Forge.[8] His descriptions
of Lafayette and Baron von Steuben are worthy.[9]
Again and again he attacks the militia,[10] and is merciless in his criticism of the slip-shod, happy-go-

Enticks Dictionary, Murrays Grammar, Enfield's Speaker, Best
Books on Surveying, D? on Navigation, Misses Magazine, Vicar of
Wakefield, Robinson Crusoe, Divine Songs for Children, Pamela
Small." In this letter forty-four different titles are called for.

[1] Weems to Wayne, Jan. 28, 1804, and Aug. 25, 1806, Dreer MSS.
loc. cit.

[2] Same to same, Sept. 20, 1806, Wayne MSS. *loc. cit.* This letter is
written from Augusta, Georgia. Among other books ordered in it,
Weems names twelve copies each of "Sallust, Corderius, Eutropius,
Nepos, Caesar's Commentaries, Virgil Delph., Horace Delphini, Ci-
cero D?, Ovid D?"; and nine copies each of "Greek Grammar, D?
Testament, Lucian, Xenophon."

[3] Marshall, III, 28–42.   [4] See vol. I, 93–98, 102, of this work.
[5] Marshall, III, chaps. III and IV.
[6] See vol. I, 98–101, of this work.   [7] Marshall, III, 43–48, 52.
[8] *Ib.* 319, 330, 341–50; and see vol. I, 110–32, of this work.
[9] Marshall, III, 345, 347–49.   [10] *Ib.* 50–53, 62.

lucky American military system. These shortcomings were offset, he says, only by the conduct of the enemy.[1] The treatment of American prisoners is set forth in somber words,[2] and he gives almost a half-page of text[3] and two and a half pages of appendix[4] to the murder of Miss McCrea.

The story of the battle of Monmouth in which Marshall took part is told with spirit.[5] Nineteen pages[6] are devoted to the history of the alliance with the French monarch, and no better résumé of that event, so fruitful of historic results, ever has been given. The last chapter describes the arrival of the British Commission of Conciliation, the propositions made by them, the American answer, the British attempts to bribe Congress,[7] followed by the Indian atrocities of which the appalling massacres at Kingston and Wyoming were the worst.

The long years of writing, the neglect and crudity of his first efforts, and the self-reproval he underwent, had their effect upon Marshall's literary craftsmanship. This is noticeable in his fourth volume, which is less defective than those that preceded it. His delight in verbiage, so justly ridiculed by Cal-

---

[1] Marshall, III, 59. "No species of licentiousness was unpracticed. The plunder and destruction of property was among the least offensive of the injuries sustained." The result "could not fail to equal the most sanguine hopes of the friends of the revolution. A sense of personal wrongs produced a temper, which national considerations had been found too weak to excite... The great body of the people flew to arms."

[2] *Ib.* 20, 22, 24, 27, 386. See also vol. I, 115–16, of this work, and authorities there cited.

[3] Marshall, III, 246–47.   [4] *Ib.* Notes, 4–6.

[5] *Ib.* chap. 8; and see vol. I, 134–38, of this work.

[6] Marshall, III, 366–85.   [7] *Ib.* 486–96.

lender in 1799,[1] is a little subdued, and his sense of proportion is somewhat improved. He again criticizes the American military system and traces its defects to local regulations.[2] The unhappy results of the conflict of State and Nation are well presented.[3]

The most energetic narrative in the volume is that of the treason of Benedict Arnold. In telling this story, Marshall cannot curb the expression of his intense feeling against this "traitor, a sordid traitor, first the slave of his rage, then purchased with gold." Marshall does not economize space in detailing this historic betrayal of America,[4] imperative as the saving of every line had become.

He relates clearly the circumstances that caused the famous compact between Denmark, Sweden, and Russia known as "The Armed Neutrality," formed in order to check Great Britain's power on the seas. This was the first formidable assertion of the principle of equality among nations on the ocean. Great Britain's declaration of war upon Holland, because that country was about to join "The Armed Neutrality," and because Holland appeared to be looking with favor upon a commercial treaty which the United States wished to conclude with her, is told with dispassionate lucidity.[5]

Marshall gives a compact and accurate analysis — by far the best work he has done in the whole four volumes — of the party beginnings discernible when the clouds of the Revolutionary War began to break. He had now written more than half a million words,

---

[1] See vol. II, 405, of this work.   [2] Marshall, IV, 114–15.   [3] *Ib.* 188.
[4] *Ib.* 247–65; see vol. I, 143–44, of this work.   [5] Marshall, IV, 284–88.

and this description was the first part of his work that could be resented by the Republicans. The political division was at bottom economic, says Marshall — those who advocated honest payment of public debts were opposed by those who favored repudiation; and the latter were also against military establishments and abhorred the idea of any National Government.[1]

The fourth volume ends with the mutiny of part of the troops, the suppression of it, Washington's farewell to his officers, and his retirement when peace was concluded.

Marshall's final volume was ready for subscribers and the public in the autumn of 1807, just one year before the Federalist campaign for the election of Jefferson's successor — four years later than Jefferson had anticipated.[2] It was the only political part of Marshall's volumes, but it had not the smallest effect upon the voters in the Presidential contest.

Neither human events nor Thomas Jefferson had waited upon the convenience of John Marshall. The Federalist Party was being reduced to a grumbling company of out-of-date gentlemen, leaders in a bygone day, together with a scattered following who, from force of party habit, plodded along after them, occasionally encouraged by some local circumstance or fleeting event in which they imagined an "issue" might be found. They had become anti-National, and, in their ardor for Great Britain, had all but ceased to be American. They had repudiated democracy and assumed an attitude of insolent

[1] Marshall, IV, 530–31.   [2] See Jefferson's letter to Barlow, *supra*.

superiority, mournful of a glorious past, despairing of a worthy future.[1]

Marshall could not hope to revive the fast weakening Federalist organization. The most that he could do was to state the principles upon which opposing parties had been founded, and the determinative conflicts that had marked the evolution of them and the development of the American Nation. He could only set forth, in plain and simple terms, those antagonistic ideas which had created party divisions; and although the party to which one group of those ideas had given life was now moribund, they were ideas, nevertheless, which would inevitably create other parties in the future.

The author's task was, therefore, to deal not only with the years that had gone; but, through his treatment of the past, with the years that were to come. He must expound the philosophy of Nationalism as opposed to that of Localism, and must enrich his exposition by the unwritten history of the period between the achievement of American Independence and the vindication of it in our conflict with France.

Marshall was infinitely careful that every statement in his last volume should be accurate; and, to make sure of this, he wrote many letters to those who had first-hand knowledge of the period. Among others he wrote to John Adams, requesting permission to use his letters to Washington. Adams readily agreed, although he says, "they were written," "under great agitation of mind at a time when a

[1] See *supra*, chap. III, and *infra*, chap. VI; and see especially vol. IV, chap. I, of this work.

cruel necessity compelled me to take measures
which I was very apprehensive would produce the
evils which have followed from them. If you have
detailed the events of the last years of General
Washington's Life, you must have run the Gauntlet
between two infuriated factions, armed with scor-
pions. . . It is a period which must however be in-
vestigated, but I am very confident will never be
well understood." [1]

Because of his lack of a sense of proportion in
planning his "Life of Washington," and the volumi-
nousness of the minor parts of it, Marshall had to
compress the vital remainder. Seldom has a serious
author been called upon to execute an undertaking
more difficult. Marshall accomplished the feat in
creditable fashion. Moreover, his fairness, restraint,
and moderation, even in the treatment of subjects
regarding which his own feelings were most ardent,
give to his pages not only the atmosphere of justice,
but also something of the artist's touch.

[1] Adams to Marshall, July 17, 1806, MS.

This letter is most important. Adams pictures his situation when
President: "A first Magistrate of a great Republick with a General
officer under him, a Commander in Chief of the Army, who had ten
thousand times as much Influence Popularity and Power as himself,
and that Commander in Chief so much under the influence of his
Second in command [Hamilton], . . the most treacherous, malicious,
insolent and revengeful enemy of the first Magistrate is a Picture
which may be very delicate and dangerous to draw. But it must be
drawn. . .

"There is one fact . . which it will be difficult for posterity to believe, and that is that the measures taken by Senators, Members of
the House, some of the heads of departments, and some officers of the
Army to force me to appoint General Washington . . proceeded not
from any regard to him . . but merely from an intention to employ
him as an engine to elevate Hamilton to the head of affairs civil as
well as military."

Washington's Nationalism is promptly and skill-fully brought into the foreground.[1] An excellent ac-count of the Society of the Cincinnati contains the first covert reflection on Jefferson.[2] But the state of the country under the Articles of Confederation is passed over with exasperating brevity — only a few lines are given to this basic subject.[3]

The foundation of political parties is stated once more and far better — "The one . . contemplated America as a nation," while "the other attached itself to state authorities." The first of these was made up of "men of enlarged and liberal minds . . who felt the full value of national honour, and the full obligation of national faith; and who were persuaded of the insecurity of both, if resting for their preservation on the 'concurrence of thirteen distinct sovereignties"; and with these far-seeing and upright persons were united the "officers of the army" whose experience in war had weakened "local prejudices."[4]

Thus, by mentioning the excellence of the mem-bers of one party, and by being silent upon the short-comings of those of the other party, Marshall imputes to the latter the reverse of those qualities which he praises — a method practiced throughout the book, and one which offended Jefferson and his followers more than a direct attack could have done.

He succinctly reviews the attempts at union,[5] and the disputes between America and Great Britain

---

[1] He was "accustomed to contemplate America as his country, and to consider . . the interests of the whole." (Marshall, v, 10.)
[2] *Ib.* 24–30. [3] *Ib.* 31–32. [4] *Ib.* 33–34. [5] *Ib.* 45–47.

over the Treaty of Peace;[1] he quickly swings back to
the evolution of political parties and, for the third
time, reiterates his analysis of debtor and Localist as
against creditor and Nationalist.

"The one [party] struggled . . for the exact observance of public and private engagements"; to
them "the faith of a nation, or of a private man
was deemed a sacred pledge." These men believed
that "the distresses of individuals" could be relieved
only by work and faith, "not by a relaxation of the
laws, or by a sacrifice of the rights of others." They
thought that "the imprudent and idle could not be
protected by the legislature from the consequences
of their indiscretion; but should be restrained from
involving themselves in difficulties, by the conviction
that a rigid compliance with contracts would be enforced." Men holding these views "by a natural association of ideas" were "in favour of enlarging the
powers of the federal government, and of enabling it
to protect the dignity and character of the nation
abroad, and its interests at home."[2]

With these principles Marshall sharply contrasts
those of the other party: "Viewing with extreme
tenderness the case of the debtor, their efforts were
unceasingly directed to his relief"; they were against
"a faithful compliance with contracts" — such a
measure they thought "too harsh to be insisted on . .
and one which the people would not bear." Therefore, they favored "relaxing . . justice," suspending
the collection of debts, remitting taxes. These men
resisted every attempt to transfer from their own

---

[1] Marshall, v, 65.   [2] *Ib.* 85–86.

hands into those of Congress all powers that were, in reality, National. Those who held to such "lax notions of honor," were, in many States, "a decided majority of the people," and were very powerful throughout the country. Wherever they secured control, paper money, delay of justice, suspended taxes "were the fruits of their rule"; and where they were in the minority, they fought at every election for the possession of the State Governments.

In this fashion Marshall again states those antipodal philosophies from which sprang the first two American political parties. With something like skill he emphasizes the conservative and National idea thus: "No principle had been introduced [in the State Governments] which could resist the wild projects of the moment, give the people an opportunity to reflect, and allow the good sense of the nation time for exertion." The result of "this instability in principles which ought if possible to be rendered immutable, produced a long train of ills." [1] The twin spirits of repudiation and Localism on one side, contending for the mastery against the companion spirits of faith-keeping and Nationalism on the other, were from the very first, says Marshall, the source of public ill-being or well-being, as one or the other side prevailed.

Then follows a review of the unhappy economic situation which, as Marshall leaves the reader to infer, was due exclusively to the operation of the principles which he condemns by the mere statement of them.[2] So comes the Philadelphia Convention

---

[1] Marshall, v, 85–87. [2] *Ib*. 88–89.

of 1787 that was deemed by many "an illegitimate
meeting." [1]

Although Washington presided over, and was the
most powerful influence in, the Constitutional Convention, Marshall allots only one short paragraph
to that fact. [2] He enumerates the elements that
prepared to resist the Constitution; and brings out
clearly the essential fact that the proposed government of the Nation was, by those who opposed it,
considered to be "foreign." He condenses into less
than two pages his narrative of the conflict over
ratification, and almost half of these few lines is devoted to comment upon "The Federalist."

Marshall writes not one line or word of Washington's power and activities at this critical moment.
He merely observes, concerning ratification, that
"the intrinsic merits of the instrument would not
have secured" the adoption of the Constitution, and
that even in some of the States that accepted it "a
majority of the people were in the opposition." [3]

He tells of the pressure on Washington to accept
the Presidency. To these appeals and Washington's
replies, he actually gives ten times more space than
he takes to describe the formation, submission, and
ratification of the Constitution itself. [4] After briefly
telling of Washington's election to the Presidency,
Marshall employs twenty pages in describing his
journey to New York and his inauguration.

Then, with quick, bold strokes, he lays the final

[1] Marshall, v, 105. Marshall's account of the causes and objects of
Shays's Rebellion is given wholly from the ultra-conservative view
of that important event. (*Ib.* 123.)

[2] *Ib.* 128–29.   [3] *Ib.* 132.   [4] *Ib.* 133–50.

color on his picture of the state of the country before the new government was established, and dark-
ens the tints of his portrayal of those who were
opposing the Constitution and were still its enemies.
In swift contrast he paints the beginnings of better
times, produced by the establishment of the new
National Government: "The new course of thinking
which had been inspired by the adoption of a constitution that was understood to prohibit all laws
impairing the obligation of contracts, had in a great
measure restored that confidence which is essential
to the internal prosperity of nations." [1]

He sets out adequately the debates over the first
laws passed by Congress,[2] and is generous in his
description of the characters and careers of both
Jefferson and Hamilton when they accepted places
in Washington's first Cabinet.[3] He joyfully quotes
Washington's second speech to Congress, in which
he declares that "to be prepared for war is one of
the most effectual means of preserving peace"; and
in which the people are adjured "to discriminate the
spirit of liberty from that of licentiousness." [4]

An analysis of Hamilton's First Report on the

[1] Marshall, v, 178–79. Thus Marshall, writing in 1806, states one
of the central principles of the Constitution as he interpreted it from
the Bench years later in three of the most important of American
judicial opinions — Fletcher vs. Peck, Sturgis vs. Crowninshield, and
the Dartmouth College case. (See infra, chap. x; also vol. iv, chaps.
iv and v, of this work.)

[2] Marshall, v, 198–210.

[3] Ib. 210–13. At this point Marshall is conspicuously, almost osten-
tatiously impartial, as between Jefferson and Hamilton. His description of the great radical is in terms of praise, almost laudation; the
same is true of his analysis of Hamilton's work and character. But
he gives free play to his admiration of John Adams. (Ib. 219–20.)

[4] Ib. 230–32.

Public Credit follows. The measures flowing from it "originated the first regular and systematic opposition to the principles on which the affairs of the union were administered." [1] In condensing the momentous debate over the establishment of the American financial system, Marshall gives an excellent summary of the arguments on both sides of that controversy. He states those of the Nationalists, however, more fully than the arguments of those who opposed Hamilton's plan. [2]

While attributing to Hamilton's financial measures most of the credit for improved conditions, Marshall frankly admits that other causes contributed to the new-found prosperity: By "progressive industry, . . the influence of the constitution on habits of thinking and acting," and especially by "depriving the states of the power to impair the obligation of contracts, or to make any thing but gold and silver a tender in payment of debts, the conviction was impressed on that portion of society which had looked to the government for relief from embarrassment, that personal exertions alone could free them from difficulties; and an increased degree of industry and economy was the natural consequence." [3]

Perhaps the most colorful pages of Marshall's entire work are those in which he describes the effect of the French Revolution on America, and the popular hostility to Washington's Proclamation of Neutrality [4]

---

[1] Marshall, v, 241.   [2] *Ib.* 243–58.   [3] *Ib.* 271.

[4] "That system to which the American government afterwards inflexibly adhered, and to which much of the national prosperity is to be ascribed." (*Ib.* 408.)

and to the treaty with Great Britain negotiated by John Jay.[1]

In his treatment of these subjects he reveals some of the sources of his distrust of the people. The rupture between the United States and the French Republic is summarized most inadequately. The greatest of Washington's state papers, the immortal "Farewell Address,"[2] is reproduced in full. The account of the X. Y. Z. mission is provokingly incomplete; that of American preparations for war with France is less disappointing. Washington's illness and death are described with feeling, though in stilted language; and Marshall closes his literary labors with the conventional analysis of Washington's character which the world has since accepted.[3]

Marshall's fifth volume was received with delight by the disgruntled Federalist leaders. A letter of Chancellor James Kent is typical of their comments. "I have just finished . . the last Vol. of Washington's Life and it is worth all the rest. It is an excellent History of the Government and Parties in this country from Vol. 3 to the death of the General."[4]

Although it had appeared too late to do them any harm at the election of 1804, the Republicans and Jefferson felt outraged by Marshall's history of the foundation period of the Government. Jefferson said nothing for a time, but the matter was seldom out of his thoughts. Barlow, it seems, had been laggard in writing a history from the Republican point of view, as Jefferson had urged him to do.

[1] See vol. II, chaps. I to IV, of this work.
[2] Marshall, v, 685–709.   [3] *Ib.* 773.
[4] James Kent to Moss Kent, July 14, 1807, Kent MSS. Lib. Cong.

Three years had passed since the request had been made, and Barlow was leaving for Paris upon his diplomatic mission. Jefferson writes his congratulations, "yet . . not unmixed with regret. What is to become of our past revolutionary history? Of the antidotes of truth to the misrepresentations of Marshall?" [1]

Time did not lessen Jefferson's bitterness: "Marshall has written libels on one side," [2] he writes Adams, with whom a correspondence is opening, the approach of old age having begun to restore good relations between these former enemies. Jefferson's mind dwells on Marshall's work with increasing anxiety: "On the subject of the history of the American Revolution . . who can write it?" he asks. He speaks of Botta's "History," [3] criticizing its defects; but he concludes that "the work is nevertheless a good one, more judicious, more chaste, more classical, and more true than the party diatribe of Marshall. Its greatest fault is in having taken too much from him." [4]

Marshall's "party diatribe" clung like a burr in Jefferson's mind and increased his irritation with the passing of the years. Fourteen years after Marshall's last volume appeared, Justice William Johnson of the Supreme Court published an account of the

---

[1] Jefferson to Barlow, April 16, 1811, *Works:* Ford, xi, 205.

[2] Jefferson to Adams, June 15, 1813, *ib.* 296.

[3] Botta: *History of the War of the Independence of the United States of America.* This work, published in Italian in 1809, was not translated into English until 1820; but in 1812–13 a French edition was brought out, and that is probably the one Jefferson had read.

[4] Jefferson to Adams, Aug. 10, 1815, *Works:* Ford, xi, 485.

period [1] covered by Marshall's work, and it was severely criticized in the *North American Review.* Jefferson cheers the despondent author and praises his "inestimable" history: "Let me . . implore you, dear Sir, to finish your history of parties. . . We have been too careless of our future reputation, while our tories will omit nothing to place us in the wrong." For example, Marshall's "Washington," that "five-volumed libel, . . represents us as struggling for office, and not at all to prevent our government from being administered into a monarchy." [2]

In his long introduction to the "Anas," Jefferson explains that he would not have thought many of his notes "worth preserving but for their testimony against the only history of that period which pretends to have been compiled from authentic and unpublished documents." Had Washington himself written a narrative of his times from the materials he possessed, it would, of course, have been truthful: "But the party feeling of his biographer, to whom after his death the collection was confided, has culled from it a composition as different from what Genl. Washington would have offered, as was the candor of the two characters during the period of the war.

"The partiality of this pen is displayed in lavishments of praise on certain military characters, who had done nothing military, but who afterwards, &

---

[1] Johnson: *Sketches of the Life and Correspondence of General Nathanael Greene.* This biography was even a greater failure than Marshall's *Washington.* During this period literary ventures by judges seem to have been doomed.

[2] Jefferson to Johnson, March 4, 1823, *Works:* Ford, XII, 277–78.

before he wrote, had become heroes in party, altho' not in war; and in his reserve on the merits of
others, who rendered signal services indeed, but did
not earn his praise by apostatising in peace from the
republican principles for which they had fought in
war."

Marshall's frigidity toward liberty "shews itself
too," Jefferson continues, "in the cold indifference
with which a struggle for the most animating of
human objects is narrated. No act of heroism ever
kindles in the mind of this writer a single aspiration
in favor of the holy cause which inspired the bosom,
& nerved the arm of the patriot warrior. No gloom
of events, no lowering of prospects ever excites a
fear for the issue of a contest which was to change
the condition of man over the civilized globe.

" The sufferings inflicted on endeavors to vindicate
the rights of humanity are related with all the frigid
insensibility with which a monk would have contemplated the victims of an *auto da fé*. Let no man
believe that Gen. Washington ever intended that
his papers should be used for the suicide of the cause,
for which he had lived, and for which there never
was a moment in which he would not have died."

Marshall's "abuse of these materials," Jefferson
charges, "is chiefly however manifested in the history of the period immediately following the establishment of the present constitution; and nearly
with that my memorandums [the "Anas"] begin.
Were a reader of this period to form his idea of it
from this history alone, he would suppose the republican party (who were in truth endeavoring to

keep the government within the line of the Constitution, and prevent it's being monarchised in practice) were a mere set of grumblers, and disorganisers, satisfied with no government, without fixed principles of any, and, like a British parliamentary opposition, gaping after loaves and fishes, and ready to change principles, as well as position, at any time, with their adversaries." [1]

Jefferson denounces Hamilton and his followers as "monarchists," "corruptionists," and other favorite Jeffersonian epithets, and Marshall is again assailed: "The horrors of the French revolution, then raging, aided them mainly, and using that as a raw head and bloody bones they were enabled by their stratagems of X. Y. Z. in which this historian was a leading mountebank, their tales of tub-plots, Ocean massacres, bloody buoys, and pulpit lyings, and slanderings, and maniacal ravings of their Gardiners, their Osgoods and Parishes, to spread alarm into all but the firmest breasts." [2]

Criticisms of Marshall's "Life of Washington" were not, however, confined to Jefferson and the Republicans. Plumer thought the plan of the work "preposterous." [3] The Reverend Samuel Cooper Thatcher of Boston reviewed the biography through three numbers of the *Monthly Anthology*.[4] "Every

[1] *Works:* Ford, I, 165–67. [2] *Ib.* 181–82.
[3] Plumer, March 11, 1808, "Diary," Plumer MSS. Lib. Cong.
[4] May, June, and August numbers, 1808, *Monthly Anthology and Boston Review*, v, 259, 322, 434. It appears from the minutes of the Anthology Society, publishers of this periodical, that they had a hard time in finding a person willing to review Marshall's five volumes. Three persons were asked to write the critique and declined. Finally, Mr. Thatcher reluctantly agreed to do the work.

reader is surprized to find," writes Mr. Thatcher, "the history of North America, instead of the life of an individual. . . He [Washington] is always presented . . in the pomp of the military or civil costume, and never in the ease and undress of private life." However, he considers Marshall's fifth volume excellent. "We have not heard of a single denial of his fidelity. . . In this respect . . his work [is] *unique* in the annals of political history."

Thatcher concludes that Marshall's just and balanced treatment of his subject is not due to a care for his own reputation: "We are all so full of agitation and effervescence on political topicks, that a man, who keeps his temper, can hardly gain a hearing." Indeed, he complains of Marshall's fairness: he writes as a spectator, instead of as "one, who has himself descended into the arena . . and is yet red with the wounds which he gave, and smarting with those which his enemies inflicted in return"; but the reviewer charges that these volumes are full of "barbarisms" and "grammatical impurities," "newspaper slang," and "unmeaning verbiage."

The Reverend Timothy Flint thought that Marshall's work displayed more intellect and labor than "eloquence and interest."[1] George Bancroft, reviewing Sparks's "Washington," declared that "all that is contained in Marshall is meagre and incomplete in comparison."[2] Even the British critics were not so harsh as the *New York Evening Post*, which pronounced the judgment that if the biography "bears

---

[1] Flint, in London *Athenæum* for 1835, 803.
[2] *North American Review*, XLVI, 483.

any traces of its author's uncommon powers of
mind, it is in the depths of dulness which he ex-
plored." [1]

The British critics were, of course, unsparing.
The *Edinburgh Review* called Marshall's work "un-
pardonably deficient in all that constitutes the soul
and charm of biography. . . We look in vain,
through these stiff and countless pages, for any
sketch or anecdote that might fix a distinguishing
feature of private character in the memory. . . What
seemed to pass with him for dignity, will, by his
reader, be pronounced dullness and frigidity." [2]
Blackwood's Magazine asserted that Marshall's
"Life of Washington" was "a great, heavy book. . .
One gets tired and sick of the very name of Washington before he gets half through these . . prodigious . . octavos." [3]

Marshall was somewhat compensated for the criticisms of his work by an event which soon followed
the publication of his last volume. On August 29,
1809, he was elected a corresponding member of
the Massachusetts Historical Society. In a singu-
larly graceful letter to John Eliot, corresponding
secretary of the Society at that time, Marshall ex-
presses his thanks and appreciation. [4]

As long as he lived, Marshall worried over his
biography of Washington. When anybody praised it,

[1] *New York Evening Post*, as quoted in Allibone: *Dictionary of English Literature and British and American Authors*, II, 1227.

[2] *Edinburgh Review*, Oct. 1808, as quoted in Randall, II, footnote
to 40.

[3] *Blackwood's Edinburgh Magazine*, XVII, 179.

[4] Marshall to Eliot, Sept. 20, 1809, MSS. of the Mass. Hist. Soc.

he was as appreciative as a child. In 1827, Archibald D. Murphey eulogized Marshall's volumes in an oration, a copy of which he sent to the Chief Justice, who thanks Murphey, and adds: "That work was hurried into a world with too much precipitation, but I have lately given it a careful examination and correction. Should another edition appear, it will be less fatiguing, and more worthy of the character which the biographer of Washington ought to sustain." [1]

Toilsomely he kept at his self-imposed task of revision. In 1816, Bushrod Washington wrote Wayne to send Marshall "the last three volumes in sheets (the two first he has) that he may devote this winter to their correction." [2]

When, five years later, the Chief Justice learned that Wayne was actually considering the risk of bringing out a new edition, Marshall's delight was unbounded. "It is one of the most desirable objects I have in this life to publish a corrected edition of that work. I would not on any terms, could I prevent it, consent that one other set of the first edition should be published." [3]

Finally, in 1832, the revised biography was published. Marshall clung to the first volume, which was issued separately under the title "History of the American Colonies." The remaining four volumes were, seemingly, reduced to two; but they were so closely printed and in such comparatively small

[1] Marshall to Murphey, Oct. 6, 1827, *Papers of Archibald D. Murphey:* Hoyt, i, 365–66.

[2] Washington to Wayne, Nov. 26, 1816, Dreer MSS. *loc. cit.*

[3] Marshall to Washington, Dec. 27, 1821, MS.

type that the real condensation was far less than it appeared to be. The work was greatly improved, however, and is to this day the fullest and most trustworthy treatment of that period, from the conservative viewpoint.[1]

Fortunately for Marshall, the work required of him on the Bench gave him ample leisure to devote to his literary venture. During the years he consumed in writing his "Life of Washington" he wrote fifty-six opinions in cases decided in the Circuit Court at Richmond, and in twenty-seven cases determined by the Supreme Court. Only four of them[2] are of more than casual interest, and but three of them[3] are of any historical consequence. All the others deal with commercial law, practice, rules of evidence, and other familiar legal questions. In only one case, that of Marbury *vs.* Madison, was he called upon to deliver an opinion that affected the institutions and development of the Nation.

[1] So popular did this second edition become that, three years after Marshall's death, a little volume, *The Life of Washington*, was published for school-children. The publisher, James Crissy of Philadelphia, states that this small volume is "printed from the author's own manuscript," thus intimating that Marshall had prepared it. (See Marshall, school ed.)

[2] Talbot *vs.* Seeman, United States *vs.* Schooner Peggy, Marbury *vs.* Madison, and Little *vs.* Barreme.

[3] The first three in above note.

CHAPTER VI

THE BURR CONSPIRACY

My views are such as every man of honor and every good citizen must approve. (Aaron Burr.)

His guilt is placed beyond question. (Jefferson.)

I never believed him to be a Fool. But he must be an Idiot or a Lunatic if he has really planned and attempted to execute such a Project as is imputed to him. But if his guilt is as clear as the Noonday Sun, the first Magistrate ought not to have pronounced it so before a Jury had tryed him. (John Adams.)

ON March 2, 1805, not long after the hour of noon, every Senator of the United States was in his seat in the Senate Chamber. All of them were emotionally affected — some were weeping.[1] Aaron Burr had just finished his brief extemporaneous address [2] of farewell. He had spoken with that grave earnestness so characteristic of him.[3] His remarks produced a

[1] "We were all deeply affected, and many shed tears." (Plumer to his wife, March 2, 1805, Plumer, 331; and see *Memoirs, J. Q. A.*: Adams, I, 367.)

"Tears did flow abundantly." (Burr to his daughter, March 13, 1805, Davis, II, 360.)

[2] "There was nothing written or prepared. . . It was the solemnity, the anxiety, the expectation, and the interest which I saw strongly painted in the countenances of the auditors, that inspired whatever was said." (*Ib.* 360.)

[3] The speech, records the *Washington Federalist*, which had been extremely abusive of Burr, "was said to be the most dignified, sublime and impressive that ever was uttered."

"His address . . was delivered with great force and propriety." (Plumer to his wife, March 2, 1805, Plumer, 331.)

"His speech . . was delivered with great dignity. . . It was listened to with the most earnest and universal attention." (*Memoirs, J. Q. A.*: Adams, I, 367.) Burr made a profound impression on John Quincy Adams. "There was not a member present but felt the force of this solemn appeal to his sense of duty." (J. Q. Adams to his father, March 14, 1805, *Writings, J. Q. A.*: Ford, III, 119.)

The franking privilege was given Burr for life, a courtesy never before

curious impression upon the seasoned politicians and statesmen, over whose deliberations he had presided for four years. The explanation is found in Burr's personality quite as much as in the substance of his speech. From the unprecedented scene in the Senate Chamber when the Vice-President closed, a stranger would have judged that this gifted personage held in his hands the certainty of a great and brilliant career. Yet from the moment he left the Capital, Aaron Burr marched steadily toward his doom.

An understanding of the trial of Aaron Burr and of the proceedings against his agents, Bollmann and Swartwout, is impossible without a knowledge of the events that led up to it; while the opinions and rulings of Chief Justice Marshall in those memorable controversies are robbed of their color and much of their meaning when considered apart from the picturesque circumstances that produced them. This chapter, therefore, is an attempt to narrate and condense the facts of the Burr conspiracy in the light of present knowledge of them.

Although in a biography of John Marshall it seems a far cry to give so much space to that episode, the import of the greatest criminal trial in American history is not to be fully grasped without a summary of the events preceding it. Moreover, the fact that in the Burr trial Marshall destroyed the law of "constructive treason" requires that the circumstances of the Burr adventure, as they appeared to Marshall, be here set forth.

extended except to a President of the United States and Mrs. Washington. (See Hillhouse's speech, *Annals*, 10th Cong. 1st Sess. 272.)

A strong, brave man who, until then, had served his country well, Aaron Burr was in desperate plight when on the afternoon of March 2 he walked along the muddy Washington streets toward his lodging. He was a ruined man, financially, politically, and in reputation. Fourteen years of politics had destroyed his once extensive law practice and plunged him hopelessly into debt. The very men whose political victory he had secured had combined to drive him from the Republican Party.

The result of his encounter with Hamilton had been as fatal to his standing with the Federalists, who had but recently fawned upon him, as it was to the physical being of his antagonist. What now followed was as if Aaron Burr had been the predestined victim of some sinister astrology, so utterly did the destruction of his fortunes appear to be the purpose of a malign fate.

His fine ancestry now counted for nothing with the reigning politicians of either party. None of them cared that he came of a family which, on both sides, was among the worthiest in all the country.[1] His superb education went for naught. His brilliant services as one of the youngest Revolutionary officers were no longer considered — his heroism at Quebec, his resourcefulness on Putnam's staff, his valor at Monmouth, his daring and tireless efficiency at West Point and on the Westchester lines, were, to these men, as if no such record had ever been written.

Nor, with those then in power, did Burr's notable

---

[1] His father was the President of Princeton. His maternal grandfather was Jonathan Edwards.

AARON BURR

public services in civil life weigh so much as a feather
in his behalf. They no longer remembered that only
a few years earlier he had been the leader of his
party in the National Senate, and that his appointment to the then critically important post of Minister to France had been urged by the unanimous
caucus of his political associates in Congress. None
of the notable honors that admirers had asserted
to be his due, nor yet his effective work for his party,
were now recalled. The years of provocation [1] which

---

[1] Hamilton's pursuit of Burr was lifelong and increasingly venom-
ous. It seems incredible that a man so transcendently great as Hamilton — easily the foremost creative mind in American statesmanship
— should have succumbed to personal animosities such as he displayed toward John Adams, and toward Aaron Burr.

The rivalry of Hamilton and Burr began as young attorneys at the
New York bar, where Burr was the only lawyer considered the equal
of Hamilton. Hamilton's open hostility, however, first showed itself
when Burr, then but thirty-five years of age, defeated Hamilton's
father-in-law, Philip Schuyler, for the United States Senate. The
very next year Hamilton prevented Burr from being nominated and
elected Governor of New York. Then Burr was seriously considered
for Vice-President, but Hamilton also thwarted this project.

When Burr was in the Senate, the anti-Federalists in Congress unanimously recommended him for the French Mission; and Madison and
Monroe, on behalf of their colleagues, twice formally urged Burr's
appointment. Hamilton used his influence against it, and the appointment was not made. At the expiration of Burr's term in the Senate,
Hamilton saw to it that he should not be chosen again and Hamilton's
father-in-law this time succeeded.

President Adams, in 1798, earnestly desired to appoint Burr to the
office of Brigadier-General under Washington in the provisional army
raised for the expected war with France. Hamilton objected so strenuously that the President was forced to give up his design. (See
Adams to Rush, Aug. 25, 1805, *Old Family Letters*, 77; and same to
same, June 23, 1807, *ib.* 150.)

In the Presidential contest in the House in 1801 (see vol. II, 533–38,
of this work), Burr, notwithstanding his refusal to do anything in his
own behalf (*ib.* 539–47), would probably have been elected instead of
Jefferson, had not Hamilton savagely opposed him. (*Ib.*)

When, in 1804, Burr ran for Governor of New York, Hamilton

had led, in an age of dueling,[1] to a challenge of his remorseless personal, professional, and political enemy were now unconsidered in the hue and cry raised when his shot, instead of that of his foe, proved mortal.

Yet his spirit was not broken. His personal friends stood true; his strange charm was as potent as ever over most of those whom he met face to face; and throughout the country there were thousands who still admired and believed in Aaron Burr. Particularly in the West and in the South the general sentiment was cordial to him; many Western Senators were strongly attached to him; and most of his brother officers of the Revolution who had settled beyond the Alleghanies were his friends.[2] Also, he was still in vigorous middle life, and though delicate of frame and slight of stature, was capable of greater physical exertion than most men of fewer years.

What now should the dethroned political leader do? Events answered that question for him, and,

again attacked him. It was for one of Hamilton's assaults upon him during this campaign that Burr challenged him. (See Parton: *Life and Times of Aaron Burr*, 339 *et seq.*; also Adams: *U.S.* II, 185 *et seq.*; and *Private Journal of Aaron Burr*, reprinted from manuscript in the library of W. K. Bixby, Introduction, iv-vi.) So prevalent was dueling that, but for Hamilton's incalculable services in founding the Nation and the lack of similar constructive work by Burr, the hatred of Burr's political enemies and the fatal result of the duel, there certainly would have been no greater outcry over the encounter than over any of the similar meetings between public men during that period.

[1] Dueling continued for more than half a century. Many of the most eminent of Americans, such as Clay, Randolph, Jackson, and Benton, fought on "the field of honor." In 1820 a resolution against dueling, offered in the Senate by Senator Morrill of New Hampshire, was laid on the table. (*Annals*, 16th Cong. 1st Sess. 630, 636.)

[2] McCaleb: *Aaron Burr Conspiracy*, 19; Parton: *Burr*, 382.

beckoned forward by an untimely ambition, he followed the path that ended amid dramatic scenes in
Richmond, Virginia, where John Marshall presided
over the Circuit Court of the United States.

Although at the time Jefferson had praised what
he called Burr's "honorable and decisive conduct" [1]
during the Presidential contest in the House in February of 1801, he had never forgiven his associate
for having received the votes of the Federalists,
nor for having missed, by the merest chance, election as Chief Magistrate.[2] Notwithstanding that
Burr's course as Vice-President had won the admiration even of enemies,[3] his political fall was decreed
from the moment he cast his vote on the Judiciary
Bill in disregard of the rigid party discipline that
Jefferson and the Republican leaders then exacted.[4]

Even before this, the constantly increasing frigidity of the President toward him, and the refusal of
the Administration to recognize by appointment any
one recommended by him for office in New York,[5]
had made it plain to all that the most Burr could
expect was Jefferson's passive hostility. Under these
circumstances, and soon after his judiciary vote, the
spirited Vice-President committed another impru-

[1] Vol. II, 545, of this work.   [2] Adams: *U.S.* I, 331.
[3] "His official conduct in the Senate . . has fully met my approba-
tion," testifies the super-critical Plumer in a letter to his wife March 2,
1805. (Plumer, 331.)
[4] "Burr is completely an insulated man." (Sedgwick to King, Feb.
20, 1802, King, IV, 74.)
"Burr has lost ground very much with Jefferson's sect during the
present session of Congress... He has been not a little abused . . in the
democratic prints." (Troup to King, April 9, 1802, King, IV, 103.)
Also see *supra*, chap. II; Adams: *U.S.* I, 280; and Parton: *Burr*, 309.
[5] Adams: *U.S.* I, 230–33; Channing: *Jeff. System*, 17–19.

dence. He attended a banquet given by the Federalists in honor of Washington's birthday. There he proposed this impolitic toast: "To the union of all honest men." Everybody considered this a blow at Jefferson. It was even more offensive to the Administration than his judiciary vote had been.[1]

From that moment all those peculiar weapons which politicians so well know how to use for the ruin of an opponent were employed for the destruction of Aaron Burr. Moreover, Jefferson had decided not only that Burr should not again be Vice-President, but that his bitterest enemy from his own State, George Clinton, should be the Republican candidate for that office; and, in view of Burr's strength and resourcefulness, this made necessary the latter's political annihilation.[2] "Never in the history of the United States did so powerful a combination of rival politicians unite to break down a single man as that which arrayed itself against Burr."[3]

Nevertheless, Burr, who "was not a vindictive man,"[4] did not retaliate for a long time.[5] But at last

[1] "Burr is a gone man; . . Jefferson is really in the dust in point of character, but notwithstanding this, he is looked up to . . as the Gog and Magog of his party." (Troup to King, Dec. 12, 1802, King, IV, 192–93.) See also Adams: *U.S.* I, 282.

[2] Channing: *Jeff. System*, 18–19.   [3] Adams: *U.S.* I, 332.

[4] Adams: *U.S.* II, 185.

"He was accused of this and that, through all of which he maintained a resolute silence. It was a characteristic of his never to refute charges against his name. . . It is not shown that Burr ever lamented or grieved over the course of things, however severely and painfully it pressed upon him." (McCaleb, 19.) See also Parton: *Burr*, 336.

[5] "Burr . . is acting a little and skulking part. Although Jefferson hates him as much as one demagogue can possibly hate another who is aiming to rival him, yet Burr does not come forward in an open and manly way agt. him. . . Burr is ruined in politics as well as in fortune." (Troup to King, Aug. 24, 1802, King, IV, 160.)

to retrieve himself,[1] he determined to appeal to the
people — at whose hands he had never suffered defeat — and, in 1804, he became a candidate for the
office of Governor of New York. The New York
Federalists, now reduced to a little more than a
strong faction, wished to support him, and were
urged to do so by many Federalist leaders of other
States. Undoubtedly Burr would have been elected
but for the attacks of Hamilton.

At this period the idea of secession was stirring in
the minds of the New England Federalist leaders.
Such men as Timothy Pickering, Roger Griswold,
Uriah Tracy, James Hillhouse, had even avowed
separation from the Union to be desirable and certain; and talk of it was general.[2] All these men were
warm and insistent in their support of Burr for
Governor, and at least two of them, Pickering and
Griswold, had a conference with him in New York
while the campaign was in progress.

Plumer notes in his diary that during the winter
of 1804, at a dinner given in Washington attended
by himself, Pickering, Hillhouse, Burr, and other
public men, Hillhouse "unequivocally declared that
. . the United States would soon form two distinct
and separate governments."[3] More than nine
months before, certain of the most distinguished
New England Federalists had gone to the extreme
length of laying their object of national dismemberment before the British Minister, Anthony Merry,

[1] Davis, II, 89 *et seq.*; Adams: *U.S.* I, 332–33; McCaleb, 20; Parton:
Burr, 327 *et seq.*
[2] See *supra,* 150–52, and vol. IV, chap. I, of this work.
[3] Plumer, 295.

and had asked and received his promise to aid them
in their project of secession.[1]

There was nothing new in the idea of dismembering the Union. Indeed, no one subject was more
familiar to all parts of the country. Since before the
adoption of the Constitution, it had been rife in the
settlements west of the Alleghanies.[2] The very year
the National Government was organized under the
Constitution, the settlers beyond the Alleghanies
were much inclined to withdraw from the Union because the Mississippi River had not been secured to
them.[3] For many years this disunion sentiment grew
in strength. When, however, the Louisiana Purchase
gave the pioneers on the Ohio and the Mississippi a

[1] It appears that some of the New England Federalists urged upon
the British Minister the rejection of the articles of the Boundary
Treaty in retaliation for the Senate's striking out one article of that
Convention. They did this, records the British Minister, because, as
they urged, such action by the British Government "would prove to be
a great exciting cause to them [the New England Secessionists] to go
forward rapidly in the steps which they have already commenced toward a separation from the Southern part of the Union.

"The [Federalist] members of the Senate," continues Merry, "have
availed themselves of the opportunity of their being collected here to
hold private meetings on this subject, and . . their plans and calcula-
tions respecting the event have been long seriously resolved. . . . They
naturally look forward to Great Britain for support and assistance
whenever the occasion shall arrive." (Merry to Hawkesbury, March
1, 1804, as quoted in Adams: *U.S.* II, 392.)

[2] As early as 1784, Washington declared that he feared the effect on
the Western people "if the Spaniards on their right, and Great Britain
on their left, instead of throwing impediments in their way as they
now do, should hold out lures for their trade and alliance. . . The
western settlers (I speak now from my own observations) stand as it
were, upon a pivot. The touch of a feather would turn them any way.
. . It is by the cement of interest alone we can be held together."
(Washington to the Governor of Virginia, 1784, as quoted in Marshall, v, 15–16.)

[3] Marshall, v, 179.

free water-way to the Gulf and the markets of the world, the Western secessionist tendency disappeared. But after the happy accident that bestowed upon us most of the great West as well as the mouth of the Mississippi, there was in the Eastern States a widely accepted opinion that this very fact made necessary the partitioning of the Republic.

Even Jefferson, as late as 1803, did not think that outcome unlikely, and he was prepared to accept it with his blessing: "If they see their interest in separation, why should we take sides with our Atlantic rather than our Mississippi descendants? It is the elder and the younger brother differing. God bless them both, and keep them in union, if it be for their good, but separate them, if it be better." [1]

Neither Spain nor Great Britain had ever given over the hope of dividing the young Republic and of acquiring for themselves portions of its territory. The Spanish especially had been active and unceasing in their intrigues to this end, their efforts being directed, of course, to the acquisition of the lands adjacent to them and bordering on the Mississippi and the Ohio.[2] In this work more than one American was in their pay. Chief of these Spanish agents was James Wilkinson, who had been a pensioner of Spain from 1787,[3] and so continued until at least 1807, the bribe money coming into his hands for several years

[1] Jefferson to Breckenridge, Aug. 12, 1803, *Works:* Ford, x, footnotes to 5–6.

[2] See Shepherd in *Am. Hist. Rev.* viii, 501 *et seq.*; also *ib.* ix, 748 *et seq.*

[3] Clark: *Proofs of the Corruption of Gen. James Wilkinson*, 11–12, 16, 18–24, and documents therein referred to and printed in the appendix to Clark's volume.

after he had been placed in command of the armies of the United States.[1]

None of these plots influenced the pioneers to wish to become Spanish subjects; the most that they ever desired, even at the height of their dissatisfaction with the American Government, was independence from what they felt to be the domination of the East. In 1796 this feeling reached its climax in the Kentucky secession movement, one of its most active leaders being Wilkinson, who declared his purpose of becoming "the Washington of the West." [2]

By 1805, however, the allegiance of the pioneers to the Nation was as firm as that of any other part of the Republic. They had become exasperated to the point of violence against Spanish officials, Spanish soldiers, and the Spanish Government. They regarded the Spanish provinces of the Floridas and of Mexico as mere satrapies of a hated foreign autocracy; and this indeed was the case. Everywhere west of the Alleghanies the feeling was universal

---

[1] "Wilkinson is entirely devoted to us. He enjoys a considerable pension from the King." (Casa Yrujo, Spanish Minister, to Cevallos, Jan. 28, 1807, as quoted in Adams: *U.S.* III, 342.) And see affidavits of Mercier and Derbigny, *Blennerhassett Papers:* Safford, footnotes to 429, 432.

"He [Wilkinson] had acted conformably as suited the true interests of Spain, and so I assured him for his satisfaction." (Folch, Spanish Governor of Florida, to the Governor-General of Cuba, June 25, 1807, as quoted by Cox in *Am. Hist. Rev.* x, 839.)

[2] Parton: *Burr*, 383; see also McCaleb, 4-9.

It should be borne in mind that this was the same Wilkinson who took so unworthy a part in the "Conway Cabal" against Washington during the Revolution. (See vol. I, 121-23, of this work.)

For further treatment of the Spanish intrigue, see Cox in *Am. Hist. Rev.* XIX, 794-812; also Cox in *Southwestern Historical Quarterly*, XVII, 140-87.

that these lands on the south and southwest, held in subjection by an ancient despotism, should be "revolutionized" and "liberated"; and this feeling was shared by great numbers of people of the Eastern States.

Moreover, that spirit of expansion — of taking and occupying the unused and misused lands upon our borders — which has been so marked through American history, was then burning fiercely in every Western breast. The depredations of the Spaniards had finally lashed almost to a frenzy the resentment which had for years been increasing in the States bordering upon the Mississippi. All were anxious to descend with fire and sword upon the offending Spaniards.

Indeed, all over the Nation the conviction was strong that war with Spain was inevitable. Even the ultra-pacific Jefferson was driven to this conclusion; and, in less than ten months after Aaron Burr ceased to be Vice-President, and while he was making his first journey through the West and Southwest, the President, in two Messages to Congress, scathingly arraigned Spanish misdeeds and all but avowed that a state of war actually existed.[1]

Such, in broad outline, was the general state of things when Aaron Burr, his political and personal fortunes wrecked, cast about for a place to go and for work to do. He could not return to his practice in New York; there his enemies were in absolute control and he was under indictment for having chal-

[1] Annual Message, Dec. 3, 1805, and Special Message, Dec. 6, 1805, Richardson, I, 384–85, 388–89.

lenged Hamilton. The coroner's jury also returned
an inquest of murder against Burr and two of his
friends, and warrants for their arrest were issued. In
New Jersey, too, an indictment for murder hung
over him.[1]

Only in the fresh and undeveloped West did a new
life and a new career seem possible. Many projects
filled his mind — everything was possible in that inviting region beyond the mountains. He thought of
forming a company to dig a canal around the falls
of the Ohio and to build a bridge over that river,
connecting Louisville with the Indiana shore. He
considered settling lands in the vast dominions beyond the Mississippi which the Nation had newly
acquired from Spain. A return to public life as
Representative in Congress from Tennessee passed
through his mind.

But one plan in particular fitted the situation
which the apparently certain war with Spain created. Nearly ten years earlier,[2] Hamilton had
conceived the idea of the conquest of the Spanish
possessions adjacent to us, and he had sought to
enlist the Government in support of the project of
Miranda to revolutionize Venezuela.[3] Aaron Burr
had proposed the invasion and capture of the
Floridas, Louisiana, and Mexico two years before

[1] See *Memoirs, J. Q. A.*: Adams, I, 314–15.

Burr wrote: "In New-York I am to be disfranchised, and in New-
Jersey hanged" but "you will not . . conclude that I have become
disposed to submit tamely to the machinations of a banditti." Burr
to his son-in-law, March 22, 1805, Davis, II, 365.

[2] 1797–98.

[3] Lodge: *Alexander Hamilton*, 212–15; and see Turner in *Am. Hist.
Rev.* x, 276.

Hamilton embraced the project,[1] and the desire to carry out the plan continued strong within him. Circumstances seemed to make the accomplishment of it feasible. At all events, a journey through the West would enlighten him, as well as make clearer the practicability of his other schemes.

Now occurred the most unfortunate and disgraceful incident of Burr's life. In order to get money for his Mexican adventure, Burr played upon the British Minister's hostile feelings toward America and, in doing so, used downright falsehood. Although it was unknown at the time and not out of keeping with the unwritten rules of the game called diplomacy as then played, and although it had no effect upon the thrilling events that brought Burr before Marshall, so inextricably has this shameful circumstance been woven into the story of the Burr conspiracy, that mention of it must be made. It was the first thoroughly dishonorable act of Burr's tempestuous career.[2]

[1] Davis, II, 376–79.

[2] Only one previous incident in Burr's public life can even be faintly criticized from the viewpoint of honesty. In 1799 there were in New York City but two banking institutions, and both were controlled by Federalists. These banks aided business men of the Federalist Party and refused accommodation to Republican business men. The Federalists controlled the Legislature and no State charter for another bank in New York could be had.

Burr, as a member of the State Senate, secured from the Legislature a charter for the Manhattan Company to supply pure water to the city; but this charter authorized the use by the company of its surplus capital in any lawful way it pleased. Thus was established a new bank where Republican business men could get loans. Burr, in committee, frankly declared that the surplus was to establish a bank, and Governor Jay signed the bill. Although the whole project appears to have been open and aboveboard as far as Burr was concerned, yet when the bank began business, a violent attack was made on him. (Parton: *Burr*, 237–40.)

Five months after Pickering, Griswold, and other New England Federalists had approached Anthony Merry with their plan to divide the Union, Burr prepared to follow their example. He first sounded that diplomat through a British officer, one Colonel Charles Williamson. The object of the New England Senators and Representatives had been to separate their own and other Northern States from the Union; the proposition that Williamson now made to the British Minister was that Burr might do the same thing for the Western States.[1] It was well known that the break-up of the Republic was expected and hoped for by the British Government, as well as by the Spaniards, and Williamson was not surprised when he found Merry as favorably disposed toward a scheme for separation of the States beyond the Alleghanies as he had been hospitable to the plan for the secession of New England.

Of the results of this conference Burr was advised; and when he had finished his preparations for his journey down the Ohio, he personally called upon Merry. This time a part of his real purpose was revealed; it was to secure funds.[2] Burr asked that half a million dollars be supplied him[3] for the revolutionizing of the Western States, but he did not tell of his dream about Mexico, for the realization of which the money was probably to be employed. In short, Burr lied; and in order to persuade Merry to

[1] Merry to Harrowby, Aug. 6, 1804, as quoted in Adams: *U.S.* II, 395.

[2] McCaleb, viii–ix, 20–23.

[3] Merry to Harrowby (No. 15), "most secret," March 29, 1805, as quoted in Adams: *U.S.* II, 403.

secure for him financial aid he proposed to commit treason. Henry Adams declares that, so far as the proposal of treason was concerned, there was no difference between the moral delinquency of Pickering, Griswold, Hillhouse, and other Federalists and that of Aaron Burr.[1]

The eager and credulous British diplomat promised to do his best and sent Colonel Williamson on a special mission to London to induce Pitt's Ministry to make the investment.[2] It should be repeated that Burr's consultations with the shallow and easily deceived Merry were not known at the time. Indeed, they never were fully revealed until more than three quarters of a century afterward.[3] Moreover, it has been demonstrated that they had little or no bearing upon the adventure which Burr finally tried to carry out.[4] He was, as has been said, audaciously and dishonestly playing upon Merry's well-known hostility to this country in order to extract money from the British Treasury.[5] This attempt and the later one upon the Spanish Minister, who was equally antagonistic to the United States, were revolting exhibitions of that base cunning and du-

[1] Adams: *U.S.* II, 394.   [2] Davis, II, 381; also Parton: *Burr*, 412.

[3] Henry Adams, in his researches in the British and Spanish archives, discovered and for the first time made public, in 1890, the dispatches of the British, Spanish, and French Ministers to their Governments. (See Adams: *U.S.* III, chaps. XIII and XIV.)

[4] Professor Walter Flavius McCaleb has exploded the myth as to Burr's treasonable purposes, which hitherto has been accepted as history. His book, the *Aaron Burr Conspiracy*, may be said to be the last word on the subject. The lines which Professor McCaleb has therein so firmly established have been followed in this chapter.

[5] Pitt died and Burr did not get any money from the British. (See Davis, II, 381.)

plicity which, at that period, formed so large a part of secret international intrigue.[1]

On April 10, 1805, Burr left Philadelphia on horseback for Pittsburgh, where he arrived after a nineteen days' journey. Before starting he had talked over his plans with several friends, among them former Senator Jonathan Dayton of New Jersey, who thereafter was a partner and fellow "conspirator."[2]

Another man with whom Burr had conferred was General James Wilkinson. Burr expected to meet him at Pittsburgh, but the General was delayed and the meeting was deferred. Wilkinson had just been appointed Governor of Upper Louisiana — one of the favors granted Burr during the Chase impeachment — and was the intimate associate of the fallen politician in his Mexican plan until, in a welter of falsehood and corruption, he betrayed him. Indeed, it was Wilkinson who, during the winter of 1804–05, when Burr was considering his future, proposed to him the invasion of Mexico and thus gave new life to Burr's old but never abandoned hope.[3]

On May 2, Burr started down the Ohio. When he

[1] "Burr's intrigue with Merry and Casa Yrujo was but a consummate piece of imposture." (McCaleb, viii.)

[2] Up to this time Dayton had had an honorable career. He had been a gallant officer of the Revolution; a member of the New Jersey Legislature for several years and finally Speaker of the House; a delegate to the Constitutional Convention; a Representative in Congress for four terms, during the last two of which he was chosen Speaker of that body; and finally Senator of the United States. He came of a distinguished family, was a graduate of Princeton, and a man of high standing politically and socially.

[3] See Cox in *Am. Hist. Rev.* xix, 801; also in *Southwestern Hist. Quarterly*, xvii, 174.

reached Marietta, Ohio, he was heartily welcomed.
He next stopped at an island owned by Harman
Blennerhassett, who happened to be away. While
inspecting the grounds Burr was invited by Mrs.
Blennerhassett to remain for dinner. Thus did
chance lay the foundations for that acquaintance
which, later, led to a partnership in the enterprise
that was ended so disastrously for both.

At Cincinnati, then a town of some fifteen hundred
inhabitants, the attentions of the leading citizens
were markedly cordial. There Burr was the guest
of John Smith, then a Senator from Ohio, who had
become attached to Burr while the latter was Vice-
President, and who was now one of his associates in
the plans under consideration. At Smith's house he
met Dayton, and with these friends and partners
he held a long conversation on the various schemes
they were developing.[1]

A week later found him at the "unhealthy and in-
considerable village" [2] of Louisville and from there
he traveled by horseback to Frankfort and Lexington. While in Kentucky he conferred with General
John Adair, then a member of the National Senate,

[1] That Burr, Dayton, and others seriously thought of building a
canal around the falls of the Ohio on the Indiana side, is proved by an
act passed by the Legislature of Indiana Territory in August, 1805,
and approved by Governor William Henry Harrison on the 24th of
that month. The act — entitled "An Act to Incorporate the Indiana
Canal Company" — is very elaborate, authorizes a capital of one
million dollars, and names as directors George Rogers Clark, John
Brown, Jonathan Dayton, Aaron Burr, Benjamin Hovey, Davis
Floyd, and six others. (See *Laws of the Indiana Territory, 1801–1806*,
94–108.) The author is indebted to Hon. Merrill Moores, M.C., of
Indianapolis, for the reference to this statute.

[2] Hildreth, v. 597.

who, like Smith and Dayton, had in Washington
formed a strong friendship for Burr, and was his
confidant.[1] Another eminent man with whom he
consulted was John Brown, then a member of the
United States Senate from Kentucky, also an ad-
mirer of Burr.

It would appear that the wanderer was then seriously considering the proposal, previously made by
Matthew Lyon, now a Representative in Congress
from Kentucky, that Burr should try to go to the
National House from Tennessee,[2] for Burr asked and
received from Senator Brown letters to friends in
that State who could help to accomplish that design. But not one word did Burr speak to General
Adair, to Senator Brown, or to any one else of his
purpose to dismember the Nation.

Burr arrived at Nashville at the end of the month.
The popular greeting had grown warmer with each
stage of his journey, and at the Tennessee Capital
it rose to noisy enthusiasm. Andrew Jackson, then
Major-General of the State Militia, was especially
fervent and entertained Burr at his great log house.
A "magnificent parade" was organized in his honor.
From miles around the pioneers thronged into the

---

[1] Adair had been a soldier in the Revolutionary War, an Indian
fighter in the West, a member of the Kentucky Constitutional Convention, Speaker of the House of Representatives of that State, Regis-
trar of the United States Land Office, and was one of the ablest, most
trusted, and best beloved of Kentuckians.

Adair afterward declared that "the intentions of Colonel Burr . .
were to prepare and lead an expedition into Mexico, predicated on a
war" between Spain and the United States; "without a war he knew
he could do nothing." If war did not come he expected to settle the
Washita lands. (Davis, II, 380.)

[2] See McCaleb, 25; Parton: *Burr*, 385–86.

frontier Capital. Flags waved, fifes shrilled, drums rolled, cannon thundered. A great feast was spread and Burr addressed the picturesque gathering.[1] Never in the brightest days of his political success had he been so acclaimed. Jackson, nine years before, when pleading with Congress to admit Tennessee into the Union, had met and liked Burr, who had then advocated statehood for that vigorous and aggressive Southern Territory. Jackson's gratitude for Burr's services to the State in championing its admission,[2] together with his admiration for the man, now ripened into an ardent friendship.

His support of Burr well reflected that of the people among whom the latter now found himself. Accounts of Burr's conduct as presiding officer at the trial of Chase had crept through the wilderness; the frontier newspapers were just printing Burr's farewell speech to the Senate, and descriptions of the effect of it upon the great men in Washington were passing from tongue to tongue. All this gilded the story of Burr's encounter with Hamilton, which, from the beginning, had been applauded by the people of the West and South.

Burr was now in a land of fighting men, where dueling was considered a matter of honor rather than disgrace. He was in a rugged democracy which regarded as a badge of distinction, instead of shame, the killing in fair fight of the man it had been taught to believe to be democracy's greatest foe. Here, said these sturdy frontiersmen, was the captain so long

[1] McCaleb, 26; Parton: *Life of Andrew Jackson*, I, 307–10.
[2] Parton: *Jackson*, I, 309.

sought for, who could lead them in the winning of
Texas and Mexico for America; and this Burr now
declared himself ready to do — a purpose which
added the final influence toward the conquest of the
mind and heart of Andrew Jackson.

Floating down the Cumberland River in a boat
provided by Jackson, Burr encountered nothing but
friendliness and encouragement. At Fort Massac he
was the guest of Wilkinson, with whom he remained
for four days, talking over the Mexican project. Soon
afterward he was on his way down the Mississippi
from St. Louis in a larger boat with colored sails,
manned by six soldiers — all furnished by Wilkinson. After Burr's departure Wilkinson wrote to
Adair, with whom he had served in the Indian
wars, that "we must have a peep at the unknown
world beyond me."

On June 25, 1805, Burr landed at New Orleans,
then the largest city west of the Alleghanies. There
the ovation to the "hero" surpassed even the demonstration at Nashville. Again came dinners, balls,
fêtes, and every form of public and private favor.
So perfervid was the welcome to him that the Sisters
of the largest nunnery in Louisiana invited Burr to
visit their convent, and this he did, under the conduct of the bishop.[1] Wilkinson had given him a
letter of introduction to Daniel Clark, the leading
merchant of the city and the most influential man
in Louisiana. The letter contained this cryptic sentence: "To him [Burr] I refer you for many things

---

[1] Burr to his daughter, May 23, 1805. This letter is delightful. "I
will ask Saint A. to pray for thee too. I believe much in the efficacy
of her prayers." (Davis, II, 372.)

improper to letter, and which he will not say to any other." [1]

The notables of the city were eager to befriend Burr and to enter into his plans. Among them were John Watkins, Mayor of New Orleans, and James Workman, Judge of the Court of Orleans County. These men were also the leading members of the Mexican Association, a body of three hundred Americans devoted to effecting the "liberation" of Mexico — a design in which they accurately expressed the general sentiment of Louisiana. The invasion of Mexico had become Burr's overmastering purpose, and it gathered strength the farther he journeyed among the people of the West and South. To effect it, definite plans were now made. [2]

The Catholic Bishop of New Orleans heartily approved Burr's project, and appointed three Jesuits to act as agents for the revolutionists in Mexico. The Superior of the Ursuline Nuns lent the aid of her order. Burr's vision of Spanish conquest seemed likely of realization. [3] The invasion of Mexico was in every heart, on every tongue. All that was yet lacking to make it certain was war between Spain and the United States, and every Western or Southern man believed that war was at hand.

Late in July, Burr, with justifiably high hope, left New Orleans by the overland route for Nashville, riding on horses supplied by Daniel Clark. Everywhere he found the pioneers eager for hostilities. At Natchez the people were demonstrative. By August 6, Burr was again with Andrew Jackson, having

[1] McCaleb, 27; Parton: *Burr*, 393.   [2] McCaleb, 29.   [3] *Ib.*

ridden over Indian trails four hundred and fifty
miles through the swampy wilderness.[1]

The citizens of Nashville surpassed even their
first welcome. At the largest public dinner ever
given in the West up to that time, Burr entered the
hall on Jackson's arm and was received with cheers.
Men and women vied with one another in doing him
honor. The news Burr brought from New Orleans of
the headway that was being made regarding the projected descent upon the Spanish possessions, thrilled
Jackson; and his devotion to the man whom all
Westerners and Southerners had now come to look
upon as their leader knew no bounds.[2] For days
Jackson and Burr talked of the war with Spain which
the bellicose Tennessee militia general passionately
desired, and of the invasion of Mexico which Burr
would lead when hostilities began.[3] At Lexington,
at Frankfort, everywhere, Burr was received in similar fashion. While in Kentucky he met Henry Clay,
who at once yielded to his fascination.

But soon strange, dark rumors, starting from
Natchez, were sent flying over the route Burr had
just traveled with such acclaim. They were set on
foot by an American, one Stephen Minor, who was a
paid spy of Spain.[4] Burr, it was said, was about to
raise the standard of revolution in the Western and
Southern States. Daniel Clark wished to advise
Burr of these reports and of the origin of them, but

---

[1] Burr to his daughter, May 23, 1805, Davis, II, 372.

[2] "No one equalled Andrew Jackson in warmth of devotion to
Colonel Burr." (Adams: U.S. III, 221.)

[3] Parton: *Jackson*, I, 311–12; and McCaleb, 81.

[4] McCaleb, 32–33. Minor was probably directed to do this by
Casa Yrujo himself. (See Cox: *West Florida Controversy*, 189.)

did not know where to reach him. So he hastened to write Wilkinson that Burr might be informed of the Spanish canard: "Kentucky, Tennessee, the State of Ohio, . . with part of Georgia and Carolina, are to be bribed with the plunder of the Spanish countries west of us, to separate from the Union." And Clark added: "Amuse Mr. Burr with an account of it." [1]

Wilkinson himself had long contemplated the idea of dismembering the Nation; he had even sounded some of his officers upon that subject.[2] As we have seen, he had been the leader of the secession movement in Kentucky in 1796. But if Burr ever really considered, as a practical matter, the separation of the Western country from the Union, his intimate contact with the people of that region had driven such a scheme from his mind and had renewed and strengthened his long-cherished wish to invade Mexico. For throughout his travels he had heard loud demands for the expulsion of Spanish rule from America; but never, except perhaps at New Orleans, a hint of secession. And if, during his journey, Burr so much as intimated to anybody the dismemberment of the Republic, no evidence of it ever has been produced.[3]

Ignorant of the sinister reports now on their way behind him, Burr reached the little frontier town of St. Louis early in September and again conferred with Wilkinson, assuring him that the whole South

[1] Clark to Wilkinson, Sept. 7, 1805, Wilkinson: *Memoirs of My Own Times*, II, Appendix XXXIII.

[2] Testimony of Major James Bruff, *Annals*, 10th Cong. 1st Sess. 589–609, 616–22.

[3] Except, of course, Wilkinson's story that Burr urged Western revolution, during the conference of these two men at St. Louis.

and West were impatient to attack the Spaniards, and that in a short time an army could be raised to invade Mexico.[1] According to the story which the General told nearly two years afterward, Burr informed him that the South and West were ripe for secession, and that Wilkinson responded that Burr was sadly mistaken because "the Western people . . are bigoted to Jefferson and democracy."[2]

Whatever the truth of this may be, it is certain that the rumors put forth by his fellow Spanish agent had shaken Wilkinson's nerve for proceeding further with the enterprise which he himself had suggested to Burr. Also, as we shall see, the avaricious General had begun to doubt the financial wisdom of giving up his profitable connection with the Spanish Government. At all events, he there and then began to lay plans to desert his associate. Accordingly, he gave Burr a letter of introduction to William Henry Harrison, Governor of Indiana Territory, in which he urged Harrison to have Burr sent to Congress from Indiana, since upon this "perhaps . . the Union may much depend."[3]

Mythical accounts of Burr's doings and intentions had now sprung up in the East. The universally known wish of New England Federalist leaders for a division of the country, the common talk east of the Alleghanies that this was inevitable, the vivid memory of a like sentiment formerly prevailing in Kentucky, and the belief in the seaboard States that it still continued — all rendered probable, to those liv-

---

[1] McCaleb, 34.

[2] Wilkinson's testimony, *Annals*, 10th Cong. 1st Sess. 611.

[3] McCaleb, 35; Parton: *Burr*, 401.

ing in that section, the schemes now attributed to Burr.

Of these tales the Eastern newspapers made sensations. A separate government, they said, was to be set up by Burr in the Western States; the public lands were to be taken over and divided among Burr's followers; bounties, in the form of broad acres, were to be offered as inducements for young men to leave the Atlantic section of the country for the land of promise toward the sunset; Burr's new government was to repudiate its share of the public debt; with the aid of British ships and gold Burr was to conquer Mexico and establish a vast empire by uniting that imperial domain to the revolutionized Western and Southern States.[1] The Western press truthfully denied that any secession sentiment now existed among the pioneers.

The rumors from the South and West met those from the North and East midway; but Burr having departed for Washington, they subsided for the time being. The brushwood, however, had been gathered — to burst into a raging conflagration a year later, when lighted by the torch of Executive authority in the hands of Thomas Jefferson.

During these months the Spanish officials in Mexico and in the Floridas, who had long known of the hostility of American feeling toward them, learned of Burr's plan to seize the Spanish possessions, and magnified the accounts they received of the preparations he was making.[2]

The British Minister in Washington was also in

---

[1] McCaleb, 36–37.   [2] Cox, 190; and McCaleb, 39.

spasms of nervous anxiety.[1] When Burr reached
the Capital he at once called on that slow-witted
diplomat and repeated his overtures. But Pitt had
died; the prospect of British financial assistance had
ended; [2] and Burr sent Dayton to the Spanish Minister with a weird tale [3] in order to induce that diplomat to furnish money.

Almost at the same time the South American
adventurer, Miranda, again arrived in America, his
zeal more fiery than ever, for the "liberation" of
Venezuela. He was welcomed by the Administration, and Secretary of State Madison gave him a
dinner. Jefferson himself invited the revolutionist
to dine at the Executive Mansion. Burr's hopes
were strengthened, since he intended doing in
Mexico precisely what Miranda was setting out to
do in Venezuela.

[1] McCaleb, 38.

[2] Pitt died January 6, 1806. The news reached America late in the
winter and Wilkinson learned of it some time in the spring. This fed
his alarm, first awakened by the rumors set afloat by Spanish agents
of which Clark had advised him. According to Davis and Parton,
Wilkinson's resolve to sacrifice Burr was now taken. (See Davis, II,
381–82; also Parton: *Burr*, 412.)

[3] This was that Burr with his desperadoes would seize the President
and other officers of the National Government, together with the public money, arsenals, and ships. If, thereafter, he could not reconcile
the States to the new arrangement, the bandit chief and his followers
would sail for New Orleans and proclaim the independence of Louisiana.

Professor McCaleb says that this tale was a ruse to throw Casa Yrujo
off his guard as to the now widespread reports in Florida and Texas, as
well as America, of Burr's intended descent upon Mexico. (See Mc-
Caleb, 54–58.) It should be repeated that the proposals of Burr and
Dayton to Merry and Casa Yrujo were not publicly known for many
years afterward.

Wilkinson had coached Dayton and Burr in the art of getting money
by falsehood and intrigue. (*Ib.* 54.)

In February, 1806, Miranda sailed from New York upon his Venezuelan undertaking. His openly avowed purpose of forcibly expelling the Spanish Government from that country had been explained to Jefferson and Madison by the revolutionist personally. Before his departure, the Spanish filibuster wrote to Madison, cautioning him to keep "in the deepest secret" the "important matters" which he (Miranda) had laid before him.[1] The object of his expedition was a matter of public notoriety. In New York, in the full light of day, he had bought arms and provisions and had enlisted men for his enterprise.

Excepting for Burr's failure to secure funds from the British Government, events seemed propitious for the execution of his grand design. He had written to Blennerhassett a polite and suggestive letter, not inviting him, however, to engage in the adventure; [2] the eager Irishman promptly responded, begging to be admitted as a partner in Burr's enterprises, and pledging the services of himself and his friends.[3] Burr, to his surprise, was cordially received by Jefferson at the White House where he had a private conference of two hours with the President.

The West openly demanded war with Spain; the whole country was aroused; in the House, Randolph offered a resolution to declare hostilities; everywhere the President was denounced for weakness and delay.[4] If only Jefferson would act — if only the people's earnest desire for war with Spain were granted —

---

[1] Adams: *U.S.* III, 189–91.   [2] *Blennerhassett Papers:* Safford, 115.
[3] Blennerhassett to Burr, Dec. 21, 1805, *ib.* 118; and see Davis, II, 392.
[4] McCaleb, 50–53.

Burr could go forward.   But the President would
make no hostile move — instead, he proposed to buy
the Floridas. Burr, lacking funds, thought for a moment of abandoning his plans against Mexico, and
actually asked Jefferson for a diplomatic appointment, which was, of course, refused.[1]

The rumor had reached Spain that the Americans
had actually begun war. On the other hand, the
report now came to Washington that the Spaniards
had invaded American soil. The Secretary of War
ordered General Wilkinson to drive the Spaniards
back. The demand for war throughout the country
grew louder. If ever Burr's plan of Mexican conquest was to be carried out, the moment had come
to strike the blow. His confederate, Wilkinson, in
command of the American Army and in direct contact with the Spaniards, had only to act.

The swirl of intrigue continued. Burr tried to get
the support of men disaffected toward the Administration. Among them were Commodore Truxtun,
Commodore Stephen Decatur, and "General"[2]
William Eaton. Truxtun and Decatur were writhing
under that shameful treatment by which each of
these heroes had been separated, in effect removed,
from the Navy. Eaton was cursing the Administration for deserting him in his African exploits, and
even more for refusing to pay several thousand
dollars which he claimed to have expended in his
Barbary transactions.[3]

[1] Plumer, 348; Parton: *Burr*, 403–04.

[2] Eaton assumed this title during his African career. He had no
legal right to it.

[3] Eaton had done good work as American Consul to Algiers, a post

Truxtun and Burr were intimate friends, and the Commodore was fully told of the design to invade Mexico in the event of war with Spain; should that not come to pass, Burr advised Truxtun that he meant to settle lands he had arranged to purchase beyond the Mississippi. He tried to induce Truxtun to join him, suggesting that he would be put in command of a naval force to capture Havana, Vera Cruz, and Cartagena. When Burr "positively" informed him that the President was not a party to his enterprise, Truxtun declined to associate himself with it. Not an intimation did Burr give Truxtun of any purpose hostile to the United States. The two agreed in their contemptuous opinion of Jefferson and his Administration.[1] To Commodore Decatur, Burr talked in similar fashion, using substantially the same language.

But to "General" Eaton, whom he had never be-

to which he was appointed by President Adams. In 1804, Jefferson appointed him United States Naval Agent to the Barbary States. With the approval of the Administration, Eaton undertook to overthrow the reigning Pasha of Tripoli and restore to the throne the Pasha's brother, whom the former had deposed. In executing this project Eaton showed a resourcefulness, persistence, and courage as striking as the means he adopted were bizarre and the adventure itself fantastic. (Allen: *Our Navy and the Barbary Corsairs*, 227 *et seq.*)

Eaton charged that the enterprise failed because the American fleet did not properly coöperate with him, and because Tobias Lear, American Consul-General to Algiers, compromised the dispute with the reigning Bey whom Eaton's nondescript "army" was then heroically fighting. (Eaton to the Secretary of the Navy, Aug. 9, 1805, *Eaton:* Prentiss, 376.)

Full of wrath he returned to the United States, openly denouncing all whom he considered in any way responsible for the African *débâcle*, and demanding payment of large sums which he alleged had been paid by him in advancing American interests in Africa. (*Ib.* 393, 406; also see Allen, 265.)

[1] See Truxtun's testimony, *infra*, 459–60.

fore met, Burr unfolded plans more far-reaching and
bloody, according to the Barbary hero's account of
the revelations.[1] At first Burr had made to Eaton
the same statements he had detailed to Truxtun
and Decatur, with the notable difference that he
had assured Eaton that the proposed expedition was
"under the authority of the general government."
Notwithstanding his familiarity with intrigue, the
suddenly guileless Eaton agreed to lead a division
of the invading army under Wilkinson who, Burr
assured him, would be "Chief in Command."

But after a while Eaton's sleeping perception was
aroused. Becoming as sly as a detective, he resolved
to "draw Burr out," and "listened with seeming
acquiescence" while the villain "unveiled himself"
by confidences which grew ever wilder and more irra-
tional: Burr would establish an empire in Mexico
and divide the Union; he even "meditated overthrowing the present Government" — if he could secure Truxtun, Decatur, and others, he "*would turn
Congress neck and heels out of doors, assassinate the
President, seize the treasury and Navy; and declare
himself the protector of an energetic government.*"

Eaton at last was "shocked" and "dropped the
mask," declaring that the one word, "*Usurper,*"
would destroy" Burr. Thereupon Eaton went to
Jefferson and urged the President to appoint Burr
American Minister to some European government
and thus get him out of the country, declaring that
"*if Burr were not in some way disposed of we should*

---

[1] The talks between Burr and Eaton took place at the house of Sergeant-at-Arms Wheaton, where Burr boarded. (*Annals*, 10th Cong.
1st Sess. 510.)

*within eighteen months have an insurrection if not a
revolution on the waters of the Mississippi.*" The
President was not perturbed — he had too much
confidence in the Western people, he said, "to admit
an *apprehension* of that kind." But of the horrid
details of the murderous and treasonable villain's
plans, never a word said Eaton to Jefferson.[1]

However, the African hero did "detail the whole
projects of Mr. Burr" to certain members of Congress.[2] "They believed Col. Burr capable of anything — and agreed that *the fellow ought to be
hanged*"; but they refused to be alarmed — Burr's
schemes were "too chimerical and his circumstances
too desperate to . . merit of serious consideration." [3]
So for twelve long months Eaton said nothing more
about Burr's proposed deviltry. During this time
he continued alternately to belabor Congress and the
Administration for the payment of the expenses of
his Barbary exploits.[4]

Andrew Jackson, while entertaining Burr on his

[1] See Eaton's deposition, *Eaton:* Prentiss, 396–403; 4 Cranch, 462–
67. (Italics are Eaton's.)

[2] Samuel Dana and John Cotton Smith. (See Eaton's testimony,
Annals, 10th Cong. 1st Sess. 512; and *Eaton:* Prentiss, 396–403.)

That part of Eaton's account of Burr's conversation which differs
from those with Truxtun and Decatur is simply unaccountable. That
Burr was capable of anything may be granted; but his mind was
highly practical and he was uncommonly reserved in speech. Undoubtedly Eaton had heard the common talk about the timidity and
supineness of the Government under Jefferson and had himself used
language such as he ascribed to Burr.

Whichever way one turns, no path out of the confusion appears.
But for Burr's abstemious habits (he was the most temperate of all
the leading men of that period) an explanation might be that he and
Eaton were very drunk — Burr recklessly so — if he indulged in this
uncharacteristic outburst of loquacity.

[3] *Eaton:* Prentiss, 402.   [4] McCaleb, 62.

first Western journey, had become the most promising, in practical support, of all who avowed themselves ready to follow Burr's invading standard into Mexico; and with Jackson he had freely consulted about that adventure. From Washington, Burr now wrote the Tennessee leader of the beclouding of their mutually cherished prospects of war with Spain.

But hope of war was not dead, wrote Burr — indeed, Miranda's armed expedition "composed of American citizens, and openly fitted out in an American port," made it probable. Jackson ought to be attending to something more than his militia offices, Burr admonished him: "Your country is full of fine materials for an army, and I have often said a brigade could be raised in West Tennessee which would drive double their number of Frenchmen off the earth." From such men let Jackson make out and send to Burr "a list of officers from colonel down to ensign for one or two regiments, composed of fellows fit for business, and with whom you would trust your life and your honor." Burr himself would, "in case troops should be called for, recommend it to the Department of War"; he had "reason to believe that on such an occasion" that department would listen to his advice.[1]

[1] Burr to Jackson, March 24, 1806, Parton: *Jackson*, I, 313–14.

Burr also told Jackson of John Randolph's denunciation of Jefferson's "duplicity and imbecility," and of small politics receiving "more of public attention than all our collisions with foreign powers, or than all the great events on the theatre of Europe." He closed with the statement, then so common, that such "things begin to make reflecting men think, many good patriots to doubt, and some to despond." (See McCaleb, 51.)

At last Burr, oblivious to the danger that Eaton might disclose the deadly secrets which he had so imprudently confided to a dissipated stranger, resolved to act and set out on his fateful journey. Before doing so, he sent two copies of a cipher letter to Wilkinson. This was in answer to a letter which Burr had just received from Wilkinson, dated May 13, 1806, the contents of which never have been revealed. Burr chose, as the messenger to carry overland one of the copies, Samuel Swartwout, a youth then twenty-two years of age, and brother of Colonel John Swartwout whom Jefferson had removed from the office of United States Marshal for the District of New York largely because of the Colonel's lifelong friendship for Burr. The other copy was sent by sea to New Orleans by Dr. Justus Erich Bollmann.[1]

No thought had Burr that Wilkinson, his ancient army friend and the arch conspirator of the whole plot, would reveal his dispatch. He and Wilkinson were united too deeply in the adventure for that to be thinkable. Moreover, the imminence of war appeared to make it certain that when the General received Burr's cipher, the two men would be comrades in arms against Spain in a war which, it cannot

[1] This man, then thirty-five years of age, and "engaging in . . appearance" (*Blennerhassett Papers:* Safford, 434), had had a picturesque career. A graduate of Göttingen, he lived in Paris during the Revolution, went to London for a time, and from there to Vienna, where he practiced medicine as a cover for his real design, which was to discover the prison where Lafayette was confined and to rescue him from it. This he succeeded in doing, but both were taken soon afterward. Bollmann was imprisoned for many months, and then released on condition that he leave Austria forever. He came to the United States and entered into Burr's enterprise with unbounded enthusiasm. His name often appears as "Erick Bolman" in American records.

be too often repeated, it was believed Wilkinson could bring on at any moment.

Nevertheless, Burr and Dayton had misgivings that the timorous General might not attack the Spaniards. They bolstered him up by hopeful letters, appealing to his cupidity, his ambition, his vanity, his fear. Dayton wrote that Jefferson was about to displace him and appoint another head of the army; let Wilkinson, therefore, precipitate hostilities — "You know the rest. . . Are you ready? Are your numerous associates ready? Wealth and glory! Louisiana and Mexico!" [1]

In his cipher dispatch to Wilkinson, Burr went to even greater lengths and with reason, for the impatient General had written him another letter, urging him to hurry: "I fancy Miranda has taken the bread out of your mouth; and I shall be ready for the grand expedition before you are." [2] Burr then assured Wilkinson that he was not only ready but on his way, and tried to strengthen the resolution of the shifty General by falsehood. He told of tremendous aid secured in far-off Washington and New York, and intimated that England would help. He was coming himself with money and men, and details were given. Bombastic sentences — entirely unlike any language appearing in Burr's voluminous correspondence and papers — were well chosen for their effect on Wilkinson's vainglorious mind: "The gods invite us to glory and fortune; it remains to be seen whether we deserve the boon. . . Burr guarantees

---

[1] Dayton to Wilkinson, July 24, 1806, *Annals*, 10th Cong. 1st sess. 560.

[2] See testimony of Littleton W. Tazewell, John Brokenbrough, and Joseph C. Cabell. (*Annals*, 10th Cong. 1st Sess. 630, 675, 676).

his the result with life and honor, with the lives and
honor and the fortunes of hundreds, the best blood
of our country." [1]

Fatal error! The sending of that dispatch was to
give Wilkinson his opportunity to save himself by
assuming the disguise of patriotism and of fealty
to Jefferson, and, clad in these habiliments, to denounce his associates in the Mexican adventure as
traitors to America. Soon, very soon, Wilkinson was
to use Burr's letter in a fashion to bring his friend
and many honest men to the very edge of execution
— a fate from which only the fearlessness and pene-
trating mind of John Marshall was to save them.

But this black future Burr could not foresee. Certain, as were most men, that war with Spain could
not be delayed much longer, and knowing that Wilkinson could precipitate it at any moment, Burr's
mind was at rest. At the beginning of August, 1806,
he once more journeyed down the Ohio. On the way
he stopped at a settlement on the Monongahela, not
far from Pittsburgh, where he visited one Colonel
George Morgan. This man afterward declared that
Burr talked mysteriously — the Administration was
contemptible, two hundred men could drive the
Government into the Potomac, five hundred could
take New York; and, Burr added laughingly,
even the Western States could be detached from the
Union. Most of this was said "in the presence of a
considerable company." [2]

---

[1] For Burr's cipher dispatch see Appendix D.

[2] *Annals*, 10th Cong. 1st sess. 424–28 and see McCaleb, 77.

Professor McCaleb evidently doubts the disinterestedness of Morgan and his sons. He shows that they had been in questionable land

The elder Morgan, who was aged and garrulous,[1] pieced together his inferences from Burr's meaning looks, jocular innuendoes, and mysterious statements,[2] and detected a purpose to divide the Nation. Deeply moved, he laid his deductions before the Chief Justice of Pennsylvania and two other gentlemen from Pittsburgh, a town close at hand; and a letter was written to Jefferson, advising him of the threatened danger.[3]

From Pittsburgh, Burr for the second time landed on the island of Harman Blennerhassett, who was eager for any adventure that would restore his declining fortunes. If war with Spain should, after all, not come to pass, Burr's other plan was the purchase of the enormous Bastrop land grant on the Washita River. Blennerhassett avidly seized upon both projects.[4] From that moment forward, the settlement of this rich and extensive domain in the then untouched and almost unexplored West became the alternative purpose of Aaron Burr in case the

transactions and, at this moment, were asking Congress to grant them a doubtful land claim. (See McCaleb, footnote to 77.)

[1] Testimony of Morgan's son, *Annals*, 10th Cong. 1st Sess. 424.

[2] "Colonel Burr, on this occasion as on others, comported himself precisely as a man having 'treasonable' designs would *not* comport himself, unless he were mad or intoxicated." (Parton: *Burr*, 415.) Professor McCaleb's analysis of the Morgan incident is thorough and convincing. (See McCaleb, 76–78.)

[3] Nevill and Roberts to Jefferson, Oct. 7, 1806, "Letters in Relation to Burr Conspiracy," MSS. Lib. Cong. This important letter set out that "to give a correct written statement of those [Burr's] conversations [with the Morgans] . . would be difficult . . and indeed, according to our informant, much more was to be collected, from the *manner* in which certain things were said, and hints given than from words used."

[4] McCaleb, 78–79; Parton: *Burr*, 411.

desire of his heart, the seizure of Mexico, should fail.[1]

Unfortunately Blennerhassett who, as his friends declared, "had all kinds of sense, except common sense,"[2] now wrote a series of letters for an Ohio country newspaper in answer to the articles appearing in the Kentucky organ of Daveiss and Humphrey Marshall, the *Western World*. The Irish enthusiast tried to show that a separation of the Western States from "Eastern domination" would be a good thing. These foolish communications were merely repetitions of similar articles then appearing in the Federalist press of New England, and of effusions printed in Southern newspapers a few years before. Nobody, it seems, paid much attention to these vagaries of Blennerhassett. It is possible that Burr knew of them, but proof of this was never adduced. When the explosion came, however, Blennerhassett's maunderings were recalled, and they became another one of those evidences of Burr's guilt which, to the public mind, was "confirmation strong as holy writ."

Burr and his newly made partner contracted for the building of fifteen boats, to be delivered in four months; and pork, meal, and other provisions were purchased. The island became the center of operations. Soon a few young men from Pittsburgh joined the enterprise, some of them sons of Revolutionary officers, and all of them of undoubted loyalty

---

[1] McCaleb, 83–84; Parton: *Burr*, 412–13.

At this time Burr also wrote to William Wilkins and B. H. Latrobe calling their attention to his Bastrop speculation. (Miscellaneous MSS. N.Y. Pub. Lib.)

[2] See testimony of Dudley Woodbridge, *infra*, 489.

to the Nation. To each of these one hundred acres of land on the Washita were promised, as part of their compensation for participating in the expedition, the entire purpose of which was not then explained to them.[1]

Burr again visited Marietta, where the local militia were assembled for their annual drill, and put these rural soldiers through their evolutions, again fascinating the whole community.[2] At Cincinnati, Burr held another long conference with his partner, Senator John Smith, who was a contractor and general storekeeper. The place which the Washita land speculation had already come to hold in his mind is shown by the conversation — Burr talked as much of that project as he did of war with Spain and his great ambition to invade Mexico; [3] but of secession, not a syllable.

Next Burr hurried to Nashville and once more became the honored guest of Andrew Jackson, whom he frankly told of the modification of his plans. His immediate purpose, Burr said, now was to settle the Washita lands. Of course, if war should break out he would lead a force into Texas and Mexico. Burr kept back only the part Wilkinson was to play in precipitating hostilities; and he said nothing of his efforts to bolster up that frail warrior's resolution.[4]

In Tennessee and Kentucky the talk was again of war with Spain. Indeed, it was now the only talk.[5]

---

[1] McCaleb, 80.   [2] Parton: *Burr*, 415–16.   [3] McCaleb, 81.
[4] *Ib.*; and see Parton: *Jackson*, I, 318.
[5] "There were not a thousand persons in the United States who did not think war with Spain inevitable, impending, begun!" (Parton: *Burr*, 407; McCaleb, 110.)

For the third time in the Tennessee Capital a public
banquet was given to the hero by whom the people
expected to be led against the enemy. Soon afterward Jackson issued his proclamation to the Tennessee militia calling them to arms against the hated
Spaniards, and volunteered his services to the National Government. Jefferson answered in a letter
provoking in its vagueness.[1]

At Lexington, Kentucky, Burr and Blennerhassett now purchased from Colonel Charles Lynch,
the owner of the Bastrop grant, several hundred
thousand acres on the Washita River in Northern
Louisiana.[2]

To many to whom Burr had spoken of his scheme
to invade Mexico he gave the impression that his
designs had the approval of the Administration; to
some he actually stated this to be the fact. In case
war was declared, the Administration, of course,
would necessarily support Burr's attack upon the
enemy; if hostilities did not occur, the "Government might overlook the preparations as in the case
of Miranda." [3] It is hard to determine whether the
project to invade Mexico — of which Burr did not
inform them, but which they knew to be his purpose — or the plan to settle the Washita lands, was
the more attractive to the young men who wished
to join him. Certainly, the Bastrop grant was so

[1] See Jefferson to Jackson, Dec. 3, 1806, as quoted in McCaleb, 82.
[2] See testimony of Colonel Charles Lynch, *Annals*, 10th Cong.
1st Sess. 656–58; and that of Thomas Bodley, Clerk of the Circuit
Court, *ib.* 655–56. The statements of these men are also very important as showing Burr's plans and preparations at this time.
[3] McCaleb, 84–85.

placed as to afford every possible lure to the youthful, enterprising, and adventurous.[1]

At this moment Wilkinson, apparently recovered from the panic into which Clark's letter had thrown him a year before, seemed resolved at last to strike. He even wrote with enthusiasm to General John Adair: "The time long looked for by many & wished for by more has now arrived, for subverting the Spanish government in Mexico — be ready & join me; we will want little more than light armed troops. . . More will be done by marching than by fighting. . . We cannot fail of success.[2] Your military talents are requisite. Unless you fear to join a Spanish intriguer [Wilkinson] come immediately — without your aid I can do nothing."[3] In reply Adair wrote Wilkinson that "the United States had not declared war against Spain and he did not believe they would." If not, Adair would not violate the law by joining Wilkinson's projected attack on Spain.[4]

By the same post Wilkinson wrote to Senator John Smith a letter bristling with italics: "I shall assuredly push them [the Spaniards] over the Sabine . . as that you are alive. . . *You must speedily send me a force* to

[1] The Bastrop grant was accessible to the markets of New Orleans; it was surrounded by Indian tribes whose trade was valuable; its forests were wholly unexplored; it was on the Spanish border, and therefore an admirable point for foray or retreat. (See McCaleb, 83; and Cox in *Southwestern Hist. Quarterly*, XVII, 150.)

[2] Wilkinson to Adair, Sept. 28, 1806, as quoted in open letter of Adair to the *New Orleans Gazette*, May 16, 1807, "Letters in Relation," MSS. Lib. Cong.

[3] Wilkinson to Adair, Sept. 28, 1806, as quoted by Plumer, Feb. 20, 1807, "Register," Plumer MSS. Lib. Cong.

[4] Adair to Wilkinson, Oct. or Nov. 1806, as quoted by Plumer, Feb. 20, 1807, "Register," Plumer MSS. Lib. Cong.

support our pretensions . . 5000 *mounted infantry . .
may suffice to carry us forward as far as Grand River*
[the Rio Grande], *there we shall require 5000 more to
conduct us to Mount el Rey . . after which from* 20 to
30,000 *will be necessary to carry our conquests to Cali-
fornia* and the *Isthmus of Darien. I write in haste,
freely* and *confidentially,* being ever your friend." [1]

In Kentucky once more the rumors sprang up
that Burr meant to dismember the Union, and these
were now put forward as definite charges. For
months Joseph Hamilton Daveiss, a brother-in-law
of John Marshall — appointed at the latter's instance by President Adams as United States Attorney for the District of Kentucky [2] — had been
writing Jefferson exciting letters about some kind of
conspiracy in which he was sure Burr was engaged.
The President considered lightly these tales written
him by one of his bitterest enemies.

With the idea of embarrassing the Republican
President, by connecting him, through the Administration's seeming acquiescence in Burr's projects
as in the case of the Miranda expedition, Daveiss
and his relative, former Senator Humphrey Marshall — both leaders of the few Federalists now remaining in Kentucky — welded together the rumors
of Burr's Mexican designs and those of his treasonable plot to separate the Western States from the
Union. These they published in a newspaper which
they controlled at Frankfort. [3]

[1] Wilkinson to Smith, Sept. 28, 1806, "Letters in Relation," MSS.
Lib. Cong.

[2] See vol. II, 560, of this work.

[3] The *Western World,* edited by the notorious John Wood, author of

The moss was removed from the ancient Spanish intrigues; Wilkinson was truthfully denounced as a pensioner of Spain; but the plot, it was charged, had veered from a union of the West with the Spanish dominions, to the establishment, by force of arms, of an independent trans-Alleghany Government.[1] The Federalist organs in the East adopted the stories related in the *Western World*, and laid especial emphasis on the disloyalty of the Western States, particularly of Kentucky.

The rumors had so aroused the people living near Blennerhassett's island that Mrs. Blennerhassett sent a messenger to warn Burr that he could not, in safety, appear there again. Learning this from the bearer of these tidings, Burr's partner, Senator John Smith, demanded of his associate an explanation. Burr promptly answered that he was "greatly surprised and really hurt" by Smith's letter. "If," said Burr, "there exists any design to separate the Western from the Eastern States, I am totally ignorant of it. I never harbored or expressed any such intention to any one, nor did any person ever intimate such design to me."[2]

the *History of the Administration of John Adams*, which was suppressed by Burr. (See vol. II, 380, of this work.) Wood was of the same type of irresponsible pamphleteer and newspaper hack as Callender and Cheetham. His so-called "history" was a dull, untruthful, scandalous diatribe; and it is to Burr's credit that he bought the plates and suppressed the book. Yet this action was one of the reasons given for the remorseless pursuit of him, after it had been determined to destroy him.

[1] McCaleb, 172–75.

[2] Adams: *U.S.* III, 276. This was a falsehood, since Burr had proposed Western secession to the British Minister. But he knew that no one else could have knowledge of his plot with Merry. It is both

Daveiss and Humphrey Marshall now resolved to stay the progress of the plot at which they were convinced that the Republican Administration was winking. If Jefferson was complacent, Daveiss would act and act officially; thus the President, by contrast, would be fatally embarrassed. Another motive, personal in its nature, inspired Daveiss. He was an able, fearless, passionate man, and he hated Burr violently for having killed Hamilton whom Daveiss had all but worshiped.[1]

Early in November the District Attorney moved the United States Court at Frankfort to issue compulsory process for Burr's apprehension and for the attendance of witnesses. Burr heard of this at Lexington and sent word that he would appear voluntarily. This he did, and, the court having denied Daveiss's motion because of the irregularity of it, the accused demanded that a public and official investigation be made of his plans and activities. Accordingly, the grand jury was summoned and Daveiss given time to secure witnesses.

On the day appointed Burr was in court. By his side was his attorney, a tall, slender, sandy-haired

interesting and important that to the end of his life Burr steadily maintained that he never harbored a thought of dismembering the Nation.

[1] (Clay to Pindell, Oct. 15, 1828, *Works of Henry Clay:* Colton, IV, 206; also *Private Correspondence of Henry Clay:* Colton, 206–08.)

So strong was his devotion to Hamilton, that "after he had attained full age," Daveiss adopted the name of his hero as part of his own, thereafter signing himself Joseph Hamilton Daveiss and requiring everybody so to address him. "Chiefly moved . . by his admiration of Colonel Hamilton and his hatred of Colonel Burr," testifies Henry Clay, Daveiss took the first step in the series of prosecutions that ended in the trial of Burr for treason. (*Ib.*)

young man of twenty-nine who had just been appointed to the National Senate. Thus Henry Clay
entered the drama. Daveiss failed to produce a
single witness, and Burr, "after a dignified and grave
harangue," was discharged, to the tumultuous delight of the people.[1]

Two weeks later the discomfited but persistent
and undaunted District Attorney again demanded of
Judge Innes the apprehension of the "traitor." Clay
requested of Burr a written denial of the charges so
incessantly made against him. This Burr promptly
furnished.[2] Clay was so convinced of Burr's integrity that he declared in court that he "could pledge

[1] Adams: *U.S.* III, 278.

[2] "I have no design, nor have I taken any measure to promote a
dissolution of the Union, or a separation of any one or more States
from the residue. I have neither published a line on this subject nor
has any one, through my agency, or with my knowledge. I have
no design to intermeddle with the Government or to disturb the
tranquillity of the United States, or of its territories, or any part
of them.

"I have neither issued, nor signed, nor promised a commission to
any person for any purpose. I do not own a musket nor a bayonet,
nor any single article of military stores, nor does any person for me,
by my authority or with my knowledge.

"My views have been fully explained to, and approved by, several
of the principal officers of Government, and, I believe, are well understood by the administration and seen by it with complacency. They
are such as every man of honor and every good citizen must approve."
(Burr to Clay, Dec. 1, 1806, *Priv. Corres.*: Colton, 13–14.)

Parton says that this was substantially true: "Jefferson and his
cabinet undoubtedly knew . . that he was going to settle in the western country, and that if the expected war should break out, he would
head an onslaught upon the Dons.

"His *ulterior* views may have been known to one, or even two,
members of Jefferson's cabinet, for anything that can *now* be ascertained. The moment the tide really turned against this fated man, a
surprising ignorance overspread many minds that had before been
extremely well-informed respecting his plans." (Parton: *Burr*, 422–23;
see also McCaleb, 191.)

his own honor and innocence" for those of his client. Once more no witnesses were produced; once more the grand jury could not return an indictment; once more Burr was discharged. The crowd that packed the court-room burst into cheers.[1] That night a ball, given in Burr's honor, crowned this second of his triumphs in the United States Court.[2]

Thereafter Burr continued his preparations as if nothing had happened. To all he calmly stated the propriety of his enterprise. To his fellow adventurer, Senator John Smith, he was again particularly explicit and clear: "If there should be a war between the United States and Spain, I shall head a corps of volunteers and be the first to march into the Mexican provinces. If peace should be proffered, which I do not expect, I shall settle my Washita lands, and make society as pleasant as possible. . . I have been persecuted, shamefully persecuted." [3] As to dividing the Union, Burr told Smith that "if Bonaparte with all his army were in the western country with the object . . he would never see salt water again." [4]

While Burr was writing this letter, Jefferson was signing a document that, when sent forth, as it immediately was, ignited all the rumors, reports, accusations, and suspicions that had been accumulating,

---

[1] "When the grand jury returned the bill of indictment not true, a scene was presented in the Court-room which I had never before witnessed in Kentucky. There were shouts of applause from an audience, not one of whom . . would have hesitated to level a rifle against Colonel Burr, if he believed that he aimed to dismember the Union, or sought to violate its peace, or overturn its Constitution." (Clay to Pindell, Oct. 15, 1828, *Priv. Corres.*: Colton, 207.)

[2] Adams: *U.S.* III, 282–83; McCaleb, 192–93; Parton: *Burr*, 418–22.

[3] Burr to Smith, as quoted in McCaleb, 183.   [4] Parton: *Burr*, 423.

and set the country on fire with wrath against the disturber of our national bliss.

When Wilkinson received Burr's cipher dispatch, he took time to consider the best methods for saving himself, filling his purse, and brightening his tarnished reputation.[1] The faithful and unsuspecting young Swartwout, Burr's messenger, was persuaded to remain in Wilkinson's camp for a week after the delivery of the fatal letter. He was treated with marked friendliness, and from him the General afterward pretended to have extracted frightful details of Burr's undertaking.[2]

---

[1] The Spanish Minister accurately explained to his home Government the motives that now animated the commander of the American Army:

"Wilkinson is entirely devoted to us. He enjoys a considerable pension from the King. . . He anticipated . . the failure of an expedition of this nature [Burr's invasion of Mexico]. Doubtless he foresaw from the first that the improbability of success in case of making the attempt would leave him like the dog in the fable with the piece of meat in his mouth; that is, that he would lose [both] the honorable employment . . [as American Commander] and the generous pension he enjoys from the King. These considerations, secret in their nature, he could not explain to Burr; and when the latter persisted in an idea so fatal to Wilkinson's interests, nothing remained but to take the course adopted.

"By this means he assures his pension; and will allege his conduct on this occasion as an extraordinary service, either for getting it increased, or for some generous compensation.

"On the other hand this proceeding secures his distinguished rank in the military service of the United States, and covers him with a popularity which may perhaps result in pecuniary advantages, and in any case will flatter his vanity.

"In such an alternative he has acted as was to be expected; that is, he has sacrificed Burr in order to obtain, on the ruins of Burr's reputation, the advantages I have pointed out." (Casa Yrujo to Cevallos, Jan. 28, 1807, as quoted in Adams: *U.S.* III, 342–43.)

[2] Swartwout, under oath, denied that he had told Wilkinson this story. Swartwout's affidavit is important. He swears that he never heard of the revolutionizing of "the N[ew] O[rleans] Territory" until

Seven more days passed, and at last, two weeks
after he had received Burr's cipher dispatch, Wilkinson wrote Jefferson that "a Numerous and powerful Association, extending from New York to . .
the Mississippi had been formed to levy & rendezvous eight or Ten Thousand Men in New Orleans . .
& from thence . . to carry an Expedition against
Vera Cruz." Wilkinson gave details — dates and
places of assembling troops, methods of invasion,
etc., and added: "It is unknown under what Authority this Enterprize has been projected, from where
the means of its support are derived, or what may
be the intentions of its leaders in relation to the
Territory of Orleans." [1]

Surprising as this was, the General supported it
by a "confidential" and personal letter to Jefferson [2]
still more mysterious and disquieting: "The mag-

Wilkinson mentioned it — "I first heard of such a project from Wilkinson"; that Burr never had spoken of attacking Mexico except "in
case of war with Spain"; that if there were no war, Burr intended to
settle the Washita lands. (See Henshaw in *Quarterly Pub. Hist. and
Phil. Soc. Ohio*, IX, Nos. 1 and 2, 53–54.)

This young man made a deep impression of honesty and straight-
forwardness on all who came in contact with him. (See testimony of
Tazewell, Cabell, and Brokenbrough, *Annals*, 10th Cong. 1st Sess.
633.) "Swartwout is a fine genteel intelligible young man." (Plumer
to Mason, Jan. 30, 1807, Plumer MSS. Lib. Cong.)

Notwithstanding his frank and engaging manner, Swartwout was
at heart a basely dishonest person. Thirty years later, when Collector
of the Port of New York, he embezzled a million and a quarter
dollars of the public funds. (Bassett: *Life of Andrew Jackson*, II,
452–53.)

[1] Wilkinson's dispatch, Oct. 20, 1806, "Letters in Relation," MSS.
Lib. Cong. Wilkinson's dispatch to Jefferson was based on the revelations which he pretended to have drawn from Swartwout.

[2] The dispatch would go on file in the War Department; the "personal and confidential" communication to Jefferson would remain
in the President's hands.

nitude of the Enterprize, the desperation of the Place, and the stupendous consequences with which it seems pregnant, stagger my belief & excite doubts of the reality, against the conviction of my Senses; & it is for this reason I shall forbear to commit Names. .. I have never in my whole Life found myself in such circumstances of perplexity and Embarrassment as at present; for I am not only uninformed of the prime mover and Ultimate Objects of this daring Enterprize, but am ignorant of the foundation on which it rests."

Wilkinson went on to say that, as an inducement for him to take part in it, he had been told that "you [Jefferson] connive at the combination and that our country will justify it." If this were not true, "then I have no doubt the revolt of this Territory will be made an auxiliary step to the main design of attacking Mexico." So he thought he ought to compromise with the Spaniards and throw himself with his "little Band into New Orleans, to be ready to defend that Capitol against Usurpation and violence."

He wrote more to the same effect, and added this postscript: "Should Spain be disposed to War seriously with us, might not some plan be adopted to correct the delirium of the associates, and by a pitiable appeal to their patriotism to engage them in the service of their Country. I merely offer the suggestion as a possible expedient to prevent the Horrors of a civil contest, and I do believe that, with competent authority I could accomplish the object." [1]

[1] Wilkinson to Jefferson, Oct. 21, 1806, "Letters in Relation," MSS. Lib. Cong.

This was the letter which a few months later caused Chief Justice John Marshall to issue a subpœna *duces tecum* directed to President Thomas Jefferson in order to have it produced in court.[1]

Jefferson had known of the rumors about Burr — George Morgan, Joseph H. Daveiss, and William Eaton had put him on the track of the "traitor." Others had told of the American Catiline's treasonable plans; and the newspapers, of which he was a studious reader, had advised the President of every sensation that had appeared. Jefferson and his Cabinet had nervously debated the situation, decided on plans to forestall the conspiracy, and then hurriedly abandoned them;[2] evidently they had no faith in the lurid stories of Burr's treasonable purposes and preparations.

Letters to Jefferson from the West, arriving October 24, 1806, bore out the disbelief of the President and his Cabinet in Burr's lawless activities; for these advices from the President's friends who, on the ground, were closely watching Burr, contained "not one word . . of any movements by Colonel Burr. This total silence of the officers of the Government, of the members of Congress, of the newspapers, proves he is committing no overt act against law," Jefferson wrote in his Cabinet Memorandum.[3] So the President and his Cabinet decided to do nothing further at that time than to order John Graham, while on his way to assume the office of

---

[1] See *infra*, chap. viii.

[2] Jefferson's Cabinet Memorandum, Oct. 22, 1806, as quoted in Adams: *U.S.* iii, 278–80.

[3] *Ib.* Oct. 25, 1806, as quoted in Adams: *U.S.* iii, 281.

Secretary of the Orleans Territory, to investigate Burr's activities.

But when the mysterious warnings from Wilkinson reached Jefferson, he again called his Cabinet into consultation and precipitate action was taken. Orders were dispatched to military commanders to take measures against Burr's expedition; Wilkinson was directed to withdraw his troops confronting the Spaniards and dispose of them for the defense of New Orleans and other endangered points.

Most important of all, a Presidential Proclamation was issued to all officials and citizens, declaring that a conspiracy had been discovered, warning all persons engaged in it to withdraw, and directing the ferreting out and seizure of the conspirators' "vessels, arms and military stores." [1] Graham preceded the Proclamation and induced Governor Tiffin and the Ohio Legislature to take action for the seizure of Burr's boats and supplies at Marietta; and this was done.

On December 10, 1806, Comfort Tyler of Onondaga County, New York, one of the minor leaders of the Burr expedition,[2] arrived at Blennerhassett's island with a few boats and some twenty young men who had joined the adventure. There were a half-

[1] Jefferson's Proclamation, Nov. 27, 1806, *Works*, Ford, x, 301-02; Wilkinson: *Memoirs*, II, Appendix XCVI.

[2] Tyler had been in the New York Legislature with Burr and there became strongly attached to him. (See Clark: *Onondaga*.) He went to Beaver, Pennsylvania, in the interests of Burr's enterprise, and from there made his way to Blennerhassett's island. Tyler always maintained that the sole object of the expedition was to settle the Washita lands. (See his pathetic letter asserting this to Lieutenant Horatio Stark, Jan. 23, 1807, "Letters in Relation," MSS. Lib. Cong.)

dozen rifles among them, and a few fowling pieces. With these the youths went hunting in the Ohio forests. Blennerhassett, too, had his pistols. This was the whole of the warlike equipment of that militant throng — all that constituted that "overt act of treason by levying war against the United States" which soon brought Burr within the shadow of the gallows.

Jefferson's Proclamation had now reached Western Virginia, and it so kindled the patriotism of the militia of Wood County, within the boundaries of which the island lay, that that heroic host resolved to descend in its armed might upon the embattled "traitors," capture and deliver them to the vengeance of the law. The Wood County men, unlike those of Ohio, needed no act of legislature to set their loyalty in motion. The Presidential Proclamation, and the sight of the enemies of the Nation gathered in such threatening and formidable array on Blennerhassett's island, were more than enough to cause them to spring to arms in behalf of their imperiled country.

Badly frightened, Blennerhassett and Tyler, leaving Mrs. Blennerhassett behind, fled down the river with thirty men in six half-equipped boats. They passed the sentries of the Wood County militia only because those ministers of vigilance had got thoroughly drunk and were sound asleep. Next day, however, the militia invaded the deserted island and, finding the generously stocked wine cellar, restored their strength by drinking all the wine and whiskey on the place. They then demonstrated their abhorrence of treason by breaking the windows, demolishing the furniture, tearing the pictures, trampling the flower-beds, burning the fences, and insulting Mrs. Blennerhassett.[1]

Graham procured the authorities of Kentucky to take action similar to that adopted in Ohio. Burr, still ignorant of Jefferson's Proclamation, proceeded to Nashville, there to embark in the boats Jackson was building for him, to go on the last river voyage of his adventure.

Jackson, like Smith and Clay, had been made uneasy by the rumors of Burr's treasonable designs. He had written Governor Claiborne at New Orleans a letter of warning, particularly against Wilkinson, and not mentioning Burr by name.[2] When Burr arrived at the Tennessee Capital, Jackson, his manner now cold, demanded an explanation. Burr, "with his usual dignified courtesy, instantly complied." [3] It would seem that Jackson was satisfied by his reassurance, in spite of the President's Proclamation which reached Nashville three days before Burr's departure; [4] for not only did Jackson permit him to proceed, but, when the adventurer started down the Cumberland in two of the six boats which he had built on Burr's previous orders, consented that a nephew of his wife should make one of the ten or fifteen young men who accompanied the expedi-

---

[1] Hildreth, v, 619; Parton: *Burr*, 436–38.

[2] Jackson to Claiborne, Nov. 12, 1806, Parton: *Jackson*, I, 319; and see McCaleb, 253.

[3] Adams: *U.S.* III, 287; Parton: *Jackson*, I, 320–21.

[4] Parton inaccurately says that the Proclamation reached Nashville after Burr's departure. (Parton: *Jackson*, I, 322.)

tion. He even gave the boy a letter of introduction to Governor Claiborne at New Orleans.[1]

After the people had recovered from the shock of astonishment that Jefferson's Proclamation gave them, the change in them was instantaneous and extreme.[2] The President, to be sure, had not mentioned Burr's name or so much as hinted at treason; all that Jefferson charged was a conspiracy to attack the hated Spaniards, and this was the hope and desire of every Westerner. Nevertheless, the public intelligence penetrated what it believed to be the terrible meaning behind the President's cautious words; the atrocious purpose to dismember the Union, reports of which had pursued Burr since a Spanish agent had first set the rumor afoot a year before, was established in the minds of the people.

Surely the President would not hunt down an American seeking to overthrow Spanish power in North America, when a Spanish "liberator" had been permitted to fit out in the United States an expedition to do the same thing in South America. Surely Jefferson would not visit his wrath on one whose only crime was the gathering of men to strike at Spain with which power, up to that very moment, everybody supposed war to be impending and, indeed, almost begun. This was unthinkable. Burr must be guilty of a greater crime — the greatest of

[1] Adams: *U.S.* III, 288; Parton: *Jackson*, I, 321.

[2] For instance, at Nashville, Burr was burnt in effigy in the public square. (Parton: *Jackson*, I, 322.) At Cincinnati an amusing panic occurred: three merchant scows loaded with dry goods were believed to be a part of Burr's flotilla of war vessels about to attack the town. The militia was called out, citizens organized for defense, the adjacent country was appealed to for aid. (See McCaleb, 248–49.)

crimes. In such fashion was public opinion made ready to demand the execution of the "traitor" who had so outrageously deceived the people; and that popular outcry began for the blood of Aaron Burr by which John Marshall was assailed while presiding over the court to which the accused was finally taken.

From the moment that Wilkinson decided to denounce Burr to the President, his language became that of a Bombastes Furioso, his actions those of a military ruffian, his secret movements matched the cunning of a bribe-taking criminal. By swiftest dispatch another message was sent to Jefferson. "My doubts have ceased," wrote Wilkinson, concerning "this deep, dark, wicked, and wide-spread conspiracy, embracing the young and the old, the democrat and the federalist, the native and the foreigner, the patriot of '76 and the exotic of yesterday, the opulent and the needy, the ins and the outs."

Wilkinson assured Jefferson, however, that he would meet the awful emergency with "indefatigable industry, incessant vigilance and hardy courage"; indeed, declared he, "I shall glory to give my life" to defeat the devilish plot. But the numbers of the desperadoes were so great that, unless Jefferson heavily reinforced him with men and ships, he and the American army under his command would probably perish.[1]

As the horse bearing the messenger to Jefferson disappeared in the forests, another, upon which rode

---

[1] Wilkinson to Jefferson, Nov. 12, 1806, Wilkinson: *Memoirs*, ii, Appendix c.

a very different agent, left Wilkinson's camp and
galloped toward the Southwest. The latter agent
was Walter Burling, a corrupt factotum of Wilkinson's, whom that martial patriot sent to the Spanish
Viceroy at Mexico City to advise him of Wilkinson's
latest service to Spain in thwarting Burr's attack
upon the royal possessions, and in averting war between the United States and His Catholic Majesty.
For these noble performances Wilkinson demanded
of the Spanish Viceroy more than one hundred and
ten thousand dollars in cash, together with other
sums which "he [had] been obliged to spend in order
to sustain the cause of good government, order and
humanity." [1]

Wilkinson had asked the Viceroy to destroy the
letter and this was accordingly done in Burling's
presence. The Royal representative then told Burling that he knew all about Burr's plans to invade
Mexico, and had long been ready to repel a much
larger force than Wilkinson stated Burr to be leading. "I thanked him for his martial zeal and insinuated that I wished him happiness in the pursuit of
his righteous intentions," wrote the disgusted and
sarcastic Viceroy in his report to the Government at

[1] Iturrigaray to Cevallos, March 12, 1807, as quoted in McCaleb,
169; and see Shepherd in *Am. Hist. Rev.* IX, 533 *et seq.*

The thrifty General furnished Burling with a passport through the
posts he must pass. ("Letters in Relation," as quoted in McCaleb,
166.)

Credentials to the Spanish official were also given Burling by one of
Wilkinson's friends, Stephen Minor of Natchez, the man who had
first set on foot the rumor of Burr's secession intentions. He was also
in the pay of Spain. (*Ib.* 166–67.)

The Spaniards aided Burling on his journey in every way possible.
(Herrera to Cordero, Dec. 1, 1806, as quoted in *ib.* 167–68.)

Madrid.[1] With this Wilkinson had to be content, for
the Viceroy refused to pay him a peso.

Upon Burling's return, the vigilant American
Commander-in-Chief forwarded to Jefferson a report of conditions in Mexico, as represented by
Burling, together with a request for fifteen hundred dollars to pay that investigator's expenses.[2]
The sole object of Burling's journey was, Wilkinson
informed the President, to observe and report upon
the situation in the great Spanish Vice-royalty as
recent events had affected it, with respect to the
interests of the United States; and Jefferson was assured by the General that his agent was the soundest and most devoted of patriots.[3]

To back up the character he was now playing,
Wilkinson showered warnings upon the officers of
the Army and upon government officials in New
Orleans. "The plot thickens. . . My God! what a
situation has our country reached. Let us save it if
we can. . . On the 15th of this month [November],
Burr's declaration is to be made in Tennessee and
Kentucky; hurry, hurry after me, and, if necessary,
let us be buried together, in the ruins of the place we
shall defend." This was a typical message to Colonel
Cushing.[4]

Wilkinson dispatched orders to Colonel Freeman
at New Orleans to repair the defenses of the city;
but "be you as silent as the grave. . . You are sur-

[1] Iturrigaray to Cevallos, March 12, 1807, as quoted in McCaleb,
168–69.   [2] *Ib*. 171.

[3] Wilkinson to Jefferson, March 12, 1807, "Letters in Relation,"
MSS. Lib. Cong.

[4] Wilkinson to Cushing, Nov. 7, 1806, Wilkinson: *Memoirs*, II,
Appendix xcix.

rounded by secret agents." [1] He informed Governor
Claiborne that "the storm will probably burst in
New Orleans, where I shall meet it and triumph or
perish." [2] Otherwise "the fair fabric of our inde-
pendence . . will be prostrated, and the Goddess of
Liberty will take her flight from the globe forever."
Again and again, Wilkinson sounded the alarm.
"Burr with rebellious bands may soon be at hand."
Therefore, "civil institutions must . . yield to the
strong arm of military law." [3] But Claiborne must
"not breathe or even hint" that catastrophe was
approaching.

At last, however, Wilkinson unbosomed himself to
the merchants of New Orleans whom he assembled
for that purpose. Agents of the bandit chief were all
around them, he said — he would have arrested
them long since had he possessed the power. The
desperadoes were in larger force than he had at first
believed — "by all advices the enemy, at least 2000
strong," would soon reach Natchez. They meant,
first, to sack New Orleans and then to attack Mexico
by land and sea. If successful in that invasion, "the
Western States were then to be separated from the
Union." But Wilkinson would "pledge his life in the
defense of the city and his country." [4]

At that moment Burr had not even started down
the Mississippi with his nine boats manned by sixty
young men.

[1] Wilkinson to Freeman, Wilkinson: *Memoirs*, ii, Appendix xcix.
[2] Wilkinson to Claiborne, Nov. 12, 1806, *ib.* 328.
[3] Wilkinson to Claiborne, Dec. 6 and 7, 1806, as quoted in McCaleb,
205–06.
[4] *Ib.* 209–10.

For a time the city was thrown into a panic.[1] But Wilkinson had overblustered. The people, recovered from their fright, began to laugh. Thousands of fierce Vandals, brandishing their arms, on their way to take New Orleans, capture Mexico, destroy the Union! And this mighty force not now far away! How could that be and no tidings of it except from Wilkinson? That hero witnessed with dismay this turn of public sentiment. Ruthless action, then, or all his complicated performances would go for naught. Ridicule would be fatal to his plans.

So General James Wilkinson, as head of the Army of the United States, began a reign of lawless violence that has no parallel in American history. To such base uses can authority be put — with such peril to life and liberty is it invested — when unchecked by Constitutional limitation enforced by fearless and unprejudiced judges! Men were arrested and thrown into prison on Wilkinson's orders, wholly without warrant of law. The first thus to be seized were Samuel Swartwout and Dr. Justus Erich Bollmann. Their papers were confiscated; they were refused counsel, were even denied access to the courts. Soldiers carried them to a warship in the river which at once set sail with orders from Wilkinson for the delivery of the prisoners to the President at Washington.[2]

---

[1] Wilkinson to Clark, Dec. 10, 1806, Clark: *Proofs*, 150; also McCaleb, 212; and see Wilkinson to Claiborne, Dec. 15, 1806, as quoted in McCaleb, 213–14.

[2] Swartwout was treated in a manner peculiarly outrageous. Before his arrest Wilkinson had borrowed his gold watch, and afterward refused to return it. When the soldiers seized Swartwout they "hurried"

Another man similarly arrested was Peter V. Ogden of New York, nephew of Jonathan Dayton, who had been the companion of Swartwout in his long overland journey in quest of Wilkinson. Public-spirited lawyers swore out writs of habeas corpus for these three men. Not a syllable of evidence was adduced against Ogden, who by some mischance had not been transported with Bollmann and Swartwout, and the court discharged him.

In response to the order of the court to produce the bodies of Bollmann and Swartwout, Wilkinson sent his aide with the General's return to the process. As the "Commander of the Army of the United States," he said, he took on himself "all responsibility . . resulting from the arrest of Erick Bollmann, who is accused of being guilty of the crime of treason against the government and the laws of the United States," and he had "taken opportune measures to warrant his safe delivery into the hands of the President."

This had been done, avowed Wilkinson, solely in

him across the river, lodged him "for several days & nights in a poor inhospitable shed— & deprived of the necessaries of life."

Finally, when ordered to march with his guard — and being refused any information as to where he was to be taken — the prisoner declared that he was to be murdered and leapt into the river, crying, "I had as well die here as in the woods," whereupon "the L^t drew up his file of six men & ordered them to shoot him. The soldiers directed their guns at him & snapt them, but owing to the great rain, 3 of the guns flashed in the pan, & the other's would not take fire. The men pursued & took him. But for the wetness of the powder this unfortunate young man must have be[en] murdered in very deed."

Swartwout was not permitted to take his clothing with him on the ship that carried him to Baltimore; and the officer in charge of him was under orders from Wilkinson to put his prisoner in chains during the voyage. (Plumer, Feb. 21, 1807, "Register," Plumer MSS. Lib. Cong.)

order "to secure the nation which is menaced to its foundations by a band of traitors associated with Aaron Burr." To that end he would, he defiantly informed the court, "arrest, without respect to class or station, all those against whom [he had] positive proof of being accomplices in the machinations against the state." [1] This defiance of the courts was accompanied by a copy of Wilkinson's version of Burr's cipher letter and some memoranda by Bollmann, together with Wilkinson's assertion that he had certain evidence which he would not, at that time, disclose.

Jefferson had long demanded of Wilkinson a copy of the incriminating Burr letter, and this was now forwarded, together with the General's account of the arrest of Bollmann, Swartwout, and Ogden. In his report to the President, Wilkinson accused the judge who had released Ogden of being an associate of Burr in his "treasonable combinations," and characteristically added that he would "look to our country for protection" in case suit for damages was brought against him by Bollmann and Swartwout. [2]

While Bollmann and Swartwout, in close confinement on the warship, were tossing on the winter seas, the saturnalia of defiance of the law continued in New Orleans. Ogden was again seized and incarcerated. So was his friend, James Alexander of New

---

[1] Wilkinson's return reported in the *Orleans Gazette*, Dec. 18, 1806, as quoted in McCaleb, 217. It does not appear what return was made in the matter of the application for a writ of habeas corpus in favor of Swartwout.

[2] Wilkinson to Jefferson, printed in *National Intelligencer*, Jan. 23, 1807, as quoted in McCaleb, 218.

York, who had displeased Wilkinson by suing out
the writs of habeas corpus. Both were shortly taken
to a military prison. Judges, leading lawyers, prominent citizens — all protested in vain. New writs of
habeas corpus were issued and ignored. Edward
Livingston sued out a writ of attachment [1] against
Wilkinson. It was defied. The civil governor was
appealed to; he was cowed and declined to act in
this "delicate as well as dangerous" state of things.
In despair and disgust Judge James Workman adjourned the Orleans County Court *sine die* and resigned from the Bench;[2] he too was seized by Wilkinson's soldiers, and recovered his liberty only by
the return of the Judge of the United States District
Court, who dared the wrath of the military tyrant
in order to release his imprisoned fellow judge.[3]

In the midst of this debauch of military lawless-
ness, General John Adair, late one afternoon, rode
into New Orleans. He had come on business, having
sent three thousand gallons of whiskey and two boat-
loads of provisions to be sold in the city, and expecting also to collect a debt of fifteen hundred dollars
due him at that place; he had also intended to make
some land deals.

The moment Wilkinson heard of the arrival of his
old friend and comrade, the General ordered "a captain and one hundred soldiers" to seize Adair. This
was done so peremptorily that he was not allowed to
dine, "altho the provision was ready on the table";

[1] This was one cause of Jefferson's hatred of Livingston. For the
celebrated litigation between these men and the effect of it on Marshall and Jefferson, see vol. IV, chap. II, of this work.
[2] McCaleb, 219–21.   [3] Hildreth, v, 613.

he was denied medicine, which on account of illness
he wished to take with him; he was refused extra
clothing and was not even allowed "to give directions respecting his horses which cost him $700 in
Kentucky." Then the bewildered Adair was hurried
on board a schooner and taken "down the river 25
miles, landed on the other side . . and placed under
a tent in a swamp."

After he had been kept six days under guard
in this situation, Adair "was shipped aboard the
schooner Thatcher for Baltimore . . in the custody
of Lt. Luckett." Wilkinson ordered the lieutenant to
keep Adair in close confinement and to resist "with
force and arms" any civil officer who might attempt
to take Adair "by a writ of habeas corpus." [1]

The reason for this particular atrocity was that
Wilkinson had written Adair the letters quoted
above, and unless his correspondent were discredited and disgraced, he could convict Wilkinson of
the very conspiracy with which Burr was being
charged.[2] During his reign of terror to put down

[1] Plumer's résumé of a letter from Adair to Clay. (Feb. 20, 1807,
"Register," Plumer MSS. Lib. Cong.)

For this outrage Adair, within a year, brought suit against Wilkinson for false imprisonment. This was bitterly fought for ten years, but
finally Adair secured judgment for $2500, "against which Wilkinson
was indemnified by Congress." (Hildreth, v, 627.)

For three or four years Adair continued in public disfavor solely
because of his supposed criminal connection with Burr, of which his
arrest by Wilkinson convinced the inflamed public mind. He slowly
recovered, however, rendered excellent service as an officer in the War
of 1812, and under Jackson commanded the Kentucky troops at the
battle of New Orleans with distinguished gallantry. In 1820 the old
veteran was elected Governor of Kentucky. Afterward he was chosen
Representative in Congress from his district.

[2] Plumer's résumé of Adair's letter to Clay, *supra*, note 1. Every

"treason," the General was in secret communication with the Spaniards, earning the bribe money which he was, and long had been, receiving from them.[1]

While Wilkinson at New Orleans was thus openly playing despot and secretly serving Spain, the President's Annual Message was read to Congress.

In this document Jefferson informed the National Legislature of the advance of the Spaniards toward American territory, the alarming posture of affairs, the quick response of the pioneers to the call of the Government for volunteers. "Having received information," he said, "that, in another part of the United States, a great number of private individuals were combining together, arming and organizing themselves contrary to law, to carry on a military expedition against the territories of Spain [he] thought it necessary to take measures . . for suppressing this enterprise . . and bringing to justice

---

word of Adair's startling account of his arrest was true. It was never even denied. John Watkins told Wilkinson of a conversation with Adair immediately after the latter's arrival which showed that nobody had reason to fear Burr: "He [Adair] observed . . that the bubble would soon burst & signified that the claims were without foundation & that he had seen nothing like an armament or preparations for a warlike expedition." (Watkins to Wilkinson, Jan. 14, 1807, Wilkinson MSS. Chicago Hist. Soc.)

Professor Cox has suggested to the author that Wilkinson's summary arrest of Adair was to prevent the further circulation of his statement.

[1] "During the disturbances of Burr the aforesaid general [Wilkinson] has, by means of a person in his confidence, constantly maintained a correspondence with me, in which he has laid before me not only the information which he acquired, but also his intentions for the various exigencies in which he might find himself." (Folch to the Governor-General of Cuba, June 25, 1807, as quoted by Cox in *Am. Hist. Rev.* x, 839.)

its authors and abettors." [1] Such was the slight reference made to the Burr "conspiracy." Thanks to the President's Proclamation, the "treasonable" plot of Aaron Burr was already on every tongue; but here, indeed, was an anti-climax.

The Senate referred the brief paragraph of the President's Message relating to the conspiracy to a special committee. The committee took no action. Everybody was in suspense. What were the facts? Nobody knew. But the air was thick with surmise, rumor, conjecture, and strange fancies — none of them bearing the color of truth. [2] Marshall was then

---

[1] Jefferson's Message, Dec. 2, 1806, *Annals*, 9th Cong. 2d Sess. 12; Richardson, I, 406.

[2] "We have been, & still are, both amused & perplexed with the rumours, reports, & conjectures respecting Aaron Burr. They are numerous, various, & contradictory. . . I must have plenary evidence before I believe him capable of committing the hundredth part of the absurd & foolish things that are ascribed to him. . . The president of the United States, a day or two since, informed me that he knew of no evidence sufficient to convict him of either high crimes or misdemeanors." (Plumer to Jeremiah Mason, Jan. 4, 1807, Plumer MSS. Lib. Cong.) See also Plumer to Langdon, Dec. 1806, and to Livermore, Jan. 19, 1807, Plumer MSS. *loc. cit.*

These letters of Plumer's are most important. They state the general opinion of public men, especially Federalists, as expressed in their private conversations.

"I never believed him to be a Fool," wrote John Adams to his most intimate friend. "But he must be an Idiot or a Lunatick if he has really planned and attempted to execute such a Project as is imputed to him." Politicians have "no more regard to Truth than the Devil. . . I suspect that this Lying Spirit has been at Work concerning Burr. . . But if his guilt is as clear as the Noon day Sun, the first Magistrate ought not to have pronounced it so before a Jury had tryed him." (Adams to Rush, Feb. 2, 1807, *Old Family Letters*, 128–29.) See also Adams to Pickering, Jan. 1, 1807, Pickering MSS. Mass. Hist. Soc.; and Peters to Pickering, Feb. 1807, Pickering MSS. *loc. cit.*

Marshall undoubtedly shared the common judgment, as his conduct at Burr's trial abundantly shows.

in Washington and must have heard all these tales
which were on every tongue.

In two weeks from the time Jefferson's Message
was read to Congress, John Randolph rose in his
place in the House, and in a speech of sharp criticism both of Spain and of the President, demanded
that the President lay before Congress any information in his possession concerning the conspiracy and
the measures taken to suppress it.[1]

A heated debate followed. Jefferson's personal
supporters opposed the resolution. It was, however,
generally agreed, as stated by George W. Campbell
of Tennessee, that "this conspiracy has been painted
in stronger colors than there is reason to think it deserves." There was no real evidence, said Campbell;
nothing but "newspaper evidence." [2] Finally that
part of the resolution calling for the facts as to the
conspiracy was passed by a vote of 109 yeas to 14
nays; while the clause demanding information as to
the measures Jefferson had taken was carried by 67
yeas to 52 nays.[3]

A week later the President responded in a Special
Message. His information as to the conspiracy was,
he said, a "voluminous mass," but there was in it
"little to constitute legal evidence." It was "chiefly
in the form of letters, often containing such a mixture of rumors, conjectures, and suspicions, as renders it difficult to sift out the real facts." On November 25, said Jefferson, he had received Wilkinson's
letter exposing Burr's evil designs which the General, "with the honor of a soldier and fidelity of a

[1] *Annals*, 9th Cong. 2d Sess. 336.   [2] *Ib.* 347.   [3] *Ib.* 357–58.

good citizen," had sent him, and which, "when brought together" with some other information, "developed Burr's general designs." [1]

The President assured Congress that "one of these was the severance of the Union of these States beyond the Alleghany mountains; the other, an attack on Mexico. A third object was provided . . the settlement of a pretended purchase of a tract of country on the Washita." But "this was merely a pretext." Burr had soon found that the Western settlers were not to be seduced into secession; and thereupon, said Jefferson, the desperado "determined to seize upon New Orleans, plunder the bank there, possess himself of the military and naval stores, and proceed on his expedition to Mexico." For this purpose Burr had "collected . . all the ardent, restless, desperate, and disaffected persons" within his reach.

Therefore the President made his Proclamation of November 27, which had thwarted Burr's purposes. In New Orleans, however, General Wilkinson had been forced to take extreme measures for the defense of the country against the oncoming plunderers. Among these was the seizure of Bollmann and Swartwout who were "particularly employed in the endeavor to corrupt the General and the Army of the United States," and who had been sent oversea by Wilkinson for "ports in the Atlantic states, probably on the consideration that an impartial trial could not be expected . . in New

---

[1] *Annals*, 9th Cong. 2d Sess. 39–41. Jefferson's Message, Jan. 22, 1807, Richardson, I, 412–17.

Orleans, and that the city was not as yet a safe place of confinement." [1]

As to Burr, Jefferson assured Congress that his *"guilt is placed beyond question."* [2]

With this amazing Message the President sent an affidavit of Wilkinson's, as well as two letters from that veracious officer, [3] and a copy of Wilkinson's version of Burr's letter to him from which the General had carefully omitted the fact that the imprudent message was in answer to a dispatch from himself. But Jefferson did not transmit to Congress the letter, dated October 21, 1806, which he had received from Wilkinson.

Thoughtful men, who had personally studied Burr for years and who were unfriendly to him, doubted the accuracy of Wilkinson's version of the Burr dispatch: "It sounds more like Wilkinson's letter than Burr's," Senator Plumer records in his diary. "There are . . some things in it quite irrelevant. . . Burr's habits have been never to trust himself on paper, if he could avoid it — when he wrote, it was with great caution. . .Wilkinson is not an accurate correct man." [4]

No such doubts, however, assailed the eager multitude. The awful charge of treason had now been

---

[1] *Annals*, 9th Cong. 2d Sess. 43; Richardson, I, 416.

[2] *Annals*, 9th Cong. 2d Sess. 40. (Italics the author's.)

[3] "Wilkinson's letter is a curiosity. . . Tis Don Adriano de Armado the second." (J. Q. Adams to L. C. Adams, Dec. 8, 1806, *Writings, J. Q. A.*: Ford, III, footnote to 157.)

[4] Plumer, Jan. 22, 1807, "Diary," Plumer MSS. Lib. Cong.

Senator Plumer wrote his son, concerning Wilkinson's account of Burr's letter: "I am satisfied he has not accurately decyphered it. There is more of Wilkinsonism than of Burrism in it." (Plumer to his son, Jan. 24, 1807, Plumer MSS. Lib. Cong.)

formally made against Burr by the President of the
United States. This, the most sensational part of
Jefferson's Message, at once caught and held the attention of the public, which took for granted the
truth of it. From that moment the popular mind was
made up, and the popular voice demanded the life of
Aaron Burr. No mere trial in court, no adherence to
rules of evidence, no such insignificant fact as the
American Constitution, must be permitted to stand
between the people's aroused loyalty and the miscreant whom the Chief Executive of the Nation had
pronounced guilty of treason.

CHAPTER VII

THE CAPTURE AND ARRAIGNMENT

It was President Jefferson who directed and animated the prosecution.
(Winfield Scott.)

The President's popularity is unbounded and his will is that of the nation.
(Joseph Nicholson.)

The press from one end of the continent to the other has been enlisted to excite prejudices against Colonel Burr.   (John Wickham.)

Two thirds of our speeches have been addressed to the people.   (George Hay.)

It would be difficult or dangerous for a jury to acquit Burr, however innocent they might think him.   (Marshall.)

WHILE Washington was still agitated by the President's Special Message, the long winter voyage of Bollmann and Swartwout ended at Baltimore, and Burr's dazed dispatch-bearers were brought by military guards to the National Capital. There, on the evening of January 22, they were thrown into the military prison at the Marine Barracks, and "guarded, night and day, by an officer & 15 soldiers of the Marine Corps." [1]

The ship bearing James Alexander had made a swift passage. On its arrival, friends of this prisoner applied to Joseph F. Nicholson, now United States Judge at Baltimore, for a writ of habeas corpus. Alexander was at once set free, there being not the slightest evidence to justify his detention.[2]

[1] Plumer, Jan. 30, 1807, "Diary," Plumer MSS. Lib. Cong. Senator Plumer adds: "The government are apprehensive that the arts & address of *Bollman*, who effected the liberation of the Marquis de Lafayette from the strong prison of Magdeburge, may now find means to liberate himself."

[2] Clay to Prentiss, Feb. 15, 1807, *Priv. Corres.*: Colton, 15; also *Works:* Colton, IV, 14.

A week or two later the schooner Thatcher, on board which was the disconsolate and dumbfounded General Adair — Wilkinson's fourth prisoner to be sent to Jefferson — tied up to its dock at Baltimore and he was delivered "over to the commander of the fort at that city." But a passenger on the vessel, "a stranger . . of his own accord . . assured [Adair] he would procure a writ of Habeas Corpus for him." Adair also was "immediately liberated, . . there being no evidence against him."[1]

After the incarceration of Bollmann and Swartwout in Washington, attorneys were secured for them and an application was made to Judge William Cranch, United States Judge for the District of Columbia, for a writ of habeas corpus in their behalf, directed to Colonel Wharton, who was in command at Washington. Wharton brought the luckless prisoners into court and stated that "he held them under the orders of his superior officer. They were then taken upon a bench warrant charging them with treason which superseded the writ. A motion was made by the prisoners council . . that they be discharged. The Court required evidence of their probable guilt."[2]

Jefferson now took a hand in the prosecution. He considered Wilkinson's affidavit insufficient[3] to hold Bollmann and Swartwout, and, in order to

---

[1] Plumer, Feb. 20, 1807, "Register," Plumer MSS. Lib. Cong.

[2] Plumer to Mason, Jan. 30, 1807, Plumer MSS. Lib. Cong.

Plumer's account of the proceedings is trustworthy. He was an eminent lawyer himself, was deeply interested in the case, and was writing to Jeremiah Mason, then the leader of the New England bar.

[3] *Eaton: Prentiss*, 396.

strengthen the case against them, secured from Eaton an affidavit stating the dire revelations which Eaton alleged Burr had made to him a year before.[1] Eaton's theatrical story was thus given to the press,[2] and not only fortified the public conviction that a conspiracy to destroy the Union had been under way, but also horrified the country by the account of Burr's intention to assassinate Jefferson.

The Attorney-General and the United States District Attorney, representing the Government, demanded that Bollmann and Swartwout be held; Charles Lee, Robert Goodloe Harper, and Francis S. Key, attorneys for the prisoners, insisted that they be released. Long was the argument and "vast" the crowd that heard it; "collected & firm" was the appearance of the accused men.[3] So universal was

[1] See *supra*, 303–05.

Three days before he made oath to the truth of this story, Eaton's claim against the Government was referred to a committee of the House (see *Annals*, 9th Cong. 2d Sess. 383), and within a month from the time the historic affidavit was made, a bill was passed, without debate, "authorizing the settlement of the accounts between the United States and William Eaton."

John Randolph was suspicious: "He believed the bill had passed by surprise. It was not so much a bill to settle the accounts of William Eaton, as to rip up the settled forms of the Treasury, and to transfer the accountable duties of the Treasury to the Department of State. It would be a stain upon the Statute Book." (*Ib.* 622.)

The very next week after the passage of this measure, Eaton received ten thousand dollars from the Government. (See testimony of William Eaton, *Trials of Colonel Aaron Burr*: Robertson, stenographer, I, 483.)

[2] "Eaton's story .. has now been served up in all the newspapers. . . The amount of his narrative is, that he advised the President to send Burr upon an important embassy, BECAUSE!!! he had discovered the said Burr to be a *Traitor to his country*." (J. Q. Adams to L. C. Adams, Dec. 8, 1806, *Writings*, J. Q. A.: Ford, III, footnote to 157.)

[3] Plumer, Jan. 30, 1807, "Diary," Plumer MSS. Lib. Cong.

the curiosity, says John Quincy Adams, that the Senate was "scarcely able here to form a quorum . . and the House . . actually adjourned." [1] The court decided that Bollmann and Swartwout should be sent back to prison "for trial without bail or mainprize." For the first time in our history a National court divided on political grounds. Judge Cranch, a Federalist first appointed by President Adams,[2] thought that the prisoners should be discharged, but was overruled by his associates, Judges Nicholas Fitzhugh and Allen Bowie Duckett, Republicans appointed by Jefferson.[3]

But John Marshall and the Supreme Court had yet to be reckoned with. Counsel for the reimprisoned men at once applied to that tribunal for a writ of habeas corpus, and Marshall directed process to the jailer to show cause why the writ should not issue.

An extreme and violent step was now taken to end the proceedings in court. On Friday, January 23, 1807, the day after the President's Special Message denouncing Burr had been read in the Senate, Senator Giles, who, it should be repeated, was Jefferson's personal representative in that body, actually moved the appointment of a committee to draft a bill "to suspend the privilege of the writ of habeas

[1] J. Q. Adams to his father, Jan. 30, 1807, *Writings, J. Q. A.*: Ford, III, 159.

[2] Feb. 28, 1801, *Journal Exec. Proc. Senate*, I, 387. Cranch was so excellent a judge that, Federalist though he was, Jefferson reappointed him February 21, 1806. (*Ib.* II, 21.)

[3] Jefferson appointed Nicholas Fitzhugh of Virginia, November 22, 1803 (*ib.* I, 458), and Allen Bowie Duckett of Maryland, February 28, 1806 (*ib.* II, 25).

corpus." Quickly Giles himself reported the measure, the Senate suspended its rules, and the bill was hurriedly passed, only Bayard of Delaware voting against it.[1] More astounding still, Giles recommended, and the Senate adopted, a special message to the House, stating the Senate's action "which they think expedient to communicate to you in confidence," and asking the popular branch of Congress to pass the Senate bill without delay.[2]

Immediately after the House convened on Monday, January 26,[3] Senator Samuel Smith of Maryland appeared on the floor and delivered this "confidential message," together with the Senate bill, which provided that "in all cases, where any person or persons, charged on oath with treason, misprision of treason, or other high crime or misdemeanor . . shall be arrested or imprisoned . . the privilege of the writ of habeas corpus shall be . . suspended, for and during the term of three months."[4]

The House was astounded. Party discipline was, for the moment, wrathfully repudiated. Mr. Philip R. Thompson of Virginia instantly moved that the "message and the bill received from the Senate ought not to be kept secret and that the doors be opened." Thompson's motion was adopted by 123 yeas to 3 nays.

Then came a motion to reject the bill, followed by a brief and almost one-sided debate, which was little

[1] J. Q. Adams to his father, Jan. 27, 1807, *Writings, J. Q. A.*: Ford, III, 158.

[2] *Annals*, 9th Cong. 2d Sess. 44.

[3] On Friday afternoon the House adjourned till Monday morning.

[4] *Annals*, 9th Cong. 2d Sess. 402.

more than the angry protest of the representatives of the people against the proposed overthrow of this last defense of liberty. William A. Burwell of Virginia asked whether there was any danger "to justify this suspension of this most important right of the citizen. . . He could judge from what he had already seen that men, who are perfectly innocent, would be doomed to . . undergo the infamy of the dungeon." [1] "Never," exclaimed John W. Eppes of the same State, "under this Government, has personal liberty been held at the will of a single individual." [2]

On the other hand, Joseph B. Varnum of Massachusetts said that Burr's "insurrection" was the worst in all history.[3] James Sloan of New Jersey made a similar statement.[4] But the House promptly rejected the Senate bill by 113 yeas to 19 nays. The shameful attempt to prevent John Marshall from deciding whether Bollmann and Swartwout were entitled to the benefit of the most sacred writ known to the law was thereby defeated and the Chief Justice was left free to grant or reject it, as justice might require.

The order of the court of the District of Columbia was that Bollmann and Swartwout "be committed to prison of this court, to take their trial for treason against the United States, by levying war against them." [5] In the Supreme Court the prisoners and the Government were represented by the same counsel who had argued the case below, and Luther Martin

---

[1] *Annals*, 9th Cong. 2d Sess. 404–05.
[2] *Ib.* 410. Eppes was Jefferson's son-in-law.
[3] *Ib.* 412.   [4] *Ib.* 414–15.   [5] 4 Cranch, 76.

also appeared in behalf of the men whose long-continued and, as he believed, wholly illegal suffering had aroused the sympathies of that admirable lawyer.

The Supreme Court first decided that it had jurisdiction. The application for the writs of habeas corpus was, in effect, an appeal from the decision of the District Court. On this point Justice Johnson delivered a dissenting opinion, observing, as an aside, that the argument for the prisoners had shown "an unnecessary display of energy and pathos." [1] The affidavit of General Wilkinson and his version of the Burr letter, concerning which "the court had difficulty," were admitted by a vote of the majority of the Justices. At noon on the twenty-first day of February, 1807, Marshall delivered the opinion of the majority of the court upon the main question,[2] "whether the accused shall be discharged or held to trial."

The specific charge was that of "treason in levying war against the United States." This, declared Marshall, was the most serious offense of which any man can be accused: "As there is no crime which can more excite and agitate the passions of men than treason, no charge demands more from the tribunal before which it is made a deliberate and temperate inquiry. Whether this inquiry be directed to the fact or to the law, none can be more solemn, none more

[1] 4 Cranch, 107. Justice Chase, who was absent because of illness, concurred with Johnson. (Clay to Prentiss, Feb. 15, 1807, *Priv. Corres.*: Colton, 15; also *Works:* Colton, IV, 15.)

Cæsar A. Rodney, Jefferson's Attorney-General, declined to argue the question of jurisdiction.

[2] 4 Cranch, 125–37.

important to the citizen or to the government; none can more affect the safety of both."

In order that it should never be possible to extend treason "to offenses of minor importance," the Constitution "has given a rule on the subject both to the legislatures and the courts of America, which neither can be permitted to transcend." Marshall then read, with solemn impressiveness, these words from the Constitution of the United States: "Treason against the United States shall consist only in levying war against them, or in adhering to their enemies, giving them aid and comfort."

To support the charge against Bollmann and Swartwout, said Marshall, "war must be actually levied. . . To conspire to levy war, and actually to levy war, are distinct offenses. The first must be brought into open action by the assemblage of men for a purpose treasonable in itself, or the fact of levying war cannot have been committed." It was not necessary for the commission of this crime that a man should actually "appear in arms against his country. . . If a body of men be actually assembled for the purpose of effecting by force a treasonable purpose; all those who perform any part, however minute, or however remote from the scene of the action, and who are actually leagued in the general conspiracy, are to be considered as traitors."[1] This passage was soon to cause Marshall great embarrassment when he was confronted with it in the trial of Aaron Burr at Richmond.

Did this mean that men who go to the very edge

[1] 4 Cranch, 125-26.

of legal boundaries — who stop just short of committing treason — must go scathless? By no means! Such offenses could be and must be provided for by statute. They were not, like treason, Constitutional crimes. "The framers of our Constitution . . must have conceived it more safe that punishment in such cases should be ordained by general laws, formed upon deliberation, under the influence of no resentments, and without knowing on whom they were to operate, than that it should be inflicted under the influence of those passions which the occasion seldom fails to excite, and which a flexible definition of the crime, or a construction which would render it flexible, might bring into operation."

This was a direct rebuke to Jefferson. There can be no doubt that Marshall was referring to the recent attempt to deprive Bollmann and Swartwout of the protection of the courts by suspending the writ of habeas corpus. "It is, therefore, more safe," continued Marshall, "as well as more consonant to the principles of our constitution, that the crime of treason should not be extended by construction to doubtful cases; and that crimes not clearly within the constitutional definition should receive such punishment as the legislature in its wisdom may provide."

What do the words "levying war" mean? To complete that crime, Marshall repeated, "there must be an actual assemblage of men for the purpose of executing a treasonable design . . but no conspiracy for this object, no enlisting of men to effect it, would be an actual levying of war."[1] He then

[1] 4 Cranch, 127.

applied these principles to the testimony. First he took up the deposition of Eaton [1] which, he said, indicated that the invasion of Mexico "was the immediate object" [2] that Burr had in mind.

But, asked the Chief Justice, what had this to do with Bollmann and Swartwout? The prosecution connected the prisoners with the statements made in Eaton's deposition by offering the affidavit of General Wilkinson, which included his version of Burr's celebrated letter. Marshall then overruled the "great and serious objections made" to the admission of Wilkinson's affidavit. One of these objections was to that part which purported to set out the Wilkinson translation of the Burr cipher, the original letter not having been presented. Marshall announced that "a division of opinion has taken place in the court," two of the Judges believing such testimony totally inadmissible and two others holding that it was proper to consider it "at this incipient stage of the prosecution."

Thereupon Marshall analyzed Wilkinson's version of Burr's confidential cipher dispatch.[3] It was so vague, said the Chief Justice, that it "furnishes no distinct view of the design of the writer." But the "coöperation" which Burr stated had been secured "points strongly to some expedition against the territories of Spain."

---

[1] See *supra*, 303–05.   [2] 4 Cranch, 128–29.
[3] See Appendix D.

In his translation Wilkinson carefully omitted the first sentence of Burr's dispatch: "Yours, post-marked 13th of May, is received." (Parton: *Burr*, 427.) This was not disclosed until the fact was extorted from Wilkinson at the Burr trial. (See *infra*, chap. VIII.)

Marshall then quoted these words of Burr's famous message: "'Burr's plan of operations is to move down rapidly from the falls on the 15th of November, with the first 500 or 1,000 men in the light boats now constructing for that purpose, to be at Natchez between the 5th and 15th of December, there to meet Wilkinson; then to determine whether it will be expedient in the first instance to seize on, or to pass by, Baton Rouge. The people of the country to which we are going are prepared to receive us. Their agents now with Burr say that if we will protect their religion, and will not subject them to a foreign power, in three weeks all will be settled.'"

This language was, said Marshall, "rather more explicit." But "there is no expression in these sentences which would justify a suspicion that any territory of the United States was the object of the expedition. For what purpose seize on Baton Rouge? Why engage Spain against this enterprise, if it was designed against the United States?" [1]

Burr's statement that "the people of the country to which we are going are prepared to receive us," was, said Marshall, "peculiarly appropriate to a foreign country." And what was the meaning of the statement: "Their agents now with Burr say, that if we will protect their religion, and will not subject them to a foreign power, in three weeks all will be settled"? It was not probable that this referred to American citizens; but it perfectly fitted the Mexicans. "There certainly is not in the letter delivered to General Wilkinson . . one syllable which has a

[1] 4 Cranch, 131–32.

necessary or a natural reference to an enterprise against the territory of the United States."

According to Wilkinson's affidavit, Swartwout knew the contents of the dispatch he was carrying; Wilkinson had deposed that Burr's messenger had frankly said so. Without stating that, in his long journey from New York through the Western States and Territories in quest of Wilkinson, he had "performed on his route any act whatever which was connected with the enterprise," Swartwout had declared "their object to be 'to carry an expedition to the Mexican provinces.'"[1] This, said Marshall, was "explanatory of the letter of Col. Burr, if the expressions of that letter could be thought ambiguous."

But Wilkinson declared in his affidavit that Swartwout had also told him that "this territory would be revolutionized where the people were ready to join them, and that there would be some seizing, he supposed at New Orleans."[2] If this meant that

---

[1] 4 Cranch, 132–33.

[2] Wilkinson declared in his affidavit that he "drew" from Swartwout the following disclosures: "Colonel Burr, with the support of a powerful association, extending from New York to New Orleans, was levying an armed body of seven thousand men from the state of New York and the Western states and Territories" to invade Mexico which "would be revolutionized, where the people were ready to join them."

"There would be some seizing, he supposed at New Orleans"; he "knew full well" that "there were several millions of dollars in the bank of this place," but that Burr's party only "meant to borrow and would return it — they must equip themselves at New Orleans, etc., etc." (*Annals*, 9th Cong. 2d Sess. 1014–15.)

Swartwout made oath that he told Wilkinson nothing of the kind. The high character which this young man then bore, together with the firm impression of truthfulness he made on everybody at that time and during the distracting months that followed, would seem to suggest the conclusion that Wilkinson's story was only another of the brood of falsehoods of which that fecund liar was so prolific.

the Government in any American territory was to be revolutionized by force, "although merely as a .. means of executing some greater projects, the design was unquestionably treasonable," said Marshall; "and any assemblage of men for that purpose would amount to a levying of war." It was, then, of first importance to discover the true meaning of the youthful and indiscreet messenger.

For the third time the court divided. "Some of the judges," Marshall explained, suppose that these words of Swartwout "refer to the territory against which the expedition was intended; others to that in which the conversation was held. Some consider the words, if even applicable to a territory of the United States, as alluding to a revolution to be effected by the people, rather than by the party conducted by Col. Burr."

Swartwout's statement, as given in Wilkinson's affidavit, that Burr was assembling thousands of armed men to attack Mexico, did not prove that Burr had gathered an army to make war on the United States.[1] If the latter were Burr's purpose, it was not necessary that the entire host should have met at one spot; if detachments had actually formed and were marching to the place of rendezvous, treason had been committed. Following his tedious habit of repeating over and over again, often in identical language, statements already clearly made, Marshall for the fourth time asserted that there must be "unequivocal evidence" of "an actual assemblage."

[1] 4 Cranch, 133-34.

The mere fact that Burr "was enlisting men in his service .. would not amount to levying war." That Swartwout meant only this, said Marshall, was "sufficiently apparent." If seven thousand men had actually come together in one body, every one would know about it; and surely, observed Marshall, "some evidence of such an assembling would have been laid before the court."

Burr's intention to do certain "seizing at New Orleans" did not amount to levying war from anything that could be inferred from Swartwout's statement. It only "indicated a design to rob." Having thus examined all the testimony before the court, Marshall announced the opinion of the majority of the Justices that there was not "sufficient evidence of his [Swartwout's] levying war against the United States to justify his commitment on the charge of treason." [1]

The testimony against Bollmann was, if possible, still weaker. There was, indeed, "no evidence to support a charge of treason" against him. Whoever believed the assertions in Wilkinson's affidavit could not doubt that both Bollmann and Swartwout "were engaged in a most culpable enterprise against the dominions of a power at peace with the United States"; but it was apparent that "no part of this crime was committed in the District of Columbia." They could not, therefore, be tried in that District.

Upon that point the court was at last unanimous. The accused men could have been tried in New Orleans — "there existed a tribunal in that city,"

---

[1] 4 Cranch, 135.

sarcastically observed Marshall; but to say that citizens might be seized by military power in the jurisdiction where the alleged crime was committed and thereafter tried "in any place which the general might select, and to which he might direct them to be carried," was not to be thought of — such a thing "would be extremely dangerous." So the long-suffering Bollmann and Swartwout were discharged.[1]

Thus, by three different courts, five of the "conspirators" had successively been released. In the case of Ogden, there was no proof; of Alexander, no proof; of Adair, no proof; of Bollmann and Swartwout, no proof. And the Judges had dared to set free the accused men — had refused to consign them to prison, despite public opinion and the desire of the Administration. Could anything be more undemocratic, more reprehensible? The Supreme Court, especially, should be rebuked.

On learning of that tribunal's action, Giles adjourned the meeting of his committee on the treason bill in order to secure immediately a copy of Marshall's opinion. In a true Virginian rage, Giles threatened to offer an amendment to the Constitution "taking away *all* jurisdiction of the Supreme Court in criminal cases." There was talk of impeaching every occupant of the Supreme Bench.[2]

More news had now reached Washington concerning the outrages committed at New Orleans; and on the day that the attorneys for Bollmann and Swart-

---

[1] 4 Cranch, 136.
[2] Feb. 21, 1807, *Memoirs, J. Q. A.*: Adams, i, 459.

wout applied to the Supreme Court for writs of habeas corpus, James M. Broom of Delaware rose in the House, and introduced a resolution "to make further provision for securing the privilege of the writ of habeas corpus to persons in custody under or by color of the authority of the United States."[1] While the cases were being argued in the Supreme Court and the divided Judges were wrangling over the disputed points, a violent debate sprang up in the House over Broom's resolution. "If, upon every alarm of conspiracy," said Broom, "our rights of personal liberty are to be entrusted to the keeping of a military commander, we may prepare to take our leave of them forever."[2] All day the debate continued; on the next day, February 18, while Marshall was delivering his opinion that the Supreme Court had jurisdiction of the application of Bollmann and Swartwout, the controversy in the House was renewed.

James Elliot of Vermont said that "most of the privileges intended to be secured" by the Fourth, Fifth, and Sixth Amendments[3] "have recently been

[1] *Annals*, 9th Cong. 2d Sess. 472.   [2] *Ib.* 506.

[3] They are: "Article IV. The right of the people to be secure in their persons, houses, papers and effects, against unreasonable searches and seizures, shall not be violated, and no warrants shall issue but upon probable cause, supported by oath or affirmation, and particularly describing the place to be searched, and the persons or things to be seized.

"Article V. No person shall be held to answer for a capital or otherwise infamous crime, unless on a presentment or indictment of a grand jury, except in cases arising in the land or naval forces, or in the militia when in actual service in time of war or public danger; nor shall any person be subject for the same offence to be twice put in jeopardy of life or limb; nor shall be compelled, in any criminal case, to be witness against himself, nor be deprived of life, liberty, or prop-

denied .. at the point of the bayonet, and under
circumstances of peculiar violence." He read Wilkinson's impertinent return to the Orleans County
Court. This, said Elliot, was "not obedience to
the laws .. but .. defiance... What necessity could
exist for seizing one or two wandering conspirators,
and transporting them fifteen hundred or two thousand miles from the Constitutional scene of inquisition and trial, to place them particularly under the
eye of the National Government"? [1] Not only was
the swish of the party whip heard in the House,
he asserted, but members who would not desert
the fundamentals of liberty must "be prepared for
the insinuation that we countenance treason, and
sympathize with traitors." [2]

The shrill voice of John Randolph was heard.
Almost his first sentence was a blow at Jefferson. If
the President and his party "ever quit the ground of
trial by jury, the liberty of the press, and the subor-
dination of the military to the civil authority, they
must expect that their enemies will perceive the desertion and avail themselves of the advantage." [3]
Randolph assailed the recent attempt to suspend
the writ of habeas corpus which, he said, "was in-

erty, without due process of law; nor shall private property be taken
for public use without just compensation.

"Article VI. In all criminal prosecutions the accused shall enjoy
the right to a speedy and public trial, by an impartial jury of the
state and district wherein the crime shall have been committed,
which district shall have been previously ascertained by law, and to
be informed of the nature and cause of the accusation; to be confronted with the witnesses against him; to have compulsory process
for obtaining witnesses in his favour, and to have the assistance of
counsel for his defence."

[1] *Annals*, 9th Cong. 2d Sess. 531.   [2] *Ib.* 532–33.   [3] *Ib.* 535.

tended . . to cover with a mantle the most daring usurpation which ever did, will, or can happen, in this or any country. There was exactly as much right to shoot the persons in question as to do what has been done." [1] The Declaration of Independence had assigned wrongs of precisely the kind suffered by Bollmann and Swartwout "as one of the grievances imposed by the British Government on the colonies. Now, it is done under the Constitution," exclaimed Randolph, "and under a republican administration, and men are transported without the color of law, nearly as far as across the Atlantic." [2]

Again and again angry speakers denounced the strenuous attempts of the Administration's supporters to influence Republican votes on partisan grounds. Only by the most desperate efforts was Jefferson saved from the rebuke and humiliation of the passage of the resolution. But his escape was narrow. Indefinite postponement was voted by the dangerous majority of 2 out of a total of 118 members. [3]

While Burr's messengers were on the high seas, prisoners of war, and Wilkinson at New Orleans was saving the Republic by rending its laws, Burr himself, ignorant of all, was placidly making his way down the Ohio and Mississippi with his nine boats and sixty adventurers, mostly youths, many only boys. He had left Jackson at Nashville on December 22, and floating down the Cumberland in two unarmed boats, had joined the remainder of the little expedition.

---

[1] *Annals*, 9th Cong. 2d Sess. 536.   [2] *Ib*. 537–38.   [3] *Ib*. 589.

He then met for the first time the young adventurers whom Blennerhassett, Comfort Tyler of Syracuse, New York, and Davis Floyd of the tiny settlement of New Albany, Indiana Territory, had induced to join the expedition. On a cold, rainy December morning they were drawn up in a semi-circle on a little island at the mouth of the Cumberland River, and Burr was introduced to each of them. Greeting them with his customary reserved friendliness, he told them that the objects of the expedition not already disclosed to them would be revealed at a more opportune time.[1]

Such was the second "overt act" of the gathering of an armed host to "levy war" on the United States for which Jefferson later fastened the charge of treason upon Aaron Burr.

As it floated down the Ohio and Mississippi, the little flotilla[2] stopped at the forts upon the river bluffs, and the officers proffered Burr all the courtesies at their command. Seven days after Burr had left Fort Massac, Captain Bissel, in answer to a letter of inquiry from Andrew Jackson, assured him that "there has nothing the least alarming appeared"; Burr had passed with a few boats "having nothing on board that would even suffer a conjecture, more than a man bound to market."[3] John

---

[1] Nearly all the men had been told that they were to settle the Washita lands; and this was true, as far as it went. (See testimony of Stephen S. Welch, Samuel Moxley, Chandler Lindsley, John Mulhollan, Hugh Allen, and others, *Annals*, 10th Cong. 1st Sess. 463 *et seq.*)

[2] The boats were very comfortable. They were roofed and had compartments for cooking, eating, and sleeping. They were much like the modern house boat.

[3] Bissel to Jackson, Jan. 5, 1807, *Annals*, 9th Cong. 2d Sess. 1017–18.

Murrell of Tennessee, sent on a secret mission of investigation, reported to Jackson that, pursuant to instructions, he had closely followed and examined Burr's movements on the Cumberland; that he had heard reports that Burr "had gone down the river with one thousand armed men"; but Murrell had found the fact to be that there were but ten boats with only "sixty men on board," and "no appearance of arms." [1]

During the week when John Randolph, in the House, was demanding information of the President, and Wilkinson, in New Orleans, was making his second series of arrests, Burr, with his little group of boats and small company of men — totally unequipped for anything but the settlement of the Washita lands, and poorly supplied even for that — serenely drew up to the landing at the small post of Bayou Pierre in the Territory of Mississippi. He was still uninformed of what was going forward at New Orleans and at Washington — still unconscious of the storm of hatred and denunciation that had been blown up against him.

At the little settlement, Burr learned for the first time of the fate prepared for him. Bloody and violent were the measures he then adopted! He wrote a letter to Cowles Mead, Acting Governor of the Territory, stating that rumors he had just heard were untrue; that "his object is agriculture and his boats are the vehicles of immigration." But he "hinted at resistance to any attempt to coerce him." [2]

---

[1] Murrell to Jackson, Jan. 8, 1807, *Annals*, 9th Cong. 2d Sess. 1017.
[2] Mead to the Secretary of War, Jan. 13, 1807, *ib.* 1018.

What followed was related by Mead himself. As directed by the War Department, he had prorogued the Legislature, put the Territory in a state of defense, and called out the militia. When Burr's letter came, Mead ordered these frontier soldiers to "rendezvous at certain points. . . With the promptitude of Spartans, our fellow-citizens shouldered their firelocks, and in twenty-four hours I had the honor to review three hundred and seventy-five men at Natches, prepared to defend their country." Mead sent two aides to Burr, "who tendered his respects to the civil authority." The Acting Governor himself then saw Burr, whereupon the desperado actually "offered to surrender himself to the civil authority of the Territory, and to suffer his boats to be searched." This was done by "four gentlemen of unquestionable respectability, with a detachment of thirty men." Burr readily went into court and awaited trial.

"Thus, sir," concludes Governor Mead, "this mighty alarm, with all its exaggeration, has eventuated in nine boats and one hundred men,[1] and the major part of these are boys, or young men just from school," wholly unaware of Burr's evil designs.[2]

The Legislature of the Territory of Orleans had just convened. Governor Claiborne recommended that a law be passed suspending the writ of habeas corpus. Behind closed doors the Representatives

[1] Burr had picked up forty men on his voyage down the Mississippi.

[2] Mead to the War Department, Jan. 19, 1807, *Annals*, 9th Cong. 2d Sess. 1019.

were harangued by Wilkinson on the subject of the
great conspiracy. All the old horrors were again
paraded to induce the legislators to support Wilkinson in his lawless acts. Instead, that body denied the
existence of treason in Louisiana, expressed alarm at
the "late privation" of the rights of American citizens, and determined to investigate the "measures
and motives" of Wilkinson. A memorial to Congress
was adopted, denouncing "the acts of high-handed
military power . . too notorious to be denied, too
illegal to be justified, too wanton to be excused," by
which "the temple of justice" had been "sacrile-
giously rifled." [1]

In Mississippi, Burr calmly awaited his trial before the United States Court of that Territory. Bail
in the sum of five thousand dollars had been furnished by Colonel Benijah Osmun and Lyman Harding, two Revolutionary comrades of Burr, who years
before had emigrated to Mississippi and developed
into wealthy planters. Colonel Osmun invited Burr
to be his guest. Having seen the ogre and talked with
him, the people of the neighborhood became Burr's
enthusiastic friends.

Soon the grand jury was impaneled to investigate
Burr's "crimes" and indict him for them if a true
bill could be found. This body outdid the performance of the Kentucky grand jury nine weeks earlier.
The grand jurors asserted that, after examining the

[1] McCaleb, 233–36. For the discussion over this resolution see
*Debate in the House of Representatives of the Territory of Orleans, on a
Memorial to Congress, respecting the illegal conduct of General Wilkinson.* Both sides of the question were fully represented. See also Cox,
194, 200, 206–08.

evidence, they were "of the opinion that Aaron Burr has not been guilty of any crime or misdemeanor against the laws of the United States or of this Territory or given any just alarm or inquietude to the good people of this Territory." Worse still followed — the grand jury formally presented as "a grievance" the march of the militia against Burr, since there had been no prior resistance by him to the civil authorities. Nor did the grand jurors stop there. They also presented "as a grievance, destructive of personal liberty," Wilkinson's military outrages in New Orleans.[1]

When the grand jury was dismissed, Burr asked to be discharged and his sureties released from his bond. The judge was Thomas Rodney, the father of Cæsar A. Rodney whom Jefferson soon afterward appointed Attorney-General. Judge Rodney out-Wilkinsoned Wilkinson; he denied Burr's request and ordered him to renew his bond or go to jail. This was done despite the facts that the grand jury had refused to indict Burr and that there was no legal charge whatever before the court.

Wilkinson was frantic lest Burr escape him. Every effort was made to seize him; officers in disguise were sent to capture him,[2] and men "armed with Dirks & Pistolls" were dispatched to assassinate him.[3] Burr consulted Colonel Osmun and other

[1] Return of the Mississippi Grand Jury, Feb. 3, reported in the *Orleans Gazette*, Feb. 20, 1807, as quoted in McCaleb, 272-73.

[2] *Annals*, 10th Cong. 1st Sess. 528-29, 536, 658-61.

[3] Deposition of George Peter, Sept. 10, 1807, *Am. State Papers, Misc.* I, 566; and see *Quarterly Pub. Hist. and Phil. Soc. of Ohio*, IX, Nos. 1 and 2, 35-38; McCaleb, 274-75; Cox, 200-08.

friends, who advised him to keep out of sight for a
time. So he went into hiding, but wrote the Governor that he would again come before the court
when he could be assured of being dealt with legally.

Thereupon the bond of five thousand dollars,
which Judge Rodney had compelled Burr to give,
was declared forfeited and a reward of two thousand
dollars was offered for his apprehension. From his
place of retreat the harried man protested by letter.
The Governor would not relent. Wilkinson was raging in New Orleans. Illegal imprisonment, probably
death, was certain for Burr if he should be taken.
His friends counseled flight, and he acted on their
judgment.[1]

But he would not go until he had seen his disconsolate followers once more. Stealthily visiting his
now unguarded flotilla, he told his men to take for
themselves the boats and provisions, and, if they
desired, to proceed to the Washita lands, settle
there, and keep as much as they wanted. He had
stood his trial, he said, and had been acquitted; but
now he was to be taken by unlawful violence, and
the only thing left for him to do was to "flee from
oppression." [2]

Colonel Osmun gave him the best horse in his
stables. Clad "in an old blanket-coat begirt with a
leathern strap, to which a tin cup was suspended on
the left and a scalping knife on the right," Aaron
Burr rode away into the wilderness.

At ten o'clock of a rainy night, on the very day
when Marshall delivered his first opinion in the case

---

[1] McCaleb, 277.   [2] *Ib.*

of Bollmann and Swartwout, Burr was recognized at a forest tavern in Washington County,[1] where he had stopped to inquire the way to the house of Colonel Hinson, whom he had met at Natchez on his first Western journey and who had invited Burr to be his guest if he ever came to that part of the Territory. "Major" Nicholas Perkins, a burly backwoods lawyer from Tennessee, penetrated the disguise,[2] because of Burr's fine eyes and erect carriage.

Perkins hurried to the cabin of Theodore Brightwell, sheriff of the county, and the two men rode after Burr, overtaking him at the residence of Colonel Hinson, who was away from home and whose wife had prepared supper for the wanderer. Brightwell went inside while Perkins remained in the downpour watching the house from the bushes.

Burr so won the hearts of both hostess and sheriff that, instead of arresting him, the officer proposed to guide the escaping criminal on his way the next morning.[3] The drenched and shivering Perkins, feeling that all was not right inside the cabin, hastened by horse and canoe to Fort Stoddert and told Captain Edward P. Gaines of Burr's whereabouts. With a file of soldiers the captain and the lawyer set off to find and take the fugitive. They soon met him with the sheriff, who was telling Burr the roads to follow.

Exclusively upon the authority of Jefferson's Proc-

---

[1] In that part of the Territory which is now the State of Alabama.

[2] Perkins had read and studied the description of Burr in one of the Proclamations which the Governor of Mississippi had issued. A large reward for the capture of Burr was also offered, and on this the mind of Perkins was now fastened.

[3] Pickett: *History of Alabama*, 218–31.

lamation, Burr was arrested and confined in the fort.
With quiet dignity, the "traitor" merely protested
and asked to be delivered to the civil courts. His
arrest was wholly illegal, he correctly said; let a
judge and jury again pass on his conduct. But seizure and incarceration by military force, utterly without warrant of law, were a denial of fundamental
rights — rights which could not be refused to the
poorest citizen or the most abandoned criminal.[1]

Two weeks passed before Burr was sent northward. During this period all within the stockades
became his friends. The brother of Captain Gaines
fell ill and Burr, who among other accomplish-
ments knew much about medicine, treated the sick
man and cheered him with gay conversation. The
soldiers liked Burr; the officers liked him; their
wives liked him. Everybody yielded to his strange
attractiveness.

Two weeks after Marshall discharged Bollmann
and Swartwout at Washington, Burr was delivered
by Captain Gaines to a guard of nine men organized
by Perkins; and, preceded and followed by them, he
began the thousand-mile journey to Washington.
For days torrential rains fell; streams were swollen;
the soil was a quagmire. For hundreds of miles the
only road was an Indian trail; wolves filled the forest; savage Indians were all about.[2] At night the

---

[1] Yet, five months afterward, Jefferson actually wrote Captain
Gaines: "That the arrest of Colo. B. was military has been disproved;
but had it been so, every honest man & good citizen is bound, by any
means in his power, to arrest the author of projects so daring & dangerous." (Jefferson to Gaines, July 23, 1807, *Works:* Ford, x, 473.)

[2] Pickett, 224-25.

party, drenched and chilled, slept on the sodden earth. Burr never complained.

After ten days the first white settlements appeared. In two days more, South Carolina was reached. The cautious Perkins avoided the larger settlements, for Burr was popular in that State and his captor would run no risks of a rescue. As the prisoner and his convoy were passing through a village, a number of men were standing before a tavern. Burr suddenly threw himself from his horse and cried: "I am Aaron Burr, under military arrest, and claim the protection of the civil authorities."

Before any one could move, Perkins sprang to Burr's side, a pistol in each hand, and ordered him to remount. Burr refused; and the gigantic frontier lawyer lifted the slight, delicate prisoner in his hands, threw him into his saddle, and the sorry cavalcade rode on, guards now on either side, as well as before and behind their charge. Then, for the first and last time in his life, Burr lost his composure, but only for a moment; tears filled his eyes, but instantly recovering his self-possession, he finished the remainder of that harrowing trip as courteous, dignified, and serene as ever.[1]

At Fredericksburg, Virginia, Perkins received orders from the Government to take his prisoner to Richmond instead of to Washington. John Randolph describes the cavalcade: "Colonel Burr . . passed by my door the day before yesterday under a strong guard. . . To guard against enquiry as

[1] For the account of Burr's arrest and transfer from Alabama to Richmond, see Pickett, 218–31. Parton adopts Pickett's narrative, adding only one or two incidents; see Parton: *Burr*, 444–52.

much as possible he was accoutred in a shabby suit of homespun with an old white hat flopped over his face, the dress in which he was apprehended." [1]

In such fashion, when the candles were being lighted on the evening of Thursday, March 26, 1807, Aaron Burr was brought into the Virginia Capital, where, before a judge who could be neither frightened nor cajoled, he was to make final answer to the charge of treason.

Burr remained under military guard until the arrival of Marshall at Richmond. The Chief Justice at once wrote out,[2] signed, and issued a warrant by virtue of which the desperate yet composed prisoner was at last surrendered to the civil authorities, before whom he had so long demanded to be taken.

During the noon hour on Monday, March 30, Marshall went to "a retired room" in the Eagle Tavern. In this hostelry Burr was confined. Curious citizens thronged the big public room of the inn and were "awfully silent and attentive" as the pale and worn conspirator was taken by Major Joseph Scott, the United States Marshal, and two deputies through the quiet but hostile assemblage to the apartment where the Chief Justice awaited him. To the disappointment of the crowd, the door was closed and Aaron Burr stood before John Marshall.[3]

George Hay, the United States District Attorney, had objected to holding even the beginning of the preliminary hearing at the hotel, because the great

---

[1] Randolph to Nicholson, March 25, 1807, Adams: *Randolph*, 220.

[2] The warrant was written by Marshall himself. (MS. Archives of the United States Court, Richmond, Va.)

[3] *Burr Trials*, I, 1.

number of eager and antagonistic spectators could not be present. Upon the sentiment of these, as will be seen, Hay relied, even more than upon the law and the evidence, to secure the conviction of the accused man. He yielded, however, on condition that, if any discussion arose among counsel, the proceedings should be adjourned to the Capitol.[1]

It would be difficult to imagine two men more unlike in appearance, manner, attire, and characteristics, than the prisoner and the judge who now confronted each other; yet, in many respects, they were similar. Marshall, towering, ramshackle, bony, loose-jointed, negligently dressed, simple and unconventional of manner; Burr, undersized and erect, his apparel scrupulously neat,[2] his deportment that of the most punctilious society. Outwardly, the two men resembled each other in only a single particular: their eyes were as much alike as their persons were in contrast.[3] Burr was fifty years of age, and Marshall was less than six months older.

Both were calm, admirably poised and self-possessed; and from the personality of each radiated a strange power of which no one who came near either of them could fail to be conscious. Intellectually, also, there were points of remarkable similarity. Clear, cold logic was the outstanding element of their minds.

[1] *Burr Trials*, I, 1.

[2] The first thing that Burr did upon his arrival at Richmond was to put aside his dirty, tattered clothing and secure decent attire.

[3] Marshall's eyes were "the finest ever seen, except Burr's, large, black and brilliant beyond description. It was often remarked during the trial, that two such pairs of eyes had never looked into one another before." (Parton: *Burr*, 459.)

The two men had the gift of lucid statement, although Marshall indulged in tiresome repetition while Burr never restated a point or an argument. Neither ever employed imagery or used any kind of rhetorical display. Notwithstanding the rigidity of their logic, both were subtle and astute; it was all but impossible to catch either off his guard. But Marshall gave the impression of great frankness; while about every act and word of Burr there was the air of mystery. The feeling which Burr's actions inspired, that he was obreptitious, was overcome by the fascination of the man when one was under his personal influence; yet the impression of indirectness and duplicity which he caused generally, together with his indifference to slander and calumny,[1] made it possible for his enemies, before his Western venture, to build up about his name a structure of public suspicion, and even hatred, wholly unjustified by the facts.

The United States District Attorney laid before Marshall the record in the case of Bollmann and Swartwout in the Supreme Court, and Perkins proudly described how he had captured Burr and brought him to Richmond. Hay promptly moved to commit the accused man to jail on the charges of treason and misdemeanor. The attorneys on both sides agreed that on this motion there must be argument. Marshall admitted Burr to bail in the sum of five thousand dollars for his appearance the next day at the court-room in the Capitol.

When Marshall opened court the following morn-

[1] It was a rule of Burr's life to ignore attacks upon him. (See *supra*, 280.)

ing, the room was crowded with spectators, while hundreds could not find admittance. Hay asked that the court adjourn to the House of Delegates, in order that as many as possible of the throng might hear the proceedings. Marshall complied, and the eager multitude hurried pell-mell to the big ugly hall, where thenceforth court was held throughout the tedious, exasperating months of this historic legal conflict.

Hay began the argument. Burr's cipher letter to Wilkinson proved that he was on his way to attack Mexico at the time his villainy was thwarted by the patriotic measures of the true-hearted commander of the American Army. Hay insisted that Burr had intended to take New Orleans and "make it the capital of his empire." The zealous young District Attorney "went minutely into . . the evidence." The prisoner's stealthy "flight from justice" showed that he was guilty.

John Wickham, one of Burr's counsel, answered Hay. There was no testimony to show an overt act of treason. The alleged Mexican project was not only "innocent, but meritorious"; for everybody knew that we were "in an intermediate state between war and peace" with Spain. Let Marshall recall Jefferson's Message to Congress on that point. If war did not break out, Burr's expedition was perfectly suitable to another and a wholly peaceful enterprise, and one which the President himself had "recommended" — namely, "strong settlements beyond the Mississippi." [1]

[1] *Burr Trials*, I, 5.

Burr himself addressed the court, not, he said, "to remedy any omission of his counsel, who had done great justice to the subject," but "to repel some observations of a personal nature." Treason meant deeds, yet he was being persecuted on "mere conjecture." The whole country had been unjustly aroused against him. Wilkinson had frightened the President, and Jefferson, in turn, had alarmed the people.

Had he acted like a guilty man, he asked? Briefly and modestly he told of his conduct before the courts and grand juries in Kentucky and Mississippi, and the result of those investigations. The people among whom he journeyed saw nothing hostile or treasonable in his expedition.

His "flight"? That had occurred only when he was denied the protection of the laws and when armed men, under illegal orders of an autocratic military authority, were seeking to seize him violently. Then, and only then, acting upon the advice of friends and upon his own judgment, had he "abandoned a country where the laws ceased to be the sovereign power." Why had the guards who brought him from Alabama to Richmond "avoided every magistrate on the way"? Why had he been refused the use of pen, ink, and paper — denied even the privilege of writing to his daughter? It was true that when, in South Carolina, the soldiers chanced upon three civilians, he did indeed "demand the interposition of the civil authority." Was that criminal? Was it not his right to seek to be delivered from "military despotism, from the tyranny

of a military escort," and to be subjected only to
" the operation of the laws of his country"? [1]

On Wednesday, April 1, Marshall delivered the
second of that series of opinions which established
the boundaries of the American law of treason and
rendered the trial of Aaron Burr as notable for the
number and the importance of decisions made from
the bench during the progress of it, as it was famous
among legal duels in the learning, power, and eloquence of counsel, in the influences brought to bear
upon court and jury, and in the dramatic setting
and the picturesque incidents of the proceedings.

Marshall had carefully written his opinion. At
the close of court on the preceding day, he had announced that he would do this in order "to prevent
any misrepresentations of expressions that might
fall on him." He had also assured Hay that, in case
he decided to commit Burr, the District Attorney
should be heard at any length he desired on the
question of bail.

Thus, at the very beginning, Marshall showed
that patience, consideration, and prudence so characteristic of him, and so indispensable to the conduct of this trial, if dangerous collisions with the
prevailing mob spirit were to be avoided. He had in
mind, too, the haughty and peremptory conduct of
Chase, Addison, and other judges which had given
Jefferson his excuse for attacking the Judiciary, and
which had all but placed that branch of the Government in the absolute control of that great practical
genius of political manipulation. By the gentleness

[1] *Burr Trials*, I, 6–8.

of his voice and manner, Marshall lessened the excuse which Jefferson was eagerly seeking in order again to inflame the passions of the people against the Judiciary.

Proof strong enough to convict "on a trial in chief," or even to convince the judge himself of Burr's guilt, was not, said Marshall, necessary to justify the court in holding him for the action of the grand jury; but there must be enough testimony "to furnish good reason to believe" that Burr had actually committed the crimes with which he stood charged.

Marshall quoted Blackstone to the effect that a prisoner could be discharged only when it appeared that the suspicion against him was "wholly groundless," but this did not mean that "the hand of malignity may grasp any individual against whom its hate may be directed or whom it may capriciously seize, charge him with some secret crime and put him on the proof of his innocence."

Precisely that "hand of malignity," however, Burr was feeling by orders of Jefferson. The partisans of the President instantly took alarm at this passage of Marshall's opinion. Here was this insolent Federalist Chief Justice, at the very outset of the investigation, presuming to reflect upon their idol. Such was the indignant comment that ran among the Republicans who packed the hall; and reflect upon the President, Marshall certainly did, and intended to do.

The softly spoken but biting words of the Chief Justice were unnecessary to the decision of the

question before him; they accurately described the
conduct of the Administration, and they could
have been uttered only as a rebuke to Jefferson or
as an attempt to cool the public rage that the President had aroused. Perhaps both motives inspired
Marshall's pen when he wrote that statesmanlike
sentence.[1]

On the whole, said Marshall, probable cause to
suspect Burr guilty of an attempt to attack the
Spanish possessions appeared from Wilkinson's affidavit; but the charge of treason was quite another
matter. "As this is the most atrocious offence which
can be committed against the political body, so it is
the charge which is most capable of being employed
as the instrument of those malignant and vindictive
passions which may rage in the bosoms of contending parties struggling for power." Treason is the
only crime specifically mentioned in the Constitution — the definition of all others is left to Congress.
But the Constitution itself carefully and plainly describes treason and prescribes just how it must be
proved.

Did the testimony show probable grounds for believing that Burr had committed treason? Marshall
analyzed the affidavits of Eaton and Wilkinson,
which constituted all of the "evidence" against
Burr; and although the whole matter had been ex-

[1] At the noon hour "a friend" told the Chief Justice of the impression produced, and Marshall hastened to forestall the use that he
knew Jefferson would make of it. Calling the reporters about him, he
"explicitly stated" that this passage in his opinion "had no allusion
to the conduct of the government in the case before him." It was, he
assured the representatives of the press, "only an elucidation of
Blackstone." (*Burr Trials*, I, footnote to 11.)

amined by the Supreme Court in the case of Bollmann and Swartwout, he nevertheless went over the
same ground again. No impatience, no hasty or
autocratic action, no rudeness of manner, no harsh-
ness of speech on his part should give politicians a
weapon with which once more to strike at judges
and courts.

Where, asked Marshall, was the evidence that
Burr had assembled an army to levy war on the
United States? Not before the court, certainly.
Mere "suspicion" was not to be ignored when means
of proving the suspected facts were not yet secured;
but where the truth could easily have been established, if it existed, and yet no proof of it had been
brought forward, everybody "must admit that the
ministers of justice at least ought not officially to
entertain" unsupported conjectures or assertions.

"The fact to be proved . . is an act of public notoriety. It must exist in the view of the world, or it
cannot exist at all. . . Months have elapsed since the
fact did occur, if it ever occurred. More than five
weeks have elapsed since the . . supreme court has
declared the necessity of proving the fact, if it exists.
Why is it not proved?" It is, said Marshall, the
duty of the Executive Department to prosecute
crimes. "It would be easy" for the Government
"to procure affidavits" that Burr had assembled
troops five months ago. Certainly the court "ought
not to believe that there had been any remissness"
on the part of the Administration; and since no
evidence had been presented that Burr had gathered
soldiers, "the suspicion, which in the first instance

might have been created, ought not to be continued, unless this want of proof can be in some manner accounted for."

Marshall would, therefore, commit Burr for high misdemeanor, but not for treason, and must, of consequence, admit the prisoner to bail. The Chief Justice suggested the sum of ten thousand dollars as being "about right." [1] Hay protested that the amount was too small. Burr "is here among strangers," replied Wickham. He has fewer acquaintances in Richmond than anywhere in the country. To be sure, two humane men had saved the prisoner "from the horrors of the dungeon" when he arrived; but the first bail was only for two days, while the present bail was for an indefinite period. "Besides," asserted Wickham, "I have heard several gentlemen of great respectability, who did not doubt that colonel Burr would keep his recognisance, express an unwillingness to appear as bail for him, lest it might be supposed they were enemies to their country." [2]

Thus were cleverly brought into public and official view the conditions under which this trial, so vital to American liberty, was to be held. Burr was a "traitor," asserted Jefferson. "Burr a traitor!" echoed the general voice. That all who befriended Burr were, therefore, also "traitors at heart," was the conclusion of popular logic. Who dared brave the wrath of that blind and merciless god, Public Prejudice? From the very beginning the prosecution invoked the power of this avenging and re-

[1] *Burr Trials*, I, 11–18.   [2] *Ib.* 19.

morseless deity, while the defense sought to break that despotic spell and arouse the spirit of opposition to the tyranny of it. These facts explain the legal strategy of the famous controversy — a controversy that continued throughout the sweltering months of the summer and far into the autumn of 1807.

Hay declared that he had been "well informed that Colonel Burr could give bail in the sum of one hundred thousand dollars." Gravely Burr answered that there was serious doubt whether bail in any sum could be procured; "gentlemen are unwilling to expose themselves to animadversions" which would be the result of their giving bail for him. He averred that he had no financial resources. "It is pretty well known that the government has ordered my property seized, and that the order has been executed." He had thus lost "upwards of forty thousand dollars," and his "credit had consequently been much impaired." [1]

Marshall, unmoved by the appeals of either side, fixed the bail at ten thousand dollars and adjourned court until three o'clock to enable Burr to procure sureties for that amount. At the appointed hour the prisoner came into court with five men of property who gave their bond for his appearance at the next term of the United States Circuit Court, to be held at Richmond on May 22.

For three precious weeks at least Aaron Burr was free. He made the best of his time, although he

[1] *Burr Trials*, I, 20. His "property," however, represented borrowed money.

could do little more than perfect the plans for his defense. His adored Theodosia was in alternate rage and despair, and Burr strove to cheer and steady her as best he might. Some of "your letters," he writes, "indicate a sort of stupor"; in others "you rise into phrenzy." He bids her come "back to reason. . . Such things happen in all democratic governments." Consider the "vindictive and unrelenting persecution" of men of "virtue, . . independence and . . talents in Greece and Rome." Let Theodosia "amuse" herself by collecting instances of the kind and writing an essay on the subject "with reflections, comments and applications." The perusal of it, he says, will give him "great pleasure" if he gets it by the time court opens in May.[1]

Burr learned the names of those who were to compose the grand jury that was to investigate his misdeeds. Among them were "twenty democrats and four federalists," he informs his daughter. One of "the former is W. C. Nicholas my vindictive . . personal enemy — the most so that could be found in this state. The most indefatigable industry is used by the agents of government, and they have money at command without stint. If I were possessed of the same means, I could not only foil the prosecutors, but render them ridiculous and infamous. The democratic papers teem with abuse of me and my counsel, and even against the chief justice. Nothing is left undone or unsaid which can tend to prejudice the public mind, and produce a conviction without evidence. The machinations of

[1] Burr to his daughter, May 15, 1807, Davis, ii, 405–06.

this description which were used against Moreau in
France were treated in this country with indignation.
They are practiced against me in a still more impudent degree, not only with impunity, but with
applause; and the authors and abettors suppose,
with reason, that they are acquiring favour with the
administration." [1]

Every word of this was true. The Republican
press blazed with denunciation of "the traitor."
The people, who had been led to believe that the
destruction of their "liberties" had been the object
at which Burr ultimately aimed, were intent on the
death of their would-be despoiler. Republican politicians were nervously apprehensive lest, through
Marshall's application of the law, Burr might escape
and the Administration and the entire Republican
Party thereby be convicted of persecuting an innocent man. They feared, even more, the effect on
their political fortunes of being made ridiculous.

Giles was characteristically alert to the danger.
Soon after Marshall had declined to commit Burr
for treason and had released him under bail to appear on the charge of misdemeanor only, the Republican leader of the Senate, then in Virginia, wrote
Jefferson of the situation.

The preliminary hearing of Burr had, Giles stated,
greatly excited the people of Virginia and probably
would "have the same effect in all parts of the
United States." He urged the President to take
"all measures necessary for effecting . . a full and
fair judicial investigation." The enemies of the Ad-

[1] Burr to his daughter, May 15, 1807, Davis, II, 405–06.

ministration had gone so far as to "suggest doubts" as to the "measures heretofore pursued in relation to Burr," and had dared to "intimate that the executive are not possessed of evidence to justify those measures" — or, if there was such evidence, that the prosecution had been "extremely delinquent in not producing it at the examination." Nay, more! "It is even said that General Wilkinson will not be ordered to attend the trial." That would never do; the absence of that militant patriot "would implicate the character of the administration, more than they can be apprised of." [1]

But Jefferson was sufficiently alarmed without any sounding of the tocsin by his Senatorial agent. "He had so frightened the country .. that to escape being overwhelmed by ridicule, he must get his prisoner convicted of the fell designs which he had publically attributed to him." [2] It is true that Jefferson did not believe Burr had committed treason; [3] but he had formally declared to Congress and the country

[1] Giles to Jefferson, April 6, 1807, Anderson, 110. The date is given in Jefferson to Giles, April 20, 1807, *Works:* Ford, x, 383.

[2] Parton: *Burr,* 455.

[3] "Altho' at first he proposed a separation of the Western country, .. yet he very early saw that the fidelity of the Western country was not to be shaken and turned himself wholly towards Mexico and so popular is an enterprize on that country in this, that we had only to be still, & he could have had followers enough to have been in the city of Mexico in 6. weeks." (Jefferson to James Bowdoin, U.S. Minister to Spain, April 2, 1807, *Works:* Ford, x, 381–82.)

In this same letter Jefferson makes this amazing statement: "If we have kept our hands off her [Spain] till now, it has been purely out of respect for France. . . We expect therefore from the friendship of the emperor [Napoleon] that he will either compel Spain to do us justice, or abandon her to us. We ask but one month to be in .. the city of Mexico."

that Burr's "guilt is placed beyond question," and, at any cost, he must now make good that charge.[1]

From the moment that he received the news of Marshall's decision to hold Burr for misdemeanor and to accept bail upon that charge, the prosecution of his former associate became Jefferson's ruling thought and purpose. It occupied his mind even more than the Nation's foreign affairs, which were then in the most dangerous state.[2] Champion though he was of equal rights for all men, yet any opposition to his personal or political desires or interests appeared to madden him.[3] A personal antagonism, once formed, became with Thomas Jefferson a public policy.

He could see neither merit nor honesty in any act or word that appeared to him to favor Burr. Anybody who intimated doubt of his guilt did so, in Jefferson's opinion, for partisan or equally unworthy reasons. "The fact is that the Federalists make Burr's cause their own, and exert their whole influence to shield him," he asserted two days after Marshall had admitted Burr to bail.[4] His hatred of the National Judiciary was rekindled if, indeed, its fires ever had died down. "It is unfortunate that federalism is still predominant in our judiciary department, which is consequently in opposition to the legislative & Executive branches & is able to

[1] McCaleb, 325.

[2] See *infra*, 476–77; also vol. IV, chap. I, of this work.

[3] See Nicholson to Monroe, April 12, 1807, Adams: *Randolph*, 216–18. Plumer notes "the rancor of his personal and political animosities." (Plumer, 356.)

[4] Jefferson to James Bowdoin, U.S. Minister to Spain, April 2, 1807, *Works:* Ford, x, 382.

baffle their measures often," he averred at the same time, and with reference to Marshall's rulings thus far in the Burr case.

He pours out his feelings with true Jeffersonian bitterness and passion in his answer to Giles's letter. No wonder, he writes, that "anxiety and doubt" had arisen "in the public mind in the present defective state of the proof." This tendency had "been sedulously encouraged by the tricks of the judges to force trials before it is possible to collect the evidence dispersed through a line of two thousand miles from Maine to Orleans."

The Federalists too were helping Burr! These miscreants were "mortified only that he did not separate the Union and overturn the government." The truth was, declares Jefferson, that the Federalists would have joined Burr in order to establish "their favorite monarchy" and rid themselves of "this hated republic," if only the traitor had had "a little dawn of success." Consider the inconsistent attitude of these Federalists. Their first "complaint was the supine inattention of the administration to a treason stalking through the land in the open light of day; the present one, that they [the Administration] have crushed it before it was ripe for execution, so that no overt acts can be proved."

Jefferson confides to Giles that the Government may not be able to establish the commission of overt acts; in fact, he says, "we do not know of a certainty yet what will be proved." But the Administration is already doing its very best: "We have set on foot an inquiry through the whole of the country which has been the scene of these transactions to be able to prove to the courts, if they will give time, or to the public by way of communication to Congress, what the real facts have been" — this three months after Jefferson had asserted, in his Special Message on the conspiracy, that Burr's "guilt is placed beyond question."

In this universal quest for "the facts," the Government had no help from the National courts, complains the President: "Aided by no process or facilities from Federal Courts,[1] but frowned on by their new-born zeal for the liberty of those whom we would not permit to overthrow the liberties of their country, we can expect no revealments from the accomplices of the chief offender." But witnesses would be produced who would "satisfy the world if not the judges" of Burr's treason. Jefferson enumerates the "overt acts" which the Administration expected to prove.[2]

Marshall, of course, stood in the way, for it was

[1] This was flatly untrue. No process to obtain evidence or to aid the prosecution in any way was ever denied the Administration. This statement of the President was, however, a well-merited reflection on the tyrannical conduct of the National judges in the trials of men for offenses under the Sedition Law and even under the common law. (See *supra*, chap. I.) But, on the one hand, Marshall had not then been appointed to the bench and was himself against the Sedition Law (see vol. II, chap. XI, of this work); and, on the other hand, Jefferson had now become as ruthless a prosecutor as Chase or Addison ever was.

[2] These were: "1. The enlistment of men in a regular way; 2. the regular mounting of guard round Blennerhassett's island; .. 3. the rendezvous of Burr with his men at the mouth of the Cumberland; 4. his letter to the acting Governor of Mississippi, holding up the prospect of civil war; 5. his capitulation, regularly signed, with the aides of the Governor, as between two independent and hostile commanders."

plain that "the evidence cannot be collected under
4 months, probably 5." Jefferson had directed his
Attorney-General, "unofficially," but "expressly,"
to "inform the Chief Justice of this." With what
result? "Mr. Marshall says, 'more than 5 weeks
have elapsed since the opinion of the Supreme Court
has declared the necessity of proving the overt
acts if they exist. Why are they not proved?' In
what terms of decency," growls Jefferson, "can we
speak of this? As if an express could go to Natchez
or the mouth of the Cumberland and return in 5
weeks, to do which has never taken less than
twelve."

Jefferson cannot sufficiently criticize Marshall's
opinion: "If, in Nov. or Dec. last, a body of troops
had assembled on the Ohio, it is impossible to suppose the affidavits establishing the fact could not
have been obtained by the last of March," he quotes
from Marshall's ruling. "I ask the judge where
they [the affidavits] should have been lodged? At
Frankfort? at Cincinnati? at Nashville? St. Louis?
. . New Orleans? . . Where? At Richmond he certainly meant, or meant only to throw dust in the
eyes of his audience." [1]

As his pen flew over the burning page, Jefferson's

[1] The affidavits in regard to what happened on Blennerhassett's
island would necessarily be lodged in Richmond, since the island was
in Virginia and the United States Court for the District of that State
alone had jurisdiction to try anybody for a crime committed within its
borders.

Even had there been any doubt as to where the trial would take
place, the Attorney-General would have held the affidavits pending
the settlement of that point; and when the place of trial was determined upon, promptly dispatched the documents to the proper district attorney.

anger grew. Marshall's love of monarchy was at the bottom of his decision: "All the principles of law are to be perverted which would bear on the favorite offenders who endeavor to overrun this odious Republic."

Marshall's refinements as to proof required to establish probable cause to believe Burr guilty, particularly irritated Jefferson. "As to the overt acts, were not the bundle of letters of information in Mr. Rodney's hands, the letters and facts published in the local newspapers, Burr's flight, & the universal belief or rumor of his guilt, probable ground for presuming the facts .. so as to put him on trial? Is there a candid man in the U S who does not believe some one, if not all, of these overt acts to have taken place?"

How dare Marshall require legal evidence when "letters, newspapers and rumors" condemned Burr! How dare he, as a judge, not heed "the universal belief," especially when that general public opinion had been crystallized by Jefferson himself!

That Marshall was influenced by politics and was of a kidney with the whole breed of National judges up to that time, Jefferson had not the slightest doubt. "If there ever had been an instance in this or the preceding administrations, of federal judges so applying principles of law as to condemn a federal or acquit a republican offender, I should have judged them in the present case with more charity."

But the conduct of the Chief Justice will be the final outrage which will compel a great reform. "The nation will judge both the offender & judges for themselves . . the people . . will see . . & amend the error in our Constitution, which makes any branch independent of the nation. . . One of the great co-ordinate branches of the government, setting itself in opposition to the other two, and to the common sense of the nation, proclaims impunity to that class of offenders which endeavors to overturn the Constitution, and are themselves protected in it by the Constitution itself; for impeachment is a farce which will not be tried again."

Thus Jefferson extracts some comfort from Marshall's refusal to obey popular clamor and condemn on "rumor." If Marshall's "protection of Burr produces this amendment,[1] it will do more good than his condemnation would have done. Against Burr, personally," audaciously adds Jefferson, "I never had one hostile sentiment." [2]

Such was the state of the President's mind when he learned of Marshall's ruling on the Government's motion to commit Burr to jail upon the charges of treason and high misdemeanor. Jefferson felt that he himself was on trial; he knew that he must make good his charges or suffer a decline in the popularity which he prized above all else in life. He proposed that, at the very least, the public should be on his side, and he resolved to exert the utmost efforts of the National Government to bend Marshall to his will.

---

[1] The reference is to the amendment to the Constitution urged by Jefferson, and offered by Randolph in the House, providing that a judge should be removed by the President on the address of both Houses of Congress. (See *supra*, chap. IV, 221.)

[2] Jefferson to Giles, April 20, 1807, *Works:* Ford, x, 383–88.

Thus the President of the United States became the leading counsel in the prosecution of Aaron Burr, as well as the director-general of a propaganda planned to confirm public opinion of Burr's treason, and to discredit Marshall should his decisions from the bench result in the prisoner's escape from the gallows.[1] Jefferson ordered his Attorney-General, Cæsar A. Rodney, to direct justices of the peace throughout the country to examine everybody supposed to have any knowledge of Burr, his plans, movements, or conversations. Long lists of questions, designed to elicit replies that would convict Burr, were sent to these officials on printed forms. A vast drag-net was spread over almost the whole of the United States and drawn swiftly and remorselessly to Washington.

The programme for the prosecution became the subject of anxious Cabinet meetings, and the resources of every department of the Executive branch of the Government were employed to overwhelm the accused man. Jefferson directed Madison as Secretary of State "to take the necessary measures," including the advance of money for their expenses, to bring to Richmond witnesses "from great distances."

Five thousand dollars, in a single warrant, was given to the Attorney-General for use in supporting

[1] See Parton: *Burr*, 456–57. "The real prosecutor of Aaron Burr, throughout this business, was Thomas Jefferson, President of the United States, who was made President of the United States by Aaron Burr's tact and vigilance, and who was able therefore to wield against Aaron Burr the power and resources of the United States." (*Ib.* 457.) And see McCaleb, 361.

the Administration's case.[1] The total amount of the public money expended by Jefferson's orders to secure Burr's conviction was $11,721.11, not a dollar of which had been appropriated for that purpose. "All lawful expenses in the prosecution of Burr were audited, and paid in full," under a law which provided for the conduct of criminal cases; the sums spent by direction of the President were in addition to the money dispensed by authority of that law.[2]

When Bollmann had been brought to Washington, he had read with rage and amazement the newspaper accounts that Burr had led two thousand armed men in a violent and treasonable attack upon the United States. Accordingly, after Marshall released him from imprisonment, he hastened to Jefferson and tried to correct what he declared to be "false impressions" concerning Burr's treason. Bollmann also wished to convince the President that war with Spain was desirable, and to get his support of Burr's expedition. Jefferson, having taken the precaution to have the Secretary of State present at the interview, listened with apparent sympathy. The following day he requested Bollmann to write out and deliver to him his verbal statements, "Thomas Jefferson giving him *his word of honour* that they should never be used against himself [Bollmann] and *that the paper shall never go out of his* [Jefferson's] *hand.*"[3]

---

[1] Jefferson to the Secretary of State, April 14, 1807, *Works:* Ford, x, 383.

[2] Jenkinson: *Aaron Burr*, 282–83.

[3] Jefferson to "Bollman," Jan. 25, 1807, Davis, ii, 388.

The confiding Bollmann did as the President requested, his whole paper going "to disprove treason,
and to show the expediency of war." Because of unfamiliarity with the English language "one or two
expressions" may have been "improperly used." [1]
Bollmann's statement Jefferson now transmitted to
the District Attorney at Richmond, in order, said
the President, "that you may know how to examine
him and draw everything from him."

Jefferson ordered Hay to show the paper only to
his associate counsel; but, if Bollmann "should pre-
varicate," the President adds, "ask him whether he
did not say so and so to Mr. Madison and myself."
The President assures Hay that "in order to let
him [Bollmann] see that his prevarication will be
marked, Mr. Madison will forward [Hay] a pardon
for him, which we mean should be delivered previously." Jefferson fears that Bollmann may not
appear as a witness and directs Hay to "take effectual measures to have him immediately taken into
custody."

Nor was this all. Three months earlier, Wilkinson had suggested to Jefferson the base expedient
of offering pardons to Burr's associates, in order to
induce them to betray him and thus make certain
his conviction.[2] Apparently this crafty and sinister
advice now recurred to Jefferson's mind — at least
he followed it. He enclosed a sheaf of pardons and
directed Hay to fill them out "at [his] discretion, if
[he] should find a defect of evidence, & believe that
this would supply it, by avoiding to give them to

[1] Bollmann's narrative, Davis, II, 389.   [2] McCaleb, 331.

the gross offenders, unless it be visible that the principal will otherwise escape." [1]

In the same letter Jefferson also sent to Hay the affidavit of one Jacob Dunbaugh, containing a mass of bizarre falsehoods, as was made plain during the trial. Dunbaugh was a sergeant who had been arrested for desertion and had been pardoned by Wilkinson on condition that he would give suitable testimony against Burr. "If," continues Jefferson, "General Wilkinson gets on in time,[2] I expect he will bring Dunbaugh with him. At any rate it [Dunbaugh's affidavit] may be a ground for an arrest & committment for treason."

Vividly alive to the forces at work to doom him, Burr nevertheless was not dismayed. As a part of his preparation for defense he exercised on all whom he met the full power of his wonderful charm; and if ever a human being needed friends, Aaron Burr needed them in the Virginia Capital. As usual, most of those who conversed with him and looked into his deep, calm eyes became his partisans. Gradually, a circle of men and women of the leading families of Richmond gathered about him, supporting and comforting him throughout his desperate ordeal.

Burr's attorneys were no longer merely his counsel performing their professional duty; even before the preliminary hearing was over, they had

[1] Jefferson to the United States District Attorney for Virginia, May 20, 1807, *Works:* Ford, x, 394–401.

Bollmann, in open court, scornfully declined to accept the pardon. (See *infra*, 452.)

[2] Wilkinson was then *en route* by sea to testify against Burr before the grand jury.

become his personal friends and ardent champions. They were ready and eager to go into court and fight for their client with that aggressiveness and enthusiasm which comes only from affection for a man and a faith in his cause. Every one of them not only had developed a great fondness for Burr, but earnestly believed that his enterprise was praiseworthy rather than treasonable.

One of them, John Wickham, was a commanding figure in the society of Richmond, as well as the leader of the Virginia bar at that time.[1] He was a close friend of Marshall and lived in an imposing house near him. It was to Wickham that Marshall had left the conduct of his cases in court when he went to France on the X. Y. Z. mission.

Dinners were then the principal form of social intercourse in Richmond, and were constantly given. The more prominent lawyers were particularly devoted to this pleasing method of cheer and relaxation. This custom kept the brilliant bar of Richmond sweet and wholesome, and nourished among its members a mutual regard, while discouraging resentments and animosities. Much of that courtesy and deference shown to one another by the lawyers of that city, even in the most spirited encounters in court, was due to that esteem and fellowship which their practice of dining together created.

Of the dispensers of such hospitality, Marshall and Wickham were the most notable and popular. The "lawyer dinners" given by Marshall were famous; and the tradition of them still casts a

[1] Mordecai: *Richmond in By-Gone Days*, 68.

warm and exhilarating glow. The dinners, too, of John Wickham were quite as alluring. The food was as plentiful and as well prepared, the wines as varied, select, and of as ancient vintage, the brandy as old and "sound," the juleps as fragrant and seductive; and the wit was as sparkling, the table talk as informing, the good humor as heartening. Nobody ever thought of declining an invitation to the house of John Wickham.

All these circumstances combined to create a situation for which Marshall was promptly denounced with that thoughtlessness and passion so characteristic of partisanship — a situation that has furnished a handle for malignant criticism of him to this day. During the interval between the preliminary hearing and the convening of court in May, Wickham gave one of his frequent and much-desired dinners. As a matter of course, Wickham's intimate friend and next-door neighbor was present — no dinner in Richmond ever was complete without the gentle-mannered, laughter-loving John Marshall, with his gift for making everybody happy and at ease. But Aaron Burr was also a guest.

Aaron Burr, "the traitor," held to make answer to charges for his infamous crimes, and John Marshall, the judge before whom the miscreant was to be tried, dining together! And at the house of Burr's chief counsel! Here was an event more valuable to the prosecution than any evidence or argument, in the effect it would have, if rightly employed, on public opinion, before which Burr had been and was arraigned far more than before the court of justice.

Full use was made of the incident. The Republican organ, the Richmond *Enquirer*, promptly exposed and denounced it. This was done by means of two letters signed "A Stranger from the Country," who "never had any, the least confidence in the political principles of the chief justice" — none in "that noble candor" and "those splendid . . even god-like talents which many of all parties ascribe to him." Base as in reality he was, Marshall might have "spared his country" the "wanton insult" of having "feasted at the same convivial board with Aaron Burr." What excuse was there for "conduct so grossly indecent"? To what motive should Marshall's action be ascribed? "Is this charity, hypocracy, or federalism?" Doubtless he "was not actuated by any corrupt motive," and "was unapprised of the invitation of B."[1] However, the fact is, that the judge, the accused, and his attorney, were fellow guests at this "treason rejoicing dinner."[2]

---

[1] According to a story, told more than a century after the incident occurred, Marshall did not know, when he accepted Wickham's invitation, that Burr was to be a guest, but heard of that fact before the dinner. His wife, thereupon, advised him not to go, but, out of regard for Wickham, he attended. (Thayer: *John Marshall*, 80–81.)

This tale is almost certainly a myth. Professor Thayer, to whom it was told by an unnamed descendant of Marshall, indicates plainly that he had little faith in it.

The facts that, at the time, even the *Enquirer* acquitted Marshall of any knowledge that Burr was to be present; that the prudence of the Chief Justice was admitted by his bitterest enemies; that so gross an indiscretion would have been obvious to the most reckless; that Marshall, of all men, would not have embarrassed himself in such fashion, particularly at a time when public suspicion was so keen and excitement so intense — render it most improbable that he knew that Burr was to be at the Wickham dinner.

[2] *Enquirer*, April 10 and 28, 1807.

Thus the great opinions of John Marshall, delivered during the trial of Aaron Burr, were condemned before they were rendered or even formed. With that lack of consideration which even democracies sometimes display, the facts were not taken into account. That Marshall never knew, until he was among them, who his fellow guests were to be; that Wickham's dinner, except in the presence of Burr, differed in no respect from those constantly given in Richmond; that Marshall, having arrived, could do nothing except to leave and thus make the situation worse; — none of these simple and obvious facts seemed to have occurred to the eager critics of the Chief Justice.

That Marshall was keenly aware of his predicament there can be no doubt. He was too good a politician and understood too well public whimsies and the devices by which they are manipulated, not to see the consequences of the innocent but unfortunate evening at Wickham's house. But he did not explain; he uttered not a syllable of apology. With good-natured contempt for the maneuvers of the politicians and the rage of the public, yet carefully and coolly weighing every element of the situation, John Marshall, when the appointed day of May came around, was ready to take his seat upon the bench and to conduct the historic trial of Aaron Burr with that kindly forbearance which never deserted him, that canny understanding of men and motives which served him better than learning, and that placid fortitude that could not be shaken.

CHAPTER VIII

ADMINISTRATION VERSUS COURT

In substance Jefferson said that if Marshall should suffer Burr to escape, Marshall himself should be removed from office. (Henry Adams.)

It becomes our duty to lay the evidence before the public. Go into any expense necessary for this purpose. (Jefferson.)

The President has let slip the dogs of war, the hell-hounds of persecution, to hunt down my friend. (Luther Martin.)

If you cannot exorcise the demon of prejudice, you can chain him down to law and reason. (Edmund Randolph.)

On May 22, 1807, the hall of the House of Delegates at Richmond was densely crowded long before the hour of half-past twelve, when John Marshall took his seat upon the bench and opened court. So occupied was every foot of space that it was with difficulty that a passage was opened through which the tall, awkwardly moving, and negligently clad Chief Justice could make his way. By Marshall's side sat Cyrus Griffin, Judge of the District Court, who throughout the proceedings was negligible.

The closely packed spectators accurately portrayed the dress, manners, and trend of thought of the American people of that period. Gentlemen in elegant attire — hair powdered and queues tied in silk, knee breeches and silver buckles, long rich cloth coats cut half away at the waist, ruffled shirts and high stocks — were conspicuous against the background of the majority of the auditors, whose apparel, however, was no less picturesque.

This audience was largely made up of men from the smaller plantations, men from the mountains, men from the backwoods, men from the frontiers. Red woolen shirts; rough homespun or corduroy trousers, held up by "galluses"; fringed deerskin coats and "leggings" of the same material kept in place by leather belts; hair sometimes tied by strings in uncouth queues, but more often hanging long and unconfined — in such garb appeared the greater part of the attendance at the trial of Aaron Burr. In forty years there had been but little change in the general appearance of Virginians [1] except that fewer wore the old dignified and becoming attire of well-dressed men.

Nearly all of them were Republicans, plain men, devoted to Jefferson as the exponent of democracy and the heaven-sent leader of the people. Among these Jeffersonians, however, were several who, quite as much as the stiffest Federalists, prided themselves upon membership in the "upper classes."

Nearly all of the Republicans present, whether of the commonalty or the gentry, were against Aaron Burr. Scattered here and there were a few Federalists — men who were convinced that democracy meant the ruin of the Republic, and who profoundly believed that Jefferson was nothing more than an intriguing, malicious demagogue — most of whom looked upon Burr with an indulgent eye. So did an occasional Republican, as now and then a lone Federalist denounced Burr's villainy.

The good-sized square boxes filled with sand that were placed at infrequent intervals upon the floor of the improvised court-room were too few to receive

[1] See vol. I, 201, of this work.

the tobacco juice that filled the mouths of most of
the spectators before it was squirted freely upon the
floor and wall. Those who did not chew the weed
either smoked big cigars and fat pipes or contented
themselves with taking snuff.[1] Upon recess or adjournment of court, all, regularly and without loss of
time, repaired to the nearest saloons or taverns and
strengthened themselves, with generous draughts of
whiskey or brandy, taken "straight," for a firmer,
clearer grasp of the points made by counsel.

Never, in its history, had Richmond been so
crowded with strangers. Nearly five thousand
people now dwelt in the Virginia Capital, the site of
which was still "untamed and broken" by "inac-
cessible heights and deep ravines."[2] Thousands of
visitors had come from all over the country to witness the prosecution of that fallen angel whose dark
deeds, they had been made to believe, had been in
a fair way to destroy the Nation. The inns could
shelter but an insignificant fraction of them, and few
were the private houses that did not take in men
whom the taverns could not accommodate. Hundreds
brought covered wagons or tents and camped under
the trees or on the river-banks near the city. Corre-
spondents of the press of the larger cities were present,
among them the youthful [3] Washington Irving, who
wrote one or two articles for a New York paper.

---

[1] Tobacco chewing and smoking in court-rooms continued in most
American communities in the South and West down to a very recent
period.

[2] Address of John Tyler on "Richmond and its Memories," Tyler,
I, 219.

[3] Irving was twenty-four years old when he reported the Burr trial.

In the concourse thus drawn to Richmond, few there were who were not certain that Burr had planned and attempted to assassinate Jefferson, overthrow the Government, shatter the Nation, and destroy American "liberty"; and so vocal and belligerent was this patriotic majority that men who at first held opinions contrary to the prevailing sentiment, or who entertained doubts of Burr's guilt, kept discreetly silent. So aggressively hostile was public feeling that, weeks later, when the bearing and manners of Burr, and the devotion, skill, and boldness of his counsel had softened popular asperity, Marshall declared that, even then, "it would be difficult or dangerous for a jury to venture to acquit Burr, however innocent they might think him." [1] The prosecution of Aaron Burr occurred when a tempest of popular prejudice and intolerance was blowing its hardest.

The provision concerning treason had been written into the American Constitution "to protect the people against that horrible and dangerous doctrine of constructive treason which had stained the English records with blood and filled the English valleys with innocent graves." [2]

The punishment for treason in all countries had been brutal and savage in the extreme. In Eng-

---

[1] *Blennerhassett Papers:* Safford, 465. Marshall made this avowal to Luther Martin, who personally told Blennerhassett of it.

[2] Judge Francis M. Finch, in Dillon, i, 402.

" The men who framed that instrument [Constitution] remembered the crimes that had been perpetrated under the pretence of justice; for the most part they had been traitors themselves, and having risked their necks under the law they feared despotism and arbitrary power more than they feared treason." (Adams: *U. S.* iii, 468.)

land, that crime had not perhaps been treated with such severity as elsewhere. Yet, even in England, so harsh had been the rulings of the courts against those charged with treason, so inhuman the execution of judgments upon persons found guilty under these rulings, so slight the pretexts that sent innocent men and women to their death,[1] that the framers of our fundamental law had been careful to define treason with utmost clearness, and to declare that proof of it could only be made by two witnesses to the same overt act or by confession of the accused in open court.[2]

That was one subject upon which the quarreling members of the Constitutional Convention of 1787 had been in accord, and their solution of the question had been the one and the only provision of which no complaint had been made during the struggle over ratification.

Every member of that Convention — every officer and soldier of the Revolution from Washington down to private, every man or woman who had given

---

[1] A favorite order from the bench for the execution of the condemned was that the culprit should be drawn prostrate at the tails of horses through the jagged and filthy streets from the court-room to the place of execution; the legs, arms, nose, and ears there cut off; the intestines ripped out and burned "before the eyes" of the victim; and finally the head cut off. Details still more shocking were frequently added. See sentences upon William, Lord Russell, July 14, 1683 (*State Trials Richard II to George I*, vol. 3, 660); upon Algernon Sidney, November 26, 1683 (*ib.* 738); upon William, Viscount Stafford, December 7, 1680 (*ib.* 214); upon William Stayley, November 21, 1678 (*ib.* vol. 2, 656); and upon other men condemned for treason.

[2] Even in Philadelphia, after the British evacuation of that place during the Revolution, hundreds were tried for treason. Lewis alone, although then a very young lawyer, defended one hundred and fifty-two persons. (See *Chase Trial*, 21.)

succor or supplies to a member of the patriot army, everybody who had advocated American independence — all such persons could have been prosecuted and might have been convicted as "traitors" under the British law of constructive treason.[1] "None," said Justice James Iredell in 1792, "can so highly . . prize these provisions [of the Constitution] as those who are best acquainted with the abuses which have been practised in other countries in prosecutions for this offence. . . We . . hope that the page of American history will never be stained with prosecutions for treason, begun without cause, conducted without decency, and ending in iniquitous convictions, without the slightest feelings of remorse."[2]

Yet, six years later, Iredell avowed his belief in the doctrine of constructive treason.[3] And in less than seventeen years from the time our National Government was established, the reasons for writing into the Constitution the rigid provision concerning treason were forgotten by the now thoroughly partisanized multitude, if, indeed, the people ever knew those reasons.

Moreover, every National judge who had passed upon the subject, with the exception of John Mar-

[1] "In the English law . . the rule . . had been that enough heads must be cut off to glut the vengeance of the Crown." (Isaac N. Phillips, in Dillon, ii, 394.)

[2] Iredell's charge to the Georgia Grand Jury, April 26, 1792, *Iredell:* McRee, ii, 349; and see Iredell's charge to the Massachusetts Grand Jury, Oct. 12, 1792, *ib.* 365.

[3] See his concurrence with Judge Peters's charge in the Fries case, Wharton: *State Trials,* 587–91; and Peters's opinion, *ib.* 586; also see Chase's charge at the second trial of Fries, *ib.* 636.

shall, had asserted the British doctrine of constructive treason. Most of the small number who realized the cause and real meaning of the American Constitutional provision as to treason were overawed by the public frenzy; and brave indeed was he who defied the popular passion of the hour or questioned the opinion of Thomas Jefferson, then at the summit of his popularity.[1]

One such dauntless man, however, there was among the surging throng that filled the Capitol Square at Richmond after the adjournment of court on May 22, and he was a vigorous Republican, too. "A tall, lank, uncouth-looking personage, with long locks of hair hanging over his face, and a queue down his back tied in an eel-skin, his dress singular, his manners and deportment that of a rough backwoodsman,"[2] mounted the steps of a corner grocery and harangued the glowering assemblage that gathered in front of him.[3] His daring, and an unmistakable air that advertised danger to any who disputed him, prevented that violent interruption certain to have been visited upon one less bold and formidable. He praised Burr as a brave man and a patriot who would have led Americans against the hated Spanish; he denounced Jefferson as a persecutor who sought the ruin of one he hated. Thus Andrew Jackson of Tennessee braved and cowed the hostile mob that was demanding and impatiently awaiting the condemnation and execution of the

[1] "The President's popularity is unbounded, and his will is that of the nation. . . Such is our present infatuation." (Nicholson to Randolph, April 12, 1807, Adams: *Randolph*, 216–17.)

[2] Hildreth, IV, 692.   [3] Parton: *Burr*, 458.

one who, for the moment, had been made the object of the country's execration.[1]

Jackson had recovered from his brief distrust of Burr, and the reaction had carried his tempestuous nature into extreme championship of his friend. "I am more convinced than ever," he wrote during the trial, "that treason was never intended by Burr."[2] Throughout the extended and acrimonious contest, Jackson's conviction grew stronger that Burr was a wronged man, hounded by betrayers, and the victim of a political conspiracy to take his life and destroy his reputation. And Jackson firmly believed that the leader of this cabal was Thomas Jefferson. "I am sorry to say," he wrote, "that this thing [the Burr trial] has . . assumed the shape of a political persecution."[3]

The Administration retaliated by branding Andrew Jackson a "malcontent"; and Madison, because of Jackson's attitude, prevented as long as possible the military advancement of the refractory Tennesseean during the War of 1812.[4] On the other hand, Burr never ceased to be grateful to his frontiersman adherent, and years later was one of those who set in motion the forces which made Andrew Jackson President of the United States.[5]

Nor was Jackson the only Republican who considered Jefferson as the contriving and energizing hand of the scheme to convict Burr. Almost riotous

---

[1] Parton: *Jackson*, I, 333.
[2] Jackson to Anderson, June 16, 1807, *ib*. 334.
[3] *Ib*. 335.   [4] *Ib*. 334–36.
[5] Parton: *Burr*, 606–08; see also Parton: *Jackson*, II, 258–59, 351–54; and Davis, II, 433–36.

were the efforts to get into the hall where the trial
was held, though it was situated on a steep hill and
"the ascent to the building was painfully laborious." [1]
Old and eminent lawyers of Richmond could not
reach the bar of the court, so dense was the throng.

One youthful attorney, tall and powerful, "the
most magnificent youth in Virginia," determined to
witness the proceedings, shouldered his way within
and "stood on the massive lock of the great door"
of the chamber.[2] Thus Winfield Scott got his first
view of that striking scene, and beheld the man
whose plans to invade Mexico he himself, more
than a generation afterward, was to carry out as
Commander of the American Army. Scott, there
and then, arrived at conclusions which a lifetime of
thought and experiences confirmed. "It was President Jefferson who directed and animated the prosecution," he declares in his "Memoirs." Scott records
the political alignment that resulted: "Hence every
Republican clamored for execution. Of course, the
Federalists . . compacted themselves on the other
side." [3]

Of all within the Hall of Delegates, and, indeed,
among the thousands then in Richmond, only two
persons appeared to be perfectly at ease. One of
them was John Marshall, the other was Aaron Burr.
Winfield Scott tells us of the manner of the imperiled man as he appeared in court on that sultry mid-
day of May: "There he stood, in the hands of power,
on the brink of danger, as composed, as immovable,

[1] Address of John Tyler, "Richmond and its Memories," Tyler, I, 219.
[2] Parton: *Burr*, 459.   [3] *Memoirs of Lieut.-General Scott*, I, 13.

as one of Canova's living marbles." But, says Scott, "Marshall was the master spirit of the scene." [1]

Gathered about Burr were four of his counsel, the fifth and most powerful of his defenders, Luther Martin, not yet having arrived. The now elderly Edmund Randolph, bearing himself with "over-awing dignity"; John Wickham, whose commanding presence corresponded well with his distinguished talents and extensive learning; Benjamin Botts, a very young lawyer, but of conceded ability and noted for a courage, physical and moral, that nothing could shake; and another young attorney, John Baker, a cripple, as well known for his wit as Botts for his fearlessness — this was the group of men that appeared for the defense.

For the prosecution came Jefferson's United States District Attorney, George Hay — eager, nervous, and not supremely equipped either in mind or attainments; William Wirt — as handsome and attractive as he was eloquent and accomplished, his extreme dissipation [2] now abandoned, and who, by his brilliant gifts of intellect and character, was beginning to lay the solid foundations of his notable career; and Alexander MacRae, then Lieutenant-Governor of Virginia — a sour-tempered, aggressive, well-informed, and alert old Scotchman, pitiless in his use of sarcasm, caring not the least whom he

---

[1] *Memoirs of Lieut.-General Scott,* I, 13, 16.

[2] See *Great American Lawyers:* Lewis, II, 268–75.

Kennedy says that the stories of Wirt's habits of intoxication were often exaggerated (Kennedy, I, 68); but see his description of the bar of that period and his apologetic reference to Wirt's conviviality (*ib.* 66–67).

offended if he thought that his affronts might help
the cause for which he fought. David Robertson,
the stenographer who reported the trial, was a
scholar speaking five or six languages.[1]

With all these men Marshall was intimately acquainted, and he was well assured that, in making
up his mind in any question which arose, he would
have that assistance upon which he so much relied
— exhaustive argument and complete exposition of
all the learning on the subject to be decided.

Marshall was liked and admired by the lawyers
on both sides, except George Hay, who took Jefferson's view of the Chief Justice. Indeed, the ardent
young Republican District Attorney passionately
espoused any opinion the President expressed. The
whole bar understood the strength and limitations
of the Chief Justice, the power of his intellect no
less than his unfamiliarity with precedents and the
learning of the law. From these circumstances, and
from Marshall's political wisdom in giving the lawyers a free hand, resulted a series of forensic encounters seldom witnessed or even tolerated in a
court of justice.

The first step in the proceedings was the examination by the grand jury of the Government's witnesses, and its return, or refusal to return, bills of
indictment against Burr. When the clerk had called
the names of those summoned on the grand jury,
Burr arose and addressed the court. Clad in black
silk, hair powdered and queue tied in perfect fashion,
the extreme pallor of his face in striking contrast to

[1] *Blennerhassett Papers:* Safford, 426.

his large black eyes, he made a rare picture of elegance and distinction in the uncouth surroundings of that democratic assemblage.

The accused man spoke with a quiet dignity and an "impressive distinctness" which, throughout the trial, so wrought upon the minds of the auditors that, fifty years afterward, some of those who heard him could repeat sentences spoken by him.[1] Burr now objected to the panel of the grand jury. The law, he said, required the marshal to summon twenty-four freeholders; if any of these had been struck off and others summoned, the act was illegal, and he demanded to know whether this had been done.[2]

For an hour or more the opposing counsel wrangled over this point. Randolph hints at the strategy of the defense: "There never was such a torrent of prejudice excited against any man, before a court of justice, as against colonel Burr, and by means which we shall presently unfold." Marshall sustained Burr's exception: undoubtedly the marshal had acted "with the most scrupulous regard to what he believed to be the law," but, if he had changed the original panel, he had transcended his authority.[3] It was then developed that the panel had been changed, and the persons thus illegally placed on the grand jury were dismissed.[4]

"With regret," Burr demanded the right to challenge the remainder of the grand jury "for favour." [5] Hay conceded the point, and Burr challenged Sena-

---

[1] Parton: *Burr*, 461.   [2] *Burr Trials*, I, 31–32.   [3] *Ib.* 37.   [4] *Ib.* 38.

[5] Meaning the partiality of the persons challenged, such as animosity toward the accused, conduct showing bias against him, and the like. See *Bouvier's Law Dictionary:* Rawle, 3d revision, II, 1191.

tor William Branch Giles. Merely upon the documents in Jefferson's Special Message to Congress, Giles had advocated that the writ of habeas corpus be suspended, and this, argued Burr, he could have done only if he supposed "that there was a rebellion or insurrection, and a public danger, of no common kind." This action of Giles was a matter of record; moreover, he had publicly made statements to the same effect.[1]

Senator Giles admitted that he had acted and spoken as Burr charged; and while denying that he held any "personal resentments against the accused," and asserting that he could act fairly as a grand juror, he graciously offered to withdraw. Marshall mildly observed that "if any gentleman has made up and declared his mind, it would be best for him to withdraw." With superb courtesy, Burr disavowed any reflection on Giles; it was merely above "human nature" that he should not be prejudiced. "So far from having any animosity against him, he would have been one of those whom I should have ranked among my personal friends."

Burr then challenged Colonel Wilson Cary Nicholas,[2] who spiritedly demanded the objections to him. Nicholas "entertained a bitterly personal animosity" against him, replied Burr. He would not, however, insist upon "further inquiry" if Nicholas would withdraw as Giles had done. Nicholas then addressed the court: He had been a member of the National House, he said, "when the attempt was made to elect colonel Burr president," and every-

---

[1] *Burr Trials*, I, 38–39.　　　　[2] *Ib.* 41–42.

body knew how he felt about that incident. He had
been in the Senate for three years "while colonel
Burr was president of that body," and had done all
he could to nominate Clinton in Burr's stead.

His suspicions had been "very much excited"
when Burr made his Western journey, and he had
openly stated his "uncommon anxiety" concerning
"not only the prosperity, but the union of the
states." Therefore, he had not desired to serve on
the grand jury and had asked the marshal to excuse
him. He had finally consented solely from his delicate sense of public duty. Also, said Nicholas, he
had been threatened with the publication of one of
the "most severe pieces" against him if he served
on the grand jury; and this inclined him to "defy
[his] enemies [rather] than to ask their mercy or
forbearance."

His friends had advised him not to make mention
of this incident in court; but, although he was "not
scrupulous of acquiring, in this way, a reputation of
scrupulous delicacy," and had determined to heed
the counsel of his friends, still, he now found himself
so confused that he did not know just what he ought
to do. On the whole, however, he thought he would
follow the example of Senator Giles and withdraw.[1]

At that very moment, Nicholas was a Republican
candidate for Congress and, next to Giles, Jefferson's
principal political agent in Virginia. Four days after
Burr had been brought to Richmond, Jefferson had
written Nicholas a letter of fulsome flattery "be-
seeching" him to return to the National House in

[1] *Burr Trials*, I, 41–42.

the place of the President's son-in-law, Thomas
Mann Randolph, who had determined to retire, and
assuring him of the Republican leadership if he
would do so.[1]

Thus, for a moment, was revealed a thread of
that web of intrigue and indirect influence which,
throughout the trial, was woven to enmesh judge,
jury, and public. Burr was instantly upon his feet
denouncing in his quiet but authoritative manner
the "attempt to intimidate" Nicholas as "a con-
trivance of some of [his] enemies for the purpose of
irritating" the hot-blooded Republican politician
"and increasing the public prejudice against [Burr];
since it was calculated to throw suspicion on [his]
cause." Neither he nor his friends had ever "sanctioned" such an act; they were wholly ignorant of
it, and viewed it "with indignation."[2]

Mr. Joseph Eggleston, another of the grand jurors,
now asked to be excused because he had declared his
belief of Burr's guilt; but he admitted, in answer to
Marshall's questions, that he could act justly in the
impending investigation. Burr said that he would
not object to Eggleston: "the industry which has
been used through this country [Virginia] to prejudice
my cause, leaves me very little chance, indeed, of
an impartial jury." Eggleston's "candour . . in
excepting to himself" caused Burr to hope that he
would "endeavour to be impartial." But let Marshall decide — Burr would be "perfectly passive."[3]
The scrupulous grand juror was retained.

---

[1] Jefferson to Nicholas, Feb. 28, 1807, *Works: Ford*, x, 370–71.
[2] *Burr Trials*, I, 43.   [3] *Ib.* 44.

John Randolph and Dr. William Foushee were
then added to the grand jury panel and Marshall
appointed Randolph foreman.[1] He promptly asked
to be excused because of his "strong prepossession."
"Really," observed Burr, "I am afraid we shall not
be able to find any man without this prepossession."
Marshall again stated "that a man must not only
have formed but declared an opinion in order to
excuse him from serving on the jury." So Randolph
was sworn as foreman, the oath administered to all,
and at last the grand jury was formed.[2]

Marshall then instructed the jury, the substance of
his charge being to the same effect as his opinion in
the case of Bollmann and Swartwout. Burr asked
the Chief Justice also to advise the men who were to
decide the question of his indictment "as to the ad-
missability of certain evidence" which he supposed
Hay would lay before them. The District Attorney
objected to any favor being shown Burr, "who," he
declared, "stood on the same footing with every
other man charged with crime."

For once Burr unleashed his deep but sternly

[1] In view of the hatred which Marshall knew Randolph felt toward Jefferson, it is hard to reconcile his appointment with the fairness which Marshall tried so hard to display throughout the trial.
However, several of Jefferson's most earnest personal friends were
on the grand jury, and some of them were very powerful men. Also
fourteen of the grand jury were Republicans and only two were Federalists.

[2] *Burr Trials*, I, 45–46. This grand jury included some of the foremost citizens of Virginia. The sixteen men who composed this body
were: John Randolph, Jr., Joseph Eggleston, Joseph C. Cabell, Littleton W. Tazewell, Robert Taylor, James Pleasants, John Brockenbrough, William Daniel, James M. Garnett, John Mercer, Edward
Pegram, Munford Beverly, John Ambler, Thomas Harrison, Alexander Shephard, and James Barbour.

repressed feeling: "Would to God," he cried, his voice vibrant with emotion, "that I did stand on the same ground with every other man. This is the first time [since the military seizure] that I have been permitted to enjoy the rights of a citizen. How have I been brought hither?" Marshall checked this passionate outburst: it was not proper, he admonished both Hay and Burr, to "go into these digressions."

His composure restored, Burr insisted that he should be accorded "the same privileges and rights which belonged to every other citizen." He would not now urge his objections to Marshall's opinion in the Bollmann-Swartwout case; [1] but he pointed out "the best informed juryman might be ignorant of many points .. relating to testimony, .. for instance, as to the article of papers," and he wished Marshall to inform the jury on these matters of law.

A brief, sharp debate sprang up, during which Burr's counsel spoke of the "host of prejudices raised against [their] client," taunted Hay with his admission "that there was no man who had not formed an opinion," and denounced "the activity of the Government." [2] Upon Hay's pledging himself that he would submit no testimony to the grand jury "without notice being first given to Colonel Burr and his counsel," Marshall adjourned the court that the attorneys might prepare for "further

---

[1] Marshall's error in this opinion, or perhaps the misunderstanding of a certain passage of it (see *supra*, 350), caused him infinite perplexity during the trial; and he was put to his utmost ingenuity to extricate himself. The misconstruction by the grand jury of the true meaning of Marshall's charge was one determining cause of the grand jury's decision to indict Burr. (See *infra*, 466.)

[2] *Burr Trials*, I, 47–48.

discussion." The Government was not ready to present any testimony on either the following day or on Monday because its principal witness, General Wilkinson, had not arrived.

Hay now sent Jefferson his first report of the progress of the case. Burr had steadily been making friends, and this irritated the District Attorney more than the legal difficulties before him. "I am surprised, and afflicted, when I see how much, and by how many, this man has been patronised and supported." Hay assured Jefferson, however, that he would "this day move to commit him for treason." [1] Accordingly, he announced in the presence of the grand jury that he would again ask the court to imprison Burr on that accusation. In order, he said, that the impropriety of mentioning the subject in their presence might be made plain, Burr moved that the grand jury be withdrawn. Marshall sustained the motion; and after the grand jury had retired, Hay formally moved the court to order Burr's incarceration upon the charge of treason. [2]

Burr's counsel, surprised and angered, loudly complained that no notice had been given them. With a great show of generosity, Hay offered to delay his motion until the next day. "Not a moment's postponement," shouted Botts, his fighting nature thoroughly aroused. Hay's "extraordinary application," he said, was to place upon the court the functions of the grand jury. Burr wanted no delay. His dearest wish was to "satisfy his country . . and even

[1] Hay to Jefferson, May 25, 1807, Jefferson MSS. Lib. Cong.
[2] Burr Trials, I, 48–51.

his prosecutors, that he is innocent." Was ever a man so pursued? He had been made the victim of unparalleled military despotism; his legal rights had been ignored; his person and papers unlawfully seized. The public had been excited to anger. Through newspaper threats and "popular clamor" attempts had been made to intimidate every officer of the court. Consider "the multitude around us" — they must not be further infected "with the poison already too plentifully infused."

Did Hay mean to "open the case more fully?" inquired Marshall. No, answered Hay; but Wilkinson's arrival in Virginia might be announced before he reached Richmond. Who could tell the effect on Burr of such dread tidings? The culprit might escape; he must be safely held.[1] "The bets were against Burr that he would abscond, should W. come to Richmond." [2]

If Wilkinson is so important a witness, "why is he not here?" demanded Wickham. Everybody knew that "a set of busy people .. are laboring to ruin" Burr. "The press, from one end of the continent to the other, has been enlisted .. to excite prejudices" against him. Let the case be decided upon "the evidence of sworn witnesses" instead of "the floating rumours of the day."

Did the Government's counsel wish that "the multitude around us should be prejudiced by garbled evidences?" Wickham avowed that he could not understand Hay's motives, but of this he was sure —

[1] *Burr Trials*, I, 53–54.
[2] Irving to Paulding, June 22, 1807, *Life and Letters of Washington Irving:* Irving, I, 145.

that if, thereafter, the Government wished to oppress any citizen, drag him by military force over the country, prejudice the people against him, it would "pursue the very same course which has now been taken against colonel Burr." The prosecution admitted that it had not enough evidence to lay before the grand jury, yet they asked to parade what they had before the court. Why? — "to nourish and keep alive" the old prejudices now growing stale.[1]

Wirt answered at great length. He understood Wickham's purpose, he said. It was to "divert the public attention from Aaron Burr," and "shift the popular displeasure . . to another quarter." Wickham's speech was not meant for the court, exclaimed Wirt, but for "the people who surround us," and so, of course, Marshall would not heed it. Burr's counsel "would convert this judicial inquiry into a political question . . between Thomas Jefferson and Aaron Burr."

Not to be outdone by his gifted associate, Hay poured forth a stream of words: "Why does he [Burr] turn from defending himself to attack the administration?" he asked. He did not answer his own question, but Edmund Randolph did: "An order has been given to treat colonel Burr as an outlaw, and to burn and destroy him and his property." Jefferson, when requested, had furnished the House information; — "would to God he had stopped here, as an executive officer ought to have done!" But instead he had also pronounced Burr guilty — an opinion calculated to affect courts, juries, the people.

[1] *Burr Trials*, I, 57–58.

Wickham detailed the treatment of Burr, "the only man in the nation whose rights are not secure from violation." [1]

Burr himself closed this unexpected debate, so suddenly thrust upon his counsel and himself. His speech is a model of that simple, perspicuous, and condensed statement of which he was so perfectly the master. He presented the law, and then, turning to Hay, said that two months previous the District Attorney had declared that he had enough evidence to justify the commitment, and surely he must have it now. Nearly half a year had elapsed since Jefferson had "declared that there was a crime," and yet, even now, the Government was not ready. Nevertheless, the court was again asked to imprison him for an alleged offense for which the prosecution admitted it had not so much as the slight evidence required to secure his indictment by the grand jury.

Were the Government and he "on equal terms?" Far from it. "The United States [could] have compulsory process" to obtain affidavits against him; but he had "no such advantage." So the prosecution demanded his imprisonment on *ex parte* evidence which would be contradicted by his own evidence if he could adduce it. Worse still! The Government affidavits against him "are put into the newspapers, and they fall into the hands of the grand jury." Meanwhile, he was helpless. And now the opinion of the court was also to be added to the forces working to undo him.

[1] *Burr Trials*, I, 58–76.

Wirt and Hay had charged his counsel "with declamation against the government." Certainly nobody could attribute "declamation" to him; but, said Burr, his restrained voice tense with suppressed emotion, "no government is so high as to be beyond the reach of criticism" — that was a fundamental principle of liberty. This was especially true when the Government prosecuted a citizen because of "the vast disproportion of means which exists between it and the accused." And "if ever there was a case which justified this vigilance, it is certainly the present one"; let Marshall consider the "uncommon activity" of the Administration.

Burr would, he said, "merely state a few" of the instances of "harrassing, . . contrary to law" to which he had been subjected. His "friends had been every where seized by the military authority," dragged before "particular tribunals," and forced to give testimony; his papers taken; orders to kill him issued; post-offices broken open and robbed —⁣ "nothing seemed too extravagant to be forgiven by the amiable morality of this government." Yet it was for milder conduct that Americans rightly condemned "European despotisms."

The President was a great lawyer; surely "he ought to know what constitutes war. Six months ago he proclaimed that there was a civil war. And yet, for six months they have been hunting for it and cannot find one spot where it existed. There was, to be sure, a most terrible war in the newspapers; but no where else." He had been haled before the court in Kentucky — and no proof; in Mississippi — and no proof. The Spaniards actually invaded American territory — even then there was no war.

Thus early the record itself discloses the dramatic, and, for Marshall, perilous, conditions under which this peculiar trial was to be conducted. The record makes clear, also, the plan of defense which Burr and his counsel were forced to adopt. They must dull the edge of public opinion sharpened to a biting keenness by Jefferson. They must appeal to the people's hatred of oppression, fear of military rule, love of justice. To do this they must attack, attack, always attack.

They must also utilize every technical weapon of the law. At another time and place they could have waived, to Burr's advantage, all legal rights, insisted upon his indictment, and gone to trial, relying only upon the evidence. But not in the Virginia of 1807, with the mob spirit striving to overawe jury and court, and ready to break out in violent action — not at the moment when the reign of Thomas Jefferson had reached the highest degree of popular idolatry.

Just as Hay, Wirt, and MacRae generally spoke to the spectators far more than to the Bench, so did Wickham, Randolph, Botts, and Martin.[1] Both sides so addressed the audience that their hearers were able to repeat to the thousands who could not get into the hall what had been said by the advocates.

[1] "I .. contented myself .. with .. declaring to the Audience (for two thirds of our speeches have been addressed to the people) that I was prepared to give the most direct contradiction to the injurious Statements." (Hay to Jefferson, June 14, 1807, giving the President an account of the trial, Jefferson MSS. Lib. Cong.)

From the very first the celebrated trial of Aaron
Burr was a contest for the momentary favor of public opinion; and, in addition, on the part of Burr, an
invoking of the law to shield him from that popular wrath which the best efforts of his defenders
could not wholly appease.

Marshall faced a problem of uncommon difficulty.
It was no small matter to come between the popu-
lace and its prey — no light adventure to brave the
vengeance of Thomas Jefferson. Not only his public
repute [1] — perhaps even his personal safety [2] and
his official life [3] — but also the now increasing influence and prestige of the National Judiciary were
in peril. However, he must do justice no matter
what befell — he must, at all hazards, pronounce
the law truly and enforce it bravely, but with elas-
tic method. He must be not only a just, but also
an understanding, judge.

When court opened next morning, Marshall was
ready with a written opinion. Concisely he stated
the questions to be decided: Had the court the power
to commit Burr, and, if so, ought the circumstances
to restrain the exercise of it? Neither side had made
the first point, and Marshall mentioned it only
"to show that it [had] been considered." Briefly he
demonstrated that the court was clothed with authority to grant Hay's motion. Should that power,

---

[1] He was hanged in effigy soon after the trial. (See *infra*, 539.)

[2] It must be remembered that Marshall himself declared, in the
very midst of the contest, that it would be dangerous for a jury to
acquit Burr. (See *supra*, 401.)

[3] He had narrowly escaped impeachment (see *supra*, chap. IV), and
during the trial he was openly threatened with that ordeal (see *infra*,
500).

then, be exerted? Marshall thought that it should. The Government had the right to ask Burr's incarceration at any time, and it was the duty of the court to hear such a motion.

Thus far spoke Marshall the judge. In the closing sentences the voice of the politician was heard: "The court perceives and regrets that the result of this motion may be publications unfavourable to the justice, and to the right decision of the case"; but this must be remedied "by other means than by refusing to hear the motion." Every honest and intelligent man extremely deplored "any attempt . . to prejudice the public judgment, and to try any person," not by the law and the evidence, but "by public feelings which may be and often are artificially excited against the innocent, as well as the guilty, . . a practice not less dangerous than it is criminal." Nevertheless he could not "suppress motions, which either party may have a legal right to make." So, if Hay persisted, he might "open his testimony." [1]

While Marshall, in Richmond, was reading this opinion, Jefferson, in Washington, was writing directions to Hay. He was furious at "the criminal and voluntary retirement" of Giles and Nicholas from the grand jury "with the permission of the court." The opening of the prosecution had certainly begun "under very inauspicious circumstances." One thing was clear: "It becomes our duty to provide that full testimony shall be laid before the Legislature, and through them the public."

[1] *Burr Trials*, I, 79–81.

If the grand jury should indict Burr, then Hay must furnish Jefferson with all the evidence, "taken as verbatim as possible." Should Burr not be indicted, and no trial held and no witnesses questioned in court, then Hay must "have every man privately examined by way of affidavit," and send Jefferson "the whole testimony" in that form. "This should be done before they receive their compensation, that they may not evade examination. Go into any expense necessary for this purpose,[1] & meet it from the funds provided to the Attorney general for the other expenses." [2]

Marshall's decision perplexed Hay. It interfered with his campaign of publicity. If only Marshall had denied his motion, how effectively could that incident have been used on public sentiment. But now the Republican press could not exclaim against Marshall's "leniency" to "traitors" as it had done. The people were deprived of fresh fuel for their patriotic indignation. Jefferson would be at a loss for a new pretext to arouse them against the encroachments of the courts upon their "liberties."

Hay strove to retrieve the Government from this disheartening situation. He was "struck," he said, with Marshall's reference to "publications." To avoid such newspaper notoriety, he would try to arrange with Burr's counsel for the prisoner's appearance under additional bail, thus avoiding insistence upon the Government's request for the imprisonment of the accused. Would Marshall adjourn

---

[1] See *supra*, 390–91.
[2] Jefferson to Hay, May 26, 1807, *Works:* Ford, x, footnote to 394–95.

court that this amicable arrangement might be brought about? Marshall would and did.

But next day found Hay unrelieved; Burr's counsel had refused, in writing, to furnish a single dollar of additional bail. To his intense regret, Hay lamented that he was thus forced to examine his witnesses. Driven to this unpleasant duty, he would follow the "chronological order — first the depositions of the witnesses who were absent, and afterwards those who were present." [1]

The alert Wickham demanded "strict legal order." The Government must establish two points: the perpetration of an overt act, and "that colonel Burr was concerned in it." [2] Hay floundered — there was one great plot, he said, the two parts of it "intimately blended"; the projected attack on Spain and the plot to divide the Union were inseparable — he must have a free hand if he were to prove this wedded iniquity. Was Burr afraid to trust the court?

Far from it, cried Wickham, "but we do fear to prejudicate the mind of the grand jury. . . All propriety and decorum have been set at naught; every idle tale which is set afloat has been eagerly caught at. The people here are interested by them; and they circulate all over the country." [3] Marshall interrupted: "No evidence certainly has any bearing . . unless the overt act be proved." Hay might, however, "pursue his own course."

A long altercation followed. Botts made an extended speech, in the course of which he discredited

[1] *Burr Trials*, I, 81–82.   [2] *Ib.* 82.   [3] *Ib.* 84–85.

the Government's witnesses before they were introduced. They were from all over the country, he said, their "names, faces and characters, are alike unknown to colonel Burr." To what were they to testify? Burr did not know — could not possibly ascertain. "His character has long been upon public torture; and wherever that happens . . the impulses to false testimony are numerous. Sometimes men emerge from the sinks of vice and obscurity into patronage and distinction by circulating interesting tales, as all those of the marvelous kind are. Others, from expectation of office and reward, volunteer; while timidity, in a third class, seeks to guard against the apprehended danger, by magnifying trifling stories of alarm. . . When they are afterwards called to give testimony, perjury will not appal them, if it be necessary to save their reputations." Therefore, reasoned Botts — and most justly — strict rules of evidence were necessary.[1]

Hay insisted that Wilkinson's affidavit demonstrated Burr's intentions. That "goes for nothing," said Marshall, "if there was no other evidence to prove the overt act." Therefore, "no part of it [was] admissible at this time."[2] Thrice Marshall patiently reminded Government counsel that they charged an overt act of treason and must prove it.[3]

Hay called Peter Taylor, Blennerhassett's former gardener, and Jacob Allbright, once a laborer on the eccentric Irishman's now famous island. Both were illiterate and in utter terror of the Government. Allbright was a Dutchman who spoke Eng-

[1] *Burr Trials*, I, 91.   [2] *Ib.* 94.   [3] *Ib.* 95–96.

lish poorly; Taylor was an Englishman; and they told stories equally fantastic. Taylor related that Mrs. Blennerhassett had sent him to Kentucky with a letter to Burr warning him not to return to the island; that Burr was surprised at the people's hostility; that Blennerhassett, who was also in Kentucky, confided they were going to take Mexico and make Burr king, and Theodosia queen when her father died; also that Burr, Blennerhassett, and their friends had bought "eight hundred thousand acres of land" and "wanted young men to settle it," and that any of these who should prove refractory, he [Blennerhassett] said, "by God, .. I will stab"; that Blennerhassett had also said it would be a fine thing to divide the Union, but Burr and himself could not do it alone.

Taylor further testified that Blennerhassett once sent him with a letter to a Dr. Bennett, who lived in Ohio, proposing to buy arms in his charge belonging to the United States — if Bennett could not sell, he was to tell where they were, and Blennerhassett "would steal them away in the night"; that his employer charged him "to get [the letter] back and burn it, for it contained high treason"; and that the faithful Taylor had done this in Bennett's presence.

Taylor narrated the scene on the island when Blennerhassett and thirty men in four boats fled in the night: some of the men had guns and there was some powder and lead.[1]

Jacob Allbright told a tale still more marvelous.

[1] *Burr Trials*, I, 492–97.

Soon after his employment, Mrs. Blennerhassett had come to this dull and ignorant laborer, while he was working on a kiln for drying corn, and confided to him that Burr and her husband "were going to lay in provisions for an army for a year"; that Blennerhassett himself had asked Allbright to join the expedition which was going "to settle a new country." Two men whom the Dutch laborer met in the woods hunting had revealed to him that they were "Burr's men," and had disclosed that "they were going to take a silver mine from the Spanish"; that when the party was ready to leave the island, General Tupper of Ohio had "laid his hands upon Blennerhassett and said, 'your body is in my hands in the name of the commonwealth,'" whereupon "seven or eight muskets [were] levelled" at the General; that Tupper then observed he hoped they would not shoot, and one of the desperadoes replied, "I'd as lieve as not"; and that Tupper then "changed his speech," wished them "to escape safe," and bade them Godspeed.

Allbright and Taylor were two of the hundreds to whom the Government's printed questions had been previously put by agents of the Administration. In his answers to these, Allbright had said that the muskets were pointed at Tupper as a joke.[1] Both Taylor and he swore that Burr was not on the island when Blennerhassett's men assembled there and stealthily departed in hasty flight.

To the reading of the deposition of Jacob Dunbaugh, Burr's counsel strenuously objected. It was

[1] *Burr Trials*, I, 509–14.

not shown that Dunbaugh himself could not be produced; the certification of the justice of the peace, before whom the deposition was taken, was defective. For the remainder of the day the opposing lawyers wrangled over these points. Marshall adjourned court and "took time to consider the subject till the next day"; when, in a long and painfully technical opinion, he ruled that Dunbaugh's affidavit could not be admitted because it was not properly authenticated.[1]

May 28, when the court again convened, was made notable by an event other than the reading of the unnecessarily long opinion which Marshall had written during the night: the crimson-faced, bellicose superman of the law, Luther Martin, appeared as one of Burr's counsel.[2] The great lawyer had formed an ardent admiration and warm friendship for Burr during the trial of the Chase impeachment,[3] and this had been intensified when he met Theodosia, with whom he became infatuated.[4] He had voluntarily come to his friend's assistance, and soon threw himself into the defense of Burr with all the passion of his tempestuous nature and all the power and learning of his phenomenal intellect.

After vexatious contendings by counsel as to whether Burr should give additional bail,[5] Marshall declared that "as very improper effects on the public mind [might] be produced," he wished that no opinion would be required of him previous to the action of

[1] *Burr Trials*, I, 97–101. [2] *Ib.* 97.
[2] *Md. Hist. Soc. Fund-Pub. No. 24*, 22.
[4] *Blennerhassett Papers:* Safford, 468–69.
[5] *Burr Trials*, I, 101–04.

LUTHER MARTIN

the grand jury; and that the "appearance of colonel
Burr could be secured without . . proceeding in this
inquiry." Burr denied the right of the court to hold
him on bail, but said that if Marshall was "embarrassed," he voluntarily would furnish additional bail,
"provided it should be understood that no opinion
on the question even of probable cause was pronounced by the court." [1] Marshall agreed; and Burr
with four sureties, among whom was Luther Martin,
gave bond for ten thousand dollars more. [2]

Day after day, court, grand jury, counsel, and
spectators awaited the coming of Wilkinson. The
Government refused to present any testimony to
the grand jury until he arrived, although scores of
witnesses were present. Andrew Jackson was very
much in town, as we have seen. So was Commodore
Truxtun. And "General" William Eaton was also
on hand, spending his time, when court was not in
session, in the bar-rooms of Richmond.

Wearing a "tremendous hat," clad in gay colored coat and trousers, with a flaming Turkish belt
around his waist, Eaton was already beginning to
weaken the local hatred of Burr by his loud blustering against the quiet, courteous, dignified prisoner. [3]
Also, at gambling-tables, and by bets that Burr
would be convicted, the African hero was making
free with the ten thousand dollars paid him by the
Government soon after he made the bloodcurdling

[1] *Burr Trials*, I, 105.

[2] The men who went on this second bail bond for Burr were: William Langburn, Thomas Taylor, John G. Gamble, and Luther Martin.
(*Ib.* 106.)

[3] *Blennerhassett Papers:* Safford, 315–16.

affidavit [1] with which Jefferson had so startled Congress and the country.

While proceedings lagged, Marshall enjoyed the dinners and parties that, more than ever, were given by Richmond society. On one of these occasions that eminent and ardent Republican jurist, St. George Tucker, was present, and between him and Marshall an animated discussion grew out of the charge that Burr had plotted to cause the secession of the Western States; it was a forecast of the tremendous debate that was to end only at Appomattox. "Judge Tucker, though a violent Democrat," records Blennerhassett, "seriously contended .. with Judge Marshall .. that any State in the Union is at any time competent to recede from the same, though Marshall strongly opposed this doctrine." [2]

Hay wrote Jefferson of the slow progress of the case, and the President "hastened" to instruct his district attorney: If the grand jury should refuse to indict Burr, Hay must not deliver the pardon to Bollmann; otherwise, "his evidence is deemed entirely essential, & .. his pardon is to be produced before he goes to the book." Jefferson had become more severe as he thought of Bollmann, and now actually directed Hay to show, in open court, to this new object of Presidential displeasure, the "sacredly confidential" statement given Jefferson under pledge of the latter's "word of honor" that it should never leave his hand. Hay was directed to ask Bollmann whether "it was not his handwriting." [3]

---

[1] *Eaton: Prentiss*, 396–403; 4 Cranch, 463–66.
[2] *Blennerhassett Papers: Safford*, 425.
[3] Jefferson to Hay, May 28, 1807, *Works: Ford*, x, 395–96.

With the same ink on his pen the President wrote his son-in-law that he had heard only of the first day of the trial, but was convinced that Marshall meant to do all he could for Burr. Marshall's partiality showed, insisted Jefferson, "the original error of establishing a judiciary independent of the nation, and which, from the citadel of the law can turn it's guns on those they were meant to defend, & controul & fashion their proceedings to it's own will." [1]

Hay quickly answered Jefferson: The trial had "indeed commenced under inauspicious circumstances," and doubtless these would continue to be unfavorable. Nobody could predict the outcome. Hay was so exhausted and in such a state of mind that he could not describe "the very extraordinary occurrences in this very extraordinary examination." Burr's "partizans" were gloating over the failure of Wilkinson to arrive. Bollmann would neither accept nor reject the pardon; he was "as unprincipled as his leader." Marshall's refusal to admit Dunbaugh's affidavit was plainly illegal — "his eyes [were] almost closed" to justice. [2]

Jefferson now showered Hay with orders. The reference in argument to Marshall's opinion in Marbury *vs*. Madison greatly angered him: "Stop . . citing that case as authority, and have it denied to be law," he directed Hay, and gave him the arguments to be used against it. An entire letter is devoted to this one subject: "I have long wished for a proper occasion to have the gratuitous opinion in Marbury

---

[1] Jefferson to Eppes, May 28, 1807, *Works:* Ford, x, 412–13.
[2] Hay to Jefferson, May 31, 1807, Jefferson MSS. Lib. Cong.

v. Madison brought before the public, & denounced
as not law; & I think the present a fortunate one,
because it occupies such a place in the public
attention."

Hay was openly to declare that the President
rejected Marshall's opinion in that case as having
been "given extra-judicially & against law," and
that the reverse of it would be Jefferson's "rule of
action." If necessary, Hay might state that the
President himself had said this.[1]

Back and forth went letters from Hay to Jefferson
and from Jefferson to Hay,[2] the one asking for instructions and the other eagerly supplying them.
To others, however, the President explained that he
could take no part in any judicial proceeding, since
to do so would subject him to "just censure."[3]

In spite of the abundance of Government witnesses available, the prosecution refused to go on
until the redoubtable savior of his country had arrived from New Orleans. Twice the grand jury had
to be dismissed for several days, in order, merrily
wrote Washington Irving, "that they might go
home, see their wives, get their clothes washed, and
flog their negroes."[4] A crowd of men ready to testify
was held. The swarms of spectators waited with
angry impatience. "If the great hero of the South
does not arrive, it is a chance if we have any trial
this term,"[5] commented Irving.

---

[1] Jefferson to Hay, June 2, 1807, *Works:* Ford, x, 396–97.

[2] Same to same, June 5, 1807, *ib.* 397–98; Hay to Jefferson, same
date, Jefferson MSS. Lib. Cong.; and others cited, *infra.*

[3] Jefferson to Dayton, Aug. 17, 1807, *Works:* Ford, x, 478.

[4] Irving to Mrs. Hoffman, June 4, 1807, Irving, I, 142.   [5] *Ib.*

During this period of inaction and suspense, suddenly arose one of the most important and exciting questions of the entire trial. On June 9, while counsel and court were aimlessly discussing Wilkinson's journey to Richmond, Burr arose and said that he had a "proposition to submit" to the court. The President in his Message to Congress had made mention of the letter and other papers dated October 21, which he had received from Wilkinson. It had now become material that this letter should be produced in court.

Moreover, since the Government had "attempted to infer certain intentions on [his] part, from certain transactions," such as his flight from Mississippi, it had become necessary to prove the conditions that forced him to attempt that escape. Vital among these were orders of the Government to the army and navy "to destroy" Burr's "person and property." He had seen these orders in print,[1] and an officer had assured him that such instructions had actually been issued. It was indispensable that this be established. The Secretary of the Navy had refused to allow him or his counsel to inspect these orders. "Hence," maintained Burr, "I feel it necessary . . to call upon [the court] to issue a subpoena to the President of the United States, with a clause, requiring him to produce certain papers; or in other words, to issue the subpoena *duces tecum.*" If Hay would agree to produce these documents, the motion would not be made.[2]

[1] Burr had seen the order in the *Natchez Gazette*. It was widely published.
[2] *Burr Trials*, I, 113-14.

Hay was sadly confused. He would try to get all the papers wanted if Marshall would say that they were material. How, asked Marshall, could the court decide that question without inspecting the papers? "Why .. issue a subpœna to the President?" inquired Hay. Because, responded Marshall, "in case of a refusal to send the papers, the officer himself may be present to show cause. This subpœna is issued only where fears of this sort are entertained."

Counsel on both sides became angry. Hay denied the authority of the court to issue such a writ. Marshall called for argument, because, he said, "I am not prepared to give an opinion on this point." [1] Thus arose the bitter forensic struggle that preceded Marshall's historic order to Jefferson to come into court with the papers demanded, or to show cause why he should not do so.

Hay instantly dispatched the news to Jefferson; he hoped the papers would be "forwarded without delay," because "detention of them will afford [Burr] pretext for clamor." Besides, "L. Martin has been here a long time, perfectly inactive"; he was yearning to attack Jefferson and this would "furnish a topic." [2]

The President responded with dignified caution: "Reserving the necessary right of the President of the U S to decide, independently of all other authority, what papers, coming to him as President, the public interests permit to be communicated, & to whom, I assure you of my readiness under that

---

[1] *Burr Trials*, I, 115–18.
[2] Hay to Jefferson, June 9, 1807, Jefferson MSS. Lib. Cong.

restriction, voluntarily to furnish on all occasions, whatever the purposes of justice may require." He had given the Wilkinson letter, he said, to the Attorney-General, together with all other documents relating to Burr, and had directed the Secretary of War to search the files so that he (Jefferson) could "judge what can & ought to be done" about sending any order of the Department to Richmond.[1]

When Marshall opened court on June 10, Burr made affidavit that the letters and orders might be material to his defense. Hay announced that he had written Jefferson to send the desired papers and expected to receive them within five days. They could not, however, be material, and he did not wish to discuss them. Martin insisted that the papers be produced. Wickham asked what Hay was trying to do — probably trying to gain time to send to Washington for instructions as to how the prosecution should now act.

Was not "an accused man . . to obtain witnesses in his behalf?" Never had the denial of such a right been heard of "since the declaration of American Independence." The despotic treatment of Burr called aloud not only for the court's protection of the persecuted man, but "to the protection of every citizen in the country as well." [2] So it seemed to that discerning fledgling author, Washington Irving. "I am very much mistaken," he wrote, "if the most underhand . . measures have not been observed toward him. He, however, retains his serenity." [3]

[1] Jefferson to Hay, June 12, 1807, *Works:* Ford, x, 398–99.
[2] *Burr Trials,* i, 124–25.
[3] Irving to Mrs. Hoffman, June 4, 1807, Irving, i, 143.

Luther Martin now took the lead: Was Jefferson "a kind of sovereign?" No! "He is no more than a servant of the people." Yet who could tell what he would do? In this case his Cabinet members, "under presidential influence," had refused copies of official orders. In another case "the officers of the government screened themselves . . under the sanction of the president's name." [1] The same might be done again; for this reason Burr applied "directly to the president." The choleric legal giant from

---

[1] Martin here refers to what he branded as "the farcical trials of Ogden and Smith." In June and July, 1806, William S. Smith and Samuel G. Ogden of New York were tried in the United States Court for that district upon indictments charging them with having aided Miranda in his attack on Caracas, Venezuela. They made affidavit that the testimony of James Madison, Secretary of State, Henry Dearborn, Secretary of War, Robert Smith, Secretary of the Navy, and three clerks of the State Department, was necessary to their defense. Accordingly these officials were summoned to appear in court. They refused, but on July 8, 1806, wrote to the Judges — William Paterson of the Supreme Court and Matthias B. Talmadge, District Judge — that the President "has specially signified to us that our official duties cannot . . be at this juncture dispensed with." (*Trials of Smith and Ogden:* Lloyd, stenographer, 6–7.)

The motion for an attachment to bring the secretaries and their clerks into court was argued for three days. The court disagreed, and no action therefore was taken. (*Ib.* 7–90.) One judge (undoubtedly Paterson) was "of opinion, that the absent witnesses should be laid under a rule to show cause, why an attachment should not be issued against them"; the other (Talmadge) held "that neither an attachment in the first instance, nor a rule to show cause ought to be granted." (*Ib.* 89.)

Talmadge was a Republican, appointed by Jefferson, and charged heavily against the defendants (*ib.* 236–42, 287); but they were acquitted.

The case was regarded as a political prosecution, and the refusal of Cabinet officers and department clerks to obey the summons of the court, together with Judge Talmadge's disagreement with Justice Paterson — who in disgust immediately left the bench under plea of ill-health (*ib.* 90) — and the subsequent conduct of the trial judge, were commented upon unfavorably. These facts led to Martin's reference during the Burr trial.

Maryland could no longer restrain his wrath: "This is a peculiar case," he shouted. "The president has undertaken to prejudice my client by declaring, that 'of his guilt there can be no doubt.' He has assumed to himself the knowledge of the Supreme Being himself, and pretended to search the heart of my highly respected friend. He has proclaimed him a traitor in the face of that country, which has rewarded him. He has let slip the dogs of war, the hell-hounds of persecution, to hunt down my friend."

"And would this president of the United States, who has raised all this absurd clamor, pretend to keep back the papers which are wanted for this trial, where life itself is at stake?" That was a denial of "a sacred principle. Whoever withholds, wilfully, information that would save the life of a person, charged with a capital offence, is substantially a murderer, and so recorded in the register of heaven." Did Jefferson want Burr convicted? Impossible thought! "Would the president of the United States give his enemies . . the proud opportunity of saying that colonel Burr is the victim of anger, jealousy and hatred?" Interspersed with these outbursts of vitriolic eloquence, Martin cited legal authorities. Never, since the days of Patrick Henry, had Richmond heard such a defiance of power.[1]

Alexander MacRae did his best to break the force of Martin's impetuous attack. The present question was "whether this court has the right to issue a subpœna *duces tecum*, addressed to the president of

[1] *Burr Trials*, I, 127–28.

the United States." MacRae admitted that "a subpœna may issue against him as well as against any other man." Still, the President was not bound to disclose "confidential communications." Had not Marshall himself so ruled on that point in the matter of Attorney-General Lincoln at the hearing in Marbury *vs.* Madison? [1]

Botts came into the fray with his keen-edged sarcasm. Hay and Wirt and MacRae had "reprobated" the action of Chase when, in the trial of Cooper, that judge had refused to issue the writ now asked for; yet now they relied on that very precedent. "I congratulate them upon their dereliction of the old democratic opinions." [2]

Wirt argued long and brilliantly. What were the "orders," military and naval, which had been described so thrillingly? Merely to "apprehend Aaron Burr, and *if . . necessary . . to destroy his boats.*" Even the "sanguinary and despotic" orders depicted by Burr and his counsel would have been a "great and glorious virtue" if Burr "was aiming a blow at the vitals of our government and liberty." Martin's "fervid language" had not been inspired merely by devotion to "his honourable friend," said Wirt. It was the continued pursuit of a "policy settled . . before Mr. Martin came to Richmond." Burr's counsel, on the slightest pretext, "flew off at a tangent . . to launch into declamations against the government, exhibiting the prisoner continually as a persecuted patriot: a Russell or a Sidney, bleeding under the scourge of a despot, and dying for virtue's sake!"

[1] *Burr Trials,* I. 130–33.   [2] *Ib.* 134–35.

He wished to know "what gentlemen can intend, expect, or hope, from these perpetual philippics against the government? Do they flatter themselves that this court feel political prejudices which will supply the place of argument and of innocence on the part of the prisoner? Their conduct amounts to an insinuation of the sort." What would a foreigner "infer from hearing . . the judiciary told that the administration are 'blood hounds,' hunting this man with a keen and savage thirst for blood," and witnessing the court receive this language "with all complacency?" Surely no conclusion could be made very "honourable to the court. It would only be inferred, while they are thus suffered to roll and luxuriate in these gross invectives against the administration, that they are furnishing the joys of a Mahomitan paradise to the court as well as to their client." [1]

Here was as bold a challenge to Marshall as ever Erskine flung in the face of judicial arrogance; and it had effect. Before adjourning court, Marshall addressed counsel and auditors: he had not interfered with assertions of counsel, made "in the heat of debate," although he had not approved of them. But now that Wirt had made "a pointed appeal" to the court, and the Judges "had been called upon to support their own dignity, by preventing the government from being abused," he would express his opinion. "Gentlemen on both sides had acted improperly in the style and spirit of their remarks; they had been to blame in endeavoring to excite the prejudices

[1] *Burr Trials*, I, 137-45.

of the people; and had repeatedly accused each other
of doing what they forget they have done themselves." Marshall therefore "expressed a wish that
counsel . . would confine themselves on every occasion to the point really before the court; that their
own good sense and regard for their characters required them to follow such a course." He "hoped
that they would not hereafter deviate from it." [1]

His gentle admonition was scarcely heeded by the
enraged lawyers. Wickham's very "tone of voice,"
exclaimed Hay, was "calculated to excite irritation,
and intended for the multitude." Of course, Jefferson *could* be subpœnaed as a witness; that was in the
discretion of the court. But Marshall ought not to
grant the writ unless justice required it. The letter
might be "of a private nature"; if so, it ought not
to be produced. Martin's statement that Burr had a
right to resist was a "monstrous . . doctrine which
would have been abhorred even in the most turbulent
period of the French revolution, by the jacobins
of 1794!"

Suppose, said Hay, that Jefferson had been "mis-
led," and that "Burr was peaceably engaged in the
project of settling his Washita lands!" Did that
give him "a right to resist the president's orders to
stop him?" Never! "This would be treason." The
assertion of the right to disobey the President was
the offspring of "a new-born zeal of some of the
gentlemen, in defence of the rights of man." [2]

Why await the arrival of Wilkinson? asked Edmund Randolph. What was expected of "that great

[1] *Burr Trials*, I, 147–48.   [2] *Ib.* 148–52.

accomplisher of all things?'' Apparently this: "He is to support . . the *sing-song* and the ballads of treason and conspiracy, which we have heard delivered from one extremity of the continent to the other. The funeral pile of the prosecution is already prepared by the hands of the public attorney, and nothing is wanting to kindle the fatal blaze but the torch of James Wilkinson,'' who "is to officiate as the high priest of this human sacrifice. . . Wilkinson will do many things rather than disappoint the wonder-seizing appetite of America, which for months together he has been gratifying by the most miraculous actions.'' If Burr were found guilty, Wilkinson would stand acquitted; if not, then "the character, the reputation, every thing . . will be gone for ever from general Wilkinson.''

Randolph's speech was a masterpiece of invective. "The President testifies, that Wilkinson has testified to him fully against Burr; then let that letter be produced. The President's declaration of Burr's guilt is unconstitutional.'' It was not the business of the President "to give opinions concerning the guilt or innocence of any person.'' Directly addressing Marshall, Randolph continued: "With respect to your exhortation,'' that Burr's appeal was to the court alone, "we demand justice only, and if you cannot exorcise the demon of prejudice, you can chain him down to law and reason, and then we shall have nothing to fear.'' [1]

The audacious Martin respected Marshall's appeal to counsel even less than Hay and Randolph had

[1] *Burr Trials*, i, 153–64.

done. The prosecution had objected to the production of Wilkinson's mysterious letter to Jefferson because it might contain confidential statements. "What, sir," he shouted, "shall the cabinet of the United States be converted into a lion's mouth of Venice, or into a *repertorium* of the inquisition? Shall envy, hatred, and all the malignant passions pour their poison into that cabinet against the character and life of a fellow citizen, and yet that cabinet not be examined in vindication of that character and to protect that life?"

Genuine fury shook Martin. "Is the life of a man, lately in high public esteem . . to be endangered for the sake of punctilio to the president?" Obey illegal orders! "If every order, however arbitrary and unjust, is to be obeyed, we are slaves as much as the inhabitants of Turkey. If the presidential edicts are to be the supreme law, and the officers of the government have but to register them, as formerly in France, . . we are as subject to despotism, as . . the subjects of the former '*Grands Monarques*.'" [1]

Now occurred as strange a mingling of acrimony and learning as ever enlightened and enlivened a court. Burr's counsel demanded that Marshall deliver a supplementary charge to the grand jury. Marshall was magnificently cautious. He would, he said, instruct the jury as confused questions arose. On further reflection and argument — Marshall's dearly beloved argument — he wrote additional instructions,[2] but would not at present announce them. There must be an actual "levying of war"; the overt

---

[1] *Burr Trials*, I, 164–67.   [2] *Ib.* 173–76.

act must be established; no matter what suspicions were entertained, what plans had been formed, what enterprises had been projected, there could be "no treason without an overt act." [1]

In such would-and-would-not fashion Marshall contrived to waive this issue for the time being. Then he delivered that opinion which proved his courage, divided Republicans, stirred all America, and furnished a theme of disputation that remains fresh to the present day. He decided to grant Burr's demand that Jefferson be called into court with the papers asked for.

The purpose of the motion was, said Marshall, to produce copies of the army and navy orders for the seizure of Burr, the original of Wilkinson's letter to Jefferson, and the President's answer. To accomplish this object legally, Burr had applied for the well-known subpœna *duces tecum* directed to the President of the United States.

The objection that until the grand jury had indicted Burr, no process could issue to aid him to obtain testimony, was, Marshall would not say new elsewhere, but certainly it had never before been heard of in Virginia. "So far back as any knowledge of our jurisprudence is possessed, the uniform practice of this country [Virginia] has been, to permit any individual . . charged with any crime, to prepare for his defence and to obtain the process of the court, for the purpose of enabling him so to do." An accused person must expect indictment, and has a right to compel the attendance of witnesses to meet it. It

[1] *Burr Trials*, I, 177.

was perhaps his duty to exercise that right: "The genius and character of our laws and usages are friendly, not to condemnation at all events, but to a fair and impartial trial."

In all criminal prosecutions the Constitution, Marshall pointed out, guarantees to the prisoner "a speedy and public trial, and to compulsory process for obtaining witnesses in his favour." The courts must hold this "sacred," must construe it "to be something more than a dead letter." Moreover, the act of Congress undoubtedly contemplated "that, in all capital cases, the accused shall be entitled to process before indictment found." Thus "immemorial usage," the language of the Constitution, the National statute, all combined to give "any person, charged with a crime in the courts of the United States, . . a right, before, as well as after indictment, to the process of the court to compel the attendance of his witnesses."

But could "a subpœna *duces tecum* be directed to the president of the United States?" If it could, ought it to be "in this case"? Neither in the Constitution nor in an act of Congress is there any exception whatever to the right given all persons charged with crime to compel the attendance of witnesses. "No person could claim an exemption." True, in Great Britain it was considered "to be incompatible with his dignity" for the King "to appear under the process of the court." But did this apply to the President of the United States? Marshall stated the many differences between the status of the British King and that of the American President.

The only possible ground for exempting the President "from the general provisions of the constitution" would be, of course, that "his duties . . demand his whole time for national objects. But," continued Marshall, "it is apparent, that this demand is not unremitting" — a statement at which Jefferson took particular offense.[1] Should the President be so occupied when his presence in court is required, "it would be sworn on the return of the subpœna, and would rather constitute a reason for not obeying the process of the court, than a reason against its being issued."

To be sure, any court would "much more cheerfully" dispense with the duty of issuing a subpœna to the President than to perform that duty; "but, if it be a duty, the court can have no choice" but to perform it.

If, "as is admitted by counsel for the United States," the President may be "summoned to give his personal attendance to testify," was that power nullified because "his testimony depends on a paper in his possession, not on facts which have come to his knowledge otherwise than by writing?" Such a distinction is "too much attenuated to be countenanced in the tribunals of a just and humane nation." [2] The character of the paper desired as evidence, and not "the character of the person who holds it," determines "the propriety of introducing any paper . . as testimony."

It followed, then, that "a subpœna *duces tecum* may issue to any person to whom an ordinary subpœna

[1] See *infra*, 455–56.   [2] *Burr Trials*, I, 181–83.

may issue." The only difference between the two writs is that one requires only the attendance of the witness, while the other directs also "bringing with him a paper in his custody."

In many States the process of subpœna *duces tecum* issues of course, and without any action of the judge. In Virginia, however, leave of the court is required; but "no case exists . . in which the motion . . has been denied or in which it has been opposed," when "founded on an affidavit."

The Chief Justice declared that he would not issue the writ if it were apparent that the object of the accused in applying for it was "not really in his own defence, but for purposes which the court ought to discountenance. The court would not lend its aid to motions obviously designed to manifest disrespect to the government; but the court has no right to refuse its aid to motions for papers to which the accused may be entitled, and which may be material in his defence." If this was true in the matter of Burr's application, "would it not be a blot in the page, which records the judicial proceedings of this country, if, in a case of such serious import as this, the accused should be denied the use" of papers on which his life might depend?

Marshall carefully examined a case cited by the Government[1] in which Justice Paterson had presided, at the same time paying to the memory of the deceased jurist a tribute of esteem and affection. He answered with tedious particularity the objections to the production of Wilkinson's letter to Jeffer-

[1] United States *vs*. Smith and Ogden. (See *supra*, 436, foot-note.)

son, and then referred to the "disrespect" which the
Government counsel had asserted would be shown
to the President if Marshall should order him to
appear in court with the letters and orders.

"This court feels many, perhaps peculiar motives,
for manifesting as guarded respect for the chief
magistrate of the Union as is compatible with its
official duties." But, declared Marshall, "to go
beyond these . . would deserve some other appellation than the term respect."

If the prosecution should end, *"as is expected"* by
the Government, those who withheld from Burr any
paper necessary to his defense would, of course, bitterly regret their conduct. "I will not say, that this
circumstance would . . tarnish the reputation of the
Government; but I will say, that it would justly
tarnish the reputation of the court, which had given
its sanction to its being withheld."

With all that impressiveness of voice and manner
which, on occasion, so transformed Marshall, he
exclaimed: "Might I be permitted to utter one sentiment, with respect to myself, it would be to deplore,
most earnestly, the occasion which should compel
me to look back on any part of my official conduct
with so much self-reproach as I should feel, could I
declare, on the information now possessed, that the
accused is not entitled to the letter in question, if
it should be really important to him."

Let a subpœna *duces tecum*, therefore ruled the
Chief Justice, be issued, directed to Thomas Jefferson, President of the United States.[1]

[1] *Burr Trials*, I, 187-88.

Nothing that Marshall had before said or done so highly excited counsel for the prosecution as his assertion that they "expected" Burr's conviction. The auditors were almost as deeply stirred. Considering the peculiarly mild nature of the man and his habitual self-restraint, Marshall's language was a pointed rebuke, not only to the Government's attorneys, but to the Administration itself. Even Marshall's friends thought that he had gone too far.

Instantly MacRae was on his feet. He resented Marshall's phrase, and denied that the Government or its counsel "wished" the conviction of Burr — such a desire was "completely abhorrent to [their] feelings." MacRae hoped that Marshall did not express such an opinion deliberately, but that it had "accidentally fallen from the pen of [his] honor."

Marshall answered that he did not intend to charge the Administration or its attorneys with a desire to convict Burr "whether he was guilty or innocent"; but, he added dryly, "gentlemen had so often, and so uniformly asserted, that colonel Burr was guilty, and they had so often repeated it before the testimony was perceived, on which that guilt could alone be substantiated, that it appeared to him probable, that they were not indifferent on the subject." [1]

Hay, in his report to Jefferson, gave more space to this incident than he did to all other features of the case. He told the President that Marshall had issued the dreaded process and then quoted the offensive sentence. "This expression," he relates,

[1] *Burr Trials*, I, 189.

"produced a very strong & very general sensation. The friends of the Judge, both personal & political, Condemned it. Alex⸢ M⸢c⸣Rae rose as soon as he had finished, and in terms mild yet determined, demanded an explanation of it. The Judge actually blushed." And, triumphantly continues the District Attorney, "he did attempt an explanation. . . I observed, with an indifference which was not assumed, that I had endeavored to do my duty, according to my own judgment and feelings, that I regretted nothing that I had said or done, that I should pursue the same Course throughout, and that it was a truth, that I cared not what *any man* said or thought about it."

Marshall himself was perturbed. "About three hours afterwards," Hay tells Jefferson, "when the Crowd was thinned, the Judge acknowledged the impropriety of the expression objected to, & informed us from the Bench that 'he had erased it." The Chief Justice even apologized to the wrathful Hay: "After he had adjourned the Court, he descended from the Bench, and told me that he regretted the remark, and then by way of apology said, that he had been so pressed for time, that he had never read the opinion, after he had written it." Hay loftily adds: "An observation from me that I did not perceive any connection between my declarations & his remark, or how the former could regularly be the Cause of the latter, closed the Conversation." [1]

Hay despondently goes on to say that "there never was such a trial from the beginning of the

[1] Hay to Jefferson, June 14, 1807, Jefferson MSS. Lib. Cong.

world to this day." And what should he do about
Bollmann? That wretch "resolutely refuses his
pardon & is determined not to utter a word, if he can
avoid it. The pardon lies on the clerks table. The
Court are to decide whether he is really pardoned or
not. Martin says he is not pardoned. Such are the
questions, with which we are worried. If the Judge
says that he is not pardoned, I will take the pardon
back. What shall I then do with him?"

The immediate effect of Marshall's ruling was the
one Jefferson most dreaded. For the first time, most
Republicans approved of the opinion of John Marshall. In the fanatical politics of the time there was
enough of honest adherence to the American ideal,
that all men are equal in the eyes of the law, to justify the calling of a President, even Thomas Jefferson,
before a court of justice.

Such a militant Republican and devotee of Jefferson as Thomas Ritchie, editor of the Richmond
Enquirer, the party organ in Virginia, did not criticize Marshall, nor did a single adverse comment on
Marshall appear in that paper during the remainder
of the trial. Not till the final verdict was rendered
did Ritchie condemn him.[1]

Before he learned of Marshall's ruling, Jefferson
had once more written the District Attorney giving
him well-stated arguments against the issuance of
the dreaded subpœna.[2] When he did receive the
doleful tidings, Jefferson's anger blazed — but this
time chiefly at Luther Martin, who was, he wrote,

---

[1] Ambler: *Thomas Ritchie — A Study in Virginia Politics*, 40–41.
[2] Jefferson to Hay, June 17, 1807, *Works:* Ford, x, 400–01.

an "unprincipled & impudent federal bull-dog."
But there was a way open to dispose of him: Martin
had known all about Burr's criminal enterprise.
Jefferson had received a letter from Baltimore stating that this had been believed generally in that city
"for more than a twelve-mouth." Let Hay subpœna as a witness the writer of this letter — one
Greybell.

Something must be done to "put down" the
troublesome "bull-dog": "Shall L M be summoned
as a witness against Burr?" Or "shall we move to
commit L M as *particeps criminis* with Burr? Greybell will fix upon him misprision of treason at least
.. and add another proof that the most clamorous
defenders of Burr are all his accomplices."

As for Bollmann! "If [he] finally rejects his pardon, & the Judge decides it to have no effect ..
move to commit him immediately for treason or
misdemeanor." [1] But Bollmann, in open court, had
refused Jefferson's pardon six days before the President's vindictively emotional letter was written.

After Marshall delivered his opinion on the question of the subpœna to Jefferson, Burr insisted, in
an argument as convincing as it was brief, that the
Chief Justice should now deliver the supplementary
charge to the grand jury as to what evidence it could
legally consider. Marshall announced that he would
do so on the following Monday.[2]

Several witnesses for the Government were sworn,
among them Commodore Thomas Truxtun, Com-

---

[1] Jefferson to Hay, June 19, 1807, *Works:* Ford, x, 402–03.
[2] *Burr Trials*, I, 190.

modore Stephen Decatur, and "General" William
Eaton. When Dr. Erich Bollmann was called to the
book, Hay stopped the administration of the oath.
Bollmann had told the Government all about Burr's
"plans, designs and views," said the District Attorney; "as these communications might criminate
doctor Bollman before the grand jury, the president has communicated to me this pardon" — and
Hay held out the shameful document. He had already offered it to Bollmann, he informed Marshall,
but that incomprehensible person would neither
accept nor reject it. His evidence was "extremely
material"; the pardon would "completely exonerate
him from all the penalties of the law." And so, exclaimed Hay, "in the presence of this court, I offer
this pardon to him, and if he refuses, I shall deposit
it with the clerk for his use." Then turning to Bollmann, Hay dramatically asked:

"Will you accept this pardon?"

"No, I will not, sir," firmly answered Bollmann.

Then, said Hay, the witness must be sent to the
grand jury "with an intimation, that he has been
pardoned."

"It has always been doctor Bollman's intention
to refuse this pardon," broke in Luther Martin.
He had not done so before only "because he wished
to have this opportunity of publicly rejecting it."

Witness after witness was sworn and sent to the
grand jury, Hay and Martin quarreling over the
effect of Jefferson's pardon of Bollmann. Marshall
said that it would be better "to settle . . the validity
of the pardon before he was sent to the grand jury."

Again Hay offered Bollmann the offensive guarantee of immunity; again it was refused; again Martin protested.

"Are you then willing to hear doctor Bollman indicted?" asked Hay, white with anger. "Take care," he theatrically cried to Martin, "in what an awful condition you are placing this gentleman."

Bollmann could not be frightened, retorted Martin: "He is a man of too much honour to trust his reputation to the course which you prescribe for him."

Marshall "would perceive," volunteered the nonplussed and exasperated Hay, "that doctor Bollman now possessed so much zeal, as even to encounter the risk of an indictment for treason."

The Chief Justice announced that he could not, "at present, declare, whether he be really pardoned or not." He must, he said, "take time to deliberate."

Hay persisted: "Categorically then I ask you, Mr. Bollman, do you accept your pardon?"

"I have already answered that question several times. I say no," responded Bollmann. "I repeat, that I would have refused it before, but that I wished this opportunity of publicly declaring it." [1]

Bollmann was represented by an attorney of his own, a Mr. Williams, who now cited an immense array of authorities on the various questions involved. Counsel on both sides entered into the discussion. One "reason why doctor Bollman has refused this pardon" was, said Martin, "that it would

[1] *Burr Trials*, I, 191–93.

be considered as an admission of guilt." But "doctor Bollman does not admit that he has been guilty. He does not consider a pardon as necessary for an innocent man. Doctor Bollman, sir, knows what he has to fear from the persecution of an angry government; but he will brave it all."

Yes! cried Martin, with immense effect on the excited spectators, "the man, who did so much to rescue the marquis la Fayette from his imprisonment, and who has been known at so many courts, bears too great a regard for his reputation, to wish to have it sounded throughout Europe, that he was compelled to abandon his honour through a fear of unjust persecution." Finally the true-hearted and defiant Bollmann was sent to the grand jury without having accepted the pardon, and without the legal effect of its offer having been decided.[1]

When the Richmond *Enquirer*, containing Marshall's opinion on the issuance of the subpœna *duces tecum*, reached Washington, the President wrote to Hay an answer of great ability, in which Jefferson the lawyer shines brilliantly forth: "as is usual where an opinion is to be supported, right or wrong, he [Marshall] dwells much on smaller objections, and passes over those which are solid. . . He admits no exception" to the rule "that all persons owe obedience to subpœnas . . unless it can be produced in his law books."

"But," argues Jefferson, "if the Constitution enjoins on a particular officer to be always engaged in a particular set of duties imposed on him, does not

---

[1] *Burr Trials*, I, 193-96.

this supersede the general law, subjecting him to minor duties inconsistent with these? The Constitution enjoins his [the President's] constant agency in the concerns of 6. millions of people. Is the law paramount to this, which calls on him on behalf of a single one?"

Let Marshall smoke his own tobacco: suppose the Sheriff of Henrico County should summon the Chief Justice to help " quell a riot "? Under the "general law" he is "a part of the *posse* of the State sheriff"; yet, "would the Judge abandon major duties to perform lesser ones?" Or, imagine that a court in the most distant territory of the United States "commands, by subpœnas, the attendance of all the judges of the Supreme Court. Would they abandon their posts as judges, and the interests of millions committed to them, to serve the purposes of a single individual?"

The Judiciary was incessantly proclaiming its "independence," and asserting that "the leading principle of our Constitution is the independence of the Legislature, executive and judiciary of each other." But where would be such independence, if the President "were subject to the *commands* of the latter, & to imprisonment for disobedience; if the several courts could bandy him from pillar to post, keep him constantly trudging from north to south & east to west, and withdraw him entirely from his constitutional duties?"

Jefferson vigorously resented Marshall's personal reference to him. "If he alludes to our annual retirement from the seat of government, during the

sickly season," Hay ought to tell Marshall that
Jefferson carried on his Executive duties at Monticello.[1]

Crowded with sensations as the proceedings had
been from the first, they now reached a stage of thrilling movement and high color. The long-awaited and
much-discussed Wilkinson had at last arrived "with
ten witnesses, eight of them Burr's select men," as
Hay gleefully reported to Jefferson.[2] Fully attired
in the showy uniform of the period, to the last item
of martial decoration, the fat, pompous Commanding General of the American armies strode through
the crowded streets of Richmond and made his way
among the awed and gaping throng to his seat by
the side of the Government's attorneys.

Washington Irving reports that "Wilkinson strutted into the Court, and .. stood for a moment
swelling like a turkey cock." Burr ignored him
until Marshall "directed the clerk to swear General
Wilkinson; at the mention of the name Burr turned
his head, looked him full in the face with one of his
piercing regards, swept his eye over his whole person
from head to foot, as if to scan its dimensions, and

---

[1] Jefferson to Hay, June 20, 1807, *Works:* Ford, x, 403–05.

[2] Hay to Jefferson, June 11, 1807, Jefferson MSS. Lib. Cong. This
letter announced Wilkinson's landing at Hampton Roads.

Wilkinson reached Richmond by stage on Saturday, June 13. He
was accompanied by John Graham and Captain Gaines, the ordinary
witnesses having been sent ahead on a pilot boat. (Graham to Madison, May 11, 1807, "Letters in Relation," MSS. Lib. Cong.) Graham
incorrectly dated his letter May 11 instead of June 11. He had left
New Orleans in May, and in the excitement of landing had evidently
forgotten that a new month had come.

Wilkinson was "too much fatigued" to come into court. (*Burr
Trials,* i, 196.) By Monday, however, he was sufficiently restored to
present himself before Marshall.

then coolly . . went on conversing with his counsel as tranquilly as ever." [1]

Wilkinson delighted Jefferson with a different description: "I saluted the Bench & in spite of myself my Eyes darted a flash of indignation at the little Traitor, on whom they continued fixed until I was called to the Book– here Sir I found my expectations verified– This Lyon hearted Eagle Eyed Hero, sinking under the weight of conscious guilt, with haggard Eye, made an Effort to meet the indignant salutation of outraged Honor, but it was in vain, his audacity failed Him, He averted his face, grew pale & affected passion to conceal his perturbation." [2]

But the countenance of a thin, long-faced, roughly garbed man sitting among the waiting witnesses was not composed when Wilkinson appeared. For three weeks Andrew Jackson to all whom he met had been expressing his opinion of Wilkinson in the unrestrained language of the fighting frontiersman; [3] and he now fiercely gazed upon the creature whom he regarded as a triple traitor, his own face furious with scorn and loathing.

Within the bar also sat that brave and noble

---

[1] Irving to Paulding, June 22, 1807, Irving, I, 145.

[2] Wilkinson to Jefferson, June 17, 1807, "Letters in Relation," MSS. Lib. Cong.

The court reporter impartially states that Wilkinson was "calm, dignified, and commanding," and that Burr glanced at him with "haughty contempt." (*Burr Trials*, I, footnote to 197.)

[3] "Gen: Jackson of Tennessee has been here ever since the 22ᵈ [of May] denouncing Wilkinson in the coarsest terms in every company." (Hay to Jefferson, June 14, 1807, Jefferson MSS. Lib. Cong.)

Hay had not the courage to tell the President that Jackson had been as savagely unsparing in his attacks on Jefferson as in his thoroughly justified condemnation of Wilkinson.

man whose career of unbroken victories had made
the most brilliant and honorable page thus far in
the record of the American Navy — Commodore
Thomas Truxtun. He was dressed in civilian attire.[1]
By his side, clad as a man of business, sat a brother
naval hero of the old days, Commodore Stephen Decatur.[2] A third of the group was Benjamin Stoddert,
the Secretary of the Navy under President Adams.[3]

[1] Truxtun left the Navy in 1802, and, at the time of the Burr trial,
was living on a farm in New Jersey. No officer in any navy ever made
a better record for gallantry, seamanship, and whole-hearted devotion
to his country. The list of his successful engagements is amazing. He
was as high-spirited as he was fearless and honorable.

In 1802, when in command of the squadron that was being equipped
for our war with Tripoli, Truxtun most properly asked that a captain
be appointed to command the flagship. The Navy was in great disfavor with Jefferson and the whole Republican Party, and naval affairs
were sadly mismanaged or neglected. Truxtun's reasonable request
was refused by the Administration, and he wrote a letter of indignant
protest to the Secretary of the Navy. To the surprise and dismay of
the experienced and competent officer, Jefferson and his Cabinet construed his spirited letter as a resignation from the service, and, against
Truxtun's wishes, accepted it as such. Thus the American Navy
lost one of its ablest officers at the very height of his powers. Truxtun
at the time was fifty-two years old. No single act of Jefferson's
Administration is more discreditable than this untimely ending of a
great career.

[2] This man was the elder Decatur, father of the more famous officer
of the same name. He had had a career in the American Navy as
honorable but not so distinguished as that of Truxtun; and his service
had been ended by an unhappy circumstance, but one less humiliating
than that which severed Truxtun's connection with the Navy.

The unworthiest act of the expiring Federalist Congress of 1801,
and one which all Republicans eagerly supported, was that authorizing most of the ships of the Navy to be sold or laid up and most of the
naval officers discharged. (Act of March 3, 1801, *Annals*, 6th Cong.
1st and 2d Sess. 1557–59.) Among the men whose life profession was
thus cut off, and whose notable services to their country were thus
rewarded, was Commodore Stephen Decatur, who thereafter engaged in business in Philadelphia.

[3] It was under Stoddert's administration of the Navy Department
that the American Navy was really created. Both Truxtun and
Decatur won their greatest sea battles in our naval war with France.

In striking contrast with the dignified appearance and modest deportment of these gray-haired friends was the gaudily appareled, aggressive mannered Eaton, his restlessness and his complexion advertising those excesses which were already disgusting even the hard-drinking men then gathered in Richmond. Dozens of inconspicuous witnesses found humbler places in the audience, among them Sergeant Jacob Dunbaugh, bearing himself with mingled bravado, insolence, and humility, the stripes on the sleeve of his uniform designating the position to which Wilkinson had restored him.

Dunbaugh had gone before the grand jury on Saturday, as had Bollmann; and now, one by one, Truxtun, Decatur, Eaton, and others were sent to testify before that body.

Eaton told the grand jury the same tale related in his now famous affidavit.[1]

Commodore Truxtun testified to facts as different from the statements made by "the hero of Derne"[2] as though Burr had been two utterly contrasted persons. During the same period that Burr had seen Eaton, he had also conversed with him, said Truxtun. Burr mentioned a great Western land speculation, the digging of a canal, and the building of a bridge. Later on Burr had told him that "in the event of a

while Stoddert was Secretary. The three men were close friends and all of them warmly resented the demolition of the Navy and highly disapproved of Jefferson, both as an individual and as a statesman. They belonged to the old school of Federalists. Three more upright men did not live.

[1] See *supra*, 304–05.

[2] A popular designation of Eaton after his picturesque and heroic Moroccan exploit.

war with Spain, which he thought inevitable, . . he
contemplated an expedition to Mexico," and had
asked Truxtun "if the Havanna could be easily
taken . . and what would be the best mode of attacking Carthagena and La Vera Cruz by land and
sea." The Commodore had given Burr his opinion
"very freely," part of it being that "it would require a naval force." Burr had answered that "*that*
might be obtained," and had frankly asked Truxtun if he "would take the command of a naval expedition."

"I asked him," testified Truxtun, "if the executive of the United States were privy to, or concerned
in the project? He answered *emphatically* that he
was not: . . I told Mr. Burr that I would have nothing to do with it. . . He observed to me, that in the
event of a war [with Spain], he intended to establish
an independent government in Mexico; that Wilkinson, the army, and many officers of the navy
would join. . . Wilkinson had projected the expedition, and he had matured it; that many greater
men than Wilkinson would join, and that thousands
to the westward would join."

In some of the conversations "Burr mentioned to
me that the government was weak," testified Truxtun, "and he wished me to get the navy of the United
States out of my head; [1] . . and not to think more of
those men at Washington; that he wished to *see* or

---

[1] Truxtun at the time of his conversations with Burr was in
the thick of that despair over his cruel and unjustifiable separation
from the Navy, which clouded his whole after life. The longing to
be once more on the quarter-deck of an American warship never left
his heart.

make me, (I do not recollect which of those two terms he used) an Admiral."

Burr wished Truxtun to write to Wilkinson, to whom he was about to dispatch couriers, but Truxtun declined, as he "had no subject to write about." Again Burr urged Truxtun to join the enterprise — "several officers would be pleased at being put under my command. . . The expedition could not fail — the Mexicans were ripe for revolt." Burr "was sanguine there would be war," but "if he was disappointed as to the event of war, he was about to complete a contract for a large quantity of land on the Washita; that he intended to invite his friends to settle it; that in one year he would have a thousand families of respectable and fashionable people, and some of them of considerable property; that it was a fine country, and that they would have a charming society, and in two years he would have doubled the number of settlers; and being on the frontier, he would be ready to move whenever a war took place. . .

"All his conversations respecting military and naval subjects, and the Mexican expedition, were in the event of a war with Spain." Truxtun testified that he and Burr were "very intimate"; that Burr talked to him with "no reserve"; and that he "never heard [Burr] speak of a division of the union."

Burr had shown Truxtun the plan of a "kind of boat that plies between Paulus-Hook and New-York," and had asked whether such craft would do for the Mississippi River and its tributaries, especially on voyages upstream. Truxtun had said they would. Burr had asked him to give the plans to "a naval constructor to make several copies," and Truxtun had done so. Burr explained that "he intended those boats for the conveyance of agricultural products to market at New-Orleans, and in the event of war [with Spain], for transports."

The Commodore testified that Burr made no proposition to invade Mexico "whether there was war [with Spain] or not." He was so sure that Burr meant to settle the Washita lands that he was "astonished" at the newspaper accounts of Burr's treasonable designs after he had gone to the Western country for the second time.

Truxtun had freely complained of what amounted to his discharge from the Navy, being "pretty full" himself of "resentment against the Government," and Burr "joined [him] in opinion" on the Administration.[1]

Jacob Dunbaugh told a weird tale. At Fort Massac he had been under Captain Bissel and in touch with Burr. His superior officer had granted him a furlough to accompany Burr for twenty days. Before leaving, Captain Bissel had "sent for [Dunbaugh] to his quarters," told him to keep "any secrets" Burr had confided to him, and "advised" him "never to forsake Col. Burr"; and "at the same time he made [Dunbaugh] a present of a silver breast plate."

After Dunbaugh had joined the expedition, Burr had tried to persuade him to get "ten or twelve

---

[1] *Burr Trials*, I, 486–91. This abstract is from the testimony given by Commodore Truxtun before the trial jury, which was substantially the same as that before the grand jury.

of the best men" among his nineteen fellow soldiers then at Chickasaw Bluffs to desert and join
the expedition; but the virtuous sergeant had refused. Then Burr had asked him to "steal from the
garrison arms such as muskets, fusees and rifles,"
but Dunbaugh had also declined this reasonable
request. As soon as Burr learned of Wilkinson's
action, he told Dunbaugh to come ashore with him
armed "with a rifle," and to "conceal a bayonet under
[his] clothes. . . He told me he was going to tell me
something I must never relate again, . . that General Wilkinson had betrayed him . . that he had
played the devil with him, and had proved the
greatest traitor on the earth."

Just before the militia broke up the expedition,
Burr and Wylie, his secretary, got "an axe, auger
and saw," and "went into Colonel Burr's private
room and began to chop," Burr first having "ordered no person to go out." Dunbaugh did go out,
however, and "got on the top of the boat." When
the chopping ceased, he saw that "a Mr. Pryor and
a Mr. Tooly got out of the window," and "saw two
bundles of arms tied up with cords, and sunk by
cords going through the holes at the gunwales of
Colonel Burr's boat." The vigilant Dunbaugh also
saw "about forty or forty-three stands [of arms],
besides pistols, swords, blunderbusses, fusees, and
tomahawks"; and there were bayonets too.[1]

Next Wilkinson detailed to the grand jury the
revelations he had made to Jefferson. He produced
Burr's cipher letter to him, and was forced to admit

[1] *Annals*, 10th Cong. 1st Sess. 452–63. See note 1, next page.

that he had left out the opening sentence of it —
"Yours, postmarked 13th of May, is received" —
and that he had erased some words of it and substituted others. He recounted the alarming disclosures
he had so cunningly extracted from Burr's messenger, and enlarged upon the heroic measures he had
taken to crush treason and capture traitors. For
four days [1] Wilkinson held forth, and himself escaped indictment by the narrow margin of 7 to 9 of
the sixteen grand jurymen. All the jurymen, however, appear to have believed him to be a scoundrel.[2]

"The mammoth of iniquity escaped," wrote John
Randolph in acrid disgust, "not that any man pretended to think him innocent, but upon certain wire-
drawn distinctions that I will not pester you with.
Wilkinson is the only man I ever saw who was from
the bark to the very core a villain. . . Perhaps you
never saw human nature in so degraded a situation
as in the person of Wilkinson before the grand jury,
and yet this man stands on the very summit and
pinnacle of executive favor."[3]

[1] Wilkinson's testimony on the trial for misdemeanor (*Annals*,
10th Cong. 1st Sess, 520–22) was the same as before the grand jury.

"Wilkinson is now before the grand jury, and has such a mighty
mass of *words* to deliver himself of, that he claims at least two days
more to discharge the wondrous cargo." (Irving to Paulding, June 22,
1807, Irving, I, 145.)

[2] See McCaleb, 335. Politics alone saved Wilkinson. The trial was
universally considered a party matter, Jefferson's prestige, especially,
being at stake. Yet seven out of the sixteen members of the grand
jury voted to indict Wilkinson. Fourteen of the jury were Republicans, and two were Federalists.

[3] Randolph to Nicholson, June 25, 1807, Adams: *Randolph*, 221–
22. Speaking of political conditions at that time, Randolph observed:
"Politics have usurped the place of law, and the scenes of 1798 [re-
ferring to the Alien and Sedition laws] are again revived."

Samuel Swartwout, the courier who had delivered Burr's ill-fated letter, "most positively denied" that he had made the revelations which Wilkinson claimed to have drawn from him.[1] The youthful Swartwout as deeply impressed the grand jury with his honesty and truthfulness as Wilkinson impressed that body with his untrustworthiness and duplicity.[2]

Peter Taylor and Jacob Allbright then recounted their experiences.[3] And the Morgans told of Burr's visit and of their inferences from his mysterious tones of voice, glances of eye, and cryptic expressions. So it was, that in spite of overwhelming testimony of other witnesses,[4] who swore that Burr's purposes were to settle the Washita lands and in the event of war with Spain, and only in that event, to invade Mexico, with never an intimation of any project hostile to the United States — so it was that bills of indictment for treason and for misdemeanor were, on June 24, found against Aaron Burr of New York and Harman Blennerhassett of Virginia. The indictment for treason charged that on December 13, 1806, at Blennerhassett's island in Virginia, they

[1] Testimony of Joseph C. Cabell, one of the grand jury. (*Annals*, 10th Cong. 1st Sess. 677.)

[2] "Mr. Swartwout . . discovered the utmost frankness and candor in his evidence. . . The very frank and candid manner in which he gave his testimony, I must confess, raised him very high in my estimation, and induced me to form a very different opinion of him from that which I had before entertained." (Testimony of Littleton W. Tazewell, one of the grand jury, *Annals*, 10th Cong. 1st Sess. 633.)

"The manner of Mr. Swartwout was certainly that of conscious innocence." (Testimony of Joseph C. Cabell, one of the grand jury, *ib.* 677.)

[3] See *supra*, 426–27.

[4] Forty-eight witnesses were examined by the grand jury. The names are given in Brady: *Trial of Aaron Burr*, 69–70.

had levied war on the United States; and the one for misdemeanor alleged that, at the same time and place, they had set on foot an armed expedition against territory belonging to His Catholic Majesty, Charles IV of Spain.[1]

This result of the grand jury's investigations was reached because of that body's misunderstanding of Marshall's charge and of his opinion in the Bollmann and Swartwout case.[2]

John Randolph, as foreman of the grand jury, his nose close to the ground on the scent of the principal culprit, came into court the day after the indictment of Burr and Blennerhassett and asked for the letter from Wilkinson to Burr, referred to in Burr's cipher dispatch to Wilkinson, and now in the possession of the accused. Randolph said that, of course, the grand jury could not ask Burr to appear before them as a witness, but that they did want the letter.

Marshall declared "that the grand jury were perfectly right in the opinion." Burr said that he could not reveal a confidential communication, un-

[1] *Burr Trials*, I, 305–06; also "Bills of Indictment," MSS. Archives of the United States Court, Richmond, Va.

The following day former Senator Jonathan Dayton of New Jersey, Senator John Smith of Ohio, Comfort Tyler and Israel Smith of New York, and Davis Floyd of the Territory of Indiana, were presented for treason. How Bollmann, Swartwout, Adair, Brown, and others escaped indictment is only less comprehensible than the presentment of Tyler, Floyd, and the two Smiths for treason.

[2] *Blennerhassett Papers:* Safford, 314. "Two of the most respectable and influential of that body, since it has been discharged, have declared they mistook the meaning of Chief Justice Marshall's opinion as to what sort of acts amounted to treason in this country, in the case of Swartwout and Ogden [Bollmann]; that it was under the influence of this mistake they concurred in finding such a bill against A. Burr, which otherwise would have probably been ignored."

less "the extremity of circumstances might impel him to such a conduct." He could not, for the moment, decide; but that "unless it were extorted from him by law" he could not even "deliberate on the proposition to deliver up any thing which had been confided to his honour."

Marshall announced that there was no "objection to the grand jury calling before them and examining any man .. who laid under an indictment." Martin agreed "there could be no objection."

The grand jury did not want Burr as a witness, said John Randolph. They asked only for the letter. If they should wish Burr's presence at all, it would be only for the purpose of identifying it. So the grand jury withdrew.[1]

Hay was swift to tell his superior all about it, although he trembled between gratification and alarm. "If every trial were to be like that, I am doubtful whether my patience will sustain me while I am wading thro' this abyss of human depravity."

Dutifully he informed the President that he feared that "the Gr: Jury had not dismissed all their suspicions of Wilkinson," for John Randolph had asked for his cipher letter to Burr. Then he described to Jefferson the intolerable prisoner's conduct: "Burr rose immediately, & declared that no consideration, no calamity, no desperation, should induce *him* to betray a letter confidentially written. He could not even allow himself to deliberate on a point, where his conduct was prescribed by the clearest principles of honor &c. &c. &c."

[1] *Burr Trials*, I, 327-28.

Hay then related what Marshall and John Randolph had said, underscoring the statement that "the Gr: Jury *did not want A. B. as a witness*." Hay did full credit, however, to Burr's appearance of candor: "The attitude & tone assumed by Burr struck everybody. There was an appearance of *honor* and magnanimity which brightened the countenances of the phalanx who daily attend, for his encouragement & support." [1]

Day after day was consumed in argument on points of evidence, while the grand jury were examining witnesses. Marshall delivered a long written opinion upon the question as to whether a witness could be forced to give testimony which he believed might criminate himself. The District Attorney read Jefferson's two letters upon the subject of the subpœna *duces tecum*. No pretext was too fragile to be seized by one side or the other, as the occasion for argument upon it demanded — for instance, whether or not the District Attorney might send interrogatories to the grand jury. Always the lawyers spoke to the crowd as well as to the court, and their passages at arms became ever sharper.[2]

Wilkinson is "an honest man and a patriot" — no! he is a liar and a thief; Louisiana is a "poor, unfortunate, enslaved country"; letters had been seized by "foulness and violence"; the arguments of Burr's attorneys are "mere declamations"; the Government's agents are striving to prevent Burr

---

[1] Hay to Jefferson, June 25, 1807, Jefferson MSS. Lib. Cong.
[2] *Burr Trials*, I, 197–357.

from having "a fair trial .. the newspapers and
party writers are employed to *cry* and *write* him
down; his counsel are denounced for daring to defend him; the passions of the grand jury are endeavored to be excited against him, at all events"; [1]
Hay's mind is "harder than Ajax's seven fold shield
of bull's hide"; Edmund Randolph came into court
"with mysterious looks of awe and terror .. as if he
had something to communicate which was too horrible to be told"; Hay is always "on his heroics";
he "hopped up like a parched pea"; the object of
Burr's counsel is "to prejudice the surrounding
multitude against General Wilkinson"; one newspaper tale is "as impudent a falsehood as ever malignity had uttered" — such was the language with
which the arguments were adorned.   They were,
however, well sprinkled with citations of authority. [2]

---

[1] This was one of Luther Martin's characteristic outbursts.   Every
word of it, however, was true.

[2] *Burr Trials*, I, 197–357.

CHAPTER IX

WHAT IS TREASON?

No person shall be convicted of Treason unless on the Testimony of two Witnesses to the same overt Act, or on Confession in open Court.

(Constitution, Article III, Section 3.)

Such are the jealous provisions of our laws in favor of the accused that I question if he can be convicted. (Jefferson.)

The scenes which have passed and those about to be transacted will hereafter be deemed fables, unless attested by very high authority. (Aaron Burr.)

That this court dares not usurp power is most true. That this court dares not shrink from its duty is no less true. (Marshall.)

WHILE the grand jury had been examining witnesses, interesting things had taken place in Richmond. Burr's friends increased in number and devotion. Many of them accompanied him to and from court each day.[1] Dinners were given in his honor, and Burr returned these courtesies, sometimes entertaining at his board a score of men and women of the leading families of the city.[2] Fashionable Richmond was rapidly becoming Burr-partisan. In society, as at the bar, the Government had been maneuvered into defense. Throughout the country, indeed, Burr's numerous adherents had proved stanchly loyal to him.

"I believe," notes Senator Plumer in his diary, "even at this period, that no man in this country, has more personal friends or who are more firmly attached to his interests — or would make greater

---

[1] *Blennerhassett Papers:* Safford, 298.

Blennerhassett wrote this comment when the trial was nearly over. He said that two hundred men acted as a bodyguard to Burr on his way to court each day.

[2] Parton: *Burr*, 481.

sacrifices to aid him than this man." [1] But this availed Burr nothing as against the opinion of the multitude, which Jefferson manipulated as he chose. Indeed, save in Richmond, this very fidelity of Burr's friends served rather to increase the public animosity; for many of these friends were persons of standing, and this fact did not appeal favorably to the rank and file of the rampant democracy of the period.

In Richmond, however, Burr's presence and visible peril animated his followers to aggressive action. On the streets, in the taverns and drinking-places, his adherents grew bolder. Young Swartwout chanced to meet the bulky, epauletted Wilkinson on the sidewalk. Flying into "a paroxysm of disgust and rage," Burr's youthful follower [2] shouldered the burly general "into the middle of the street." Wilkinson swallowed the insult. On learning of the incident Jackson "was wild with delight." [3] Burr's enemies were as furious with anger. To spirited Virginians, only treason itself was worse than the refusal of Wilkinson, thus insulted, to fight.

Swartwout, perhaps inspired by Jackson, later confirmed this public impression of Wilkinson's cowardice. He challenged the General to a duel; the hero refused — "he held no correspondence with traitors or conspirators," he loftily observed; [4] whereupon the young "conspirator and traitor" denounced, in the public press, the commander of the American armies as guilty of treachery, perjury,

---

[1] April 1, 1807, "Register," Plumer MSS. Lib. Cong.
[2] Swartwout was then twenty-four years old.
[3] Parton: *Jackson*, I, 335.
[4] Swartwout challenged Wilkinson after the trial was over.

forgery, and cowardice.[1] The highest officer in the
American military establishment "posted for cow-
ardice" by a mere stripling! More than ever was
Swartwout endeared to Jackson.

Soon after his arrival at Richmond, and a week
before Burr was indicted, Wilkinson perceived, to
his dismay, the current of public favor that was beginning to run toward Burr; and he wrote to Jefferson in unctuous horror: "I had anticipated that a
deluge of Testimony would have been poured forth
from all quarters, to overwhelm Him [Burr] with
guilt & dishonour – . . To my Astonishment I found
the Traitor vindicated & myself condemned by a
Mass of Wealth Character-influence & Talents–
merciful God what a Spectacle did I behold– Integrity & Truth perverted & trampled under foot
by turpitude & Guilt, Patriotism appaled & Usurpation triumphant."[2]

Wilkinson was plainly weakening, and Jefferson
hastened to comfort his chief witness: "No one is
more sensible than myself of the injustice which has
been aimed at you. Accept I pray, my salutations
and assurances of respect and esteem."[3]

---

[1] See brief account of this incident, including Swartwout's open letter to Wilkinson, in *Blennerhassett Papers:* Safford, footnote to 459–60.

[2] Wilkinson to Jefferson, June 17, 1807, "Letters in Relation,"
MSS. Lib. Cong.

[3] Jefferson to Wilkinson, June 21, 1807, Wilkinson: *Memoirs,* ii,
Appendix xxx. Jefferson's letter also contains the following: "You
have, indeed, had a fiery trial at New Orleans, but it was soon apparent that the clamorous were only the criminal, endeavouring to turn
the public attention from themselves, and their leader, upon any other
object. . . Your enemies have filled the public ear with slanders, and
your mind with trouble, on that account. The establishment of their
guilt, will . . place you on higher ground in the public estimate, and
public confidence."

Before the grand jury had indicted Burr and Blennerhassett, Wilkinson suffered another humiliation. On the very day that the General sent his wailing cry of outraged virtue to the President, Burr gave notice that he would move that an attachment should issue against Jefferson's hero for "contempt in obstructing the administration of justice" by rifling the mails, imprisoning witnesses, and extorting testimony by torture.[1] The following day was consumed in argument upon the motion that did not rise far above bickering. Marshall ruled that witnesses should be heard in support of Burr's application, and that Wilkinson ought to be present.[2] Accordingly, the General was ordered to come into court.

James Knox, one of the young men who had accompanied Burr on his disastrous expedition, had been brought from New Orleans as a witness for the Government. He told a straightforward story of brutality inflicted upon him because he could not readily answer the printed questions sent out by Jefferson's Attorney-General.[3] By other witnesses it appeared that letters had been improperly taken from the post-office in New Orleans.[4] An argument followed in which counsel on both sides distinguished themselves by the learning and eloquence they displayed.[5]

It was while Botts was speaking on this motion to attach Wilkinson, that the grand jury returned the bills of indictment.[6] So came the dramatic climax.

[1] *Burr Trials*, I, 227–53.
[2] *Ib.* 257–67. Wilkinson was then giving his testimony before the grand jury.
[3] *Ib.* 268–72. [4] *Ib.* 276–77. [5] *Ib.* 277–305. [6] See *supra*, 455–56.

Instantly the argument over the attachment of Wilkinson was suspended. Burr said that he would "prove that the indictment against him had been obtained by perjury"; and that this was a reason for the court to exercise its discretion in his favor and to accept bail instead of imprisoning him.[1] Marshall asked Martin whether he had "any precedent, where a court has bailed for treason, after the finding of a grand jury," when "the testimony .. had been impeached for perjury," or new testimony had been presented to the court.[2] For once in his life, Martin could not answer immediately and offhand. So that night Aaron Burr slept in the common jail at Richmond.

"The cup of bitterness has been administered to him with unsparing hand," wrote Washington Irving.[3] But he did not quail. He was released next morning upon a writ of habeas corpus;[4] the argument on the request for the attachment of Wilkinson was resumed, and for three days counsel attacked and counter-attacked.[5] On June 26, Burr's attorneys made oath that confinement in the city jail was endangering his health; also that they could not, under such conditions, properly consult with him about the conduct of his case. Accordingly, Marshall ordered Burr removed to the house occupied by Luther Martin; and to be confined to the front room, with the window shutters secured by bars, the door by a padlock, and the building guarded by seven men. Burr pleaded not guilty to the indictments

---

[1] *Burr Trials*, i, 306.   [2] *Ib.* 308.
[3] Irving to Miss Fairlie, July 7, 1807, Irving, i, 152.
[4] *Burr Trials*, i, 312.   [5] *Ib.* 313-50.

against him, and orders were given for summoning the jury to try him.[1]

Finally, Marshall delivered his written opinion upon the motion to attach Wilkinson. It was unimportant, and held that Wilkinson had not been shown to have influenced the judge who ordered Knox imprisoned or to have violated the laws intentionally. The Chief Justice ordered the marshal to summon, in addition to the general panel, forty-eight men to appear on August 3 from Wood County, in which Blennerhassett's island was located, and where the indictment charged that the crime had been committed.[2]

Five days before Marshall adjourned court in order that jurymen might be summoned and both prosecution and defense enabled to prepare for trial, an event occurred which proved, as nothing else could have done, how intent were the people on the prosecution of Burr, how unshakable the tenacity with which Jefferson pursued him.

On June 22, 1807, the British warship, the Leopard, halted the American frigate, the Chesapeake, as the latter was putting out to sea from Norfolk. The British officers demanded of Commodore James Barron to search the American ship for British deserters and to take them if found. Barron refused. Thereupon the Leopard, having drawn alongside the American vessel, without warning poured broadsides into her until her masts were shot away, her rigging destroyed, three sailors killed and eighteen wounded. The Chesapeake had not been fitted out, was unable

[1] *Burr Trials*, I, 350-54. [2] *Ib.* 354-57.

to reply, and finally was forced to strike her colors. The British officers then came on board and seized the men they claimed as deserters, all but one of whom were American-born citizens.[1]

The whole country, except New England, roared with anger when the news reached the widely separated sections of it; but the tempest soon spent its fury. Quickly the popular clamor returned to the "traitor" awaiting trial at Richmond. Nor did this "enormity," as Jefferson called the attack on the Chesapeake,[2] committed by a foreign power in American waters, weaken for a moment the President's determination to punish the native disturber of our domestic felicity.

The news of the Chesapeake outrage arrived at Richmond on June 25, and John Randolph supposed that, of course, Jefferson would immediately call Congress in special session.[3] The President did nothing of the kind. Wilkinson, as Commander of the Army, advised him against armed retaliation. The "late outrage by the British," wrote the General, "has produced . . a degree of Emotion bordering on rage– I revere the Honourable impulse but fear its Effects– . . The present is no moment for precipitancy or a stretch of power– on the contrary the British being prepared for War & we not, a sudden appeal to hostilities will give them a great advantage– . . The efforts made here [Richmond] by a band of depraved Citizens, in conjunction with an

---

[1] See Adams: *U.S.* II, chap. I; Channing: *Jeff. System*, 189–94; Hildreth, III, 402; and see vol. IV, chap. I, of this work.

[2] Jefferson's Proclamation, July 2, 1807, *Works:* Ford, x, 434.

[3] Randolph to Nicholson, June 25, 1807, Adams: *John Randolph*, 222.

audacious phalanx of insolent exotics, to save Burr, will have an ultimate good Effect, for the national Character of the *Ancient dominion* is in display, and the honest impulses of true patriotism will soon silence the advocates of usurpation without & conspiracy within."

Wilkinson tells Jefferson that he is coming to Washington forthwith to pay his "respects," and concludes: "You are doubtless well advised of proceedings here in the case of Burr— to me they are incomprehensible as I am no Jurist— The Grand Jury actually made an attempt to present me for Misprision of Treason—.. I feel myself between 'Scylla and Carybdis' the Jury would Dishonor me for failing of my Duty, and Burr & his Conspirators for performing it—"[1]

Not until five weeks after the Chesapeake affair did the President call Congress to convene in special session on October 26 — more than four months after the occurrence of the crisis it was summoned to consider.[2] But in the meantime Jefferson had sent a messenger to advise the American Minister in London to tell the British Government what had happened, and to demand a disavowal and an apology.

Meanwhile, the Administration vigorously pushed the prosecution of the imprisoned "traitor" at Richmond.[3] Hay was dissatisfied that Burr should

[1] Wilkinson to Jefferson, June 29, 1807, "Letters in Relation," MSS. Lib. Cong.

[2] Jefferson to Congress, *Annals*, 10th Cong. 1st Sess. 9.

[3] At this time Jefferson wrote curious letters, apparently to explain, by inference, to his friends in France his want of energy in the Chesapeake affair and the vigor he displayed in the prosecution of Burr. "Burr's conspiracy has been one of the most flagitious of which his-

remain in Martin's house, even under guard and with windows barred and door locked; and he obtained from the Executive Council of Virginia a tender to the court of "apartments on the third floor" of the State Penitentiary for the incarceration of the prisoner. Burr's counsel strenuously objected, but Marshall ordered that he be confined there until August 2, at which time he should be returned to the barred and padlocked room in Martin's house.[1]

In the penitentiary, "situated in a solitary place among the hills" a mile and a half from Richmond,[2] Burr remained for five weeks. Three large rooms were given him in the third story; the jailer was considerate and kind; his friends called on him every day;[3] and servants constantly "arrived with messages, notes, and inquiries, bringing oranges, lemons, pineapples, raspberries, apricots, cream, butter, ice and some ordinary articles."[4]

tory will ever furnish an example. . . Yet altho' there is not a man in the U S who is not satisfied of the depth of his guilt, such are the jealous provisions of our laws in favor of the accused, . . that I question if he can be convicted." (Jefferson to De Nemours, July 14, 1807, *Works:* Ford, x, 461; also see same to Lafayette, same date, *ib.* 463.) It will be observed that in these letters Jefferson condemns the laxity of American laws instead of blaming Marshall.

[1] *Burr Trials,* I, 357–59.

[2] Irving to Miss Fairlie, July 7, 1807, Irving, I, 153. "The only reason given for immuring him in this abode of thieves, cut-throats, and incendiaries," says Irving, "was that it would save the United States a couple of hundred dollars (the charge of guarding him at his lodgings), and it would insure the security of his person."

[3] "Burr lives in great style, and sees much company within his gratings, where it is as difficult to get an audience as if he really were an Emperor." (*Blennerhassett Papers:* Safford, 324.) At first, however, his treatment was very severe. (See Irving to Miss Fairlie, July 7, 1807, Irving, I, 153.)

[4] Burr to his daughter, July 3, 1807, Davis, II, 409.

Burr wrote Theodosia of his many visitors, women as well as men: "It is well that I have an ante-chamber, or I should often be *gêné* with visiters." If Theodosia should come on for the trial, he playfully admonishes her that there must be "no agitations, no complaints, no fears or anxieties on the road, or I renounce thee." [1]

Finally Burr asked his daughter to come to him: "I want an independent and discerning witness to my conduct and that of the government. The scenes which have passed and those about to be transacted will exceed all reasonable credibility, and will hereafter be deemed fables, unless attested by very high authority. . . I should never invite any one, much less those so dear to me, to witness my disgrace. I may be immured in dungeons, chained, murdered in legal form, but I cannot be humiliated or disgraced. If absent, you will suffer great solicitude. In my presence you will feel none, whatever be the *malice* or the *power* of my enemies, and in both they abound." [2]

Theodosia was soon with her father. Her husband, Joseph Alston, now Governor of South Carolina, accompanied her; and she brought her little son, who, almost as much as his beautiful mother, was the delight of Burr's heart.

During these torrid weeks the public temper throughout the country rose with the thermometer.[3]

[1] Burr to his daughter, July 6, 1807, Davis, II, 410.

[2] Same to same, July 24, 1807, *ib.* 410.

[3] At a Fourth of July celebration in Cecil County, Maryland, toasts were proposed wishing for the grand jury "a crown of immortal glory" for "their zeal and patriotism in the cause of liberty"; hoping that

The popular distrust of Marshall grew into open hostility. A report of the proceedings, down to the time when Burr was indicted for treason, was published in a thick pamphlet and sold all over Virginia and neighboring States. The impression which the people thus acquired was that Marshall was protecting Burr; for had he not refused to imprison him until the grand jury indicted the "traitor"?

The Chief Justice estimated the situation accurately. He knew, moreover, that prosecutions for treason might be instituted thereafter in other parts of the country, particularly in New England. The Federalist leaders in that section had already spoken and written sentiments as disloyal, essentially, as those now attributed to Burr; and, at that very time, when the outcry against Burr was loudest, they were beginning to revive their project of seceding from the Union.[1] To so excellent a politician and so far-seeing a statesman as Marshall, it must have seemed probable that his party friends in New England might be brought before the courts to answer to the same charge as that against Aaron Burr.

At all events, he took, at this time, a wise and characteristically prudent step. Four days after the news of the Chesapeake affair reached Richmond, the Chief Justice asked his associates on the Supreme Bench for their opinion on the law of treason as pre-

Martin would receive "an honorable coat of tar, and a plumage of feathers" as a reward for "his exertions to preserve the Catiline of America"; and praying that Burr's treachery to his country might "exalt him to the scaffold, and hemp be his escort to the republic of dust and ashes." (Parton: *Burr*, 478.)

[1] See vol. IV, chap. I, of this work. Also *supra*, chap. III.

sented in the case of Aaron Burr. "I am aware,"
he wrote, "of the unwillingness with which a judge
will commit himself by an opinion on a case not
before him, and on which he has heard no argument.
Could this case be readily carried before the Supreme Court, I would not ask an opinion in its present stage. But these questions must be decided
by the judges separately on their respective circuits,
and I am sure that there would be a strong and
general repugnance to giving contradictory decisions
on the same points. Such a circumstance would be
disreputable to the judges themselves as well as to
our judicial system. This suggestion suggests the
propriety of a consultation on new and different
subjects and will, I trust, apologize for this letter." [1]

'Whether a consultation was held during the five
weeks that the Burr trial was suspended is not known.
But if the members of the Supreme Court did not
meet the Chief Justice, it would appear to be certain
that they wrote him their views of the American law
of treason; and that, in the crucial opinion which
Marshall delivered on that subject more than two
months after he had written to his associates, he
stated their mature judgments as well as his own.

It was, therefore, with a composure, unwonted
even for him, that Marshall again opened court on
August 3, 1807. The crowd was, if possible, greater
than ever. Burr entered the hall with his son-in-law,
Governor Alston. [2] Not until a week later was coun-

---

[1] Marshall to the Associate Justices of the Supreme Court, June
29, 1807, as quoted by Horace Gray, Associate Justice of the Supreme
Court, in Dillon, I, 72.

[2] Parton: *Burr*, 483.

sel for the Government ready to proceed. When at
last the men summoned to serve on the petit jury
were examined as to their qualifications, it was all
but impossible to find one impartial man among
them — utterly impossible to secure one who had
not formed opinions from what, for months, had
been printed in the newspapers.

Marshall described with fairness the indispensable qualifications of a juror.[1] Men were rejected as
fast as they were questioned — all had read the stories and editorial opinions that had filled the press,
and had accepted the deliberate judgment of Jefferson and the editors; also, they had been impressed
bv the public clamor thus created, and believed
Burr guilty of treason. Out of forty-eight men examined during the first day, only four could be
accepted.[2]

While the examination of jurors was in progress,
one of the most brilliant debates of the entire trial
sprang up, as to the nature and extent of opinions
formed which would exclude a man from serving on
a jury.[3]

When Marshall was ready to deliver his opinion,
he had heard all the reasoning that great lawyers
could give on the subject, and had listened to acute
analyses of all the authorities. His statement of the
law was the ablest opinion he had yet delivered during the proceedings, and is an admirable example of
his best logical method. It appears, however, to have
been unnecessary, and was doubtless delivered as a
part of Marshall's carefully considered plan to go to

[1] *Burr Trials*, I, 369-70.   [2] *Ib.* 370-85.   [3] *Ib.* 385-414.

the extreme throughout the trial in the hearing and examination of every subject.[1]

For nearly two weeks the efforts to select a jury continued. Not until August 15 were twelve men secured, and most of these avowed that they had formed opinions that Burr was a traitor. They were accepted only because impartial men could not be found.

When Marshall finished the reading of his opinion, Hay promptly advised Jefferson that "the [bi]as of Judge Marshall is as obvious, as if it was [stam]ped upon his forehead. . . [He is] endeavoring to work himself up to a state of [f]eeling which will enable [him] to aid Burr throughout the trial, without appearing to be conscious of doing wrong. He [Marshall] seems to think that his reputation is irretrievably gone, and that he has now nothing to lose by doing as he pleases. — His concern for Burr is wonderful. He told me many years ago, when Burr was rising in the estimation of the republican party, that he was as profligate in principle, as he was desperate in fortune. I remember his words. They astonished me.

"Yet," complained Hay, "when the Gr: Jury brought in their bill the Chief Justice gazed at him, for a long time, without appearing conscious that he was doing so, with an expression of sympathy & sorrow as strong, as the human countenance can exhibit without *palpable* emotion. If Mr. Burr has any feeling left, yesterday must have been a day of agonizing humiliation," because the answers of the

[1] *Burr Trials*, I, 414-20.

jurors had been uniformly against him; and Hay gleefully relates specimens of them.

"There is but one chance for the accused," he continued, "and that is a good one because it rests with the Chief Justice. It is already hinted, but not by himself [that] the decision of the Supreme Court will no[t be] deemed binding. If the assembly of men on [Blennerhassett's is]land, can be pronounced 'not an overt act' [it will] be so pronounced." [1]

Hay's opening statement to the jury was his best performance of the entire proceedings. He described Burr's purpose in almost the very words of Jefferson's Special Message. The gathering on Blennerhassett's island was, he said, the overt act; Burr, it was true, was not there at the time, but his presence was not necessary. Had not Marshall, in the Bollmann and Swartwout case, said that "if war be actually levied, . . *all those who perform any part, however minute, or however remote from the scene of action,* and who are actually *leagued in the general conspiracy, are to be considered* as *traitors*"? [2]

The examination of the Government's witnesses began. Eaton took the stand; but Burr insisted that the overt act must be proved before collateral testimony could be admitted. So came the first crossing of swords over the point that was to save the life of Aaron Burr. The arguments of counsel were brilliant; but neither side forgot the public. They must thrill the audience as well as convince the court. "There had been a great deal of war in the news-

---

[1] Hay to Jefferson, Aug. 11, 1807, Jefferson MSS. Lib. Cong.
[2] *Burr Trials*, I, 433-51.

papers," said Wickham, but everybody knew "that there had been no war in fact." Wirt insisted on "unfolding events as they occurred"; that was "the lucid order of nature and reason." Martin pointed out that Eaton's testimony did not "relate to any *acts* committed any where, but to mere declarations out of the district." [1] Let the evidence be pertinent. The indictment charged a specific act, and it must be proved as charged. No man could be expected suddenly to answer for every act of his life. If Burr had planned to free Mexico and had succeeded, "he would have merited the applause of the friends of liberty and of posterity; . . but his friends may now pray that he may not meet the fate that Washington himself would have met, if the revolution had not been established."

A mass of decisions, English as well as American, were cited by both Wirt and Martin; [2] and when, that night, Marshall began to write his opinion on whether the overt act must be proved before other testimony could be received, all authorities had been reviewed, all arguments made.

Must the overt act be proved before hearing collateral testimony? The question, said Marshall, was precisely the same as that raised and decided on the motion to commit Burr. But it came up now under different circumstances — an indictment had been found "specifying a charge which is to be proved," and thus "an issue made up which presents a point to which all the testimony must apply." So Mar-

[1] Hay had announced that Eaton's testimony would be to the same effect as his deposition.

[2] *Burr Trials*, i, 452–69.

shall could now "determine, with some accuracy, on the relevancy of the testimony."

The prosecution contended that the crime consisted of "the fact and the intention," and that the Government might first prove either of these; the defense insisted that the overt act must be shown before any testimony, explanatory or confirmatory of that fact, can be received. To prove first the fact charged was certainly "the most useful . . and . . natural order of testimony"; but no fixed rule of evidence required it, and no case had been cited in which any court had ever "forced" it on counsel for the prosecution.

The different impressions made upon the minds of the jury by the order of testimony was important, said Marshall: "Although human laws punish actions, the human mind spontaneously attaches guilt to intentions." When testimony had prepared the mind to look upon the prisoner's designs as criminal, a jury would consider a fact in a different light than if it had been proved before guilty intentions had been shown. However, since no rule prevented the prosecution from first proving either, "no alteration of that arrangement . . will now be directed."

But, continued Marshall, "the intention which is . . relevant in this stage of the inquiry is the intention which composes a part of the crime, the intention with which the overt act itself was committed; not a general evil disposition, or an intention to commit a distinct [different] fact." Testimony as to such intentions, "if admissible at all, is received as corroborative or confirmatory testimony," and could not precede "that which it is to corroborate or confirm."

Apply this rule to Eaton's testimony: it would be admissible only "so far as his testimony relate[d] to the fact charged in the indictment, . . to levying war on Blennerhassett's island," and the "design to seize on New-Orleans, or to separate by force, the western from the Atlantic states"; but "so far as it respect[ed] other plans to be executed in the city of Washington, or elsewhere," Eaton's story would be at best merely "corroborative testimony," and, "if admissible at any time," could be received only "after hearing that which it is to confirm."

So let Hay "proceed according to his own judgment." Marshall would not exclude any testimony except that which appeared to be irrelevant, and upon this he would decide when it was offered.[1]

Again Eaton was called to the stand. Before he began his tale, he wished to explain "the motives" of his "own conduct." Marshall blandly suggested that the witness stick to Burr's revelations to him. Then, said Eaton, "concerning any overt act, which goes to prove Aaron Burr guilty of treason I know nothing. . . But concerning Colonel Burr's expressions of treasonable intentions, I know much."

Notwithstanding Marshall's intimation that Eaton must confine his testimony to Burr, "the hero of Derne" was not to be denied his self-vindication; not even the Chief Justice should check his recital of his patriotism, his glories, his wrongs. Burr had good reasons for supposing him "disaffected toward

[1] *Burr Trials*, I, 469–72.

the Government"; he then related at length his services in Africa, the lack of appreciation of his ability and heroism, the preferment of unworthy men to the neglect of himself. Finally, Eaton, who "strutted more in buskin than usual," to the amusement of "the whole court,"[1] delivered his testimony, and once more related what he had said in his deposition. Since Marshall had "decided it to be irrelevant," Eaton omitted the details about Burr's plans to murder Jefferson, turn Congress out of the Capitol, seize the Navy, and make himself ruler of America at one bold and bloody stroke.[2]

Commodore Truxtun then gave the simple and direct account, already related, of Burr's conversation with him;[3] Peter Taylor and Jacob Allbright once more told their strange tales; and the three Morgans again narrated the incidents of Burr's incredible acts and statements while visiting the elder Morgan at Morganza.[4]

William Love, an Englishman, formerly Blennerhassett's servant — a dull, ignorant, and timorous creature — testified to the gathering of "about betwixt twenty and twenty-five" men at his employer's island, some of whom went "out a gunning." He saw no other arms except those belonging to his

---

[1] *Blennerhassett Papers:* Safford, 343.

[2] It was this farrago, published in every newspaper, that had influenced the country only less than Jefferson's Special Message to Congress.

[3] Commodore Decatur's testimony was almost identical with that of Truxtun. More convincing still, General Adair, writing before the trial began, told substantially the same story. (Adair's statement, March, 1807, as quoted in Parton: *Burr,* footnote to 493.)

[4] For the full Morgan testimony, see *Burr Trials,* I, 497–506.

master, nor did he "see any guns presented," as Allbright had described. Blennerhassett told him that
if he would go with him to the Washita, he should
have "a piece of land." Love "understood the object of the expedition was to settle Washita lands." [1]

Dudley Woodbridge, once a partner of Blennerhassett, told of Burr's purchase from his firm of a
hundred barrels of pork and fifteen boats, paid by
a draft on Ogden of New York; of Blennerhassett's
short conversation with Woodbridge about the enterprise, from which he inferred that "the object
was Mexico"; of his settlement with Blennerhassett
of their partnership accounts; of Blennerhassett's
financial resources; and of the characteristics of the
man — "very nearsighted," ignorant of military
affairs, a literary person, a chemist and musician,
with the reputation of having "every kind of sense
but common sense."

The witness related his observation of the seizure
at Marietta of Burr's few boats and provisions by
the Ohio militia, and the sale of them by the Government; of the assemblage of the twenty or thirty
men on Blennerhassett's island; of their quiet, orderly conduct; of Comfort Tyler's declaration "that
he would not resist the constituted authorities, but
that he would not be stopped by a mob"; of Mrs.
Blennerhassett's taking part of her husband's library with her when she followed him, after the flight
of the terrified little band from the island; and of the
sale of the remainder of the cultivated visionary's
books. [2]

---

[1] *Burr Trials*, i, 514–18. [2] *Ib.* 518–26.

Simeon Poole, who had been sent by Governor Tiffin of Ohio to arrest Blennerhassett, said that he was not on the island, but from dusk until ten o'clock watched from a concealed place on the Ohio shore. He saw a few men walking about, who during the night kindled a fire, by the light of which it seemed to Poole that some of them were "armed." He could not be sure from where he watched, but they "looked like sentinels." However, Poole "could not say whether the persons . . were not merely loitering around the fire." There were some boats, he said, both big and little. Also, when anybody wanted to cross from the Ohio side, the acute Poole thought that "a watchword" was given. The night was cold, the rural sleuth admitted, and it was customary to build fires on the river-bank. He observed, however, another suspicious circumstance — "lanterns were passing . . between the house and boats. . . Most of the people were without guns," he admitted; but, although he could not see clearly, he "apprehended that some of them had guns." [1]

Morris P. Belknap, an Ohio business man, testified that he had hailed a boat and been taken to the island on the night when the gathering and flight took place.[2] He saw perhaps twenty men in the house; "two or three . . near the door, had rifles, and appeared to be cleaning them. These were all the arms I saw." He also observed two or three boats.[3]

---

[1] *Burr Trials*, I, 527–28.

[2] Belknap was undoubtedly one of those whom Poole saw cross the stream. Woodbridge and Dana were the others.

[3] *Burr Trials*, I, 529.

Edmund P. Dana testified that, with two other young men, he had gone in a skiff to the island on that war-levying night.[1] In the hall he saw about "fifteen or sixteen" men — "one of them was running some bullets." Dana was shown to another room where he met "colonel Tyler, Blennerhassett, Mr. Smith of New-York . . and three or four other gentlemen." He had met Tyler the day before, and was now "introduced to Mr. Smith and Doctor M'Castle[2] who had his lady . . there." The men in the hall "did not appear to be alarmed" when Dana and his companions came in. Dana "never saw colonel Burr on the island."[3]

The Government's counsel admitted that Burr was in Kentucky at that time.[4]

Such was the testimony, and the whole of it, adduced to support the charge that Burr had, at Blennerhassett's island, on December 13, 1806, levied war against the United States. Such was the entire proof of that overt act as laid in the indictment when Marshall was called upon to make that momentous decision upon which the fate of Aaron Burr depended.

The defense moved that, since no overt act was proved as charged, collateral testimony as to what had been said and done elsewhere should not be received. Wickham opened the argument in an address worthy of that historic occasion. For nearly two days this superb lawyer spoke. Burr's counsel would, he said, have preferred to go on, for they

---

[1] These young men were thinking of joining the expedition.
[2] The physician who accompanied the party.
[3] *Burr Trials*, I, 528–29. [4] *Ib.* 529.

could "adduce . . conclusive testimony" as to Burr's innocence. But only seven witnesses out of "about one hundred and forty" summoned by the Government had been examined, and it was admitted that these seven had given all the testimony in existence to prove the overt act.

If that overt act had not been established and yet the more than one hundred and thirty remaining witnesses were to be examined, it was manifest that "weeks, perhaps months," would elapse before the Government completed its case. It was the unhealthy season, and it was most probable that one or more jurors would become ill. If so, said Wickham, "the cause must lie over and our client, innocent, may be subjected to a prolongation of that confinement which is in itself . . punishment." Yet, after all this suffering, expense, and delay, the result must be the same as if the evidence were arrested now, since there was no testimony to the overt act other than that already given.

Did that testimony, then, prove the overt act of levying war on the United States? Those who wrote the Constitution "well knew the dreadful punishments inflicted and the grievous oppressions produced by [the doctrine of] constructive treasons in other countries." For this reason, truly declared Wickham, the American Constitution explicitly defined that crime and prescribed the only way it could be proved. This could not be modified by the common law, since the United States, as a Nation, had not adopted it; and the purpose of the Constitution was to destroy, as far as America was concerned,

the British theory of treason. The Constitution
"explains itself," said Wickham; under it treason is
a newly created offense against a newly created government. Even the Government's counsel "will not
contend that the words [in the Constitution concerning treason] used in their natural sense," can
embrace the case of a person who never committed
an act of hostility against the United States and
was not even present when one was committed;[1]
otherwise what horrible cruelties any Administration could inflict on any American citizen.

The Supreme Court, in the case of Bollmann and
Swartwout, had, indeed, pronounced a *"dictum"* to
the contrary, said Wickham, but that had been in
a mere case of commitment; the present point did
not then come before the court; it was not argued
by counsel. So Marshall's objectionable language
in that case was not authority.[2]

It was only by the doctrine of constructive treason
that Burr could be said to be at Blennerhassett's
island at the time charged — the doctrine that "in
treason all are principals," and that, by "construction of law," he was present, although in reality he
was hundreds of miles away. But this was the very
doctrine which the Constitution prohibited from
ever being applied in America.

If Burr "conspired to levy war against the United
States, and . . the war was carried on by others in
his absence, his offense can only be punished by *a
special indictment charging the facts as they existed.*"
The prosecution "should at once withdraw their

---

[1] *Burr Trials*, I, 533–34.   [2] *Ib.* 555–56.

indictment as it does not contain a specification that can be supported by the evidence." [1]

Edmund Randolph followed Wickham, but added nothing to his rich and solid argument. Addressing Marshall personally, Randolph exclaimed: "Amidst all the difficulties of the trial, I congratulate Your Honour on having the opportunity of fixing the law, relative to this peculiar crime, on grounds which will not deceive, and with such regard for human rights, that we shall bless the day on which the sentence was given, to prevent the fate of Stafford." [2]

When Randolph closed, on Friday, August 21, Hay asked Marshall to postpone further discussion until Monday, that counsel for the Government might prepare their arguments. [3] Burr's attorneys stoutly objected, but Marshall wisely granted Hay's request. [4] "Did you not do an unprecedented thing," a friend asked Marshall, "in suspending a criminal prosecution and granting two days, in the midst of the argument on a point then under discussion, for counsel to get ready to speak upon it?" "Yes," replied the Chief Justice, "I did and I knew it. But if I had not done so I should have been reproached with not being *disposed* to give the prosecutors an opportunity to answer." [5]

Saturday and Sunday were more than time enough to light the fires of MacRae's Scotch wrath. His anger dominated him to such an extent that he became almost incoherent. [6] Burr not a principal! "Let all who are in any manner concerned in treason

---

[1] *Burr Trials*, I, 557.   [2] *Ib.* II, 3–12.   [3] *Ib.* 25.   [4] *Ib.* 26–27.
[5] *Blennerhassett Papers:* Safford, 354–55.
[6] Alston's description in *ib.* 360.

be principals," and treason will be suppressed.[1] Mac-
Rae, speaking the language of Jeffreys, had, in his
rage, forgotten that he had immigrated to America.

On Tuesday, August 25, although the court
opened at nine o'clock,[2] the heat was so oppressive
that nothing but the public interest — now reaching
the point of hysteria — could have kept the densely
packed audience in the stifling hall.[3] But the spectators soon forgot their discomfort. The youthful,
handsome William Wirt enraptured them with an
eloquence which has lived for a century. It is impossible to give a faithful condensation of this
charming and powerful address, the mingled courtesy and boldness of it, the apt phrase, the effective
imagery, the firm logic, the wealth of learning. Only
examples can be presented; and these do scant justice to the young lawyer's speech.

"When we speak of treason, we must call it treason. . . Why then are gentlemen so sensitive . . as if
instead of a hall of justice, we were in a drawing-
room with colonel Burr, and were barbarously violating towards him every principle of decorum and
humanity?[4] This motion [to arrest the testimony]
is a bold and original stroke in the noble science of
defence," made to prevent the hearing of the evidence. But he knew that Marshall would not "sacrifice public justice, committed to [his] charge, by
aiding this stratagem to elude the sentence of the
law."[5]

[1] *Burr Trials*, II, 42. [2] *Blennerhassett Papers:* Safford, 360.
[3] The temperature was very high throughout the trial. One night
Blennerhassett was overcome by it. (*Ib.* 319.)
[4] *Burr Trials*, II, 57. [5] *Ib.* 57–59.

Why had Wickham said so little of American and so much of British precedents, vanishing "like a spirit from American ground and .. resurging by a kind of intellectual magic in the middle of the 16th century, complaining most dolefully of my lord Coke's bowels." It was to get as far as possible away from Marshall's decision in the case of Bollmann and Swartwout. If Marshall's opinion had been favorable, Wickham "would not have .. deserted a rock so broad and solid, to walk upon the waves of the Atlantic." Wirt made the most of Marshall's careless language.[1]

The youthful advocate was impressing Marshall as well as jury and auditors. "Do you mean to say," asked the Chief Justice, "that it is not necessary to state in the indictment in what manner the accused, who it is admitted was absent, became connected with the acts on Blennerhassett's island?" In reply Wirt condensed the theory of the prosecution: "I mean to say, that the *count* is *general* in modern cases; that we are endeavoring to make the accused a traitor by connection, by stating the act which was done, and which act, from his conduct in the transaction, he made his own; that it is sufficient to make this charge generally, not only because it is authorized by the constitutional definition, but because it is conformable to modern cases, in which the indictments are pruned of all needless luxuriances." [2]

Burr's presence at the island necessary! If so, a man might devise and set in motion "the whole mechanism" of treason, "go a hundred miles" away,

[1] *Burr Trials*, II, 61-65.　　　　[2] *Ib.* 92.

let it be operated by his agents, "and he is innocent,
. . while those whom he has deluded are to suffer the
death of traitors." How infamous! Burr only the
accessory and Blennerhassett the principal! "Will
any man believe that Burr who is a soldier bold,
ardent, restless and aspiring, the great actor whose
brain conceived and whose hand brought the plot
into operation, should sink down into an accessory
and Blennerhassett be elevated into a principal!"

Here Wirt delivered that passage which for nearly
a hundred years was to be printed in American
schoolbooks, declaimed by American youth, and to
become second only to Jefferson's Proclamation,
Messages, and letters, in fixing, perhaps irremovably,
public opinion as to Aaron Burr and Harman Blennerhassett.[1] But his speech was not all rhetoric.
Indeed, no advocate on either side, except John
Wickham and Luther Martin, approached him in
analyses of authorities and closeness of reasoning.[2]

"I cannot promise you, sir, a speech manufac-
tured out of tropes and figures," remarked Botts in
beginning his reply. No man better could have been
found to break the force of the address of his young
brother of the bar. Wirt had defaced his otherwise
well-nigh perfect address by the occasional use of
extravagant rhetoric, some of which, it appears, was

---

[1] See *Burr Trials*, II, 96–98.

For this famous passage of Wirt's speech, see Appendix E.

Burr was vastly amused by it and it became "a standing joke with
him for the rest of his life." (See Parton: *Burr*, 506.) But it was no
"joke" — standing or otherwise — to the people. They believed
Wirt's imagery to be a statement of the facts.

[2] "Wirt raised his reputation yesterday, as high as MacRae sunk
his the day before." (*Blennerhassett Papers*: Safford, 366.)

not reported. Botts availed himself of one such display to make Wirt's argument seem absurd and trivial: "Instead of the introduction of a sleeping Venus with all the luxury of voluptuous and wanton nakedness to charm the reason through the refined medium of sensuality, and to convince us that the law of treason is with the prosecution by leading our imaginations to the fascinating richness .. of heaving bosom and luscious waist, I am compelled to plod heavily and meekly through the dull doctrines of Hale and Foster." Botts continued, with daring but brilliant satire, to ridicule Wirt's unhappy rhetoric.[1] Soon spectators, witnesses, jury, were in laughter. The older lawyers were vastly amused. Even Marshall openly enjoyed the humor.

His purpose thus accomplished, Botts now addressed himself to the evidence, to analyze which he had been assigned. And a perfect job he made of it. He spoke with impetuous rapidity.[2] He reviewed the events at Blennerhassett's island: "There *was war*, when there was confessedly no war; and it happened although it was prevented!" As to arms: "No arms were necessary .. they might make war with their fingers." Yes, yes, "a most bloody war indeed — and ten or twelve boats." Referring to the flight from Blennerhassett's island, the sarcastic lawyer observed: "If I run away and hide to avoid a beating I am guilty and may be convicted of assault and battery!" What "simpletons" the people of Kentucky and Mississippi had been! "They hunted but

---

[1] *Burr Trials*, II, 123–24.

[2] See Hay's complaint that Botts talked so fast that he could not make notes on his points. (*Ib.* 194.)

could not find the war," although there it was, right among them![1]

What was the moving force back of the prosecution? It was, charged Botts, the rescue of the prestige of Jefferson's Administration. "It has not only been said here but published in all the newspapers throughout the United States, that if Aaron Burr should be acquitted it will be the severest satire on the government; and that the people are called upon to support the government by the conviction of colonel Burr; . . even jurymen have been taught by the common example to insult him."

No lie was too contemptible to be published about him. For instance, "when the grand jury returned a true bill, he was firm, serene, unmoved, composed — no change of countenance. . . Yet the next day they announced in the newspapers," declared Botts, "that he was in a state of indescribable consternation and dismay." Worse still, "every man who dares to look at the accused with a smile or present him the hand of friendship" is "denounced as a traitor."[2]

Black but faithful was the picture the fearless lawyer drew of the Government's conduct.[3] He dwelt on the devices resorted to for inflaming the people against Burr, and after they had been

---

[1] *Burr Trials*, II, 128-35.

[2] *Ib.* 168. Another story "propagated through the crowd" was that Burr had, by his "emissaries," attempted to poison with laudanum one of the Government's witnesses — this although the particular witness had been brought to Richmond to testify only that Wilkinson was not in the pay of Spain. (*Blennerhassett Papers:* Safford, 367.)

[3] *Burr Trials*, II, 164-73.

aroused, the demand that public sentiment be heeded and the accused convicted. Was that the method of justice! If so, where was the boasted beneficence of democracies? Where the righteousness and wisdom of the people? What did history tell us of the justice or mercy of the people? It was the people who forced Socrates to drink hemlock, banished Aristides, compelled the execution of Admiral Byng. "Jefferson was run down in 1780 [1] by the voice of the people." If the law of constructive treason were to be adopted in America and courts were to execute the will of the people, alas for any man, however upright and innocent, whom public opinion had been falsely led to condemn.[2]

Hay, who had been ill for several days [3] and was badly worn, spoke heavily for the greater part of two days.[4] His address, though dull, was creditable; but he added nothing in thought or authorities to Wirt's great speech. His principal point, which he repeated interminably, was that the jury must decide both law and fact. In making this contention he declared that Marshall was now asked by Burr's counsel to do the very thing for which Chase had been impeached.[5] Time and again the District Attorney insinuated that impeachment would be Marshall's fate if he did not permit the jury to hear all the testimony.[6]

Charles Lee, Attorney-General under President

---

[1] Botts here refers to the public outcry against Jefferson, while Governor during the Revolution, that nearly resulted in his impeachment. (See vol. I, 143–44, of this work.)

[2] *Burr Trials*, II, 135–92.　　　[3] *Ib.* 224.

[4] *Ib.* 192–236.　　　[5] *Ib.* 193–94.　　　[6] *Ib.* 200–19, 235.

Adams, and an intimate friend of Marshall,[1] had joined Burr's legal forces some time before. In opening his otherwise dry argument, Lee called Marshall's attention to Hay's threat of impeachment. The exhausted District Attorney finally denied that he meant such a thing, and Marshall mildly observed: "I did not consider you as making any personal allusion, but as merely referring to the law."[2] Thus, with his kindly tactfulness, Marshall put the incident aside.

On August 28, Luther Martin closed the debate. He had been drinking even more than usual throughout the proceedings;[3] but never was he in more perfect command of all his wonderful powers. No outline of his address will be attempted; but a few quotations may be illustrative.

It was the admitted legal right and "indispensable duty" of Burr's counsel, began Martin, to make the motion to arrest the testimony; yet for doing so "we have been denounced throughout the United States as attempting to suppress the truth." Our act "has been held up to the public and to this jury as conclusive proof of our guilt." Such, declared the great lawyer, were the methods used to convict Burr.[4] He had been in favor, he avowed, of waiving

---

[1] See vol. II, 201, 428, of this work.   [2] *Burr Trials*, II, 237–80.

[3] Blennerhassett, in his diary, makes frequent mention of Martin's drinking: "Martin was both yesterday and to-day more in his cups than usual, and though he spared neither his prudence nor his feelings, he was happy in all his hits." (*Blennerhassett Papers:* Safford, 438.)

"I . . recommended our brandy . . placing a pint tumbler before him. No ceremonies retarded the libation." (*Ib.* 377.)

"Luther Martin has just made his final immersion into the daily bath of his faculties." (*Ib.* 463.)

[4] *Burr Trials*, II, 260.

"obvious and undeniable rights," and of going on with the trial because he was convinced that all the evidence would not only clear "his friend," but remove the groundless prejudices which had so wickedly been excited against Burr. But he had yielded to the judgment of his associates that the plan adopted was more conformable to law.

"I shall ever feel the sincerest gratitude to heaven, that my life has been preserved to this time, and that I am enabled to appear . . in his defense." And if his fellow counsel and himself should be "successful in rescuing a gentleman, for whom I with pleasure avow my friendship and esteem, from the fangs of his persecutors . . what dear delight will my heart enjoy!"[1] Martin thanked Heaven, too, for the boon of being permitted to oppose the "destructive" doctrine of treason advanced by the Government. For hours he analyzed the British decisions which he "thanked God . . are not binding authority in this country." He described the origin and growth of the doctrine of constructive treason and defined it with clearnèss and precision.[2] It was admitted that Burr was not actually present at the time and place at which the indictment charged him with having committed the crime; but, according to the Government, he was "constructively" present.

With perfect fearlessness Martin attacked Marshall's objectionable language in the Bollmann and Swartwout opinion from the Supreme Bench: "As a binding judicial opinion," he accurately declared, "it ought to have no more weight than the ballad of

[1] *Burr Trials*, II, 262.   [2] *Ib.* 275–79; see also 339–42, 344–48.

Chevy Chase." [1] Deftly he impressed upon Marshall, Hay's threat of impeachment if the Chief Justice should presume to decide in Burr's favor.[2] Lamenting the popular hostility toward Burr, Martin defied it: "I have with pain heard it said [3] that such are the public prejudice against colonel Burr, that a jury, even should they be satisfied of his innocence, must have considerable firmness of mind to pronounce him *not guilty*. I have not heard it without horror.

"God of Heaven! have we already under our form of government (which we have so often been told is best calculated of all governments to secure all our rights) arrived at a period when a trial in a court of justice, where life is at stake, shall be but . . a mere idle . . ceremony to transfer innocence from the gaol to the gibbet, to gratify popular indignation excited by bloodthirsty enemies!"

Martin closed by a personal appeal to Marshall: "But if it require in such a situation firmness in a jury, so does it equally require fortitude in judges to perform their duty. . . If they do not and the prisoner fall a victim, they are guilty of murder in *foro cœli* whatever their guilt may be in *foro legis*. . . May that God who now looks down upon us, and who has in his infinite wisdom called you into existence and placed you in that seat to dispense justice to your fellow citizens, to preserve and protect innocence against persecution — may that God so illuminate your understandings that you may *know* what

[1] *Burr Trials*, II, 334.   [2] *Ib.* 377.
[3] One of those who told Martin this was Marshall himself. See *supra*, 401.

is right; and may he nerve your souls with firmness and fortitude to *act* according to that knowledge." [1]

The last word of this notable debate had been spoken.[2] The fate of Aaron Burr and of American liberty, as affected by the law of treason, now rested in the hands of John Marshall.

On Monday morning, August 31, the Chief Justice read his opinion. All Richmond and the multitude of strangers within her gates knew that the proceedings, which for four months had enchained the attention of all America, had now reached their climax. Burr's friends were fearful, and hoped that the laudanum calumny [3] would "strengthen" Marshall to do his duty.[4] For the moment the passions of the throng were in abeyance while the breathless spectators listened to Marshall's calm voice as it pronounced the fateful words.

The opinion of the Chief Justice was one of the longest ever rendered by him, and the only one in which an extensive examination of authorities is made. Indeed, a greater number of decisions, treatises, and histories are referred to than in all the rest of Marshall's foremost Constitutional opinions. Like every one of these, the Burr opinion was a state paper of first importance and marked a critical phase in the development of the American Nation.

Marshall stated the points first to be decided: under the Constitution can a man be convicted of treason in levying war who was not present when

[1] *Burr Trials*, II, 377–78.
[2] Randolph made another speech, but it was of no moment.
[3] See *supra*, footnote to 499.
[4] *Blennerhassett Papers: Safford*, 367.

the war was levied; and, if so, can testimony be received "to charge one man with the overt acts of others until those overt acts as laid in the indictment be proved to the satisfaction of the court"? He made clear the gravity of the Constitutional question: "In every point of view in which it can be contemplated, [it] is of infinite moment to the people of this country and their government." [1]

What was the meaning of the words, "'levying war'? . . Had their first application to treason been made by our constitution they would certainly have admitted of some latitude of construction." Even so it was obvious that the term "levying war" literally meant raising or creating and making war. "It would be affirming boldly to say that those only who actually constituted a portion of the military force appearing in arms could be considered as levying war."

Suppose the case of "a commissary of purchases" for an army raised to make war, who supplied it with provisions; would he not "levy war" as much as any other officer, although he may never have seen the army? The same was true of "a recruiting officer holding a commission in the rebel service, who, though never in camp, executed the particular duty assigned to him."

But levying war was not for the first time designated as treason by the American Constitution. "It is a technical term," borrowed from an ancient English statute [2] and used in the Constitution in the sense understood in that country and this at the time our fundamental law was framed.

[1] *Burr Trials*, II, 401; also in 4 Cranch, 470.   [2] 25th, of Edward III.

Not only British decisions, but "those celebrated elementary writers" whose "books are in the hands of every student," and upon which "legal opinions are formed" that are "carried to the bar, the bench and the legislature " — all must be consulted in ascertaining the import of such terms.[1]

Marshall reviewed Coke, Hale, Foster, and Blackstone, and found them vague upon the question "whether persons not in arms, but taking part in a rebellion, could be said to levy war independent of that legal rule [of constructive treason] which attaches the guilt of the principal to an accessory." Nor were the British decisions more satisfactory: "If in adjudged cases this question [has] been . . directly decided, the court has not seen those cases." [2] To trace the origin of "the doctrine that in treason all are principals" was unimportant. However "spurious," it was the British principle settled for ages.

The American Constitution, however, "comprizes no question respecting principal and accessory"—the traitor must "truly and in fact levy war." He must "perform a part in the prosecution of the war." [3]

Marshall then gingerly takes up the challenge of his opinion in the case of Bollmann and Swartwout. Since it had been upon the understanding by the grand jury of his language in that opinion that Burr had been indicted for treason, and because the Government relied on it for conviction so far as the prosecution depended on the law, the Chief Justice took pains to make clear the disputed passages.

[1] *Burr Trials*, II, 402–03; 4 Cranch, 470.
[2] *Burr Trials*, II, 403; 4 Cranch, 471.
[3] *Burr Trials*, II, 404–05; 4 Cranch, 472.

"Some gentlemen have argued as if the supreme court had adopted the whole doctrine of the English books on the subject of accessories to treason.[1] But certainly such is not the fact. Those only who perform a part, and who are leagued in the conspiracy, are declared to be traitors. To complete the definition *both* circumstances must occur. They must 'perform a part' which will furnish the overt act; and they must be 'leagued in the conspiracy.'"

Did the things proved to have happened on Blennerhassett's island amount to the overt act of levying war? He had heard, said Marshall, that his opinion in Bollmann and Swartwout was construed as meaning that "any assemblage whatever for a treasonable purpose, whether in force or not in force, whether in a condition to use violence or not in that condition, is a levying of war." That view of his former opinion had not, indeed, "been expressly advanced at the bar"; but Marshall understood, he said, that "it was adopted elsewhere." [2]

Relying exclusively on reason, all would agree, he continued, "that war could not be levied without the employment and exhibition of force... Intention to go to war may be proved by words," but the actual going to war must "be proved by open deed." [3]

---

[1] The doctrine that accessories are as guilty as principals.

[2] *Burr Trials*, II, 406–08; 4 Cranch, 476. This reference is to Jefferson's explanation of Marshall's opinion in Bollmann and Swartwout, which Giles and other Republican leaders were proclaiming throughout Virginia. It had been adopted by the grand jury; and it was this construction of Marshall's language under which they returned the bills of indictment for treason. Had the grand jury understood the law to be as Marshall was now expounding it, Burr would not have been indicted for treason.

[3] *Burr Trials*, II, 409; 4 Cranch, 476.

This natural and reasonable understanding of the term was supported by the authorities. Marshall then made specific reference to the opinions of a large number of British writers and judges, and of all American judges who had passed upon the question. In none of these, he asserted, had "the words 'levying war' . . received a technical different from their natural meaning" [1] — that is, "the employment and exhibition of force."

Had he overruled all these opinions in the Bollmann-Swartwout case? Had he, in addition, reversed the natural interpretation of the Constitution which reason dictated? Surely not! Yet this was what he was now charged with having done.

But, said Marshall, "an opinion which is to overrule all former precedents, and to establish a principle never before recognized, should be expressed in plain and explicit terms." A mere implication was not enough. Yet this was all there was to justify the erroneous construction of his opinion in the case of Bollmann and Swartwout — "the omission of the court to state that the assemblage which constitutes the fact of levying war ought to be in force." [2]

Marshall then went into an extended and minute analysis of his misunderstood opinion, and painfully labored to show that he then intended to say, as he now did say: that the act of levying war required "an assemblage in force," and not merely "a secret furtive assemblage without the appearance

---

[1] *Burr Trials*, II, 409–13; 4 Cranch, 477–80.
[2] *Burr Trials*, II, 415; 4 Cranch, 481.

of force." The gathering "must be such as to prove
that [war] is its object." If it was not "a military
assemblage in a condition to make war, it was not a
levying of war." [1]

The indictment charged Burr with having levied
war at a specific place and stated the exact manner
in which the act had been done; this was necessary;
otherwise the accused could not make adequate defense. So the indictment "must be proved as laid";
otherwise "the charge of an overt act would be a
mischief instead of an advantage to the accused,"
and would lead him from the true cause and nature of the accusation instead of informing him
respecting it. [2]

The Government insisted that, although Burr
"had never been with the party . . on Blennerhassett's island, and was, at the time, at a great distance
and in a different state, . . he was yet legally present,
and therefore may properly be charged in the indictment as being present in fact." Thus, the question
arose "whether in this case the doctrine of constructive presence can apply." In answering it, John
Marshall ended the contention that so cruel a dogma
can ever be applied in America. This achievement
was one of his noblest services to the American
people. [3]

Again an imposing array of precedents was examined. "The man, who incites, aids, or procures
a treasonable act," is not, merely on that account,

[1] *Burr Trials*, II, 415–23; 4 Cranch, 482–88.
[2] *Burr Trials*, II, 425; 4 Cranch, 490.
[3] This part of Marshall's opinion (*Burr Trials*, II, 425–34; 4 Cranch,
490–504) is reproduced in full in Appendix F.

"legally present when that act is committed."[1] Of course, other facts might require that a man should be considered to be present although really absent; for example, if he were on the way there for the purpose of taking part in the specific act charged, or if he were stationed near in order to coöperate with those who actually did the deed, he would be of them and associated with them in the perpetration of that particular act.[2] But otherwise he could not be said to be present.

If this were not so, then a man levying war in one part of the country might be construed to be present at and taking part in hostilities at the most distant point of the Republic — a participator in "every overt act performed anywhere"; and he would be liable to trial and conviction "in any state on the continent where any overt act has been committed" by anybody. "He may be proved to be guilty of an overt act laid in the indictment in which he had no personal participation, by proving that he advised it, or that he committed other acts."[3]

If Burr were guilty of treason in connection with the assemblage on Blennerhassett's island, it was only because Burr procured the men to meet for the purpose of levying war against the United States. But the fact that he did procure the treasonable assemblage must be charged in the indictment and proved by two witnesses, precisely as must actual physical presence — since the procuring of the assemblage takes the place of presence at it. "If in

[1] *Burr Trials*, ii, 426; 4 Cranch, 492.

[2] *Burr Trials*, ii, 429; 4 Cranch, 494.

[3] *Burr Trials*, ii, 430; 4 Cranch, 495.

one case," declared Marshall, "the presence of the individual make the guilt of the assemblage his guilt, and in the other case the procurement by the individual make the guilt of the assemblage his guilt, then presence and procurement are equally component parts of the overt act, and equally require two witnesses." [1]

Neither presence nor procurement could, therefore, be proved by collateral testimony: "No presumptive evidence, no facts from which presence may be conjectured or inferred will satisfy the constitution and the law." And "if procurement take the place of presence and become part of the overt act, then no presumptive evidence, no facts from which the procurement may be conjectured, or inferred, can satisfy the constitution and the law.

"The mind is not to be led to the conclusion that the individual was present by a train of conjectures, of inferences, or of reasoning; the fact must be proved by two witnesses," as required by the Constitution. "Neither, where procurement supplies the want of presence, is the mind to be conducted to the conclusion that the accused procured the assembly, by a train of conjectures or inferences or of reasoning; the fact itself must be proved by two witnesses." [2]

To the objection that this could "scarcely ever" be done, since "the advising or procurement of treason is a secret transaction," the answer was,

---

[1] *Burr Trials*, II, 436; 4 Cranch, 500.

[2] *Burr Trials*, II, 436–37; 4 Cranch, 500. These paragraphs furnish a perfect example of Marshall's method of statement and logic — the exact antithesis plainly put, the repetition of precise words with only the resistless monosyllables, "if" and "then," between them.

said Marshall, "that the difficulty of proving a fact will not justify conviction without proof." And most "certainly it will not justify conviction without [one] direct and positive witness in a case where the constitution requires two." The true inference from "this circumstance" was "that the advising of the fact is not within the constitutional definition of the crime. To advise or procure a treason . . is not treason in itself." [1]

The testimony which the Government now proposed to offer was to "prove — what? the overt act laid in the indictment? that the prisoner was one of those who assembled at Blennerhassett's island? No!" But, instead, "evidence [of] subsequent transactions at a different place and in a different state." But such "testimony was not relevant." If it could be introduced at all, it would be "only in the character of corroborative or confirmatory testimony, after the overt act has been proved by two witnesses in such a manner that the question of fact ought to be left with the jury." [2]

Before closing, Marshall answered the threats of Hay and Wirt that, if he decided in favor of Burr, he would be impeached: "That this court dares not usurp power is most true. That this court dares not shrink from its duty is not less true. . . No man is desirous of becoming the peculiar subject of calumny. No man, might he let the bitter cup pass from him without self reproach, would drain it to the bottom. But if he have no choice in the case, if there

---

[1] *Burr Trials*, II, 437; 4 Cranch, 501.
[2] *Burr Trials*, II, 443; 4 Cranch, 506.

be no alternative presented to him but a dereliction of duty or the opprobrium of those who are denominated the world, he merits the contempt as well as the indignation of his country who can hesitate which to embrace." [1]

Let the jury apply the law as announced to the facts as proved and "find a verdict of guilty or not guilty as their own consciences shall direct."

The next morning the petit jury retired, but quickly returned. Marshall's brother-in-law, Colonel Edward Carrington, foreman, rose and informed the court that the jury had agreed upon a verdict.

"Let it be read," gravely ordered Marshall.

And Colonel Carrington read the words of that peculiar verdict:

"We of the jury say that Aaron Burr is not proved to be guilty under this indictment by any evidence submitted to us. We therefore find him not guilty." [2]

Instantly Burr, Martin, Wickham, and Botts were on their feet protesting. This was no verdict, according to law. It was informal, irregular. In such cases, said Burr, the jury always was sent back to alter it or else the court itself corrected it; and he accurately stated the proper procedure.

Discussion followed. Hay insisted that the verdict be received and recorded as returned. "It was like the whole play," exclaimed Martin, "Much Ado About Nothing." Of course the verdict must be corrected. Did the jury mean to "censure . . the court for suppressing irrelevant testimony?" Un-

---

[1] *Burr Trials*, II, 444–45; 4 Cranch, 507.   [2] *Burr Trials*, II, 446.

thinkable! And if not, they ought to answer simply
"Guilty" or "Not Guilty." [1]

Colonel Carrington informed the court that,
among themselves, the jury had said that "they
would alter the verdict if it was informal — it was
in fact a verdict of acquittal." Richard E. Parker,
also of the jury, said he never would agree to change
the form — they knew what they were about when
they adopted it. Parker was "a violent Jeffersonian
partisan," and Burr's friends had reproved him for
accepting such a man as a member of the jury. [2]

Soothingly Marshall directed that the verdict
"stand on the bill" as the jury wished it; but, since
it was "in effect a verdict of acquittal," let "an
entry be made on the record of 'Not Guilty.'"

The Chief Justice "politely thanked the jury for
their patient attention during the whole course of
this long trial, and then discharged them." [3]

A week before Marshall delivered his opinion, an
attempt was made to induce Blennerhassett to betray Burr. On August 23 William Duane, editor of
the *Aurora*, and an intimate friend, supporter, and
agent of Jefferson, approached Blennerhassett for
that purpose, and offered to go to Washington, "now
or at any time hereafter," in his behalf. Duane assured him that the Administration would refuse him
(Duane) "nothing he should ask." But Blennerhassett repulsed Duane's advances. [4]

---

[1] *Burr Trials*, II, 446–47. Martin was right; the verdict should have
been either "guilty" or "not guilty."

[2] *Blennerhassett Papers:* Safford, 339.

[3] *Burr Trials*, II, 447.

[4] *Blennerhassett Papers:* Safford, 356–58; and see Adams: *U.S.* III,

Hay, angry and discomfited, entered a *nolle prosequi* to the indictments of Dayton, Blennerhassett, and the others for the same crime; but, in obedience to Jefferson's orders, demanded that all of them, Burr included, be still held under the charge of treason, that they might be sent for trial to some place where an overt act might have been committed.[1] Marshall, after enduring another long argument, gently put the application aside because all the conspirators were now to be tried upon the charge of misdemeanor under the second indictment.[2]

Marshall's motives were clearer than ever to Jefferson. "The event has been what was evidently intended from the beginning of the trial; . . not only to clear Burr, but to prevent the evidence from ever going before the world. But this latter case must not take place." Hay must see to it that "not a single witness be paid or permitted to depart until his testimony has been committed to writing. . . These whole proceedings will be laid before Congress, that they may . . provide the proper remedy."[3]

Jefferson ordered Hay to press for trial on the indictment for misdemeanor, not with the expectation of convicting Burr, but in the hope that some sort of

---

448, 464–65. Duane was known to have unbounded influence with Jefferson, who ascribed his election to the powerful support given him by the *Aurora*.

Government agents also tried to seduce Colonel de Pestre, another of Burr's friends, by insinuating "how handsomely the Col. might be provided for in the army, if his principles . . were not adverse to the administration." De Pestre's brother-in-law "had been turned out of his place as Clerk in the War Office, because he could not accuse the Col. of Burr-ism." (*Blennerhassett Papers:* Safford, 328–29.)

[1] *Burr Trials*, II, 448–49.   [2] *Ib.* 455.

[3] Jefferson to Hay, Sept. 4, 1807, as quoted in Adams, *U.S.* III, 470; and see *Jefferson:* Randolph, IV, 102.

testimony would be brought out that would convict Marshall in the court of public opinion, and perhaps serve as a pretext for impeaching him. Thus, in the second trial of which we are now to be spectators, "the chief-justice was occupied in hearing testimony intended for use not against Burr, but against himself." [1] It was for this reason that Marshall, when the trial for misdemeanor began, threw open wide the doors to testimony. [2]

Burr's counsel, made unwise by victory, insisted that he should not be required to give bail, and Marshall, although the point had been decided and was not open to dispute, permitted and actually encouraged exasperatingly extended argument upon it. [3] Burr had submitted to give bail at the beginning, said Botts, not because it was "demandable of right," but because he and his counsel "had reason to apprehend danger . . from the violence and turbulence of the mob." [4]

Marshall was careful to deliver another long and, except for the political effect, wholly unnecessary opinion; nor was it directly on the matter at issue. Counsel floundered through a tangle of questions, Marshall exhibiting apparent indecision by manifesting great concern, even on the simplest points.

---

[1] Adams: *U.S.* III, 470.   [2] See *infra*, 524.

[3] *Burr Trials*, II, 473–80.

[4] *Ib.* 480. This statement of Botts is of first importance. The whole proceeding on the part of the Government was conspicuously marked by a reliance upon public sentiment to influence court and jury through unceasing efforts to keep burning the fires of popular fear and hatred of Burr, first lighted by Jefferson's Proclamation and Message. Much repetition of this fact is essential, since the nature and meaning of the Burr trial rests upon it.

JOHN MARSHALL
Painted by Robert Matthew Sully

Finally, he ordered that Burr "be acquitted and discharged" as to the indictment for treason, but to be held in five thousand dollars bail under the indictment for misdemeanor. Jonathan Dayton and William Langbourne offered themselves and were accepted as sureties; and on September 3, after nearly nine weeks of imprisonment, Burr walked out of court unhindered, no longer to be under lock and bar and armed guard.[1]

Merry were the scenes in the houses of Richmond society that night; hilarious the rejoicing about the flowing board of Luther Martin; and, confused and afflicted with a blurred anger, the patriotic multitude talked resentfully of Marshall's decision. On one side it was said that justice had prevailed and persecution had been defeated; on the other, that justice had been mocked and treason protected. Hay, Wirt, and MacRae were bitter and despondent; Edmund Randolph, Botts, Martin, and Burr, jubilant and aggressive.

Many conflicting stories sprang up concerning Marshall — his majestic bearing on the bench, his servility, his courage, his timidity. One of these has survived: "Why did you not tell Judge Marshall that the people of America demanded a conviction?" a disgusted Republican asked of Wirt. "Tell *him* that!" exclaimed Wirt. "I would as soon have gone to Herschel, and told him that the people of America insisted that the moon had horns as a reason why he should draw her with them." [2]

[1] *Burr Trials*, ii, 481–503.
[2] Van Santvoord: *Sketches of the Lives and Judicial Services of the*

The captain of the "conspiracy" had never lost heart, and, save when angered by Marshall's seeming inconsistency and indecision, had continued to be cheery and buoyant. Steadily he had assured his friends that, when acquitted, he would again take up and put through his plans. This thought now dominated him. Blennerhassett, upon visiting his chief, found Burr "as gay as usual, and as busy in speculations on reorganizing his projects for action as if he had never suffered the least interruption," with better prospects for success than ever.[1]

Quick to press his advantage, Burr the next morning demanded the production of the letters called for in the subpœna *duces tecum* to Jefferson. These had not been forthcoming, and Burr asserted the President to be in contempt of court and subject to punishment therefor.[2] Once more altercation flared up in debate. Hay said he had one of the letters; that it had not "the most distant bearing on the subject," and that he might prefer "to be put in prison" rather than disclose its contents.[3]

Jefferson had become very nervous about Marshall's order and plainly feared that the Chief Justice might attempt to enforce it. The thought frightened him; he had no stomach for a direct encounter. At last he wished to compose the differences between himself and the obstinate and fearless, if gentle-mannered, Marshall. So the President directed his

Chief-Justices of the United States, 379. Yet popular sentiment was the burden of many of the speeches of Government counsel throughout the trial.

[1] *Blennerhassett Papers:* Safford, 402.
[2] *Burr Trials*, ii, 504.   [3] *Ib.* 511.

district attorney to tell the United States Marshal to obey no order of the court and to intimate to the Chief Justice the wisdom of deferring the vexed question until the next session of Congress.

He wrote, said Jefferson, "in a spirit of conciliation and with the desire to avoid conflicts of authority between the high branches of the government which would discredit equally at home and abroad." Naturally Burr and his counsel would like "to convert this trial into a contest between the judiciary & Exve Authorities"; but he had not "expected . . that the Ch. Justice would lend himself to it." Surely Marshall's "prudence and good sense" would not "permit him to press it."

But if Marshall was determined to attack Jefferson and "issue any process which [would] involve any act of force to be committed on the persons of the Exve or heads of departs," Hay was to give Jefferson "instant notice, and by express if you find that can be done quicker than by post; and . . moreover . . advise the marshal on his conduct as he will be critically placed between us."

The "safest way" for that officer to pursue "will be to take no part in the exercise of any act of force ordered in this case. The powers given the Exve by the constn are sufficient to protect the other branches from judiciary usurpation of pre-eminence, & every individual also from judiciary vengeance, and the marshal may be assured of it's effective exercise to cover him."

Such was Jefferson's threat to use force against the execution of the process of the National courts.

But the President went on: "I hope however that the discretion of the C. J. will suffer this question to lie over for the present, and at the ensuing session of the legislature [Congress] he may have means provided for giving individuals the benefit of the testimony of the Exve functionaries in proper cases, without breaking up the government. *Will not the associate judge* [Cyrus Griffin] *assume to divide his court and procure a truce at least in so critical a conjuncture?*"[1]

When Hay acknowledged that he had one of the letters from Wilkinson to Jefferson, a subpœna *duces tecum* was served on the District Attorney, notwithstanding his gallant declaration that he would not produce it even if he were sent to jail for not doing so. Hay then returned a copy of such parts of the letter as he thought "material for the purposes of justice," declining to give those passages which Jefferson deemed "confidential."[2] Burr insisted on the production of the entire letter.

Botts moved that the trial be postponed "till the letter shall be produced." Another of that unending series of arguments followed,[3] and still another of Marshall's cautious but convincing opinions came

[1] Jefferson to Hay, no date; but Paul Leicester Ford fixes it between August 7 and 20, 1807. It is, says Ford, "the mere draft of a letter .. which may never have been sent, but which is of the utmost importance." (*Works:* Ford, x, 406–07.) It would seem that Jefferson wrote either to Marshall or Judge Griffin personally, for the first words of his astounding letter to Hay were: "The *enclosed letter* is written in a spirit of conciliation," etc., etc. Whether or not the President actually posted the letter to Hay, the draft quoted in the text shows the impression which Marshall's order made on Jefferson. (Italics the author's.)

[2] *Burr Trials*, ii, 513–14.   [3] *Ib.* 514–33.

forth. Jefferson, he said, had not forbidden the production of the letter — the President, in response to the subpœna upon him, had sent the document to Hay, leaving to the discretion of the District Attorney the question as to what should be done with it. Of course if, for public reasons, Jefferson had declined to produce the letter, his "motives may [have been] such as to restrain the court" from compelling him to do so.[1] At least Burr might see the letter now; consideration of the other features of the controversy would be deferred.[2]

The distracted Hay, his sour temper made more acid by a "greatly aggravated influenza," wrote Jefferson of the Government's predicament; Marshall's remarks from the bench had not been explicit, he said, and "it is impossible to foresee what his opinion will be unless I could foresee what will be the state of his nerves. Wirt, who has hitherto advocated the *integrity* of the Chief Justice, now abandons him."

The District Attorney dolefully tells the President that he is "very decidedly of the opinion, that these prosecutions will terminate in nothing." He thinks the Government will be defeated on the trials for misdemeanor, and believes the indictments for that offense should be dismissed and motion made for the commitment of Burr, Blennerhassett, and Smith to be transferred to some spot where their crime

[1] This remark of Marshall would seem to indicate that Hay had tried to patch up "a truce" between the President and the Chief Justice, as Jefferson desired him to do. If so, it soon expired.

[2] *Burr Trials*, II, 533–37.

might be proved. "Instruct me," he begs Jefferson, "specially on this point." [1]

Jefferson, now on his vacation at Monticello, directed Hay to press at Richmond the trial of Burr for misdemeanor. "If defeated it will heap coals of fire on the head of the judge; if convicted, it will give them time to see whether a prosecution for treason can be instituted against him in any, and what court." A second subpœna *duces tecum* seems to have been issued against Jefferson,[2] and he defiantly refused to "sanction a proceeding so preposterous," by "any notice" of it.[3] And there this heated and dangerous controversy appears to have ended.[4]

Finally, the hearing of evidence began on the in-dictment against Burr for misdemeanor — for having conducted an attack upon Mexico. For seven weeks the struggle went on. The Government's attorneys showed the effects of the long and losing fight. Many witnesses were sent home unexamined or merely leav-ing their affidavits. Hay acted like the sick man he really was. The dour MacRae appeared "utterly chop-fallen; an object of disgust to his friends, and pity to his enemies." [5] Only Wirt, with his fine gal-lantry of spirit, bore himself manfully. Motions,

---

[1] Hay to Jefferson, Sept. 5, 1807, Jefferson MSS. Lib. Cong.

[2] The printed record does not show this, but Jefferson, in his letter to Hay, September 7, says: "I received, late last night, your favor of the day before, and now re-enclose you the subpœna."

[3] Jefferson to Hay, Sept. 7, 1807, *Works:* Ford, x, 408.

[4] For some reason the matter was not again pressed. Perhaps the favorable progress of the case relieved Burr's anxiety. It is possible that the "truce" so earnestly desired by Jefferson was arranged.

[5] *Blennerhassett Papers:* Safford, 394.

arguments, opinions continued. One of Marshall's rulings on the admissibility of evidence moved Blennerhassett to ecstasies.[1]

More than fifty witnesses were examined, the heavy preponderance of the evidence clearly showing that Burr's purpose and expectations had been to settle the Washita lands and, in case the United States went to war with Spain, and *only in that event*, to lead a force against the Spaniards. No testimony whatever was given tending to disclose any hostile plans against the United States, or even for an attack upon Mexico without war between America and Spain, except that of Wilkinson, Eaton, Taylor, Allbright, and the Morgans, as already set out. One witness also told of a wild and fanciful talk by the eccentric and imaginative Blennerhassett.[2]

The credibility of Dunbaugh was destroyed. Wilkinson was exposed in a despicable light,[3] and Eaton appeared more fantastic than ever; but both these heroes put on looks of lofty defiance. The warrior-diplomat of Algerian fame had now fallen so low in the public esteem that one disgusted Virginian had threatened to kick him out of a room.[4]

On September 15, 1807, the District Attorney, by

[1] "Today, the Chief Justice has delivered an able, full, and luminous opinion as ever did honor to a judge, which has put an end to the present prosecution." (*Blennerhassett Papers:* Safford, 403.)

[2] *Annals*, 10th Cong. 1st Sess. 416–19.

[3] This appears from the record itself. (See Wilkinson's testimony, *ib.* 512–44; also testimony of Major James Bruff, *ib.* 589–90.) Blennerhassett, who usually reported faithfully the general impression, notes in his diary: "The General exhibited the manner of a sergeant under a courtmartial, rather than the demeanor of an accusing officer confronted with his culprit." (*Blennerhassett Papers:* Safford, 422.)

[4] *Ib.* 418.

attempting to enter a *nolle prosequi* on the indictment of Burr for misdemeanor, tried to prevent
the jury from rendering a verdict.[1] One member
of the jury wanted that body to return a special
finding; but his associates would have none of it,
and in half an hour they reported a straight verdict
of "Not Guilty."[2]

Hay dismissed further proceedings against Smith
and Blennerhassett on the indictments for misdemeanor, and then moved to commit Burr and his
associates upon the charge of treason by "levying
war" within the jurisdiction of the United States
Court for the District of Ohio.[3] On this motion,
Marshall, as an examining magistrate, gave the
Government wide scope in the introduction of testimony, to the immense disgust of the triply accused
men. Blennerhassett thought that Marshall was
conciliating "public prejudice."[4] Burr told his
counsel that the Chief Justice "did not for two days
together understand either the questions or himself
. . and should in future be put right by strong language." So angered was he with Marshall's "wavering," that at times "Burr . . would not trust
himself to rise up to sum up and condense the forces
displayed by his counsel, into compact columns,
after the engagement, toward the close of the day,
as is generally his practice."[5]

Just at this time appeared a pamphlet[6] by Mar-

---

[1] Record, MSS. Archives U.S. Circuit Court, Richmond, Va.

[2] *Blennerhassett Papers:* Safford, 404.

[3] *Ib.* 409–10.   [4] *Ib.* 416.   [5] *Ib.* 412–13.

[6] Daveiss: "A View of the President's Conduct Concerning the
Conspiracy of 1806."

shall's brother-in-law, Joseph Hamilton Daveiss.
Jefferson had removed him from the office of United
States Attorney for the District of Kentucky because of Daveiss's failure in his attacks on Burr,
and the revengeful Federalist lawyer and politician
retaliated by abusing the President, Wilkinson, and
Burr equally. Between Daveiss's pamphlet and
Marshall's sudden admission of evidence, some saw
a direct connection; the previous knowledge Marshall must have had of his brother-in-law's intended
assault, inferred because of "the well-known spirit of
clanship and co-operation with which the Marshalls
and all their connections are so uniformly animated,"
showed, it was alleged, that the Chief Justice was
working with his kinsman to bring down in indiscrim-
inate ruin, Jefferson, Burr, and Wilkinson together.

The last volume of Marshall's "Life of Washington," that "five volumed libel," as Jefferson
branded the biography, had recently appeared.
Blennerhassett, who, in expressing his own opinions,
usually reflected those of his associates, had "no
doubt" that the President's perusal of Marshall's
last volume and Daveiss's pamphlet "inspired Jefferson with a more deadly hatred of the Marshall
faction than he has ever conceived of all the Burrites
he ever heard of." [2]

The President's partisans in Virginia were prompt
to stoke the furnace of his wrath. William Thompson of Petersburgh [3] wrote a brief "view" of the

---

[1] *Blennerhassett Papers:* Safford, 465–66.   [2] *Ib.* 502.

[3] The brother of John Thompson, author of "The Letters of Curtius" which attacked Marshall in 1798. (See vol. II, 395–96, of this
work.)

Burr trial and sent "the first 72. pages" to Jefferson, who read them "with great satisfaction" and clamored for more.[1] Marshall's conduct should indeed fill everybody "with alarm," wrote Jefferson in reply. "We had supposed we possessed fixed laws to guard us equally against treason & oppression. But it now appears we have no law but the will of the judge. Never will chicanery have a more difficult task than has been now accomplished to warp the text of the law to the will of him who is to construe it. Our case too is the more desperate as to attempt to make the law plainer by amendment is only throwing out new materials for sophistry."[2]

The Federalists in Washington, fast dwindling in power and number, experienced as much relief as their chronic melancholia permitted them to enjoy. "Had the late vice president and two senators been convicted and executed for treason, it would in the opinion of Europe, have reflected disgrace upon our country," notes Senator Plumer in his diary.[3]

Hay, on the other hand, thought that "a correct and perspicuous legal history of this trial would be a valuable document in the hands of intelligent legislators," but that "among others it might perhaps do mischief. It might produce a sentiment toward all judicial system and law itself, the operation of which might perhaps be fatal to the tranquillity and good order of Society."[4]

[1] Thompson's "view" was published as a series of letters to Marshall immediately after the trial closed. (See *infra*, 533–35.)

[2] Jefferson to Thompson, September 26, 1807, *Works: Ford*, x, 501–02.

[3] Plumer, Aug. 15, 1807, "Diary," Plumer MSS. Lib. Cong.

[4] Hay to Jefferson, Oct. 15, 1807, Jefferson MSS. Lib. Cong.

On October 20, Marshall delivered his last opinion in the Burr trials. It was upon the Government's motion to commit Burr and his associates for treason and misdemeanor committed on the dismal island at the mouth of the Cumberland, where Burr had first greeted his little band of settlers and potential adventurers. He must grant the motion, Marshall said, "unless it was perfectly clear that the act was innocent." If there was any doubt, the accused must be held. The Chief Justice then carefully analyzed all the evidence.[1] He concluded that Burr's purposes were to settle the Washita lands and to invade Mexico if opportunity offered, perhaps, however, only in the event of war with Spain. But whether this was so ought to be left to the jury; Marshall would "make no comment upon it which might, the one way or the other, influence their judgment."[2] He therefore would commit Burr and Blennerhassett "for preparing and providing the means for a military expedition" against Spain.

"After all, this is a sort of drawn battle," Burr informed Theodosia. "This opinion was a matter of regret and surprise to the friends of the chief justice and of ridicule to his enemies — all believing that it was a sacrifice of principle to conciliate *Jack Cade*. Mr. Hay immediately said that he should advise the government to *desist from further prosecution*."[3]

[1] This statement is lucid, conspicuously fair, and, in the public mind, would have cleared Burr of any taint of treason, had not Jefferson already crystallized public sentiment into an irrevocable conviction that he was a traitor. (See *Annals*, 10th Cong. 1st Sess. 766–78.)

[2] *Ib.*

[3] Burr to his daughter, Oct. 23, 1807, Davis, ii, 411–12.

If Marshall disappointed Burr, he infuriated Jefferson. In the closing words of his opinion the Chief Justice flung at the President this challenge: "If those whose province and duty it is to prosecute offenders against the laws of the United States shall be of the opinion that a crime of a deeper dye has been committed, it is at their choice to act in conformity with that opinion" — in short, let Jefferson now do his worst.

Marshall's final opinion and his commitment of Burr, under bail, to be tried in Ohio for possible misdemeanor at the mouth of the Cumberland should a grand jury indict him for that offense, disgusted Burr. Indeed he was so "exasperated" that "he was rude and insulting to the Judge." [1] Nor did Marshall's friends in Richmond feel differently. They "are as much dissatisfied," records Blennerhassett, "with his opinion yesterday as Government has been with all his former decisions. He is a good man, and an able lawyer, but timid and yielding under the fear of the multitude, led . . by the vindictive spirit of the party in power." [2]

Burr gave the bond of five thousand dollars required by Marshall, but in Ohio the Government declined to pursue the prosecution. [3] Burr put the

[1] Hay to Jefferson, Oct. 21, 1807, Jefferson MSS. Lib. Cong.

[2] *Blennerhassett Papers:* Safford, 301. If this were only the personal opinion of Burr's gifted but untrustworthy associate, it would not be weighty. But Blennerhassett's views while at Richmond, as recorded in his diary, were those of all of Burr's counsel and of the Richmond Federalists.

[3] No wonder the Government abandoned the case. Nearly all the depositions procured by Hay under Jefferson's orders demonstrated that Burr had not the faintest intention of separating the Western

whole matter out of his mind as a closed incident, left Richmond, and started anew upon the execution of his one great plan as though the interruption of it had never happened.

Marshall hurried away to the Blue Ridge. "The day after the commitment of Col°. Burr for a misdemeanor I galloped to the mountains," he tells Judge Peters. During the trial Peters had sent Marshall a volume of his admiralty decisions; and when he returned from his belated vacation, the Chief Justice acknowledged the courtesy: "I have as yet been able only to peep into the book. . . I received it while fatigued and occupied with the most unpleasant case which has ever been brought before a Judge in this or perhaps any other country, which affected to be governed by laws, since the decision of which I have been entirely from home. . . I only returned in time to perform my North Carolina Circuit which terminates just soon enough to enable me to be here to open the Court for the antient dominion. Thus you perceive I have sufficient bodily employment to prevent my mind from perplexing itself about the attentions paid me in Baltimore and elsewhere.[1]

"I wish I could have had as fair an opportunity to let the business go off as a jest here as you seem to have had in Pennsylvania: but it was most deplorably serious & I could not give the subject a different

States from the Union, or even of attacking Mexico unless war broke out between Spain and the United States. See particularly deposition of Benjamin Stoddert of Maryland, October 9, 1807 (*Quarterly Pub. Hist. and Phil. Soc. Ohio*, ix, nos. 1 and 2, 7–9); of General Edward Tupper of Ohio, September 7, 1807 (*ib.* 13–27); and of Paul H. M. Prevost of New Jersey, September 28, 1807 (*ib.* 28–30).

[1] See *infra*, 536.

aspect by treating it in any manner which was in my power. I might perhaps have made it less serious to my self by obeying the public will instead of the public law & throwing a little more of the sombre upon others." [1]

While Marshall was resting in the mountains, Jefferson was writing his reply to the last challenge of the Chief Justice.[2] In his Message to Congress which he prepared immediately after the Burr trials, he urged the House to impeach Marshall. He felt it to be his duty, he said, to transmit a record of the Burr trial. "*Truth & duty alone extort the observation that wherever the laws were appealed to in aid of the public safety, their operation was on behalf of those only against whom they were invoked.*" From the record "you will be enabled to judge whether the defect was in the testimony, or in the laws, or *whether there is not a radical defect* in the administration of the law? And wherever it shall be found the legislature alone can apply or originate the remedy.

"The framers of our constitution certainly supposed they had guarded, as well their government against destruction by treason, as their citizens against oppression under pretence of it: and if *the pliability of the law as construed in the case of Fries,*[3] *and it's wonderful refractoriness as construed in that of Burr, shew that neither end has been attained, and induce an awful doubt whether we all live under the*

---

[1] Marshall to Peters, Nov. 23, 1807, Peters MSS. Pa. Hist. Soc.

[2] Hay, for the moment mollified by Marshall's award of two thousand dollars as his fee, had made no further complaint for several days.

[3] See *supra*, chap. I, 35–36; also vol. II, 429–30, of this work.

same law. The right of the jury too to decide law as well as fact seems nugatory without the evidence pertinent to their sense of the law. If these ends are not attained it becomes worthy of enquiry by what means more effectual they may be secured?" [1]

On the advice of his Cabinet,[2] Jefferson struck out from the Message the sentences italicized above. But even with this strong language omitted, Congress was told to impeach Marshall in far more emphatic terms than those by which Jefferson had directed the impeachment of Pickering — in plainer words, indeed, than those privately written to Nicholson ordering the attack upon Chase. Jefferson's attack on Marshall was also inserted in a Message dealing with probable war against Great Britain and setting out the continuance of our unhappy relations with Spain, "to our former grounds of complaint" against which country had "been added a very serious one." [3]

Had these grave conditions not engaged the instant attention of Congress, had public sentiment — even with part of its fury drawn from Burr to Great Britain — been heeded at the National Capital,

[1] Jefferson's Seventh Annual Message, first draft, *Works:* Ford, x, 523–24.

[2] See notes of Gallatin and Rodney, *Works:* Ford, x, footnotes to 503–10.

[3] Jefferson's Seventh Annual Message, second draft, *Works:* Ford, x, 517. Blennerhassett, and probably Burr, would not have grieved had Marshall been impeached. It would be "penance for that timidity of conduct, which was probably as instrumental in keeping him from imbruing his hands in our blood as it was operative in inducing him to continue my vexations [the commitment of the conspirators to be tried in Ohio], to pacify the menaces and clamorous yells of the cerberus of Democracy with a sop which he would moisten, at least, with the tears of my family." (*Blennerhassett Papers:* Safford, 465.)

there can be little doubt that John Marshall would have been impeached by the House that was now all but unanimously Republican, and would have been convicted by the overwhelmingly Jeffersonian Senate.

Well for Marshall's peace of mind that he had secluded himself in the solitudes of the Blue Ridge, for never was an American judge subjected to abuse so unsparing. The Jeffersonian press, particularly the *Aurora* and the *Enquirer*, the two leading Republican papers, went to the limits of invective. "Let the judge be impeached," said the *Enquirer;* the Wickham dinner was recalled — why had Marshall attended it? His speech on the Jonathan Robins case [1] — "the price of his seat on the bench" — was "a lasting monument of his capacity to defend error."

Marshall's "wavering and irresolute spirit" manifested throughout the trial had disgusted everybody. His attempt to make his rulings "palatable to all parties" had "so often wrapt them in obscurity" that it was hard "to understand on which side the court had decided." His conduct had been inspired by "power illicitly obtained." And think of his encouragement to Burr's counsel to indulge in "unbounded . . slander and vilification" of the President! Callender's libel on Adams was insipid compared with Martin's vulgar billingsgate toward Jefferson! But that "awful tribunal" — the people — would try Marshall; before it "evidence

---

[1] See vol. II, 464–71, of this work.

will neither be perverted nor suppressed... The character of the Chief Justice awaits the issue." [1]

Another attack soon followed. Marshall's disgraceful conduct "has proved that the Judges are too independent of the people." Let them be made removable by the President on the address of Congress. The Chase trial had shown that impeachment could not be relied on to cleanse the bench of a judge no matter how "noxious," "ridiculous," "contemptible," or "immoral" he might be. But "shall an imposter be suffered to preside on the bench of justice?.. Are we to be eternally pestered with that most ridiculous and dangerous cant; that the people .. are incompetent to their own government: and that matters must be set over them and that barriers are to be raised up to protect those matters from the vengeance of the people?" [2]

Next came a series of "Letters to John Marshall," which appeared simultaneously in the *Aurora* and the *Enquirer*. They were written by William Thompson under the *nom de guerre* of "Lucius"; he undoubtedly was also the author of the earlier attacks on the Chief Justice in the *Enquirer*. They were widely copied in the Republican press of the country, and were a veracious expression of public sentiment.

"Your country, sir, owes you a debt of gratitude for former favors," which cannot be paid because

---

[1] "Portrait of the Chief Justice," in the Richmond *Enquirer*, Nov. 6, 1807. This article fills more than two closely printed columns. It discusses, and not without ability, the supposed errors in Marshall's opinions.

[2] *Enquirer*, Nov. 24, 1807.

"the whole stock of national indignation and contempt would be exhausted, before the half of your just claim could be discharged." Marshall had earned "infamy and detestation" by his efforts to erect "tyranny upon the tomb of freedom." His skill "in conducting the manouvres of a political party," his "crafty cunning" as a diplomat, had been perpetuated by the "genius" of John Thompson, whose "literary glory . . will shine when even the splendour of your talents and your crimes shall have faded forever. When your volumes of apology for British insolence and cruelty [1] shall be buried in oblivion, the 'Letters of Curtius ' [2] will . . 'damn you to everlasting fame.'" Marshall's entire life, according to Lucius, had been that of a sly, bigoted politician who had always worked against the people. He might have become "one of the boasted patriots of Virginia," but now he was "a disgrace to the bench of justice." He was a Jeffreys, a Bromley, a Mansfield. [3]

Quickly appeared a second letter to Marshall, accusing him of having "prostrated the dignity of the chief justice of the United States." Lucius goes into a lengthy analysis of Marshall's numerous opinions in the Burr trials. A just review of the proceedings, he said, demonstrates that the Chief Justice had "exhibited a culpable partiality towards the accused, and a shameless solicitude . . to implicate the government . . as negligent of their duty" —

[1] Marshall's *Life of Washington.*
[2] See vol. II, 395-96, of this work.
[3] "Letters to John Marshall, Chief Justice of the United States," in the *Aurora,* reprinted in the *Enquirer,* Dec. 1, 1807.

something that "a less malicious magistrate" never
would have dared to display.[1] A third letter continued the castigation of Marshall and the defense
of Jefferson. Closing an extended argument on
this joint theme, Lucius addressed Marshall thus:
"Common sense, and violated justice, cry aloud
against such conduct; and demand against you the
enforcement of these laws, which you refuse to administer." [2]

All these arraignments of Marshall had, as we
have seen,[3] been submitted to Jefferson. They rose
in the final letter to a climax of vituperation: "Could
I be instrumental in removing you from the elevation which you have dishonored by . . your crimes, I
would still trace you . . for screening a criminal and
degrading a judge" by the "juggle of a judicial
farce." Marshall and Burr were alike "morally
guilty," alike "traitors in heart and in fact. . . Such
a criminal and such a judge, few countries ever produced. . . You are forever doomed to blot the fair
page of American history, to be held up, as examples
of infamy and disgrace, of perverted talents and unpunished criminality, of foes to liberty and traitors
to your country." [4]

Incited by similar attacks in the Republican press
of Baltimore,[5] the more ardent patriots of that
place resolved publicly to execute Marshall in effigy, along with Burr, Blennerhassett, and Martin.
On the morning of November 3, satirical handbills,

---

[1] *Enquirer*, Dec. 4, 1807.
[2] *Ib.* Dec. 8, 1807. [3] See *supra*, 525–26.
[4] *Enquirer*, Dec. 12, 1807.
[5] *Blennerhassett Papers:* Safford, 475.

announcing this act of public justice, were scattered over the city:

AWFUL!!!

"The public are hereby notified that four 'choice spirits' are this afternoon, at 3 o'clock, to be marshaled for execution by the hangman, on Gallows Hill, in consequence of the sentence pronounced against them by the unanimous voice of every honest man in the community.

"The respective crimes for which they suffer are thus stated in the record:

"First, Chief Justice M. for a repetition of his X.Y.Z. tricks, which are said to be much aggravated by his *felonins* [*sic*] capers in open Court, on the plea of irrelevancy;

"Secondly, His Quid Majesty [Burr], charged with the trifling fault of wishing to divide the Union, and farm *Baron* Bastrop's grant;

"Thirdly, B[lennerhassett], the chemist, convicted of conspiracy to destroy the tone of the public Fiddle;

"Fourthly, and lastly, but not least, *Lawyer* Brandy-Bottle, for a false, scandalous, malicious Prophecy, that, before six months, 'Aaron Burr would divide the Union.'

"N.B. The execution of accomplices is postponed to a future day." [1]

Martin demanded of the Mayor the protection of the law. In response, police were sent to his house and to the Evans Hotel where Blennerhassett was

---

[1] *Blennerhassett Papers:* Safford, 477.

staying. Burr and the faithful Swartwout, who had accompanied his friend and leader, were escorted by a guard to the stage office, where they quickly left for Philadelphia.[1] Martin's law students and

[1] Gathering a few dollars from personal friends, Burr sailed for England, hoping to get from the British Government support for his plans to revolutionize Mexico. At first all went well. Men like Jeremy Bentham and Sir Walter Scott became his friends and admirers. But the hand of Jefferson followed him; and on representations of the American Minister, the British Government ordered him to leave the United Kingdom immediately.

Next he sought the ear of Napoleon; but again he was flouted and insulted by the American diplomatic and consular representatives — he was, they said, "a fugitive from justice." His last sou gone, ragged and often hungry, he managed at last, by the aid of one John Reeves, to secure passage for Boston, where he landed May 4, 1812. Then he journeyed to New York, where he arrived June 30 in abject poverty and utterly ruined. But still his spirit did not give way.

Soon, however, fate struck him the only blow that, until now, ever had brought this iron man to his knees. His passionately beloved little grandson, Aaron Burr Alston, died in June. In December, another and heavier stroke fell. His daughter sailed from Charleston, South Carolina, to join and comfort her father and be comforted by him. Her ship was lost in a storm, and Theodosia the beautiful, the accomplished, the adored, was drowned. Then, at last, the heart of Aaron Burr was broken.

Of the many ridiculous stories told of Burr and his daughter, one was that her ship was captured by pirates and she, ordered to walk the plank, did so with her child in her arms "without hesitation or visible tremor." This absurdity was given credit and currency by Harriet Martineau. (See Martineau: *Western Travels*, II, 291–92.) Theodosia's child had died six months before she sailed from Charleston to go to her father, and she embarked in a pilot boat, about which no pirate would have troubled himself.

The remainder of Burr's long life was given to the practice of his profession. His industry, legal learning, and ability, once more secured for him a good business. In 1824, Marshall ruled on an application to restore an attorney named Burr to the bar of the Circuit Court of the District of Columbia from which he had been suspended for unprofessional conduct. (*Ex parte* Burr, 9 Wheaton, 529–31.) It has often been erroneously supposed that this applicant was Aaron Burr: he was, however, one Levi Burr, a local practitioner, and not related to Aaron Burr.

It is characteristic of Burr that he remembered the great lawyer

other friends armed themselves to resist violence to him.

A policeman named Goldsmith notified Blenner-

who voluntarily had hastened to defend him at Richmond, and Luther Martin — aged, infirm, and almost deranged — was taken to the home of Aaron Burr and tenderly cared for until he died. Burr's marriage, at the age of seventy-eight, to Madame Jumel was, on his part, inexplicable; it was the only regrettable but not unworthy incident of the latter years of his life. (See Shelton: *Jumel Mansion*, 170–74.)

Burr's New York friends were loyal to him to his very last day. His political genius never grew dim. He early suggested and helped to bring about the nomination of Andrew Jackson for the Presidency. Thus did he pay the debt of gratitude for the loyalty with which the rugged Tennesseean had championed his cause against public opinion and Administration alike.

During the summer of 1836 his last illness came upon him. When his physician said that he could live but a few hours longer, a friend at his bedside asked the supposedly expiring man "whether in the expedition to the Southwest he had designed a separation of the Union." Believing himself to be dying, Burr replied: "No! I would as soon have thought of taking possession of the moon and informing my friends that I intended to divide it among them." To a man, his most intimate friends believed this statement to be true.

Finally, on September 14, 1836, Aaron Burr died and was buried near his father at Princeton, New Jersey, where the parent had presided over, and the son had attended, that Alma Mater of so many patriots, soldiers, and statesmen.

For two years his burial place was unmarked. Then, at night-time, unknown friends erected over his grave a plain marble shaft, bearing this inscription:

AARON BURR

Born Feb. 6, 1756
Died Sept. 14, 1836
Colonel in the Army of the Revolution
Vice-President of the United States from 1801 to 1805

(*Gulf States Historical Magazine*, II, 379.)

Parton's *Life of Burr* is still the best story of this strange life. But Parton must be read with great care, for he sometimes makes statements which are difficult of verification.

A brief, engaging, and trustworthy account of the Burr episode is *Aaron Burr*, by Isaac Jenkinson. Until the appearance of Professor McCaleb's book, *The Aaron Burr Conspiracy*, Mr. Jenkinson's little

hassett that a great mob was gathering, "had everything prepared for tarring and feathering and would,
.. if disappointed or opposed, tear Martin [and
Blennerhassett] to pieces." The manager of the
hotel begged Blennerhassett to hide in the garret
of the hostelry. This the forlorn Irishman did,
and beheld from a window in the attic what passed
below.

Shouting and huzzaing men poured by, headed
by fifers and drummers playing the "Rogue's
march." Midway in the riotous throng were drawn
two carts containing effigies of Chief Justice Marshall
and the other popularly condemned men "habited
for execution. . . Two troops of cavalry patrolled
the streets, not to disperse the mob, but to follow
and behold their conduct." At Martin's house the
crowd stopped for a moment, hurling threats and
insults, jeering at and defying the armed defenders
within and "the cavalry without."

Making "as much noise as if they were about to
destroy the city," these devotees of justice and liberty proceeded to the place of public execution.
There, amid roars of approval, the effigy of John
Marshall, Chief Justice of the United States, was
hanged by the neck until the executioner pronounced
the stuffed figure to be dead. About him dangled
from the gibbet the forms of the "traitors" — Aaron
Burr and Harman Blennerhassett — and also that
of Luther Martin, who had dared to defend them

volume was the best on that subject. Professor McCaleb's thorough
and scholarly study is, however, the only exhaustive and reliable
narrative of that ambitious plan and the disastrous outcome of the
attempted execution of it.

and had thus incurred the malediction of Thomas Jefferson and "the people." [1]

In the Senate Giles reported a bill to punish as traitors persons who permitted or aided in the perpetration of certain acts, "although not personally present when any such act was done"; and he supported it in an argument of notable ability. He powerfully attacked Marshall, analyzed his opinions in the Burr case, contrasted them with those of other National judges, and pointed out the resulting confusion in the interpretation of the law. All this was spoken, however, with careful regard to the rules of parliamentary discussion. [2]

Legislation was necessary, said Giles; as matters stood, the decisions of judges on treason were like Congress "enacting our speeches, interspersed with our laws." With what result? No two judges have yet delivered the same opinion upon some of the most essential features of treason. Take for example the British doctrine that, in treason, accessories are principals. Were they in America? "Judge Chase and others say they are. Judge Marshall says he does not know whether they are or not, but his reasoning would go to show that they are not." [3]

Solely to gratify *vox populi*, the Senate next indulged in a doubtful performance. An attempt was made to expel Senator John Smith of Ohio. With

---

[1] *Blennerhassett Papers:* Safford, 480–82; also see *Baltimore American*, Nov. 4, 5, 6, 1807.

[2] *Annals*, 10th Cong. 1st Sess. 108–27.

[3] The bill passed the Senate, but foreign affairs, and exciting legislation resulting from these, forced it from the mind of the House. (See vol. IV, chap. I, of this work.)

only a partial examination, and without allowing him to call a single witness in his own behalf beforehand, a special Senate Committee[1] presented a report concluding with a resolution to expel Smith because of "his participation in the conspiracy of Aaron Burr against the peace, union and liberties of the people of the United States." [2] This surprising document was the work of John Quincy Adams,[3] who apparently adopted the ideas and almost the language of Lucius.

Burr's conspiracy, wrote Adams, was so evil and was "established by such a mass of concurring and mutually corroborative testimony" that the "honor" of the Senate and "the deepest interests of this

[1] John Quincy Adams of Massachusetts, Samuel Maclay of Pennsylvania, Jesse Franklin of North Carolina, Samuel Smith of Maryland, John Pope of Kentucky, Buckner Thruston of Kentucky, and Joseph Anderson of Tennessee. (*Annals*, 10th Cong. 1st Sess. 42.)

[2] Smith had been indicted for treason and misdemeanor, but Hay had entered a *nolle prosequi* on the bills of indictment after the failure of the Burr prosecution. (*Memoirs, J. Q. A.*: Adams, I, 481.)

[3] Adams had been indulging in political maneuvers that indicated a courtship of the Administration and a purpose to join the Republican Party. His course had angered and disgusted most of his former Federalist friends and supporters, who felt that he had deserted his declining party in order to advance his political fortunes. If this were true, his performance in writing the Committee report on the resolution to expel Smith was well calculated to endear him to Jefferson. Adams expressed his own views thus: "On most of the great national questions now under discussion, my sense of duty leads me to support the administration, and I find myself of course in opposition to the federalists in general. . . My political prospects are declining." (*Memoirs, J. Q. A.*: Adams, I, 497–98.)

The Federalist Legislature of Massachusetts grossly insulted Adams by electing his successor before Adams's term in the Senate had expired. Adams resigned, and in March, 1809, President Madison appointed him Minister to Russia, and later Minister to Great Britain. President Monroe made the former Federalist his Secretary of State. No Republican was more highly honored by these two Republican Presidents than was John Quincy Adams.

nation" required that nobody connected with it should be a member of Congress. After an unctuous recitation of accepted generalities and a review of the expulsion of Senator Blount, together with an excellent statement of the law of parliamentary bodies in such cases, Adams got down to the business of destroying John Marshall.[1]

Marshall had "withheld from the jury . . a great part of the testimony which was essential to [Burr's] conviction. . . In consequence of this suppression of evidence" the trial jury had not been allowed to find a verdict of guilty against the traitor. Marshall's "decisions, forming the basis of the issue upon the trials of Burr . . were the sole inducements upon which the counsel for the United States abandoned the prosecution against him" (Smith). An American grand jury had charged Senator Smith with being "an accomplice" of these diabolical plans, and the safety which Marshall's decisions in the Burr trial had thrown around Smith and other associates of the traitor "cannot, in the slightest degree, remove the imputation" which the indictment of Smith had brought to his door.

---

[1] Adams did not, of course, mention Marshall by name. His castigation of the Chief Justice, however, was the more severe because of the unmistakable designation of him. (See *Writings*, *J. Q. A.*: Ford, III, 173–84; also *Annals*, 10th Cong. 1st Sess. 56–63.)

It must be remembered, too, that this attack upon Marshall comes from the son of the man who, on January 20, 1801, appointed Marshall Chief Justice. (See vol. II, 552–53, of this work.) But John Quincy Adams soon came to be one of the stanchest supporters and most ardent admirers that Marshall ever had. It was peculiarly characteristic of Marshall that he did not resent the attack of Adams and, for the only time in his judicial career, actually interested himself in politics in behalf of Adams. (See vol. IV, chap. IX, of this work.)

"If," wrote Adams, "the daylight of evidence combining one vast complicated intention, with overt acts innumerable, be not excluded from the mind by the curtain of artificial rules, the simplest understanding cannot but see what the subtlest understanding cannot disguise, crimes before which ordinary treason whitens into virtue" and beyond "the ingenuity of a demon."

Adams continued: "Whether the transactions proved against Aaron Burr did or did not amount, in technical language, to an overt act of levying war, your committee have not a scruple of doubt .. that, but for the vigilance and energy of the government, and of faithful citizens under its directions .. in crushing his designs, they would .. have terminated not only in war, but in a war of the most horrible description, . . at once foreign and domestic."

To such lengths can popular demand, however unjust, drive even cold, unemotional, and upright men who are politically ambitious. Adams's Federalist confrères reacted quickly;[1] and the *New*

---

[1] Adams's colleague Senator Pickering was, of course, disgusted (see his letter to King, Jan. 2, 1808, King, v, 44), and in a pamphlet entitled "A Review of the Correspondence Between the Hon. John Adams and the late William Cunningham, Esq." which he published in 1824, Pickering wrote that the resolution "outraged .. every distinguished lawyer in America" (see p. 41 of pamphlet). King thought Adams "indiscreet" (see his letter to Pickering, Jan. 7, 1808, King, v, 50). Plumer declared that the report "had given mortal offence" in New Hampshire (see *Mass. Historical Society Proceedings*, XLV, 357). John Lowell asserted that "justice .. was to be dragged from her seat .. and the eager minister of presidential vengeance seemed to sigh after the mild mercies of the star chamber, and the rapid movements of the revolutionary tribunal" (see his "Remarks" as quoted in *Writings*, *J. Q. A.*: Ford, III, footnote to 184).

York Evening Post sharply criticized him.[1] When
the report came up in the Senate, James A. Bayard
of Delaware, and James Hillhouse of Connecticut,
attacked it and its author with "unusual virulence."
Bayard was especially severe.[2] Thus assailed, Adams
was cast into black depression: "It is indeed a fiery
ordeal I have to go through. God speed me through
it!" he wrote in his diary that night.[3]

William Branch Giles cast the deciding vote which
defeated Adams's resolution — the Senate refusing
to expel Smith by a vote of 19 yeas to 10 nays,[4] just
one short of the necessary two thirds. The Virginia
Republican Senator attacked the resolution with
all his fiery eloquence, and compelled the admiration
even of Adams himself.[5] "I shall vote against the
resolution," Giles concluded, "solely from the conviction of the innocence of the accused." [6]

Herefrom one may judge the temper of the times
and the perilous waters through which John Marshall
had been compelled to pilot the craft of justice. If
that "most deliberative legislative body" in our
Government, and the one least affected by popular
storms, was so worked upon, one can perceive the

[1] Jan. 28, 1808, *Memoirs, J. Q. A.*: Adams, I, 508; see also *Writings,
J. Q. A.*: Ford, III, footnote to 184.

[2] "He poured himself forth in his two speeches to-day. . . It was
all a phillipic upon me." (Jan. 7, 1808, *Memoirs, J. Q. A.*: Adams,
I, 501.)

[3] *Ib.*   [4] *Annals*, 10th Cong. 1st Sess. 324.

[5] "Mr. Giles, in one of the most animated and eloquent speeches I
ever heard him make, declared himself . . against the resolution for
expulsion. He argued the case of Mr. Smith with all his eloquence,
and returned to the charge with increasing warmth until the last
moment." (April 9, 1808, *Memoirs, J. Q. A.*: Adams, I, 528.)

[6] *Annals*, 10th Cong. 1st Sess. 321–24.

conditions that surrounded the Chief Justice in overcrowded Richmond during the trial of Aaron Burr, and the real impending danger for Marshall, after the acquittal of the man whom Jefferson and the majority had branded with the most hideous infamy.

Fortunate, indeed, for the Chief Justice of the United States, and for the stability of American institutions, that the machinery of impeachment was, during these fateful months, locked because the President, Congress, and the Nation were forced to give their attention to the grave foreign situation which could no longer be ignored.

Going about his duties in Washington, or, at home, plodding out to the farm near Richmond, joking or gossiping with friends, and caring for his afflicted wife, Marshall heard the thunders of popular denunciation gradually swallowed up in the louder and ever-increasing reverberations that heralded approaching war with Great Britain. Before the clash of arms arrived, however, his level common sense and intelligent courage were again called upon to deal with another of those perplexing conditions which produced, one by one, opinions from the Supreme Bench that have become a part of the living, growing, yet stable and enduring Constitution of the American Nation.

CHAPTER X

FRAUD AND CONTRACT

If I were to characterize the United States, it should be by the appellation of the land of speculation.   (William Priest.)

By the God of Heaven, if we go on in this way, our nation will sink into disgrace and slavery.   (John Tyler.)

Millions of acres are easily digested by such stomachs. They buy and sell corruption in the gross. (John Randolph.)

When a law is in its nature a contract, when absolute rights have vested under that contract, a repeal of the law cannot divest those rights. The people can act only by their agents and, within the powers conferred upon them, their acts must be considered as the acts of the people.   (Marshall.)

THE Honorable William Longstreet was an active and influential member of the Georgia Legislature during the winter of 1794–95. He was also a practical man. An important bill was then before that body, and Mr. Longstreet employed effective methods to forward its passage. The proposed legislation was to authorize the sale to four speculating land companies [1] of most of that territory which comprises the present States of Alabama and Mississippi.

"Why are you not in favor of selling the western lands?" frequently asked Representative Longstreet of his fellow member, Clem Lanier. "Because I do not think it right to sell to companies of speculators," was the answer. "Better vote for the bill," observed his seat mate, Representative Henry Gindrat, one day as they sat chatting before the Speaker of the House took the chair. "It will be worth your while. Senator Thomas Wylly says that he can have eight or ten likely negroes for his part."

[1] See *infra*, 550.

That afternoon Senator Wylly came to Lanier and began to talk of the land bill. A Mr. Dennison sauntered up. Wylly left, and the newcomer remarked that, of course, he advised no legislator how to vote, but he could not help noticing that all who favored the sale of the lands "were handsomely provided for." If Lanier should support the bill, he would be taken care of like the rest. He was buying, Dennison said, from members who wished to sell lands allotted to them for agreeing to support the measure.

Once more came Longstreet, who "presented a certificate entitling the bearer to two shares of twenty-five thousand acres each," as security that Lanier would be rewarded if he voted for the sale bill. The obdurate Representative, who wished to probe the depths of the plot, objected, and Longstreet assured him that he would immediately procure "another certificate . . for the same number of acres." But Lanier finally declined the bribe of seventy-five thousand acres of land.[1]

Representative Gindrat had offered to sell his shares for one thousand dollars, the price generally given; but, securing "a better market," declined that sum.[2] Representative Lachlan M'Intosh received six shares in one of the land companies, which he sold at a premium of two hundred and fifty dollars each.[3]

After the bill had passed, Senator Robert Thomas,

[1] Affidavit of Clem Lanier, *Am. State Papers, Public Lands*, i, 145.
[2] Affidavit of Peter L. Van Allen, *ib.*
[3] *Ib.* It would appear that one hundred and fifty thousand acres were allotted to the thrifty Scotch legislator. He sold them for $7500.

who had no means of acquiring ready cash,[1] brought
two thousand dollars to the house where he boarded
and asked Philip Clayton, the owner, to keep it for
him. Clayton was curious — did Senator Thomas
get the money for his share of the lands? he inquired.
"It is nothing to you; take care of it," answered the
suddenly affluent legislator, smiling.[2]

Representative Longstreet offered Representative
John Shepperd one hundred thousand acres, but
Shepperd was not interested; then Philip Clayton,
the tavern-keeper, offered him seventy pounds to go
home for the session.[3]

A saturnalia of corruption was in progress in the
little village of Augusta, where the Legislature of
Georgia was in session.[4] The leading men of that
and neighboring States were on the ground urging
the enactment of the law in which all were interested.
Wade Hampton of South Carolina was on hand.
State and National judges were present. James
Wilson of Pennsylvania, Associate Justice of the
Supreme Court of the United States, was there
with twenty-five thousand dollars in bank bills.[5]

---

[1] Affidavit of John Thomas, Jr., *Am. State Papers, Public Lands*,
I, 148.

[2] Affidavit of Philip Clayton, *ib.* 146.

[3] Affidavit of John Shepperd, *ib.*

[4] About sixty affidavits were made to show the venality of members
of the Legislature. Of these, twenty-one are printed in *ib.* 144–49.

[5] Harris: *Georgia from the Invasion of De Soto to Recent Times*,
127–28; White: *Statistics of the State of Georgia*, 50; Chappell: *Miscellanies of Georgia*, 93–95.

These writers leave the unjust inference that Wilson was one of
those who were corrupting the Legislature. This is almost certainly
untrue. For a quarter of a century Wilson had been a heavy speculator
in Indian lands, and it appears reasonable that he took this money
to Augusta for the purpose of investment. When the deal was con-

William Smith, Judge of the Superior Court of
Georgia, added his influence, receiving for his services as lobbyist thirteen thousand dollars. Nathaniel Pendleton, Judge of the United States Court for
that district, urged the legislation and signed and
issued the certificates for shares that were given
to the members for their votes.[1] Directing all
was General James Gunn, United States Senator
from Georgia: his first term in the National Senate
about to expire, he was now reëlected by this very
Legislature.[2]

A majority of Georgia's lawmaking body thus
became financially interested in the project, and
the bill passed both houses. But Governor George
Mathews vetoed the measure, because he thought
the time not propitious for selling the lands, the price
too low, the reservations for Georgians too small,
and the principle of monopoly wrong.[3] Another bill
was prepared to meet some of the Governor's objections. This was introduced as a supplement to a law
just enacted to pay the State troops.[4] Again every
possible influence was brought upon the Legislature
to pass this bill with utmost dispatch.[5] Some mem-

summated, the Justice held shares to the amount of at least three
quarters of a million of acres. (Chappell, 94.)

[1] *Ib.* 95.

[2] Gunn's reëlection was the first step in the conspiracy. Not until
that was accomplished was a word said about the sale of the lands.
Immediately after the Legislature had chosen Gunn for a second term
in the National Senate, however, the bill was introduced and the
campaign of intimidation and bribery launched, to force its passage.
(*Ib.* 82–83.)

[3] See Mathews's reasons, as quoted in the Rescinding Act of 1796,
Am. State Papers, Public Lands, I, 156.

[4] Chappell, 86.

[5] The claims of Spain to the territory had been a serious cloud on

bers, who would not support it, were induced to leave the tiny Georgia Capital; others, who were recalcitrant, were browbeaten and bullied.

Senator Gunn, the field marshal of this legislative campaign, strode about the village arrayed in broadcloth, top boots, and beaver hat, commending those who favored the bill, abusing those who opposed it. In his hand he carried a loaded whip, and with this the burly Senator actually menaced members who objected to the scheme.[1] In a little more than one week the bill was rushed through both houses. This time it received the reluctant approval of the Governor, and on January 7, 1795, became a law.

In such fashion was enacted the legislation which disposed of more than thirty-five million acres of fertile, well-watered, heavily wooded land at less than one and one half cents an acre.[2] The purchasers were four companies known as The Georgia Company, The Georgia Mississippi Company, The Tennessee Company, and The Upper Mississippi Company. The total purchase price was five hundred thousand dollars in specie or approved currency, one fifth to be deposited with the State Treasurer before the passage of the act, and the remainder to

the title. In October, 1795, the treaty with the Spanish Government, which removed this defect, was published. Senator James Gunn had knowledge that the treaty would be negotiated long before it was made known to the world or even concluded. This fact was one of the reasons for the mad haste with which the corrupt sale act was rushed through the Georgia Legislature. (See Chappell, 72–73.)

[1] Gunn was a perfect example of the corrupt, yet able, bold, and demagogical politician. He was a master of the arts alike of cajolery and intimidation. For a vivid account of this man see Chappell, 99–105.

[2] Haskins: *Yazoo Land Companies*, 24.

be paid on or before November 1, 1795. The Governor was directed to execute a deed in fee-simple to the men composing each company as tenants in common; and the deferred payments were secured by mortgages to the Governor, to be immediately foreclosed upon default of payment, and the one fifth already deposited to be forfeited to the State.

Two million acres were reserved for exclusive entry by citizens of Georgia, and the land companies were bound to form settlements within five years after the Indian titles had been extinguished. The lands were declared free of taxation until they should be so occupied that the settlers were represented in the Legislature.[1] Governor Mathews executed deeds in compliance with the law, and, the entire amount of the purchase money having been paid into the State Treasury before November 1, the mortgages were canceled and the transaction was closed in accordance with the provisions of the statute. So far as that legislation and the steps taken in pursuance of it could bring about such a result, the legal title to practically all of the domain stretching from the present western boundary of Georgia to the Mississippi River, and from the narrow strip of Spanish territory on the Gulf to the Tennessee line, was transferred to the men composing these four land companies. The greatest real estate deal in history was thus consummated.

But even while this bill was before the Legislature, popular opposition to it began. A young man of twenty-three was then teaching in a little school-

[1] *Am. State Papers, Public Lands*, I, 151-52.

house at Augusta, but he was destined to become
United States Senator, Minister to France, Secretary of the Treasury, and candidate for President.
Enraged at what he believed the despoiling of the
people by a band of robbers using robbers' methods,
young William H. Crawford hurried to his home in
Columbia County, got up a petition to the Governor
to reject the bill again, and hurried to the Capital
where he presented it to the Chief Executive of the
State.[1] But Governor Mathews, against whom no
man, then or thereafter, charged corrupt motives,
persisted in signing the measure.

And it must be said that the bill was not without
merit. Georgia was but thinly populated, not more
than fifty thousand human beings inhabiting its
immense extent of savanna and forest. Most of
these people were very poor[2] and unable to pay any
public charges whatever. The State Treasury was
empty; the State troops, who had been employed in
the endless Indian troubles, were unpaid and clamoring for the money long due them; the State currency had so depreciated that it was almost without
value. No commonwealth in the Union was in worse
financial case.[3]

Moreover, the titles of the Indians, who occupied
the country and who were its real owners, had not
been extinguished. Under the Constitution, the National Government alone could deal with the tribes,

---

[1] Chappell, 87.

[2] "A small smoky cabin with a dirt floor was the home of most of
them." (Smith: *Story of Georgia and the Georgia People*, 181.) For
a good description of pioneer houses and manner of living, see Ramsey: *Annals of Tennessee to the End of the Eighteenth Century*, 715–16.

[3] Smith, 170–71.

and it had long been urging Georgia to cede her claims to the United States, as Virginia and Connecticut had done. Indeed, the State had once offered to make this cession, but on such terms that Congress had refused to accept it. The purchasers now took whatever title Georgia had, subject to these burdens, the State to be saved from all annoyance on account of them.

The tribes were powerful and brave, and they had been prompt and bold in the defense of their lands. The Creeks alone could put nearly six thousand fighting men in the field, and the Choctaws had more than four thousand trained warriors.[1] The feeble and impoverished State had never been able to subdue them, or to enforce in the slightest degree the recognition of the State's title to the country they inhabited. Georgia's right to their lands "depended on her power to dispossess the Indians; but however good the title might be, the State would have been fortunate to make it a free gift to any authority strong enough to deal with the Creeks and Cherokees alone."[2]

The sale of the territory was not a new or novel project. Six years earlier the State had disposed of twenty-five million five hundred thousand acres of the same territory to four land companies on much poorer terms.[3] Jefferson, then Secretary of State, rendered a careful opinion on the right of Georgia to

[1] Morse's *American Gazetteer*, as quoted in Bishop: *Georgia Speculation Unveiled*, 3–4.

[2] Adams: *U.S.* i, 303.

[3] The South Carolina Yazoo Company, 10,000,000 acres for $66,964; The Virginia Yazoo Company, 11,400,000 acres for $93,741; The Tennessee Company, 4,000,000 acres for $46,875. (Haskins, 8.)

make the grant.[1] These purchasers had tendered
payment in South Carolina and Continental scrip
that was practically worthless; the Treasurer of
Georgia had properly refused to accept it; and there
ended the transaction as far as the State was concerned. A suit was later brought against Georgia by
the grantees [2] to compel the performance of the contract; but the Eleventh Amendment of the Constitution, which this litigation produced, thwarted that
legal plan. So these speculators dropped the matter
until the sale just described was made to the new
companies six years later.

The most active promoters of the first purchasing
companies, in 1789, were mere adventurers, although
at first Patrick Henry and other men of honor and
repute were interested in the speculation. Henry,
however, soon withdrew.[3] The consummation of
their deal with Georgia required the payment of
sound money and *bona-fide* settlement by actual
tillers of the soil. Also, the adventurers got into
trouble with the Indians, became gravely involved
in Spanish intrigue, and collided with the National
Government;[4] so the enterprise lost, for a time, all
attractiveness for these speculators.

The new land companies, on the other hand, were
for the most part composed of men of excellent reputations.[5] At the head of the largest, The Georgia

[1] *Works:* Ford, vi, 55–57.
[2] Chisholm *vs.* Georgia, 2 Dallas, 419; and see vol. ii, 83–84, of
this work.
[3] Chappell, 92–93.   [4] *Ib.* 67–68; Haskins, 13–15.
[5] "No men stood higher in Georgia than the men who composed
these several companies and the members of the Legislature who made
the sale." (Smith, 173.)

Company, were United States Senator James Gunn and United States Attorney for the District of Georgia, Mathew McAlister; associated with them, in addition to Judges Stith and Pendleton, and Justice Wilson, were Robert Goodloe Harper, Representative in Congress from Maryland, Robert Morris, the financier of the Revolution, and others of substance and position.[1] Also, as has been stated, they paid for their lands in the money called for by the act — the best money then circulating in America. The first sales of Indian lands to which Georgia claimed title were known as the "Yazoo" speculation, and this designation stuck to the second transaction.

In the six years that had intervened between the sales to the irresponsible land-jobbers of 1789 and the solvent investors of 1795, an event of world importance had occurred which doubled and trebled the value of all cotton-bearing soil. Eli Whitney, a Connecticut school-teacher twenty-seven years of age, had gone to Georgia in 1792 to act as a private tutor. Finding the position taken, he studied law while the guest of the widow of General Nathanael Greene. This discerning woman, perceiving that the young man was gifted with inventive genius, set him to work on a device for separating cotton from the seed. The machine was built, and worked perfectly. The news of it traveled with astonishing rapidity throughout Georgia and the South. The model was stolen; and so simple was the construction of it that everywhere in cotton-growing lands it

[1] See Haskins, 25, and sources there cited.

was freely reproduced by planters great and small.
The vast sweep of territory stretching from Georgia
to the Father of Waters, the best cotton land in the
world, thus rose in value as if the wand of a financial
deity had been waved over it. Settlers poured into
Georgia by the thousand, and Indian atrocities were
now as little feared as Indian rights were respected.[1]

The purchase of the unoccupied Georgia lands by
the *bona-fide*, if piratical, land companies of 1795
became, therefore, an adventure far more valuable
in possibilities for the investors, and incomparably
more attractive in the probability of political advantage to those who resisted it, than the innocuous and
unopposed sale to the Yazoo swindlers of six years
previous.

So it fell out that the mechanical genius of Eli
Whitney, in 1793, called into action, exactly eighteen
years afterward, the judicial genius of John Marshall.
His opinion in Fletcher *vs.* Peck was one of the first
steps toward the settling of the law of public contract in the riotous young Republic — one of the
earliest and strongest judicial assertions of the supremacy of Nationalism over Localism. And never
more than at that particular time did an established
rule on these vital subjects so need to be announced
by the highest judicial authority.

Since before the Revolution, all men had fixed
their eyes, hopes, and purposes upon land. Not the

---

[1] The effect of Whitney's invention is shown in striking fashion
by the increase of cotton exports. In 1791 only 189,500 pounds were
exported from the entire United States. Ten years later Georgia alone
exported 3,444,420 pounds. (Jones and Dutcher: *Memorial History
of Augusta, Georgia,* 165.)

humble and needy only, but the high-placed and
opulent, had looked to the soil — the one as their
chief source of livelihood, and the other as a means
of profitable speculation. Indeed, dealing in land
was the most notable economic fact in the early
years of the American Nation. "Were I to characterize the *United States*," chronicles one of the
most acute British travelers and observers of the
time, "it should be by the appellation of the *land of
speculation*." [1]

From the Nation's beginning, the States had lax
notions as to the sacredness of public contracts, and
often violated the obligations of them. [2] Private
agreements stood on a somewhat firmer basis, but
even these were looked upon with none too ardent
favor. The most familiar forms of contract-breaking
were the making legal tender of depreciated paper,
and the substitution of property for money; but other
devices were also resorted to. So it was that the provision, "no state shall pass any law impairing the
obligation of contracts," was placed in the Constitution. [3] The effect of this on the public mind, as re-

[1] Priest: *Travels in the United States*, 132; and see Haskins, 3.
Otis speaks of the "land jobbing prospectors," and says that
"money is the object here [Boston] with all ranks and degrees."
(Otis to Harper, April 10, 1807, Morison: *Otis*, I, 283.)
The national character "is degenerated into a system of stock-
jobbing, extortion and usury. . . By the God of Heaven, if we go on
in this way, our nation will sink into disgrace and slavery." (Tyler
to Madison, Jan. 15, 1810, Tyler, I, 235.)

[2] See vol. I, 428, of this work.

[3] It was, however, among the last items proposed to the Convention, which had been at work more than three months before the
"contract clause" was suggested. Even then the proposal was only
as to *new* States. The motion was made by Rufus King of New York
on August 28. Gouverneur Morris objected. "This would be going

ported by conservatives like Marshall, is stated in the *Commercial Gazette* of Boston, January 28, 1799: "State laws protected debtors" when they "were citizens .. [and] the creditors foreigners. The federal constitution, prohibiting the states to clear off debts *without payment*, by exacting *justice*, seemed .. to establish *oppression*." The debtors, therefore, "pronounced .. the *equal* reign of law and debt-compelling justice, the beginning of an insidious attack on liberty and the erection of aristocracy."

too far," he said. George Mason of Virginia said the same thing. Madison thought "a negative on the State laws could alone secure the effect." James Wilson of Pennsylvania warmly supported King's motion. John Rutledge of South Carolina moved, as a substitute for King's proposition, that States should not pass "bills of attainder nor retrospective laws." (*Records, Fed. Conv.*: Farrand, II, 440.) This carried, and nothing more appears as to the contract clause until it was included by the Committee on Style in its report of September 12. (*Ib.* 596–97.) Elbridge Gerry of Massachusetts strongly favored it and even wanted Congress "to be laid under the like prohibitions." (*Ib.* 619.) The Convention refused to insert the word "previous" before "obligation." (*Ib.* 636.)

In this manner the provision that "no state shall pass any law impairing the obligation of contracts" was inserted in the Constitution. The framers of that instrument apparently had in mind, however, the danger of the violation of contracts through depreciated paper money rather than the invalidation of agreements by the direct action of State Legislatures. (See speech of William R. Davie in the North Carolina Convention, July 29, 1788, *ib.* III, 349–50; speech of James McHenry before the Maryland House of Delegates, Nov. 29, 1787, *ib.* 150; and speech of Luther Martin before same, same date, *ib.* 214; also see Madison to Ingersoll, Feb. 2, 1831, *ib.* 495.)

Madison best stated the reason for the adoption of the contract clause: "A violations [*sic*] of Contracts had become familiar in the form of depreciated paper made a legal tender, of property substituted for money, of Instalment laws, and of the occlusions of the Courts of Justice; although evident that all such interferences affected the rights of other States, relatively Creditor, as well as Citizens Creditors within the State." (*Ib.* 548.) Roger Sherman and Oliver Ellsworth explained briefly that the clause "was thought necessary as a security to commerce." (Letter to the Governor of Connecticut, Sept. 26, 1787, *ib.* 100.)

The "contract clause" of the Constitution was
now to be formally challenged by a "sovereign"
State for the first time since the establishment of
the National Government. Georgia was to assert
her "sovereignty" by the repudiation of her laws
and the denial of contractual rights acquired under
them. And this she was to do with every apparent
consideration of morality and public justice to support her.

The tidings of the corruption attending the second
"Yazoo" sale were carried over the State on the
wings of fury. A transaction which six years before
had met with general acquiescence,[1] now received
deep-throated execration. The methods by which
the sale was pushed through the Legislature mad-
dened the people, and their wrath was increased by
the knowledge that the invention of the Connecticut
schoolmaster had tremendously enhanced the value
of every acre of cotton-bearing soil.

Men who lived near Augusta assembled and
marched on the Capital determined to lynch their
legislative betrayers. Only the pleadings of members
who had voted against the bill saved the lives of
their guilty associates.[2] Meetings were held in every
hamlet. Shaggy backwoodsmen met in "old-field"
log schoolhouses and denounced "the steal." The
burning in effigy of Senator Gunn became a favorite
manifestation of popular wrath. The public indignation was strengthened by the exercise of it. Those
responsible for the enactment of the law found it
perilous to be seen in any crowd. One member left

[1] Chappell, 67.   [2] Harris, 130.

the State. Another escaped hanging only by precipitate flight.[1] Scores of resolutions were passed by town, rural, and backwoods assemblages demanding that the fraudulent statute be rescinded. Petitions, circulated from the "mansion" of the wealthy planter to the squalid cabin of the poorest white man, were signed by high and low alike. The grand juries of every county in Georgia, except two, formally presented as a grievance the passage of the land sale act of 1795.

Among other things, the land sale act required the Senators and Representatives of Georgia in Congress to urge the National Government to speed the making of a treaty with the Indian tribes extinguishing their title to the lands which the State had sold. Upon receiving a copy of the nefarious law, Senator James Jackson of Georgia laid it before the Senate, together with a resolution declaring that that body would "advise and consent" to the President's concluding any arrangement that would divest the Indians of their claims.[2]

But although he had full knowledge of the methods by which the act was passed, the records do not show that Jackson then gave the slightest expression to that indignation which he so soon thereafter poured forth. Nor is there any evidence that he said a word on the subject when, on March 2, 1795, Georgia's title again came before the Senate.[3]

---

[1] Harris, 131.

[2] Feb. 27, 1795, *Annals*, 3d Cong. 1st and 2d Sess. 838–39.

[3] *Ib.* 844–45. The silence of Jackson at this time is all the more impressive because the report of the Attorney-General would surely be used by the land companies to encourage investors to buy. Both

Some time afterward, however, Senator Jackson
hurried home and put himself at the head of the
popular movement against the "Yazoo Frauds."
In every corner of the State, from seaport to re-
motest settlement, his fiery eloquence roused the
animosity of the people to still greater frenzy. In two
papers then published in Georgia, the *Savannah
Gazette* and the *Augusta Chronicle*, the Senator, under the *nom de guerre* of "Sicillius," published a series
of articles attacking with savage violence the sale
law and all connected with the enactment of it.[1]

It came out that every member of the Legislature
who had voted for the measure, except one,[2] had
shares of stock in the purchasing companies.[3] Stories of the extent of the territory thus bartered away
kept pace with tales of the venality by which the
fraud was effected. Bad as the plain facts were,
they became simply monstrous when magnified by
the imagination of the public.

Nearly every man elected[4] to the new Legislature
was pledged to vote for the undoing of the fraud in
any manner that might seem the most effective.
Senator Jackson had resigned from the National
Senate in order to become a member of the Georgia
House of Representatives; and to this office he
was overwhelmingly elected. When the Legislature

Jackson and Gunn were present when King offered his resolution.
(*Annals*, 3d Cong. 1st and 2d Sess. 846.) Jackson declined to vote
on the passage of a House bill "making provision for the purposes of
treaty" with the Indians occupying the Yazoo lands. (*Ib.* 849–50.)

[1] Smith, 174.   [2] Robert Watkins.
[3] See Report of the Commissioners, *Am. State Papers, Public
Lands*, I, 132–35.
[4] The "Yazoo men" carried two counties.

convened in the winter of 1795–96, it forthwith went about the task of destroying the corrupt work of its predecessor. Jackson was the undisputed leader;[1] his associates passed, almost unanimously, and Governor Irwin promptly approved, the measure which Jackson wrote.[2] Thus was produced that enactment by a "sovereign" State, the validity of which John Marshall was solemnly to deny from the Supreme Bench of the Nation.

Jackson's bill was a sprightly and engaging document. The preamble was nearly three times as long as the act itself, and abounded in interminable sentences. It denounced the land sale act as a violation of both State and National Constitutions, as the creation of a monopoly, as the dismemberment of Georgia, as the betrayal of the rights of man. In this fashion the "whereases" ran on for some thousands of words. On second thought the Legislature concluded that the law was worse than unconstitutional — it was, the "whereases" declared, a "usurped act." That part of the preamble dealing with the mingled questions of fraud and State sovereignty deserves quotation in full:

"And Whereas," ran this exposition of Constitutional law and of the nature of contracts, "divested

---

[1] Chappell, 126.

[2] The outgoing Governor, George Mathews, in his last message to the Legislature, stoutly defended his approval of the sale act. He attributed the attacks upon him to "base and malicious reports," inspired by "the blackest and the most persevering malice aided by disappointed avarice." The storm against the law was, he said, due to "popular clamour." (Message of Governor Mathews, Jan. 28, 1796, Harper: *Case of the Georgia Sales on the Mississippi Considered*, 92–93.)

of all fundamental and constitutional authority which the said usurped act might be declared by its advocates, and those who claim under it, to be founded on, fraud has been practised to obtain it and the grants under it; and it is a fundamental principle, both of law and equity, that there cannot be a wrong without a remedy, and the State and the citizens thereof have suffered a most grievous injury in the barter of their rights by the said usurped act and grants, and there is no court existing, if the dignity of the State would permit her entering one, for the trial of fraud and collusion of individuals, or to contest her sovereignty with them, whereby the remedy for so notorious an injury could be obtained; and it can no where better lie than with the representatives of the people chosen by them, after due promulgation by the grand juries of most of the counties of the State, of the means practised, and by the remonstrances of the people of the convention, held on the 10th day of May, in the year 1795, setting forth the atrocious peculation, corruption, and collusion, by which the usurped act and grants were obtained." [1]

At last the now highly enlightened Legislature enacted "that the said usurped act . . be declared null and void," and that all claims directly or indirectly arising therefrom be "annulled." The lands sold under the Act of 1795 were pronounced to be "the sole property of the State, subject only to the right of treaty of the United States, to enable the State to purchase, under its pre-emption right, the Indian title to the same." [2]

[1] *Am. State Papers, Public Lands*, I, 157.   [2] *Ib.* 158.

Such was the law which John Marshall was to declare invalid in one of the most far-reaching opinions ever delivered from the Supreme Bench.

The Legislature further enacted that the "usurped act" and all "records, documents, and deeds" connected with the Yazoo fraud, "shall be expunged from the face and indexes of the books of record of the State, and the enrolled law or usurped act shall then be publicly burnt, in order that no trace of so unconstitutional, vile, and fraudulent a transaction, other than the infamy attached to it by this law, shall remain in the public offices thereof." County officials were, under the severest of penalties for disobedience, directed to "obliterate" all records of deeds or other instruments connected with the anathematized grants, and courts were forbidden to receive any evidence of title of any kind whatever to lands from the grantees under the "usurped act." [1]

The Governor was directed to issue warrants for repayment to those who, in good faith, had deposited their purchase money, with this reservation, however: "Provided the same shall be now therein." [2] After six months all moneys not applied for were to become the property of Georgia. To prevent frauds upon individuals who might otherwise purchase lands from the pirate companies, the Governor was directed to promulgate this brief and simple act "throughout the United States."

[1] *Am. State Papers, Public Lands*, i, 158.

[2] The punctilious Legislature failed to explain that one hundred thousand dollars of the purchase money had already been appropriated and expended by the State. This sum they did not propose to restore.

A committee, appointed to devise a method for destroying the records, immediately reported that this should be done by cutting out of the books the leaves containing them. As to the enrolled bill containing the "usurped act," an elaborate performance was directed to be held: "A fire shall be made in front of the State House door, and a line formed by the members of both branches around the same. The Secretary of State [1] .. shall then produce the enrolled bill and usurped act from among the archives of the State and deliver the same to the President of the Senate, who shall examine the same, and shall then deliver the same to the Speaker of the House of Representatives for like examination; and the Speaker shall then deliver them to the Clerk of the House of Representatives, who shall read aloud the title to the same, and shall then deliver them to Messenger of the House, who shall then pronounce — 'GOD SAVE THE STATE!! AND LONG PRESERVE HER RIGHTS!! AND MAY EVERY ATTEMPT TO INJURE THEM PERISH AS THESE CORRUPT ACTS NOW DO!!!!'" [2]

Every detail of this play was carried out with all theatrical effect. Indeed, so highly wrought were the imaginations of actors and onlookers that, at the last moment, a final dash of color was added. Some one gifted with dramatic genius suggested that the funeral pyre of such unholy legislation should not be lighted by earthly hands, but by fire from Heaven. A sun-glass was produced; Senator Jackson held it

[1] "Or his deputy."

[2] Report of the joint committee, as quoted in Stevens: *History of Georgia from its First Discovery by Europeans to the Adoption of the Present Constitution in 1798*, II, 491–92.

above the fagots and the pile was kindled from "the burning rays of the lidless eye of justice." [1]

While the State was still in convulsions of anger, a talented young Virginian of impressionable temperament went to Georgia upon a visit to a college friend, Joseph Bryan, and was so profoundly moved by accounts of the attempt to plunder the State, that a hatred of the corrupt plot and of all connected with it became an obsession that lasted as long as he lived. [2] Thus was planted in the soul of John Randolph that determination which later, when a member of Congress, caused him to attack the Administration of Thomas Jefferson. [3]

Swift as was the action of the people and legislature of Georgia in attempting to recover the Yazoo lands, it was not so speedy as that of the speculators in disposing of them to purchasers in other States. Most of these investors bought in entire good faith and were "innocent purchasers." Some, however, must have been thoroughly familiar with the fraud. [4]

---

[1] Stevens, 492–93. Stevens says that there is no positive proof of this incident; but all other writers declare that it occurred. See Knight: *Georgia's Landmarks, Memorials and Legends*, I, 152–53; also Harris, 135.

[2] Adams: *Randolph*, 23; also Garland: *Life of John Randolph of Roanoke*, I, 64–68.

[3] See *infra*, 577–81; and *supra*, chap. IV.

[4] For instance, Wade Hampton immediately sold the entire holdings of The Upper Mississippi Company, 138,000 acres, to three South Carolina speculators, and it is quite impossible that they did not know of the corruption of the Georgia Legislature. Hampton acquired from his partners, John B. Scott and John C. Nightingale, all of their interests in the company's purchase. This was done on January 16 and 17, immediately after Governor Mathews had signed the deed from the State. Seven weeks later, March 6, 1795, Hampton conveyed all of this land to Adam Tunno, James Miller, and James Warrington. (*Am. State Papers, Public Lands*, I, 233.) Hampton was a member of Congress from South Carolina.

The most numerous sales were made in the Middle States and in New England. The land companies issued a prospectus,[1] setting out their title, which appeared to be, and indeed really was, legally perfect. Thousands of copies of this pamphlet were scattered among provident and moneyed people. Agents of the companies truthfully described the Yazoo country to be rich, the climate mild and healthful, and the land certain of large and rapid rise in value.

Three of the companies[2] opened an office in Boston, where the spirit of speculation was rampant. Then ensued an epidemic of investment. Throngs of purchasers gathered at the promoters' offices. Each day prices rose and the excitement increased. Buying and selling of land became the one absorbing business of those who had either money or credit. Some of the most prominent and responsible men in New England acquired large tracts.[3] The companies received payment partly in cash, but chiefly in notes which were speedily sold in the market for commercial paper. Sales were made in other Northern cities, and many foreigners became purchasers. The average price received was fourteen cents an acre.[4]

[1] State of Facts, shewing the Right of Certain Companies to the Lands lately purchased by them from the State of Georgia.

[2] The Georgia Mississippi Company, The Tennessee Company, and The Georgia Company. (See Haskins, 29.)

[3] Eleven million acres were purchased at eleven cents an acre by a few of the leading citizens of Boston. This one sale netted the Yazoo speculators almost a million dollars, while the fact that such eminent men invested in the Yazoo lands was a strong inducement to ordinary people to invest also. (See Chappell, 109.)

[4] See Chappell, 110–11.

Some New Englanders were suspicious. "The Georgia land speculation calls for vigor in Congress. Near fifty millions acres sold . . for a song," wrote Fisher Ames.[1] But such cautious men as Ames were few in number and most of them were silent. By the time reports reached Boston that the Legislature of Georgia was about to repeal the act under which the companies had bought the lands, numerous sales, great and small, had been made. In that city alone more than two millions of dollars had been invested, and this had been paid or pledged by "every class of men, even watch-makers, hair-dressers, and mechanics." The Georgia Company conveyed eleven million acres on the very day that the Legislature of Georgia passed the bill declaring the "usurped act" to be null and void and asserting the title of the whole territory still to be in the State.[2]

Three weeks later, the news of the enactment of the rescinding law was published in the New England metropolis. Anger and apprehension seized the investors. If this legislation were valid, all would lose heavily; some would be financially ruined. So a large number of the purchasers organized the New England Mississippi Company for the purpose of defending their interests. A written opinion upon the validity of their titles was procured from Alexander Hamilton, who was then practicing law in New York and directing the Federalist Party throughout

[1] Ames to Gore, Feb. 24, 1795, Ames, i, 168. Ames's alarm, however, was that the Georgia land sale " threatens Indian, Spanish, and civil, wars." The immorality of the transaction appears to have been unknown to him.

[2] Haskins, 30.

the Nation. He was still regarded by most Federalists, and by nearly all moneyed men, as the soundest lawyer, as well as the ablest statesman, in America.

Hamilton's opinion was brief, simple, convincing, and ideally constructed for perusal by investors. It stated the facts of the enactment of the sale law, the fulfillment of the conditions of it by the purchasers, and the passage of the rescinding act. Hamilton declared this latter act to be invalid because it plainly violated the contract clause of the Constitution. "Every grant . . whether [from] . . a state or an individual, is virtually a contract." The rescinding act was therefore null, and "the courts of the United States . . will be likely to pronounce it so." [1]

Soon after its passage, President Washington had received a copy of the Georgia land sale act. He transmitted it to Congress with a short Message,[2] stating that the interests of the United States were involved. His principal concern, however, and that of Congress also, was about the Indians. It was feared that depredations by whites would cause another outbreak of the natives. A resolution was adopted authorizing the President to obtain from Georgia the cession of her "claim to the whole or any part of the land within the . . Indian boundaries," and recommending that he prevent the making of treaties by individuals or States "for the extinguishment of the Indian title." But not a word was said in Washington's Message, or in the debate in Con-

[1] Harper, 109. Hamilton's opinion is dated March 25, 1796. In Harper's pamphlet it is incorrectly printed 1795.

[2] *Annals*, 3d Cong. 1st and 2d Sess. 1231.

gress, about the invalidity of the Georgia sale law or the corrupt methods employed to secure the enactment of it.[1]

Two bills to protect the Indians failed of passage.[2] Just before adjournment the House adopted a Senate resolution which had been offered by Senator Rufus King of New York, requesting that the Attorney-General report to the Senate all data bearing on Georgia's title to the territory sold to the land companies; but again the invalidity of the sale law was not even suggested, and the corruption of the Georgia Legislature was not so much as referred to.[3]

A year later, Charles Lee, Washington's Attorney-General, transmitted to Congress an exhaustive report containing all facts.[4] This report was referred to a special committee, headed by Senator Aaron Burr of New York, who, on May 20, 1796, reported a resolution authorizing the President to treat with Georgia for the cession of the territory.[5] Once more no attention was paid to the fraud in the sale act, or to the rescinding act of the Georgia Legislature.

But when the public finally learned of the "Yazoo Fraud" and of the repudiation by the Georgia Legislature of the corrupt law, the whole country was deeply stirred. A war of pamphlets broke out and was waged by both sides with vigor and ability. Abraham Bishop of Hartford, Connecticut, wrote a comprehensive answer to the prospectus of the land companies, and copies of this pamphlet, which

---

[1] *Annals*, 3d Cong. 1st and 2d Sess. 1251–54. The Georgia act was transmitted to Washington privately.

[2] *Ib.* 1255, 1262–63. [3] *Ib.* 1282–83.

[4] *Am. State Papers, Public Lands*, I, 341. [5] *Ib.* 71.

appeared in four parts, were widely circulated.[1]
Georgia had no fee in the lands, said Bishop.[2] Sales
to "innocent purchasers" could not give them what
Georgia had no right to sell. Neither could such a
device validate fraud. Much litigation had already
grown out of the swindle, and the Georgia rescinding
act had "brought . . matters to a crisis, and one
decision of the supreme court of the United States
may probably influence the decisions of lower
courts."[3] Bishop discussed brilliantly, and at length,
every possible question involved. The power of the
State to pass and repeal laws was "wholly uncontrol-
able,"[4] he asserted. The history of other dishonest
and imprudent speculations was examined — the
South Sea Bubble, the Mississippi Bubble,[5] and the
interposition of the legislative power of Great Britain
in the one case and of France in the other. Should
like power be denied in America? Georgia's rescinding act "nipt in the bud a number of aspiring swindlers."[6] Courts could not overthrow such legislation.
The "sacredness of contracts" was the favorite cloak
of fraud. Bishop urged buyers to resist the recovery of money pledged in their purchase notes and,
by so doing, to restore "millions of dollars . . to the
channels of industry."[7]

Hard upon the publication of the first number of
Bishop's pamphlet followed one for the land companies and investors. This had been written by
Robert Goodloe Harper of Maryland a few months
after Hamilton had rendered his opinion that the

[1] Bishop's pamphlet was called *Georgia Speculation Unveiled.*
[2] Bishop, 6. [3] *Ib.* 11. [4] *Ib.* [5] *Ib.* 29-32. [6] *Ib.* 92. [7] *Ib.* 144.

Georgia grant was inviolable.[1] It was an able and learned performance. The title of Georgia to the lands was carefully examined and held to be indefeasible. The sale of 1795 was set forth and the fact disclosed that Georgia had appropriated one hundred thousand dollars of the purchase money immediately upon the receipt of it.[2] It was pointed out that the rescinding act ignored this fact.[3]

Harper argued that only the courts could determine the validity and meaning of a law, and that no Legislature could annul a grant made by a previous one. To the Judiciary alone belonged that power.[4] The sale law was a contract, fully executed; one party to it could not break that compact.[5] If Georgia thought the sale act unconstitutional, she should have brought suit in the United States Court to determine that purely judicial question. The same was true as to the allegations of fraud and corruption in the passage of the measure. If any power could do so, the courts and they alone could decide the effect of fraud in procuring the enactment of a law. But even the courts were barred from investigating that question: if laws could be invalidated because of the motives of members of lawmaking bodies, "what a door would be opened to fraud and uncertainty of every kind!"[6]

[1] Harper's opinion bears, opposite his signature, this statement: "Considered at New-York August 3d, 1796." Beyond all doubt it had been submitted to Hamilton — perhaps prepared in collaboration with him. Harper was himself a member of one of the purchasing companies and in the House he later defended the transaction. (See *Annals*, 5th Cong. 2d Sess. 1277.)

[2] Harper, 16.   [3] *Ib.* 14.   [4] *Ib.* 49–50.

[5] *Ib.* 50. Here Harper quotes Hamilton's opinion.

[6] *Ib.* 50–53. Harper's pamphlet is valuable as containing, in com-

Finally, after a long altercation that lasted for nearly three years, Congress enacted a law authorizing the appointment of commissioners to settle the disputes between the National Government and Georgia, and also to secure from that truculent sovereignty the cession to the Nation of the lands claimed by the State.[1] In the somewhat extended debate over the bill but little was said about the invalidity of the Yazoo sale, and the corruption of the Legislature that directed it to be made was not mentioned.[2]

Under this act of Congress, Georgia ceded her rights over the disputed territory for one million, two hundred and fifty thousand dollars; provided, however, that the Nation should extinguish the Indian titles, settle British and Spanish claims, ulti-

pact form, all the essential documents relating to Georgia's title as well as the sale and rescinding acts. Other arguments on both sides appeared. One of the ablest of these was a pamphlet by John E. Anderson and William J. Hobby, attorneys of Augusta, Georgia, and published at that place in 1799 "at the instance of the purchasers." It is entitled: *The Contract for the Purchase of the Western Territory Made with the Legislature of Georgia in the Year 1795, Considered with a Reference to the Subsequent Attempts of the State to Impair its Obligations.*

[1] See report of Attorney-General Charles Lee, April 26, 1796, *Am. State Papers, Public Lands*, I, 34; report of Senator Aaron Burr, May 20, 1796, *ib.* 71; report of Senator James Ross, March 2, 1797, *ib.* 79.

[2] Except by John Milledge of Georgia, who declared that "there was no legal claim upon . . any part of that territory." Robert Goodloe Harper said that that question "must be determined in a Court of Justice," and argued for an "amicable settlement" of the claims. He himself once had an interest in the purchase, but had disposed of it three years before when it appeared that the matter must come before Congress (*Annals*, 5th Cong. 2d Sess. 1277–78); the debate occupied parts of two days (see also *ib.* 1298–1313). In view of the heated controversy that afterward occurred, it seems scarcely credible that almost no attention was given in this debate to the fraudulent character of the transaction.

mately admit the vast domain as a State of the
Union, and reserve five million acres for the purpose
of quieting all other demands. A later law [1] directed
the National commissioners, who had negotiated this
arrangement with Georgia, to investigate and report
upon the claims of individuals and companies to
lands within the territory thus ceded to the United
States.

At once the purchasers from the land companies,
especially the New England investors, besieged Congress to devote part of this five million acres to the
salvage of their imperiled money. The report of the
commissioners [2] was wise, just, and statesmanlike.
It was laid before the House on February 16, 1803.
Although the titles of the claimants could "not be
supported," still, because most of the titles had been
acquired in good faith, and because it would be injurious to everybody, including the Nation, to leave
the matter unsettled, the report recommended the
accommodation of the dispute on terms that would
save innocent purchasers at least a part of the
money they had paid or legally engaged to pay. [3]

When a bill to carry out the recommendations of
the commission for the payment of the Yazoo claim-

[1] May 10 1800, Sess. i, chap. 50, *U.S. Statutes at Large*, ii, 69.

[2] The entire commission was composed of three of the five members
of Jefferson's Cabinet, to wit: James Madison, Secretary of State;
Albert Gallatin, Secretary of the Treasury; and Levi Lincoln, Attorney-General.

[3] Report of the Commissioners, *Am. State Papers, Public Lands*, i,
132–35. "The interest of the United States, the tranquillity of those
who may hereafter inhabit that territory, and various equitable considerations which may be urged in favor of most of the present claimants, render it expedient to enter into a compromise on reasonable
terms."

ants came before the House, John Randolph offered
a resolution that went directly to the heart of the
controversy and of all subsequent ones of like nature.
It declared that "when the governors of any people
shall have betrayed" their public trust for their own
corrupt advantage, it is the "inalienable right" of
that people "to abrogate the act thus endeavoring
to betray them." Accordingly the Legislature of
Georgia had passed the rescinding act. This was
entirely legal and constitutional because "a subsequent Legislature of an individual State has an undoubted right to repeal any act of a preceding Legislature, provided such repeal be not forbidden by the
constitution of such State, or of the United States."
Neither the fundamental law of Georgia nor of the
Nation forbade the repeal of the corrupt law of 1795.
Claims under this nullified and "usurped" law were
not recognized by the compact of cession between
Georgia and the United States, "nor by any act
of the Federal Government." Therefore, declared
Randolph's resolution, "no part of the five millions
of acres reserved for satisfying and quieting claims
. . shall be appropriated to quiet or compensate any
claims" derived under the corrupt legislation of the
Georgia Legislature of 1795.[1] After a hot fight, consideration of the resolutions was postponed until the
next session; but the bill authorizing the commissioners to compromise with the Yazoo claimants also
went over.[2]

The matter next came up for consideration in the
House, just before the trial in the Senate of the

[1] *Annals*, 8th Cong. 1st Sess. 1039–40.   [2] *Ib.* 1099–1122, 1131–70.

impeachment of Justice Samuel Chase. A strong and influential lobby was pressing the compromise. The legislative agents of the New England Mississippi Company [1] presented its case with uncommon ability. In a memorial to Congress [2] they set forth their repeated applications to President, Congress, and the commissioners for protection. They were, they said, "constantly assured" that the rights of the claimants would be respected; and that it was expressly for this purpose that the five million acres had been reserved. For years they had attended sittings of the commissioners and sessions of Congress "at great cost and heavy expense."

Would not Congress at last afford them relief? If a "judicial decision" was desired, let Congress enact a law directing the Supreme Court to decide as to the validity of their title and they would gladly submit the matter to that tribunal. It was only because Congress seemed to prefer settlement by compromise that they again presented the facts and reasons for establishing their rights. So once more every aspect of the controversy was discussed with notable ability and extensive learning in Granger and Morton's brochure. [3]

[1] Perez Morton and Gideon Granger. Morton, like Granger, was a Republican and a devoted Jeffersonian. He went annually to Washington to lobby for the Yazoo claimants and assiduously courted the President. In Boston the Federalists said that his political activity was due to his personal interest in the Georgia lands. (See *Writings, J. Q. A.*: Ford, III, 51–53.)

[2] *Memorial of the Agents of the New England Mississippi Company to Congress, with a Vindication of their Title at Law annexed.*

[3] This document, issued in pamphlet form in 1804, is highly important. There can be little doubt that Marshall read it attentively, since it proposed a submission of the acrimonious controversy to the Supreme Court.

The passions of John Randolph, which had never grown cold since as a youth, a decade previously, he had witnessed the dramatic popular campaign in Georgia — and which during 1804 had been gathering intense heat — now burst into a furious flame. Unfortunately for Jefferson, the most influential agent of the New England claimants was the one Administration official who had most favors to bestow — Gideon Granger of Massachusetts, the Postmaster-General.[1] He was the leader of the lobby which the New England Mississippi Company had mustered in such force. And Granger now employed all the power of his department, so rich in contracts and offices, to secure the passage of a bill that would make effectual the recommendations of Jefferson's commissioners.

As the vote upon it drew near, Granger actually appeared upon the floor of the House soliciting votes for the measure. Randolph's emotions were thus excited to the point of frenzy — the man was literally beside himself with anger. He needed to husband all his strength for the conduct of the trial of Chase[2] and to solidify his party, rather than to waste his physical resources, or to alienate a single Republican. On the report of the Committee of Claims recommending the payment of the Yazoo claimants, one of the most virulent and picturesque debates in the history of the American Congress began.[3] Randolph took the floor, and a "fire and brimstone speech"[4] he made.

---

[1] The Postmaster-General was not made a member of the Cabinet until 1829.

[2] See *supra*, chap. iv.

[3] *Annals*, 8th Cong. 2d Sess. 1023.   [4] Cutler, ii, 182.

"Past experience has shown that this is one of those subjects which pollution has sanctified," he began. "The press is gagged." The New England claimants innocent purchasers! "Sir, when that act of stupendous villainy was passed in 1795 . . it caused a sensation scarcely less violent than that produced by the passage of the stamp act." Those who assert their ignorance of "this infamous act" are gross and willful liars.[1] To a "monstrous anomaly" like the present case, cried Randolph, "narrow maxims of municipal jurisprudence ought not, and cannot be applied. . . Attorneys and judges do not decide the fate of empires." [2]

Randolph mercilessly attacked Granger, and through him the Administration itself. Granger's was a practiced hand at such business, he said. He was one of "the applicants by whom we were beset" in the Connecticut Reserve scheme, "by which the nation were swindled out of some three or four millions of acres of land, which, like other bad titles, had fallen into the hands of innocent purchasers." Granger "seems to have an unfortunate knack of buying bad titles. His gigantic grasp embraces with one hand the shores of Lake Erie,[3] and stretches with the other to the Bay of Mobile.[4] Millions of

---

[1] *Annals*, 8th Cong. 2d Sess. 1024. To such extravagance and inaccuracy does the frenzy of combat sometimes drive the most honest of men. When he made these assertions, John Randolph knew that scores of purchasers from the land companies had invested in absolute good faith and before Georgia had passed the rescinding act. His tirade done, however, this inexplicable man spoke words of sound though misapplied statesmanship.

[2] *Ib.* 1029–30.

[3] Referring to Granger's speculations in the Western Reserve.

[4] The Yazoo deal.

acres are easily digested by such stomachs. . . They buy and sell corruption in the gross." They gamble for "nothing less than the patrimony of the people." Pointing his long, bony finger at Granger, Randolph exclaimed: "Mr. Speaker, . . this same agent is at the head of an Executive department of our Government. . . This officer, possessed of how many snug appointments and fat contracts, let the voluminous records on your table, of the mere names and dates and sums declare, . . this officer presents himself at your bar, at once a party and an advocate." [1]

The debate continued without interruption for four full days. Every phase of the subject was discussed exhaustively. The question of the power of the Legislature to annul a contract; of the power of the Judiciary to declare a legislative act void because of corruption in the enactment of it; the competency of Congress to pass upon such disputed points — these questions, as well as that of the innocence of the purchasers, were elaborately argued.

The strongest speech in support of the good faith of the New England investors was made by that venerable and militant Republican and Jeffersonian, John Findley of Pennsylvania.[2] He pointed out that the purchase by members of the Georgia Legislature of the lands sold was nothing unusual — everybody knew "that had been the case in Pennsylvania and other states." Georgia papers did not circulate in

---

[1] *Annals*, 8th Cong. 2d Sess. 1031.

[2] Findley was one of those who led the fight against the ratification of the Constitution in the Pennsylvania Convention. (See vol. I, 327–38, of this work.)

New England; how could the people of that section know of the charges of corruption and the denial of the validity of the law under which the lands were sold?

Those innocent purchasers had a right to trust the validity of the title of the land companies — the agents had exhibited the deeds executed by the Governor of Georgia, the law directing the sale to be made, and the Constitution of the State. What more could be asked? "The respectability of the characters of the sellers" was a guarantee "that they could not themselves be deceived and would not deceive others." Among these, said Findley, was an eminent Justice of the Supreme Court,[1] a United States Senator,[2] and many other men of hitherto irreproachable standing. Could people living in an old and thickly settled State, far from the scene of the alleged swindle, with no knowledge whatever that fraud had been charged, and in need of the land offered — could they possibly so much as suspect corruption when such men were members of the selling companies?

Moreover, said Findley — and with entire accuracy — not a Georgia official charged with venality had been impeached or indicted. The truth was that if the Georgia Legislature had not passed the rescinding act the attention of Congress would never have been called to the alleged swindle. Then, too, everybody knew "that one session of a Legislature cannot annul the contracts made by the preceding session"; for did not the National Constitution

---

[1] James Wilson.   [2] James Gunn.

forbid any State from passing a law impairing the obligation of contracts? [1]

Randolph outdid himself in daring and ferocity when he again took the floor. His speech struck hostile spectators as "more outrageous than the first." [2] He flatly charged that a mail contract had been offered to a member of the House, who had accepted it, but that it had been withdrawn from him when he refused to agree to support the compromise of the Yazoo claims. Randolph declared that the plot to swindle Georgia out of her lands "was hatched in Philadelphia and New York (and I believe Boston . .) and the funds with which it was effected were principally furnished by moneyed capitalists in those towns." [3]

At last the resolution was adopted by a majority of 63 to 58,[4] and Randolph, physically exhausted and in despair at his overthrow as dictator of the House, went to his ineffective management of the Chase impeachment trial.[5] He prevented for the time being, however, the passage of the bill to carry out the compromise with the Yazoo claimants. He had mightily impressed the people, especially those of Virginia. The Richmond *Enquirer*, on October 7, 1806, denounced the Yazoo fraud and the compromise of the investors' claims as a "stupendous scheme of plunder." Senator Giles, in a private conversation with John Quincy Adams, asserted that "not a man from that State, who should give any

---

[1] *Annals*, 8th Cong. 2d Sess. 1080–89.
[2] Cutler, II, 182.
[3] *Annals*, 8th Cong. 2d Sess. 1100–08.
[4] *Ib.* 1173.   [5] See *supra*, chap. IV.

countenance to the proposed compromise, could obtain an election after it." He avowed that "nothing since the Government existed had so deeply affected him." [1]

The debate was published fully in the newspapers of Washington, and it is impossible that Marshall did not read it and with earnest concern. As has already been stated, the first sale of these very Georgia lands had brought about the Eleventh Amendment to the Constitution, abolishing the right to sue a State in the National courts. Moreover, Marshall was profoundly interested in the stability of contractual obligations. The repudiation of these by the Legislature of Virginia had powerfully and permanently influenced his views upon this subject. [2] Also, Marshall's own title to part of the Fairfax estate had more than once been in jeopardy. [3] At that very moment a suit affecting the title of his brother to certain Fairfax lands was pending in Virginia courts, and the action of the Virginia Court of Appeals in one of these was soon to cause the first great conflict between the highest court of a State and the supreme tribunal of the Nation. [4] No man in America, therefore, could have followed with deeper anxiety the Yazoo controversy than did John Marshall.

Again and again, session after session, the claimants presented to Congress their prayers for relief. In 1805, Senator John Quincy Adams of Massachu-

---

[1] *Memoirs, J. Q. A.*: Adams, i, 343.
[2] See vol. i, 224–41, of this work.
[3] *Ib.* 191, 196; and vol. ii, 206.
[4] Martin *vs.* Hunter's Lessees; see vol. iv, chap. iii, of this work.

setts and Senator Thomas Sumter of South Carolina
urged the passage of a bill to settle the claims. This
led Senator James Jackson of Georgia to deliver "a
violent invective against the claims, without any
specific object." [1] After Jackson's death the measure
passed the Senate by a vote of 19 to 11, but was
rejected in the House by a majority of 8 out of a
total of 116. [2]

Among the lawyers who went to Washington for
the New England Mississippi Company was a young
man not yet thirty years of age, Joseph Story of
Massachusetts, who on his first visit spent much
time with Madison, Gallatin, and the President. [3]
On a second visit, Story asked to address the House
on the subject, but that body refused to hear him. [4]

From the first the New England investors had
wished for a decision by the courts upon the validity
of their titles and upon the effect of the rescinding
act of the Georgia Legislature; but no way had
occurred to them by which they could secure such
a determination from the bench. The Eleventh
Amendment prevented them from suing Georgia;
and the courts of that State were, as we have seen,
forbidden by the rescinding act from entertaining
such actions.

To secure a judicial expression, the Boston claimants arranged a "friendly" suit in the United States

[1] *Memoirs, J. Q. A.*: Adams, I, 381; also see *ib.* 389, 392, 404–05,
408–09, 417–19.
[2] Haskins, 38.
[3] Story to Fay, May 30, 1807, Story, I, 150–53; and see Cabot to
Pickering, Jan. 28, 1808, Lodge: *Cabot,* 377.
[4] *Annals,* 10th Cong. 1st Sess. 1601–13.

Court for the District of Massachusetts. One John Peck of Boston had been a heavy dealer in Georgia lands.[1] On May 14, 1803, he had either sold or pretended to sell to one Robert Fletcher of Amherst, New Hampshire, fifteen thousand acres of his holdings for the sum of three thousand dollars. Immediately Fletcher brought suit against Peck for the recovery of this purchase money; but the case was "continued by consent" for term after term from June, 1803, until October, 1806.[2]

The pleadings[3] set forth every possible phase of the entire subject which could be considered judicially. Issues were joined on all points except that of the title of Georgia to the lands sold.[4] On this question a jury, at the October term, 1806, returned as a special verdict a learned and bulky document. It recited the historical foundations of the title to the territory in dispute; left the determination of the question to the court; and, in case the judge should decide that Georgia's claim to the lands sold was not valid, found for the plaintiff and assessed his damages at the amount alleged to have been paid to Peck.

Thereafter the case was again "continued by consent" until October, 1807, when Associate Justice William Cushing of the Supreme Court, sitting as Circuit Judge, decided in Peck's favor every question raised by the pleadings and by the jury's special verdict. Fletcher sued out a writ of error to the

---

[1] See Abstract, *Am. State Papers, Public Lands*, i, 220–34.

[2] Records, U.S. Circuit Court, Boston.

[3] Judge Chappell asserts that the pleadings showed, on the face of them, that the case was feigned. (See Chappell, 135–36.)

[4] Fletcher *vs.* Peck, 6 Cranch, 87–94.

Supreme Court of the United States, and so this controversy came before John Marshall. The case was argued twice, the first time, March 1-4, 1809, by Luther Martin for Fletcher and by Robert Goodloe Harper and John Quincy Adams for Peck. There was no decision on the merits because of a defect of pleadings which Marshall permitted counsel to remedy.[1]

During this argument the court adjourned for two hours to attend the inauguration of James Madison. For the third time Marshall administered the Presidential oath. At the ball that night, Judge Livingston told Adams that the court had been reluctant "to decide the case at all, as it appeared manifestly made up for the purpose of getting the Court's judgment upon all the points." The Chief Justice himself had mentioned the same thing to Cranch.

Adams here chronicles an incident of some importance. After delivering the court's opinion on the pleadings, Marshall "added verbally, that, circumstanced as the Court are, only five judges attending,[2] there were difficulties which would have prevented them from giving any opinion at this term had the pleadings been correct; and the Court the more readily forbore giving it, as from the complexion of the pleadings they could not but see that at the time when the covenants were made the parties had notice of the acts covenanted against." [3]

The cause was argued again a year later. This

---

[1] Fletcher *vs.* Peck, 6 Cranch, 127.

[2] Justices Chase and Cushing were absent because of illness.

[3] *Memoirs, J. Q. A.*: Adams, I, 546-47.

time Joseph Story, so soon thereafter appointed an Associate Justice, took the place of John Quincy Adams. Martin's address was technical and, from the record, appears to have been perfunctory.[1] On behalf of Peck, two thirds of the argument for the soundness of his title was devoted to the demonstration of the validity of that of Georgia. If that were sound, said Story, the Legislature had a right to sell the land, and a subsequent Legislature could not cancel the contract when executed. The Judiciary alone could declare what a law is or had been. Moreover, the National Constitution expressly forbade a State to pass an act impairing the obligation of contracts. To overthrow a law because it was corruptly enacted "would open a source of litigation which could never be closed." However, "the parties now before the court are innocent of the fraud, if any has been practiced. They were bona fide purchasers, for a valuable consideration, without notice of fraud. They cannot be affected by it." [2]

On March 16, 1810, Marshall delivered the opinion of the majority of the Supreme Court. In this he laid the second stone in the structure of American Constitutional law which bears his name. He held that the Georgia rescinding act was a violation of the contract clause of the Constitution, and in doing so asserted that courts cannot examine the motives

---

[1] *Memoirs, J. Q. A.*: Adams, i, 115.

On this occasion Martin was so drunk that the court adjourned to prevent him from completing his argument. (See *Md. Hist. Soc. Fund-Pub. No. 24*, 35.) This was the first time that drink seems to have affected him in the discharge of his professional duties. (See *supra*, footnote to 185–86.)

[2] 6 Cranch, 123.

that induce legislators to pass a law. In arriving at these profoundly important conclusions his reasoning was as follows:

Did the Georgia sale act of 1795 violate the Constitution of that State? An act of a legislature was not to be set aside "lightly" on "vague conjecture" or "slight implication." There was no ground for asserting that the Georgia Legislature transcended its constitutional powers in passing the sale act.[1] Had the corruption of the Legislature destroyed the title of Peck, an innocent purchaser? It was, cautiously said Marshall, doubtful "how far the validity of a law depends upon the motives of its framers," particularly when the act challenged authorized a contract that was executed according to the terms of it. Even if such legislation could be set aside on the ground of fraud in the enactment of it, to what extent must the impurity go?

"Must it be direct corruption, or would interest or undue influence of any kind be sufficient? Must the vitiating cause operate on a majority, or on what number of the members? Would the act be null, whatever might be the wish of the nation, or would its obligation or nullity depend upon the public sentiment?"

The State of Georgia did not bring this action; nor, "by this count" of the complaint, did it appear that the State was dissatisfied. On the face of the pleadings a purchaser of Georgia land declares that the seller had no title because "some of the members of the legislature were induced to vote in favor

[1] 6 Cranch, 128–29.

of the law, which constituted the contract [with the original grantees], by being promised an interest in it, and that therefore the act is a mere nullity." A tribunal "sitting as a court of law" cannot decide, in a suit between private parties, that the law of a State "is a nullity in consequence of the impure motives which influenced certain members of the legislature which passed the law."[1] Conceding, for the sake of argument, that "the original transaction was infected with fraud," the purchasers from the land companies were innocent according to the records before the court. Yet, if the rescinding act were valid, it "annihilated their rights. . . The legislature of Georgia was a party to this transaction; and for a party to pronounce its own deed invalid" was an assertion "not often heard in courts of justice." It was true, as urged, that "the real party . . are the people"; but they can act only through agents whose "acts must be considered as the acts of the people." Should these agents prove unfaithful, the people can choose others to undo the nefarious work, "if their contracts be examinable" by legislation.[2]

Admit that the State "might claim to itself the power of judging in its own case, yet there are certain great principles of justice . . that ought not to be entirely disregarded." Thus, at first, Marshall rested his opinion on elementary "principles of justice," rather than on the Constitution. These "principles" required that an innocent purchaser should not suffer. "If there be any concealed defect, arising from the conduct of those who had held the

[1] 6 Cranch, 130–31.   [2] *Ib.* 132–33.

property long before he acquired it, of which he had no notice, that concealed defect cannot be set up against him. He has paid his money for a title good at law; he is innocent, whatever may be the guilt of others, and equity will not subject him to the penalties attached to that guilt. All titles would be insecure, and the intercourse between man and man would be very seriously obstructed, if this principle be overturned." The John Marshall who sat in the Virginia Legislature [1] is speaking now.

Even if the Legislature could throw aside all "rules of property," still the rescinding act is "supported by its power alone, and the same power may divest any other individual of his lands, if it shall be the will of the legislature so to exert it." To make this perfectly clear, Marshall defined the theory relied upon by the opponents of the Yazoo fraud — "The principle is this: that a legislature may, by its own act, divest the vested estate of any man whatever, for reasons which shall, by itself, be deemed sufficient." [2]

Supposing that the Georgia sale act had been procured by fraud; nevertheless, "the grant, when issued, conveyed an estate in fee-simple to the grantee, clothed with all the solemnities which law can bestow. This estate was transferable; and those who purchased parts of it were not stained by that guilt which infected the original transaction." They could not, therefore, be made to suffer for the wrong of another.

Any legislature can, of course, repeal the acts of a

[1] See vol. I, 202, of this work.   [2] 6 Cranch, 133–34.

preceding one, and no legislature can limit the powers of its successor. "But, if an act be done under a law, a succeeding legislature cannot undo it. The past cannot be recalled by the most absolute power." The purchase of estates from the land companies was, by virtue of law, "a fact, and cannot cease to be a fact," even if the State should deny that it was a fact.

"When, then, a law is in its nature a contract, where absolute rights have vested under that contract, a repeal of the law cannot divest those rights." If it can, such a power is "applicable to the case of every individual in the community." Regardless of written constitutions, the "nature of society and of government" prescribes "limits to the legislative power." But "where are they to be found, if the property of an individual, fairly and honestly acquired, may be seized without compensation?" Again Marshall founds his reasoning, not on the Constitution, but on fundamental principles. At last, however, he arrives at the Constitution.

Georgia was not a single sovereign power, but "a part of a large empire, . . a member of the American Union; and that Union has a constitution . . which imposes limits to the legislatures of the several states, which none claim a right to pass." Had the Legislature of Georgia overstepped those limits? "Is a grant a contract?" The answer to that depended upon the definition of a contract. On this decisive point Marshall cited Blackstone: "A contract executed . . differs in nothing from a grant." This was the exact case presented by the Georgia sale act and the fulfillment, by the purchasers, of the conditions of it. "A party is, therefore, always estopped by his own grant," one obligation of which is that he shall never attempt "to re-assert that right" thus disposed of.

By this reasoning Marshall finally came to the conclusion that the Constitution plainly covered the case. That instrument did not distinguish between grants by individuals and those by States. If a State could not pass a law impairing the obligation of contracts between private persons, neither could it invalidate a contract made by itself.

Indeed, as everybody knew, said Marshall, "the framers of the constitution viewed, with some apprehension, the violent acts which might grow out of the feelings of the moment; and that the people of the United States, in adopting that instrument, have manifested a determination to shield themselves and their property from the effects of those sudden and strong passions to which men are exposed." Therefore, it was provided in America's fundamental law that "no state shall pass any bill of attainder, ex post facto law, or law impairing the obligation of contracts." [1]

Such limitations, declared Marshall, constitute a bill of rights for the people of each State. Would any one pretend to say that a State might enact an *ex post facto* law or pass a bill of attainder? Certainly not! How then could anybody pretend that a State could by legislation annul a contract?

Thus far the opinion of the court was unanimous. [2]

[1] 6 Cranch, 137–38.   [2] *Ib.* 139.

As to the Indian title, Justice Johnson dissented. On the want of power of the Georgia Legislature to annul the sale act of 1795, the Republican Associate Justice was, however, even more emphatic than the soft-spoken Federalist Chief Justice. But he ended by a rebuke which, if justified, and if the case had not been so important and the situation so critical, probably would have required the peremptory dismissal of the appeal and the disbarment of counsel appearing in the cause. Justice Johnson intimated — all but formally charged — that the case was collusive.

"I have been very unwilling," he said, "to proceed to the decision of this cause at all. It appears to me to be[ar] strong evidence, upon the face of it, of being a mere feigned case. It is our duty to decide upon the rights but not upon the speculations of parties. My confidence, however, in the respectable gentlemen who have been engaged for the parties, had induced me to abandon my scruples, in the belief that they would never consent to impose a mere feigned case upon this court." [1]

One cannot patiently read these words. Far better had Justice William Johnson denounced Fletcher *vs*. Peck for what everybody believed it to be, and what it really was, or else had refrained from raising the question, than in these unctuous sentences to have shifted the responsibility upon the shoulders of the attorneys who appeared before the Supreme Bench. The conclusion seems inescapable that had not Jefferson, who placed Johnson on the

[1] 6 Cranch, 147–48.

Supreme Bench, and Jefferson's Secretary of State
and political legatee, James Madison, ardently desired the disposition which Marshall made of the
case, Justice Johnson would have placed on record
a stronger statement of the nature of this litigation.

The fact that Marshall rendered an opinion, under
the circumstances, is one of the firmest proofs of his
greatness. As in Marbury *vs.* Madison, the supremacy
of the National Judiciary had to be asserted or its
inferiority conceded, so in Fletcher *vs.* Peck, it was
necessary that the Nation's highest court should
plainly lay down the law of public contract, notify
every State of its place in the American system, and
announce the limitations which the National Constitution places upon each State.

Failure to do this would have been to sanction
Georgia's rescinding act, to encourage other States
to take similar action, and to render insecure and
litigious numberless titles acquired innocently and
in good faith, and multitudes of contracts entered
into in the belief that they were binding. A weaker
man than John Marshall, and one less wise and cour-
ageous, would have dismissed the appeal or decided
the case on technical points.

Marshall's opinion did more than affect the controversy in Congress over the Yazoo lands. It announced fundamental principles for the guidance of
the States and the stabilizing of American business.[1]

[1] At the risk of iteration, let it again be stated that, in Fletcher *vs.*
Peck, Marshall declared that a grant by a State, accepted by the
grantees, is a contract; that the State cannot annul this contract, because the State is governed by the National Constitution which forbids any State to pass any law "impairing the obligation of contracts";

It increased the confidence in him of the conservative elements and of all Nationalists. But, for the
same reason, it deepened the public distrust of him
and the popular hostility toward him.

Although Marshall's opinion gave steadiness to
commercial intercourse at a time when it was sadly
needed, checked for the moment a flood of contract-
breaking laws, and asserted the supremacy of Nationalism over Localism, it also strengthened many
previous speculations that were at least doubtful
and some that were corrupt.[1] Moreover, it furnished
the basis for questionable public grants in the future.
Yet the good effects of it fairly outweighed the bad.
Also it taught the people to be careful in the choice
of their representatives in all legislative bodies; if
citizens will not select honest and able men as their
public agents, they must suffer the consequences of
their indifference to their own affairs.

Whatever may be thought of other aspects of this
case, it must be conceded that Marshall could not
have disobeyed the plain command of the Constitution which forbids any State to impair the obligation of contracts. That the Georgia Legislature was
guilty of such violation even Jefferson's appointee,
Justice Johnson, declared more emphatically than

that even if the contract clause were not in the Constitution, fundamental principles of society protect vested rights; and that the courts
cannot inquire into the motives of legislators no matter how corrupt
those motives may be.

[1] For the first two decades of the National Government land frauds
were general. See, for example, letter of Governor Harrison of Indiana, Jan. 19, 1802, *Am. State Papers, Public Lands*, I, 123; report of
Michael Leib, Feb. 14, 1804, *ib.* 189; and letter of Amos Stoddard,
Jan. 10, 1804, *ib.* 193-94.

did Marshall himself. If Johnson had asserted that a legislative grant, accepted by the grantee, was not a contract, Marshall's opinion would have been fatally wounded.

It had now been Marshall's fate to deliver opinions in three cases [1] which helped to assure his future fame, but which, at the moment, were highly unwelcome to the people. Throughout the country, at the end of the first decade of the nineteenth century, a more unpopular person could not have been found than that wise, brave, gentle man, the Chief Justice of the United States.

Marshall's opinion and the decision of the court had no practical effect whatever, so far as the legal result of it was concerned, but it had some influence in the settlement of the controversy by Congress. The Eleventh Congress was in session when Fletcher *vs.* Peck was decided, and the New England Yazoo claimants immediately presented another petition for relief. Soon after Marshall's opinion was published, Randolph moved that the New England memorial be referred to the Committee of Claims with instructions to report to the House. The matter, he said, must not go by default. He wanted nothing "done, directly or indirectly, by any act of commission or omission, that should give any the slightest degree of countenance to that claim."

Randolph thus brought Marshall's opinion before the House: "A judicial decision, of no small importance, had, during the present session of Congress, taken place in relation to that subject." To let the

---

[1] Marbury *vs.* Madison, the Burr trial, and Fletcher *vs.* Peck.

business rest, particularly at this time, "would wear the appearance abroad of acquiescence [by the House] in that judicial decision." The Yazoo claimants must not be allowed to profit in this way by the action of the Supreme Court as they would surely do if not prevented, since "never has a claim been pressed upon the public with such pertinacity, with such art, with such audacity." [1]

George M. Troup of Georgia, slender, handsome, fair-haired, [2] then thirty years old and possessing all the fiery aggressiveness of youth, sprang to his feet to add his reproof of Marshall and the Supreme Court. He declared that the opinion of the Chief Justice, in Fletcher *vs.* Peck, was a pronouncement "which the mind of every man attached to Republican principles must revolt at." [3]

Because the session was closing and from pressure of business, Randolph withdrew his motion to refer the memorial to the Committee, and offered another: "That the prayer of the petition of the New England Mississippi Land Company is unreasonable, unjust, and ought not to be granted." This, if passed, would amount to a condemnation by the House of the decision of the Supreme Court of the United States. All Federalists and conservative Republicans combined to defeat it, and the resolution was lost by a vote of 46 yeas to 54 nays. [4]

But Troup would not yield. On December 17 he insisted that the National Government should resist by force of arms the judgment of the Supreme

---

[1] *Annals*, 11th Cong. 2d Sess. 1881.
[2] Harden: *Life of George M. Troup*, 9.
[3] *Annals*, 11th Cong. 2d. Sess. 1882.   [4] *Ib.*

Court. The title to the lands was in the United States, he said, yet the court had decided it to be in the Yazoo claimants. "This decision must either be acquiesced in or resisted by the United States. . . If the Government . . would not submit to this decision, . . what course could be taken but to employ the whole military force . . to eject all persons not claiming under the authority of the United States?" Should those "in whose behalf" Marshall's opinion was rendered, take possession, either the National Government must "remove them by . . military power, or tamely acquiesce in the lawless aggression." [1]

But Marshall and the Supreme Court were to be attacked still more openly and violently. Strengthened by the decision in Fletcher *vs.* Peck, the Yazoo claimants pressed Congress harder than ever for payment. On January 20, 1813, a bill from the Senate providing for the payment of the claims came up for consideration in the House.

Troup instantly took the floor, moved its rejection and delivered such an excoriation of the Supreme Court as never before was or has since been heard in Congress. He began by reciting the details of the "hideous corruption." Such legislation was void *ab initio*. The original speculators had made fortunes out of the deal, and now Congress was asked to make the fortunes of the second-hand speculators. For years the House had, most righteously, repelled their audacious assaults; but now they had devised a new weapon of attack.

[1] *Annals*, 11th Cong. 3d Sess. 415.

They had secured the assistance of the Judiciary. "Two of the speculators combined and made up a fictitious case, a feigned issue for the decision of the Supreme Court," asserted Troup. "They presented precisely those points for the decision of the Court which they wished the Court to decide, and the Court did actually decide them as the speculators themselves would have decided them if they had been in the place of the Supreme Court.

"The first point was, whether the Legislature of Georgia had the *power* to sell the territory.

"Yes, said the Judges, they had.

"Whether by the Yazoo act an estate did vest in the original grantees?

"Yes, said the Judges, it did.

"Whether it was competent to any subsequent Legislature to set aside the act on the ground of fraud and corruption?

"No, said the Judges, it was not. . . No matter, say the Judges, what the nature or extent of the corruption, . . be it ever so nefarious, it could not be set aside. . .

"The [legal] maxim that third purchasers without notice shall not be affected by the fraud of the original parties" had, declared Troup, been wielded by the Judges for the benefit of the speculators and to the ruin of the country.

"Thus, sir, by a maxim of English law are the rights and liberties of the people of this country to be corruptly bartered by their Representatives.

"It is this decision of the Judges which has been made the basis of the bill on your table — a decision shocking to every free Government, sapping the foundations of all your constitutions, and annihilating at a breath the best hope of man.

"Yes, sir," exclaimed the deeply stirred and sincerely angered Georgian, "it is proclaimed by the Judges, and is now to be sanctioned by the Legislature, that the Representatives of the people may corruptly betray the people, may corruptly barter their rights and those of their posterity, and the people are wholly without any kind of remedy whatsoever.

"It is this monstrous and abhorrent doctrine which must startle every man in the nation, that you ought promptly to discountenance and condemn."

In such fashion the enraged Troup ran on; and he expressed the sentiments of the vast majority of the inhabitants of the United States. The longer the Georgia champion of popular justice and the rights of the States talked, the more unrestrained became his sentiments and his expression of them: "If, Mr. Speaker, the arch-fiend had in . . his hatred to mankind resolved the destruction of republican government on earth, he would have issued a decree like that of the judges" — the opinion of John Marshall in Fletcher *vs*. Peck. "Why . . do the judges who passed this decision live and live unpunished? . . The foundations of the Republic are shaken and the judges sleep in tranquillity at home. . . The question . . had been so often discussed" that it was "well understood by every man in the nation." Troup prophesied, therefore, that "no party in this country, however deeply seated in power, can long survive the adoption of this measure." [1]

[1] *Annals*, 12th Cong. 2d Sess. 856–59.

But the Federalist-Jeffersonian Yazoo coalition held firm and Troup's motion to reject the Senate Yazoo bill was lost by a vote of 55 to 59.[1] The relief bill was delayed, however, and the claimants were compelled to nurse their eighteen-year-old disappointment until another session of Congress convened.

The following year the bill to settle the Yazoo claims was again introduced in the Senate and passed by that body without opposition. On February 28, 1814, the measure reached the House.[2] On the second reading of it, Troup despairingly moved that the bill be rejected. The intrepid and resourceful John Randolph had been beaten in the preceding Congressional election, the House no longer echoed with his fearless voice, and his dominant personality no longer inspired his followers or terrified his enemies. Troup could not bend the mighty bow that Randolph had left behind and that he alone could draw. But the dauntless Georgian did his best. Once more he went over the items of this "circle of fraud," as he branded it. Success of the "plunderers" now depended on the affirmation by Congress of Marshall's opinion, which, said Troup, "overturns Republican Government. You cannot, you dare not, sanctify this doctrine." If you do so, then "to talk of the rights of the people after this is insult and mockery."[3]

Long did Troup argue and denounce. He could not keep his eager fingers from the throat of John Marshall and the Supreme Court. "The case of

---

[1] *Annals*, 12th Cong. 2d Sess. 860.
[2] *Annals*, 13th Cong. 2d Sess. 1697.   [3] *Ib.* 1840–42.

Fletcher and Peck was a decision of a feigned issue, made up between two speculators, to decide certain points, in the decision of which they were interested. . . Whenever it is conceded that it is competent to the Supreme Court, in a case between A and B, to take from the United States fifty [*sic*] millions of acres of land, it will be time for the Government to make a voluntary surrender of the public property to whosoever will have it. . . Sir, I am tired and disgusted with this subject." [1]

Robert Wright of Maryland urged the passage of the bill. "He . . dwelt . . on the sanctity of the title of the present claimants under the decision of the Supreme Court, against whose awards he hoped never to see the bayonet employed. He feared not to advocate this bill on account of the clamor against it. Let justice be done though the heavens fall." [2]

Weaker and ever weaker grew the assaults of the opponents against Marshall's opinion and the bill to reimburse the Yazoo claimants. In every case the speakers supported or resisted the bill solely according to the influence of their constituents. Considerations of local politics, and not devotion to the Constitution or abhorrence of fraud, moved the Representatives. The House voted, 56 to 92, against Troup's motion to reject the bill. [3] Finally the measure was referred to a select committee, with instructions to report. [4] Almost immediately this committee reported in favor of the Yazoo claimants. [5] No time was lost and the friends of the bill now crowded

---

[1] *Annals*, 13th Cong. 2d Sess. 1848. [2] *Ib.* 1850.
[3] *Ib.* 1855. [4] *Ib.* 1858–59. [5] *Ib.* 1873–75.

the measure to a vote with all the aggressive confidence of an assured majority. By a vote of 84 yeas to 76 nays, five millions of dollars were appropriated for reimbursement to the purchasers of the Yazoo lands.[1]

Daniel Webster, who was serving his first term in the House and supported the bill, thus describes the situation at the time of its passage: "The Yazoo bill is through, passed by eight majority. It excited a great deal of feeling. All the Federalists supported the bill, and some of the Democrats. Georgians, and some Virginians and Carolinians, opposed it with great heat. . . Our feeling was to get the Democratic support of it." [2]

Thus John Marshall's great opinion was influential in securing from Congress the settlement of the claims of numerous innocent investors who had, in good faith, purchased from a band of legislative corruptionists. Of infinitely more importance, however, is the fact that Marshall's words asserted the power of the Supreme Court of the United States to annul State laws passed in violation of the National Constitution, and that throughout the Republic a fundamental principle of the law of public contract was established.

[1] *Annals*, 13th Cong. 2d Sess. 1925; see also Sess. I, chap. 39, March 31, 1814, *U.S. Statutes at Large*, III, 117.

[2] Daniel to Ezekiel Webster, March 28, 1814, *Private Correspondence of Daniel Webster:* Webster, 244.

END OF VOLUME III

APPENDIX

APPENDIX A

THE PARAGRAPH OMITTED FROM THE FINAL DRAFT OF
JEFFERSON'S MESSAGE TO CONGRESS, DECEMBER 8, 1801[1]

APPLICATIONS from different persons suffering prosecution under the act usually called the Sedition act, claimed my early attention to that instrument. our country has thought proper to distribute the powers of it's government among three equal & independent authorities, constituting each a check on one or both of the others, in all attempts to impair it's constitution. to make each an effectual check, it must have a right in cases which arise within the line of it's proper functions, where, equally with the others, it acts in the last resort & without appeal, to decide on the validity of an act according to it's own judgment, & uncontrouled by the opinions of any other department. we have accordingly, in more than one instance, seen the opinions of different departments in opposition to each other, & no ill ensue. the constitution moreover, as a further security for itself, against violation even by a concurrence of all the departments, has provided for it's own reintegration by a change of the persons exercising the functions of those department. Succeeding functionaries have the same right to judge of the conformity or non-conformity of an act with the constitution, as their predecessors who past it. for if it be against that instrument it is a perpetual nullity. uniform decisions indeed, sanctioned by successive functionaries, by the public voice, and by repeated elections would so strengthen a construction as to render highly responsible a departure from it. On my accession to the administration, reclamations against the Sedition act were laid before me by individual citizens, claiming the protection of the constitution against the Sedition act. called on by the position in which the nation had placed me, to exercise in their behalf my free & independent judgment, I took the act into consideration, compared it with the constitution, viewed it under every aspect of which I thought it susceptible, and gave to it all the attention which the magnitude of the case demanded. on mature deliberation, in the presence of the nation, and under the tie of the solemn oath which binds

[1] See 51–53 of this volume.

me to them & to my duty, I do declare that I hold that act to be in palpable & unqualified contradiction to the constitution. considering it then as a nullity, I have relieved from oppression under it those of my fellow-citizens who were within the reach of the functions confided to me. in recalling our footsteps within the limits of the Constitution, I have been actuated by a zealous devotion to that instrument. it is the ligament which binds us into one nation. It is, to the national government, the law of it's existence, with which it began, and with which it is to end. infractions of it may sometimes be committed from inadvertence, sometimes from the panic, or passions of a moment. to correct these with good faith, as soon as discovered, will be an assurance to the states that, far from meaning to impair that sacred charter of it's authorities, the General government views it as the principle of it's own life.[1]

[1] Jefferson MSS. Lib. Cong.

APPENDIX B

LETTER OF JOHN TAYLOR "OF CAROLINE" TO JOHN BRECKEN-
RIDGE CONTAINING ARGUMENTS FOR THE REPEAL OF THE
FEDERALIST NATIONAL JUDICIARY ACT OF 1801[1]

VIRGINIA — CAROLINE — Decr 22^d 1801

DEAR SIR

An absence from home, when your letter arrived, has been the cause which delayed this answer.

I confess that I have not abstracted myself from the political world, but I must at the same time acknowledge, that this kind of world, of which I am a member, is quite distinct from that in which your country has placed you. Mine is a sort of meta-physical world, over which the plastick power of the imagi-nation is unlimited — yours, being only physical, cannot be modulated by fancy. The ways of mine are smooth & soft; of yours, rugged & thorny. And a most prosperous traveller into the political world which I inhabit, generally becomes unfortunate if he wanders into the region of which you are now a resident. Yet, as a solicitation for the continuance of your correspondence, I will venture upon a short excursion out of my own atmosphere, in relation to the subject you state.

By way of bringing the point into plain view, I will suppose some cases. Suppose a congress and president should conspire to erect five times as many courts & judges, as were made by the last law, meerely for the sake of giving salaries to themselves or their friends, and should annex to each office, a salary of 100,000 dollars. Or suppose a president in order to reward his counsel on an impeachment, and the members of the senate who voted for his acquittal, had used his influence with the legisla-ture to erect useless tribunals, paid by him in fees or bribes. Or, lastly, suppose a long list of courts and judges to be estab-lished, without any ill intention, but meerly from want of intel-lect in the legislature, which from experience are found to be useless, expensive and unpopular. Are all these evils originat-ing either in fraud or error, remediless under the principles of your constitution?

[1] See footnote to 58 of this volume.

The first question is, whether the *office* thus established, is to continue.

The second, whether the officer is to continue, after the office is abolished, as being unnecessary.

Congress are empowered "from *time to time* to ordain & establish inferior courts."

The law for establishing the present inferior courts, is a legislative construction, affirming that under this clause, congress may *abolish* as well as create these *judicial offices;* because it does expressly *abolish* the then existing inferior courts, for the purpose of making way for the present.

It is probable that this construction is correct, but it is equally pertinent to our object, whether it is or not. If it is, then the present inferior courts may be abolished, as constitutionally as the last; if it is not, then the law for abolishing the former courts, and establishing the present, was unconstitutional, and being so, is undoubtedly repealable.

Thus the only ground which the present inferior courts can take, is, that congress may from time to time, regulate, create or abolish such courts, as the public interest may dictate, because such is the very tenure under which they exist.

The second question is, whether the officer is to continue after the office is abolished, as being useless or pernicious.

The constitution declares "that the judge shall hold his *office* during good behavior." Could it mean, that he should hold this *office* after it was *abolished?* Could it mean that his tenure should be limited by behaving well in an office, which did not exist?

It must either have intended these absurdities, or admit of a construction which will avoid them. This construction obviously is, that the officer should hold that which he might hold, namely, an existing office, so long as he did that which he might do, namely, his duty in that office; and not that he should hold an office, which did not exist, or perform duties not sanctioned by law. If therefore congress can abolish the courts, as they did by the last law, the officer dies with his office, unless you allow the constitution to intend impossibilities as well as absurdities. A construction bottomed upon either, overthrows the benefits of language and intellect.

The article of the constitution under consideration closes with an idea, which strongly supports my construction.

The salary is to be paid "during their continuance in office."

This limitation of salary is perfectly clear and distinct. It literally excludes the idea of paying a salary, when the officer is not in office; and it is undeniably certain, that he cannot be in office, when there is no office. There must have been some other mode by which the officer should cease to be in office, than that of *bad behaviour*, because, if this had not been the case, the constitution would have directed "that the judges should hold their offices *and salaries* during good behaviour," instead of directing "that they should" hold the salaries during *their continuance* in office. This could only be an abolition of the office itself, by which the salary would cease with the office, tho' the judge might have conducted himself unexceptionably.

This construction certainly coincides with the public opinion, and the principles of the constitution. By neither is the idea for a moment tolerated, of maintaining burthensome sinecure offices, to enrich unfruitful individuals.

Nor is it incompatible with the "good behaviour" tenure, when its origin is considered. It was invented in England, to counteract the influence of the crown over the judges, and we have rushed into the principle with such precipitancy, in imitation of this our general prototype, as to have outstript monarchists, in our efforts to establish a judicial oligarchy; their judges being removable by a joint vote of Lords & commons, and ours by no similar or easy process.

The tenure however is evidently bottomed upon the idea of securing the honesty of Judges, whilst exercising the office, and not upon that of sustaining useless or pernicious offices, for the sake of Judges. The regulation of offices in England, and indeed of inferior offices in most or all countries, depends upon the legislature; it is a part of the detail of the government, which necessarily devolves upon it, and is beyond the foresight of a constitution, because it depends on variable circumstances. And in England, a regulation of the courts of justice, was never supposed to be a violation of the "good behaviour" tenure.

If this principle should disable congress from erecting tribunals which temporary circumstances might require, without entailing them upon the society after these circumstances by ceasing, had converted them in grievances, it would be used in a mode, contemplated neither in its original or duplicate.

Whether courts are erected by regard to the administration of justice, or with the purpose of rewarding a meritorious faction, the legislature may certainly abolish them without infringing the constitution, whenever they are not required by the administration of justice, or the merit of the faction is exploded, and their claim to reward disallowed.

With respect to going into the judiciary system farther at present, the length of this trespass forbids it, and perhaps all ideas tending towards the revision of our constitution would be superfluous, as I fear it is an object not now to be attained. All my hopes upon this question rest I confess with Mr: Jefferson, and yet I know not how far he leans towards the revision. But he will see & the people will feel, that his administration bears a distinct character, from that of his predecessor, and of course discover this shocking truth, that the nature of our government depends upon the complection of the president, and not upon the principles of the constitution. He will not leave historians to say "this was a good president, but like a good Roman Emperor he left the principles of the government unreformed, so that his country remained exposed to eternal repetitions of those oppressions after his death, which he had himself felt and healed during his life."

And yet my hopes are abated by some essays signed "Solon" published at Washington, and recommending amendments to the constitution. They are elegantly written, but meerly skim along the surface of the subject, without touching a radical idea. They seem to be suggested by the pernicious opinion, that the administration only has been chargeable with the defectiveness of our operating government heretofore. Who is the author of these pieces?

Nothing can exceed our exultation on account of the president's message, and the countenance of congress — nothing can exceed the depression of the monarchists. They deprecate political happiness — we hope for the president's aid to place it on a rock before he dies.

It would have given me great pleasure to have seen you here, and I hope it may be still convenient for you to call. I close with your proposal to correspond, if the political wanderings of a man, almost in a state of vegitation, will be accepted for that interesting detail of real affairs, with which you propose occasionally to treat me. I am, with great regard, Dr Sir

Yr: mo: ob.^t Sev.^t
JOHN TAYLOR[1]

---

[1] Breckenridge MSS. Lib. Cong.

APPENDIX C

Holmes *vs.* Walton (November, 1779, New Jersey), before Chief Justice David Brearly. (See Austin Scott in *American Historical Review*, IV, 456 *et seq.*) If Marshall ever heard of this case, it was only because Paterson, who was Associate Justice with Marshall when the Supreme Court decided Marbury *vs.* Madison, was attorney-general in New Jersey at the time Holmes *vs.* Walton was decided. Both Brearly and William Paterson were members of the Constitutional Convention of 1787. (See Corwin, footnote to 41–42.)

Commonwealth *vs.* Caton (November, 1782, 4 Call, 5–21), a noted Virginia case. (See Tyler, I, 174–75.) The language of the court in this case is merely *obiter dicta;* but George Wythe and John Blair were on the Bench, and both of them were afterwards members of the Constitutional Convention. Blair was appointed by President Washington as one of the Associate Justices of the Supreme Court.

As to the much-talked-of Rhode Island case of Trevett *vs.* Weeden (September, 1786; see Arnold: *History of Rhode Island*, II, 525–27, Varnum's pamphlet, *Case of Trevett vs. Weeden*, and Chandler's *Criminal Trials*, II, 269–350), it is improbable that Marshall had any knowledge whatever of it. It arose in 1786 when the country was in chaos; no account of it appeared in the few newspapers that reached Virginia, and Varnum's description of the incident — for it can hardly be called a case — could scarcely have had any circulation outside of New England. It was referred to in the Constitutional Convention at Philadelphia in 1787, but the journals of that convention were kept secret until many years after Marbury *vs.* Madison was decided.

It is unlikely that the recently discussed case of Bayard *vs.* Singleton (North Carolina, November, 1787, 1 Martin, 48–51), ever reached Marshall's attention except by hearsay.

[1] See 118–19 of this volume.

The second Hayburn case (August, 1792, 2 Dallas, 409; and see *Annals*, 2d Cong. 2d Sess. 1319–22). For a full discussion of this important case see particularly Professor Max Farrand's analysis in the *American Historical Review* (XIII, 283–84), which is the only satisfactory treatment of it. See also Thayer: *Cases on Constitutional Law* (1, footnote to 105).

Kamper *vs.* Hawkins (November, 1793, 1 Va. Ca. 20 *et seq.*), a case which came directly under Marshall's observation.

Van Horne's Lessee *vs.* Dorrance (April, 1795, 2 Dallas, 304), in which Justice Paterson of the Supreme Court said all that Marshall repeated in Marbury *vs.* Madison upon the power of the Judiciary to declare legislation void.

Calder *vs.* Bull (August, 1798, 3 Dallas, 386–401), in which, however, the Court questioned its power to annul legislation. Cooper *vs.* Telfair (February, 1800, 4 Dallas, 14). These last two cases and the Hayburn Case had been decided by justices of the Supreme Court.

Whittington *vs.* Polk (Maryland, April, 1802, 1 Harris and Johnson, 236–52). Marshall surely was informed of this case by Chase who, as Chief Justice of Maryland, decided it. The report, however, was not published until 1821. (See McLaughlin: *The Courts, the Constitution, and Parties*, 20–23.) In his opinion in this case Justice Chase employed precisely the same reasoning used by Marshall in Marbury *vs.* Madison to show the power of courts to declare invalid legislative acts that violate the Constitution.

The old Court of Appeals, under the Articles of Confederation, denounced as unconstitutional the law that assigned circuit duties to the judges of that appellate tribunal; and this was cited by Thomas Morris of New York and by John Stanley of South Carolina in the judiciary debate of 1802.[1]

As to the statement of Chief Justice, later Governor Thomas Hutchinson of Massachusetts, in 1765, and the ancient British precedents, cited by Robert Ludlow Fowler in the *American Law Review* (XXIX, 711–25), it is positive that Marshall never had an intimation that any such pronouncements ever had been made.

Neither, in all likelihood, had Marshall known of the highly advertised case of Rutgers *vs.* Waddington, decided by a New York justice of the peace in 1784 (see *American Law Review*, XIX, 180), and the case of Bowman *vs.* Middleton (South Caro-

[1] See footnote 5 to p. 74 of this volume.

lina, May, 1792, 1 Bay, 252–55) which was not printed until
1809. (See McLaughlin, 25–26.) The same may be said of the
North Carolina controversy, State *vs.* ——, decided in April,
1794 (1 Haywood, 28–40), and of Lindsay *et al vs.* Commissioners (South Carolina, October, 1796, 2 Bay, 38–62), the report of which was not printed until 1811.

For a scholarly treatment of the matter from an historical
and legally professional point of view, see *Doctrine of Judicial
Review* by Professor Edward S. Corwin of the Department of
History and Politics, Princeton University; also *The Courts, the
Constitution, and Parties,* by Professor Andrew C. McLaughlin
of the Department of History, University of Chicago. The
discussion by these scholars is thorough. All cases are critically examined, and they omit only the political exigency that
forced Marshall's opinion in Marbury *vs.* Madison.

The student should also consult the paper of William M.
Meigs, "The Relation of the Judiciary to the Constitution,"
in the *American Law Review* (xix, 175–203), and that of Frank
E. Melvin, "The Judicial Bulwark of the Constitution," in the
American Political Science Review (viii, 167–203).

Professor Charles A. Beard's *The Supreme Court and the Constitution* contains trustworthy information not readily accessible
elsewhere, as well as sound comment upon the whole subject.

Judicial Power and Unconstitutional Legislation, by Brinton
Coxe, although published in 1893, is still highly valuable. And
Power of Federal Judiciary over Legislation, by J. Hampden
Dougherty, will be profitable to the student.

Marbury *vs.* Madison is attacked ably, if petulantly, by
Dean Trickett, "Judicial Nullification of Acts of Congress,"
in the *North American Review* (clxxxv, 848 *et seq.*), and also
by James B. McDonough, "The Alleged Usurpation of Power
by the Federal Courts," in the *American Law Review* (xlvi,
45–59). An ingenious and comparatively recent dissent from
the theory of judicial supervision of legislation is the argument
of Chief Justice Walter Clark of the Supreme Court of North
Carolina, "Government by Judges." (See Senate Document
No. 610, 63d Congress, 2d Session.)

With regard to the possible effect on American law of foreign
assertions of the supremacy of the Judiciary, particularly that
of France, the Address of James M. Beck of the New York Bar,
before the Pennsylvania Bar Association on June 29, 1915, and
reported in the Twenty-first Annual Report of that Association (222–51), is a careful and exhaustive study.

APPENDIX D

TEXT, AS GENERALLY ACCEPTED, OF THE CIPHER LETTER OF
AARON BURR TO JAMES WILKINSON, DATED JULY 29, 1806[1]

YOUR letter postmarked thirteenth May, is received. At
length I have obtained funds, and have actually commenced.
The Eastern detachments, from different points and under
different pretences, will rendezvous on the Ohio first of November. Everything internal and external favors our views. Naval
protection of England is secured. Truxtun is going to Jamaica
to arrange with the admiral on that station. It will meet us
at the Mississippi. England, a navy of the United States, are
ready to join, and final orders are given to my friends and followers. It will be a host of choice spirits. Wilkinson shall be
second to Burr only; Wilkinson shall dictate the rank and promotion of his officers. Burr will proceed westward first August,
never to return. With him goes his daughter; her husband will
follow in October, with a corps of worthies. Send forthwith an
intelligent and confidential friend with whom Burr may confer;
he shall return immediately with further interesting details;
this is essential to concert and harmony of movement. Send a
list of all persons known to Wilkinson west of the mountains
who could be useful, with a note delineating their characters.
By your messenger send me four or five commissions of your
officers, which you can borrow under any pretence you please;
they shall be returned faithfully. Already are orders given to
the contractor to forward six months' provisions to points
Wilkinson may name; this shall not be used until the last moment, and then under proper injunctions. Our object, my dear
friend, is brought to a point so long desired. Burr guarantees
the result with his life and honor, with the lives and honor and
the fortunes of hundreds, the best blood of our country. Burr's
plan of operation is to move down rapidly from the Falls, on
the fifteenth of November, with the first five hundred or a
thousand men, in light boats now constructing for that purpose;
to be at Natchez between the fifth and fifteenth of December,
there to meet you; there to determine whether it will be expedient in the first instance to seize on or pass by Baton Rouge.

[1] See 307–09, 352–55, of this volume.

On receipt of this send Burr an answer. Draw on Burr for all expenses, etc. The people of the country to which we are going are prepared to receive us; their agents, now with Burr, say that if we will protect their religion, and will not subject them to a foreign Power, that in three weeks all will be settled. The gods invite us to glory and fortune; it remains to be seen whether we deserve the boon. The bearer of this goes express to you. He is a man of inviolable honor and perfect discretion, formed to execute rather than project, capable of relating facts with fidelity, and incapable of relating them otherwise; he is thoroughly informed of the plans and intentions of Burr, and will disclose to you as far as you require, and no further. He has imbibed a reverence for your character, and may be embarrassed in your presence; put him at ease, and he will satisfy you.

APPENDIX E

APPENDIX

Excerpt from Speech of William Wirt at the Trial of Aaron Burr[1]

Who is Blennerhassett? A native of Ireland, a man of letters, fled from the storms of his own country to find quiet in ours. His history shows that war is not the natural element of his mind. If it had been, he never would have exchanged Ireland for America. So far is an army from furnishing the society natural and proper to Mr. Blennerhassett's character, that on his arrival in America, he retired even from the population of the Atlantic States, and sought quiet and solitude in the bosom of our Western forests.

But he carried with him taste and science and wealth; and lo, the desert smiled! Possessing himself of a beautiful island in the Ohio, he rears upon it a palace and decorates it with every romantic embellishment of fancy. A shrubbery, that Shenstone might have envied, blooms around him. Music, that might have charmed Calypso and her nymphs, is his. An extensive library spreads its treasures before him. A philosophical apparatus offers to him all the secrets and mysteries of nature. Peace, tranquillity, and innocence shed their mingled delights around him. And to crown the enchantment of the scene, a wife, who is said to be lovely even beyond her sex and graced with every accomplishment that can render it irresistible, had blessed him with her love and made him the father of several children. The evidence would convince you, that this is but a faint picture of the real life.

In the midst of all this peace, this innocent simplicity and this tranquillity, this feast of the mind, this pure banquet of the heart, the destroyer comes; he comes to change this paradise into a hell. Yet the flowers do not wither at his approach. No monitory shuddering through the bosom of their unfortunate possessor warns him of the ruin that is coming upon him. A stranger presents himself. Introduced to their civilities by the high rank which he had lately held in his country, he soon finds his way to their hearts, by the dignity and elegance of his demeanor, the light and beauty of his conversation and the seductive and fascinating power of his address.

[1] See 495–97 of this volume.

The conquest was not difficult. Innocence is ever simple and credulous. Conscious of no design itself, it suspects none in others. It wears no guard before its breast. Every door and portal and avenue of the heart is thrown open, and all who choose it enter. Such was the state of Eden when the serpent entered its bowers.

The prisoner, in a more engaging form, winding himself into the open and unpractised heart of the unfortunate Blenner-hassett, found but little difficulty in changing the native character of that heart and the objects of its affection. By degrees he infuses into it the poison of his own ambition. He breathes into it the fire of his own courage; a daring and desperate thirst for glory; an ardour panting for great enterprises, for all the storm and bustle and hurricane of life.

In a short time the whole man is changed, and every object of his former delight is relinquished. No more he enjoys the tranquil scene; it has become flat and insipid to his taste. His books are abandoned. His retort and crucible are thrown aside. His shrubbery blooms and breathes its fragrance upon the air in vain; he likes it not. His ear no longer drinks the rich melody of music; it longs for the trumpet's clangor and the cannon's roar. Even the prattle of his babes, once so sweet, no longer affects him; and the angel smile of his wife, which hitherto touched his bosom with ecstasy so unspeakable, is now unseen and unfelt.

Greater objects have taken possession of his soul. His imagination has been dazzled by visions of diadems, of stars and garters and titles of nobility. He has been taught to burn with restless emulation at the names of great heroes and conquerors. His enchanted island is destined soon to relapse into a wilderness; and in a few months we find the beautiful and tender partner of his bosom, whom he lately permitted not the winds of summer to visit too roughly, we find her shivering at midnight, on the winter banks of the Ohio and mingling her tears with the torrents, that froze as they fell.

Yet this unfortunate man, thus deluded from his interest and his happiness, thus seduced from the paths of innocence and peace, thus confounded in the toils that were deliberately spread for him and overwhelmed by the mastering spirit and genius of another — this man, thus ruined and undone and made to play a subordinate part in this grand drama of guilt and treason, this man is to be called the principal offender,

while *he*, by whom he was thus plunged in misery, is comparatively innocent, a mere accessory! Is this reason? Is it law?
Is it humanity? Sir, neither the human heart nor the human understanding will bear a perversion so monstrous and absurd!
So shocking to the soul! So revolting to reason! Let Aaron Burr
then not shrink from the high destination which he has courted,
and having already ruined Blennerhassett in fortune, character
and happiness forever, let him not attempt to finish the tragedy
by thrusting that ill-fated man between himself and punishment.[1]

[1] *Burr Trials*, II, 96-98.

APPENDIX F

THE place in which a crime was committed is essential to an indictment, were it only to shew the jurisdiction of the court. It is also essential for the purpose of enabling the prisoner to make his defence. . . This necessity is rendered the stronger by the constitutional provision that the offender "shall be tried in the state and district wherein the crime shall have been committed," and by the act of congress which requires that twelve petty jurors at least shall be summoned from the county where the offence was committed.

A description of the particular manner in which the war was levied seems also essential to enable the accused to make his defence. The law does not expect a man to be prepared to defend every act of his life which may be suddenly and without notice alleged against him. In common justice the particular fact with which he is charged ought to be seated, and stated in such a manner as to afford a reasonable certainty of the nature of the accusation and the circumstances which will be adduced against him.

. . . .

Treason can only be established by the proof of overt acts; and . . those overt acts only which are changed in the indictment can be given in evidence, unless perhaps as corroborative testimony after the overt acts are proved. That clause in the constitution too which says that in all criminal prosecutions the accused shall enjoy the right "to be informed of the nature and cause of the accusation" is considered as having a direct bearing on this point. It secures to him such information as will enable him to prepare for his defence.

It seems then to be perfectly clear that it would not be sufficient for an indictment to allege generally that the accused had levied war against the United States. The charge must be more particularly specified by laying what is termed an overt act of levying war. . .

[1] See *supra*, chap IX.

If it be necessary to specify the charge in the indictment, it would seem to follow, irresistibly, that the charge must be proved as laid. . . Might it be otherwise, the charge of an overt act would be a mischief instead of an advantage to the accused. It would lead him from the true cause and nature of the accusation instead of informing him respecting it.

But it is contended on the part of the prosecution that, although the accused had never been with the party which assembled at Blennerhassett's island, and was, at the time, at a great distance, and in a different state, he was yet legally present, and therefore may properly be charged in the indictment as being present in fact.

It is therefore necessary to inquire whether in this case the doctrine of constructive presence can apply.

It is conceived by the court to be possible that a person may be concerned in a treasonable conspiracy and yet be legally, as well as actually absent while some one act of the treason is perpetrated. If a rebellion should be so extensive as to spread through every state in the union, it will scarcely be contended that every individual concerned in it is legally present at every overt act committed in the course of that rebellion. It would be a very violent presumption indeed, . . to presume that even the chief of the rebel army was legally present at every such overt act.

If the main rebel army, with the chief at its head, should be prosecuting war at one extremity of our territory, say in New-Hampshire — if this chief should be there captured and sent to the other extremity for the purpose of trial — if his indictment instead of alleging an overt act, which was true in point of fact, should allege that he had assembled some small party, which in truth he had not seen, and had levied war by engaging in a skirmish in Georgia at a time when in reality he was fighting a battle in New-Hampshire — if such evidence would support such an indictment by the fiction that he was legally present though really absent, all would ask to what purpose are those provisions in the constitution, which direct the place of trial and ordain that the accused shall be informed of the nature and cause of the accusation?

But that a man may be legally absent, who has counselled or procured a treasonable act, is proved by all those books which treat upon the subject; and which concur in declaring that such a person is a principal traitor, not because he was legally present, but because in treason all are principals. Yet the indictment, speaking upon general principles, would charge him according to the truth of the case. . .

If the conspirator had done nothing which amounted to levying of war, and if by our constitution the doctrine that an accessory becomes a principal be not adopted, in consequence of which the conspirator could not be condemned under an indictment stating the truth of the case, it would be going very far to say that this defect, if it be termed one, may be cured by an indictment stating the case untruly.

. . . .

In point of law then, the man, who incites, aids, or procures a treasonable act, is not merely in consequence of that incitement, aid or procurement, legally present when that act is committed.

If it do not result, from the nature of the crime, that all who are concerned in it are legally present at every overt act, then each case depends upon its own circumstances; and to judge how far the circumstances of any case can make him legally present, who is in fact absent, the doctrine of constructive presence must be examined.

. . . .

The whole treason laid in this indictment is the levying of war in Blennerhassett's island; and the whole question to which the inquiry of the court is now directed is whether the prisoner was legally present at that fact.

I say this is the whole question; because the prisoner can only be convicted on the overt act laid in the indictment. With respect to this prosecution, it is as if no other overt act existed.

If other overt acts can be inquired into, it is for the sole purpose of proving the particular fact charged. It is as evidence of the crime consisting of this particular fact, not as establishing the general crime by a distinct fact.

The counsel for the prosecution have charged those engaged in the defence with considering the overt act as the treason, whereas it ought to be considered solely as the evidence of the treason; but the counsel for the prosecution seem themselves not to have sufficiently adverted to this clear principle; that though the overt act may not be itself the treason, it is the sole act of that treason which can produce conviction. It is the sole point in issue between the parties. And the only division of that point, if the expression be allowed, which the court is now examining, is the constructive presence of the prisoner at the fact charged. . .

Had the prisoner set out with the party from Beaver for Blennerhassett's island, or perhaps had he set out for that place, though not from Beaver, and had arrived in the island, he would have been present at the fact. Had he not arrived in the island, but had taken a position near enough to coöperate with those on the island, to assist them in any act of hostility, or to aid them if attacked, the question whether he was constructively present would be a question compounded of law and fact, which would be decided by the jury, with the aid of the court, so far as respected the law. In this case the accused would have been of the particular party assembled on the island, and would have been associated with them in the particular act of levying war said to have been committed on the island.

But if he was not with the party at any time before they reached the island — if he did not join them there, or intend to join them there — if his personal coöperation in the general plan was to be afforded elsewhere, at a great distance, in a different state — if the overt acts of treason to be performed by him were to be distinct overt acts — then he was not of the particular party assembled at Blennerhassett's island, and was not constructively present, aiding and assisting in the particular act which was there committed.

The testimony on this point, so far as it has been delivered, is not equivocal. There is not only no evidence that the accused was of the particular party which assembled on Blennerhassett's island; but the whole evidence shows he was not of that party.

In felony then, admitting the crime to have been completed on the island, and to have been advised, procured, or commanded by the accused, he would have been incontestably an accessory and not a principal.

But in treason, it is said, the law is otherwise, because the theatre of action is more extensive.

The reasoning applies in England as strongly as in the United States. While in '15 and '45 the family of Stuart sought to regain the crown they had forfeited, the struggle was for the whole kingdom; yet no man was ever considered as legally present at one place, when actually at another; or as aiding in one transaction, while actually employed in another.

With the perfect knowledge that the whole nation may be

the theatre of action, the English books unite in declaring that he, who counsels, procures or aids treason, is guilty accessorially and solely in virtue of the common law principle, that what will make a man an accessory in felony makes him a principal in treason. So far from considering a man as constructively present at every overt act of the general treason in which he may have been concerned, the whole doctrine of the books limits the proof against him to those particular overt acts of levying war with which he is charged.

What would be the effect of a different doctrine? Clearly that which has been stated. If a person levying war in Kentucky, may be said to be constructively present and assembled with a party carrying on war in Virginia at a great distance from him, then he is present at every overt act performed anywhere. He may be tried in any state on the continent, where any overt act has been committed. He may be proved to be guilty of an overt act laid in the indictment in which he had no personal participation, by proving that he advised it, or that he committed other acts.

This is, perhaps, too extravagant to be in terms maintained. Certainly it cannot be supported by the doctrines of the English law.

.   .   .   .

In conformity with principle and with authority then, the prisoner at the bar was neither legally nor actually present at Blennerhassett's island; and the court is strongly inclined to the opinion that without proving an actual or legal presence by two witnesses, the overt act laid in this indictment cannot be proved.

But this opinion is controverted on two grounds.

The first is, that the indictment does not charge the prisoner to have been present.

The second, that although he was absent, yet if he caused the assemblage, he may be indicted as being present, and convicted on evidence that he caused the treasonable act.

The first position is to be decided by the indictment itself. . . The court understands it to be directly charged that the prisoner did assemble with the multitude and did march with them. . . The charges of this special indictment therefore must be proved as laid, and no evidence which proves the crime in a form substantially different can be received. . .

But suppose the law to be as is contended by the counsel for the United States. Suppose an indictment, charging an individual with personally assembling among others and thus levying war, may be satisfied with the proof that he caused the assemblage. What effect will this law have upon this case?

The guilt of the accused, if there be any guilt, does not consist in the assemblage; for he was not a member of it. The simple fact of assemblage no more affects one absent man than another.

His guilt then consists in procuring the assemblage, and upon this fact depends his criminality. The proof relative to the character of an assemblage must be the same whether a man be present or absent. In general, to charge any individual with the guilt of an assemblage, the fact of his presence must be proved: it constitutes an essential part of the overt act.

If then the procurement be substituted in the place of presence, does it not also constitute an essential part of the overt act? must it not also be proved? must it not be proved in the same manner that presence must be proved?

If in one case the presence of the individual make the guilt of the assemblage his guilt, and in the other case the procurement by the individual make the guilt of the assemblage his guilt, then presence and procurement are equally component parts of the overt act, and equally require two witnesses.

Collateral points may, say the books, be proved according to the course of the common law; but is this a collateral point? Is the fact, without which the accused does not participate in the guilt of the assemblage if it were guilty, a collateral point? This cannot be.

The presence of the party, where presence is necessary, being a part of the overt act must be positively proved by two witnesses. No presumptive evidence, no facts from which presence may be conjectured or inferred will satisfy the constitution and the law.

If procurement take the place of presence and become part of the overt act, then no presumptive evidence, no facts from which the procurement may be conjected or inferred, can satisfy the constitution and the law.

The mind is not to be led to the conclusion that the individual was present by a train of conjectures, of inferences or of reasoning; the fact must be proved by two witnesses.

Neither, where procurement supplies the want of presence, is the mind to be conducted to the conclusion that the accused procured the assembly, by a train of conjectures of inferences or of reasoning; the fact itself must be proved by two witnesses, and must have been committed within the district.

If it be said that the advising or procurement of treason is a secret transaction, which can scarcely ever be proved in the manner required by this opinion, the answer which will readily suggest itself is, that the difficulty of proving a fact will not justify conviction without proof. Certainly it will not justify conviction without a direct and positive witness in a case where the constitution requires two.

The more correct inference from this circumstance would seem to be, that the advising of the fact is not within the constitutional definition of the crime. To advise or procure a treason is in the nature of conspiring or plotting treason, which is not treason in itself...

The 8th amendment to the constitution has been pressed with great force... The accused cannot be said to be "informed of the nature and cause of the accusation" unless the indictment give him that notice which may reasonably suggest to him the point on which the accusations turns [sic], so that he may know the course to be pursued in his defence.

It is also well worthy of consideration that this doctrine, so far as it respects treason, is entirely supported by the operation of the common law, which is said to convert the accessory before the fact into the principal, and to make the act of the principal his act. The accessory before the fact is not said to have levied war. He is not said to be guilty under the statute, but the common law attaches to him the guilt of that fact which he has advised or procured; and, as contended, makes it his act.

This is the operation of the common law not the operation of the statute. It is an operation then which can only be performed where the common law exists to perform: it is the creature of the common law, and the creature presupposes its creator. To decide then that this doctrine is applicable to the United States would seem to imply the decision that the United States, as a nation, have a common law which creates and defines the punishment of crimes accessorial in their nature. It would imply the further decision that these accessorial crimes are not in the case of treason excluded by the definition of treason given in the constitution...

I have said that this doctrine cannot apply to the United States without implying those decisions respecting the common law which I have stated; because, should it be true as is contended that the constitutional definition of treason comprehends him who advises or procures an assemblage that levies war, it would not follow that such adviser or procurer might be charged as having been present at the assemblage.

If the adviser or procurer be within the definition of levying war, and independent of the agency of the common law do actually levy war, then the advisement of procurement is an overt act of levying war. If it be the overt action which he is to be convicted, then it must be charged in the indictment; for he can only be convicted on proof of the overt acts which are charged.

To render this distinction more intelligible let it be recollected, that although it should be conceded that since the statutes of William and Mary he who advises or procures a treason may, in England, be charged as having committed that treason by virtue of the common law operation, which is said so far as respects the indictment to unite the accessorial to the principal offence and permit them to be charged as one, yet it can never be conceded that he who commits one overt act under the statute of Edward can be charged and convicted on proof of another overt act.

If then procurement be an overt act of treason under the constitution, no man can be convicted for the procurement under an indictment charging him with actually assembling, whatever may be the doctrine of the common law in the case of an accessorial offender.[1]

[1] *Burr Trials*, II, 424-38.

WORKS CITED IN THIS VOLUME

WORKS CITED IN THIS VOLUME

*The material given in parentheses and following certain titles indicates the form
in which those titles have been cited in the footnotes.*

Acts and Laws. *See* United States Statutes.

ADAMS, HENRY. History of the United States of America.
9 vols. New York. 1889–1911. (Adams: *U.S.*)

—— John Randolph. Boston. 1892. [American Statesmen
series.] (Adams: *Randolph.*)

—— Life of Albert Gallatin. Philadelphia. 1879. (Adams:
Gallatin.)

ADAMS, HENRY, *editor.* Documents relating to New-England
Federalism, 1800–1815. Boston. 1877. (*N.E. Federalism:*
Adams.)

ADAMS, JOHN. *See* Old Family Letters.

ADAMS, JOHN QUINCY. Memoirs. Edited by Charles Francis
Adams. 12 vols. Philadelphia. 1874–77. (*Memoirs,
J. Q. A.*: Adams.)

—— Writings. Edited by Worthington Chauncey Ford. 5
vols. New York. 1913–15. (*Writings, J. Q. A.*: Ford.)

ADDISON, ALEXANDER. Trial on an Impeachment by the
House of Representatives before the Senate of the Commonwealth of Pennsylvania. Reported by Thomas Lloyd,
stenographer. Lancaster. 1803. (*Addison Trial.*)

ALLEN, GARDNER WELD. Our Navy and the Barbary Corsairs.
Boston. 1905.

ALLIBONE, SAMUEL AUSTIN. Dictionary of English Literature
and British and American Authors. 3 vols. Philadelphia.
1870–71.

AMBLER, CHARLES HENRY. Thomas Ritchie — A Study in
Virginia Politics. Richmond. 1913.

American Historical Association. Annual Report. 1896, vol. II;
1913, vol. II. Washington, D.C.

American Historical Review. Vol. IV–XIX, inclusive, 1899–1914.
New York. (*Am. Hist. Rev.*)

American Law Review. Vol. I, 1867; Boston. Vols. XIX, XXIX,
XLVI, 1885, 1895, 1912; St. Louis. (*Am. Law Rev.*)

American Political Science Review. Vol. VIII, 1914; vol. IX,
1915. Baltimore. (*Am. Pol. Sci. Rev.*)

American State Papers. Documents, Legislative and Executive, of the Congress of the United States. Selected and edited under the Authority of Congress. 38 vols. Washington. 1832–61. [Citations in this work are from "Foreign Relations" (*Am. State Papers, For. Rel.*); "Miscellaneous." (*Am. State Papers, Misc.*); and "Public Lands."]

AMES, FISHER. Works. Edited by Seth Ames. 2 vols. Boston. 1854. (Ames.)

ANDERSON, DICE ROBINS. William Branch Giles: A Study in the Politics of Virginia and the Nation from 1790 to 1830. Menasha [Wisconsin]. 1914. (Anderson.)

ANDERSON, JOHN E., *and* HOBBY, WILLIAM J. Contract for the Western Territory made with the Legislature of Georgia in the year 1795, considered with a Reference to the subsequent Attempts of the State to impair its Obligation. Augusta. 1799.

ARNOLD, SAMUEL GREENE. History of the State of Rhode Island and Providence Plantations. 2 vols. New York. 1860.

Athenæum; Journal of Literature, Science, and the Fine Arts. (Weekly.) 1835. London.

BASSETT, JOHN SPENCER. Life of Andrew Jackson. 2 vols. New York. 1911.

BAY, ELIHU HALL. Reports of Cases argued and determined in the Superior Courts of Law in the State of South Carolina. Vols. I and II, 1809, 1811. New York.

BAYARD, JAMES ASHETON. Papers, from 1796 to 1815. Edited by Elizabeth Donnan. [Annual Report of the American Historical Association for the year 1913, vol. II.] Washington. 1915. (*Bayard Papers:* Donnan.)

BEARD, CHARLES AUSTIN. Economic Origins of Jeffersonian Democracy. New York. 1915. (Beard: *Econ. Origins Jeff. Dem.*)

—— Supreme Court and the Constitution. New York. 1912.

BEVERIDGE, ALBERT JEREMIAH. Life of John Marshall. 4 vols. Boston. 1916–19.

BIDDLE, ALEXANDER. *See* Old Family Letters.

BISHOP, ABRAHAM. Georgia Speculation Unveiled. [Two pamphlets, in two parts each.] Hartford. 1797–98. (Bishop.)

Blackwood's Magazine. Vol. XVII, 1822. Edinburgh and London.

Blennerhassett Papers, embodying the private Journal of Harman Blennerhassett. Edited by William H. Safford. Cincinnati. 1864. (*Blennerhassett Papers:* Safford.)

BOTTA, CARLO GIUSEPPE GUGLIELMO. History of the War of the Independence of the United States of America. Translated from the Italian by George Alexander Otis. 3 vols. Philadelphia. 1820.

BOUVIER, JOHN. Law Dictionary and Concise Encyclopedia. Third Revision by Francis Rawle. 3 vols. Kansas City and St. Paul. 1914.

BRADY, JOSEPH PLUNKETT. Trial of Aaron Burr. New York. 1913.

BROCKENBROUGH, WILLIAM, *and* HOLMES, HUGH. Collection of Cases decided by the General Court of Virginia, chiefly relating to the penal laws of the Commonwealth, commencing in the year 1789 and ending in 1814. [Also known as the first volume of Virginia Cases.] Philadelphia. 1815. (Va. Cases.)

BRYAN, WILHELMUS BOGART. History of the National Capital from its Foundation through the Period of the Adoption of the Organic Act. 2 vols. New York. 1914–16. (Bryan.)

BURR, AARON. Private Journal: Reprinted in full from the original manuscript in the library of William Keeney Bixby of St. Louis, Missouri. 2 vols. Rochester. 1903.

—— Trials, for Treason and for a Misdemeanor. Reported by David Robertson, stenographer. 2 vols. Philadelphia. 1808. (*Burr Trials.*)

And see Brady, Joseph Plunkett; Davis, Matthew Livingston; Jenkinson, Isaac; McCaleb, Walter Flavius; Parton, James.

CABOT, GEORGE. *See* Lodge, Henry Cabot.

CALL, DANIEL. Reports of Cases argued and decided in the Court of Appeals of Virginia. Vol. IV. Richmond. 1833. (Call.)

CARSON, HAMPTON LAWRENCE. Supreme Court of the United States: Its History. 2 vols. Philadelphia. 1891. (Carson.)

CHANDLER, PELEG WHITMAN. American Criminal Trials. 2 vols. Boston. 1844.

CHANNING, EDWARD. History of the United States. Vols. 1–4. New York. 1905–17. (Channing: *U.S.*)

—— Jeffersonian System, 1801–11. [Vol. 12 of "The American Nation, a History," edited by Albert Bushnell Hart.] New York and London. 1906. (Channing: *Jeff. System.*)

CHAPPELL, ABSALOM HARRIS. Miscellanies of Georgia, Historical, Biographical, Descriptive, etc. Atlanta. 1874. (Chappell.)

CHASE, SAMUEL. Trial, before the High Court of Impeachment, composed of the Senate of the United States, for charges exhibited against him by the House of Representatives . . for high Crimes and Misdemeanors. Reported by Charles Evans, stenographer. Baltimore. 1805. (*Chase Trial.*)

CHASTELLUX, FRANÇOIS JEAN, MARQUIS DE. Travels in North America in the years 1780–81–82. New York. 1828.

CLARK, DANIEL. Proofs of the Corruption of Gen. James Wilkinson and of his Connexion with Aaron Burr. Philadelphia. 1809. (Clark: *Proofs.*)

CLARK, JOSHUA VICTOR HOPKINS. Onondaga; or Reminiscences of Earlier and Later Times; being a Series of Historical Sketches relative to Onondaga; with Notes on the Several Towns in the County, and Oswego. 2 vols. Syracuse. 1849. (Clark: *Onondaga.*)

CLAY, HENRY. Private Correspondence. Edited by Calvin Colton. New York. 1855. (*Priv. Corres.*: Colton.)

—— Works. Edited by Calvin Colton. 7 vols. New York. 1897. (*Works:* Colton.)

CLEVELAND, CATHERINE CAROLINE. Great Revival in the West, 1797–1805. Chicago. 1916.

COLTON, CALVIN, *editor. See* Clay, Henry. Private Correspondence, and Works.

CONGRESS. *See* United States Congress.

CORWIN, EDWARD SAMUEL. Doctrine of Judicial Review — Its Legal and Historical Basis and other Essays. Princeton. 1914. (Corwin.)

COX, ISAAC JOSLIN. West Florida Controversy, 1798–1813. Baltimore. 1918. (Cox.)

COXE, BRINTON. Essay on Judicial Power and Unconstitutional Legislation, being a Commentary on Parts of the Constitution of the United States. Philadelphia. 1893.

CRANCH, WILLIAM. Reports of Cases argued and adjudged in the Supreme Court of the United States, 1801–08. 6 vols. New York. 1812.

—— Same February term, 1810. Vol. VI. New York. 1812.

Also Cases argued and decided in the Supreme Court of the United States and others. [Lawyers' edition.] 1, 2, 3, 4 Cranch, Book II. 5, 6, 7, 8, 9 Cranch, Book III. Edited and annotated by Stephen K. Williams and Walter Malins Rose. Rochester. 1901. (Cranch.)

CUTLER, WILLIAM PARKER, *and* JULIA PERKINS. Life, Journals, and Correspondence of Menasseh Cutler. 2 vols. Cincinnati. 1888. (Cutler.)

DALLAS, ALEXANDER JAMES. Reports of Cases ruled and adjudged in the several Courts of the United States and of Pennsylvania. Vols. 2, 3, 4. Philadelphia. 1798, 1799, 1835.

Also Cases argued and decided in the Supreme Court of the United States and others. [Lawyers' edition.] 1, 2, 3, 4 Dallas, Book I. Edited and annotated by Stephen K. Williams and Walter Malins Rose. Rochester. 1901. (Dallas.)

DAVIS, JOHN CHANDLER BANCROFT, *reporter*. *See* United States Supreme Court.

DAVIS, MATTHEW LIVINGSTON. Memoirs of Aaron Burr. 2 vols. New York. 1836. (Davis.)

Debate in the House of Representatives of the Territory of Orleans, on a Memorial to Congress, respecting the illegal conduct of General Wilkinson. New Orleans. 1807.

Debates in the Several State Conventions. See Elliot, Jonathan.

DILLON, JOHN FORREST, *compiler and editor*. John Marshall. Life, Character, and Judicial Services, as portrayed in the Centenary Proceedings throughout the United States in Marshall's Day. 1901. 3 vols. Chicago. 1903. (Dillon.)

DODD, WILLIAM EDWARD. Life of Nathaniel Macon. Raleigh. 1903. (Dodd.)

DONNAN, ELIZABETH, *editor*. *See* Bayard Papers.

DOUGHERTY, JOHN HAMPDEN. Power of Federal Judiciary over Legislation. New York. 1912.

DWIGHT, NATHANIEL. Signers of the Declaration of Independence. New York. 1895. (Dwight.)

634 WORKS CITED IN THIS VOLUME

EATON, WILLIAM. Life, principally collected from his correspondence and other manuscripts. Edited by Charles Prentiss. Brookfield. 1813. (*Eaton:* Prentiss.)

ELLIOT, JONATHAN. Debates in the several State Conventions, on the Adoption of the Federal Constitution, as recommended by the General Convention at Philadelphia in 1787. 5 vols. Washington. 1836–45.

EVANS, CHARLES, *reporter.* *See* Chase, Samuel. Trial.

FARRAND, MAX, *editor.* *See* Records of the Federal Convention.

Federalist, The. Commentary on the Constitution of the United States from original text of Alexander Hamilton, John Jay, and James Madison. Edited by Henry Cabot Lodge. New York. 1895.

First Forty Years of Washington Society. *See* Hunt, Gaillard.

FORD, PAUL LEICESTER, *editor.* *See* Jefferson, Thomas. Works.

FORD, WORTHINGTON CHAUNCEY, *editor.* *See* Adams, John Quincy. Writings.

GALLATIN, ALBERT. *See* Adams, Henry.

GARLAND, HUGH ALFRED. Life of John Randolph of Roanoke. 2 vols. New York. 1851.

GIBBS, GEORGE, *editor.* Memoirs of the Administrations of Washington and John Adams. *See* Wolcott, Oliver.

GILES, WILLIAM BRANCH. *See* Anderson, Dice Robins.

GIRARD, STEPHEN. *See* McMaster, John Bach.

Great American Lawyers. *See* Lewis, William Draper.

Green Bag: An Entertaining Magazine for Lawyers. Edited by Horace Williams Fuller. Vol. II, 1890. Boston.

GREENE, NATHANAEL. *See* Johnson, William.

GRIGSBY, HUGH BLAIR. History of the Virginia Federal Convention of 1788, with a Biographical Sketch of the Author and Illustrative Notes. Edited by Robert Alonzo Brock. 2 vols. [Collections of the Virginia Historical Society, new series, vols. IX and X.] Richmond. 1890–91.

—— Virginia Convention of 1829–30. Richmond. 1854.

Gulf States Historical Magazine. Vol. II, 1903. Montgomery [Ala.].

HAMILTON, ALEXANDER. *See* Lodge, Henry Cabot.

HAMMOND, JABEZ DELANO. History of Political Parties in the State of New York from the Ratification of the Federal Constitution to December, 1840. Albany. 1842.

HARDEN, EDWARD JENKINS. Life of George Michael Troup. Savannah. 1859.

HARPER, ROBERT GOODLOE. Case of the Georgia Sales on the Mississippi considered with a Reference to Law Authorities and Public Acts, and an Appendix containing certain Extracts, Records, and Official Papers. Philadelphia. 1797. (Harper.)

HARRIS, JOEL CHANDLER. Georgia from the Invasion of De Soto to recent Times. New York. 1896. (Harris.)

HARRIS, THOMAS, and JOHNSON, REVERDY. Reports of Cases argued and determined in the General Court and Court of Appeals of the State of Maryland from 1800 to 1805 inclusive. Vol. I. Annapolis. 1821. (Harris and Johnson.)

HASKINS, CHARLES HOMER. Yazoo Land Companies. [Reprinted from the papers of the American Historical Association for October, 1891.] New York. 1891. (Haskins.)

HAYWOOD, JOHN. Reports of Cases adjudged in the Superior Courts of Law and Equity of the State of North Carolina from the year 1789 to the year 1798. Halifax. 1799.

HENRY, WILLIAM WIRT. Patrick Henry. Life, Correspondence and Speeches. 3 vols. New York. 1891.

HILDRETH, RICHARD. History of the United States of America. 6 vols. New York. 1854–55. (Hildreth.)

Historical and Philosophical Society of Ohio. Quarterly Publication. Vol. IX, Nos. 1 and 2; January and April, 1914. Cincinnati. (*Quarterly Pub. Hist. and Phil. Soc. Ohio.*)

HOWARD, BENJAMIN CHEW. Reports of Cases argued and adjudged in the Supreme Court of the United States, December term, 1856. Vol. XIX. Washington. 1857. (Howard.)

HOYT, WILLIAM HENRY, *editor. See* Murphey, Archibald Debow.

HUDSON, FREDERIC. Journalism in the United States from 1690 to 1872. New York. 1873. (Hudson.)

HUGHES, ROBERT WILLIAM. Reports of Cases decided in the Courts of the Fourth Judicial Circuit sitting in Admiralty. Vol. V, edited by Robert Morton Hughes. New York. 1883.

HUNT, GAILLARD, *editor*. First Forty Years of Washington Society, portrayed by the Family Letters of Mrs. Samuel Harrison Smith. New York. 1906. (Hunt.)

INDIANA TERRITORY. Laws of the Indiana Territory, 1801–06 inclusive. Paoli [Indiana]. 1886.

IREDELL, JAMES. Life and Correspondence. Edited by Griffith John McRee. 2 vols. New York. 1857–58. (*Iredell:* McRee.)

IRVING, PIERRE MUNROE. Life and Letters of Washington Irving. 4 vols. New York. 1869. (Irving.)

JACKSON, ANDREW. *See* Bassett, John Spencer; Parton, James.

JAY, JOHN. Correspondence and Public Papers. Edited by Henry Phelps Johnston. 4 vols. New York. 1890–93. [Letter-press edition.] (*Jay:* Johnston.)

JEFFERSON, THOMAS. Memoir, Correspondence, and Miscellanies. Edited by Thomas Jefferson Randolph. Charlottesville. 1829. (*Jefferson:* Randolph.)

—— Works. Edited by Paul Leicester Ford. 12 vols. New York. 1904–05. [Federal edition.] (*Works:* Ford.)

—— Writings. Edited by Henry Augustine Washington. Washington. 1853–54. (*Jefferson:* Washington.)

    See Parton, James; Randall, Henry Stephens.

JENKINSON, ISAAC. Aaron Burr. His Personal and Political Relations with Thomas Jefferson and Alexander Hamilton. Richmond [Indiana]. 1902. (Jenkinson.)

JOHNSON, ALLEN. Union and Democracy. Boston. 1915.

JOHNSON, WILLIAM. Sketches of the Life and Correspondence of Nathanael Greene. 2 vols. Charleston. 1822.

JOHNSTON, HENRY PHELPS, *editor*. *See* Jay, John.

JONES, CHARLES COLCOCK, *and* DUTCHER, SALEM. Memorial History of Augusta, Georgia. Syracuse. 1890.

KENNEDY, JOHN PENDLETON. Memoirs of the Life of William Wirt. 2 vols. Philadelphia. 1849. (Kennedy.)

KING, RUFUS. Life and Correspondence, comprising his Letters, Private and Official, his Public Documents and his Speeches. Edited by Charles Ray King. 6 vols. New York. 1894–1900. [Letterpress edition.] (King.)

KNIGHT, LUCIAN LAMAR. Georgia's Landmarks, Memorials and Legends. 2 vols. Atlanta. 1913–14.

LA ROCHEFOUCAULD-LIANCOURT, FRANÇOIS ALEXANDRE FRÉ-
DÉRIC, DUC DE. Travels through the United States of
North America. 4 vols. London. 1800. (La Roche-
foucauld-Liancourt.)
LEWIS, WILLIAM DRAPER, editor. Great American Lawyers:
A History of the Legal Profession in America. 8 vols.
Philadelphia. 1907–09. (Great American Lawyers: Lewis.)
Literary Magazine and American Register. Vol. II, April to
December, inclusive, 1804. Philadelphia.
LODGE, HENRY CABOT. Alexander Hamilton. Boston. 1882.
[American Statesmen series.]
—— Life and Letters of George Cabot. Boston. 1877.
(Lodge: Cabot.)
LODGE, HENRY CABOT, editor. See Federalist.

MCCALEB, WALTER FLAVIUS. Aaron Burr Conspiracy. New
York. 1903. (McCaleb.)
MCHENRY, JAMES. See Steiner, Bernard Christian.
MCLAUGHLIN, ANDREW CUNNINGHAM. Courts, the Constitu-
tion and Parties. Studies in Constitutional History and
Politics. Chicago. 1912. (McLaughlin.)
MACLAY, SAMUEL. Journal. Annotated by John Franklin
Meginness. Williamsport. 1887. (Maclay's Journal.)
MCMASTER, JOHN BACH. History of the People of the United
States from the Revolution to the Civil War. 8 vols.
New York. 1883–1914. (McMaster: U.S.)
—— Life and Times of Stephen Girard, Merchant and Mariner.
2 vols. Philadelphia and London. 1918.
MACON, NATHANIEL. See Dodd, William Edward.
MCREE, GRIFFITH JOHN, editor. See Iredell, James.
MANUSCRIPTS:
Breckenridge, John. Library of Congress.
Dreer, Ferdinand Julius. Pennsylvania Historical Society.
Etting, Frank Marx. Pennsylvania Historical Society.
Hopkinson, Joseph. Possession of Edward P. Hopkinson,
Philadelphia.
Jefferson, Thomas. Library of Congress.
Kent, James. Library of Congress.
Letters in Relation to the Burr Conspiracy. Library of
Congress. (Letters in Relation.)
Letters of the Corresponding Secretary. (Marshall to John
Eliot.) Massachusetts Historical Society.

Miscellaneous. New York Public Library.

Peters, Richard. Pennsylvania Historical Society.

Pickering, Timothy. Massachusetts Historical Society.

Plumer, William. Library of Congress. [The Plumer Papers are listed in several divisions, as "Congress," "Diary," "Journal," "Letters," "Register," and "Repository."]

Records of the United States Circuit Court, Boston, Mass.

Records of the United States Circuit Court, Richmond, Va.

Wilkinson, James. Chicago Historical Society.

MARSHALL FAMILY. *See* Paxton, William McClung.

MARSHALL, JOHN. Life of George Washington. [1st edition.] 5 vols. Philadelphia. 1805–07. (Marshall, 1st ed.)

—— Same. [2d edition.] 2 vols. Philadelphia. 1840. (Marshall, 2d ed.)

—— Same. [School edition.] Philadelphia. 1838. (Marshall, school ed.)

> *And see* Beveridge, Albert Jeremiah; Dillon, John Forrest; Paxton, William McClung.

MARTIN, FRANÇOIS XAVIER. Notes of a few decisions in the Superior Courts of the State of North-Carolina, and in the Circuit Court of the U[nited] States, for North-Carolina District. Newbern. 1797. (Martin.)

MARTINEAU, HARRIET. Retrospect of Western Travel. 2 vols. London and New York. 1838.

Maryland Historical Society. Fund-Publications. No. 24, 1887. Baltimore. (*Md. Hist. Soc. Fund-Pub.*)

Massachusetts Historical Society. Proceedings. Boston. (*Mass. Hist. Soc. Proc.*)

MASSACHUSETTS. Senate Journal, 1798–99. Vol. XIX. Manuscript volume, Massachusetts State Library.

MEGINNESS, JOHN FRANKLIN, *annotator.* *See* Maclay, Samuel. Journal.

Messages and Papers of the Presidents, 1789–1897. *See* Richardson, James Daniel.

Monthly Anthology and Boston Review. Vol. V. 1808. Boston.

MOORE, THOMAS. Poetical Works, collected by himself, with a Memoir. 6 vols. Boston. 1856.

MORDECAI, SAMUEL. Richmond in By-Gone Days, being the Reminiscences of An Old Citizen. Richmond. 1856. (Mordecai.)

MORISON, JOHN HOPKINS. Life of the Hon. Jeremiah Smith. Boston. 1845. (Morison: *Smith.*)

MORISON, SAMUEL ELIOT.   Life and Letters of Harrison Gray
Otis, Federalist, 1765–1848. 2 vols. Boston. 1913.
(Morison: *Otis*.)

MORRIS, GOUVERNEUR.   Diary and Letters. Edited by Anne
Cary Morris. 2 vols. New York. 1888. (Morris.)

MURPHEY, ARCHIBALD DEBOW.   Papers. Edited by William
Henry Hoyt. [Publications of the North Carolina Historical Commission.] 2 vols. Raleigh. 1914.

New England Mississippi Land Company.   Memorial of the
Agents to Congress, with a Vindication of their Title at
Law annexed. Washington. 1804.

NEWSPAPERS:

Baltimore, Md.: *American*, issues of November 4, 5, 6,
                 1807.

Boston, Mass.:   *Columbian Centinel*, issues of January
                 23, February 16, March 27, 30, 1799, Feb-
                 ruary 6, 17, April 2, 7, 1802. *Independ-
                 ent Chronicle*, issues of February 11, 14,
                 18, 25, 1799, May 12, July 10, 1800,
                 March 15, April 26, 1802, March 10,
                 June 30, 1803.
                 *J. Russell's Gazette — Commercial and Po-
                 litical* (later known as the *Boston Gazette*
                 and the *Boston Commercial Gazette*), is-
                 sue of January 28, 1799.
                 New England Palladium, issues of March
                 12, 23, 1802.

Richmond, Va.:   *Enquirer*, issues of April 10, 28, May 8,
                 November 6, 24, December 1, 4, 8, 12,
                 1807.

Washington, D.C.: *Federalist*, issues of February 13, 20, 22,
                 March 3, 1802, January 8, 1805.

New York Review. Vols. II and III. 1838. New York.

New York State Library Bulletin. Vol. IV, 1900. New York.

North American Review. Vol. 46, 1838; Boston. Vol. 185,
1907; New York.

North Carolina Booklet. Vol. XVII, 1917. Raleigh.

Old Family Letters.   Copied from the Originals for Alexander
Biddle. Series A. Philadelphia. 1892.

OTIS, HARRISON GRAY.   *See* Morison, Samuel Eliot.

PARTON, JAMES. Life and Times of Aaron Burr. New York. 1858. (Parton: *Burr*.)
—— Life of Andrew Jackson. 3 vols. New York. 1861. (Parton: *Jackson*.)
—— Life of Thomas Jefferson. Boston. 1874.

PAXTON, WILLIAM MCCLUNG. Marshall Family. Cincinnati. 1885. (Paxton.)

Pennsylvania Bar Association. Report of the Twenty-first Annual Meeting, 1915. Philadelphia.

PETERS, RICHARD, JR. Reports of Cases argued and adjudged in the Supreme Court of the United States, January term, 1828. Vol. I. Philadelphia. 1828. (Peters.)

PICKERING, TIMOTHY. Review of the Correspondence between the Hon. John Adams and the late William Cunningham, Esq., beginning in 1803 and ending in 1812. Salem. 1824

PICKETT, ALBERT JAMES. History of Alabama, and incidentally of Georgia and Mississippi, from the earliest period. 2 vols. Charleston. 1851. (Pickett.)

PLUMER, WILLIAM. Life. Begun by William Plumer, Jr., completed and edited, with a sketch of the author's life, by Andrew Preston Peabody. Boston. 1857. (Plumer.)

PRENTISS, CHARLES, *editor*. *See* Eaton, William. Life.

PRIEST, WILLIAM. Travels in the United States of America, 1793–97. London. 1802.

QUINCY, EDMUND. Life of Josiah Quincy of Massachusetts. Boston. 1867. (Quincy.)

RAMSEY, JAMES GATTYS MCGREGOR. Annals of Tennessee to the End of the Eighteenth Century. Charleston. 1853.

RANDALL, HENRY STEPHENS. Life of Thomas Jefferson. 3 vols. New York. 1858. (Randall.)

RANDOLPH, JOHN. Adams, Henry; Garland, Hugh Alfred.

RANDOLPH, THOMAS JEFFERSON, *editor*. *See* Jefferson, Thomas.

Records of the Federal Convention of 1787. Edited by Max Farrand. 3 vols. New Haven. 1911. (*Records Fed. Conv.*: Farrand.)

RICHARDSON, JAMES DANIEL, *compiler*. A Compilation of Messages and Papers of the Presidents, 1789–1897. 10 vols. Washington. 1896–99. (Richardson.)

RITCHIE, THOMAS. *See* Ambler, Charles Henry.

ROBERTSON, DAVID, *reporter*. *See* Burr, Aaron. Trials.

SAFFORD, WILLIAM HARRISON, *editor*. *See* Blennerhassett Papers.

SCOTT, LIEUT.-GENERAL [WINFIELD]. Memoirs. Written by Himself. 2 vols. New York. 1864.

SEMPLE, ROBERT BAYLOR. History of the Rise and Progress of the Baptists in Virginia. Richmond. 1810.

SHELTON, WILLIAM HENRY. Jumel Mansion, being a Full History of the House on Harlem Heights built by Roger Morris before the Revolution, together with some Account of its more Notable Occupants. Boston. 1916.

SINGLETON, ESTHER. Story of the White House. 2 vols. New York. 1907.

SMITH, GEORGE GILLMAN. Story of Georgia and the Georgia People, 1732 to 1800. Macon. 1900. (Smith.)

SMITH, JEREMIAH. *See* Morison, John Hopkins.

SMITH, MRS. SAMUEL HARRISON. *See* Hunt, Gaillard.

SMITH, WILLIAM STEUBEN, *and* OGDEN, SAMUEL GOUVERNEUR. Trials for Misdemeanors. Reported by Thomas Lloyd, stenographer. New York. 1807. (*Trials of Smith and Ogden.*)

South Carolina Historical and Genealogical Magazine. Vol. VII, 1906. Charleston.

Southwestern Historical Quarterly. Vol. XVII, 1909. Austin. (*Southwestern Hist. Quarterly.*)

SPARKS, JARED, *editor*. *See* Washington, George.

State of Facts, showing the Right of Certain Companies to the Lands lately purchased by them from the State of Georgia. United States. 1795.

State Trials. Complete Collection of State Trials and Proceedings for High-Treason, and other Crimes and Misdemeanors; from the Reign of King Richard II. to the End of the Reign of King George I. [1377–1727.] 6 vols. London. 1730. (*State Trials Richard II. to George I.*)

Statutes at Large. *See* United States Statutes.

STEINER, BERNARD CHRISTIAN. Life and Correspondence of James McHenry. Cleveland. 1907.

STEVENS, THADDEUS. *See* Woodburn, James Albert.

STEVENS, WILLIAM BACON. History of Georgia from its First Discovery by Europeans to the Adoption of the Present

Constitution in 1798.   2 vols.   Vol. I, New York, 1847. Vol. II, Philadelphia, 1859.   (Stevens.)

STORY, JOSEPH.   Life and Letters.   Edited by William Wetmore Story.   2 vols.   Boston.   1851.   (Story.)

SUPREME COURT.   *See* United States Supreme Court.

THAYER, JAMES BRADLEY.   Cases on Constitutional Law.   4 vols.   Cambridge.   1894–95.

—— John Marshall.   Boston.   1904.   [Riverside Biographical Series.]

TROUP, GEORGE MICHAEL.   *See* Harden, Edward Jenkins.

TUCKER, George.   Life of Thomas Jefferson.   2 vols.   Philadelphia.   1837.   (Tucker.)

TYLER, LYON GARDINER.   Letters and Times of the Tylers. 3 vols.   Richmond.   1884–96.   (Tyler.)

UNITED STATES CONGRESS.   Debates and Proceedings, First Congress, First Session, March 3, 1789, to Eighteenth Congress, First Session, May 27, 1824.   [Known as the Annals of Congress.]   42 vols.   Washington.   1834–56.   (*Annals.*)

—— Documents, Legislative and Executive.   *See* American State Papers.

—— History of the Last Session of Congress, which commenced on the seventh of December, 1801.   [Taken from the *National Intelligencer.*]   Washington.   1802.   (*Hist. Last Sess. Cong. which commenced 7th Dec. 1801.*)

UNITED STATES SENATE.   Document No. 610.   63d Congress, 2d Session.   Washington.   1914.

—— Journal of the Executive Proceedings of the Senate of the United States of America, from the Commencement of the First to the Termination of the Nineteenth Congress.   3 vols.   Washington.   1828.   (*Journal Exec. Proc. Senate.*)

United States Statutes at Large.   Vols. I, II, III.   Boston.   1850. (*U.S. Statutes at Large.*)

UNITED STATES SUPREME COURT.   Cases adjudged in the Supreme Court at October term, 1883.   Reported by John Chandler Bancroft Davis.   Vol. III.   New York and Albany.   1884.

    See also Cranch, William; Dallas, Alexander James; Howard, Benjamin Chew; Peters, Richard, Jr.; Wallace, John William.

VAN SANTVOORD, GEORGE. Sketches of the Lives and Judicial Services of the Chief-Justices of the Supreme Court of the United States. New York. 1854.

VARNUM, JAMES MITCHELL. The Case of Trevett against Weeden, on Information and Complaint, for refusing Paper Bills in Payment for Butcher's Meat, in Market, at par with Specie, tried before the Honourable Superior Court, in the County of Newport. Also the Case of the Judges of Said Court before the Honourable General Assembly. Providence. 1787.

VERMONT. Records of the Governor and Council of the State of Vermont. 8 vols. Montpelier. 1873–80.

VIRGINIA. Journal of the House of Delegates of the Commonwealth of Virginia. Begun and held at the Capitol in the City of Richmond on Monday, the third of December, 1798. Richmond. 1798.

Virginia Cases. *See* Brockenbrough, William, and Holmes, Hugh.

WALLACE, JOHN WILLIAM. Cases argued and adjudged in the Supreme Court of the United States, December term, 1865. Vol. III. Washington. 1866.

—— Same, December term, 1871. Vol. XIII. Washington. 1872. (Wallace.)

WARREN, CHARLES. History of the American Bar. Boston. 1911. (Warren.)

WASHINGTON, GEORGE. Writings. Selected and published from the Original Manuscripts with a Life of the Author. Edited by Jared Sparks. 12 vols. Boston. 1836.
And see Marshall, John.

WASHINGTON, HENRY AUGUSTINE, *editor*. *See* Jefferson, Thomas.

WEBSTER, DANIEL. Private Correspondence. Edited by Fletcher Webster. 2 vols. Boston. 1857.

WHARTON, ANNE HOLLINGSWORTH. Social Life in the Early Republic. Philadelphia. 1902. (Wharton: *Social Life.*)

WHARTON, FRANCIS. State Trials of the United States during the Administrations of Washington and Adams, with references. Philadelphia. 1849. (Wharton: *State Trials.*)

WHITE, GEORGE. Statistics of the State of Georgia. Savannah. 1849.

WILKINSON, JAMES. Memoirs of my Own Times. 3 vols. Philadelphia. 1816.

—— Proofs of the Corruption of. *See* Clark, Daniel.

    And see Debate in the House of Representatives of the Territory of Orleans.

WILSON, JAMES. Works. Edited by Bird Wilson. 3 vols. Philadelphia. 1804.

WIRT, WILLIAM. Letters of the British Spy. Baltimore. No date.

—— Memoirs. *See* Kennedy, John Pendleton.

WOLCOTT, OLIVER. Memoirs of the Administrations of Washington and John Adams. Edited from the papers of Oliver Wolcott by George Gibbs. 2 vols. New York. 1846. (Gibbs.)

WOODBURN, JAMES ALBERT. Life of Thaddeus Stevens. Indianapolis. 1913.

WROTH, LAWRENCE COUNSELMAN. Parson Weems, Biographical and Critical Study. Baltimore. 1911.

𝕿𝖍𝖊 𝕽𝖎𝖛𝖊𝖗𝖘𝖎𝖉𝖊 𝕻𝖗𝖊𝖘𝖘

CAMBRIDGE . MASSACHUSETTS

U . S . A